HARRY HANSEN was born in Davenport, Iowa, and received a bachelor of philosophy degree from the University of Chicago. He served as a war correspondent for the Chicago *Daily News* during World War I, and was a correspondent at the Paris Peace Conference in 1919. Mr. Hansen served as literary editor of the Chicago *Daily News,* the New York *World,* and the New York *World Telegram.* He wrote eleven books as well as numerous articles and essays, and lectured at Colombia University and the University of Chicago. A member of the Society of American Historians, he was the editor of *The World Almanac.*

DR. GARY W. GALLAGHER is the John L. Nav III Professor in the History of the American Civil War at the University of Virginia in Charlottesville, Virginia. He is also the author of *The Confederate War* and *Lee and His Army in Confederate History.*

RICHARD WHEELER is the author of *Voices of the Civil War, Witness to Gettysburg,* and other books about the Civil War and the American West.

THE
CIVIL WAR

★★★★★ *A History* ★★★★★

HARRY HANSEN

With a New Foreword by Dr. Gary Gallagher
Introduction by Richard S. Wheeler

NEW AMERICAN LIBRARY

For Carl Sandburg

New American Library
Published by New American Library, a division of
Penguin Putnam Inc., 375 Hudson Street,
New York, New York 10014, U.S.A.
Penguin Books Ltd, 80 Strand,
London WC2R ORL, England
Penguin Books Australia Ltd, Ringwood,
Victoria, Australia
Penguin Books Canada Ltd, 10 Alcorn Avenue,
Toronto, Ontario, Canada M4V 3B2
Penguin Books (N.Z.) Ltd, 182–190 Wairau Road,
Auckland 10, New Zealand

Penguin Books Ltd, Registered Offices:
Harmondsworth, Middlesex, England

Published by New American Library, a division of Penguin Putnam Inc. Previously published
in a Mentor edition.

First New American Library Trade Printing, December 2001
10 9 8 7 6 5 4 3 2 1

The maps on pages 515 and 535 are adapted with the permission of the publisher from maps
drawn by Samuel H. Bryant for *Lee's Last Campaign,* by Clifford Dowdey, published by
Little, Brown and Company.

Library of Congress Cataloging-in-Publication Data

Hansen, Harry, 1884–
    The Civil War : a history / Harry Hansen ; with a new foreword by Gary Gallagher ;
introduction by Richard S. Wheeler.
    p. cm.
    Includes index.
    ISBN 0-451-20503-0 (alk. paper)
    1. United States—History—Civil War, 1861–1865. I. Title.

E468.H3 2001
973.7—dc21   2001044781

Printed in the United States of America

CONTENTS

The author has adopted, for the most part, the topical method of carrying an action or a campaign to its conclusion in a single chapter. This necessitates an occasional departure from the chronological record.

LIST OF MAPS

INTRODUCTION

The American Civil War has given rise to a vast multitude of books which, taken together, cover events from every conceivable angle. But good one-volume histories of the conflict remain rare, since they are difficult to produce. The war was fifty years in developing, and this background period teemed with social, economic, and political complications. The war itself involved a great many battles and skirmishes.

When Harry Hansen undertook the challenge of trying to present the story of the war in a single book, he was already well advanced in years and had distinguished himself in American letters. A war correspondent during World War I, he had afterward become a literary editor, serving a series of prominent newspapers and magazines as a reviewer and a columnist. He had also turned out numerous books, articles, and essays, his topics often historical. This wealth of writing experience gave Hansen a firm basis for making a worthwhile contribution to the Civil War's centennial literature.

Upon its publication in 1961, *The Civil War* won a ready acceptance among critics and readers alike, a success that was fully merited. The book is compact, yet comprehensive. It makes a careful examination of the war's causes before it turns to the fighting, which is then covered in every aspect. The principals are deftly introduced. All in all, the reader is given an excellent understanding of this momentous period.

Harry Hansen is gone now—he died in 1977 at the age of ninety-two—but *The Civil War* endures.

—RICHARD S. WHEELER

FOREWORD

The Civil War centennial focused attention on the greatest upheaval in United States history. Between 1961 and 1965, Americans could turn to an array of publications, national and state commemorative events, television programs, and theatrical films to explore the history and meaning of a conflict that had confirmed the inviolability of the Union, killed the institution of slavery, left more than 600,000 soldiers dead and hundreds of thousands more maimed, and destroyed untold material wealth. Ulysses S. Grant III, whose grandfather had done more than anyone but Abraham Lincoln to ensure Union victory, and who chaired the National Civil War Centennial Commission, expressed widely held opinions about the war's significance. The commission sought not to find winners and losers in the conflict, remarked Grant in an article in *National Geographic,* but rather to use the hundredth anniversary to discover "a new understanding of the way in which Americans built from suffering and sacrifice an enduring nation." Echoing the many Union and Confederate veterans who had urged reconciliation in the late nineteenth and early twentieth centuries (many other veterans, it should be noted, never embraced the idea of forgiving their former enemies), Grant praised the courage of soldiers on both sides "who fought to the limit of endurance for four years . . . [but later] saw in the unity of their land something that overshadowed the bitterness of the struggle." With the conduct of his illustrious ancestor and Robert E. Lee at Appomattox in mind, Grant added, "In their great internal conflict, Americans have given the world an example not only of how to fight a war, but how to end a war. History offers few lessons more inspiring."

Life magazine opened a six-part centennial series in its January 6, 1961, issue, affirming that the "nation never faced a crisis more strange and bitter, never rang more loudly with daring or suffered more with bloodshed and hate. . . . And no other event has so compellingly kept the nation's interest or left its mark so deeply upon the nation's soul." Although *Life*'s text alluded to the sectional hatreds of the 1860s, the magazine's editors enlisted Pulitzer Prize–winning historian Bruce Catton to write a lead essay titled "Gallant Men in Deeds of Glory." Catton selected examples of heroic conduct by a number of soldiers on each side, stressing, as did U. S. Grant III, that both the Confederacy and the Union could claim their share of martial honor: "When all proper allowances have been made for stragglers and goldbricks, the Federal and Confederate soldiers of the 1860s abundantly deserve the old line: 'All the brothers were valiant.' " Had all the deserving men been awarded decorations for their valorous actions, remarked Catton, "there might not have been enough metal left for making bullets."

Most centennial-era writings that aspired to a large audience adopted the rigorously impartial stance implicit in Grant's and Catton's eagerness to accord full credit to soldiers on both sides. Careful not to alienate readers either above or below the Mason-Dixon line, authors chose the safest path of making certain that Union and Confederate leaders received their due and avoided rendering harsh judgments about the relative worthiness of the two causes. Military campaigns especially lent themselves to such treatment because they could be described and analyzed without much reference to the blighting issue of slavery, the complex story of emancipation, and the messy political debates and popular disaffection that plagued both the United States and the Confederacy.

Harry Hansen's *The Civil War: A New One-Volume History,* which appeared from New American Library in 1961 and soon was reprinted in paperback as *The Civil War: A History,* matched the impartial approach but avoided the rhetorical flourishes characteristic of many works published during the centennial. The structure and tone of *The Civil War* would not have surprised anyone familiar with Hansen's earlier publications. Born in Davenport, Iowa, in December 1884, Hansen graduated with a degree from the University of Chicago in 1909. He went to work for the Chicago *Daily News* in 1913 and the following year became head of the Berlin office of its European news service. Well positioned when World War I erupted in August 1914, Hansen traveled to the front in Belgium and filed a series of reports that established his reputation as a prominent war correspondent. He continued to write about the conflict for two more years and, in 1919, contributed a series of articles on the Versailles peace conference later collected in book form as *The Adventures of the Fourteen Points.*

Hansen left Chicago in 1926 to become literary editor of the New York *World.* Over the next twenty years, he discussed new books and explored a variety of literary topics in a daily column that reached several million readers through syndication in the Scripps Howard newspapers. He also wrote about current literature for *Harper's, Redbook,* the literary supplement of the *Chicago Tribune,* and a number of other publications. An evenhanded critic who sought to describe books as clearly as possible, Hansen prompted one author to characterize him as "a good example of the objective type of reviewer."

Hansen remained active professionally following retirement from his journalistic career in the autumn of 1948. He almost immediately assumed the editorship of the *World Almanac,* which he oversaw for seventeen years, and later took on editorial duties with the publisher Hastings House. Near the end of his life, he served as editor of revised editions of the *American Guide* state histories that had been prepared in the 1930s under the auspices of the Works Progress Administration. He died in January 1977 after suffering a heart attack. Nearly twenty-five years earlier, the author and screenwriter Ben Hecht, who also had worked at the Chicago *Daily News,* aptly described Hansen as a man devoted to books who lived and labored among them "like a pilgrim in a rain of manna."

The Civil War reflects Hansen's predilection for a straightforward, reportorial style marked by close attention to factual detail. Unlike much of the centennial literature, the narrative avoids sentimental language, gushy passages about commanders and the brave men they led, excessive use of adjectives and adverbs, and a tendency to second-guess the decisions and actions of participants. *The New York Times Book Review* called the book "a fact-packed review of the battles and leaders of the eighteen sixties," and a scholarly reviewer commented that Hansen retold the story "of combat on land and sea without much embroidery . . . [offering] detail concerning order of battle, commanders of units, and casualties . . . rarely found in one-volume histories."

Hansen's handling of Gettysburg illuminates his disinclination to wallow in historical debates. No battle spawned more literary wrangling among participants and generations of historians who assigned praise and blame to various generals. Hansen notes the controversies but almost never takes sides. Concerning Confederate corps commander Richard S. Ewell's much-discussed failure to seize high ground south of Gettysburg on the evening of July 1, for example, Hansen observes: "Ewell has been made the subject of attack by commentators seeking a reason for Lee's defeat at Gettysburg, and his delay in attacking Culp's Hill has been called catastrophic." But Union artillery chief Henry J. Hunt, added Hansen, "pointed out that Ewell's men were in no condition for an assault after the day's fighting" because of heavy casualties in some units. Having informed readers that Ewell's conduct spurred debate and offered one piece of evidence that runs counter to arguments against the general, Hansen moves on to other aspects of the battle without further comment.

The Civil War does not pretend to offer the full story of the nation's most traumatic event. It touches only briefly on sectional controversies before getting to the opening guns. Thereafter, Hansen devotes the overwhelming majority of his attention to military campaigns, ranging across geographic theaters in a largely (but not strictly) chronological narrative. Politics, the respective home fronts, foreign affairs, the process of emancipation, and other nonmilitary dimensions of the war figure only obliquely in Hansen's story. Within the military context, the eastern theater, where Robert E. Lee's famous Army of Northern Virginia contended against a succession of Union commanders who headed the Army of the Potomac, garners more attention than any other arena.

In the four decades since publication of Hansen's book, Civil War scholarship has expanded to include far more work on women, African Americans, the home fronts, the motivations and behavior of common soldiers, and the many ways in which the civilian and military spheres intersected. A number of one-volume histories have appeared, including James M. McPherson's *Battle Cry of Freedom: The Civil War Era,* which allocates approximately equal attention to the activities of soldiers and civilians, and Herman Hattaway and Archer Jones's *How the North Won: A Military History of the Civil War,* a detailed examination of strategic planning, tactics, administration, logistics, communications, and civil-military relationships.

Both McPherson's and Hattaway and Jones's books are far longer than Hansen's. Multivolume general histories by Bruce Catton, Shelby Foote, and Allan Nevins, each begun before the centennial, take readers on even more leisurely journeys across the landscape of the war. Yet for anyone new to the field seeking to establish familiarity with major military campaigns and leaders, *The Civil War* remains a lively option that conveys a sense of the immense scale and powerful drama of a seismic event.

—Dr. Gary W. Gallagher
John L. Nav III Professor in the History
of the American Civil War
University of Virginia
July 4, 2001

1

THE HISTORIC BACKGROUNDS
OF THE ISSUES OF
SECESSION AND SLAVERY

Why the War Began

The American Civil War of 1861–1865 was a conflict between Northern and Southern citizens brought about by sharp differences on political and economic issues between the two sections. In the North it was known to the generation that fought it as the War of the Rebellion, this indicating the official view that it was a revolt against the government of the United States. This term has been falling into disuse as the study of Southern grievances and Northern inflexibility has made the Southern position better understood. Southern historians began calling it the War Between the States, thus emphasizing the Southern contention that the Constitution of the United States was a contract between states, from which a sovereign state could withdraw. But although regiments were recruited by states and carried state insignia, the war was conducted by two federal regimes—the United States of America and the Confederate States of America, the latter dominating the military and economic life of the South, despite the protest of such states as Georgia and South Carolina.

The actual causes of the war extended far back in the

history of the Republic and resulted from an accentuation of sectional grievances not resolved in nearly half a century of negotiation.

The two major issues that brought on the war were the fight over state rights (or states' rights), which involved the right of secession from the Union of the states under the Constitution, and the extension of slavery to new states and territories. These long-range issues are discussed later in this chapter.

The immediate provocation for secession of the states, which led to the war, was the election of Abraham Lincoln as President of the United States in the fall of 1860, on a platform which denied the extension of slavery to new states and territories. By this time the controversy over slavery had become so intense, tempers were so inflamed, and extremists were so uncompromising that the basis for peaceful adjustment of differences was lost. South Carolina precipitated a break when, in a convention at Charleston, December 20, 1860, it adopted an ordinance of secession, repealing its 1788 ratification of the Constitution of the United States, and its governor proclaimed the act in effect on December 24, 1860.

April 12, 1861, is the date designated as the opening of hostilities, because the first gun was fired on Fort Sumter in Charleston harbor on that day, and April 26, 1865, is called the end of the war, because the last major opposition, that of Lieutenant General Joseph E. Johnston, ended on that day. There were, however, numerous overt acts before the attack on Fort Sumter, and there were capitulations by minor organizations and commanders after April 26, 1865.

The Civil War was fought by civilians hastily recruited in large numbers and commanded by officers who had been trained in both the regular army and the state militia. Many of the high-ranking commanders on both sides were graduates of the United States Military Academy at West Point and as young men had served in the Mexican War. The number of men who served in the Federal armies was reported by the Commissioner of Pensions in 1903 as 2,213,363. The number of enlistments, based on the reports of the Provost Marshal General, was 2,898,304; this was believed to include militia and short-term men, not all of whom were mustered into the United States Army, as well as re-enlistments. Of the first figure, 84,415 served in the Navy. The number in the ranks of the Confederate armies cannot be stated exactly because of lack of detailed records; informal estimates run from 600,000 to 900,000, whereas the exhaustive study of all sources by Thomas L. Livermore in *Numbers and Losses in the Civil War in America* (1900; reissue 1957) placed the total well over 1,000,000. The total number of deaths on the Union side is given officially as 364,501; on the Confederate side the estimate, in the absence of complete reports, is 133,821. These numbers represent soldiers killed in battle and dying from wounds received in battle, but they do not take into account the many premature deaths, in the decades after the war, that were legacies of exposure and disease suffered while the men were under arms.

A More—or Less—Perfect Union

The origin of the issues that precipitated the Civil War goes back to the earliest years of the Republic; in fact, to the contention that the Thirteen States that fought and won the American Revolution while bound in defensive action under the Articles of Confederation, did not yield up their sovereign rights as political entities when they adopted a better agreement in the Constitution of the United States. Under the Articles of Confederation the United States of America were former British colonies united for a common purpose; under the Constitution the United States of America soon became the name of the Federal government, which was referred to in the singular.

The preamble of the Constitution opened with "We the people of the United States, in order to form a mcre perfect union . . . ," but to many this meant a more perfect way of providing for the common defense and the general welfare, leaving much to be done by the states. The ratification of the Constitution was done by the voting in state conventions, and when the ninth state had ratified it, it was considered in operation, although the Constitution was not declared in effect until nine months later.

Ratification was not unanimous in all cases and considerable opposition had to be overcome, enough to indicate that after acceptance there remained a body of opinion opposed to its terms for one reason or another. Thus, while Delaware, New Jersey, and Georgia voted with unanimity, the other states did not, and New York had only three votes more for ratification than for rejection.

When Congress began to pass laws under the powers granted it by the Constitution there quickly arose objection that it was transgressing on the rights of the states. Among the earliest formal protests were the Virginia and Kentucky Resolutions. They were prompted by the Alien and Sedition Acts passed by the Federalist majority. The first set of Kentucky Resolutions was adopted November 16, 1798, and the second set on November 22, 1799. Though unsigned, they were later discovered to have been written by Thomas Jefferson. They pointed out that the Federal government had limited powers delegated to it by the states. The Virginia Resolutions, of the same tenor, were the work of James Madison. Jefferson pointed out that there should be a way of judging how far the Federal government had exceeded its powers, and that the states should judge this.

In the Kentucky resolutions of 1799 appeared a word that was charged with explosive force. It was "nullification," which meant nullifying a law that went beyond the powers of the Federal government. It was to turn up later in one of the great controversies that was to prove divisive. In the ensuing discussion some statesmen suggested that the Constitution itself had provided, in the judiciary, a means of judging whether or not its provisions were applied rightfully. It was the decision of Chief Justice John Marshall that the Supreme Court could pass on constitutionality, that gave the Court its superior position as the place of final appeal.

Jefferson Against Slavery

Thomas Jefferson was the great fighter against slavery in the emerging republic. He tried to combat it with his logic, and he wanted it condemned in the Declaration of

Independence. His draft blamed George III for slavery in the colonies, but this was not accepted by the Continental Congress. Virginia had passed laws against the importation of slaves and these had been vetoed by the British government, hence Jefferson's resentment. He explained in his *Memoir* concerning the Declaration: "The clause . . . reprobating the enslaving the inhabitants of Africa, was struck out in complaisance to South Carolina and Georgia, who had never attempted to restrain the importation of slaves, and who, on the contrary, still wished to continue it. Our northern brethren also, I believe, felt a little tender under those censures; for although their people had very few slaves themselves, yet they had been pretty considerable carriers of them to others."

A law governing the return of fugitive slaves had been enacted in 1793, based on Sec. 2, Art. IV of the Constitution, which provided that a person "held to service or labor" under the laws of one state and escaping to another should be returned to the person to whom he was obligated. This applied also to indentured servants.

Jefferson fought slavery relentlessly. In 1784 the Continental Congress appointed him chairman of a committee to draft a plan of administration for territories north of 31° N. Lat., including land later admitted as the states of Alabama, Mississippi, Tennessee, and Kentucky. On March 1, 1784, Jefferson made a report that included the provision that "after the year 1800 of the Christian era there shall be neither slavery nor involuntary servitude in any of the said states." This clause was rejected by a majority of one vote, causing Jefferson to write: "The voice of a single individual . . . would have prevented this abominable crime from spreading itself over the new country. Thus we see the fate of millions unborn hanging on the tongue of one man, and heaven was silent in that awful moment!"

The Continental Congress on July 13, 1787, adopted the famous Northwest Ordinance (An Ordinance for the Government of the Territory of the United States Northwest of the River Ohio). This stipulated that "there shall be neither slavery nor involuntary servitude in the said territory." This ordinance was re-adopted under the Con-

stitution, August 7, 1789. The same prohibition of slavery
was incorporated by Congress in acts creating the governments of territories of Indiana, 1800, Michigan, 1805,
Illinois, 1809, Wisconsin, 1836, and Iowa, 1838. But
when North Carolina in December, 1789, ceded its
western lands to the new federal government, it stipulated
that "no regulations made or to be made by Congress
shall tend to emancipate slaves." Congress accepted the
condition in its act for the government of the territory
south of the Ohio, and similarly kept its hands off when
creating new southern states. Five territorial acts from
1798 to 1822 either accepted or made no provision concerning slavery. By 1846 six southern states in which
slavery was permitted had been admitted without any
prohibition against slavery: Tennessee, Louisiana, Mississippi, Alabama, Arkansas, and Florida, and a seventh,
Missouri, had tricked Congress by accepting restrictions
in order to acquire statehood, and then spurning them.

The slave trade was prohibited in 1808 and slavers
became subject to seizure when caught, but they still
managed to deliver their cargoes. A number of American sloops of war were on patrol off the African West
Coast for decades before the Civil War. The USS *San
Jacinto* was returning from such a patrol when it captured the Confederate commissioners Mason and Slidell.

John C. Calhoun and Nullification

The doctrine of nullification began to find support in
South Carolina in the 1820's, and is forever associated with the name of its chief spokesman, John C. Calhoun. It grew out of the antagonism of the cotton planters to protective tariffs that were voted by Congress to
help the small industries of the North compete with foreign imports. Nullification was spelled out in a report of a
committee of the South Carolina legislature called *Exposition*, which was published unsigned for general distribution, but which Calhoun admitted in 1831 to have
written.

James Madison, fourth President of the United States,
was one of the framers of the Constitution of the United
States. When he heard the assertion that a state could

nullify an act of Congress he declared: "For this preposterous and anarchical pretension there is not a shad-
ow of countenance in the Constitution."

In essence it meant that when an act of Congress or of
the Federal government transgressed those rights that a
state considered reserved to itself, it was unconstitu-
tional and the injured state could use its power to stop enforcement of the act within its borders, thus making the
act null and void. The document set forth that the protective tariff was a geographical mistake, since it bene-
fited one section of the country against another.

The cotton planters of South Carolina may not have
suffered more severely than those of other Southern
states, but they had the most vigorous spokesmen. For a
generation the halls of the legislature resounded with de-
nunciations of the Northern leaders who had counte-
nanced such impositions as the "tariff of abominations"
of 1828. The writings of Thomas Cooper and R. J.
Turnbull were extraordinary expositions of the point of
view that the Constitution strictly limited the Federal
government from interfering with the sovereign states
over matters affecting their immediate welfare, and contributed greatly to building a body of sympathetic opinion in the South. Cooper had a remarkable career as a
lawyer, politician, professor of chemistry and min-
eralogy, and pamphleteer; he was president of South
Carolina College (later the University) 1820–1834,
and his work *On the Constitution* appeared in 1826.
Robert J. Turnbull was a Charleston lawyer who, over
the signature of "Brutus," contributed to the Charleston
Mercury a series of papers challenging the jurisdiction of
the Federal government in many matters affecting the
states, and publishing them in 1827 in a book called *The
Crisis, or Essays on the Usurpation of the Federal Government.* The reiterated contentions of these and other
political spokesmen created such intense feeling in South
Carolina more than thirty years before the state trained
its batteries on Fort Sumter that John C. Calhoun was
persuaded to present the state's position as a warning
to Congress and recommend steps toward amelioration.

Calhoun's career belongs to the period of transition
when an American nationality was developing out of

sectional loyalties. Calhoun worked for the welfare of the whole United States in his early life, but he always saw it as a union of sovereign states. He concentrated on the defenses of the whole and supported a protective tariff to encourage manufactures, but when the economic situation of the South became difficult he agreed with his South Carolinian colleagues that the tariff hurt some while aiding others. He then realized that what was necessary for the common good might injure some sections, but in 1816 he still said that "it must be submitted to as the condition of our greatness." Gradually he became convinced that the Federal government by its practices was invading the rights of his state contrary to the agreement called the Constitution.

John Caldwell Calhoun was born near Abbeville, South Carolina, March 18, 1782, was graduated from Yale College in 1804, and studied law in Litchfield, Connecticut, and Charleston, South Carolina, eventually opening a law office in Abbeville. He became a Republican (Anti-Federalist) and was elected to Congress in 1810. Here he became a strong advocate of the second war with Great Britain and after war came worked diligently for the support of American arms. After the war he supported a far-reaching program to build up the nation's strength; he wanted a powerful Navy, with "steam frigates," as early as 1816, when no steamship had ever crossed the ocean; also he asked for a standing army and permanent roads for its use, and he wanted adequate internal revenue raised by taxation and encouragement for manufacturers. Thus, thinking the economic needs of the country out for himself and before sectional influences were brought to bear, he recommended that "a certain encouragement should be extended at least to our woolen and cotton manufactures." He specifically referred to these two industries when he spoke in April in support of the New Tariff bill, when he said protective duties were necessary to help manufactures and "put them beyond the reach of contingency." Thus, far from thinking that a tariff would damage Southern agriculture, he asserted that this system would help bind together more closely "our widely spread republic," increase mutual dependence and intercourse, and "excite increased attention to internal improvements, a subject every way so intimately connected with the ultimate attainment of national strength and the perfection of our political institutions." This brought him the opposition of the "anti-protectionists," who turned out to be among his own constituents.

These were his views when he served as Secretary of War in the cabinet of President James Monroe, 1817–1824. In 1824 he was elected Vice President by popular vote, but the election of the President, John Quincy Adams, had to be effected by vote of the House of Representatives. Calhoun was re-elected Vice President when Andrew Jackson became President in 1828. By this time the fight against the tariff had become a fight against the Federal power that imposed it, and Calhoun became active in trying to find a way of reconciling two opposite positions that, he saw, held the making of a catastrophe. The nullification convention of South Carolina now met and voted the tariff null and void.

After a new protective tariff had been enacted by Congress in 1832, Calhoun amplified the doctrine of nullification in an open letter to Governor James Hamilton, once a supporter of Andrew Jackson in Congress and now bitterly opposed to the President because of the tariff. Calhoun saw no direct connection between the individual citizens of a state and the central government and wanted the state in its sovereign capacity in convention to determine the extent of obligations contracted in the Constitution. But he did not want disunion. He thought nullification would force the Federal Congress to find new ways of adjusting differences. He told Hamilton that the constitutional convention had not nationalized the government. It had only raised it from below to the level of the state. Nullification was not secession. With nullification the state was still within the Union; with secession it was beyond control. Secession freed the state from its obligations; nullification compelled "the governing agent to fulfill its obligations."

The concept of nullification took root in the minds of many South Carolinian planters and exporters, who were hurt by the protective tariff. After the tariff of 1832 was adopted and promised to compound their injuries,

South Carolina called a state convention on November 19, 1832. It passed an Ordinance of Nullification, declaring the tariff void in the state. State officials had to take an oath to obey the ordinance, and an appeal to the courts was forbidden. The ordinance was to become effective February 1, 1833, to give Congress an opportunity to reverse itself.

The Stand of Andrew Jackson

President Andrew Jackson at once became the champion of the Federal authority. He was not going to have the laws of the land treated thus by a state. He denounced nullification as rebellious treason and warned South Carolina that he would enforce the laws. He sent two warships to Charleston and troops to the border. At the same time he caused to be introduced a bill authorizing him to use the Army and the Navy to enforce the law. This became known as the Force bill. But he also urged modification of the tariff, and Senator Henry Clay of Kentucky, the Great Compromiser, carried through a revision of the tariff in 1833 before the date nullification was to come into effect. South Carolina was mollified, recalled the convention, and repealed its ordinance of nullification. But Congress did pass the Force bill demanded by President Jackson.

Tremendous significance has been ascribed by historians to President Andrew Jackson's declaration against disunion in a toast given at a dinner in celebration of Thomas Jefferson's birthday. Gerald Johnson describes it as "the most dramatic and historical toast in American history." To understand its impact we have to visualize the way political views were communicated at that time. There was no evidence to lead anyone to suspect that Andrew Jackson would not back the Union, but there were partisans, his own followers among them, who feared he would compromise with the South. It was customary at the time to have a long series of toasts, each of which expressed the mood or views of the speaker, who could expound his platform.

The Jefferson Dinner toast of Andrew Jackson had importance because with it he broke completely with John

C. Calhoun. At this distance in time the incident seems simple. When a great many lesser politicians had spoken Jackson rose and gave his toast: "Our Federal Union. It must be preserved!" He raised his glass, which meant that all would drink to it with him. John C. Calhoun was to follow. He said: "Our Union. Next to our liberty, the most dear." Jackson made no other remarks. Calhoun amplified his, saying: "May we all remember that it can only be preserved by respecting the rights of the states, and by distributing equally the benefits and burdens of the Union."

But liberty was an abstraction; it had many meanings. Abraham Lincoln was to attempt a definition a generation later when, as President, he addressed the Sanitary Fair in Baltimore. "We all declare for liberty," he said, "but in using the same word we do not mean the same thing. With some the word 'liberty' may mean for each man to do as he pleases with himself and the product of his labor; while with others the same word may mean for some men to do as they please with other men and the product of other men's labor. Here are two, not only different, but incompatible things, called by the same name, liberty. And it follows that each of the things is, by the respective parties, called by two different and incompatible names—liberty and tyranny."

Henry Clay's Two Compromises

There was slavery in the southern sections of the Louisiana Purchase Territory when it came under the United States flag in 1803. It extended into Missouri, which had been settled in part by pioneers who moved west from Virginia, Kentucky, and Tennessee. They petitioned Congress repeatedly to make Missouri a state but were ignored until 1819, when Henry Clay of Kentucky gave the proposal formal support in the House. When it was presented to the Committee of the Whole for action, Representative James Tallmadge of New York moved an amendment prohibiting any further introduction of slaves into Missouri and declaring that all children born of slave parents should be free at the age of twenty-five.

The anger and resentment that this amendment stirred up in the House showed how far apart the two sections of

the country were forty years before the Civil War. Thomas
W. Cobb, Representative from Georgia, voiced the threat
that was to be heard many times in the halls of Congress:
"If you persist the Union will be dissolved. You have kin-
dled a fire which all the waters of the ocean cannot put out,
which seas of blood can only extinguish!" Tallmadge retorted in kind: "If a dissolution of the Union must take
place, let it be so! If civil war, which gentlemen so threaten,
must come, I can only say, let it come!" Historians record
that repercussions of these debates were heard in all parts
of the country.

Late in the year a bill to admit the state of Maine was
passed by the House, but held up in the Senate, where the
South had control. The Senate would admit Maine if Congress likewise admitted Missouri without any restriction
on slavery. This caused another outbreak of vituperation
in Congress. Senator Jesse B. Thomas of Illinois then introduced an amendment to admit Missouri as a slave state,
but stating that the rest of the Louisiana Purchase north of
36° 30' N. Lat. should be forever free. Despite the violent
opposition of such leaders as John Randolph of Roanoke,
who called it an insult to the Souh, this bill managed to
pass both houses. John Randolph disputed it, and intended
to move for reconsideration, but Henry Clay, Speaker of
the House, so juggled the business of the day that the bill
had been sent to the Senate and enacted before Randolph
could get the floor.

This was the Missouri Compromise, the first major attempt to settle the issue of slavery west of the Mississippi.
Before Missouri became a state on August 10, 1821, Congress stipulated that its general assembly must not enact a
proposed law excluding free Negroes and mulattoes, since
this would violate the federal Constitution. Missouri accepted the prohibition, but after it became a state its legislature passed the law of exclusion that Congress had outlawed.

Slavery gained support when Texas was admitted to the
Union December 29, 1845, with a preponderance of slave
labor. With the cession by Mexico of the western lands, and
the rush to California following the discovery of gold in
1848, a hot battle began to organize the territories as free
or slave states. Under Henry Clay's leadership the Com-

promise of 1850 was enacted. It provided that the forming of new states out of the vast Texas area be postponed; that California be admitted as a free state; that the far-reaching western boundaries of Texas be brought east, and Texas be paid $10,000,000 compensation; that the remaining lands be organized as the territories of Utah and New Mexico, "with or without slavery, as their constitutions may prescribe at the time of their admission," and that the slave trade be abolished in the District of Columbia. With bitter opposition from the North it put teeth into the old Fugitive Slave Law by giving a Southern owner the right to reclaim a runaway slave by establishing ownership before a commissioner, instead of in a trial by jury, and denied admission of evidence in defense of the fugitive. This also threatened the liberty of free Negroes, and outraged the North.

Although Senator Jefferson Davis of Mississippi voted for the Compromise, he was one of the ten Southern senators who protested formally that admitting California as a free state was fatal "to the peace and equality" of their states, and warned that if this policy were persisted in, it would lead to dissolution of the confederacy (meaning the United States) "in which the slaveholding states have never sought more than equality, and in which they will not be content to remain with less."

Downfall of Daniel Webster

Daniel Webster (1782–1852), Massachusetts statesman, was in the forefront of the battle against slavery before the Civil War, but lost his hard-bitten antislavery constituency when he supported the Compromise of 1850, which strengthened the Fugitive Slave Law. In the House of Representatives in 1812, he suggested, in opposing the War of 1812, that a state might have the right to nullify a Federal act, but at no time did he admit a right to withdraw from the Union. As a senator he supported President Jackson in condemnation of the ordinance of nullification voted by South Carolina.

The tariff was the issue that brought about the celebrated debate in the Senate between Senator Robert Y. Hayne of South Carolina and Senator Daniel Webster of Massachusetts. Webster was a great orator and his words reverberated far beyond the halls of Congress, but the spell of his oratory is less comprehensible today when there are many avenues of communication and forums for discussion. Hayne was fighting against the "tariff of abominations" in January, 1830, predicting that it would cause the exploitation of the South. Webster was convinced that a protective tariff helped the industries of the North. He also was farsighted enough to see the South drifting away from the national Union. "It is to that Union we owe our safety at home and our consideration and dignity abroad," said Webster. He closed with a sentence that became a slogan: "Liberty and union, now and forever, one and inseparable."

But the specter of disunion haunted him and as the bitterness between the sections increased he accepted Henry Clay's Compromise of 1850 as a device to save the Union from disruption. In his "Seventh of March Speech" Webster attempted to conciliate both sections and failed. He asserted that the South had been wronged by Northern legislators and the latter's "disinclination to perform fully their constitutional duties" in the return of fugitive slaves. He also criticized extremists, thus hitting antislavery men, many of whom had considered him their champion. His advocacy of compromise lost him the support of many in the North, who remembered that in 1848 he had announced: "I shall oppose all slavery extension and all increase of slave representation, in all places, at all times, under all circumstances, even against all inducements, against all supposed limitation of great interests, against all combinations, against all compromise." To repudiate such a declaration was catastrophic.

Abolitionists took their anger out on Webster. He was a fallen idol. John Greenleaf Whittier composed a poem, "Ichabod," about him. The vote spoiled Webster's chances to be nominated for President in 1852. Later in that year he died.

The Kansas-Nebraska Act

The next big battle came when Senator Stephen A. Douglas of Illinois in 1854 presented a bill to organize the territories of Kansas and Nebraska. Southerners in Congress voted for it for two reasons: it declared he Missouri Compromise inoperative because inconsistent with the Compromise of 1850, and it left to the settlers the right to decide by vote whether the territories should be slave or free soil. This was Douglas' theory of "popular sovereignty," which his opponents derisively called "squatter sovereignty." The bill was approved May 30, 1854, by President Franklin Pierce, who then named a proslavery governor of Kansas. The hatred of slavery led to violent outbreaks (cf. *John Brown,* pp. 26-27). Bitter factional fights started when the proslavery men adopted the Lecompton Constitution for the proposed state of Kansas. Eventually Senator Douglas repudiated it and the free soil party won. The controversy split the Democratic and Whig parties and helped form the new Republican party (February-July, 1854).

2

THE POLITICAL CRISES: FROM THE DRED SCOTT DECISION TO SECESSION

The Dred Scott Decision

The controversy over slavery grew more bitter every year. It was sharpened greatly in 1857, when the United States Supreme Court handed down its famous Dred Scott decision. This was made public on March 6, 1857, two days after James Buchanan, Democrat, had become the fifteenth President of the United States. The decision, which declared that a slave was property and had no rights as a citizen, infuriated the Republicans, the antislavery Democrats, and all others who were fighting for human rights. Six justices, led by Chief Justice Roger B. Taney of Maryland, approved; three dissented. The case was Dred Scott vs. Sandford (19 Howard 393).

Dred Scott, a Negro, in 1834 was taken by his master,

Dr. Emerson, from Missouri, a slave state, to Fort Armstrong, Illinois, free territory by virtue of the Northwest Ordinance. In 1836 Emerson took Scott to Fort Snelling, in what became Minnesota, from which slavery was excluded by the Missouri Compromise. In 1838 Emerson returned to St. Louis with Scott and the wife and two daughters Scott had acquired. Emerson died and Scott in 1846 sued Mrs. Emerson for freedom on the ground that he had become free by living in nonslave territory. The lower Missouri court found in his favor; the state supreme court reversed this decision and sent the suit back to the lower court.

Mrs. Emerson in the meantime had married a representative from Massachusetts who was an abolitionist. To test Scott's case in the federal courts she "sold" Scott to her new brother-in-law, J. F. A. Sandford of New York. Dred Scott sued Sandford in the federal district court, and Sandford pleaded Scott was not a citizen because he was a Negro. Scott granted he was a Negro but denied this kept him from being a citizen. The court held that Scott's status had been determined by the laws of Missouri and properly decided by the Missouri supreme court. Scott then appealed to the U. S. Supreme Court.

Chief Justice Taney declared for the majority: Dred Scott was a slave, not a citizen, hence he had no rights under the Constitution, which was made by whites for whites. Did Scott become free when he lived at Fort Snelling, in territory where slavery was outlawed by the Missouri Compromise? No, said Taney; slaves were property, and property was protected by due process in the Fifth Amendment. An act of Congress prohibiting such ownership was not warranted by the Constitution, therefore the Missouri Compromise was void and did not apply. Justice Curtis (Mass.), dissenting, said all persons were citizens when the Constitution was adopted. Some Negroes were free at that time and recognized as citizens. The Constitution gave Congress power to make "all needful rules and regulations."

Effect of the Dred Scott decision was to becloud the Kansas–Nebraska Act of 1854, which left slavery in Kansas and Nebraska to vote of the people (squatter sovereignty), and to make slavery technically legal in the territories. However, the decision could not be enforced in the North.

On June 26 Abraham Lincoln in Springfield attacked the decision as erroneous and not valid as a precedent. By popular vote Minnesota on October 13 ratified a new constitution outlawing slavery. Ohio made it a penal offense to claim or hold slaves or carry a person of color from the state.

The Wilmot Proviso

Opponents of slavery in Congress seized every opportunity to restrict it. In August, 1846, a bill under discussion in the House proposed to appropriate $2,000,000 to buy land from Mexico in order to settle a dispute over boundaries. Representative David Wilmot, a Democrat from Pennsylvania, thereupon presented an amendment to the effect that "neither slavery nor involuntary servitude shall ever exist in any part of said territory," meaning the land acquired from Mexico. The House passed the amended bill in 1847, but the Senate adjourned two days later without acting on it. In the next session a new bill proposing to pay Mexico $3,000,000 was introduced; Representative Hannibal Hamlin of Maine offered an amendment more comprehensive than the first, outlawing slavery "in any territory on the continent of America which shall hereafter be acquired by or annexed to the United States by virtue of this appropriation or in any other manner whatever." Still called the Wilmot Proviso, it passed the House; the Senate rejected the Proviso and returned the bill; the House failed to adopt the Proviso a second time and finally voted the appropriation without prohibiting slavery.

John Brown's Raid at Harpers Ferry

Abolitionists were people who hated slavery and wanted it abolished everywhere forthwith. They were furious when Northern states were invaded by Southern constables and slaveowners who claimed escaped slaves under the Fugitive Slave Law. Such slaves were reclaimed even in Boston, where the crowds could see the spectacle of police officers handing over a cringing Negro to a white owner from the South. Hatred of slavery was fanned by Harriet Beecher Stowe's *Uncle Tom's Cabin, or Life Among the Lowly.* Wendell Phillips and William Lloyd Garrison were prominent abolitionists, and in the Senate, Charles Sumner of Massachusetts was a strong spokesman for abolition, creating such bitterness that he was beaten over the head with a cane and dangerously injured by a rabid secessionist representative from South Carolina.

Threats of leaving the Union were not confined to the South. In Boston the abolitionists under William Lloyd Garrison declared the United States Constitution protected slavery. Garrison repudiated support of the Constitution as a covenant with death and an agreement with hell. He talked of disunion because he asserted the "Southern slave power" dominated the Federal government in Washington. The idea of disunion shocked other New England leaders, who hated slavery but hoped to eradicate it without hurting the Union. Many believed Garrison was trying to attract attention to the iniquities of slavery, much as Henry Ward Beecher, pastor of Plymouth Church in Brooklyn, did when he "sold" a Negro woman from the pulpit.

A violent abolitionist with a conspiratorial bent was John Brown, some of whose activities were supported by funds from Eastern sympathizers. In 1859 John Brown turned from Kansas to Virginia to liberate slaves by force. Born in Torrington, Connecticut, May 9, 1800, he raised livestock in New York and Pennsylvania and ran a tannery in Ohio. In 1855 he went to Kansas to organize free-soil settlers to resist slavery. After proslavery bands from Missouri sacked Lawrence, Kansas, Brown's men murdered proslavery families along the Pottawatomie, May 24, 1856. With thirty followers he fought border troops at Osawatomie, Kansas, August 30, 1856. His agitation intensified hatreds and over 200 settlers were killed in "bleeding Kansas" during 13 months. He was called "Osawatomie Brown."

Getting arms from Eastern abolitionists, Brown stored them in Tabor, Iowa. He carried 11 fugitive slaves to Windsor, Ontario, Canada, 1,100 miles in 82 days. In late summer, 1859, he leased a Maryland farmhouse, five miles from Harpers Ferry (then in Virginia) and secreted his "army" there. With 16 white men, including 3 sons, and 5 Negroes, Brown seized the U.S. Armory at Harpers Ferry on October 17, 1859, killed 5 civilians, and took hostages. From Colonel Lewis W. Washington, great-grandnephew of George Washington, he took a sword Frederick the Great had sent Washington, and put it on. His men barricaded a fire-engine house.

Volunteer guards and Virginia militia were aroused. U.S. Marines arrived October 18, with Lieutenant Colonel Robert E. Lee, Second U.S. Cavalry, in command. Lieutenant J. E. B. Stuart, First U.S. Cavalry, failed to get Brown to surrender. The Marines charged and captured the raiders. One Marine was killed, one wounded. Eleven of Brown's party were killed, including two of his sons.

Brown was tried for treason to the Commonwealth of Virginia at Charleston, Virginia (now Charles Town, West Virginia) and hanged on December 2, 1859. Five others were hanged and five got away. Brown's fanaticism dramatized the intense hatred of the abolitionists for slavery. When Union soldiers marched into Virginia a few years later they sang: "John Brown's body lies a-mouldering in the grave, but his soul goes marching on."

The Crittenden Compromise

Senator John J. Crittenden, an old-line Whig, on December 18, 1860, proposed constitutional amendments in another earnest effort to hold the Union together. They provided that (1) slavery should be abolished in all territory now held or to be acquired north of Lat. 36° 30′ (the Missouri line); Congress should not interfere with it below that line; it should be protected as property by territorial government during its continuance, and states should be admitted with or without slavery as their constitutions might provide; (2) Congress could not abolish slavery in places under its exclusive jurisdiction in slave states; (3) nor in the District of Columbia without compensation and without the consent of its inhabitants and of Virginia and Maryland; (4) nor prohibit or hinder transportation of slaves between slave states and territories; (5) the government should pay owners for rescued fugitive slaves; (6) no future amendment should affect these articles or give Congress power to abolish or interfere with slavery in states where it is allowed.

Resolutions submitted by Crittenden endorsed the faithful execution of the Fugitive Slave Law, the repeal of personal-liberty laws of states, limiting the power of the marshal to call a *posse comitatus* to enforce the law, and thorough suppression of the African slave trade.

The Crittenden amendments came before the Committee of Thirteen of the Senate, comprising five Republicans, three Northern Democrats, three from border slave states, two from cotton states. Included were Senators Seward, Douglas, and Jefferson Davis. The five Republican senators voted against the first proposition, whereupon Davis and Toombs of Georgia joined them and thus defeated the compromise by 7 to 6. Behind the Republicans stood Lincoln; he was ready to see the Fugitive Slave Law enforced: "to put it in its mildest form, [it] ought not to be resisted"; but he did not countenance the extension of slavery to any territory, a basic tenet of the Republican party. "On the territorial question I am inflexible," he had written earlier to John A. Gilmer of North Carolina.

Senator Crittenden on January 3, 1861, proposed to the Senate that his Compromise be submitted to popular vote. Senator Douglas in supporting it said: "I prefer compromise to war. I prefer concession to a dissolution of the Union." The House voted for it, the Senate voted it down.

Lincoln's House Divided Speech

In 1858 Abraham Lincoln, Springfield, Illinois, lawyer and former representative in Congress, became the leading Republican fighter against slavery by his debates with Senator Stephen A. Douglas, Democrat. On June 16, 1858, the Republican state convention at Springfield nominated Lincoln for U.S. Senator to oppose Douglas. The voters were to elect members of the legislature, who would choose a senator on party lines. At the convention Lincoln gave his first version of the House Divided speech, which contained what was to become the most famous phrase of the campaign. He said:

"A house divided against itself cannot stand." I believe this government cannot endure permanently half slave and half free. I do not expect the Union to be dissolved. I do not expect the house to fall, but I do expect that it will cease to be divided. It will become all one thing or all the other.

Either the opponents of slavery will arrest the further spread of it and place it where the public mind shall rest in the belief that it is in the course of ultimate extinction, or its advocates will push it forward till it shall become alike lawful in all the states, old as well as new, North as well as South.

The Lincoln-Douglas Debates

The most famous political debates in American history were those between Abraham Lincoln and Stephen A. Douglas, when the two men campaigned in the summer of 1858 for the nomination of senator from Illinois. They did not suspect at the time that these would be memorable debates. They became important because the two men who led the nation's thinking from different points of view argued most competently the case for keeping slavery confined within certain limits.

In the campaign for senator, Lincoln challenged Douglas to divide time with him before the same Illinois audiences. Douglas agreed. The debates were held at Ottawa, August 21; Freeport, August 27; Jonesboro, September 15; Charleston, September 18; Galesburg, October 7; Quincy, October 13; Alton, October 15, 1858. The Democrats won both houses of the state legislature on November 2, making Douglas' re-election as senator certain.

Douglas had sponsored the Kansas-Nebraska Act of 1854, which proposed to admit part of the Louisiana Territory as two states and let their constitutions prescribe whether they would come into the Union as with or without slavery. This act was signed by President Pierce on May 30, 1854, and practically made the Missouri Compromise inoperative. This was known as popular sover-

eignty, in derision "squatter sovereignty," because settlers
could pack the state with partisans. It had caused bloody
rioting in Kansas when slavery men tried to drive out
free-soil men. Lincoln opposed extension of slavery to
new territories. Douglas said each state should make its
own laws and "local police regulation" could exclude
slavery under the Kansas-Nebraska act. This concession
did not please the Southern Democrats.

Lincoln declared popular sovereignty was proslavery
or noncommittal, and inconsistent with the Supreme
Court decision on Dred Scott, that a slave did not become free when taken to free states because he was
property, not a citizen. Lincoln said Chief Justice Roger
B. Taney was the first man to say the Declaration of Independence did not include Negroes when it mentioned
"all men," and Douglas was the second. Douglas accused
the Republicans of being abolitionists (for immediate
abolition of slavery). Lincoln said his House Divided
speech was not abolitionist. He intended to resist the
further spread of slavery, wanted new territories kept
free, and considered slavery a moral, social, and political
wrong.

But he had some reservations about citizenship. At the
Charleston debate he said:

"I am not in favor of making voters or jurors of Negroes, nor of qualifying them to hold office. . . . I am not
in favor of Negro citizenship."

The debates attracted national attention. A correspondent of the New York *Evening Post* observed the
tall Illinoisan at Ottawa and drew his portrait thus:

He is tall, slender and angular, awkward, even gait and
attitude. His face is sharp, large-featured, and unprepossess-
ing. His eyes are deepset, under heavy eyebrows; his forehead is high and retreating, and his hair dark and heavy. In
repose, I must confess that "Long Abe's" appearance is
not comely. But stir him up and the fire of his genius plays
on every feature. His eye glows and sparkles, every lineament,
now so ill-formed, grows brilliant and expressive, and you
have before you a man of rare power and magnetic influence.
He takes the people every time, and there is no getting away
from his good sense, his unaffected sincerity, and the unceasing play of his good humor, which accompanies his close

logic, and smooths the way to conviction. . . . He is clear, concise, logical; his language is eloquent and at perfect command.

Thousands of people came to the debates. There were bands, parades, patriotic demonstrations. After his defeat Lincoln said: "The fight must go on. The cause of civil liberty must not be surrendered at the end of one or even 100 defeats."

Senator William H. Seward, former New York governor, in 1858 supported free Kansas but endorsed popular sovereignty; in a famous speech at Rochester, October 25, he declared the country was engaged in an "irrepressible conflict" and must either become wholly slaveholding or wholly free labor.

The Campaign of 1860

Lincoln made a major speech at Cooper Institute, New York City, February 27, 1860. He had been invited by the Young Men's Central Republican Union, which opposed the faction of Senator William H. Seward and Senator Thurlow Weed, and paid him $200. Lincoln said the country could afford to let slavery alone where it was, but asked: "Can we, while our votes will prevent it, allow it to spread into the national territories and overrun us here in these free states? If our sense of duty forbids this, then let us stand by our duty, fearlessly and effectively." Horace Greeley, editor of the New York *Tribune,* called Lincoln a champion of free labor. Lincoln spoke at Hartford, Connecticut, March 5.

Senator Stephen A. Douglas had weakened his hold on the Democratic Party by refusing to tolerate secession, although he condemned Northern hostility to the Fugitive Slave Law. At the Democratic convention, April 23– May 3, 1860, the Southern minority bolted when outvoted on applying the Dred Scott decision to all states and territories. The Northern wing met June 18 in Baltimore and nominated Douglas for President. The Southern wing met June 28 in Baltimore and nominated Vice President John C. Breckinridge, of Kentucky, for President.

Conservatives, who stood for the Union and strict law

enforcement, formed the Constitution Union Party and on May 9 nominated John Bell, former senator from Tennessee, for President and Edward Everett for Vice President.

The Republican party, which had lost its first national campaign in 1856 with John C. Frémont (1813–1890) met May 16–18 in Chicago. Leading candidate was Senator William H. Seward (1801–1872). Lincoln had been endorsed by Illinois and several other states. With 233 votes needed, the first ballot gave Seward 173, Lincoln 102, Simon Cameron (Pa.) 50, Salmon P. Chase (Ohio) 49. In the second ballot Cameron's votes went to Lincoln. On the third ballot Lincoln had 231, Seward 180, Chase 24, whereupon Ohio diverted 4 Chase votes to Lincoln. Senator Hannibal Hamlin (Me.) was chosen for Vice President.

The Republican platform disavowed interference in the domestic concerns of states; demanded Kansas be admitted as a free state; repudiated the Dred Scott decision; declared freedom the normal condition of all territories; asked a protective tariff and a railway to the Pacific.

In the November election, 1,866,352 votes were cast for Lincoln and 2,810,501 against him. Of the latter, Douglas received 1,375,157; Breckinridge, 845,763; Bell, 589,581. Lincoln had 180 electoral votes, the opposition 123. The split in the Democratic Party elected Lincoln.

Senator Thurlow Weed of New York went to Springfield on December 20 and asked Lincoln to define his position on slavery. Lincoln's answer, presented to the Senate Committee on the Crisis by Senator Seward on December 24 was: Amend the Constitution to say it should never be altered to interfere with slavery; amend the Fugitive Slave Law to grant trial by jury; request the states to repeal laws that contravene constitutional acts.

Even after his election and before South Carolina had carried out its threat to secede, Lincoln tried to be conciliatory. On November 30, 1860, he wrote Alexander H. Stephens, Georgia politician who later became Vice President of the Confederate States: "Do the people of the South really entertain fears that a Republican administration would directly or indirectly interfere with their slaves or with them about their slaves? If they do, I wish to assure you . . . that there is no cause for such fears." But the South had good reason to believe the Republican party would interfere, for many of the party's members were abolitionists and more extreme than the new President.

Peace Effort by Virginia

Earnest men North and South made repeated efforts to find ways of adjusting differences while holding fast to the Union. The general assembly of Virginia, which had approved the Crittenden Compromise, invited all states to send commissioners to Washington on February 4, 1861, to meet together to "adjust the present unhappy controversies." John Tyler, former President, was appointed commissioner to see the President of the United States and to urge participation on South Carolina. Twenty-one states responded, but on the same day representatives of the seven cotton states convened in Montgomery to establish the Confederacy. Tyler was made chairman of the Washington "peace convention"; such leaders as Erastus Corning, J. S. Wadsworth, General Wool, Reverdy Johnson, Salmon P. Chase, and David Wilmot took part. The convention recommended that Congress submit a constitutional amendment to the states, but the usual effort to limit the extension of slavery did not have the support of the Southern delegates and Tyler rejected it when he returned to Virginia.

A constitutional amendment actually was recommended to the states by Congress by resolution adopted by the House on February 28, and the Senate on March 2, 1861. It read: "No amendment shall be made to the Constitution which will authorize or give to Congress the power to abolish or interfere, within any state, with the domestic institutions thereof including that of persons held to labor or service by the laws of said state."

The Virginia convention named a committee of three, Delegates Preston, Stuart, and Randolph, to ask the President what policy he intended to pursue toward the states that had seceded. President Lincoln met the delegates on April 13, 1861. They presented the resolution of the

convention, which declared that there was uncertainty
in the public mind about what Lincoln proposed to do
about "the Confederate states." Lincoln replied that he
had stated his intentions clearly in his Inaugural Address. He would spell out that he meant to repossess
the public property that had been seized, and he would
repel force by force.

Secession of the States

South Carolina voted an ordinance of secession from
the Union, repealing its 1788 ratification of the U.S.
Constitution, December 20, 1860, proclaimed in effect
December 24. Other states seceding in 1861 and their
votes in convention were:

Mississippi, January 9, 1861, by 84 to 15.

Florida, January 10, 1861, by 62 to 7.

Alabama, January 11, 1861, by 61 to 39.

Georgia, January 19, 1861, by 208 to 89.

Louisiana, January 26, 1861, by 113 to 17.

Texas, February 1, 1861, by 166 to 7, ratified by
popular vote February 23, 1861; for secession, 34,794;
against, 11,235.

Virginia had delayed action, but when President Lincoln called for troops after Sumter fell it voted for secession, April 17, 1861, by 103 to 46; ratified by popular
vote, May 23, 1861: for secession, 128,884; against,
32,134.

Arkansas, May 6, 1861, by 69 to 1.

North Carolina, May 21, 1861, voted secession but
refused by two-thirds vote to submit it to the people for
ratification.

Tennessee, May 7, 1861, entered a military league
with the Confederacy; popular vote, June 8, for secession, 104,019; against, 47,238.

Missouri Unionists stopped secession in the convention at Jefferson City, February 28, and at the second
session in St. Louis, March 9. The legislature condemned
secession on March 7. Under the protection of Confederate troops secessionist members of the legislature adopted
a resolution of secession at Neosho, October 31, 1861.
The Confederate Congress seated representatives.

Kentucky did not secede, and its government remained Unionist. In a part occupied by Confederate troops Kentuckians passed an act of secession and the Confederate Congress admitted representatives.

Maryland legislature voted against secession on April 27, 53 to 13. Delaware did not secede. Western Virginia held conventions at Wheeling, named a pro-Union governor on June 11, 1861, was admitted to the Union as West Virginia, June 30, 1863; its constitution provided for the gradual abolition of slavery.

First Confederate Congress

Forty-two delegates from South Carolina, Georgia, Alabama, Mississippi, Louisiana, and Florida met in convention at Montgomery, Alabama, February 4, 1861. Howell Cobb of Georgia was chosen to preside. On February 6, delegates from North Carolina arrived to plead in vain for conciliation. The first delegate from Texas came on February 13. The Congress adopted a provisional constitution of the Confederate States of America, February 8, 1861, and on the next day elected Jefferson Davis (Miss.), provisional President, and Alexander H. Stephens (Ga.), provisional Vice President. Davis was inducted into office at Montgomery, February 18, 1861.

The Congress adopted a flag consisting of a red field with a white stripe in the middle third and a blue jack with a circle of white stars going two-thirds of the way down the flag. The flag was unfurled in Montgomery, March 4, 1861. Later the more popular flag was the red field with blue diagonal cross bars that held thirteen white stars, designed by General Beauregard.

A permanent constitution was adopted on March 11, 1861. It provided that the President should be elected for a single term of six years and abolished the African slave trade. The Congress moved to Richmond, Virginia, July 20, 1861.

A tall, lean six-footer, with an unbending attitude and great sensitivity to criticism, was Jefferson Davis, President of the Confederate States. His experience was both military and political and he would have preferred command of an army to the Presidency. Born in Kentucky, June 3, 1808, he was fifty-three when the Civil War broke out. He was graduated from the Military Academy at West Point in 1828 and served on the Illinois and Wisconsin frontier, at Fort Winnebago and in the Black Hawk War, up to 1835. From 1835 to 1845 he had a plantation in Mississippi, and from that state he went to Congress as representative in 1843. In 1846 he led a regiment of Mississippi volunteers in the Mexican war and served with distinction under General Zachary Taylor, father of his first wife, who had died. He was appointed senator from Mississippi in 1847 and elected to that office in 1850. His views favored noninterference with slavery, and he saw no reason for excluding it from new states and territories; however, he voted for the Compromise of 1850.

After an unsuccessful attempt to be elected governor of Mississippi, Davis became Secretary of War in the cabinet of President Franklin Pierce, 1853–1857, and thus was thoroughly familiar with all phases of the military establishment of the United States. He returned to the Senate in 1857, advocated free trade as an aid to the Southern economy, and was generally looked upon as a spokesman for state rights. He did not, however, favor secession, and hoped until the last that a compromise might be effected. But when Mississippi joined in secession he resigned and on January 21, 1861, made a moving address when taking leave of the Senate. Once in office as President of the Confederate States (chosen by the congress in Montgomery, Alabama, February, 1861; elected October, 1861; inaugurated February 22, 1862, in Richmond) he became an uncompromising defender of the idea of Southern nationality and would enter into no negotiations that did not start with recognition of the Confederacy as a nation. He admitted privately that slavery was doomed. As a military man he considered himself the equal of the Confederate commanders, if not superior to some of them, and his relations with Generals Beauregard and Joseph E. Johnston were often unfriendly. Despite frequent disagreements with the Confederate Congress over policy, he was the principal force holding the Confederacy to its military objectives, to the point of exhaustion of the treasure of the Southern people, many of whom would have favored an earlier peace. His principal accomplishment was giving a fairly free hand to General Robert E. Lee, and their good relations were due in part to the remarkable tact with which Lee handled Jefferson Davis.

3

THE FALL OF FORT SUMTER, APRIL 14, 1861

Charleston, South Carolina, where Fort Sumter was located, possesses one of the finest harbors of the South. The city has Cooper River on the north and Ashley River on the south, and the harbor is bounded by islands that extend miles into the sea. To the south lies James Island, on which South Carolina in 1861 was building a battery called Fort Johnson, and Morris Island, which has a fishhook extending north to Cummings Point, on which was located an ironclad battery. Opposite Charleston at the mouth of Cooper River was Castle Pinckney, an old fortification with only a caretaker until the Confederates occupied it. Beyond toward the sea extend the larger Hog Island and Sullivan's Island. At the harbor tip of Sullivan's was Fort Moultrie, a sea battery with walls not over ten feet tall, based on works built during the American Revolution. On a shoal in the middle of the channel, about equally distant from Moultrie and Cummings Point, stood Fort Sumter, an isolated fortification of masonry and brick that rose sixty feet above the water line.

Forts Moultrie and Sumter had been neglected until the final months of Buchanan's administration, when the Secretary of War, John B. Floyd, obtained appropriations to complete work on the forts on the pretext that the nation might face war with England over the Mexican situation. Floyd was openly secessionist in his sympathies and was accused later of having diverted military supplies to Southern locations, but this charge was set aside by a Congressional inquiry. Fort Sumter had been reconstructed only partially and much work remained to be done. Several hundred laborers, chiefly from Maryland, were at work on the forts.

Fort Moultrie had hardly more than a token garrison, for it was down to two companies of United States Artillery and a band of eight men, totaling seventy-three, when Major Robert Anderson of the Regular Army assumed command on November 21, 1860. Among his officers were Captain Abner Doubleday, later major general of volunteers and designated, long after his death, as the originator of baseball, an extremely doubtful claim; also Lieutenant Jefferson Columbus Davis, no kin of the Confederate President, who became a brigadier general of Indiana volunteers and later major general commanding a corps in Sherman's march to the sea. Davis was extremely unpopular a few years later, after he shot down and killed a fellow general in a personal quarrel.

The Palmetto Flag of South Carolina was hoisted over the batteries of Charleston harbor on November 9, 1861. On December 20 the state convention passed an ordinance of secession, declaring South Carolina "a separate, sovereign, free and independent state."

Major Anderson kept the Federal government informed of events in the harbor. He sent word on November 23 that "Forts Sumter and Pinckney must be garrisoned immediately if the Government determines to keep command of this harbor." He argued that weakness invited disaster. To the adjutant general of the U.S. Army he wrote:

I need not say how anxious I am—indeed, determined, so far as honor will permit—to avoid collision with the citizens of South Carolina. Nothing, however, will be better calcu-

lated to prevent bloodshed than our being found in such an
attitude that it would be madness and folly to attack us.
There is not so much of feverish excitement as there was
last week, but that there is a settled determination to leave
the Union and to obtain possession of this work, is apparent to all.

Hostile preparations were visible everywhere; South
Carolina was building batteries and training recruits, and
its patrols were watching Moultrie. Despite their vigilance
Major Anderson on the evening of December 26 transferred his men and supplies by boats to Fort Sumter. A
guard left behind spiked the guns at Moultrie, burned the
carriages of guns facing Sumter, and cut down the flagstaff.

Major Anderson's shift to Sumter caused a sensation
in Charleston and an outburst of anger among secessionists. They realized that, although a Kentuckian, Anderson
was not going to favor them. Governor Pickens of South
Carolina sent messengers ordering Major Anderson to return to Fort Moultrie. The Major replied that he was a
Southern man, but he had been assigned to defend
Charleston harbor and intended to do so. He promptly
put his men to work erecting defenses in Fort Sumter.
Most of the guns were not in place. By hard work the
men raised two ten-inch columbiads to the top tier.
These could fire 28-pound projectiles, and a test showed
that they could reach Charleston, over three miles away.

On December 27, the day after Major Anderson had
transferred his forces from Moultrie to Sumter, South
Carolina seized Fort Moultrie and other posts of the
United States government.

The first overt act of the war took place in Charleston
harbor, January 8, 1861, when a merchant vessel, the
Star of the West, arrived with reinforcements for Fort
Sumter. To avoid sending a warship General Scott had
leased the steamship and put on board 200 soldiers and
ammunition. When the ship was within two miles of
Fort Sumter a battery on Morris Island fired one shot
at it, as also did Fort Moultrie. Then five rounds were fired
from Morris Island, and the ship was struck twice. The
ship hoisted the United States ensign, but getting no

signals from Sumter turned around and headed back to New York. Major Anderson sent a protest to Governor Pickens, who assumed responsibility and asserted the government was "imposing upon this state the condition of a conquered province."

Secretary of the Interior Jacob Thompson, a Mississippi man who stood accused of informing the South Carolinians of the ship's errand, now resigned. Senator Jefferson Davis called on President Buchanan and protested against the sending of the vessel, but the President, who belatedly had adopted a firmer attitude toward the South, gave him no satisfaction. Davis harangued the Senate, asserting the Constitution never contemplated using the U.S. Army against a state, for "a state exercising the sovereign function of secession is beyond the reach of the Federal government, unless we woo her with the voice of fraternity." Senator Davis wanted concessions from the Federal government because he hoped to avert secession, but when his own state, Mississippi, seceded and joined the Confederacy, Davis on January 21 resigned from the Senate and left for the South.

South Carolina took the position that Sumter belonged to the state and that the United States government should get out. The state and later the Confederate government at Montgomery, Alabama, wanted the fort evacuated peacefully and sent commissioners to Washington. After March 4 Abraham Lincoln was President. But although Secretary of State Seward misled Southern sympathizers by mentioning the possibility of evacuation without actually stating this might take place, President Lincoln took plenty of time to investigate and consider the alternatives. He had said that he was pledged to guard the property of the United States, and the forts, especially Sumter at Charleston and Pickens at Pensacola, were United States property. He didn't like what his general in chief, General Winfield Scott, told him—that Sumter and Pickens ought to be evacuated. Scott at first favored letting "the wayward sisters go in peace," but in the crisis his military ardor returned and he saw his duty to uphold the army.

Then the President, on March 15, wrote a note to the members of his cabinet: "Assuming it to be possible to now provision Fort Sumter, under all the circumstances is it wise to attempt it? Please give me your opinion in writing on this question." Like General Scott, Secretary Welles of the Navy was for evacuating Fort Sumter and Secretary of War Cameron called it "an inevitable necessity." Secretary Seward agreed. But Postmaster General Blair was angered that anyone should propose evacuation.

President Lincoln sent Captain Gustavus V. Fox, soon to become Assistant Secretary of the Navy, to Sumter to size up the situation. Fox reported that Sumter could be reinforced, and his report led Lincoln to believe Major Anderson could hold out until April, "without any great inconvenience."

Lincoln also sent his friend and former law partner, Ward H. Lamon, and Stephen A. Hurlbut informally to Charleston to sound out the officials on their determination to leave the Union. They returned convinced that compromise was impossible. Lamon appears to have told both Governor Pickens and Major Anderson that Sumter was to be evacuated, but he was giving his impression rather than precise information.

Despite the fact that the seceding states were appropriating United States property right and left, and the President had sworn to protect the property, Lincoln still adopted a conciliatory tone when dealing with the governor of South Carolina and the tense situation at Fort Sumter. The Confederate general Braxton Bragg, who had taken charge of government works at Pensacola, Florida, on March 18 ordered no supplies of any kind delivered to Fort Pickens there, or to armed vessels of the United States lying at anchor. In reply the Federal government equipped the sloops *Pawnee* and *Bhatan* and six transports with men and supplies and landed some of them at Fort Pickens. But the President adopted a milder tone toward South Carolina. He ordered a vessel with supplies for Fort Sumter to sail April 6 and then sent emissaries to Governor Pickens—Robert S. Chew of the State Department and Captain Talbot of the War Department— who read a message from Lincoln, who said an attempt would be made to supply Fort Sumter with provisions only, and that "if such attempt be not resisted, no effort to throw in men, arms or ammunition will be made, without further notice or in case of an attack upon the fort."

Before this word reached Charleston the Confederate government in Montgomery, Alabama, ordered Brigadier General Pierre G. T. Beauregard to stop all intercourse between Sumter and the city of Charleston, and to intercept Major Anderson's official letters and send them to Montgomery. Sumter had been getting fresh provisions from the city, and this was not interdicted. When Chew and Talbot brought President Lincoln's word on April 8, the governor and Beauregard referred the message to the Confederate government. The members of its cabinet recognized at once that they faced a hard decision. The effort to supply the fort meant that Washington was delaying action on evacuation. The alternative was to stop supplies, which meant the use of force. Secretary of State Toombs saw that the South was on the brink of war and reacted against it. He advised against force; it was murder, suicide. Said he: "It puts us in the wrong. It is fatal." This is an example of the varieties of attitudes that existed among the Confederates themselves. But President Jefferson Davis had now adopted the premise that the Confederate States had created a nation, and that as executive of that nation he had a duty that transcended sentiment. If necessary, he would endorse force. He sent an order to Charleston: Beauregard was to demand evacuation of the fort and "if this is refused, proceed in such manner as you may determine to reduce it."

President Davis' order had more behind it than appears. It was, in fact, the first military order to go out from the Confederate government, and it made clear to all that the executive would take charge of military affairs. Governor Pickens had initiated the crisis with his South Carolina militia, but the Montgomery office had quickly convinced him that the state had to yield warmaking to the common authority, just as the Thirteen Colonies had given the Continental Congress disposition of their troops under the Articles of Confederation. On February 26 Davis had talked military matters over with Louisiana's Creole warrior, Pierre G. T. Beauregard, and the next day named him the Confederacy's first brigadier general and sent him to take command over all military forces at Charleston.

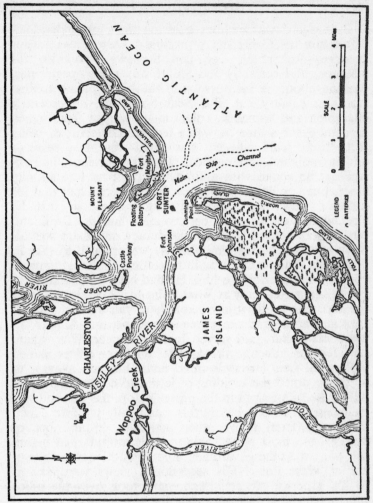

Fort Sumter in Charleston Harbor
April 12, 1861

Beauregard was without question the most individualistic figure the Confederacy produced. Others had greater prestige—Robert E. Lee and Stonewall Jackson, for instance, and certainly Jeb Stuart was more spectacular, dashing about on his horse with the black plume trailing from his cavalry hat. But Beauregard had an eccentric character and romantic coloration given by his French descent. At this time he was a few months short of being forty-three years old. He was slight—five feet seven— and he weighed 150 pounds. He was courteous, but unsmiling; he spoke with a French accent; he was socially aloof, but popular with women. He was confident that his military views were the only right ones, so that he clashed often with other commanders and the President, but he was needed by the Confederacy and there was always a command for him when he was minded to take it.

At this time, with a war in the offing, the most unusual conduct was ascribed to him. He had been graduated from the Military Academy at West Point in 1838, second from the top. His artillery instructor there was Robert Anderson, and after graduating Beauregard became Anderson's assistant. Beauregard served in the Mexican War, where he filled assignments with another engineer officer named Robert E. Lee. His agile mind made him an inventor of sorts; he urged the building of jetties to control the channel of the Mississippi in the passes before the war and was ridiculed for it long before this was finally put into effect. But aside from many other activities, in and out of politics, the most remarkable was his attitude just before the war, when the government appointed him superintendent at West Point. His secessionist views were known to his superior officers. Beauregard took over the office on January 23; the next day the government removed him, and he left on January 28. He explained to his superior, General Totten, that he had intended to keep his opinions to himself and give up his commission only in the event Louisiana went to war. T. Harry Williams, latest biographer of the general (*Beauregard: Napoleon in Gray*), remarks on the curious influence that "state rights legalism" had attained over the Southern mind, for Beauregard, ready to make war against the United States if his state did, not only berated the government for removing him but put in a bill for mileage to pay for his return trip from West Point to New Orleans. The government naturally refused to pay.

So here was Beauregard, in command of the guns trained on Fort Sumter, confronting his former artillery teacher, who could make Sumter's guns speak in return. Acting on Jefferson Davis' order, Beauregard sent his aides Colonel James R. Chesnut and Captain Stephen D. Lee, accompanied by Lieutenant A. R. Chisholm, on April 11 to present the ultimatum to Major Anderson. Beauregard would facilitate removal of the garrison, with arms and property, and send private property to any place desired. Anderson might even salute the flag, "which you have upheld so long and with so much fortitude." Major Anderson was greatly agitated, but regretted that his sense of honor and obligations to his government prevented his compliance. He said: "Gentlemen if you do not batter the fort to pieces about us, we shall be starved out in a few days."

The reply and the added comment were conveyed to Montgomery. Confederate Secretary of War Walker replied:

Do not desire needlessly to bombard Fort Sumter. If Major Anderson will state the time at which, as indicated by him, he will evacuate, and agree that in the meantime he will not use his guns against us, unless ours should be employed against Fort Sumter, you are thus authorized to avoid the effusion of blood. If this, or its equivalent, be refused, reduce the fort as your judgment decides to be most practicable.

Major Anderson replied at 3:15 A.M. that he would "if provided with the proper and necessary means of transportation, evacuate Fort Sumter by noon of the 15th," if he had not received "prior to that time, controlling instructions . . . or additional supplies." General Beauregard knew that supplies were on the way, so he had authorized his aides to give a negative reply. In the presence of Major Anderson and some of his officers Colonel Chesnut dictated the reply to Captain Lee and both signed it. The formality of their language discloses that they recognized the significance of the occasion. The note read:

FORT SUMTER, S. C., April 12, 3:20 A.M. SIR: By authority of Brigadier General Beauregard commanding the Provisional Forces of the Confederate States, we have the honor to notify you that he will open the fire of his batteries on Fort Sumter in one hour from this time. We have the honor to be, very respectfully, Your obedient servants, JAMES CHESNUT, JR., aide de camp. STEPHEN D. LEE, Captain C.S. Army, aide de camp.

Captain Lee wrote later that Major Anderson "was much affected." Pressing their hands cordially in farewell, he said: "If we never meet in this world again, God grant that we may meet in the next." The men picked up Roger A. Pryor, who had been waiting on the wharf because his state, Virginia, had not seceded, and rowed to Fort Johnson on James Island, where Captain George S. James was to fire the signal gun at 4:30 A.M.

The first shot came from a mortar and the gunners at the other batteries joined with alacrity. Soon the firing became general. Fort Sumter did not reply until 7:30 A.M. Firing continued during that day and the next night, and a great deal of damage was done to the inside of the fort, where very few guns were in working order. On the morning of April 13 the flagstaff was shot down. The Confederates, observing that the flag was missing, and that the barracks were on fire, sent a mission of three men, Captain Stephen D. Lee, William P. Miles, and Roger A. Pryor, to the fort. They had almost reached it when a new staff was raised with the Stars and Stripes floating from it. They turned back, but then saw a white flag go up and once more proceeded to Sumter.

The white flag had been raised by Major Anderson to learn what the men wanted, and when they told him that Beauregard wished to give him assistance in putting out the fire he thanked them but said he had no need of it. Learning that they came from Beauregard, he said Colonel Wigfall of Beauregard's staff, former senator from Texas, had come to the fort alone a short time before and asked Anderson to stop firing because "there has been enough bloodshed already." Wigfall had offered the original terms but Anderson had refused them. Pryor and his companions said Wigfall had come without authority from Beauregard. While they were discoursing with Anderson another emissary, Major D. R. Jones of Beauregard's staff, arrived and repeated the terms, and this time Major Anderson accepted them.

No lives were lost on either side during the bombardment. The terms called for evacuation by Major Anderson and his garrison, taking their possessions and such provisions as were left and embarking on a steamer furnished by Beauregard, which took them to ships of the United States fleet outside the harbor. Before leaving they raised the United States flag and gave it a formal salute, and then hauled it down. During the salute a gun burst, killing one man. Four years were to pass before that flag was raised again, on the anniversary of its surrender, April 14, by the hands of General Robert Anderson who, as major, had hauled it down.

4

THE ISSUES IN WASHINGTON AND RICHMOND IN 1861

First Call for Troops

Abraham Lincoln took office as President of the United States on March 4, 1861. The breach over the issue of secession had brought him the support of his principal political opponent of years, Stephen A. Douglas, who had been the candidate of the Democratic party of the North in the 1860 election. Douglas attended the inauguration, which took place in front of the Capitol, still in the process of building, with the dome incomplete. The oath of office was administered by the Chief Justice of the United States, Roger B. Taney, who had written the Dred Scott decision that Lincoln had denounced in his debates with Douglas.

Lincoln spoke calmly and without rancor. He repeated his declaration that he had no purpose to interfere with slavery in the states where it existed. He would execute the laws in all the states, since he considered the Union unbroken. He would hold, occupy, and possess property and places belonging to the government, and collect duties and imports, but he was quite willing to let some of this slide for the time being if hostility was so great that the resident officials could not function. He would not force strangers on them. He would continue the mails, unless repelled. All this was conciliatory.

But also he reminded the public that for a minority to secede rather than acquiesce meant the possibility of further splits among the seceders; a majority held in restraint by checks and balances, susceptible to changes of opinion, was the true sovereign, whereas "the central idea of secession is the essence of anarchy."

None of the earlier provocations—the seizure of arsenals and post offices—had led to forceful retaliation. But when Fort Sumter fell after a bombardment the government's attitude changed. On April 15 President Lincoln issued a call for 75,000 militia. He set the term of service at ninety days, a circumstance that was to make a great deal of trouble for the government. The term was based on an earlier act that limited the executive, so that troops could not serve longer than one month after the meeting of Congress. President Lincoln then called an emergency session of Congress for July 1.

In a few weeks the President saw the need of bringing the regular military service up to the full strength. On May 3 he called for 40,034, because he wished to increase the Regular Army by 22,714 and the Navy by the remainder.

On April 16, the day after President Lincoln called for his first defenders, the Confederate government voted conscription, affecting all white males eighteen to thirty-five years old, who were to serve for three years unless exempted. The provisions for exemption were quite liberal and favored the professions and men in essential business and industrial positions and officeholders.

To protect the national capital was the immediate concern of the authorities in Washington. The first troops to reach Washington were a Pennsylvania regiment; the second came from Massachusetts. Both changed trains in Baltimore, the first without incident; it was the second that was to make its mark on the history of the war.

Sixth Massachusetts in Baltimore

The Sixth Massachusetts Infantry Regiment, comprising eleven companies, reached Baltimore on the morning of April 19, 1861, over the Philadelphia, Wilmington & Baltimore Railroad, on the way to join the defense of Washington. At Baltimore they were transferred to the tracks of the Baltimore & Ohio Railroad. There was a great deal of sympathy for the South in Baltimore; Lincoln's call for volunteers was deeply resented and the citizens did not wish to have troops move through their streets. The colonel of the Massachusetts regiment had been warned to look out for trouble, and consequently the regiment was expected to mind its own business.

The first seven companies moved successfully from one railroad to the other, but the crowd increased and showed its hostility, as the four remaining companies were marched through the streets in double quick time. The troops were assailed by sticks and stones and at one point had to cross a partially burned bridge. Someone fired and killed a soldier and the soldiers retaliated. The officers hurried their men into the coaches and pulled the blinds, but the attacks continued. One soldier, firing from the train, killed a bystander who was a prominent Baltimorean. The attempt of the mayor to calm the rioters failed. The regiment had four killed and thirty-six wounded; Baltimore police reported nine killed and many wounded. A large public protest meeting was held in Baltimore, and the mayor as well as the governor of Maryland appealed to the Federal government to send no more troops through Baltimore. The state administration was trying to keep Maryland out of the Confederacy and wanted to remove all provocation for violence.

Privateers Versus the Blockade

President Jefferson Davis of the Confederate States on April 17, 1861, turned his attention to the commerce of the United States. In a proclamation asserting the United States was making war upon the South, he invited shipowners to help "resist aggression" by taking as prizes

49

the vessels engaged in the sea-borne trade of the North. He invited owners to apply for letters of marque and reprisal giving them the authority of the Confederate States to seize ships and cargoes. An owner must post a bond of $5,000 if he employed up to 150 hands and $10,000 if he employed more. The Confederate government would pay 20 per cent on the value of every vessel of war taken or destroyed, giving 8 per cent bonds of the Confederacy.

President Lincoln lost no time replying to this announcement. On April 19 he ordered a blockade of the ports in the states of South Carolina, Georgia, Alabama, Florida, Mississippi, Louisiana, and Texas. Ten days later he extended the blockade to ports of Virginia and North Carolina, these states having seceded in the interim. Hostile vessels attempting to leave or enter the blockaded ports would be duly warned on the first attempt; on the second the vessel would be captured and taken into port for possible seizure of ship and cargo, after court action. If anyone under the "pretended authority" of the Confederate States molested a vessel of the United States, he would be held amenable to the laws for prevention and punishment of piracy.

The Confederate Congress supported President Davis' proclamation by adopting on May 6 an act giving private armed vessels letters of marque and reprisal, with the right to roam the seas and capture ships of the United States and, in case of ships flying a neutral flag, to seize cargo owned by merchants of the United States. The act would permit Northern vessels then in Southern ports to leave within thirty days if privately owned and not ships of war. To crews that took part in an engagement in which armed ships of the United States were burned or destroyed the Confederate government would pay a bounty of $20 per person, and it would give prize money of $25 for each prisoner brought in.

One of the first vessels to obtain letters of marque from the Confederate government was the schooner *Savannah*, T. Harrison Baker, owner. In a matter of weeks it was captured by the blockading ships off Charleston and its crew was taken to New York. This led to a direct protest by Davis to President Lincoln. Davis declared he had heard that members of the crew were put in irons and jailed. The Confederacy had treated its prisoners with "the greatest humanity and leniency," but if the United States persisted in this treatment the Confederacy would retaliate in kind. It had given its prisoners the same rations as were received by its army, but now had put prisoners in strict confinement.

Seward Gives Advice to Lincoln

When President Lincoln on March 15 asked the members of his cabinet to write him whether or not it would be wise to attempt to provision Fort Sumter, he apparently gave one member the impression that he welcomed guidance in the conduct of his office. This was Secretary of State William H. Seward, who went into the cabinet with a high opinion of his own ability, and thought less of the Executive's. Two weeks after Lincoln had consulted the cabinet on Sumter, Secretary Seward decided to tell Lincoln how the affairs of the country ought to be conducted, and what attitude the Administration should take toward foreign nations. Although both Seward's letter and Lincoln's reply throw an interesting light on the thinking and personality of the two policy-making leaders, the correspondence did not become public until John G. Nicolay and John Hay published their *Complete Works of Abraham Lincoln* in 1894, twenty-two years after Seward's death.

Seward told Lincoln that as the administration had neither a foreign nor a domestic program, it was necessary to start one without delay, and he proposed that applicants for office be dismissed and local appointments made, leaving foreign or general ones for later action. Policy at home should "change the question before the public from one upon slavery or about slavery for a question upon union or disunion, in other words, from what would be regarded as a party question, to one of patriotism or union." The occupation or evacuation of Fort Sumter was regarded as a slavery or party question, so he would "terminate it as a safe means for changing the issue," but defend and reinforce all ports in the Gulf, put the island of Key West under martial law, and recall the Navy from foreign stations to be prepared for a blockade. "I would maintain every fort and possession in the South," said Seward.

Turning to foreign affairs, Secretary Seward adopted a peremptory tone. "I would demand explanations from Spain and France, categorically, at once," he wrote.

I would seek explanations from Great Britain and Russia and send agents into Canada, Mexico, and Central America to rouse a vigorous continental spirit of independence on this continent against European intervention. And if satisfactory explanations are not received from Spain and France, would convene Congress and declare war against them. But whatever policy we adopt, there must be an energetic prosecution of it. For this purpose it must be somebody's business to pursue and direct it incessantly. Either the President must do it himself, and be all the while acting in it, or devolve it on some member of his cabinet. Once adopted, debates on it must end, and all agree and abide. It is not in my special province; but I neither seek to evade nor assume responsibility.

On the day that Lincoln received Seward's letter, April 1, 1861, he wrote a calm and dignified reply. He said he thought his inaugural address had made clear that he meant to hold the government's property in the South, and that this had Seward's approval. He had begun the domestic policy now urged by Seward, except that he did not propose to abandon Fort Sumter. He thought the administration had been preparing instructions to its ministers abroad "all in perfect harmony." As to the energetic prosecution of whatever policy was adopted, Lincoln felt he must pursue it himself. "I apprehend there is no danger of its being changed without a good reason, or continuing to be a subject of unnecessary debate; still, upon points arising in its progress I wish, and suppose I am entitled to have, the advice of all the cabinet."

As the year went on Seward began to appreciate that Lincoln was the real maker of policy, however much he might consult others. Seward became a loyal supporter of the President's aims.

Queen Victoria's Neutrality

Under the title of the Queen's Proclamation of Neutrality the British government on May 13, 1861, expressed its official attitude toward the war in America. The proclamation took note of the hostilities and announced "a strict and impartial neutrality" in the contest between the contending parties. This meant that Britain saw the Confederate states as belligerents, although it did not recognize the Confederacy as a nation. In placing both the United States and the Confederacy on an equal footing, instead of treating the Southerners as rebels to a constituted authority, the British incurred the displeasure of the North, which had hoped that Britain's antislavery sentiments would cause it to favor the United States. A practical result of the proclamation would be that vessels accepting letters of marque from the Confederate government would be treated as privateers, instead of as pirates, and thus circumvented President Lincoln's proclamation of April 19.

Southern leaders were gratified when they were accepted as belligerents by the British, which meant that other European nations would grant them the same status. They were encouraged to hope for more when Earl John Russell, foreign minister, talked informally with their commissioners in London, although Russell would not receive the men officially. Earl Russell was in favor of the Southern states' striking out for themselves, but he could not condone slavery; he spoke in public of "that cursed institution" and blamed it for the war. Workingmen were bitter when mills had to close down for want of cotton, but they did not approve the Southern tolerance of slavery. The Britons who were in a fair way to make a profit on the war were builders of ships and marine machinery, for within the year the Confederacy was placing large orders for both at Liverpool and Glasgow. But the vigilance of the American minister, Charles Francis Adams, who warned the British government of the danger of alienating the United States by making warships for the South, caused the cabinet to watch its neutrality and place obstacles in the way of the delivery of ships carrying arms.

The Times of London was the great conservative organ and its ridicule of President Lincoln and antagonism to the North caused much anger in the United States, but it did print what its correspondent, William H. Russell, wrote even when it was prejudicial to the South. Russell was revolted when he saw a slave sold on the auction block in Montgomery, Alabama, near the building in which the Confederate Congress was then meeting. He wrote in his correspondence:

I tried in vain to make myself familiar with the fact that I could, for the sum of $975, become as absolutely the owner of that mass of blood, bones, sinew, flesh and brains as of the horse which stood by my side. . . . Here it grated on my ear to listen to the familiar tones of the English tongue as the medium by which the transfer was effected, and it was painful to see decent-looking men in European garb engaged in the work before me.

In early September, 1862, when the Federals had just suffered new reverses, Lord Palmerston, prime minister, asked Lord Russell whether the time had come for England and France to offer mediation and "recommend an arrangement upon the basis of separation." Lord Russell was for this immediately, wanted to get France and then Russia and the other powers to join, and saw the move as leading to recognition of Southern independence. But Palmerston was cautious; he knew that "a great conflict" was going on to the northwest of Washington, and it might be well to "wait and see"; if the Federals were defeated the time for mediation might be nearer.

It was fortunate that Palmerston delayed, for even while he and Russell were exchanging letters McClellan was fighting at Antietam and the North regained prestige. Within a few weeks the cabinet was embarrassed by rather free remarks by William E. Gladstone, chancellor of the exchequer, who said in a Newcastle speech that there was no doubt Jefferson Davis and the South had made an army and were making a navy, "and they have made what is more than either, they have made a nation." This led Lord Russell to admonish him that he went too far when he said Jefferson Davis had made a nation: "Recognition would seem to follow, and for that step

I think the cabinet is not prepared." Emperor Napoleon III of France was eager for intervention. Russia expressed friendship for the North, but advised the Federals to set their house in order.

The United States government was already provoked by the interference of France in Mexico, which grew out of a dispute over foreign loans. Mexico, which was torn by factional strife, had suspended payment on foreign loans. Great Britain, France, and Spain decided to enforce payment. In order to avert such action the United States proposed to finance Mexico's indebtedness, taking as security a lien on public lands and mineral rights in Lower California, Chihuahua, Sonora, and Sinaloa, with absolute rights to the lands if the debt were not reimbursed in six years. This fell through and in December, 1861, Britain, France, and Spain asked the United States to join in an action against Mexico to collect their debts. This the United States turned down, and when, early in 1862, the State Department learned that the powers might make Mexico a monarchy and place a foreign prince on the throne, Secretary Seward served notice that no such government could be permanent in a land dedicated to democratic principles and that American sympathy and interests would be with the republican system of government in Mexico.

Despite this France marched into Mexico in July, 1862, and French troops supported the Austrian Archduke Maximilian on the shaky throne of the new Mexican monarchy. The intensification of the revolution and the Mexican hatred of monarchy became clear to all while the United States carried its civil war to a close. In February, 1866, Secretary Seward was able to demand that France immediately withdraw its troops from Mexico and, like the United States, respect the Mexicans' "self-established sovereignty and independence."

Last Warnings by Stephen A. Douglas

On June 3, 1861, Stephen A. Douglas, who had defeated Lincoln for the Senate nomination and had been defeated by Lincoln for the Presidency, died in Chicago, forty-eight years old. A wave of intense sorrow swept the country, for in the nation's crisis Douglas had backed Lincoln in the fight to preserve the Union. The Lincoln-Douglas debates in 1858 had shown the country the weakness of Douglas' proposal to let the new territories of Kansas and Nebraska determine whether they should be free-soil or slave. He had called the device "popular sovereignty," but when the sympathizers with slavery voted the Lecompton constitution for Kansas, he saw that democracy was being misused and turned against them. In the Presidential campaign he led the Northern Democrats on an antislavery platform. When the bitter controversy threatened disruption of the Union, he came forward wholeheartedly for the unbroken United States. In putting himself against disunion he stood with Lincoln. On his return to Illinois from Washington he made several public addresses in support of the government. When he reached Chicago, May 1, a vast crowd greeted him in the Wigwam, the wooden hall on Lake Street and the river, where Lincoln had been nominated in 1860. Here he made his last public speech, stirring the crowd with these ringing lines: "Every man must be for the United States or against it. There can be no neutrals in this war; only patriots or traitors." As he lay dying he composed a message to his sons, away at college: "Tell them to obey the laws and support the Constitution of the United States." This message was cut in stone over his tomb, which stands today in Douglas Park in Chicago. Douglas was widely mourned, and it was believed that had he lived, he would have played an important part in keeping public morale high during the war.

Congress Votes More Men and Money

President Lincoln, in his first message to Congress, July 4, 1861, told why the nation had gone to war. He took up the subject of the discontented minority, which had forced the issue—immediate dissolution or blood. "It presents to the whole family of man the question whether a constitutional republic or democracy, a government of the people by the same people, can or can not maintain its territorial integrity against its own domestic foes. It presents the question whether discontented individuals,

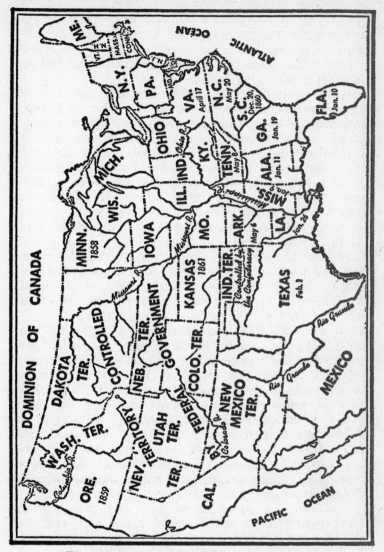

The Alignment of the States in 1861 with
dates of Secession from the Union

too few in numbers to control the Administration according to the organic law in any case, can always . . . break up their government and thus practically put an end to free government upon the earth."

The contention of the Southern states that a state could lawfully and peacefully withdraw from the Union, Lincoln called a sophism. He pointed out that the original Thirteen Colonies had been designated states first in the Declaration of Independence, when they declared not for independence of one another but for mutual action. Two years later they designated the union as perpetual. They were never states outside of the Union; the Union created them as states and "the Union, and not themselves separately, procured their independence and their liberty by conquest or purchase."

President Lincoln asked Congress to help make the war short and decisive by giving the government control of "at least 400,000 men and $400,000,000"; he estimated the number of men to be one-tenth of those available within the age limits. Congress did better; it voted authority for calling 500,000 volunteers and $500,000,000 on July 22, the day after the Battle of Bull Run put fear for the safety of the capital and of the nation in their hearts, and demonstrated that no puny effort would restore peace. Congress also authorized not over $250,000,000 for a national bond issue of twenty years at 7 per cent, or three-year $50 notes at 7.3 per cent. In August it adopted new taxes to raise $20,000,000, and added new tariffs; it voted a Confiscation Act and legalized the emergency acts of the President. One of the latter was the suspension of *habeas corpus,* by which persons thought "dangerous to the public safety" could be arrested without the ordinary processes of law. This placed great power into the hands of the executive, and some of those who opposed the war argued that it was being abused, but President Lincoln explained that it had been used "very sparingly."

President Jefferson Davis announced in his message to the first session of the Confederate Congress at Richmond, July 20, 1861, that the "enormous preparations in men and money" of the United States government was "an avowal" that the United States was "engaged in a conflict with a great and powerful nation," and that "the ancient Union has been dissolved." He declared it had recognized the separate existence of the Confederate States by its embargo and blockade on commerce by sea and land and had "repudiated the foolish conceit that the inhabitants of the Confederacy are still citizens of the United States, by waging an indiscriminate war upon them all with savage ferocity unknown in modern civilization."

Colonel Ellsworth of the Zouaves

When Virginia on May 23, 1861, voted to ratify its ordinance of secession from the Union, troops that had been stationed in Washington were ordered to Alexandria, Virginia, where demonstrations in favor of secession had given offense to the authorities in Washington. Most conspicuous among the soldiers who went there was a regiment of Fire Zouaves of New York, which had been raised among New York firemen by Colonel Elmer E. Ellsworth, a young man of twenty-four who had acquired national fame in exhibiting the popular Zouaves in military drill.

Ellsworth was a native of Saratoga County, New York, who had become a friend of Abraham Lincoln in Springfield, Illinois, accompanied the Lincolns to Washington, and was known and liked by John Hay, Lincoln's secretary, and other public men. Originally he had organized the U.S. Zouave Cadets, a Chicago organization that excelled in military evolutions so intricate that the complete drill took four and a half hours and comprised more than 500 movements and figures. The Cadets had adopted the picturesque Zouave costume that was worn by some troops in Europe and had been widely copied. As designed for Ellsworth's men it consisted of scarlet headgear and blouse, short blue jacket with gold trim, and three-quarter-length baggy red trousers.

By the time Lincoln was elected, Ellsworth had given up his Cadets; but when the President issued his first call for volunteers Ellsworth went to New York and raised a regiment of 1,100 firemen and called them the Fire Zouaves. The extreme costume that had been so picturesque on tour was now modified, gray jackets and trousers being substituted for those of blue and red. Ellsworth's recruiting in New York was no modest matter; it became a social event and when the Fire Zouaves marched out to take a steamship for Washington, New York staged a great farewell affair for the boys. At a formal ceremony silk flags were presented by Mrs. John Jacob Astor, Jr., and by the actress Laura Keene. In Washington shelter was so scarce that the Zouaves had to be lodged in the House of Representatives of the Capitol. Ellsworth was a welcome visitor at the White House, and his men were extremely popular with the ladies.

The Confederates had adopted a flag at Montgomery, Alabama, and at least one appeared on a rooftop of Alexandria, where it could be seen from Washington. On May 24 troops were ordered to move into Alexandria and police it. Among those sent were Ellsworth and his Fire Zouaves, who thus became a part of the "invasion" of Virginia.

Colonel Ellsworth on his part indulged in a warlike gesture that probably was a greater handicap to the Union than to the Virginians. He sent some of his men to tear up the tracks of the railroad to Richmond. Passing through the heart of Alexandria with his staff and several newspaper correspondents, he saw a Confederate flag flying above the three-story Marshall House. Ellsworth and several of his men entered the hotel and he and his aide, Lieutenant H. J. Winser, climbed to the roof, where Ellsworth hauled down the flag. As he was descending a man on the second floor gave him a blast from a shotgun at close range. As Ellsworth collapsed, fatally hit, Corporal Brownell shot the assassin and then plunged his bayonet into him. The man was James W. Jackson, proprietor of the hotel.

The grief and anger displayed by the Zouaves at Ellsworth's death was violent and some of the men had to be deterred from setting fire to the town. Lincoln could not restrain his tears when he heard the news and was said to have exclaimed: "My boy! My boy! was it necessary this sacrifice should be made?" He ordered a White House funeral, and as the body lay in the East Room generals and diplomats passed the bier.

The tears and lamentations over the death of Ellsworth came to a climax at his funeral. The public exhibition happened, of course, in Victorian times, when it was fashionable to display deep emotion on the slightest provocation. Women wept for both sorrow and joy, and if they were supposed to be shocked they fainted. But even men wept and at Ellsworth's funeral tears were, to use a later and irreverent phrase, in full supply. An account of what took place at Ellsworth's funeral is preserved in a letter written by Clara Barton, which was found by Dr. William E. Barton, the historian, when he came to write her biography. She described the double lines of spectators that filled the streets, the companies and regiments of "sturdy soldiers" who marched with arms reversed, drums muffled, banners furled and draped, in a slow procession. Four white horses drew the coffin of "the gallant dead"; his pall was the country's flag; six bearers walked beside the hearse and then came a small band of Zouaves from his regiment—only a few could be spared, for there was much work to be done in Alexandria. We are told that they were entirely weaponless, walking with heads bowed in grief, eyes fixed on the coffin, and "the great tears rolling down their swarthy cheeks"; then the riderless horse and the bloodstained Confederate flag that Ellsworth had taken down, followed by the official train led by President Lincoln and his cabinet. First losses are always bitter; the time was to come, very soon, when thousands were to die in an afternoon, and be shoveled under without record of their identities, without a public show.

Money to Pay for the War

The American people did not pay a tax on income to the Federal government in Lincoln's day. Every man's income was his own affair and never announced in public. Business was transacted with specie currency. The mounting expense of the military measures cleaned out the Treasury. On the last business day of 1861 the New York banks had used up their specie and had to suspend payment in coin. The war was costing $2,000,000 a day and the government had to find a way of paying it.

With great reluctance Secretary Chase of the Treasury

agreed that it had become necessary to make U.S. Treasury notes legal tender. Congress voted the act and President Lincoln approved it on February 25, 1862. It provided for a bond issue of $500,000,000 at 5.20 per cent, the interest to be paid in coin, which was to be obtained from currency paid as duty on imports. President Lincoln, in his annual message transmitted to Congress at the opening of the Second Session of the Thirty-seventh Congress, December 1, 1862, said:

The suspension of specie payments by the banks . . . made large issues of United States notes unavoidable. In no other way could the payment of troops and the satisfactions of the other just demands be so economically or so well provided for. The judicious legislation of Congress, securing the receivability of these notes for loans and internal duties and making them a legal tender for other debts has made this an universal currency, and has satisfied, partially at least . . . the long felt want of an uniform circulating medium, saving thereby to the people immense sums in discounts and exchanges. A return to specie payments, however, at the earliest period compatible with due regard to all interests concerned, should ever be kept in view.

President Lincoln's Cabinet

The first change in Lincoln's cabinet took place January 11, 1862, when Simon Cameron resigned as Secretary of War and Edwin M. Stanton took his place. Caleb B. Smith, Secretary of the Interior, resigned to become judge of the District Court of Indiana and was succeeded January 8, 1863, by John P. Usher of Indiana. Salmon P. Chase, Secretary of the Treasury, who had ambitions to become President, resigned June 30, 1864, because of a disagreement with President Lincoln over a political appointment for New York City and was succeeded by William P. Fessenden, senator from Maine. On September 23, 1864, the President asked for the resignation of Montgomery Blair as Postmaster General; Mr. Blair had brought much support to the Lincoln Administration, but in recent months had made speeches in which he took a stand on slavery that was out of keeping with the President's views on emancipation, and embarrassing because considered a reflection of the President's thinking. He was succeeded by William Dennison, former governor of Ohio, who had presided over the National Union convention that renominated Lincoln. Attorney General Edward Bates, of Missouri, resigned as of December 1, 1864, in order to be relieved of the burdens of office, which he had accepted at the urgent request of the President; he was considered a strong supporter of the Administration. He was succeeded by James Speed, of Kentucky.

5

ROBERT E. LEE AND THE OFFER OF THE UNITED STATES COMMAND

When the Southern states were adopting ordinances of secession and the Confederate States of America were preparing a system of defense, two incidents happened that were to have a tremendous influence on the development of the war. They were the decisions by Robert E. Lee and Thomas J. Jackson to fight for Virginia. The great military ability of these two commanders was accentuated when compared with that of their opponents, but even without this advantage they rank high among the men who achieved military distinction in American history.

Of the two, Robert E. Lee was by far the most remarkable personality because he exhibited at their best the traits of a Virginia gentleman, and also because he represented the loyalty of a family to the political unit—Virginia—under which it had lived for 160 years. The decision of Lee, a man who abhorred slavery and saw no profit in secession, to fight for his state against "invasion," can be understood properly only when it is seen that coercion of his state was to him like coercion of his family and thus had to be opposed. This decision came from the heart, but as he followed where he felt his duties led, he echoed in time Jefferson Davis' insistence that the Confederate States were a new nation, and should be recognized as such by foreign states and by what to him was another nation—the United States of America.

Robert E. Lee was born in 1807 and was fifty-four when the Civil War broke out. He was born in Stratford Hall, in Westmoreland County, Virginia, now more re-nowned for his few years of childhood there than for the birth and presence of other distinguished Lees who lived there a large part of their lives. His father, Henry Lee, was Light-Horse Harry of the American Revolution, intimate friend of George Washington and governor of Virginia; he also had been a member of the Continental Congress and had voted to approve the Constitution of the United States. The elder's bad in-vestments and hard luck had reduced his family to straitened circumstances, and Robert Edward Lee grew up amid much family tradition and little else. His mother was a Carter and hence related to many other first families of Virginia. Lee entered the United States Military Academy at West Point, was graduated in 1829 and be-came a lieutenant of engineers. In 1831 he was married to Mary Anne Randolph Custis, great-granddaughter of Martha Washington, at the Custis mansion at Arlington, across the Potomac River from Washington, D.C., which in time became the home of his family. From 1829 to 1846 Lee was assigned to engineering projects, in-cluding supervising improvements in the channel of the Mississippi River and work at Fort Hamilton and Fort Lafayette, located at the Narrows of New York harbor. During this tenure Lee and his growing family lived in-termittently on government grounds near Fort Hamilton and at Arlington. Among the men with whom Lee was in contact at Fort Hamilton were John Sedgwick and Henry J. Hunt who were to fight him later.

When the Mexican War began Captain Lee was asso-ciated first with Brigadier General John E. Wool and after January 16, 1847, with Lieutenant General Winfield Scott. With him in the Corps of Engineers and the topographical engineers were Second Lieutenant George B. McClellan, then twenty, P. G. T. Beauregard, Joseph E. Johnston, and George Gordon Meade. At this time General Scott gained great respect for the ability and character of Lee.

After the Mexican War, Lee was the engineer in charge

of the erection of Fort Carroll at Baltimore. On September 1, 1852, as Colonel Lee by brevet, he became superintendent of the Military Academy at West Point. During his tenure there the cadets included his son Custis, John Pegram, W. D. Pender, J. E. B. Stuart, and C. O. Howard. One of his tasks was to rule against a reconsideration of the case of James A. McNeill Whistler, who was dismissed because of low grades and no indications of improvement. One of Whistler's lapses was his reply when asked to describe silicon: "Silicon is a gas." As Whistler put it years later: "If silicon had been a gas, I would have become a major general." Lee's work at West Point ended in March, 1855. Two regiments of cavalry had been authorized and Jefferson Davis, Secretary of War in Pierce's cabinet, made Albert Sidney Johnston colonel and Robert E. Lee lieutenant colonel of the Second United States Cavalry.

In this rank Lee served in Indian country and in Texas. On October 17, 1859, when he was in the East, he was ordered to take command with the brevet rank of colonel of troops ordered to Harpers Ferry to repel what seemed an armed insurrection there. Lieutenant J. E. B. Stuart obtained permission to go with him. A detachment of Marines from the Washington Navy Yard was already on the way; Colonel Lee ordered them to stop at Sandy Hook, near Harpers Ferry, and await him there. He then commanded the operations against the engine house in which John Brown had barricaded himself with his band, and captured them. In February, 1860, he was made temporary commander of the Department of Texas at San Antonio, a post he held for a year and two months. He was ordered back to Washington by April 1, 1861.

It now becomes pertinent to determine why this officer, who had loyally served the United States government and held a commission in its army for thirty-two years, became the principal general of the Confederacy, responsible for the major part of its military successes. He is quoted in authenticated records as viewing the drift to hostilities as a departure from reasonable behavior and as hoping an adjustment of grievances could be made. Colonel Lee had no partiality for extremists of the North or of the South. He did not favor secession and disunion and hoped some way might be found of saving the country. However, he endorsed President Buchanan's proposal, favorable to the South, that the Constitution be amended to recognize the right of property in slavery where it existed and might exist thereafter, the duty of protecting this right in territories and until the territories were admitted as states, with or without slavery, as their constitutions might prescribe, as well as enforcement of the Fugitive Slave Law. These were propositions that all Northern men who hated slavery opposed. Lee was definitely against the plea of some Southern hotheads to renew the slave trade, and said he would free his slaves if that would help to save the Union. His wife had inherited sixty-three slaves from her father, George Washington Parke Custis, who had made arrangements in his will to have them manumitted. Colonel Lee had felt responsibility for them, and not having work for all of them at Arlington, had hired some of them out. Two had run away to Philadelphia and had been brought back; this led to sharp criticism of Lee as a slaveholder in Northern newspapers.

Lee's stand against secession and nullification was quite clear even three months before the war; he considered the Constitution intended for a perpetual union, meant to establish a government, and not a compact, but thought it could be dissolved only by a revolution or the consent of all the people meeting in convention. He spoke frequently of his loyalty to the state of Virginia, and in Texas said that if the Union were dissolved and the government disrupted, he would return to his native state and share the miseries of his people, and "save in defense will draw my sword on none." On several occasions he spoke of being unable to fight his state. He had no suggestions to make on how the grievances of the South were to be adjusted and how the Union was to be saved from disruption; here his recourse was to his faith in God and his hope "that a kind Providence has not yet turned the current of His blessings from us."

Lee returned to his family at Arlington, March 1. Douglas Southall Freeman, who has carefully traced the course of Lee during these crowded weeks, writes at length of the intense distress suffered by Lee in Texas and en route home because of the political crisis. He was torn by anxiety for the future of his family, his state, and his country. He had made no statement about choosing sides and ostensibly was hoping for the controversy to find a settlement. His first act in Washington was to call on General-in-Chief Scott. What was said at that interview was not reported by either of the principals.

On March 16 Colonel E. V. Sumner of the First U.S. Cavalry was named brigadier general, and Colonel Lee was made a full colonel and given command of the First. Lee received the commission, signed by Abraham Lincoln as President, March 28, and accepted it.

On April 12 Fort Sumter was attacked and on April 14 it surrendered. On April 15 President Lincoln called for 75,000 troops. On April 17 Lee received a note from his cousin, John Lee, asking him to call the following morning at the house of Francis Preston Blair, and a letter from General Scott, asking him to call at his office April 18. It is stated in *Abraham Lincoln, a History,* by Nicolay and Hay, that President Lincoln had asked Blair to sound out Lee on his attitude toward the command of the United States Army. Blair, who was the father of the Postmaster General, Montgomery Blair, wrote an account of his interview which is quoted by James Ford Rhodes in his *History of the United States.* Blair reported that he had been authorized to talk with Lee about this by Secretary of War Cameron and also had talked with President Lincoln on two or three different occasions to this end. "The President and Secretary Cameron expressed themselves as anxious to give the command of our army to Robert E. Lee. I considered myself as authorized to inform Lee of that fact." Blair said he told Lee "what President Lincoln wanted him to do," and that Lee said he was devoted to the Union and would do everything in his power to save it but could not draw his sword against his native state. Also he could not consent to supersede his old commander, General Scott, and would not decide until he could see him.

Freeman, weighing this and other less direct reports, doubted that there had been any hesitation on the part of Lee. He found that only once had Lee been quoted directly on this incident, and that was to Reverdy Johnson in 1868, quoted by Johnson in *Robert E. Lee, Jr.* This statement was explicit; Lee said: "I never intimated to anyone that I desired the command of the United States Army; nor did I ever have a conversation with but one gentleman, Mr. Francis Preston Blair, on the subject, which was at his invitation, and, as I understood, at the instance of President Lincoln. After listening to his remarks, I declined the offer he made me, to take command of the army that was to be brought into the field; stating, as candidly and as courteously as I could, that, though opposed to secession, and deprecating war, I could take no part in an invasion of the Southern States." Freeman comments: "This is first-hand evidence and the only first-hand evidence of what occurred."

Lee then went to see General Scott and presumably told him what he had told Blair. Scott is supposed to have told him he was making the greatest mistake of his life and suggested that if he intended to resign from the army, he should do so at once.

On April 19 Lee learned that Virginia had passed an ordinance of secession. He is quoted as having said, while paying a bill in a drugstore: "I must say that I am one of those dull creatures that cannot see the good of secession." The remark was written down by the druggist to be recorded in John S. Mosby's *Memoirs,* a bit roundabout, but it has an authentic ring. On April 20 Lee sent the following to Secretary of War Cameron: "I have the honor to tender the resignation of my commission as Colonel of the 1st Regt. of Cavalry." He then wrote a letter of friendship and regret to General Scott, in which he repeated his former statement: "Save in defense of my native State, I never desire again to draw my sword."

Governor Letcher of Virginia invited Lee to come to Richmond, and he went, arriving there April 22. The governor tendered Lee the command of the military and naval forces of Virginia with the rank of major general, an office created by the state convention two days before. Lee accepted and on April 23 appeared before the convention in the state capitol and replied briefly to the welcome of its president. He was fifty-four years old and stood on the threshold of military fame.

6

THE FIRST BATTLE OF
BULL RUN, OR MANASSAS

Johnston Eludes Patterson

Arlington House, with its portico of eight white Doric columns on a hill above the Potomac River, was a conspicuous landmark that could be seen from Washington. The mansion of the George Washington Custis plantation, it had been the home, until late in April, 1861, of Colonel Robert E. Lee of the United States Cavalry and his family.

On May 7 soldiers occupied Arlington Heights and the Custis-Lee plantation. They were members of the Virginia state militia and they acknowledged no allegiance to the United States government. On that day Virginia became a member of the Confederate States of America, and its troops became part of the military forces of the Confederacy. On May 24 the Federal government ordered its army into Virginia, to clear out troops at Arlington and Alexandria that did not belong to the United States. Major Irvin McDowell had been made a brigadier general on May 14 and on May 27 was given command of the Department of Northeastern Virginia. He marched with his staff to Arlington, and the house of Robert E. Lee became a military headquarters of the United States Army.

General McDowell was a native of Ohio, forty-three years old, who was graduated from West Point Military Academy in 1838 and had served with distinction on the staff of General Winfield Scott in the Mexican War. General Scott asked McDowell to draw up a plan of action

against the Confederate position at Bull Run, and Mc-
Dowell estimated he would need 30,000 men and a
reserve of 10,000. He thought the Confederates would
concentrate about 35,000 men under General Beauregard,
and said: "If General J. E. Johnston's force is kept engaged by Major General Patterson, and Major General
Butler occupies the force now in his vicinity, I think
they will not be able to bring up more than 10,000 men,
so we may calculate upon having to do with about
35,000 men." General Scott commented: "If Johnston
joins Beauregard, he shall have Patterson at his heels."

The Confederate base was around Manassas, Virginia, and for this reason their reports speak of the
Battle of Manassas, instead of Bull Run. Manassas was a
small railroad station at the junction of the Orange &
Alexandria Railroad and the Manassas Gap Railroad,
about twenty-five miles southwest of Washington. It had
a one-story warehouse and several cottages in a farming
country. The Orange Railroad led from Alexandria via
Gordonsville to Richmond; the Manassas Gap Railroad
led to Winchester and the valley of the Shenandoah. Both
provided easy access to the interior of Virginia, a condition known and valued by the military authorities of both
North and South.

The battlefield of Bull Run pivots around the inter-
section of Warrenton Turnpike and the Sudley Road. Bull
Run is a meandering stream flowing southeast at the east
of the field; it has fords and is crossed by three major
roads, one at Blackburn Ford, one the Warrenton Turnpike over the Stone Bridge, and one leading to New
Market, near Manassas Junction. A smaller run, Young's
Branch, winds around the base of the hill on which
stood the Henry and Robinson houses. It did not impede
the troops nor prove valuable for defensive action.

The Confederates expected the growing forces of the
Union to use these routes and as early as May 6, 1861,
General Robert E. Lee ordered troops sent to Manassas
to impede such a possibility. Only a few hundred recruits from Alexandria were immediately available, but
the Confederates continued to send men and within a
few weeks the area became a sprawling camp. Brigadier
General Pierre G. T. Beauregard arrived on June 1 to as-

sume supreme command and by June 25 had received so many reinforcements that he was able to organize six brigades and locate units at strategic points. In anticipation of a mass attack by the Union army from Washington, which had been agitated for some time there, Beauregard began entrenchments along Bull Run from Union Mills at the south of his line extending north to the Stone Bridge, over which passed the Warrenton Turnpike to Washington. To give the artillery clear command over the approaches he had caused trees to be felled.

McDowell's forces marched out of the camps around Alexandria with three days' rations, July 16, and on July 18 congregated at Centreville, twenty-seven miles from Washington and about seven miles northeast of Manassas Junction. That morning McDowell instructed Brigadier General Daniel Tyler of the First Division to feel out the front without bringing on a general engagement. He was to "keep up the impression that we are moving on Manassas." Tyler sent Colonel Israel R. Richardson with two infantry regiments of the Fourth Brigade, a squadron of cavalry, and two guns toward Blackburn's Ford. Here was fired the first gun against the Confederates. Richardson penetrated far enough to bring a powerful response from Confederate brigades under Brigadier General M. L. Bonham and Brigadier General James Longstreet, with some help from Colonel Jubal A. Early. They drove back the Federals. Although the Federals had only nineteen dead out of eighty-three casualties, the shock to the raw troops was such that men of the Fourth Pennsylvania Infantry and Varian's New York Battery, whose three-month enlistments were presumably up, clamored for their discharge.

While General McDowell was training his army near Washington and Confederate military contingents were converging on Manassas, two important bodies of troops were watching each other in the Shenandoah Valley. Virginia militia had taken over Harpers Ferry on April 18, 1861, under Major General Kenton Harper; the Federal guard of forty-five men under Lieutenant Roger Jones had fired the government arsenal and destroyed 20,000 rifles and pistols before retreating into Maryland. Harper was superseded by Colonel Thomas J. Jackson, by order

of Governor Letcher of Virginia, and Jackson organized
the troops, among other acts forming a regiment of cavalry under Lieutenant Colonel J. E. B. Stuart. On May
23, 1861, the top command was taken over by Brigadier
General Joseph E. Johnston, who formed the troops into
brigades, placed the Virginia Brigade under the command of Colonel Jackson, and had him commissioned
brigadier general. This was the beginning of the Army of
the Shenandoah, which eventually had 9,000 men under
arms.

Opposed to General Johnston's force were Federal
troops under Major General Robert Patterson, a Pennsylvania militia general who had been given command of the
Department of Pennsylvania on April 27. Patterson was
sixty-nine years old and had served in the War of 1812.
When he moved down from Chambersburg his object was
to keep Maryland free from Confederate control. On June
13 he sent Colonel Lew Wallace with the Eleventh Indiana Zouaves to push 500 Confederates out of Romney,
which Wallace did. Patterson's force at this time was
estimated at 18,000 and after he was joined by General
McClellan he would have a formidable force from which
General Scott expected important action. In his command were men who would play big roles in the war,
especially Fitz John Porter, who was a staff officer, and
George H. Thomas, who had a brigade. General Johnston
did not think he could hold Harpers Ferry against Patterson and evacuated it June 15.

When Patterson advanced into Virginia, Colonel
J. E. B. Stuart's cavalry discovered the movement in
time for Johnston to send Colonel Jackson to the vicinity
of Martinsburg to harass small bodies but to retire under
cover of the cavalry if the Union troops reacted in force.
At Falling Waters, Jackson impeded part of Patterson's
advance and suffered eleven men wounded and nine missing. Stuart by personal daring cut a group of Federal
infantry out of a column and bagged forty-nine prisoners.
Patterson moved to Bunker Hill, nine miles from Winchester, on July 15, and on the 17th he went to North-
field. Neither of these moves deterred Johnston, who
was able to get his troops out of Winchester by a forced
march to Piedmont. Realizing that marching on foot would

not get him to Manassas in time, Johnston commandeered rolling stock of the railroad and entrained his troops.

This resourceful act was not reported to Patterson. While Johnston's troops hurried to Manassas by rail and turned the tide of battle at Bull Run, Patterson's men marked time, deprived of vital information. Thus the difficulties of the Federals at Bull Run can be ascribed in part to Patterson's dilatory movements, for his reinforcements would have been vital to McDowell.

On the Henry House Hill

The battle of Bull Run began at 5:15 A.M. on Sunday, July 21, when a thirty-pounder Parrott gun, largest weapon in the Federal artillery, sent a shell across the Run near the Stone Bridge toward the Confederate lines. This gun and other units of the U.S. Artillery were attached to Brigadier General Daniel Tyler's First Division, which was deployed on both sides of the Warrenton Turnpike. The Confederate front extended for a long distance on the other side of Bull Run, and it was General McDowell's purpose to have Tyler keep the opposition occupied in the vicinity of the bridge while he mounted a flank attack. McDowell ordered the divisions of Colonel David Hunter and Colonel Samuel P. Heintzelman to march two miles northwest along the river to cross Bull Run at Sudley Springs Ford and then advance on the flank of the Confederates in the region of the Warrenton Turnpike.

This was a long and dusty detour, justified only if McDowell would profit by the element of surprise. This might have been accomplished on a gray, misty morning, but the sun came to the aid of the Confederates. They had had the good sense to send a signal detachment to a high hill that dominated the environs and placed an engineer, Captain Edward P. Alexander, in charge. As the sun rose in the sky he discerned repeated flashes in the northeast as the rays of the sun hit bayonets and brass cannon. His flags wigwagged to the Confederate commander on the Turnpike, Colonel Nathan G. Evans: "Look out for your left; you are turned." Evans left four regiments and two guns to occupy Tyler, who had brought his infantry closer to the Run, and pushed the bulk of his

command forward half a mile past the area where the
Warrenton Turnpike meets the Manassas-Sudley Road. On
the Henry House plateau behind the Turnpike, Brigadier
General Barnard E. Bee faced to the north with the
Third Brigade of Johnston's army, composed of Alabama,
Mississippi, and North Carolina regiments, with Captain
John D. Imboden's battery of four six-pounders support-
ing the brigade ready to shell the oncoming Federals.

Thus instead of catching the Confederates napping, the
Federal advance was precipitated at once into a furious
infantry battle, while guns began shelling them from the
hill. In the van was the Second Brigade, First Division,
of New Hampshire, New York, and Rhode Island troops,
led by Colonel Ambrose E. Burnside. Next came Colonel Andrew Porter's First Brigade, mostly regiments of
New York militia, and a regiment of Colonel Heintzelman's Third Division.

Burnside's brigade was accompanied by the Rhode
Island battery of sixteen thirteen-pounder rifles, which
attempted to reach the Confederate line from the hill on
which stood a house owned by a free Negro named
Robinson, and became the target of sharpshooters. As
Colonel Andrew Porter's brigade came up Griffin's regular artillery of six Parrott rifles trained on Imboden's position, and shortly the battery of the First U.S. Artillery,
under James B. Ricketts, added six ten-pounder Parrotts.

Directly in front and almost parallel with the Turnpike
ran Young's Branch, flowing easterly around Robinson's
hill. Here the Confederates made a stand as they moved
back to the pressure of Federal forces. The Federal troops
were raw, but rushed into action with such energy that
Evans' troops were pushed back and made him send hurried calls for brigades from General Johnston's newly arrived army, which had formed a second line on the high
ground of the Henry plateau.

When Imboden was forced to move back his guns he
maneuvered the teams so that the Henry farmhouse
would be between him and the Federals. The latter, suspecting the house was being used by riflemen, sent shells into
the building. The Confederates pulled back to the protection of a grove and there occurred a lull in the fighting, during which they re-formed their lines under the

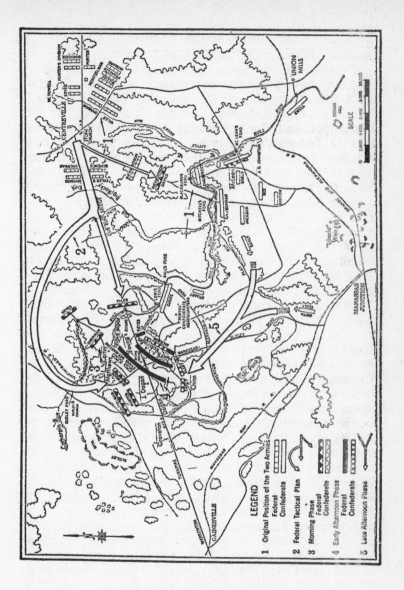

The First Battle of Bull Run
(Manassas)

direction and command of General Jackson.

Foremost among the commanders who were trying to rally their troops as they moved back in disorder behind the Henry House plateau was Brigadier General Barnard E. Bee of Johnston's Army of the Shenandoah. As he rode back he met Jackson calmly lining up his troops and ordering the placing of guns. According to legend Bee called out: "General, they are beating us back." Jackson replied: "Sir, we'll give them the bayonet." Then, continues the legend, Bee managed to get some of his troops together behind Jackson's line and seeing the calm, resolute attitude of the latter shouted to his men: "There is Jackson standing like a stone wall." As Beauregard ordered the troops forward to sweep the Federals off the plateau, Bee was in front of his ranks and was struck down by a bullet. So, too, was the commander of the Second Brigade of Georgians, Colonel Francis S. Bartow.

General Bee's speech became famous in a few weeks. Douglas Southall Freeman wrote in *Lee's Lieutenants,* Volume I, that the Richmond correspondent of the Charleston *Mercury* printed the story on July 25. As told there the episode seems embellished; General Bee is described as trying to rally his troops and going up to Jackson in desperation, saying: "General, they are beating us back," whereupon Jackson replied: "Sir, we'll give them the bayonet." Then Bee is described as turning to his brigade and saying: "There is Jackson standing like a stone wall. Let us determine to die here, and we will conquer. Follow me!" Another version says that he added, after the first sentence, "Rally behind the Virginians!" Whatever the true version, it gave Jackson a name by which he is known to history. There were, however, men who doubted the remark was meant as a compliment. D. H. Hill called it a "sheer fabrication." Freeman found a different version in the manuscript reminiscences of Colonel J. C. Haskell. Colonel Haskell wrote that Major Rhett, Johnston's chief of staff, who was with Bee until he died a few hours after the battle, told him Bee related that when he and Bartow were hard-pressed Jackson had refused to move to their relief and Bee in an outburst had derided him for standing like a stone wall. Colonel Haskell wrote that Bee's anger was con-

firmed by Johnston's engineer officer, Brigadier General
W. H. C. Whitney and by James Hill, Bee's brother-in-
law, who was with him when he fell. Freeman offers no
comment on this "entirely different theory" but accepts
the popular version. Whatever may have been Bee's
intention, the historical fact is that both Jackson and his
troops, and later the whole Confederate army, considered the phrase a compliment.

Then, on the Federal side, occurred an error of
judgment that aided materially to defeat the Federals
when victory was still possible. General McDowell decided the Confederates ought to be shelled from close
quarters and ordered his artillery adjutant, Major William
F. Barry, to post two batteries on the Henry House
plateau. Major Barry directed Captain Charles Griffin and
Captain J. B. Ricketts to take their guns up from the Sud-
ley-Manassas Road to a spot near the Henry House. This
was an open field that had brought disaster to both friend
and foe, and Griffin, who saw that the order was unjusti-
fied militarily, wanted to know what infantry support he
would have. Major Barry said the Eleventh New York
Zouave Regiment would be sent there, and Griffin objected that they would not stand the fire. He also declared
that an exposed position on the open field would make
the batteries easy targets.

Barry refused to modify the order and the eleven
pieces that Griffin and Ricketts had were taken to the spot
indicated. Opposed were fifteen guns of the Confederates,
who went eagerly to work. To make the situation worse, a
line of the Thirty-third Virginia in blue was mistaken
by the Federals for possible support until a deadly volley cut down the cannoneers. The Virginians charged;
the New York Zouaves and a battalion of U.S. Marines,
which had just come on the field, were routed. Colonel
Stuart's cavalry pursued the Zouaves, of whom a few
turned and brought down some of Stuart's horsemen. For
a short time Federals and Confederates fought over the
fieldpieces. The horses being destroyed, soldiers tried
to drag the guns, but Griffin managed to save only two of
his five.

On orders from McDowell, Colonel William T. Sherman's Third Brigade of Tyler's division moved up to as-

sist Colonel David Hunter, commanding the Second Division. With the Sixty-ninth New York Regiment, under Colonel James Corcoran, leading, the troops ascended a sharp bluff, but considering it impassable for artillery, Sherman ordered Captain R. B. Ayres to use his discretion. Ayres remained on the east bank of Bull Run and shelled the Confederate lines from there.

On orders from McDowell, Sherman's regiments moved up the ridge beyond which the Confederates were retreating, passed the point where Ricketts' battery was destroyed, and met the New York Zouaves and the battalion of U.S. Marines as they were being driven off the field. The regiments used the shelter of the sunken road as long as they could in advancing. When the Second Wisconsin Regiment was ordered up to the plateau and was twice repulsed it caused confusion among the Union ranks because its troops were uniformed in gray "and there was a universal cry that they were being fired on by our own men." Sherman reported that the Sixty-ninth New York charged across the hill several times but finally broke. The Federals recovered the Henry and Robinson houses and the guns that had been taken, but had no cannoneers or horses to serve them.

Union Retreat from Bull Run

After 3 P.M., when General McDowell was making a strong effort against the Confederate left and pushing it back, the Confederates received more help when Brigadier General Kirby-Smith arrived with the Fourth Brigade of Johnston's army from Manassas Junction. Johnston directed him to move against McDowell's right, which extended to the Chinn house on the hill, where Howard and Sykes were posted. Almost immediately Kirby-Smith was wounded and the command fell upon Colonel Arnold Elzey. Kershaw's Second South Carolina and Cash's Eighth South Carolina led with Kemper's battery in support. Johnston also ordered Colonel Jubal Early to take his troops around the Confederate left and fall upon McDowell's right flank; to his forces were added two companies of Stuart's cavalry and a battery under Lieutenant Peckham.

Then occurred the crisis of the day, when the troops, which had stood up unflinchingly under fire despite their inexperience, found the intense destruction meted out by small arms at close range too great to be borne. As men fell dead and wounded about them, they drew back in great confusion. Sherman reported:

Colonel Cameron had been mortally wounded, was carried to an ambulance and reported dying. Many other officers were reported dead or missing, and many of the wounded were making their way, with more or less assistance, to the buildings used as hospitals, on the ridge to the West. We succeeded in partially reforming the regiments, but it was manifest that they would not stand, and I directed Colonel Corcoran to move along the ridge to the rear. . . . General McDowell was there in person and used all possible efforts to reassure the men. By the active exertions of Colonel Corcoran we formed an irregular square against the cavalry . . . and we began our retreat toward the same ford of Bull Run by which we had approached the field of battle. There was no positive order to retreat, although for an hour it had been going on by the operation of the men themselves.

In the words of Captain James B. Fry, McDowell's assistant adjutant general, "the men quietly walked off." Neither commands nor the courageous example of steady units could halt the infantrymen who had fought back and forth over the field without food or water in the torrid July sun; they turned toward the highway to cross Bull Run. Caught in the jam were the carriages of sight-seers—politicians, civilians with their wives from Washington—whose curiosity had impelled them to "see the battle," and who now were dusty and bedraggled, and at times terrified when small bodies of Confederate cavalry dashed across the fields to harass them.

At Cub Run the tragedy was intensified. Edmund Ruffin was a Virginia agronomist and secessionist, who asserted he had the "honor" of firing the first gun in the attack on Fort Sumter, presumably from Morris Island after the first signal gun from Fort Moultrie. He found a battery of the Seventh Virginia Regiment of Colonel J. L. Kemper and demanded the privilege of taking a shot at the Union stragglers. At Cub Run he trained a gun on the suspension bridge and hit it just as a wagon was crossing. This and subsequent shots wrecked the bridge, piled up wagons, and added to the panic of the retreat.

To the trained military men no episode of the war was so baffling, so mortifying to their pride, as the general movement among the Federal troops on the Henry plateau to head for home. It seemed as catching as an insidious disease. When officers tried to stop them with appeals and harangues, the enlisted men moved past them as if they had not heard or seen, and had other business to perform. Evidently convinced they had done all that could be expected of them, individuals and groups turned around and walked off the field. It was what civilians would have done and these men in blue uniforms were still civilians, not yet made over into automatons who obeyed orders, even orders that sent them against musketry and cannon shot.

A civilian tragedy took place in the Henry farmhouse. When the Federal attack began on the far side of the Warrenton Turnpike, Mrs. Judith Henry, an aged bedridden woman, was removed from the house by members of her family and carried to a ravine below the Sudley Road. A short time later the house was considered safer and she was returned to it. In the afternoon, when Griffin's battery was shelling the Confederates on the Henry house hill, the guns of the Staunton Artillery were hustled back toward the Robinson house and in doing so dodged behind the Henry house for shelter. Shells from Griffin's battery passed through the house. Mrs. Henry received five wounds from shell fragments and died soon after the battle.

Sherman, in his *Memoirs* (1875), recalled some personal sensations of the day: "when for the first time I saw cannonballs strike men and crash through the trees and saplings above and around us"; the action of Lieutenant Colonel Haggerty of the Sixty-ninth, who "without orders, rode out alone and endeavored to intercept [the enemy's] retreat. One of the enemy, in full view, at short range, shot Haggerty and he fell dead from his horse." Also "the terrible scare of a poor Negro who was caught between our lines."

The Union men who insisted they be released because they had now served the ninety days specified when they volunteered, provided an embarrassment to the War Department, which was in danger of losing a big slice of its army before it could replace the men. Hastily it decided that the men were not technically in the army until they had been mustered in, and as most of them had marked time for a month to six weeks before that formality, the government was able to move the expiration date into August.

Sherman told how one of his men, who had given up a law practice to enlist, asked to be released because his time was up and he had work to do in his office. Sherman refused to let him go and said that if he attempted to leave without orders he would shoot the man down like a dog. That afternoon President Lincoln and Secretary Seward came by Fort Corcoran, where the troops were encamped. The young lawyer approached the President's carriage and complained that Sherman had threatened to shoot him. Lincoln turned the matter into a joke by whispering: "Well, if I were you and he threatened to shoot, I would not trust him, for I believe he would do it." The bystanders laughed and the complainant withdrew.

But dissatisfaction persisted in the ranks and Sherman said "the spirit of mutiny" was common and was not subdued until "several regiments or parts of regiments" had been sent as punishment to Fort Jefferson, Florida.

General McDowell had a large body of unused troops at Centreville and called a conference of commanders there to decide whether to make a new stand or to retreat. The officers voted to retire, but, as one expressed it, the men already had made their own decision. McDowell assigned brigades to cover the retreat and they stood by their posts; at midnight he ordered them, too, to withdraw by way of Fairfax Court House and Annandale to their Washington camp.

Of the Union army of approximately 35,000, only 18,572 officers and men and 24 pieces of artillery crossed Bull Run. Several divisions remained in reserve at Centreville. The Union had 2,896 casualties, of which 460 were killed, 1,124 wounded, and 1,312 captured or missing. The Confederate totals, estimated by General

Thomas Jordan, onetime adjutant general for Beauregard, for the editors of the *Century*, twenty years after the battle, showed Beauregard's Army of the Potomac to have had 21,900 effectives and 27 guns, of which 9,713 men and 17 guns were actively engaged; the Army of the Shenandoah was estimated to have had 8,340 engaged, making the Confederates on the field 18,053. Their casualties numbered 1,982, of which 387 were killed, 1,582 wounded, and 13 missing; of those killed 282 were lost by Johnston's army. Two brigade commanders were killed: Colonel F. S. Bartow and Brigadier General B. E. Bee, both of the Army of the Shenandoah. General Johnston said the Confederates captured about 5,000 muskets, 500,000 cartridges, 28 pieces of artillery, 64 artillery horses with harness, 26 wagons, and a large amount of clothing and camp equipment.

The first Battle of Bull Run showed that it would take months of stern discipline to harden the farm hands, store clerks, bookkeepers, brakemen, and teamsters so that they would stand in the face of fire. The situation in the Confederate ranks was not much better; by the end of the afternoon the brigades were so confused that their officers could not get them lined up to pursue the disorganized Federals, who could have been hurt badly on the clogged roads.

Jefferson Davis, President of the Confederacy, took a train from Richmond and arrived at Manassas Junction just as the battle ended. Meeting some retreating Confederate soldiers as he approached the field, he thought they had lost the battle. In later years his biographer wrote that Davis arrived in time to rally the men and that they were inspired by his presence. This irritated General Johnston, who called such statements "fancies." When Davis arrived none of the enemy was within cannon shot, according to Johnston; there was no opportunity for Davis to influence the troops by "his name and bearing."

A Committee on the Conduct of the War met in Washington and heard testimony from commanding officers concerning the battle. It concluded: "The principal cause of the defeat . . . was the failure of General Patterson to hold the forces of Johnston in the Valley of the Shenandoah."

The disaster at Bull Run brought about an immediate reorganization of the Federal armies. General McDowell was considered more unlucky than inefficient; he was removed from top command but not from the army. On the day after Bull Run, Major General George B. McClellan, then at Beverly, Virginia, received orders to place Major General William S. Rosecrans or some other general in charge of his Department and come at once to Washington. He arrived there the following Friday and received command of the Army of the Potomac. At the same time General Rosecrans took McClellan's former command in Western Virginia; Major General Nathaniel P. Banks took the place of General Patterson as commander of the army at Harpers Ferry, and Major General John A. Dix took the command in Baltimore held until that time by General Banks.

7

MASON AND SLIDELL:
CONFEDERATE DIPLOMACY ABROAD

On a stormy night in October, 1861, the little steamship *Theodora* left Charleston and slipped through the Union blockade headed for the West Indies. On board were two men entrusted by the Confederate government with the highly important task of establishing diplomatic relations with Great Britain and France. Foremost in their list of duties was obtaining full recognition of the Confederate States as a nation, thus paving the way for the exchange of ministers and consuls and making trade agreements. The two men were former United States Senators James M. Mason of Virginia and John Slidell of Louisiana, and with them on board were their families and their secretaries.

Both Mason and Slidell were well known in American political life. Mason, sixty-three years old, was a grandson of the famous George Mason of Revolutionary times, who had helped put the Bill of Rights into both the Virginia and the United States Constitutions. At the start of the war Mason had resigned from the Senate, where he had sponsored the Fugitive Slave Act of 1850. Slidell, sixty-eight, had been in the confidence of Presidents Polk and Buchanan, and had resigned from the Senate when Louisiana voted for secession. Their destination was first London, then Paris, and to get there they had to make a detour to Havana, where they were to transfer to the British Royal Mail steamer *Trent,* Captain Moir. The *Trent* was to make a stop at St. Thomas, Danish West Indies, on its way to England.

The United States not only kept the blockade going; it had a network of alert agents in foreign ports. Thus when the U.S. naval sloop *San Jacinto,* back from the west coast of Africa, called at St. Thomas for coal, its master learned that a Confederate privateer, the *Sumter,* Captain Raphael Semmes, was preying on American shipping in the Caribbean. The master of the *San Jacinto* was Captain Charles Wilkes, already famous as navigator and explorer, who pioneered in delineating parts of the Antarctic continent. He took up the trail at once and while at Cienfuegos, Cuba, received word from the American consul general at Havana of the mission of Mason and Slidell.

Captain Wilkes had no authority to pursue the men, but the interests of his country were his primary concern. He determined to intercept the *Trent* after it left St. Thomas and to do so placed the *San Jacinto* in that part of the Bahama Channel where it is only fifteen miles wide. Here he found his quarry, and warning it with a shot across the bow, he had it heave to and sent his executive officer, Lieutenant D. MacNeill Fairfax, to arrest the commissioners, obtain their baggage and take the ship as a prize. The order was performed with a show of courtesy on both sides. The British captain protested, but did not interfere; Mason and Slidell identified themselves and with their secretaries were taken to the *San Jacinto.* There were cries of "Pirates!" and "Throw the damned fellow overboard!" from passengers on the *Trent,* and Mrs. Slidell, learning that the Union captain was a former friend, exclaimed: "He is playing into our hands."

Slidell said to his wife in farewell: "Goodbye, my dear, we shall meet in Paris in sixty days." The ship was allowed to sail on.

The capture of the commissioners caused an international sensation. Northern cities, deprived of military successes to cheer about, gave vent to an excess of jubilation. Wilkes had not only seized two of Jefferson Davis' precious agents—he had taken them right under the nose of the British lion, which many Americans loved to deride. As the *San Jacinto* proceeded first to New York and then to Boston, to deliver its four prisoners to Fort Warren in Boston harbor, there were parades for the crew and dinners for the officers, who received the welcome reserved for eminent leaders in the city hall of New York. The Secretary of the Navy, Gideon Welles, published an order congratulating Captain Wilkes. The House voted unanimously to thank him. The Confederacy, in turn, was vociferous in denouncing his ruthlessness and illegality, and Richmond hoped the stopping of a British steamer would create complications for Washington and increase antagonism to the United States in Britain.

Such results followed quickly. British newspapers began denouncing the affront to the British flag, and crowds voiced their hatred of the Yankees. The American minister in London, Charles Francis Adams, reported the anger of the British ministry. War talk was heard on both sides, and a resolution introduced in the House of Representatives called on the President not to yield "to any menace or demand of the British Government," but it found no support. The British government prohibited further export of arms and ordered 8,000 troops to embark for Canada. But in Washington the White House took a serious view of the incident. The President realized that Wilkes had been given no authority to remove Mason and Slidell from the *Trent,* and this was conveyed informally to the prime minister, Lord Palmerston. The British government instructed its minister in Washington to demand release of the men and an apology, and to close his legation and return home if a reply was not forthcoming in seven days.

The point at issue was whether Captain Wilkes had violated international procedures by forcibly removing from a foreign ship passengers who were not in uniform nor engaged in illegal acts. The British point of view was that he should have seized the ship and taken it into port for a prize court to adjudicate. Captain Wilkes evidently had this in mind and was circumvented by Lieutenant Fairfax, who explained that he was aware of the hostility against the United States in foreign parts and that such seizure would have been interpreted as an act of war.

President Lincoln said: "One war at a time." Secretary Seward, who had not wished to surrender Mason and Slidell, had to reverse his stand and make the necessary amends. His explanation reads more like a lawyer's argument than an apology. He stretched the word "contraband" to include persons as well as property, saying it meant "contrary to proclamation, prohibited, illegal, unlawful." By not taking the vessel before a prize court Captain Wilkes had prevented the "judicial examination." Seward then declared that he had found the American point of view and that of the British identical; but he was defending not an exclusively British interest but principles that guided the United States. "If I decide this case in favor of my own government, I must disavow its most cherished principles, and reverse and forever abandon its essential policy. The country cannot afford the sacrifice. If I maintain those principles, and adhere to that policy, I must surrender the case itself. It will be seen therefore, that this government could not deny the justice of the claim presented to us in this respect upon its merits. We are asked to do to the British nation just what we have always insisted all nations ought to do to us." Secretary Seward said the four persons in military custody would be "cheerfully liberated."

When Mason and Slidell were released from custody at Fort Warren in Boston harbor they were taken by a tug to Provincetown, Massachusetts, and placed on board the British steam frigate *Rinaldo*. Treated as distinguished guests, they were conveyed to Bermuda, where the flagship of the British admiral at that station, the *Nile*, saluted them by having the band play *Dixie*. They were then transferred to St. Thomas, Danish West Indies, and sailed on the Royal Mail steamer *La Plata* for England.

As commissioners of the Confederacy, Mason and Slidell had as their primary object the attainment of recognition of the Confederate States as a nation by Britain and France. Although the Federal government in Washington considered the British government, from Queen Victoria down, pro-South, the commissioners were greatly disillusioned by the formal and correct "neutrality" of the British ministers.

Lord Russell, minister of foreign affairs, was friendly, but would not receive Mason as commissioner; he invited Mason to call on him at his home instead of the Foreign Office. Russell listened intently as Mason explained the position of the Confederacy as an independent nation no longer associated with the United States, but made no comment. Mason found members of the House of Commons more partial to the Confederate arguments, and at first was told that recognition doubtless would come in the form of a resolution appended to an address, but when this did not take place he was told that the Members did not wish to begin any controversies that might distress the Queen, who was immersed in sorrow over the death of the Prince Consort.

Mason and Slidell put in many hours in London and Paris trying to impress their points of view on the ministers. They had three important objects: (1) recognition of the Confederacy as a nation; (2) condemnation of the blockade, which was resented in Europe, and, being only partially effective, was not entitled to be tolerated under international usage; (3) mediation by the European powers to stop the war.

The argument against the Federal blockade was the strongest because Britain especially was being deprived of cotton. As mills shut down for lack of it unemployment caused disaffection and anger against the United States. But Britain began importing cotton from India and after a year or two had regained much of its imports.

The Confederate government tried to convince the European nations that the United States blockade of Southern ports was not effective. Secretary of State Judah P. Benjamin sent Mason lists of vessels that had evaded the blockade, in order for him to present it to Lord Russell. Mason attempted again and again to get Russell to withdraw recognition of the blockade, on the basis of the Paris Treaty of 1856. But the British were evasive. In official papers published by the British the Confederate President was shocked to read that Britain did not object to a few loopholes in the blockade. Lord Russell had written to the British ambassador in Washington on February 15, 1862:

Her Majesty's Government are of the opinion that, assuming that the blockade was duly notified and also that a number of ships is stationed and remains at the entrance of a port sufficient really to prevent access to it, or to create an evident danger of entering it or leaving it, and that these ships do not voluntarily permit ingress or egress, the fact that various ships may have successfully escaped through it (as in the particular instances referred to) will not of itself prevent the blockade from being an effectual one by international law.

When the commissioners urged mediation they received a response they had not bargained for. As an inspired statement in a Brussels newspaper put it: "To the friends of liberty and of the dignity of man we repeat it—mediation is the best guaranty of the abolition of slavery." This emphasis shocked the Confederates, and their agent in Brussels warned the Richmond government that the issue of independence was likely to be submerged and slavery made the object of reform. This was the main reason why they dropped appeals for mediation and concentrated their efforts on recognition.

As the months dragged with no gains by the commissioners (although the Confederate agents who were placing orders for ships were doing a big business) Mason and Slidell sent home bitter reports. They accused the British cabinet of insincerity and of being afraid that the United States might start war if the cabinet favored the South openly. They also reported that Charles Francis Adams, the United States minister in London, had a network of spies that watched every movement made by Confederate commissioners and agents. They also noted that the foreign attitude toward them changed like a barometer with Southern victories and defeats. Despite the most elaborate explanations by President Jefferson Davis of the future economic independence of the Confederacy, they made no headway.

By February, 1865, the military and naval situation of the Confederacy had deteriorated to such an extent that the British ministry suddenly dropped its conciliatory attitude and called the Confederacy sharply to account for certain depredations. It presented its list of grievances to the Confederate commissioners in Europe, James M. Mason, John Slidell and A. Dudley Mann. By a peculiar roundabout maneuver the Foreign Office also gave a copy of the document, signed by Lord Russell, to Secretary of State William H. Seward in Washington, with the request that it be conveyed through the military lines to Richmond. Thus the Federal government was not only given the text of the complaint but in effect was apprised of the British hostility to the Confederate regime. This gesture was not lost on either the United States or the Confederacy.

Lord Russell complained first of shipbuilding for the Confederate account, which actually had been welcomed by British shipbuilders. He said that "the unwarrantable practice of building ships in this country to be used as vessels of war against a state with whom Her Majesty is at peace still continues," by means of "evasion and subtlety." The paper also cited the use of Canadian soil for warlike purposes and the attempts to seize shipping on Lake Erie. The raid on St. Albans, Vermont, from across the Canadian border, was mentioned; this occurred on October 19, 1863, when Confederate guerrillas surprised this country town, robbed its banks, and killed several persons, afterward fleeing across the border.

The Confederate commissioners replied to Lord Russell with a general denial of the facts, but their report to Secretary of State Benjamin recognized the change in the British attitude. They reported that the British and French stand was based on the reverses of the Confederate armies and the fear that the United States, if successful, would retaliate by making war against them. The French were already worried because their Mexican adventure with Maximilian was running great risks.

The State Department in Washington was unaware of what other channels Lord Russell was using to communicate with Richmond and complied with his request by asking General Grant to transmit the document through the lines. Grant sent it by flag of truce to General Lee, with a covering letter from Secretary Seward explaining why. Ten days later Grant received a formal letter from Lee returning the British paper with this note:

I am directed to say that the Government of the Confederate States can not recognize as authentic a paper which is neither an original nor attested as a copy, nor could they under any circumstances consent to hold intercourse with a neutral nation through the medium of open dispatches sent through hostile lines after being read and approved by the enemies of the Confederacy.

This gave Richmond an opportunity to deliver a slap at Washington, but Mason, Slidell, and Mann attested to the authenticity of the message. In making their final appraisal of the sentiment of Europe toward the Confederacy, Colonel Mann said that among the impediments to recognition were slavery and the fear of a war with the United States, and possibly the desire to profit by the exhaustion of a competitor.

After the surrender of the Confederate armies, Mason and Slidell packed their bags preparatory to returning in a roundabout manner to the States. They had served four years as diligent representatives of the Confederacy, always conscious of being watched. Their activities had been extensive. Moving about in social circles of London and Paris, and keeping friendly relations with important ministers, they had publicized the announcements of President Jefferson Davis and attempted to minimize Southern setbacks. They spoke of the internal dissensions, incapacity, and near-bankruptcy of the United States and warned bondholders that they must expect huge losses. They pictured the Middle West as full of opponents of the Lincoln administration, who were on the verge of rising against it. When the Democrats of the North in 1864 nominated McClellan on a platform that practically repudiated the war, they welcomed it, but when McClellan announced his loyalty and determination to defeat the Confederacy they echoed the conclusion of Richmond that nothing was to be expected from McClellan. When Lincoln was reelected Mason and Slidell disseminated the view that

this had been done by Lincoln's tyrannous control of
the army votes. They reported many expressions of sympathy for the South from foreign officials, especially
from the Emperor Napoleon, whose ministers, however,
were too cautious to commit France to any pro-Confeder-
ate policy so long as the end was not clear. For a time
they made great efforts to condemn the United States
in the eyes of Europe as the employer of mercenaries,
for agents were soliciting laborers to emigrate to the
United States, obviously to have them join the armies
of the North. Later, however, when Polish volunteers
offered to come to the South in numbers the commissioners abetted attempts to accommodate them.

8

DU PONT'S SQUADRON
AT PORT ROYAL

President Lincoln could proclaim a blockade of Southern ports, but it took a navy to enforce it, and the United
States Navy had to be rebuilt almost from the waterline.
During the first summer of the war Confederate traders
moved in and out of Southern harbors without opposition, but after that it took an able master mariner to
chart a course that would run the blockade. The first important step in controlling the coast line came when the
South Atlantic Squadron, under Flag Officer Samuel F.
Du Pont, successfully reduced the forts erected by the
Confederates at the entrance to Port Royal, South Carolina, on November 7, 1861.

This was a cooperative effort of the Army and the
Navy. The South Atlantic Squadron was the counterpart
of the North Atlantic Squadron, Flag Officer Silas H.
Stringham, which managed to reduce a Confederate "fort"
at Hatteras Inlet a week before the attack on Port Royal.
The hastily thrown-up earthwork at Hatteras was no
match for Stringham and troops furnished by General

Benjamin F. Butler; yet they banged away at the fort for two days before they landed 315 troops and bagged 678 prisoners.

The demarcation between the North Atlantic and the South Atlantic Squadrons was the boundary between North Carolina and South Carolina. Secretary Gideon Welles chose Port Royal as an objective because the two major ports of Charleston and Savannah were too strong. Port Royal, lying midway between them, would provide a base of operations. Brigadier General Thomas W. Sherman of Rhode Island was ordered on August 2, 1861, to join Flag Officer Du Pont in organizing an expedition of 12,000 men, but he was advised to let the Navy direct the movements of the ships. It took a lot of transports to carry these troops, their supplies, and a number of horses. The squadron that Welles and Du Pont assembled was as variegated and patchy as a circus parade. Among the "ships of war" was a new sloop, the *Tuscarora*, built in fifty-eight days at Philadelphia; Du Pont expressed his amazement when he said: "Her keel was growing in Sussex County, Delaware, seventy days ago." There were ferryboats, river steamers, frigates with sail and steam, and a number of "ninety-day gunboats." Du Pont said: "It is like altering a vest into a shirt to convert a trading steamer into a man-of-war."

The squadron assembled at Hampton Roads and sailed south October 29. Its destination was a great secret; Secretary Welles had talked openly about a number of harbors, omitting Port Royal. Off Cape Hatteras the ships met heavy weather and had hard going; the *Isaac Smith* had to throw overboard all ordnance except one thirty-pounder; the *Governor* foundered and all but seven of its crew were transferred on the seas; four steamers loaded with stores went down, and later one transport loaded with horses ran ashore and was captured by Confederates. The rest of the ships reached Port Royal. The Confederates had two forts with earthworks, Fort Walker on Hilton Head and Fort Beauregard on Bay Point. They also relied on three converted river steamers commanded by Commodore Josiah Tattnall, formerly of the United States Navy.

The Federal squadron had forty-five fighting ships and

a large number of transports. When they moved close to the forts the latter started firing on November 7; the ships then moved past the forts, firing as they did so, and some were able to get into position to enfilade the forts. Tattnall's gunboats made a sortie or two but quickly fled out of range. The forts were evacuated, the Marines under General H. G. Wright landed and raised the Stars and Stripes. On November 8 the *Seneca* ran up the Beaufort River as far as Beaufort and reported that the white citizens had set fire to bales of cotton and departed. The Confederate forces under Brigadier General Thomas F. Drayton managed to get away without interference from the Federals. The ships reported eight killed, thirty wounded. The Confederates reported eleven killed. Flag Officer Du Pont became a rear admiral July 16, 1862.

9

THE BATTLE FOR MISSOURI

Dissension at St. Louis

Control of the Mississippi River all the way down to the Gulf became a dire necessity for the Union the moment war broke out. The Confederates were not less vigilant. Cairo, at the confluence of the Ohio and the Mississippi, became a major port of embarkation for Federal troops and a supply base, but the adjacent countryside swarmed with dissidents of all varieties of opinion. Of the trans-Mississippi states Missouri was in an uproar because its allegiance was not yet fixed. It had entered the Union as a slave state and had numerous slaveholders; it had men who endorsed the rights of states to secede but who abhorred slavery; it had free-soil men who wanted to keep Missouri in the Union but did not want fighting on its soil, and finally it had a strong body of militant Unionists, reinforced by a large German element, that was eager to drive the secessionists out of the state with arms if necessary.

The governor, Claiborne F. Jackson, had been elected on Stephen A. Douglas' Democratic ticket in 1860; he urged secession on the state assembly, which on New Year's Eve presented the Federal government with the warning that if it tried to coerce South Carolina or any other slave state with force Missouri would join the South and "resist the invaders to the last extremity." Sure of his strength, Governor Jackson brought about a state convention with the object of having it declare for secession, but the conservative delegates, led by Francis P. Blair, Jr., whose brother was Postmaster General in Lincoln's cabinet, stifled all mention of secession.

At St. Louis the United States had an important arsenal with a large stand of arms, which the secessionists planned to seize. This was frustrated by the quick action of Captain Nathaniel Lyon. Blair had been organizing the Home Guard out of the Wide Awakes who had campaigned for Lincoln; Lyon equipped the Guard with guns and sent the remaining arms to Illinois.

The Southern sympathizers established Camp Jackson near St. Louis, raised the Confederate flag, and began to drill volunteers. They obtained fieldpieces from the Confederate government. Captain Lyon raided the camp May 10 and made the occupants prisoners. As they were being marched through the streets to be held at the Arsenal a large crowd sympathetic with the prisoners collected. Two military leaders have written about the resultant incident in their memoirs: U. S. Grant and William T. Sherman.

Grant had not yet been made a colonel. He relates that he was a spectator of the hauling down of the Confederate flag at the secession headquarters and that he saw an ill-tempered crowd, but he does not mention any shooting. Whereas Sherman, who was out walking with his boy with the object of watching the prisoners, relates that a rowdy had an altercation with a soldier and fired a pistol, hitting one of the Home Guards; the Guards then began shooting at the crowd. Twenty-eight persons are supposed to have been killed at that time. Sherman says most of the people were merely curious spectators. He had been offered a commission as brigadier general by Francis P. Blair, Jr., and had refused it; the appointment then had gone to Lyon.

The next day Brigadier General W. S. Harney, who had command of the Department of the West, arrived in St. Louis to conciliate the factions. On May 21 he made an agreement with Brigadier General Sterling Price, who had become commander of the pro-secession State Guard, that he would recognize the state government as the agency to keep order and would make no military movements to create further division. This was contrary to the policy pursued by Lyon and Blair and was quickly reported to Washington. The Federal government, unwilling to treat with a state administration that was openly working for secession, repudiated the agreement and on May 31 put Lyon in temporary command of Missouri with the rank of brigadier general.

Lyon was a Connecticut-born West Point graduate who had served in the Seminole and Mexican wars and in Indian troubles on the Pacific Coast. When he became commander Governor Jackson and General Price made one further effort to get an understanding with him. Lyon rejected all cooperation and declared for open war to hold Missouri for the Union.

Colonel Thomas L. Snead, at one time acting adjutant general of Missouri, and later in the Confederate Army, saw Lyon as a "little, rough-visaged, red-bearded, weather-beaten Connecticut captain" who "by his intelligence, his ability, his energy and his zeal" acquired the command of all Union troops in Missouri in five months and made himself respected, if not feared, by his enemies.

General Price on June 12 called for 50,000 men to repel the "invasion" of Missouri. On the Union side German settlers raised a regiment of volunteers under Franz Sigel, who had been teaching in a German institute in St. Louis. General Lyon marched on Jefferson City, the capital, and when the governor and his staff departed for Boonville, dislodged the state troops there and pushed them into the southwestern part of the state. Colonel Sigel attempted to intercept them, but at Carthage was outnumbered four to one and had to retreat.

In July, Unionists formed a provisional state government with Hamilton R. Gamble as governor, and Major General John C. Frémont took command of the Department of the West in St. Louis.

John C. Frémont, whose military actions in California had made him a controversial figure, and who had been the candidate for President of the new Republican party in 1854, was named major general in the regular army at the same time as George B. McClellan. President Lincoln gave him command of the Department of the West, comprising Illinois and all states west of the Mississippi to the Rockies, including New Mexico.

Frémont took command at St. Louis on July 25 and found Confederate flags flying from houses and recruiting offices and the state "in active rebellion." Reports from southwest Missouri told Frémont that General Price and his Missouri Confederates were receiving substantial reinforcements and that General Lyon's position at Springfield was unsafe. General Frémont also was responsible for the defense of Cairo, where Brigadier General L. M. Prentiss was expecting to be attacked by Confederates under General Gideon Pillow. Confederates also were threatening Cape Girardeau and Ironton.

The Federal troops lacked arms and equipment and Frémont was keeping the wires hot calling on Midwestern governors for regiments and on the Washington government for guns. Making St. Louis the base for reserves, he started fortifications at Girardeau, Ironton, Rolla, and Jefferson City, the last three terminals of railroads that could be served quickly from St. Louis. He ordered two regiments to support Lyon, who, despite his patriotic ardor, was doubtful that he could hold against the increasing numbers confronting him.

Price's Missouri regiments were augmented by a brigade of Arkansas state troops under General N. B. Pearce and about 3,000 men under General Ben McCulloch, Texan scout, who had been organizing Confederates in Western Arkansas. Although Price was by far the most experienced officer, top command went to General McCulloch on his insistence, and the army camped on a ridge above Wilson's Creek, 10 miles south of Springfield, with 10,775 men and 15 guns. Many of the men, however, had no guns or tents; the others carried all sorts of ancient firearms. On August 10, General Lyon and Sigel, now a brigadier general, divided their forces of fewer than 6,000 men, 15 guns; Sigel attacked the camp at dawn from the rear and Lyon came on at the front.

The ensuing battle was the first major clash west of the Mississippi, with regiments from Iowa, Kansas, and Missouri in the Union ranks. The Southerners, rallied by McCulloch and Price, stood firm; the issue was hotly contested with cavalry and bayonet charges. Sigel's wing was repulsed. Lyon, who had been greatly handicapped by lack of supplies, threw all his effectives into the fight; his horse was shot under him and he was wounded in the head, but he mounted another horse and "swinging his hat in the air, called on his men to follow." He was shot through the heart, after which the Federal attack collapsed, and the army withdrew to Springfield and later to Rolla. The casualties reached over 1,200 on both sides, with 233 killed on the Union side and 265 on the Confederate.

General Frémont and Slavery

Frémont had been a free-soil senator from California, one of the first two seated when the state entered the Union as a free state. He had refused to work his mines with slaves. In Missouri his strong antislavery sentiments quickly found opportunity for expression in action. Faced with the fact that the civil authorities in many places were too weak to cope with marauders, General Frémont decided to adopt tough measures. Therefore on August 30 he issued an order that was to have dire consequences for himself. In it he set forth that the "helplessness of civil authority, the total insecurity of life and devastation of property by bands of murderers and marauders" made him declare martial law and give the military authorities power to enforce existing laws and "supply such deficiencies as the conditions of war demand."

The drastic part of his proclamation ordered "all persons who shall be taken with arms in their hands within these lines [of army occupation] shall be tried by court martial, and if found guilty will be shot. Real and

personal property of those who take up arms against
the United States, or who shall be directly proven to
have taken an active part with their enemies in the field,
is declared confiscated to public use and their slaves,
if any they have, are hereby declared free men." General
Frémont then added that anyone who destroyed railroads, bridges, or telegraph lines would get the extreme
penalty; those engaging in treasonable correspondence
or circulating false reports were warned of consequences.
Those who were "led away from their allegiance" were
to return to their homes. To implement the order Frémont named a commission to hear evidence with power
to grant manumission to slaves.

Like other commanding generals of departments Frémont was not guided by precedents but had to improvise often to cope with new situations. When, on
leaving the White House in July, he had asked President
Lincoln for further instructions, the latter had replied:
"I have given you *carte blanche*. You must use your
own judgment and do the best you can." In his own eyes
Frémont was now doing the best he could. A friend to
whom he read the proclamation warned: "Mr. Seward
will never allow this. He intends to wear down the South
by steady pressure, not by blows, and then make himself
the arbitrator." Frémont replied: "It is for the North to
say what it will or will not allow, and whether it will
arbitrate, or whether it will fight."

The friend was right; not merely Seward but Lincoln
reacted negatively, but abolitionists, radical leaders
like Senator Charles Sumner, the press that wanted heavy
blows struck against slavery, and even Secretary of War
Cameron applauded the order with enthusiasm. Against
the crowd stood Lincoln, weighing the effect of such an
order on the border states, especially Kentucky, which
he was trying to hold in the Union, with a plan for future
compensation for slaves developing in the back of his
mind. He addressed Frémont in his usual tactful manner "in a spirit of caution and not of censure," objecting
to two points:

First. Should you shoot a man, according to the Proclamation, the Confederates would very certainly shoot our best

men in their hands in retaliation; and so, man for man, indefinitely. It is, therefore, my order that you allow no man to be shot under the proclamation without first having my approbation and consent.

Second. I think there is great danger that the closing paragraph, in relation to the confiscation of property and the liberating slaves of traitorous owners, will alarm our Southern Union friends and turn them against us; perhaps ruin our rather fair prospect for Kentucky. Allow me, therefore, to ask that you will, as of your own motion, modify that paragraph so as to conform to the first and fourth sections of the act of Congress entitled "An act to confiscate property used for insurrectionary purposes," approved August 6, 1861, a copy of which I herewith send you.

Frémont defended his action to Lincoln, saying "this is as much a movement in the war as a battle," and refused to retract his own order, because "it would imply that I myself thought it wrong." He asked the President to direct him openly to make the correction. This Lincoln did, ordering the modification to conform with the act of Congress that he had cited.

President Lincoln's modification of Frémont's abolition program caused violent dissent among Northerners who wanted slavery abolished immediately. Leaders of opinion deprecated his policy of conciliating the "contemptible state of Kentucky" and wanted to know for what purpose Union men were shedding their blood on the battlefield. In Ohio there was strong opinion that Frémont was right and that Kentucky should have been ignored. Senator Sumner of Massachusetts was greatly disturbed and in an address before the Massachusetts Republican convention at Worcester argued for emancipation of the slaves as the strongest weapon the North had. This brought him expressions of approval from Rutherford B. Hayes, Moncure D. Conway, Carl Schurz, Postmaster General Blair, and even Lincoln's former law partner, William H. Herndon, who wrote Sumner from Springfield, Illinois: "Frémont's proclamation was right. Lincoln's modification of it was wrong."

But more moderate Americans began to wonder whether Frémont was the right man for the difficult task of holding Missouri on the Union side. Soon the

conduct of his office was the subject of complaint both
in St. Louis and in Washington. He was accused of
favoring certain contractors over others and of maladmin-
istration, and was transferred to a post in the field.

Mulligan Buries a Fortune

Colonel James A. Mulligan and the Twenty-third Illinois Infantry reached Lexington, Missouri, September 8,
1861, on orders from General Frémont. Here he found
350 Home Guards and a regiment of cavalry under
Colonel Thomas A. Marshall. When joined by Colonel
Everett Peabody, who was retreating from General Price's
Confederates, there were 2,780 men, with only 40 rounds
of ammunition and a shortage of rations. Colonel Mulligan carried out an order of General Frémont and commandeered the assets of the State Bank of Lexington,
$960,159, of which sum $165,659 was in gold, in order
to keep it from being seized by Governor Jackson. Not
trusting any other spot, even with a guard, Colonel
Mulligan had a hole dug in the ground under his tent and
buried the money in it.

General Price's army arrived September 12 and
began to attack Mulligan's men, but the latter fought
back fiercely and Price was unable to rout them. The
next day came a heavy rain, and Mulligan used the time
to throw up entrenchments and to cast canister in a
foundry. New units were arriving for Price's army and by
September 18 he was said to have 18,000 troops, with
sixteen pieces of artillery. The attack now began with
redoubled fury. A hospital, filled with Mulligan's wounded,
was assaulted by Price on the ground that it was
being used by sharpshooters; he captured it and Mulligan's
troops retook it, making the same charge against the
Confederates.

Mulligan's men, though outnumbered, were crack shots,
and the Confederates dreaded their fire. When fighting
continued on the 19th, they collected bales of hemp,
saturated them with water to make them impervious to
fire, and advanced behind them. This trick brought
them close enough to storm Mulligan's meager breastworks. With ammunition practically used up and short

of food and water, Mulligan's regiment surrendered.

Colonel Mulligan was held prisoner for a month and then returned to St. Louis with an escort of forty men. He then went to Chicago, where the Irish welcomed him as a conquering hero. General Price captured the bank's money, but troops were not yet in the dire straits that befell them later in the war, and he ordered it restored to the Lexington Bank. But in the process the treasure shrank: $15,000 in notes had disappeared and could not be found. A few weeks later Governor Jackson levied on $37,000 of the gold hoard, alleging it was due the state of Missouri.

Colonel Mulligan continued his military career in Virginia and was mortally wounded at Winchester, July 24, 1864.

Battle of Pea Ridge

Major General Halleck took command of the Department of Missouri in December, 1861, succeeding General David Hunter, who had started no new campaigns during his short tenure after the removal of Major General Frémont. General Halleck ordered a reorganization and placed Brigadier General Samuel R. Curtis in command of the District of Southwest Missouri, with Brigadier General Franz Sigel second in command.

General Curtis had 10,500 men and 40 pieces of artillery when he started his campaign against General Sterling Price. Price evacuated Springfield with about 8,000 on February 13 and marched across the Arkansas border. Here he joined an army organized by Brigadier General Ben McCulloch on the far side of the Boston Mountains, which lie between the valley of the White River and the valley of the Arkansas. McCulloch had fought at Wilson's Creek. Curtis followed and established his base in the neighborhood of Bentonville, Missouri.

Brigadier General Alexander Asboth, U.S.A., led a cavalry raid into Fayetteville, Arkansas, which had been a Confederate stronghold. He raised the United States flag on the city hall as an act of defiance and then returned to his base.

The largest Confederate force ever assembled in the

Missouri-Arkansas area now came together. Colonel Albert Pike was able to recruit about 5,000 Indians of the Choctaw, Cherokee, and Chickasaw tribes, many of them armed with tomahawks and knives. Major General Earl Van Dorn, who had assumed command of the Trans-Mississippi Department of the Confederacy in January, took command of all troops. He was graduated from West Point in 1842 and had seen service in Mexico and against Indian tribes. A native of Mississippi, he left the army when his state seceded, received a Confederate commission, and accepted the surrender of Texas from the United States commander there in 1861. Van Dorn did not survive the war, for he was destined to be shot dead by a personal enemy in 1863.

The two armies clashed March 7 and 8, 1862, at Pea Ridge, and the fortunes of battle at first went against the Federal troops. But on March 8, General Curtis was able to change his front and assault at the same time that General Sigel drove the Confederates from the hills. The battle was complicated by the wild charges of the Indians, who rode about scalping wounded whites and were said to have made no distinction between friend or foe. McCulloch was killed and the Confederates were badly defeated.

Curtis' troops were composed of regiments from Missouri, Iowa, Illinois, and Indiana, and his division commanders were Colonel Peter J. Osterhaus, Brigadier General Asboth, Colonel Jefferson C. Davis, and Colonel Grenville M. Dodge. Acting as quartermaster was Captain Philip H. Sheridan. The Union losses were reported as 203 killed, 980 wounded, 201 captured or missing. The Confederates, who were said to have had 16,202 effectives, were supposed to have lost 800 casualties, in addition to over 200 taken prisoner.

10

THE CAPTURE OF FORT HENRY
AND FORT DONELSON

General Grant's First Command

The western theater of war early brought to the front two men who were able to work together and to lead the Union troops to victory. They were Ulysses Simpson Grant and William Tecumseh Sherman.

When the war broke out Grant was 39 and undistinguished. He had grown up on an Ohio farm and had been graduated at West Point in 1843. His experience under fire in the Mexican War was extensive, both under General Zachary Taylor and under General Winfield Scott, and he was promoted to captain for gallantry. He was serving at Humboldt Bay, California, when he resigned from the army on April 11, 1854, and returned to St. Louis, where his family had been living on a farm owned by his wife. There he tried to adapt himself to civilian life, with small success. He tried farming and selling wood in town; he went in with a partner to sell real estate and tried to become county engineer, but in vain.

His father had started a leather-goods store in Galena, Illinois, for two sons, and in May, 1860, Grant took a clerk's job at $600 a year and moved his family there. When the Civil War began Galena raised a company of infantry and Grant made himself useful drilling them. He accompanied them to Springfield, the state capital, and helped muster regiments in the state militia. He acted as a clerk at Camp Yates, but was eager to resume military service. For this purpose he went to Cincinnati to interview Major General George B. McClellan, who had taken a commission from the governor to organize Ohio volunteers. Grant tried for two days to see him, but was unable to reach him. He also wrote to the adjutant general of the United States Army, saying he felt competent to command a regiment, but received no reply.

After President Lincoln made his second call for troops,

Governor Richard Yates of Illinois appointed Grant colonel of the Twenty-first Regiment of Illinois Volunteer Infantry. When the regiment was mustered into the United States Army, two representatives in Congress, John A. McClernand and John A. Logan, were at the camp and addressed the troops. Logan was an orator of considerable windpower and his inspirational address pleased the men, practically all of whom entered the United States service. When Grant's turn came he stepped up and said brusquely: "Go to your quarters." His manner was in keeping with his businesslike methods; he was not an orator and military discipline was important to him.

Grant's regiment was intended for Missouri, where the Confederates were trying to take over the state. Brigadier General John Pope, whom Grant had known at West Point, was in command with headquarters at Mexico, Missouri, and Grant went there. He engaged in drilling the soldiers, but not having opened a book of instruction for fifteen years he procured one and tried to keep one day ahead of the soldiers. At Mexico he learned from a St. Louis newspaper that he was the first in a list of seven officers appointed brigadier general of volunteers by President Lincoln on recommendation of the Illinois delegation in Congress. His commission was issued August 7, 1861, and dated back to May 17. He named John A. Rawlins, a young lawyer of Galena, assistant adjutant general on his staff with the rank of captain. Rawlins remained with him during his entire career, becoming brigadier general and chief of staff to the General in Chief.

As Grant's associates became better acquainted with him they found him strictly devoted to duty, quick to assume responsibility, and not afraid of making unpopular decisions. He expected orderly behavior of soldiers toward civilians. It was said that he did not talk much, and this was true except when he was with intimates. He hated useless formalities and elaborate military uniforms, and he applied common sense to situations. It was right that his bluntness should have commended itself to Lincoln, who liked to cut across formalities himself.

For several weeks Grant was kept at routine tasks, and his work was in preparation, rather than execution. He went to Ironton and then to Jefferson City on military errands, and had not been there long enough to start a campaign when Colonel Jefferson C. Davis of the United States Army arrived with an order from headquarters relieving him and directing him to St. Louis. Major General Frémont was now in command there and he gave Grant command of the district of Southeast Missouri, which included southern Illinois. Grant proceeded to Cairo, Illinois, on September 4 to make his headquarters. On September 5 he learned from one of Frémont's scouts that a Confederate force was leaving Columbus, Kentucky, to capture Paducah at the mouth of the Tennessee River, forty-five miles away. He at once wired General Frémont that unless ordered otherwise he would proceed with troops to occupy Paducah in advance of the Confederates. He loaded two regiments and one battery on steamboats and again wired Frémont; getting no reply, he left at midnight on September 5 and reached Paducah next morning.

This action contravened the so-called neutrality that Kentucky had tried to establish for the state, as well as the hands-off policy the United States government had hoped to carry out when the war began. But the real reason for this neutrality was that many citizens of the state were sympathetic with the South and did not wish Federal armies to enter. The local officials at Paducah were not pleased when Grant ordered up additional troops from Cape Girardeau and placed Brigadier General C. F. Smith in command of the area. Grant's action also was resented by Governor Magoffin of Kentucky. But Grant was in no mood to accept an objection from a Southern sympathizer, especially one who had not objected to the use of his soil by Confederate troops already established at Columbus, Kentucky. Grant replied tartly to the governor and reported this to the legislature. Later on General Frémont approved his occupation of Paducah, but added a mild reproof, saying it was not Grant's place to correspond with the legislature.

It was Magoffin who made a sharp reply to President Lincoln in April when the President called on the governors of states to help fill his call for 75,000 volunteers from their militia. "Your dispatch is received," said

Magoffin. "In answer I say emphatically Kentucky will furnish no troops for the wicked purpose of subduing her sister Southern states." At that time the general assembly of Kentucky agreed with the governor and adopted a resolution to the effect that the state and its citizens should take no part in the war except as mediators and friends to the belligerent parties, and observe strict neutrality. The State Guard had to take an oath of allegiance to the United States, and the senate declared Kentucky would not sever its connection with the national government, "but arm herself for the preservation of peace within its borders."

The Confederates, however, felt that this stand was imposed on Kentucky by the preponderance of Union men in its legislature and disregarded it. They recognized the importance of Columbus, Kentucky, as a military post, for it could provide a barrier to Federal use of the Mississippi River. They sent a body of troops under General Gideon Pillow to occupy it and then sent Major General Leonidas Polk with a number of infantry regiments and several batteries, until there was a nucleus of about 10,000 men.

General Polk was fifty-five years old and a picturesque personality among the Confederate commanders. As a clergyman he was smooth-shaven, which set him apart from the other generals. Born in North Carolina, he was graduated at West Point in the class of 1827. In his third year there he was converted to religion and joined the "praying squad." He then entered Virginia Theological Seminary and in 1830 was ordained a priest of the Protestant Episcopal Church. After doing missionary work in the Deep South he became bishop of Louisiana in 1841. He took over a plantation in Louisiana, and when his wife inherited some slaves, he increased the number to 400. He started a Sunday school for the Negro children, and apparently believed in gradual emancipation, but he was distinctly a conservative Southerner and his principal efforts as an educator were directed toward the whites. Applying all his persuasiveness to this end, he became the principal agent in the founding of the University of the South at Sewanee, Tennessee, and in 1860 laid its cornerstone.

But under his episcopal robes was the uniform of a soldier. When war came Bishop Polk felt that his country was being invaded. His military associations were potent; he had been a classmate of Jefferson Davis and a roommate of Albert Sidney Johnston. Davis made him a major general of the Confederate Army, and after Perryville, a lieutenant general. In the army he was a moral force. He tried, during the first year of the war, to suppress vandalism and loose living among the soldiers, and in the course of exchanging prisoners he practiced the greatest civility toward "the enemy," many of whom he considered personal friends. The Kentucky legislature had asked General Polk to withdraw his troops from the state, but he replied he would withdraw if the Federals did, and by this time the latter were disinclined to believe he would go.

Grant at Belmont

When General Frémont went to Jefferson City to review the Missouri troops that were to oppose General Sterling Price, Grant received orders from headquarters to make a demonstration on both sides of the Mississippi. The object apparently was to keep the Confederates in Columbus from sending reinforcements to Sterling Price. Before Grant could act he received several additional orders: to send a force against Confederates supposed to be on the St. Francis River fifty miles southwest of Cairo, which he did by ordering Colonel Richard J. Oglesby there. Also, he was told the Confederates were about to embark on boats at Columbus, so he sent Colonel W. H. L. Wallace to reinforce Oglesby and march to New Madrid, Missouri, below Columbus. Grant then ordered General C. F. Smith to move troops toward Columbus, to make a demonstration if able to do so.

General Grant then assembled all the troops from Cairo and Fort Holt opposite, a total of 3,114, under Colonels McClernand, Buford, and Logan, and moved them down the river on steamboats, with the gunboats *Tyler* and *Lexington* as escorts. They landed on the west bank of the Mississippi about six miles above Columbus in order to attack a camp of Confederates at Belmont, opposite Columbus. Here Polk had placed one regiment of infantry, one battery, and one squadron of cavalry. The Federals pushed aside the Confederates and took the camp, but Grant's troops did not pursue because they began to plunder the camp for trophies. In the meantime Polk sent Brigadier Generals G. J. Pillow and B. F. Cheatham with approximately 3,000 troops to oppose the Federals. The fighting went on for four hours. Grant set fire to the Confederate camp and then told his men that they were surrounded; this made them more amenable to orders. They made their way back to the transports. The Confederates said the Federals were in such a hurry to board that some of the troops were pushed off the boats. Grant thought he was the last man to arrive, and he related the following experience in his *Personal Memoirs*:

I was the only man between the rebel army and our transports. The captain of a boat that had just pushed out but had not started, recognized me and ordered the engineer not to start the engine; he then had a plank run out for me. My horse seemed to take in the situation. There was no path down the bank and everyone acquainted with the Mississippi River knows that its banks in a natural state do not vary at any great angle from the perpendicular. My horse put his fore feet over the bank without hesitation or urging, and with his hind feet well under him, slid down the bank and trotted aboard the boat, twelve or fifteen feet away, over a single gang plank.

Actually General Grant was not the last man left on land: Colonel N. B. Buford and the Twenty-seventh Illinois Infantry had become detached from the troops and marched up a road some distance from the field before they could signal the boats and be taken on board, much later.

The affair at Belmont served no special purpose, although Grant said it saved Oglesby. The official figures of casualties had the Union Army with 120 killed, 383 wounded, and 104 captured; the Navy had one killed. The Confederates had 105 killed, 419 wounded, 117 missing. After the battle officers of both sides met to exchange prisoners under friendly conditions, even to the extent of eating lunch served by the Confederates.

The Attack on Fort Henry

Early in the war both the Union and the Confederacy recognized the strategic value of the Tennessee River. Flowing in a curve that takes in a large segment of northern Alabama, the Tennessee crosses both Tennessee and Kentucky in a north and northwesterly direction to reach the Ohio at Paducah. Northern generals concerned with the safety of the Ohio basin recognized it as a waterway that gave access to the Deep South, and the Confederates for the same reason exerted themselves to build defenses against such intrusion. Navigation on flat-bottomed steamboats was possible as far as Muscle Shoals, Alabama. Not far east the Cumberland River, having twisted around the Cumberland mountains in East Kentucky and traversed Tennessee in a big loop, flows through Kentucky to the Ohio almost parallel with the Tennessee, although in a much more tortuous course. At the point where the Kentucky border turns south for about twelve miles to follow the course of the Tennessee, the two rivers were only about twelve miles apart.

General Albert Sidney Johnston, Confederate commander, was anxious not to offend Kentuckians unduly, and Governor Isham Harris of Tennessee suggested that defenses be built as close to the Kentucky line as possible. He instructed General Daniel S. Donelson to pick sites for forts, and the latter located the works of Fort Henry on the big bend of the Tennessee and Fort Donelson directly east of it on the Cumberland. These posts were considered the best available, although not free from drawbacks, but the need to obstruct a Federal advance along the rivers was urgent because troops there might turn General Polk's flank. Old barges were sunk below Donelson in the Cumberland. Major Jeremy F. Gilmer, who had been graduated from West Point Academy with General Halleck in 1839, was put in charge of the engineering.

Fort Donelson, on the west bank of the Cumberland, was a few miles down the river from Dover, Tennessee, whence roads ran into the South. The fort was about eleven miles east of Fort Henry, which was built on the east bank of the Tennessee. By extending rifle pits inland the outer works of the two forts were brought within eight miles of each other and thus cooperation in defense was made possible. The location of Fort Henry was a blunder, for as soon as the heavy rains began much of its terrain became flooded; the outside became a swamp and the interior had two feet of water. The Confederates realized that the higher bank opposite commanded their works and began to fortify it, calling it Fort Heiman, but by February, 1862, it was still incomplete. Work on the forts was slow because of the shortage of labor; slave owners were reluctant to furnish slaves from their plantations, and when General Johnston ordered the impressment of 1,500 Negroes near Nashville he obtained less than 200.

Two Federal gunboats, the *Lexington* and the *Conestoga,* made several trips upriver on reconnaissance and threw shells into Fort Henry to test its resistance, once getting a brief reply. Brigadier General C. F. Smith, Flag Officer Andrew H. Foote, and Brigadier General U. S. Grant were convinced that a united movement of troops and gunboats against the forts should be undertaken without delay, but when Grant made a special trip to St. Louis to urge this on Major General Halleck the latter would not hear him out. Grant and Foote reiterated their request for urgent action and Halleck finally gave his consent. On February 2 Grant started to move 17,000 troops on steamboats, part of them from Cairo under the command of Brigadier General John A. McClernand and one division from Paducah under Brigadier General C. F. Smith.

Foote had been named flag officer of the Western Flotilla late in the fall of 1861. He had three wooden gunboats, the *Tyler, Lexington,* and *Conestoga,* which had been Ohio River steamboats. Their three decks had been cut down to one deck, boilers and engines had been lowered into the hulls, and planks of five-inch oak had been built up as bulwarks. Foote also had four armored gunboats, the *Cincinnati, St. Louis, Essex,* and *Carondelet,* which were paddle-wheel steamboats with 2½ inches of iron plate across their bows and protective plates at the sides of the boilers. Each gunboat was 175 feet long, had a beam of 51½ feet and a draft of 6 feet.

General McClernand debarked his troops about nine miles below Fort Henry on the east bank. Grant ordered General Smith to take a brigade up the west bank and capture Fort Heiman. The approach of gunboats and transports signaled to the watchers in Fort Henry that the Federals were about to attack in force. "Far as the eye could see," wrote one Confederate officer, "the course of the river could be traced by the dense volumes of smoke issuing from the flotilla." On the afternoon of February 5 three gunboats threw some shells at the fort and withdrew when the fort replied.

Grant had ordered an attack to begin at 11 A.M. February 6. The fleet was ready to act on time, but the troops were still pulling their boots out of the mud. About noon Foote started action; he led the advance with the four armored gunboats and threw shot into the fort with his bow guns. The gun crews in the fort had been ordered each to center shots on one vessel and follow that. The Federal fire put seven out of eleven usable guns out of action, but the Confederates did considerable damage to the Union boats before they had to stop. The *Carondelet* was struck in thirty places, the *Cincinnati* in thirty-two, but the *Essex* suffered the greatest casualties. A Confederate shell went through a casemate and ripped open a boiler. Two pilots were scalded to death; the acting master's mate was killed and the commander, Captain W. D. Porter, severely wounded, while on both sides the crew dived into the river to escape the steam. The flotilla had 7 killed, 27 wounded, and 5 missing at the close of the battle.

Around 2 P.M. the fort hauled down its flag and General Lloyd Tilghman was brought out in a small boat and surrendered to Flag Officer Foote. General Grant and the first troops arrived about an hour later, and then it was learned that the defense of the fort had been made by a mere handful of diehards, who had agreed to hold off the Federals for one hour to let their garrison escape, whereas they had managed to hold out for two. On the night before General Tilghman had ordered Colonel A. Heiman, Colonel Joseph Drake, and Colonel Nathan Bedford Forrest to take their 2,600 men to Fort Donelson, for he estimated that 25,000 Federals were on the

way and that the fort would be overrun. Only part of the
First Tennessee Artillery and 54 infantrymen remained
in the fort, and with the addition of workers and 16
in a hospital boat about 70 surrendered to Grant.
Only 5 of the garrison had been killed. An officer reported that when he went to haul down the flag the water
at the staff was waist-deep.

Grant sent a message to General Halleck reading:
"Fort Henry is ours. The gunboats silenced the batteries
before the investment was complete. I think the garrison
must have commenced the retreat last night. Our cavalry
followed, finding two guns abandoned in the retreat. I
shall take and destroy Fort Donelson on the 8th and
return to Fort Henry."

General Halleck congratulated Flag Officer Foote with
a warmth that may have reflected his growing irritation
with Grant. He ordered Foote to capture Fort Donelson
and Clarksville. "The taking of these places is a military
necessity," he wired.

U. S. Navy and Army at Donelson

The next day Grant reconnoitered Fort Donelson and
with a small contingent approached within a mile of the
outer works without interference. In the meantime General Halleck ordered new troops to join Grant, and a
brigade of midwestern regiments commanded by Colonel John M. Thayer arrived on steamboat transports on
February 12. Grant ordered them to turn about and proceed down the Tennessee with the gunboats, travel
three miles east on the Ohio to the mouth of the Cumberland, and then proceed up the Cumberland. Halleck
also assigned to him Lieutenant Colonel James B. Mc-
Pherson, an engineer, who, like Sherman, was to work
ably with Grant and eventually command large bodies of
troops.

Grant started his army on February 12. He had about
15,000 troops, including 8 batteries and a regiment of
cavalry. The First Division, Brigadier General John A.
McClernand commanding, took the right and moved
up to cover the roads that ran to Dover and thence out
of the state. The Second, under Brigadier General

Charles F. Smith, went to the left toward Hickman Creek. About 2,500 men from Smith's division were left at Forts Henry and Heiman under command of Brigadier General Lew Wallace. On February 13 General Wallace was ordered to take his troops to Fort Donelson, and when the brigade under Colonel Thayer finally steamed down the Cumberland it was added to Wallace's troops, and they constituted the Third Division, placed between Smith and McClernand and giving McClernand opportunity to extend his line to the left. General Grant made his headquarters at the house of a Mrs. Crisp, several miles down the river.

On the morning of the 13th the *Carondelet* engaged in a solo bombardment of the batteries of the fort, evoking a response from the Confederate gunners, who landed a hit on the gunboat. That night the area was visited by a furious storm of sleet and snow, which numbed with cold the shivering troops who were not clothed for winter weather. The next day General McClernand, harried by a Confederate battery that persistently shelled his position, sent a brigade to silence the offender. The troops had to move first down one hill and then up a stiff ascent protected by felled trees placed with their tops toward the attackers. Despite the obstructions the regiments got up to the rifle pits, but after three assaults they gave ground and moved back, suffering 49 dead and many wounded.

With the arrival of Flag Officer Foote on February 14 the gunboats went into action. The *Carondelet,* which had been using its rifled gun against the fort from a safe distance, was joined by the *St. Louis,* the *Louisville,* and the *Pittsburgh,* all ironclad. Foote brought his boats within 300 yards of the fort's batteries, which was unwise, for it not only permitted the fort to concentrate on targets close at hand but handicapped the boats because of the angle at which they had to shoot. Many of their shots went far over the target.

The Confederate gunners, though inexperienced, proved adept in taking aim. Although their 32-pounders fired only about 50 rounds each, against the 2,000 shot and shell that the Union gunboats expended, they did great damage. The *Carondelet* was hit 54 times;

one shot entered the pilothouse of the *St. Louis,* killed the pilot, wounded Foote, and smashed the wheel. The pilot of the *Louisville* was wounded and its steering ropes were shot away; when the disabled boats began to drift with the current the other two gunboats had to cover them and guide them. Men serving the guns were warned to get down away from the casemates the moment a shot was seen coming; this saved a number of lives, but when several gunners disregarded the warning a shot took off the heads of two, killed another, and disabled the gun. Two wooden gunboats, the *Tyler* and the *Conestoga,* were kept well in the rear. The Federal loss was 54 killed and wounded; the Confederates reported not a man in the batteries killed.

In reporting results of the exchange with the gunboats General Pillow wired Johnston exuberantly: "I have the utmost confidence of success," but General Floyd said more calmly: "We will endeavor to hold our position, if we are capable of doing so." General Johnston replied: "If you lose the fort, bring your troops to Nashville if possible."

Nothing was accomplished on February 14, but the Federal army grew by reinforcement. Both armies suffered another night of sleet, snow, and violent winds. During the night the Confederates planned to make a mass attack on Grant's army in the morning.

The Confederate attempt to break the ring of the investing Federals began at daybreak on February 15, under direction of General Pillow. The battle passed through three stages in some seven hours; first, the mass attack against General McClernand's position on the right, when the Confederate left threw 5,300 infantry and Forrest's cavalry against the Federals, first hitting Colonel Richard Oglesby's brigade, then Colonel McArthur's, and then that of Brigadier General W. H. L. Wallace, all Illinois regiments. Charges by Mississippi and Tennessee troops were repeatedly thrown back, but soon they were pushing McClernand against the center.

Calls for help went from McClernand to Grant, but the commanding general could not be found. He had answered a call from Flag Officer Foote to confer with him on his flagship several miles down the river. General Wallace thereupon sent Colonel Charles Cruft's brigade of Indianians against the Confederates, with some temporary success.

There was now loud talk among the raw troops that the day was lost. General Lew Wallace reported: "Some fugitives from the battle came crowding up the hill, in rear of my own line, bringing unmistakable signs of disaster. Captain Rawlings was conversing with me at the time, when a mounted officer galloped down the road, shouting: 'We are cut to pieces!' The effect was very perceptible. To prevent a panic among the regiments of my Third brigade I ordered Colonel Thayer to move on by the right flank. He promptly obeyed."

The Confederates under General Buckner had cleared the Wynn's Ferry road and the avenue for the evacuation of the fort was open, though still seriously challenged by the Federals. About this time Grant arrived from his conference with Foote; he talked with Generals McClernand and Wallace and took in the situation. It is reported that when he learned that McClernand had been driven back his face flushed and he crushed some papers he was holding; then he said quietly: "Gentlemen, the position on the right must be retaken."

Grant observed that troops had run out of ammunition and were standing out of range talking in an excited manner; they had muskets but no ammunition, yet there were "tons of it" close at hand. He heard men say the Confederates had come out with knapsacks and haversacks filled with rations. He turned to Colonel J. D. Webster of his staff: "Some of our men are pretty badly demoralized," he said, "but the enemy must be more so, for he has attempted to force his way out, but has fallen back; the one who attacks first now will be victorious, and the enemy will have to be in a hurry if he gets ahead of me."

He directed Colonel Webster to ride with him and call out: "Fill your cartridge boxes quick and get into line; the enemy is trying to escape and he must not be permitted to do so." He ordered General Smith to charge with his whole division. Smith's men worked their way through the abatis, passed the outer line of rifle pits, and fought with such vigor that they were able to camp that night inside the Confederate lines. Grant was convinced that the Confederates must surrender or be captured the next day.

Unconditional Surrender

At the close of the day's fighting the troops in the fort had suffered so severely that the commanders decided a retreat was necessary if the Federals had tightened their grip. Colonel Forrest reconnoitered the ground and reported the Federals had reoccupied their positions and increased their lines around the Confederate left. General Buckner said the only reason for holding on was to give Johnston a chance to reach Nashville, and upon being assured that Johnston had arrived there he agreed to give up. General Floyd, who had been Buchanan's Secretary of War, did not intend to be caught, so he turned the command over to Pillow. Pillow refused it and it fell to Buckner.

In the night General Floyd, accompanied by Pillow, led his regiments to Dover, where they embarked about 3,000 men on steamboats and eventually reached Nashville. Colonel Forrest, who said he and his cavalrymen would neither surrender nor be taken, led about 1,000 men across an icy slough and made his escape.

Grant received a request for terms from Buckner before daylight. Buckner asked "the appointment of commissioners to agree upon terms of capitulation of the fort and forces under my command" and suggested an armistice for this purpose until 12 noon on that day, February 16. Grant replied with a declaration that became famous. He said:

Yours of this date proposing armistice and appointment of commissioners to settle terms of capitulation is just received. No terms except an unconditional and immediate surrender can be accepted. I propose to move immediately upon your works.

Buckner had no choice. He dropped the terse sentence to justify his course and tell Grant what he thought of the terms:

The distribution of the forces under my command, incident to an unexpected change of commanders, and the overwhelming force under your command, compel me, notwithstanding the brilliant success of the Confederate arms yesterday, to accept the ungenerous and unchivalrous terms which you propose.

Grant rode to Dover and met General Buckner at his headquarters in Dover Tavern. The house is now a museum conducted by the Fort Donelson Historical Society. Grant had known Buckner for three years in West Point. Buckner thought there were not fewer than 12,000 and not more than 15,000 men in the fort, but the exact number is believed to have been around 17,000. The Federals registered 14,623 prisoners. General Pillow eventually reported 2,000 casualties. Grant said he had 27,000 men the day the fort fell, and the Union report gave the losses for army and navy as 2,886, of whom 510 were killed, 2,152 wounded, 224 missing.

Grant permitted the Confederate officers to keep their body servants, but refused to return the slaves who had labored at the fort to their masters. He said they might work for his army. He sent Major General Halleck the following despatch:

We have taken Fort Donelson and from 12,000 to 15,000 prisoners, including Generals Buckner and Bushrod Johnson, also 20,000 stand of arms, 48 pieces of artillery, 17 heavy guns, from 2,000 to 4,000 horses and large quantities of commissary stores.

Buckner's conduct at Fort Donelson won him the respect of his adversaries. It was recalled that he had taught military ethics at West Point Military Academy after completing his course there in 1844. He had served in the Mexican war, coming out with the rank of Captain. After further duties at West Point and on the frontier he resigned from the Army in 1855. His subsequent career after Fort Donelson won him the high regard of citizens of his state. The United States exchanged him in August, 1862, and he served later in the Chickamauga campaign under Bragg, advancing to the rank of lieutenant general.

[Buckner became governor of Kentucky, 1887–1891.

In 1896 came the split among the Democrats over the issue of free silver, with William Jennings Bryan nominated for President by the regular Democratic Party. Buckner followed the so-called Gold Democrats out of the party and was nominated for Vice President of the United States by the National Democratic Party. Although it took votes from Bryan, it did not attract enough to be the cause of his defeat. Buckner outlived most of the Civil War generals, dying in 1914, at the age of ninety. The high repute he had won was repeated by his son, Simon Bolivar Buckner, likewise a graduate of West Point and a lieutenant general, who commanded the Alaska Defense Force and was killed in action while commander of the 10th U.S. Army in World War II.]

The victory caused a tremendous outburst of rejoicing in the North and proportionately disheartened the South. When word of the surrender of Donelson reached Albert Sidney Johnston he sent a brief dispatch to General Beauregard: "At 2 A.M. today Fort Donelson surrendered. We lost all."

Governor Harris moved the state government of Tennessee to Memphis on February 20. The Confederacy inaugurated Jefferson Davis as President at Richmond, February 22, in low spirits and under rain-swept skies.

Davis relieved both Generals Floyd and Pillow of their commands. Evacuation of Bowling Green, Kentucky, planned before the battle, was done by February 16, the troops going to Nashville. The approach of the army of General Don Carlos Buell caused Johnston to evacuate Nashville. He gave Beauregard authority to evacuate Columbus if Richmond agreed, which it did. The Confederates evacuated their works at Columbus, Kentucky, on February 27 and moved to Island No. 10. Illinois regiments occupied Columbus, March 3. On the same day President Lincoln appointed Andrew Johnson military governor of Tennessee. He was a Democrat and the one senator who had not seceded with his state. He had been governor of Tennessee in 1848–1853. His rank was that of brigadier general.

In the North, Grant achieved a popular success. Secretary Stanton made much of his "immediate and unconditional surrender" terms, and people said Grant's initials

signified the last two words. Because a newspaper correspondent described Grant as smoking a cigar during
battle, the general became the recipient of so many
boxes of cigars that he gave up pipe smoking for cigars.

General Johnston was criticized and even reviled by
Southern partisans after the fall of Forts Henry and Donelson; officers and men, as well as civilians and even
legislators in Richmond, made him the scapegoat for
their disappointment and dismay. When he evacuated
Nashville and ordered his troops to march South, many
concluded that he was about to abandon Tennessee and,
according to his son, "wrath and terror" spread over the
whole state. "Bounds could scarcely be set to the fury and
despair of the people," wrote Colonel Johnston: "General Johnston was the special target of every accusation,
including imbecility, cowardice and treason."

Many, with a show of patriotic fervor, demanded of
President Davis that he remove Johnston, and when he
did not act the abuse was turned on him. Davis, wrote
one critic, "is motionless as a clod," also "as cold as ice."
The Confederate President appeared austere and withdrawn to the public, but to Albert Sidney Johnston he
expressed a warmth of friendly feeling not found in any
other association. Davis wrote Johnston with a display
of emotion rarely found in his letters. He explained that,
lacking a full report, the public naturally accepted suggestions and surmises, so for clarification he begged the
truth. This Johnston gave in a logical, frank exposition of
the condition of his troops. He admitted the irregularity of
transfer of command at Fort Donelson, but he did not
condemn Floyd or Pillow. "The blow was most disastrous,
almost without remedy," he wrote. "I therefore in my first
report remained silent. . . . I observed silence, as it
seemed to me to be the best way to serve the cause and
my country. . . . The test of merit in my profession is
success. It is a hard rule, but I think it right." When
President Davis acknowledged receipt of the report,
March 26, he wrote: "My confidence in you has never
wavered. . . . May God bless you is the sincere prayer of
your friend. . . ."

At this time, and for several years of the war, exchange
of prisoners was considered natural and right. Officers

had an advantage over privates and invariably got better consideration, but the poor fighting man was just a unit in the mass and making exchanges was a long and tedious business. It was also customary to parole prisoners, giving them liberty on their agreement not to fight again, and in the first months of the campaigns they were even sent on their way with a mere gesture, because the Union had no accommodations for them. But paroles were easily abused; a man released was often persuaded by appeals or threats to go back to his command to fight again, and there was no one to check on him. At Fort Donelson, Grant captured Colonels Brown, Hanson, Baldwin, and Heiman; they were released and the Confederacy promptly made them brigadier generals.

Halleck Interferes with Grant

Major General Halleck's attitude toward Grant after the victory was one of tolerance rather than commendation. When Fort Donelson fell, Halleck could not wholly ignore Grant, but he diverted credit to himself and General C. F. Smith. Thus he wired General McClellan: "Make Buell, Grant, and Pope major generals of volunteers and give me command in the West. I ask this for Forts Henry and Donelson." Two days later he added: "Brig. General Charles F. Smith, by his coolness and bravery at Fort Donelson when the battle was against us, turned the tide and carried the enemy's outworks. Make him a major general. You can't get a better one. Honor him for this victory and the whole country will applaud." The whole country at that moment was applauding Grant. The following day Halleck wired McClellan a new reminder of his ambition to obtain top command of the armies in the West. He stressed that this was the golden opportunity to strike a blow at the Confederates. He also explained to Secretary of War Stanton that he must have control of Buell's army.

There was one man in Washington who was not going to be rushed into decisions by Halleck. President Lincoln sent only Grant's name to the Senate for promotion to major general of volunteers and it was confirmed February 16. Buell and Pope had to wait until March 21.

While General Grant was active in the field during February, 1861, Major General Halleck, supervising half a dozen operations from headquarters in St. Louis, was becoming increasingly restive because he was not hearing from Grant. The latter had his orders and was not greatly concerned when he did not get regular messages from Halleck; moreover, his disposition was to work at his task and do little writing.

Major General Halleck carried a heavy load directing and coordinating the armies under his control. He was an efficient officer in some respects but he also had an overpowering self-assurance and he did not intend to let any army command become autonomous. He had small respect for Grant's easy disregard of official routine.

Gossip persisted in the army that Grant had been a hard drinker during his term of service on the Pacific Coast. When General Halleck became irritated by Grant's failure to make detailed reports during the campaign up the Tennessee and the Cumberland and filed complaints with General McClellan, he mentioned that Grant seemed to be slipping into his former bad behavior.

There must have been considerable talk of this nature, for after the battle of Shiloh a temperance committee waited on President Lincoln and asked him to remove Grant from the command because he drank too much whisky. President Lincoln is supposed to have replied: "I'd like to know where General Grant gets his whisky so that I can send a barrel to some of our other generals."

Grant had ordered Smith and his division to Clarksville, fifty miles above Fort Donelson on the way to Nashville, on February 21, and had gone to Nashville February 27 to confer with General Buell. When Halleck learned this he wanted to know by what authority this movement was made and ordered Smith back to the Tennessee. On March 4 he sent Grant the following order:

You will place Major General C. F. Smith in command of expedition, and remain yourself at Fort Henry. Why do you not obey my orders to report strength and positions of your command?

On March 6 Halleck wrote Grant: "Your going to

Nashville without authority, and when your presence
with your troops was of the utmost importance, was a
matter of very serious complaint at Washington, so
much so that I was advised to arrest you on your return."

Grant was puzzled by both orders, for Nashville was
not outside of his area of operation. He contended that
he made reports regularly, but that some orders reached
him only after long delays. For instance, a demand by
General McClellan for a report on the situation at Donelson, dated February 16, only reached Grant March 3.
Grant blamed the interference of a telegraph operator
who later deserted to the South. He turned the command
over to Smith and asked to be relieved from further duty
under Halleck.

Brigadier General W. T. Sherman, who had taken over
the Department of the Cumberland when Major General
Robert Anderson relinquished it, and whose headquarters
were at Louisville, thought that after Fort Donelson surrendered "there must have been a good deal of confusion
resulting from the necessary care of the wounded, and
disposition of prisoners, common to all such occasions,
and there was real difficulty in communicating between St.
Louis and Fort Donelson." Sherman wrote later: "Halleck
was evidently working himself into a passion, but he was
too far from the seat of war to make due allowances for
the actual state of facts. General Grant had done so much
that Halleck should have been patient."

General Halleck began sending to Sherman at Paducah messages intended for Grant, and Sherman sent
them on by steamboat. In one Halleck ordered Grant to
move up the Tennessee, destroy a railroad bridge near
Eastport and railroad connections at Corinth, Jackson,
and Humboldt. He advised Grant to avoid any general
engagements with strong forces. "It will be better to retreat than to risk a general battle." He recommended
General C. F. Smith "or some very discreet officer" for
expeditions from the river. Smith and Sherman were two
officers in whom Halleck had complete confidence.

But Sherman also had had difficulties with Washington.
In October, 1861, Secretary of War Cameron stopped in
Louisville on the return journey from St. Louis to Wash-
ington and conferred with General Sherman. Sherman

argued that unless a large force was raised to checkmate the Confederates they would be able to make a general advance toward the Ohio River and pick up at least 20,000 recruits from disloyal elements in Kentucky. Sherman estimated that about 60,000 Union troops would be needed to drive the Confederates from Kentucky, and that at least 200,000 would be absolutely necessary to carry the war to the Gulf, destroying all armed opposition in the entire Mississippi Valley.

Secretary Cameron heard him with irritation and exclaimed: "Where do you suppose all this force is to come from?" Sherman replied he did not know; to raise and organize the military was not his duty but that of the War Department; his duty was to organize campaigns and command the troops after they had been put into the field.

On his return to Washington, Secretary Cameron reported the circumstances of General Sherman's "insane request" for 200,000 men. When this was repeated in the newspapers the word spread that Sherman was crazy, insane. No doubt the obstacles put in his way were wearing him down; he was a man of quick decisions, who wanted to get action, and the incompetence of subordinates, the lack of coordination at the top, and the misuse of opportunities caused frustration that reacted on his volatile spirit. He was given a twenty-day leave of absence, and when his wife came down to be with him gossips were certain that he had experienced a mental breakdown. But Sherman came back refreshed and as ready as ever for hard work. General Halleck put no store in the damaging reports, and placed Sherman in command of Western Kentucky.

General Halleck continued to criticize Grant for failing to follow orders and for his "misbehavior," and Grant three times asked to be relieved of his command. "Thus, in less than two weeks after the victory at Donelson," wrote Grant in his *Personal Memoirs,* "the two leading generals in the army were in correspondence as to what disposition should be made of me and in less than three weeks I was virtually under arrest and without a command." Actually Grant was not under arrest nor was he removed; he was simply placed on the sidelines for ten days of inaction.

When President Lincoln demanded specific charges Halleck saw the weakness of his contentions and dodged a showdown by reporting "irregularities have now been remedied." He sent Grant a copy of his report "exonerating" him. The latter, ordered to resume his command March 15, did not know until many years later that Halleck had created the difficulties himself. The episode points out the poor liaison of the time between the top commander in St. Louis, who was responsible for the whole area, and the field commanders, who had to feel their way in a strange terrain.

While Grant was inactive and Smith was in command a momentous decision was taken, nothing less than making Pittsburg Landing, on the Tennessee, a short distance above the Mississippi border, a place of disembarkation for troops. General Sherman was at Paducah, expediting transports where ordered and organizing a division out of raw troops, which he was to command. On March 10, General Smith ordered Sherman to take his division of four brigades, move upriver, land troops, and proceed to Burnsville, to destroy railroad shops and tracks. Sherman started out but had to land his troops in a torrential rain. He then discovered that the whole region was inundated and impassable, and his men had to return to the transports.

On the way upriver the captain of the gunboat on which Sherman was riding informed him that Pittsburg Landing was the usual depot for the farmers of the area, that roads ran to Corinth, and that Confederate cavalry had been posted there. Sherman tied up at Pittsburg Landing on his return trip, looked it over, and then went to Savannah to confer with Smith. Smith ordered him to disembark his troops and those of General Hurlbut at the Landing and leave room for Smith's army. Thus the responsibility for choosing Pittsburg Landing, with its subsequent effect on the fortunes of the war, rests on Sherman's recommendation and Smith's decision, and Grant had no voice in it.

11

THE BATTLE OF SHILOH

Surprise at Pittsburg Landing

On the morning of Sunday, April 6, 1862, Major General U. S. Grant was eating breakfast at his Savannah headquarters when he heard the sound of heavy firing upstream. He immediately boarded his dispatch boat, the *Tigress,* with his staff to steam for Pittsburg Landing nine miles away, where the bulk of his army was encamped. Before leaving he wrote a terse note to Brigadier General William Nelson of Buell's army ordering him to move from Savannah to the river opposite Pittsburg, and a second note to Major General Buell, in which he said: "I have been looking for this, but did not believe the attack could be made before Monday or Tuesday."

About five miles up the river was Crump's Landing, where Major General Lew Wallace was stationed with the Third Divison of the Army of the Tennessee, guarding supplies. Grant had been more worried about the safety of these supplies than about the army at Pittsburg. He did not think the Confederates could capture either place, but he feared that a quick raid on Crump's might destroy transports and stores.

When Grant came up the river on the *Tigress* he found General Wallace waiting for him on board his own headquarters steamboat at Crump's Landing. Grant brought his boat alongside that of Wallace and the two officers stood on the hurricane decks as Grant ordered Wallace to hold his division ready to march "in any direction." Wallace replied that he had been ready since 6 A.M.

At 8 A.M. Grant reached Pittsburg Landing and discovered that his troops already were hotly engaged with the Confederates; he forthwith sent a staff officer to order Wallace "to march immediately to Pittsburg by the road nearest the river." Then mounting his horse Grant plunged into the task of directing the elements of his army to stop a concerted attack that already had pushed back the forward positions of the Federal left.

The reason Grant was not at Pittsburg Landing when the Confederates attacked was that he stayed every night at Savannah, after looking after his troops during the day. He had been expecting to confer with Major General Don Carlos Buell this very morning; the first troops of General Buell's Army of the Ohio, part of the division commanded by Brigadier General Nelson, already had arrived. Neither Grant nor Sherman, commanding Grant's Third Division, considered Pittsburg Landing anything more than a jumping-off base for an attack on Corinth; Sherman called the Federals an army of invasion, and Grant had not thought entrenching necessary.

Yet he had given attention to the skirmishing at the front and said that it had been so continuous from about April 3 on that he did not leave Pittsburg Landing at night until he felt there would be no further danger of anything serious before morning. On the night of April 4 Grant had been trying to follow the sound of firing in the impenetrable darkness during a thunderstorm, and his horse had slipped in the mire and fallen, pinning his leg under him, so that for several days he had to stumble about on crutches.

Grant had wired General Halleck from Savannah on April 5: "The main force of the enemy is at Corinth, with troops at different points east. The number of the enemy at Corinth and in supporting distance of it cannot be far from 80,000 men," which was about twice the actual number. He also told Halleck: "I have scarcely the faintest idea of an attack (general one) being made upon us, but will be prepared should such a thing take place." He also told Colonel Jacob Ammen of the Tenth Brigade, Army of the Ohio, on the 5th: "There will be no fight at Pittsburg Landing; we will have to go to Corinth where the rebels are fortified." General Sherman had similar views: "The enemy is saucy, but got the worst of it yesterday and will not press our pickets far. I do not apprehend anything like an attack on our position."

Pittsburg Landing was about thirty miles north of Corinth, Mississippi, and the place where steamboats called for produce and timber. Roads from Corinth, Hamburg, and Purdy led directly to it. There was a high bluff above the Landing, and on the tableland beyond it the troops occupied a wooded terrain broken at intervals by roads and clearings, cut by creeks swollen by the heavy rains. The Union area was roughly a triangle with the Tennessee River on the East, Snake Creek on the Northwest, Lick Creek on the Southeast, and Oak Creek flowing into Snake Creek. About two and one half miles from the Landing stood a small log house, Shiloh Church, erected by the Southern Methodists, which gave its name to Union records of the battle, although the Confederates preferred the name of Pittsburg Landing.

After the fall of Fort Donelson, Corinth, Mississippi, was the logical point for concentration of the defeated Confederate forces. Located near the big bend of the Tennessee, it was at the junction of two major railroads, the Memphis & Charleston and the Mobile & Ohio, and one smaller line. Pittsburg Landing was about thirty miles northeast on the Tennessee. General Albert Sidney Johnston had reorganized at Murfreesboro, building up his army from Bowling Green, from survivors of Crittenden's army and veterans from Fort Donelson, as well as 4,000 from Arkansas under Major General William J. Hardee. He then proceeded to Corinth over difficult roads muddied by rains. Having assigned the area west of the Tennessee to Major General Pierre G. T. Beauregard, he ordered him to gather an army at Corinth. General Johnston brought about 23,000 to Corinth of whom 16,000 were effectives.

Major General Braxton Bragg had been transferred from his command at Pensacola and ordered to join Johnston; he became the latter's chief of staff with the proviso that he retain command of his troops, numbering about 5,000. Major General Leonidas Polk brought up 17,500, and 5,000 Louisianians came from New Orleans under Brigadier General Daniel Ruggles. After Beauregard had placed about 10,000 at posts along the river he had over 30,000 and with Johnston's troops about 40,000 effectives. This coincides with the estimates in *Official Records.*

Johnston had a clear concept of how the Federal campaign to hold Kentucky and Tennessee might develop and made his plans accordingly. He took for granted that the Federals would use their gunboats and proceed by the rivers. It was related by Colonel Frank Schaller of the Twenty-second Mississippi regiment, later professor of modern languages at Sewanee, Tennessee, that when Johnston had his headquarters in Bowling Green, Kentucky, in January, 1862, he was examining a map with Colonel John S. Bowen. Pointing to a spot marked Shiloh Church by the engineers, he said: "Here the great battle of the Southwest will be fought." Three months later Schaller and Bowen met on the field of Shiloh on the afternoon of the first day's fighting and Bowen recalled the prediction.

General Sherman had made his headquarters at Shiloh Church, and his troops extended across the Corinth Road on the east to Owl Creek on the west. Brigadier General Benjamin M. Prentiss' division was to the left of Sherman's and extended across another Corinth road. On the extreme left lay the second brigade of Sherman's division, commanded by Colonel David Stuart. A short distance behind Sherman and to the left was Major General John A. McClernand with the First Division. Closer to Pittsburg Landing were the Fourth Division under Brigadier General Stephen A. Hurlbut, and to his right, or northwest, the Second Division under Brigadier General W. H. L. Wallace. This was actually the division of Major General C. F. Smith. In climbing out of a boat Smith had suffered a flesh wound on a leg; although this did not seem serious it led to incapacitation, and by the time of Shiloh he had given up his command and was lying ill in Savannah, in the house Grant was using as headquarters. The wound became infected and Smith died from it within the month.

The Federal troops had done no entrenching and thus had nothing but the natural barriers of woods and creeks to give them shelter. Grant wrote later that he considered it better to give time to drill, but the lack of trenches has been generally criticized.

The Union skirmishers and outposts had several clashes with Confederate units in the weeks preceding Shiloh. When General Sherman in March probed the Confederate area he found the Memphis road occupied in force and reported that there were probably 30,000 men along the railroad from Corinth to Iuka. On April 4 the Fifth Ohio Cavalry and some infantry units engaged a Confederate force at Monterey or Pea Ridge, and lost a number of officers and privates; on April 5, the day before the battle, Sherman reported "the enemy's cavalry was again very bold, coming well down to our front; yet I did not believe they designed anything but a strong demonstration."

Yet only a few miles farther south General Albert Sidney Johnston by April 2 had completed plans to attack Grant in force at 3 A.M. on Saturday, April 5, and was deterred only because the muddy roads and the continuing rain caused confusion and delay among the troops as they moved into position.

General Beauregard was apprehensive. Just as Grant misjudged the number of Confederates at Corinth, so Beauregard overestimated the Federals; he thought they must have 70,000 fighting men at Pittsburg Landing. He was also certain that the Federals must have found out by reconnoitering that the Confederates were preparing to attack. "There is no chance for a surprise," he argued when he had all the commanders in conference. "Now they will be entrenched up to the eyes." Johnston, Bragg, Polk, Breckinridge, and Gilmer attended the council the night before the battle, when Beauregard declared that Buell must have reinforced Grant by that time. But General Johnston was not to be stopped by Beauregard's anxiety. He swept Beauregard's argument aside with: "I would fight them if they were a million!"

Beauregard had a different plan: keep the Confederate army intact at Corinth; lure the Federals to attack far from their own base. Polk and Bragg disagreed, and Johnston announced: "We shall attack at daylight tomorrow." At dawn on April 6, when the troops were already moving forward, Beauregard renewed his objections, but Johnston, hearing the sound of firing, said: "The battle has opened, gentlemen, it is too late to change our dispositions." Observing the clear sunrise, which prompted someone to recall the sun of Austerlitz, Johnston promised his staff: "Tonight we will water our horses in the Tennessee River."

The Confederate army advanced in parallel lines extending over a wide swath of woods and occasional clearings. The front line, with 9,024 under Major General William J. Hardee, extended from Owl Creek to Lick Creek, over three miles. The second line, under Bragg, had 10,731. The third, or reserve, under Polk and Breckinridge, remained 800 yards behind Bragg; Polk had 9,136, Breckinridge 6,439. Cavalry numbering 4,300 guarded flanks and outposts. The total in battle, as estimated by Colonel William Bristow Johnston, son of General Johnston, in a later study was 39,630, close to the report of 40,335 in *Official Records*. More recent studies place the total number of Confederates engaged at 44,699.

The troops clashed first on the Corinth Road at about 5 A.M. General Prentiss had ordered three companies of the Twenty-fifth Missouri Infantry Regiment forward at dawn to ascertain the extent of the outposts. When the firing became strong, companies of the Twenty-first Missouri and the Sixteenth Wisconsin were sent to help them. When the advancing Confederates drove back the pickets General Sherman ordered all troops under arms. He posted brigades to guard the bridge over Owl Creek on the right and the ford at Lick Creek on his left, and placed batteries of the First Illinois Artillery at strategic positions with Major Ezra Taylor at Shiloh and Captain A. C. Waterhouse on a ridge to the left, and three regiments from Major General McClernand's division protecting Waterhouse and Sherman's left flank. As Sherman rode along the front with his staff, pickets on the opposite bank of a creek shot down his orderly. "At 8 A.M.," he wrote in his official report, "I saw the glistening bayonets of heavy masses of infantry to our left front in the woods . . . and became satisfied for the first time that the enemy designed a determined attack on our whole camp."

The sharpest attack now developed on Sherman's left and against Prentiss. Many of the Union soldiers were raw recruits and the intensity of the Confederate attack pushed them back until they broke and ran to cover. The third brigade of Sherman's division, chiefly Ohio troops commanded by Colonel Jesse Hildebrand, melted away, but its colonel continued fighting. The Confederates overran Prentiss' camp, and General Braxton Bragg re-

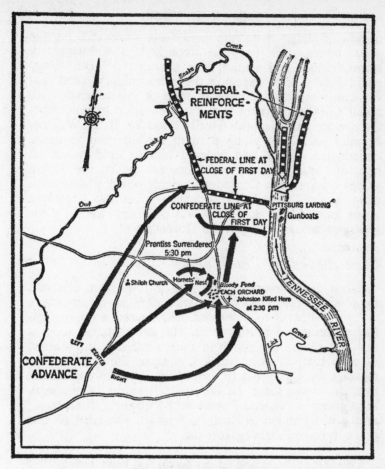

The Battle of Shiloh
April 6-7, 1862

The Confederates pushed forward three powerful prongs with the object of forcing the Union army into the Tennessee River. They moved forward rapidly against the Union right, but at left and center struck the stubborn defense at the Peach Orchard and Hornet's Nest. On the second day Grant was able to throw in the reinforcements of Generals Buell and Lew Wallace and force the Confederates off the field.

membered later that "the breakfasts were still on the
mess tables, the baggage unpacked, the knapsacks,
stores, colors and ammunition abandoned." But Bragg
could hardly have expected the extraordinary stand that
Prentiss was able to make in spite of this reverse. With
about 1,000 of his men as a core, and aided by units from
the divisions of Generals Hurlbut and W. H. L. Wallace,
Prentiss took post along a small sunken road in dense
underbrush. Grant had ordered him to hold on at all
hazards, and he held on. Here for hours the Union
troops held up the Confederate right, which was to have
piled up the Union left and pushed it into the Tennessee
River long before. So galling was their fire that the Confederates named the spot the Hornet's Nest.

Grant Looks for Lew Wallace

When Grant reached the field he rode from one unit
to another, conferred briefly with division commanders,
moved regiments to new positions, cleared ways for getting ammunition to the front. He never tarried long at
any one place, and spoke in short sentences and seemed
of even temper as he smoked a cigar. He sent another
message by steamboat to Savannah; apparently uncertain
that Buell was there, he addressed it to the "Commanding Officer, Advanced Forces near Pittsburg, Tennessee,"
and it was handed to Buell on board the steamer he had
taken to go to Pittsburg. It read:

GENERAL: The attack on my forces has been very spirited
since early this morning. The appearance of fresh troops on
the field now would have a powerful effect, both by inspiring our men and disheartening the enemy. If you will get
upon the field, leaving all your baggage on the east bank of
the river, it will be a move to our advantage, and possibly
save the day for us. The rebel forces are estimated at over
100,000 men. My headquarters will be in the log building on
the top of the hill, where you will be furnished a staff-
officer to guide you to your place on the field.

General Buell's army was already in motion. Nelson
was marching up the east bank of the Tennessee over
"a labyrinth of roads from which the overflows had ob-

literated all recent signs of travel." His artillery was
coming up by steamer. At one o'clock Buell reached the
Landing and was shocked to behold the great stream of
fugitives. He met Grant on the headquarters boat and
decided Grant lacked the air of "masterly confidence"
he was supposed to have. Buell asked Grant to bring up
Brigadier General Thomas L. Crittenden's division by
steamer, which Grant ordered done.

But where were Lew Wallace and his 5,000 men, who
ought to be coming up the river road at any moment?
Grant's order telling Wallace to come up had been
verbal; he had told Adjutant General Rawlins "to tell
Wallace to march immediately to Pittsburg by the road
nearest the river," and join the army on the right. He was
to leave a force behind to guard the stores at Crump's
Landing. The order was reduced to writing by Captain
Baxter, who carried it. Wallace had left 1,727 men behind at Crump's and started out with over 5,000, but
where was he now? Grant ordered several officers to find
out; among them was Colonel (later Major General)
John B. McPherson.

They found Wallace, but not where he was expected
to be. He was moving in a westerly direction on the
Purdy Road, evidently following the sound of guns, and
he had already covered about fourteen miles through
bogs and muddy roads: as he explained later, "for five
miles through mire so deep that the axles of my guns
left wakes behind them as if mud-scows had been
dragged that way."

General Wallace contended that he had followed orders.
The confusion seemed to have arisen because Grant's
original order was verbal and Captain Baxter later had
written his version in pencil. Wallace asserted that when
he received it at 11:30 A.M. the notation read: "You
will have a sufficient force at Crump's Landing to guard
the public property there; with the rest of the division
march and form junction with the right of the army.
Form line of battle at right angle of the river and be
governed by circumstances." When McPherson located
him he had marched past Snake Creek and Clear Creek
and was headed toward the Confederate left. Because
Wallace wanted his strongest units in front he did not

turn his troops about but countermarched them, which necessitated two columns on the road and delayed them still further. As a result Wallace did not reach the field until dusk, when Grant's army was binding its wounds in the torrential rain.

Grant was highly critical of Wallace's long march, but he respected Wallace, who had a most honorable career in the army. Wallace was one of the best writers in the army and later became famous as the author of *Ben Hur*.

There were many raw recruits at Shiloh—Grant himself said three of the five divisions were raw, hardly able to load their muskets. Consequently it was not remarkable that they should break and run at the first terrible onslaught of their experience. Grant said two colonels led their regiments from the field on first hearing the whistle of bullets. General Buell described the hordes of stragglers under the cliff at the river. Officers harangued them in vain; these lads from the farms and towns of the Midwest had never dreamed of facing such heavy volleys of gunfire. The confusion caused by disorganization of units was great; regiments were mixed up and divisions lost their separate identities. Grant had no excuses for the defecting colonels, but he understood what had happened to the young fellows who were suddenly confronted with bloodshed. He could boast later that "better troops never went upon a battlefield."

Death of Albert Sidney Johnston

At a point near the Peach Orchard, the Confederates had been unable to make headway against the Union fire. General Albert Sidney Johnston was determined to carry the position, even though it meant sending troops across an open valley between two ridges swept by rifle fire. Sizing up the situation, Johnston said to his staff: "They are offering stubborn resistance here. I shall have to put the bayonet to them." He ordered a charge, first riding up and down the line on Fire-eater, his bay, and calling out: "I will lead you!" The gray brigades bounded forward, gained the crest of the hill, and pushed back the Federal line with bayonets. The Federals retired in broken groups, turning to fire as they gave way. General Johnston's horse was hit in four places, his clothes were pierced, and the sole of one boot was torn by a Minié ball.

While he was continuing to give orders, Governor Isham Harris of Tennessee, who was acting as his aide, suddenly asked: "General, are you wounded?"

"Yes, and I fear seriously," replied Johnston.

Harris and Captain Wickham quickly led his horse under cover of the hill and lifted him from it. They found blood running into a boot from a severed leg artery. Johnston had sent his surgeon away to attend wounded men, and no one present thought of applying a tourniquet, which, according to medical opinion, would have saved his life. He bled to death without speaking again.

When General Johnston died General Pierre G. T. Beauregard took top command, with his headquarters beside Shiloh Church, which General Sherman had given up under pressure from the Confederate right. Beauregard gave General Daniel Ruggles orders to push through the Union defense at the center. Ruggles collected 62 guns and subjected the whole Union line to a continuous shelling. The Federal troops at the left and right drew back, leaving units of Prentiss and Brigadier General W. H. L. Wallace isolated in the Hornet's Nest. As the Confederates advanced they came around the flanks of these fighting troops. Thereupon Wallace ordered his troops to withdraw, and two regiments left the position by way of a ravine, subjected to Confederate fire from both sides, and since named Hell's Hollow. Here General W. H. L. Wallace received a mortal wound.

General Prentiss surrendered at about 5:30 P.M. with 2,200 officers and men. Although not a trained soldier, he had accomplished an extraordinary military feat at Shiloh by keeping the Confederates from disrupting the whole Union line. He had been fighting for eleven hours. General Beauregard, reviewing the start of the battle, mentioned Prentiss was alert as early as 3 A.M. on April 6, when he sent the Missouri companies to the front. Beauregard wrote: "But for this incident, due solely to the intelligent, soldierly forethought of an officer not trained to the business of war, the whole Federal front would have been struck wholly unawares, for nowhere else had such prudence been shown." This precautionary movement made Halleck assert that the army was not surprised.

When Prentiss surrendered, action practically stopped at that point in the Confederate line. Officers and men crowded forward to view the Yankee captives. During the night Prentiss occupied a tent with two officers, and one of them, Colonel Thomas Jordan, adjutant general of the Confederate Army, recalled Prentiss' remark: "You gentlemen have had your way today, but it will be very different tomorrow. You'll see! Buell will effect a junction with Grant tonight, and we'll turn the tables on you in the morning." Next morning, when heavy artillery fire awoke them, Prentiss exclaimed: "Ah, didn't I tell you so! There is Buell."

A deep ravine, with Dill's Branch of the Tennessee River passing through it, lay in front of the Federal left, and on the high ground behind it Colonel J. D. Webster, chief of staff, collected a score or more of batteries from various units. Brigadier General Bushrod Johnson and Brigadier General James R. Chalmers of the Confederate Army brought up segments of their commands and delivered a series of assaults on the hill, driving some gunners from their pieces, but they were unable to hold any gains. Grant described this action as "the enemy's last desperate effort to turn our flank." By this time the Thirty-sixth Indiana Infantry Regiment of Major General Buell's Army of the Ohio, under Colonel Jacob Ammen, had crossed the Tennessee and taken a position on the ridge and begun firing on the Confederates. This new support, together with the weakened character of the Confederate troops, who were running short of ammunition, caused the latter to break off the assault and discontinue the battle.

During this action the gunboats *Tyler* and *Lexington* moved up and began sending shells over the bluff to reach the Confederates, but the high elevation necessary sent the shots far over the heads of the fighters. This was not without effect, however, for as the heavy shells crashed in the Confederate rear, shattering trees in the forest, they created havoc among reserves and stragglers who were not properly coordinated with the rest of the troops. As General Bragg testified later: "To the utter dismay of the commanders on the field, the troops were seen to abandon their inspiring work, and to retire sullenly from the contest when the danger was almost past, and victory, so dearly purchased, was almost certain."

Beauregard Halts His Troops

It was now 6 P.M. on that disastrous Sunday. General Beauregard observed that Chalmers had been repulsed and that "the troops had got out of the hands either of corps, divisional and brigade commanders and for the most part at the front were out of ammunition." He dispatched orders to corps commanders to cease fighting, get the troops out from under the fire of the gunboats, and have them sleep on their arms.

This order, welcome as it must have been to soldiers who had been fighting since dawn and had seen many men killed beside them, was resented by several of the commanding officers, who looked to a united effort to defeat the Federals in the hour of daylight that still remained. Foremost among those who were aggrieved was General Braxton Bragg, who wrote in his report of April 20 that his troops were starting an attack with every hope of success when they were called off. In the controversy that developed years after the war Colonel S. H. Lockett, who had been Bragg's chief engineer at Shiloh, gave a statement to the editors of the *Century*, published also in *Battles and Leaders of the Civil War*:

I was with General Bragg and rode with him along the front of his corps. I heard him say over and over again "One more charge, my men, and we shall capture them all." While this was going on a staff officer . . . came up to General Bragg and said: "The General directs that the pursuit be stopped; the victory is sufficiently complete; it is needless to expose our men to the fire of the gunboats." General Bragg said: "My God, was a victory ever sufficiently complete?" and added: "Have you given that order to anyone else?" "Yes sir," was the reply, "to General Polk, on your left, and if you will look to the left you will see that the order is being obeyed." General Bragg looked and said, "My God, my God, it is too late!"

Bragg had a true understanding of the task before the

Confederates. Roll up Grant's army the first day; push it
into the Tennessee before Buell could arrive with
(presumably) 25,000 fresh fighters. Then, laden with
the prestige and spoils of victory, crush Buell separately,
and exploit the advantages gained to control the Middle
West. That was the master plan. It was deflected by the
stubborn defense of the Federals, who halted both cavalry
and infantry attacks as they drew back, and continued to
mount similar attacks of their own. As the Federal
front narrowed, it became harder to crack. This weakened the striking power of the Confederate units and
wore them out. Bragg thought the final push would have
knocked out the Federals; Beauregard saw his own army
weakening and judged the day's work was done.

That night someone asked Grant in the hearing of
Whitelaw Reid, newspaper correspondent: "Does not the
prospect begin to look gloomy?" "Not at all," replied
Grant. "They can't force our lines around these batteries
tonight—it is too late. Delay counts everything with us.
Tomorrow we shall attack them with fresh troops and
drive them, of course."

It rained during the night and the troops, worn down
almost beyond endurance, had a miserable time. Even
Grant had no tent over him; Sherman found him sitting
at the base of a tree, hat pulled down, coat collar turned
up. There was little rest for anyone, friend or foe, for
Colonel Webster had orders to fire guns at intervals, and
the gunboats *Lexington* and *Tyler* added to the din by
sending shells to disturb the Confederates in the far
woods, thus keeping the Federals on edge as well. Buell
visited Sherman in the evening and obtained a crude map
of the terrain that Sherman had drawn; Buell was to
find much fault with it later, but it had served its purpose.

Buell's Army to the Front

On the morning of Monday, April 7, 1862, the reinforcements were in position to attack, with General Buell's
army occupying the left wing and General Lew Wallace
posted at the extreme right. The commands, left to right,
were placed as follows: Brigadier General William Nelson
at the extreme left, then Brigadier General Thomas L.

Crittenden, and Brigadier General Alexander McCook, all of Buell's army; then Hurlbut, McClernand, and Sherman, the last adjoining Lew Wallace.

At daylight next morning General Sherman received Grant's order to advance and recapture his original camps; he lined up his troops and waited for the sound of Buell's advance on the main Corinth Road, and he took satisfaction in knowing that General Wallace was on his left flank "with his well-conducted division." The fresh troops swung quickly into action; General Sherman saw the "well ordered and compact columns of General Buell's Kentucky forces" going forward and Wallace's regiment enter a dangerous thicket "in beautiful style"; after its repulse Brigadier General Alexander McDowell McCook's division "advanced beautifully, deployed and entered this dreaded wood."

The Federals now struck with all their reserve energy. With a rush they regained the line of the Hornet's Nest and the Peach Orchard and captured more pieces of artillery than they had lost the day before. Although the whole battle line was in action Beauregard anchored his left securely at Shiloh Church and endeavored to retain control of the main road to Corinth, by which he hoped General Earl Van Dorn would arrive with reinforcements. Van Dorn, however, had been unable to get boats to ferry him across the Mississippi.

When Beauregard learned this he fought to keep the road open for retreat, and some of the hardest fighting took place around it and on a line including Water Oaks Pond. The Confederates still had formidable strength, but were being forced back. A little after 2 P.M. General Beauregard gave the order to retire. His troops moved back in orderly fashion with General Breckinridge in charge of the rearguard. They carried with them 30 Federal guns and a quantity of small arms, as well as more than 3,000 prisoners.

Grant did not pursue, even though Breckinridge's bivouac was but two miles beyond the battlefield. He noted the great fatigue of his men, and to Buell cited the instructions of Major General Halleck: not to advance beyond a point from which the troops could return in a day.

On the morning of April 8 troops from the division of

Brigadier General Thomas J. Wood of Buell's army, and the Fourth Illinois Cavalry and two brigades of General Sherman's division of Grant's army, started after the Confederates and met them at Fallen Timbers, six miles away. Here they were stopped by Confederate cavalry under Colonel Nathan Bedford Forrest, who followed the Federals until he in turn was halted by a strong unit of infantry. His troops were repulsed and he was seriously wounded.

After the second day's fighting Grant received a note from Beauregard, asking leave to send men to bury the Confederate dead. Grant chuckled over the polite wording; it began: "At the close of the conflict yesterday, my forces being exhausted by the extraordinary length of time during which they were engaged with yours . . . and it being apparent that you had received and were still receiving reinforcements, I felt it my duty to remove my troops . . ." Grant replied to the burial request: "Owing to the warmth of the weather I deemed it advisable to have all the dead of both parties buried immediately . . . now it is accomplished." Federals and Confederates were placed in separate trenches, but four years after the battle the Union dead were removed to the new national cemetery. The Confederate dead still lie in five suitably marked trenches, the largest containing 721 bodies stacked seven deep. The place is part of Shiloh National Military Park, a unit of the National Park System.

After Shiloh a bruised and battered Southern army stumbled slowly back to Corinth, Mississippi. "The whole road presents the scene of a rout," wrote General Braxton Bragg. The hospitals of both sides were jammed and urgent calls for doctors and nurses were out, but the Confederate command in Corinth found their numbers inadequate. The toll of men killed on each side, over 1,700, was as nothing to the 16,000 who, a few days before, were hale human beings and now faced amputations and festering wounds, which would carry off many of them. The Confederate doctors estimated that eight out of every ten amputations ended in death; there were no drugs to combat tetanus and gangrene and supplies of chloroform were quickly exhausted. In the yard of the Tishomingo Hotel in Corinth there was a huge and increasing pile of amputated limbs.

The number of men under arms and the casualties were never ascertained exactly. Grant spoke in general terms of 33,000 effectives, with never more than 25,000 actually fighting. Buell thought he had 25,000, with 20,000 engaged. The *Official Records* said there were 44,895 present for duty, including noncombatants. The Army of the Tennessee had 1,513 killed, 6,601 wounded, 2,830 captured or missing, total casualties 10,944. Brigadier General W. H. L. Wallace was mortally wounded; Generals Grant and Sherman were wounded (Grant when his horse fell and pinned a leg under him), and Brigadier General Prentiss was captured. The Army of the Ohio had 241 killed, 1,807 wounded, 55 missing; total casualties, 2,103. Total Union casualties were 13,047, of whom 1,754 were killed.

The Confederate losses were estimated at 1,728 killed, 8,012 wounded, and 959 captured. Major General Albert Sidney Johnston and Brigadier General A. H. Gladden were killed and Major General W. S. Cheatham and Brigadier Generals C. Clark and B. R. Johnson, and Colonel J. S. Bowen were wounded.

12

THE *MONITOR* AND THE *MERRIMACK*

The Confederate Ironclad

When it appeared that the sentiment for secession was strong in Virginia and that the state was likely to vote itself out of the Union, the Washington government became greatly concerned over the safety of military installations and supplies there. Stores could not be moved north in time, and there were no troops available to protect them. Therefore the government ordered the arsenal and armory at Harpers Ferry to be destroyed, and it was abandoned April 8, 1861.

When Virginia on April 17 voted to secede, the Federal government, alarmed by reports that armed bands were forming, decided to give up the extensive Gosport Navy Yard near Portsmouth, across the Elizabeth River from Norfolk, which naval authorities decided could not be defended. The abandonment of Gosport proved to be a major calamity. Conflicting orders over several weeks had confused the elderly commandant, Commodore Charles S. McCauley, who was considered loyal but not astute. The presence of numerous Southern sympathizers among officers and men in the navy yard was also a hazard. Although importuned to get the steam frigate *Merrimack* repaired and out of danger in time, McCauley was able to save only one sailing frigate, the *Cumberland,* by having it towed away; nine other naval vessels, from sloops to ships of the line, were scuttled and burned there. Supplies captured whole by the Confederates included 1,200 heavy guns and many shells and rounds of ammunition for small arms. A huge granite dry dock that was to have been wrecked by a mine, was left intact when the mine failed to explode.

The most remarkable windfall for the Confederates was the hull and machinery of the *Merrimack,* 3,200 tons, 275 feet long, capable of carrying 40 guns. This four-year-old ship had been sent to Gosport for repairs, and although work had been pushed the ship was only partially ready when the yard was evacuated. McCauley ordered the ship scuttled and set afire. Most of the superstructure had been burned when the Confederates arrived, but they saved the rest. They raised the hull, reconditioned the engine, and then redesigned a fighting ship such as never had been seen, and helped change the mode of naval warfare.

The rebuilt vessel was named the *Virginia,* but historians persisted in continuing to call it the *Merrimack,* spelling the name without the final *k,* and it was thus referred to even in accounts by Confederate writers. But inasmuch as the ship fought under the name of *Virginia,* and appears thus in Confederate naval records, it seems appropriate to call it that in this account of the battle.

The intense activity of the Confederates at Gosport

Navy Yard was under constant surveillance by Union sympathizers. As one alarming report after another reached Washington, the authorities awoke to the danger that threatened the Federal blockading squadron of wooden ships at Hampton Roads. For the reports said that the Confederates were building an ironclad ship, one that would withstand cannon shot. Iron plates for ships had been talked about for twenty years, and the subject now started an intensified debate. The Stevens family, of Hoboken, New Jersey, had experimented with a floating battery protected by iron plates, and Robert L. Stevens' design of 1843 had received a subsidy from Congress but remained incomplete at his death. Such floating batteries withstood the shots from land batteries in the Crimean War. In 1858 France had applied armor plate to its steam frigate *La Gloire* and was followed immediately by Great Britain, which built the *Warrior* and *Ironsides*, but in these ships the armor was only amid-ships.

In considering "iron armature for ships of war" Secretary of the Navy Gideon Welles and the Naval Board did not include the armature that was already being placed on gunboats on the Mississippi. James B. Eads, engineer and bridge builder, talked with Secretary Welles in Washington in April, 1861, about building gunboats, and in August he was awarded contracts for building seven, which were to carry 13 guns each and be plated with 2½-inch iron. They had flat sides that sloped at an angle of 35 degrees; the front and rear casemates corresponded with the sides, and the stern wheel was covered by the rear casemate. With 4,000 men engaged in construction, the first ironclad, named the *St. Louis,* and later called *Baron de Kalb,* was launched October 12, 1861, forty-five days after laying of the keel. An eighth ironclad was converted from the river snagboat *Benton.* The eight ships, however, were not entirely ready until January because of lack of funds and changes in design. Thus the slanting casemates and the use of iron plates were not original with the conversion of the *Merrimack* by the Confederates, which makes the procrastination of the naval officials in Washington all the more blameworthy.

At the beginning of 1861 the United States had 90 ships

of war of all classes, of which 50 were sailing vessels and
40 used steam. Five of the latter were not in service and
one was on the Great Lakes. Four large side-wheelers had
been completed in 1850. Seventeen ships were on foreign
missions. After the government recalled its ships and
counted its strength it had in service 30 steamships; of its
6 modern screw-frigates (sail and steam) built in
1855, the *Merrimack* alone had been left at Gosport
Navy Yard.

Charles Ellet, Jr., a Pennsylvania civil engineer who
had constructed a wire suspension bridge below Niagara
Falls in 1847, for several years before the war advised the Navy Department of the usefulness of a ram
attached to a steamship. In February, 1862, he warned
the Department that the Confederates had five steam
rams, including the one building at Norfolk, and forecast that the reconstructed *Merrimack* would be capable
of committing great depredations. His warning was ignored until after the disasters at Hampton Roads, when
Ellet was called in, given the rank of colonel of engineers, and ordered to build protected steam rams for use
on the Mississippi River.

John Taylor Wood, a lieutenant on board the *Virginia,*
later a colonel in the Confederate Army, who described
the construction of the ironclad in an article for the
Century Magazine, later reprinted in *Battles and Leaders of
the Civil War,* said it was

cut down to the old berth-deck. Both ends for seventy feet
were covered over, and when the ship was in a fighting trim
were just awash. On the midship section, 170 feet in length,
was built at an angle of 45 degrees a roof of pitch-pine and
oak 24 inches thick, extending from the water-line to a
height over the gun-deck of 7 feet. Both ends of the shield
were rounded so that the pivot-guns could be used as bow
and stern chasers or quartering. On the gun-deck was a light
grating, making a promenade of about twenty feet wide. The
wood backing was covered with iron plates, rolled at the
Tredegar works [Richmond], 2 inches thick and 8 wide.
The first tier was put on horizontally, the second up and
down—in all to the thickness of 4 inches, bolted through the
woodwork and clinched. The prow was of cast-iron, projecting 4 feet, and badly secured, as events proved. The rudder

and propeller were entirely unprotected. The pilot house was forward of the smoke-stack, and covered with the same thickness of iron as the sides. The motive power was the same that had always been in the ship. Both of the engines and boilers had been condemned on her return from her last cruise, and were radically defective. Of course the fire and sinking had not improved them. We could not depend upon them for six hours at a time.

Other authorities placed the angle of inclination of the armored walls at 35 and 38 degrees. John L. Porter, naval constructor, also said the propeller was protected. The metal ram at the prow was described as wedge-shaped, weighing 1,500 pounds, located 2 feet under water. The battery of the ship consisted of two 7-inch rifles, reinforced around the breech with 3-inch steel bands used as bow and stern pivots. There also were two 6-inch rifles and six 9-inch smoothbore guns for broadside action.

John Ericsson's Design

Word that the Confederates had salvaged the hull and engines of the *Merrimack* and were feverishly constructing an armor-clad superstructure seeped into the North and caused apprehension among Washington officials who were not quite sure what an ironclad could do. The Confederates, having no wooden navy to defend, were eager to develop a new offensive weapon, and Stephen R. Mallory, who had been chairman of the Naval Committee of the United States Senate before the war, and was now Confederate Secretary of the Navy, was convinced that the ironclad would run the Atlantic Squadron out of Hampton Roads.

Secretary Welles was convinced that ironclads were important and used his influence to get a comprehensive program adopted. When Congress met in emergency session July 4, 1861, he presented a request for a board of three naval officers to investigate the building of ironclad ships, and asked an appropriation of $1,500,000 "for the construction of one or more iron or steel-clad steamships or floating steam batteries." It took Congress one month to act on this request; it was granted, and thereupon the Navy Department advertised for plans for "vessels of iron, or iron and wood combined," in the hope of interesting naval architects.

Even after the Naval Board, after six weeks of deliberation, had decided to approve contracts for three ships that would use iron armature, it was not convinced that the experiment would pay. It reported that for coast and harbor defense ships thus protected "are undoubtedly formidable adjuncts to fortifications on land," but they were skeptical of their cruising value. Its members agreed that "no ship or floating battery, however heavily she may be plated, can cope successfully with a properly constructed fortification of masonry."

In New York at this time there was active a highly competent and energetic inventor and engineer named John Ericsson, whose head was full of mechanical ideas and whose self-confidence was based on a sure grasp of the essentials of his profession. Born in Sweden, he had tried his talents on a steam locomotive in England, becoming runner-up in a contest for a design won by George Stephenson. He had built a steam fire engine, a caloric engine, and screw propellers of various patterns. In 1837, when he was thirty-six, he had arrived in the United States; in a comparatively short time his ability was recognized and he was placing engines and propellers on small steamers. He had already anticipated the need of putting iron plates on war vessels and had proposed armored batteries to Emperor Napoleon III of France, without success.

Ericsson was not unknown to the Navy Department. As early as 1841–43 he had contributed part of his patent rights in a propeller and a semicylindrical engine to the building of the *Princeton,* and had taken charge of its construction in the Philadelphia Navy Yard. The *Princeton* has been described as the first metal-hulled, screw-propelled steamship of war, and its place in naval history is further emphasized by two remarkable incidents. In a contest for speed it outraced the famous *Great Western,* which carried both paddle wheels and sails. In 1844 it provided a national sensation. A big gun on its deck burst and killed the Secretary of State, the Secretary of the Navy, and several other prominent men while out on a test cruise attended by President Polk and, among others, Dolley Madison.

Ericsson had built the gun while disapproving of its specifications. In association with C. H. Delamater, owner of an ironworks, Ericsson had installed engines and propellers in many ships; the Treasury Department had commissioned him to convert some of its revenue cutters to steam, and the British Admiralty had used some of his engines and propellers. When the Committee on Naval Affairs of the Twenty-ninth Congress in 1846 asked for ideas on rendering an iron vessel shot-proof Ericsson submitted his ideas for a completely new type of vessel, an ironclad with engines below deck. His suggestion was shelved and he heard nothing more from Washington.

About this time the government ordered iron plates placed on the new steamer *Galena*, whereupon its builder, C. S. Bushnell, asked C. H. Delamater for some technical information. Delamater told him to call on Ericsson in New York to find out whether the ship would carry the extra weight. Ericsson gave his best engineering advice, and then brought out a dust-covered cardboard model of an ironclad that he had designed years before. He lectured Bushnell so animatedly on its possibilities that the latter became enthusiastic about it and went at once to Hartford, Connecticut, to see Secretary of the Navy Welles, who was at his home there at that moment. He urged him to give Ericsson an interview forthwith. But Welles wanted Bushnell himself to carry the design to the Naval Board. Bushnell returned to Washington, and with two influential friends managed to get an interview with President Lincoln, who went with them to the Naval Board. But the Board refused to have anything to do with the idea.

It is historic fact that Ericsson himself had to convince the Board. He went to Washington on Bushnell's urging, and finding the Board doubtful about the stability and maneuverability of his design, he gave such a detailed and impassioned exposition of its merits that the Board finally approved a test. Secretary Welles, as if to make up for earlier procrastination, gave Ericsson an order to go ahead in a brusque five-minute interview.

The Swede lost no time. He laid down the keel at

Greenpoint, Brooklyn, and assigned three establishments to build parts of the ironclad. Even when he had it started the Navy had reservations; the contract withheld 25 per cent of periodic payments until the usefulness of the vessel had been proved; if it failed Ericsson and his associates would have to refund the money paid by the government. Ericsson was so confident of the usefulness of his design, and so full of patriotic fervor that he agreed. The vessel was launched in 100 days, and because Ericsson wanted it to be a warning, or monitor, to the Confederates he called it the *Monitor,* a name that the government accepted.

When completed the *Monitor* was a strange amphibian. It was 172 feet long and 41 feet wide on its upper deck and 122 feet long and 34 feet wide on the lower. Depth was 11 feet, 2 inches, and draft at the water line 10 feet. The top deck overhung bow and stern, protecting the anchor and its gear forward and the propeller, 9 feet in diameter, aft. The central turret, 63 feet in diameter, held two 11-inch Dahlgren guns and could be made to revolve; it was built to fit tight on the deck. Forward of the turret was the pilothouse, a nearly square structure of solid blocks of wrought iron bolted together and rising 3 feet, 10 inches above the deck. Its roof was a 2-inch iron plate resting in grooves but not bolted down; the intention was to make its removal easy if the crew had to abandon ship in an emergency. The pilothouse could hold three men and the wheel, and there were narrow slits for sight holes. The vessel weighed 987 tons with guns and cost $275,000.

The *Monitor* was launched January 30, 1862, and commissioned February 28. The desperate need to check the ironclad that the Confederates were building dictated immediate orders to get under way. On March 6 the *Monitor,* with Lieutenant John L. Worden commanding and 58 officers and crew aboard, left New York harbor for Hampton Roads, towed by a tug.

The voyage along the Atlantic coast later was described by men on board as a grueling experience. The ironclad was obviously not fit for navigating the high seas. It encountered rough weather twice, when the seas swept over its low deck and water flooded in under the turret, through the hawse hole and at times even through smokestack and blower pipes. If the lines attaching the craft to the tug had broken the ironclad would have floundered helplessly. But the lines were new and held, and at about 10 P.M. on March 8 the *Monitor* reached Hampton Roads, where the burning *Congress* was still lighting up the sky. On orders it took a position near the stranded *Minnesota*. With its short draft the *Monitor* was not in danger from the shoals. It was at this time that a crewman on a harbor patrol boat called the craft "a tin can on a shingle," a phrase that stuck.

Doom of Wooden Warships

March 8, 1862, was the day of doom for the wooden warships of the United States Navy, for on that day the re-built *Merrimack,* now the Confederate ironclad *Virginia,* demonstrated the immunity of iron-plate protection.

The *Virginia* was not quite ready for its crucial test that morning, but the need of landing some blows on the Federal squadron before the well-publicized Ericsson iron-clad came down from the North forced it to start on its career. It cast off at noon and started down the Elizabeth River, and as soon as the ship was spotted by soldiers manning land batteries the long-awaited news, "She's coming out!" spread to all detachments. Unoccupied soldiers raced to the river's banks and one officer rode twelve miles in order to see the phenomenon.

The *Virginia* had had no trial trip or gunnery practice. Up to the hour of starting the ship was crowded with workmen, according to Lieutenant John Taylor Wood. He wrote later: "From the start we saw that she was slow, not over 5 knots; she steered so badly that, with her great length, it took from 30 to 40 minutes to turn. She drew 22 feet, which confined us to a comparatively narrow channel in the Roads and the engines were our weak point. She was as unmanageable as a waterlogged vessel."

Federal warships were strung out along the west coast of Hampton Roads, with the *Cumberland,* thirty guns, nearest Newport News, and the *Congress,* fifty guns, *Minnesota, Roanoke,* and *St. Lawrence* lying in the direction of Old Point Comfort. When lookouts on the *Cumber-land* observed black smoke in the distance the ship signaled the *Zouave,* a Hudson river tugboat doing auxiliary duty, to investigate. The *Zouave's* officer reported that the approaching vessel "looked like the roof of a very big barn belching forth smoke as from a chimney on fire." The Federal ships immediately cleared decks for action.

This came quickly as the *Virginia* steamed straight toward them. The ships began shelling the ironclad and were joined by the Federal land batteries near Newport News. The *Virginia* delivered a broadside at the *Congress* and steamed past to attack the *Cumberland* with its bow guns. It drove straight for the ship with its iron prow and rammed it; the implement tore a large hole in the wooden hull but broke in two. Within minutes spectators saw the masts of the *Cumberland* begin to slant as the ship started to sink. The *Cumberland* kept on firing its guns until it became submerged in thirty feet of water, with its pennant still flying on the topmost mast protruding from the water. Many of the crew saved themselves by swimming to shore, but about 100 men were reported lost.

While the attack on the *Cumberland* was in progress the Confederate flotilla of the James River steamed down to join the battle. This consisted of the *Patrick Henry,* 10 guns, the *Jamestown,* 2 guns, and the *Teazer* and *Raleigh,* 1 gun each, under Commander John R. Tucker of the *Patrick Henry.* These ships exchanged shots with the land batteries, in the course of which a shell hit a boiler on the *Patrick Henry,* scalding four seamen to death and putting it temporarily out of action.

The *Congress,* already badly hit, had observed that its guns did no damage whatever to the *Virginia.* It thereupon raised sails and prepared to get out of danger with the help of the tugboat, but grounded on a shoal. The captain of the *Zouave* reported that when he went alongside the *Congress* to attach a line blood poured out of its scupper down upon the deck of the tug. The master of the *Congress,* Commander William Smith, had been killed and the command had devolved on Lieutenant Pendergrast, who decided to surrender. Two white flags were raised on the *Congress* and the crew and officers of the damaged ship took to the boats.

The *Virginia* ordered Lieutenant Parker of the *Beaufort* to secure the officers as prisoners, obtain the flag, and allow the crew to land. Confederate seamen helped to get wounded men into boats, but only about thirty men could be rescued in this manner because the shore batteries could not be called off. Their gunners concentrated on the *Beaufort,* hitting both friend and foe and causing the Confederates to denounce the action as "vile treachery." Because of this many of the severely wounded could not be moved. The Confederate commander, unable to carry the ship off as a prize, was ordered to destroy it. When ordinary combustibles failed he sent red-hot shells fore and aft, which set it on fire.

In the meantime the *Minnesota* had grounded in shoal water halfway between Newport News and Old Point Comfort, and its captain fully expected the *Virginia* to return and polish it off. It already had suffered some damage, and one shell had passed through four cabins before exploding, wrecking all of them.

The *Virginia* also had trouble in low water and was very hard to turn around. Its commander reported years later:

To succeed in my object I was obliged to run the ship a short distance above the batteries on James River, in order to wind her. During all this time her keel was in the mud; of course she moved slowly. Thus we were subjected twice to the heavy guns of all the batteries in passing up and down the river, but it could not be avoided. We silenced several of the batteries and did much injury on shore. A large transport steamer along side of the wharf was blown up, one schooner sunk, and another captured and sent to Norfolk.

Before the *Virginia* could reach the *Minnesota* ebb tide began to set in and the pilots became wary of attempting the middle channel. At 5 P.M. the *Virginia* withdrew and steamed up the South Channel to Sewell's Point. The low water had saved the *Minnesota.*

The *Virginia* had suffered considerable damage, but although ninety-eight dents were counted in its armor, no shells had broken the plates. As Lieutenant John Taylor Wood reported, there were twenty-one casualties, including the wounded commander and the flag officer. Two guns had their muzzles shot off, and part of the iron ram had been broken off against the *Cumberland*. The smokestack, steam pipes, one anchor, railings, stanchions, and boat davits had been shot away. Several flagstaffs were destroyed and finally the colors had to be attached to a pike.

First Battle of a New Era

The first day's battle, which took place on a Saturday, was witnessed by thousands on all the surrounding shores —soldiers of both armies, and civilians. As night came on the skies were lighted by the fire raging on the *Congress,* where the flaming casemates stood out red against the darker hull. At intervals explosions took place. At 2 A.M. a tremendous blast forced the interior of the ship into the skies and the outside shell sank.

While this tragic drama was being enacted a diminutive craft, so close to the water line that it was unnoticed, slid noiselessly into the middle channel. It was the *Monitor,* too late to save two proud ships of the United States Navy, but ready to protect the rest against the destroyer.

During the night the *Virginia* transferred Commodore Franklin Buchanan and Flag Lieutenant R. D. Minor to the shore for hospitalization at Newport News. At daybreak on March 9 its men observed a strange, low craft lying between it and the *Minnesota,* and guessed, from previous reports, that the *Monitor* had finally arrived. Over breakfast they sized it up as a pygmy.

At 8:30 A.M. the *Virginia* started for the *Minnesota.* Immediately the *Monitor* left its post and steamed straight for the *Virginia,* to the great amazement of Captain Van Brunt aboard the *Minnesota.* For the Federals, no less than the Confederates, did not know what it could do.

The *Virginia* opened fire with its pivot gun, but the *Monitor* ran alongside the *Virginia,* stopped its engines, and began firing its eleven-inch guns from the revolving turret. The *Virginia* replied with a broadside, but its shots glanced off the armor of the *Monitor*. The *Monitor* made several runs past the *Virginia,* firing at about eight-minute intervals, and every shot struck. The *Virginia* then tried to ram the *Monitor,* but it had inadequate headway and the *Monitor* maneuvered out of danger and received only a glancing blow.

The *Virginia* now concentrated its fire on the pilothouse. There were three men in the pilothouse, including the commander, who communicated with the executive officer in the turret through a speaking tube. This tube was broken early in the fight and commands had to be relayed by seamen. A shell from the *Virginia,* ten yards away, struck the pilothouse above the slit, where Lieutenant Worden got the blow in his face and powder in his eyes. Bleeding and unable to see, he turned the command over to Lieutenant S. Dana Greene. The slit had been widened, contrary to the design of Ericsson, who declared no shell could have penetrated if his work had not been changed.

For six hours the two ironclads had pounded away at each other, and although their armor was dented neither gave way. At the same time shore batteries added to the din. During the fighting the *Monitor* kept the *Virginia* from approaching the *Minnesota,* and when it withdrew over the middle ground the *Virginia,* with its twenty-two-foot draft, could not follow. At 2 P.M. the *Virginia* turned around and went back to Sewell's Point.

Since the *Monitor* had not seen fit to engage it in deep water the *Virginia* claimed a victory, whereas the *Monitor's* officers, busy with overcoming the damage to their pilothouse and getting their communications in order, thought the *Virginia* had broken off the fight for its own reasons.

The first battle ever fought between ironclad warships was over and although both sides called it a victory it was more of a draw, with the prestige going to the Federals, for the *Monitor* not only had stopped the destruction of the other wooden ships but had survived the deadly blasts from the *Virginia.* Armor had proved its worth and Ericsson's design opened a new age in shipbuilding. For succeeding generations the action would be known as the battle of the *Monitor* and the *Merrimack,* for Northern historians never forgot that the *Virginia* was really their own converted vessel.

The news of the checkmate, coming to the North im-

mediately after the terrible losses of March 8, routed the
gloom and raised spirits high in Washington. In Richmond the achievements of the young Confederate Navy
caused no less satisfaction. Commodore Buchanan sent
Lieutenant Wood to President Davis with his report and
the flag of the *Congress,* which, when unrolled, was
found covered with blood. The Confederate government
promoted Buchanan to admiral and named Josiah Tattnall commander of the *Virginia.*

There was one high official of the Confederacy who had
reason to know what John Ericsson could accomplish.
This was none other than the Confederate Secretary of
the Navy, Stephen Russell Mallory, who, while United
States senator from Florida and chairman of the Naval
Committee of the Senate, in 1858 asked Congress to pay
Ericsson $13,930 for work on the USS *Princeton.* To
this Ericsson had given much of his genius, only to be
deprived of it by another man's vanity and greed.

The original features of the *Virginia* also brought distinction to the Southerners who were responsible, but a
controversy developed after the war between two men
who had most to do with its construction. Lieutenant
John M. Brooke asserted he had devised the original
when the Confederate Secretary of the Navy, Mallory,
asked him to design an ironclad and that John L. Porter,
naval constructor, was called in to help after Brooke's
plan had been adopted. Porter said he had made a
model of an ironclad as early as 1846 when he was superin-
tending building of an iron steamer in Pittsburgh, and had
used part of the design on the *Merrimack.* Obviously each
man had contributed important elements to design and
construction and there was honor enough for both.

Short Life of the Virginia

During the next few weeks, the two ships were repairing damage. The hull of the *Virginia* now received two-
inch armor below the shield, a heavier ram, iron shut-
ters for the ports, and steel-pointed solid shot. About
a hundred tons of ballast were added, increasing the
draft to twenty-three feet, hardly an advantage.

With a new commander in Josiah Tattnall, the *Virginia*

on April 11 came down the Elizabeth River attended by
six gunboats and stood off Sewell's Point, but the *Monitor,*
with steam up, remained at anchor with the United
States ships near Fort Monroe. The Confederate *James-*
town, making a sally toward Hampton, picked up two
brigs and a schooner manned by thirteen men. The
Monitor, Galena, and *Naugatuck* shelled Sewell's Point
on May 8 but withdrew when the *Virginia* appeared. The
Virginia was accompanied by four gunboats this time,
and the *Monitor's* officers were aware that their ship was
vulnerable to boarding parties. Thus the *Monitor* remained the protector of the United States ships without running any risks.

But a new situation intervened; McClellan's occupation of the York peninsula meant that Norfolk and the
Gosport Navy Yard were vulnerable to Federal guns and
had to be abandoned by the Confederates. The *Virginia*
could not navigate on the high seas nor risk grounding
near the Union batteries; on May 10, Tattnall reached
the decision that it would have to be destroyed. It was
run near the mainland at Craney Island and set on fire,
and at 5 A.M. on May 11 it blew up.

This was a disheartening incident for the Confederates,
and much surprise was expressed among officials in
Richmond, although President Davis and his cabinet were
said to have known the necessity. Tattnall was censured
by a naval board and was so angered that he demanded a
court inquiry for himself and his officers; this was given
him and he was exonerated. On May 15 Captain Catesby
ap R. Jones and the men of the *Virginia* were stationed
behind the works on Drewry's Bluff on the James River,
when it was attacked by the *Monitor,* the *Galena,* and
three other gunboats. The Confederate veterans of the
Virginia served the guns with genuine fervor, eager to
damage the *Monitor,* and they were heartened when the
Federal ships failed to reduce the batteries on the Bluff
and withdrew.

The original *Monitor* survived only nine months after
its historic duel with the *Virginia.* It was used to patrol the
James River during McClellan's Peninsular campaign, and
took part in the shelling of Fort Darling, after which it
was taken up the Potomac to Washington for repairs. On

December 29, 1862, the *Monitor* was ordered to proceed in tow to Charleston Harbor. It left Fort Monroe under command of Commander J. P. Bankhead. The *Monitor* was able to navigate safely on rivers and still waters, but, as its first experience had proved, it was at the mercy of rough weather in the open sea. It was attached by two hawsers to the USS *Rhode Island,* a sidewheeler. Off Cape Hatteras it encountered strong winds and tumbling waves. The hawsers proved a hindrance; one became entangled in the wheel of the *Rhode Island* and two men who tried to cut it loose from the *Monitor* were washed overboard. The ship was built so low that it took water in every opening. The water dampened the coal and the engineer could no longer raise steam to work the pumps. Even after the gale abated the seas remained high. The men aboard crowded the roof of the turret, for anyone on deck would be washed away. The *Rhode Island* helped to save some, but the *Monitor* went down fighting a head sea at midnight, December 31, 1862. Four officers and twelve men were lost, and forty-nine were saved. The grave of the *Monitor* was located a few years ago by the use of sonar.

Growth of the United States Navy

The growth of the United States Navy, and the change in the construction of vessels of war, were disclosed by President Lincoln when he sent his annual message to Congress, December 9, 1863. He then said the Navy had 588 vessels, completed and building, of which 75 were ironclad or armored steamers. The number of armored ships completed or building was thought to be larger than that of any other nation. Most of them were suitable for harbor defense and coastal service, but larger and stronger ships would be needed for service on the ocean. He recommended the establishment of a navy yard on the East Coast and another on a western river. The number of seamen had increased from 7,500 in the spring of 1861 to 34,000 in December, 1863, and the President asked Congress to provide more equitably for the service, since the draft and the bounties paid for army recruits worked to the disadvantage of the Navy.

13

CAPTURE OF THE RIVER FORTS
AND NEW ORLEANS

The importance of the Mississippi River to navigation and the movement of supplies from the interior was well understood by the United States government at the beginning of the Civil War, but for some reason no attention was given to forcing entry into the river from the Gulf. Projects discussed in the Navy Department invariably dealt with equipping vessels at Cairo and other northern ports and sending expeditions down the river. Also, the government considered it had interrupted trade with New Orleans when it blockaded the passes of the Mississippi. But it soon learned that this was not wholly effective. Moreover, the Confederates began fortifying points that would impede Federal control, notably Ship Island, ten or twelve miles off the coast, sixty miles from New Orleans and about the same distance from Mobile.

The Federals thereupon determined to recover Ship Island, and a force from the steamship *Massachusetts*, under Commander Melancton Smith, took possession there in September, 1861. The island had advantages as a military base and at the request of the Navy Department the government assigned Major General B. F. Butler to take charge of such troops as might be sent, the first contingent of 2,500 going to Ship Island in the *Constitution* in November. By this time the government had learned that the Confederates were building war vessels at New Orleans and had come to the conclusion that occupation of the city, with reduction of the two forts that commanded passage of the river, Fort St. Philip and Fort Jackson, was necessary to procure Federal control of the waterway.

One of the naval officers who had been active in the blockade of Gulf ports was Commander David D. Porter of the *Powhatan*. Porter had a practical knowledge of the Mississippi channel at New Orleans and the two forts, and when he brought his ship to New York in November he was ordered to report to the Navy Department. Here he found Secretary Gideon Welles interested in a project to force the passage with the cooperation of land and naval forces. Porter's knowledge was drawn on at a conference with President Lincoln, Secretary Welles, Major General Mc-Clellan, and Gustavus V. Fox, Assistant Secretary of the Navy, in the course of which he proposed the use of mortars on board vessels as auxiliary to the work of a squadron. The naval expedition was outlined; General McClellan agreed to furnish troops and the greatest secrecy was enjoined on all.

When the choice of a leader was discussed Secretary Welles's attention was drawn to Captain David Glasgow Farragut, a gunnery officer. A number of interesting matters were associated with his career. He was now sixty years old and had served in the Navy forty-nine years, having been a young midshipman on the *Essex* in the War of 1812. He was a Southern man, born in Tennessee. He was living in Norfolk when hostilities began and moved to a place on the Hudson River near New York, warning Southern partisans in the Navy that they would catch the devil before the trouble was ended. His father had performed an act of kindness in rescuing the aged grandfather of David D. Porter, and Porter's father, a captain in the Navy, had adopted young Farragut and started him on his naval career. The principal strategy for the expedition already had been decided when Secretary Welles sent for Farragut with the object of interviewing him as a prospective commander. In addition to Welles, Montgomery Blair and Assistant Secretary Fox put Farragut through an intensive examination. Farragut was enthusiastic about the prospects and certain he could get results, even with fewer mortars than were planned. When Secretary Welles had satisfied himself of Farragut's abilities and loyalty he recommended him as flag officer of the Western Gulf Blockading Squadron and commander of the expedition against the forts and New Orleans.

Fort St. Philip was located on the east bank of the Mississippi and Fort Jackson on the west bank. Fort St. Philip was an open work of brick and stone covered with sod, with fifty-two guns mounted in barbette (that is, on platforms with protective earthwork in front, and not in casemates, or enclosed chambers). It commanded both banks and some distance north and south because it stood on the interior side of a bend. Fort Jackson was a more elaborate work of stone in a star-shaped pattern with a stone citadel in the center. It had 24 guns in casemates and 42 in barbette, 2 pieces of light artillery, and a water battery of 6 guns. It had been strengthened with protective bags of sand and fully supplied with ammunition and food. The commander was Lieutenant Colonel Edward Higgins, formerly of the United States Navy. There were about 600 men in each fort, many of them Northerners and German and Irish immigrants, which proved an advantage to the Federals, since they were not die-hard Confederates.

Much of General Butler's force reached Ship Island by January, 1862, some of it under Brigadier General John W. Phelps. Commodore Farragut left Hampton Roads and arrived at Ship Island in the flagship *Hartford,* February 20.

By April, 1862, the preparations for the attack were extensive and thorough. In addition to the *Hartford,* the principal first-class screw sloops were the *Brooklyn,* Captain Thomas T. Craven; the *Richmond,* Captain James Alden; the *Pensacola,* Captain Henry W. Morris; and the *Mississippi,* a side-wheeler, Commander Melancton Smith. There were three second-class screws, nine screw gunboats, and one sailing sloop.

The mortar division under Commander David D. Porter had the *Harriet Lane* as flagship, commanded by Lieutenant J. M. Wainwright. There were 6 other gunboats and steamers, some of them ferryboats, and 19 schooners equipped with mortars. Farragut's fleet had 166 guns and 26 howitzers, a total of 192 pieces. The mortar division had 110 pieces including 19 mortars, the rest smoothbores, rifles, and howitzers. Thus the total ordnance came to 302.

The vessels prepared for the assault by carrying plenty of ammunition; the mortars alone could fire 16,800 shells. The ships were all wooden and vulnerable in a close fight. The *Brooklyn* hung chain armor on its sides to protect its boilers, and every ship was equipped to fight fires.

Farragut's plan of battle called for the Mortar Division to begin shelling the forts; when the latter had been properly reduced the flagship would show a signal—two red lights—and the squadron would move up the river in a preconceived order. Commander Porter expected the mortars to make short work of the forts. The topmasts of his schooners were bound with branches, so that to observers at the forts they would seem to merge with the trees. On April 18, 1862, the mortars began to fire—240 shells an hour. The forts replied at once, and while it took them some time to get the range, the fleet moved its ships about so that its volleys would not come from the same spot.

Hour after hour the howitzers dropped shells on the forts, working with regularity, with the firing spaced so that there were always some shells in the air. Serving the mortars was a tough assignment; when the gun was fired the men of the crew had to stand on their toes aft with their mouths open to overcome the shock of the concussion. The heavy powder smoke blackened their faces. But they hit the forts with precision. At Fort Jackson a shell tore a great hole in the earth in front of the citadel and buried two men. The citadel caught fire and the wood in it burned out.

As one day followed another the routine of attack began to wear on the men; after five days they were exhausted and Porter appealed to Farragut for a rest. The forts were still answering the fire. In addition the Confederates were sending down barges loaded with pitch pine that flamed toward the heavens and threatened to scorch any vessel they touched. But fortunately only one barge came down at a time and the vessels were able to move out of its path or push it aside. The captains surmised that if the Confederates had known enough to tie the barges together and direct them they could have done real damage.

The Confederates had not been idle in other ways. They had placed guns on gunboats, launches, and tugs. Several gunboats, like the *Manassas,* were equipped with rams. The defenders were still working feverishly to complete their ironclad, the *Louisiana;* it lacked propellers, but it carried guns, so they towed it down and anchored it under the walls of Fort St. Philip. There it was able to fire three bow guns and three starboard guns, but in one direction only; besides it was manned by inexperienced recruits and of little use in defense.

It became evident to Farragut that the mortar fleet was not reducing the forts quickly enough. He therefore called a conference of the top officers of the separate vessels on the *Hartford.* Thirteen captains responded. Commander Porter, being occupied with his duties, could not come, and sent a letter telling explicitly how he thought the attack should be conducted. Porter held strongly to the view that the mortar ships must remain in tow of the big ships when there was to be any upriver movement, for if left alone they would be helpless. He said there were two methods of attack: one, for the vessels to run past the many batteries by night or in a fog; the other, attacking the forts by laying the big ships close alongside, avoiding the casemates, firing shells, grape, and canister into the barbette, clearing the ramparts with boat guns from the tops, while smaller and more agile vessels threw in shrapnel, dismounting the guns in barbette. He said the larger ships would be anchored, the smaller ships would move about for the purpose of getting above or starting a cross fire, and the mortars would keep up a rapid and continuous fire at short range.

Commander Porter objected to running by the forts for these reasons: he suspected a chain had been placed above the forts; there would be extra batteries; and the hostile forts would remain in the rear of the ships, which could not return to bring up the mortar batteries without going through their fire. He thought a combined attack on the forts by the army and the navy was promising.

Farragut heard the paper read and then announced his own plan. He would run past the forts, for he considered the mortars as well protected by the fleet when it was above the forts as below; he also intended to cover the landing of the troops at Quarantine, five miles above. When above the forts and able to cope with the enemy, he would fight it out. Some of the officers feared the ships might get out of reach of supplies, but Farragut said ammunition was already being exhausted and that something had to be done immediately. He "believed in celerity."

Flag Officer Farragut ordered the fleet to move past

the forts the next day, and at 2:30 A.M. on April 24 they hove anchor. The fleet moved in three sections, the first led by Captain Theodorus Bailey in the *Cayuga* and comprising also the *Pensacola, Mississippi, Oneida, Varuna, Katahdin, Kineo,* and *Wissahickon.* Farragut sailed in the second section, composed of the *Hartford, Brooklyn,* and *Richmond.* The third section under Captain Henry H. Bell had the *Sciota, Iroquois, Kennebec, Pinola, Itasca,* and *Winona.* Five steamers of Commander Porter's mortar division moved up toward the water battery and shelled that, while the mortars continued to fire on the forts. The advancing vessels found that all obstructions placed by the Confederates had been washed away by the swift current, which had a strength of over three miles an hour.

The *Cayuga, Oneida,* and *Varuna* passed the forts first and engaged the enemy's gunboats above them. At daybreak the *Varuna* was rammed by the Confederate steamers *Governor Moore* and *Stonewall Jackson* and sank in shoal water, where its crew was rescued by the *Oneida.* The two Confederate rams, however, were so badly damaged that their crews set them on fire and abandoned them. It turned out that Fort St. Philip had been little damaged by the mortar shells and was able to score some hits on the ships as they passed, until Farragut in the *Hartford* made it a special target. Here a blazing fire raft was guided toward the *Hartford* by a Confederate tug, and although the Federals said the fire accomplished little more than scorching the paint of the *Hartford*'s hull, there was apparently some damage. The *Brooklyn* was rammed by the *Manassas* and hit by the guns of another vessel. The *Itasca,* one of the last vessels to pass the forts, was run ashore to prevent its sinking. Later the *Manassas* was pursued by the *Mississippi* and ran ashore, where the crew abandoned it. Farragut continued upstream and put the batteries of twenty guns at Chalmette out of action.

In the meantime Commander Porter had been viewing Farragut's defiance of the forts with mixed feelings. He congratulated Farragut on getting past them, but reminded him that he had left behind several formidable gunboats. Porter still expected Farragut to turn around and give the forts the final blow. "You will find the forts harder to take now than before unless their ammunition gives out," he warned. "I hope you will open your way down, no matter what it costs." But Farragut was not to be diverted. He judged rightly that with New Orleans in his hands the forts would not hold out long.

It turned out that they didn't, but for an unexpected reason. When Porter asked Brigadier General J. K. Duncan, commander of both places, to surrender, he replied that he would need authority from New Orleans. Porter was not putting store by that; he reopened his bombardment. Suddenly at midnight of April 28 a messenger reached the *Harriet Lane* with word that General Duncan wished to surrender. His troops had mutinied; they refused any longer to serve the guns. These were the troops that had among them a large number of recent immigrants. Next day General Duncan and Lieutenant Colonel Higgins came on board to sign articles of surrender.

While they were on the United States ship the Confederate ironclad *Louisiana* came drifting down the channel in flames, endangering the mortar flotilla. Before it reached them it blew up. It had been sent down by Commander John K. Mitchell of the Confederate naval forces. When Mitchell appeared to surrender he demanded the same terms that had been given Duncan, most of whose men had been paroled. Porter was angered because Mitchell had abused a flag of truce and refused the terms. Instead he sent Mitchell and his officers north as prisoners. When the Federals tallied losses they found they had 36 killed; the Confederates reported 185 dead.

When the Confederate commander in New Orleans, Major General Mansfield Lovell, learned that Farragut had passed the forts and was coming up the river, he marched his 3,000 troops out of town with such military supplies as they could carry and applied a torch to the levee. New Orleans people added to the destruction by setting fire to vessels, including two unfinished war craft, a ram, and an ironclad. They rolled barrels of sugar and molasses out of the warehouses and dumped them in the streets. They boasted of destroying 35,000 bales of cotton.

Farragut hoped to arrange a transfer of authority in

New Orleans without bloodshed, and for that purpose sent ashore several groups of officers to demand the surrender of the city from the mayor, John T. Monroe. The first to make the demand was Captain Theodorus Bailey, who had asked the privilege of doing so, and was accompanied through a howling mob by Lieutenant George H. Perkins. The mayor said he had no authority as long as General Lovell was there, whereas Lovell said he had sent out his troops and was about to leave the city to join them and would not surrender. The next day, April 26, Farragut sent Captain Albert Kautz of the *Hartford* ashore with a marine guard of twenty, but because of the menacing character of the mob Kautz left the guard behind and went to the City Hall in the company of one midshipman. The mayor again refused to surrender the city formally, but said that as the Federals had the power they could take possession. What happened then was described by Captain Kautz as follows:

While we were in the City Hall a mob came up from the lower part of the city with an American ensign, and when they saw us they tore the flag to shreds and threw them into the open window at us. I did not comprehend the meaning of this singular and wild demonstration at the time, but afterward learned that on the morning of this same day Farragut had instructed Captain H. W. Morris of the *Pensacola,* then at anchor abreast of the United States Mint, to hoist a flag on that building, it being United States property. Captain Morris accordingly sent Lieutenant Stillwell with officers and men from the ship and the flag was hoisted. It was up only a short time when [William] Mumford hauled it down. It was seized by the mob, which paraded it through the streets with fife and drum until they reached the City Hall, where it was destroyed. I afterward happened to be present when Farragut reported the hauling down of this flag to General Butler [who had taken charge of the city for the Army] and I heard the latter say: "I will make an example of that fellow by hanging him." Farragut smiled and remarked: "You know, General, you will have to catch him before you can hang him."

Hanging Mumford was one of the first of the acts that initiated Benjamin F. Butler's harsh rule in New Orleans and made his name odious in the South.

The passage of the forts and the capture of New Orleans caused tremendous repercussions in the South, where the Confederacy had been working against time to produce enough ironclads and fireboats to face the Federal flotilla. A Confederate court of inquiry was convened and everyone connected with building and commissioning the ships was called up for explanations. Both lack of materials and of time to complete the work were blamed for their failures. Commodore Hollin testified that he had to pay $2 and $2.50 a pound for powder purchased in New Orleans. Payment of workers had to be made in Louisiana Treasury notes, because the men would not accept Confederate paper.

The most distressing loss to the Confederates was the destruction of their new ironclad *Mississippi,* built at a cost of $400,000, which was only a few weeks short of completion and had to be set afire. The builder wept when he saw flames bursting from the portholes. The strength of the iron plates on the *Louisiana* was proved to the Confederates when, according to the testimony, the *Hartford* was unable to penetrate its armor with nine-inch shells when practically alongside. In view of the fact that one fire raft had drifted toward the *Hartford* and set part of it on fire, the Confederate naval commanders were bitter when they learned that seventeen fire rafts had been run ashore without being used. But the Confederate Navy Department remained hopeful for future success; over a year later the Secretary was still trying to arrange for the purchase of ironclads abroad because these vessels of war would "restore to us New Orleans."

Benjamin F. Butler at New Orleans

No high officer of the Civil War created so many personal enemies and caused so much ill feeling as Benjamin Franklin Butler, who was execrated in the South for his dictatorial rule of New Orleans in 1862. Butler was a Massachusetts lawyer and politician whose high rank in the armies of the United States—he was a major general of volunteers by July, 1861—is inexplicable except when his self-assurance and drive are taken into account. A Democrat, his partisanship before the war was contrary to everything Lincoln stood for. He favored the discredited Lecompton constitution for Kansas and approved the Dred Scott decision. He attended the 1860 Democratic convention as a delegate and voted to nominate Jefferson Davis for President. When the party split and the Southern Democrats named John C. Breckinridge, Butler supported him.

Thus he might have been described as a double-dyed Democrat of the Southern stripe, but when Fort Sumter was attacked he decided the Union must be saved and turned completely around. He helped recruit volunteers and led a regiment to Washington. Here his brashness and audacity won him a generalship and command of the Maryland area, with headquarters in Annapolis. He brought order to Baltimore. Carl Schurz saw him at this time and drew a portrait that shows why Butler was easy to caricature: "I found him clothed in a gorgeous militia uniform adorned with rich gold embroidery. His rotund form, his squinting eye, and the peculiar puff of his cheeks made him look a little grotesque. [He] thoroughly enjoyed his position of power . . . and keenly appreciated its theatrical possibilities."

From Annapolis, Butler was assigned to the command at Fort Monroe. It was his order that sent half a dozen regiments against the Confederates at Big Bethel, Virginia, where United States troops fired on each other in confusion and were driven off the field with 16 killed, 34 wounded—not a big action by itself but one that, by its priority, caused Washington to feel "humiliation." His expedition against Fort Hatteras brought better results, but his big opportunity came when he was assigned to command the troops in the New Orleans campaign.

It was as Federal commander in New Orleans that he acquired his unenviable repute and became known as "Beast Butler" for his ruthlessness and as "Spoons Butler" for his alleged tendency to collect silverware without reimbursing the owners. New Orleans was the largest city in the Confederacy; its citizens had French and Spanish backgrounds, and there were many Creoles who resented intrusion into their privacy. He became almost immediately the object of hatred for an act that even the North could not approve. This was the summary execution of William Mumford for taking down the United States flag, as described by Captain Kautz.

The act outraged the South. President Davis of the Confederacy gave way to violent anger. He had General Lee address a letter to Major General Halleck calling on the United States to repudiate Butler. Failing to get a reply for nearly a month, he had Lee send a second letter. To this Halleck replied that he had no authentic information but would attempt to get it. Months of silence followed. In the meantime Butler was adding to his record of suppression. Davis thereupon drew up a bill of particulars and published Butler's iniquities to the world. He had previously issued an order that if Butler were captured he was to be executed at once by hanging as an outlaw and a common enemy of mankind. He also ordered that all commissioned officers under Butler were to be considered as robbers and criminals deserving of death and that none of them when captured should be given parole before exchange until Butler had been given due punishment. Davis accused Butler of arresting citizens for selling medicine to sick Confederate soldiers, of punishing citizens by giving them ball and chain and putting them at hard labor in dungeons; he said helpless women had been arrested and insulted, and he mentioned that one woman had been exiled to an island of barren sand under the tropical sun. When Lord Palmerston, British prime minister, heard this he expressed to the American minister, Charles Francis Adams, his horror that a man of Anglo-Saxon kin should behave thus, but Adams did not think Palmerston justified on the basis of an enemy's statement.

Butler, however, continued as before. He ordered all firearms given up. He had men sentenced to take the oath of allegiance to the United States or pay a fine or be exiled to the area controlled by the Confederacy. He removed the mayor and placed a Maine general in his chair. But his real opposition came from the women.

The proud women pulled their skirts aside when passing a soldier, or took up the whole walk and made him get off. Butler himself related that when a group of women on a balcony saw him coming down the street they whirled around and "threw their skirts in a regular circle like the pirouette of a dancer. I turned to my aide, saying in full voice: 'Those women evidently know which end of theirs looks best.' "

Women spat in officers' faces, and when one woman emptied her slop jar over Farragut's full-dress uniform Butler retaliated. He published his notorious order that "when any female shall by word, gesture or movement insult or show contempt for any officer or soldier of the United States, she shall be regarded and held liable to be treated as a woman of the town plying her vocation." This order is still the best-known act of his career.

Butler was accused of harassing the owners of plantations by using their slaves on work of his own. In August, 1862, Brigadier General J. W. Phelps organized five companies of Negroes, which he wanted to equip with arms. Butler refused to approve, saying only the President had the authority to order this. In the altercation General Phelps resigned. Secretary Stanton told Butler the Negroes should be fed by the army and employed as laborers.

Despite Butler's crudities, he was admittedly a good administrator, and history mentions that he solved the sewage problem. But President Davis' proclamation, which was dated December 24, 1862, must have spurred the Federal government to make a change. Soon thereafter it removed Butler and put General Nathaniel Banks in his post. Butler, however, did not lose rank; he continued in active service, even when his leadership was unsuccessful. Eventually he commanded troops within a few miles of Richmond. He enjoyed the favor of General Grant both in and out of the army, a circumstance that puzzled such a historian as James Ford Rhodes. After the war, when he had a seat in the House of Representatives, he was looked upon as the spokesman for President Grant.

14

GEORGE B. McCLELLAN AND
THE ARMY OF THE POTOMAC

The Long Preliminaries

The stragglers from the battlefield of Bull Run had hardly caught up with their regiments when President Lincoln ordered Major General George Brinton McClellan to Washington. He arrived there on July 25, 1861, and on July 27 was placed in charge of the defense of Washington and the army that had been commanded by General McDowell. The thirty-five-year-old general of the Department of the Ohio had created an impression of firmness and energy by directing the rout of the Confederates in Western Virginia and thus helped build a strong rampart of Union support, which was to bring about the formation of the state of West Virginia. The campaign there had not been big enough to merit comparison with Bull Run; the casualties had been nominal, but the Union army had bagged about 600 prisoners when Lieutenant Pegram surrendered at Beverly on July 12, and consolidated its hold on that part of Virginia. Actions had involved mostly Ohio and Indiana state regiments and two regiments raised in Western Virginia. The Confederates had been pushed back from Philippi, Romney, Middle Creek, and Laurel Hill, with Colonel Lew Wallace of the Indiana volunteers winning advantages at Romney and Major General W. S. Rosecrans pushing the Confederates off the summit of Rich Mountain. The Confederate commander, General Robert S. Garnett, had been killed, but on the whole casualties were light. The Confederates had been directed from Richmond by the officer who had been appointed by the governor of Virginia—Major General Robert E. Lee. Some notice had come to McClellan because of a glowing proclamation to the inhabitants that he had published on entering the state.

McClellan was succeeded in Western Virginia by General Rosecrans. For the next fourteen months McClellan was to dominate military action in the East, construct a large, smooth-working organization, lead it to the brink of victory and defeat, and create such a feeling of frustration in Washington by prolonged delays in the face of Confederate activity that finally he had to be removed from the command.

There were two major campaigns during the tenure of General McClellan: the Peninsular campaign in Virginia in the spring of 1862, and the defense of Maryland against Lee's invasion in the fall of 1862. The first was brought about by McClellan's insistence that the best defense of Washington was the destruction of the Confederate army before Richmond. This failed, partly because McClellan changed his strategy abruptly in the middle of a costly expedition, and partly because the authorities lost confidence in his ability to succeed there. The second resulted in a great battle, Antietam (Sharpsburg), which held victory for the Union cause until McClellan failed to pursue and destroy the Confederate army. In between these two campaigns the Federals suffered the disaster of Second Bull Run (Manassas) under Major General John Pope.

George B. McClellan was a man of great promise when called to Washington. Born in Philadelphia in 1826, he had attended West Point and served on the staff of General Winfield Scott during the Mexican War. Scott became one of his ardent endorsers. Like Lee, McClellan specialized in engineering and became a second lieutenant in the Engineers Corps. He was an instructor in this subject at West Point; in 1851 he worked on Fort Delaware and in 1853–1854 took part in the Red River expedition in the Northwest. In 1855 Jefferson Davis, then Secretary of War in President Pierce's cabinet, made McClellan a member of a commission to study the Crimean War. Upon his return he published his observations. He became a captain in the First Regular Cavalry and invented a saddle that came to be widely used. His engineering knowledge proved useful in railroading; in 1857 he was appointed chief engineer of the Illinois Central Railroad and later vice-president and subsequently president of the Ohio & Mississippi Railroad Company.

Thus he had both organizing and administrative experience when the Civil War broke out. He determined to go to Pennsylvania and offer his services to the state, but the governor of Ohio, where he was located, invited him to become major general of volunteers and he accepted in April, 1861. On May 14, 1861, he was made a major general in the United States Army and given command of the Department of the Ohio.

There was no doubt of McClellan's ability as an organizer. He introduced strict army discipline to the regiments of easygoing recruits, some of whom were ready to leave for home when they tired of army life. He built an able corps of officers. Around Washington he erected a strong line of defenses, amplifying those begun by General McDowell's chief engineer, General John G. Barnard.

McClellan was slight of build and hence known as "Little Mac," whereas his bearing and self-sufficiency caused him to be referred to as "Young Napoleon." The President and Congress expected him to attack the Confederates without delay, but they encountered a deliberateness they could not comprehend. McClellan resented interference and ignored or evaded orders from the President and the Secretary of War. He recalled later that Edwin M. Stanton had consulted him in January on whether or not to take the post of Secretary of War. When McClellan advised him to do so Stanton had exclaimed: "Now we two will save the country!" It was not long afterward that McClellan was blaming Stanton for his difficulties with the government, saying that Stanton had turned Lincoln against him. But Lincoln's desire was action, and he would beg and beseech McClellan for it. He characterized McClellan's principal fault when he said: "He has the slows."

As the summer went by and nothing took place but drills and reviews, discontent spread from Washington to the country. The newspapers were calling: "On to Richmond!" But the army cheered when the young commander rode by on horseback. With his usual self-confidence he wrote his wife: "I shall carry this thing *en grand* and crush the rebels in one campaign." In other letters he complained about the ignorance of his superiors and especially of General Scott, whom McClellan considered an obstacle, because Scott opposed the formation of army corps, considering brigades still adequate. As he grew in his command McClellan exhibited a certain arrogance. Typical is an incident that has been described many times. President Lincoln and the Secretary of War went to McClellan's house one evening to confer with him and waited in his parlor for his return. When McClellan arrived he went upstairs without greeting his visitors. A short time later they were told that the general had gone to bed.

Washington was reminded frequently that the Confederates were not far distant. In August they placed an outpost on Munson's Hill, about seven miles outside of Washington and a spot from which they could see the city. The Federals thought it was fortified and when they approached it several weeks later found that it had been evacuated and that one log, painted to look like a cannon, had been left behind.

Fiasco at Ball's Bluff

The Confederates were posted at Leesburg on the Virginia side of the Potomac above Washington, and a number of Federal regiments patrolled the Maryland area under Brigadier General Charles P. Stone. Late in October, General McClellan sent a division upriver to Dranesville, below Leesburg, and advised General Stone of this movement. Stone decided to make a show of force to speed evacuation of Leesburg and sent regiments across the river at Edwards Ferry and Harrison's Landing on October 21, 1861. The troops climbed up Ball's Bluff, where the Confederate sharpshooters, placed higher up and in woods, easily picked off the foremost men. To extricate themselves from an untenable position the Federals had to get down the bluff in a hurry and cross the river in boats. Only five small ones were available; these were quickly swamped, and some of the soldiers were drowned. The whole assault had been badly planned and executed.

In the fighting Colonel Edward D. Baker, of the Seventy-fifth Pennsylvania, was killed. This threw a spotlight on the whole disastrous affair, for Baker was a

United States senator from Oregon, his legal residence, and a friend of President Lincoln. Taking part in the attack were the Fifteenth and Twentieth Massachusetts, the Forty-second New York "Tammany" Regiment, and a battery of Rhode Island artillery. The Union had 150 to 200 killed and drowned and 500 taken prisoner. General McClellan tried to excuse the repulse by saying 1,700 were pitted against 5,000; other reports gave the Union strength as 2,100. The blame for the disaster was placed on General Stone, who became the subject of protracted hounding by politicians. He was accused of having returned fugitive slaves to their master and of otherwise being friendly to the enemy. Accusations were made by Governor John A. Andrew of Massachusetts and a hearing was held by the Joint Committee on the Conduct of the War. Stone was arrested in January, 1862, by order of Secretary Stanton at the request of the Committee. No charges against Stone were ever made public, but his case became a subject of resentment among military officers, all of whom respected him. After being kept on the sidelines for a time he was demoted to colonel and sent to General Nathaniel Banks at New Orleans. He became Banks's chief of staff, and later Grant gave him command of a brigade in the Fifth Corps. McClellan and Hooker were strong defenders of Stone.

The Joint Committee on the Conduct of the War functioned from December, 1861, and made a number of investigations of military disasters. The senators on the committee were Benjamin F. Wade of Ohio, Zachariah Chandler of Michigan, and Andrew Johnson of Tennessee; Johnson withdrew when named military governor of Tennessee. There were also four representatives on the committee.

Lieutenant General Scott realized that his infirmities were such that he could not cope with the demands made on a general in chief and a week after the disaster of Ball's Bluff he asked to be relieved. By order of the President he was placed on the retired list with full pay. He was a Virginian, born in the eighteenth century, and now seventy-five years old. His career was indelibly a part of American history. Scott had studied law and did not attend the Military Academy at West Point. He became a captain of artillery in 1808 and fought in the War of 1812, becoming a major general and being wounded at Lundy's Lane. He settled boundary troubles and Indian risings, negotiated the treaty at the end of the Black Hawk War, and as lieutenant general conducted the Mexican War. On the day of Scott's retirement, November 1, the President designated General McClellan as general in chief, with jurisdiction over all armies except that of the Department of Virginia, the latter within sixty miles of Fort Monroe.

General McClellan was still drilling and marching his troops by January 1, 1862, without giving battle, and President Lincoln and the cabinet were wondering what the army was about. McClellan had been taken ill, but President Lincoln nevertheless called a council, which was attended by Secretaries Seward and Chase, the Assistant Secretary of War, and Generals McDowell and Franklin. Lincoln made one of his characteristic remarks when he said: "I am in great distress. If something is not done soon, the bottom will be out of the whole affair, and if General McClellan does not want to use the army, I would like to borrow it, provided I could see how it could be made to do something." He then asked the generals for their opinions, and McDowell outlined a campaign that had for its object an attack on the Confederates at Manassas Junction.

Three days later McClellan had recovered sufficiently to attend another meeting at the White House, at which Postmaster General Blair and Quartermaster General Montgomery Meigs also were present. McDowell, making a gesture of excuse toward McClellan, repeated his suggestion for a campaign, which McClellan ignored. When asked by the President what his plans were, McClellan refused to be specific, and when Secretary Chase asked him point-blank what he intended to do and when, he replied that he had some plans but did not feel called upon to expose them. Lincoln then asked whether he had set a time for putting his plans into action, and when he said he had, Lincoln closed the conference.

General McClellan's official report showed that on January 1, 1862, the army had 219,707 men, of whom 191,480 were designated as effectives, the rest being helpers of various kinds. It was pointed out that if 58,000 were assigned to defensive operations the army would still have 133,480 for offense. The exasperation of the President at the failure to make use of this great trained force was expressed in a document called President's General War Order No. 1, dated January 27, in which it was ordered that February 22, 1862, would be the day for a general movement of the land and naval forces against "the insurgent forces"; specifically, "that the Army at and about Fortress Monroe, the Army of the Potomac, the Army of Western Virginia, the Army near Mumfordsville, Kentucky, the Army and Flotilla at Cairo, and a Naval Force in the Gulf of Mexico, be ready for a movement on that day." He put this as an obligation upon all the commanding officers and ordered: "That the heads of Departments, and especially the Secretaries of War and of the Navy, with all their subordinates, and the General in Chief, with all other commanders and subordinates of land and naval forces, will severally be held to their strict and full responsibilities for the prompt execution of this order."

This extraordinary document came from a President who was determined to give the orders—in simpler phrase, to show who was boss. Lest General McClellan fail to observe that he was included, the President on January 31 delivered an order directed straight at him. He ordered that the Army of the Potomac, after providing for the defense of Washington, prepare immediately to seize and occupy a railroad point southwest of Manassas Junction, and to move on or before February 22.

In response to this order of the President, General McClellan registered objections with Secretary Stanton and in turn disclosed his own project: to move the army to Urbana, at the mouth of the Rappahannock, and advance by a rapid march via West Point, Virginia, to Richmond. If the capital was not quickly taken he proposed to cross the James River, use the river for his supply line, and attack the city from the rear, that is, the south. McClellan thought this operation would draw the Confederates out of the Shenandoah Valley and remove the threat of attack from Washington. He expected nothing to come from a movement on Manassas; the roads were bad, whereas milder weather came earlier in Virginia and the sandy soil was easier to use. He was so thoroughly convinced of the value of his plan that he declared: "I will stake my life, my reputation, on the result—more than that, I will stake upon it the success of our cause."

President Lincoln's intuition was against the plan, but he was not a military man and no equal to McClellan in argument. But he thought his own plan, moving the Army of the Potomac to a point on the railroad southwest of Manassas, was reasonable, so he wrote McClellan a letter with five specific questions: (1) Does not your plan involve a greatly larger expenditure of *time* and *money* than mine? (2) Wherein is a victory *more certain* by your plan than mine? (3) Wherein is a victory *more valuable* by your plan than mine? (4) In fact, would it not be *less* valuable in this: that it would break no great line of the enemy's communications, while mine would? (5) In case of disaster, would not a retreat be more difficult by your plan than mine?

General McClellan told Secretary Stanton that he had substantially answered the President's questions. During the month the Administration came around to his view and decided to let this huge expedition leave for the Peninsula. In the meantime McClellan investigated the situation around the upper Potomac and the Shenandoah Valley. He reported that Loudon, Bolivar Heights, and Maryland Heights at Harpers Ferry had been occupied; that he would place troops at Charlestown (now Charles Town) and Bunker Hill to cover the rebuilding of the railway, but explained he would not be able to move to Winchester and supply it for many days; if he had placed troops there they would have been at a loss for food in Virginia. Canalboats had been built for the use of the troops on the Chesapeake Canal because the left bank was too small to permit troops to use it; he now reported that the lift-lock was too small for the boats. Secretary Stanton sent a brief reply: "If the lift-lock is not big enough, why can not it be made big enough?" McClellan replied that the masonry would have to be destroyed and the lock rebuilt. The movement therefore was not made.

For months the President and his advisers had been

insisting on the organization of the army into corps, but had been unable to get General McClellan to do so. Corps commanders had a semi-independent status; they could report direct to the commander in chief. On March 8, when McClellan was about to carry out the order to move on Manassas, President Lincoln issued Order No. 2 demanding compliance "forthwith" in the organization of four army corps as follows: First Corps, Major General Irvin McDowell; Second Corps, Brigadier General E. V. Sumner; Third Corps, Brigadier General S. P. Heintzelman; Fourth Corps, Brigadier General E. D. Keyes. The divisions now commanded by these officers were to remain in their corps. Brigadier General James S. Wadsworth was placed in command of the defense of Washington and made military governor of the District of Columbia. The Fifth Army Corps was to be formed from the division of Major General Nathaniel P. Banks and from that of General Shields, lately that of General Lander, and was to be commanded by Banks.

McClellan objected strenuously to the order and telegraphed Secretary Stanton that he would either have to disregard it or suspend his movement toward Manassas. Secretary Stanton agreed to a temporary delay. McClellan occupied Centreville and Manassas on March 11.

The President then gave specific instructions to Adjutant General Thomas that the Army of the Potomac should not change its base without leaving behind a force that would make Washington entirely secure—in the opinion of the general in chief and the commanders of the army corps. He ordered that no more than two corps, about 50,000 men, should be moved en route for their new base until the Potomac down to Chesapeake Bay had been cleared of the enemy's batteries, or until the President permitted the move; that any such move should begin March 18, "and the general in chief shall be responsible that it moves as early as that day." The Army and Navy were to cooperate immediately to remove the hostile batteries on the Potomac.

While these preparations were going on in Washington the whole country was watching breathlessly the catastrophic naval battle in Hampton Roads. On March 9 the *Monitor* obstructed the progress of the Confederate ironclad *Virginia,* formerly the *Merrimack,* thereby greatly lessening the danger to McClellan's transports.

When General McClellan was in the field President Lincoln on March 11, 1862, issued an order relieving him of the command of other military departments. He created the Department of the Mississippi under Major General Henry W. Halleck, combining in it the departments of Halleck and Hunter and all of General Don Carlos Buell's lying west of a north-and-south line drawn through Knoxville, Tennessee. He also created the Mountain Department, west of the Department of the Potomac and east of the Department of the Mississippi, and gave the command to Major General Frémont.

General McClellan presented a plan agreed on by the commanders of his army corps at a council held at Fairfax Court House on March 13. It proposed operations starting from Old Point Comfort, between the York and the James rivers, provided the Confederate ironclad could be neutralized, transportation be ready at Washington and Alexandria to ship the army down the Potomac, a naval auxiliary force make an attempt to silence the Confederate batteries on the York, and a force be left to protect Washington. In the event these conditions could not be met, the generals preferred to move against the enemy behind the Rappahannock. Several generals thought 25,000 would suffice for Washington; Sumner wanted 40,000. Secretary Stanton then sent the President's order: Leave a force at Manassas Junction, provide security for Washington, move the rest of the army to a base at Fort Monroe or nearer and "at all events move the remainder of the army at once in pursuit of the enemy by some route." By now McClellan understood that the Administration wanted action. He replied that the order would be carried into effect at once.

General McClellan was now free of responsibility for the Shenandoah operations, which would proceed during March, while he was embarking for Virginia. Two new departments were now organized: the Department of the Shenandoah, comprising Virginia and Maryland lying between the Mountain Department and the Blue Ridge, under General Banks; and the Department of the Rappahannock, east of the Blue Ridge to the Potomac and the Fredericksburg & Richmond Railroad, including the District of Columbia and the country between the Potomac and the Patuxent, under General McDowell.

The Peninsular Campaign Begins

Transports were lined up at the Alexandria docks, and on March 17 the first troops, part of Major General Heintzelman's Third Corps, embarked. The original destination, the mouth of the Rappahannock, had been moved farther south, first to the York River and now to Fort Monroe above Newport News, no longer in danger from the Confederate ironclad. General McClellan reached Fort Monroe on April 2. There were 10,000 troops there under the command of Major General John E. Wool; the Department of Virginia had been placed under General McClellan's command, and he was authorized to draw on Wool's force to add to his own strength. But the day he arrived there Washington withdrew the Department from his control and advised that he would need General Wool's consent to make use of his troops. This disclosed the different influences that were operating in Washington, where, at this opening of a new campaign, there was loss of confidence in McClellan's leadership.

The adjutant general certified that the Army of the Potomac had available 158,419 troops on April 1, this including the nonfighting contingents. The adjutant general also reported that the number available to General Wadsworth for the defense of the capital was 22,410, with less than 20,000 fit for duty. The President's advisers, the adjutant general, L. Thomas, and Major General E. A. Hitchcock, called this force entirely inadequate to protect Washington, and said the President's orders had not been complied with. The President then ordered that McDowell's First Corps, which had 38,454 men enrolled, should be retained in the environs of Washington, and again urged "that General McClellan commence his forward movements from his new base at once."

McClellan replied that he was ready to move on Yorktown, where 15,000 Confederates were entrenched. But two days later he telegraphed that the Confederates were entrenched in large force across the Peninsula from Yorktown to the Warwick River, and he begged that the First Corps of McDowell be not detached and that Franklin's division be returned. "Do not force me to [fight] with diminished numbers," he protested. Secretary Stanton promised that Sumner's Second Corps would be sent; the return of April 1 showed that he had 31,037 men. Opposed to McClellan was Confederate General John B. Magruder, who had built his defensive line along the Warwick River, a tidewater branch of the James, and had connected its inundations with entrenchments at the village of Yorktown. Gloucester Point, opposite Yorktown, also was entrenched, and there were water batteries between them, covering the narrowest part of the York River, less than one mile wide. The lines near Yorktown were not completed. Magruder intended to delay the Federals until troops could be brought up in sufficient numbers. But McClellan already considered the Confederate line formidable and began placing heavy guns, as if for a siege, rather than preparing to advance. President Lincoln advised McClellan: "I think you had better break the enemy's line from Yorktown to Warwick River at once. They will probably use time as advantageously as you can." McClellan, who expressed his thoughts fully in letters to his wife, wrote her: "I was much tempted to reply that he had better come and do it himself."

General Joseph E. Johnston took command of the Confederate defense on April 17. Just before, he had attended a conference with President Jefferson Davis in Richmond at which two plans were discussed. Davis had called in George W. Randolph, Secretary of War; General Lee, who was his adviser; and Major Generals G. W. Smith and James Longstreet. Johnston had argued that the way to defeat the Federal army was to let it follow Magruder to the environs of Richmond and then fall upon it with the total Confederate strength. He would call in the available forces from North Carolina, South Carolina, and Georgia, move over the troops from Norfolk, and surprise the Federals when they were ready to besiege Richmond. They would be a hundred miles from Fort Monroe and could not escape destruction. To this both General Randolph, who had been a naval officer, and General Lee objected; Randolph did not want to lose the naval materials at the Norfolk navy yard, and Lee thought withdrawal of troops from South Carolina and Georgia would endanger Charleston and Savannah. He thought the Peninsula suited for fighting by a small army against a large one. President Davis decided in favor of Lee's view and ordered the divisions of Smith and Longstreet to join the army on the Peninsula.

In answer to McClellan's repeated requests, Washington agreed to send Franklin's division, and it reached West Point April 22. On April 7 McClellan wired that he had only 85,000 ready for duty, but on the 13th he admitted to the adjutant general that he had 117,721, with 100,970 available for duty. To show what preparation had been made, there was official record that McClellan had also received 14,592 animals (horses and mules), 1,150 wagons, 44 batteries, 74 ambulances; also pontoon bridges, telegraphic materials, and other equipment. On April 16 there was a skirmish at Lee's Mill in which the Federals came off second best, losing 35 killed and 130 wounded, otherwise nothing of consequence. But when McClellan was still calling for more guns at the end of the month President Lincoln wired: "Your call for Parrott guns from Washington alarms me chiefly because it argues indefinite procrastination. Is anything to be done?"

But something was definitely to be done, and the initiative came from the Confederates.

General Johnston had kept careful watch of Federal preparations and judged that their batteries would be ready for service in the first week in May. He feared McClellan's siege guns would demolish the Confederate water batteries. He told Richmond that he was about to abandon Yorktown and the Warwick line and again urged his favorite plan of concentrating a powerful army near Richmond. He ordered Major General Huger at Norfolk to evacuate his position and march to Richmond and Captain S. C. Lee, at Gosport navy yard, to remove as much valuable property as he could and leave. On May 3 he ordered the Confederate army to fall back by way of Williamsburg.

On that day Union Battery No. 1, located near the York River, had begun shelling the Confederate batteries opposite, preparatory to opening the river to the movement of Franklin's division up to West Point and the establishment of the Federal depot of supplies at White House Landing, above where the Pamunkey flows into the York.

Yorktown to Williamsburg

General McClellan was supervising the transport of General Franklin's troops on May 4 when the withdrawal of the Confederates was noted. General Stoneman's cavalry and the horse artillery were immediately sent in pursuit. At about 4 P.M. he clashed with General Stuart's cavalry but was stopped by a line of redoubts called Fort Magruder at the junction of two roads leading from Yorktown to Williamsburg. Brigadier General McLaws of Longstreet's division sent Semmes' and Kershaw's brigades to support the rear guard while the Federals sent the divisions of Generals Smith and Hooker to back up Stoneman. They arrived too late for action that evening. The troops were moving in heavy rain and the roads were mired.

Since McClellan was occupied with the transports at Yorktown, General Sumner took command of the field the next day. Finding two redoubts of the Confederates unoccupied, he ordered General Hancock to occupy them with a brigade and ten guns. At 7:30 A.M. General Hooker advanced from a dense wood in front of the main redoubt, which had a bastion and wide ditch in front and numerous rifle pits leading to other redoubts, as well as an abatis of felled trees. When Webber's six-gun battery was ordered up it became the target of such a heavy fire that its men were knocked out before it could open; a new crew and Bramhall's battery then opened on the Confederate position. Hooker's troops suffered losses and were to get help, but General Philip Kearny was not able to reach them until afternoon because of muddy roads and heavy rainfall. The Confederates brought up brigades of Wilcox, Pryor, Pickett, and A. P. Hill, and General Stuart sent his horse artillery under Captain John Pelham. The Federals were driven back into the woods.

On the Confederate left, however, they had better for-

tune. Here General W. S. Hancock was able to hold out
against superior numbers until supported late in the
afternoon. Confederate General Jubal A. Early, observing that one of Hancock's batteries behind a wood was
able to hit the Confederate flank, suggested an attack at a
weak spot, which was endorsed by General D. H. Hill
after a reconnaissance. General Longstreet agreed to the
attack but warned against a major involvement. The Confederates advanced through a wood with Hill and Early
in command each of two regiments. Hill's troops had to
reform after crossing a small stream, but Early did not
wait for the brigade but rushed ahead with the Twenty-
fourth Virginia regiment. The Federals, pushed back,
quickly rallied and Early's regiments were overwhelmed
before Hill could support them. General Hill wrote later:
"I cannot think of it, till this day, without horror. The
slaughter of the Fifth North Carolina regiment was one
of the most awful things I ever saw and it was caused by
a blunder." The Confederates were supposed to have lost
over 400 men in front of Hancock, who lost only 31. General McClellan, who came up to the field late in the afternoon, gave high praise to Hancock, saying "his conduct
was brilliant in the extreme," and reporting to Stanton
that he repulsed Early "by a real charge with the
bayonet." In his formal report he credited the bayonet
charge with "routing and dispersing" the whole attacking
force. To this General Early retorted: "This statement is
wholly devoid of truth . . . there was no charge by the
enemy with or without bayonets." Early blamed the repulse on the failure of D. H. Hill to follow him.

The Union army lost 456 killed, 1,410 wounded, 372
missing. The Confederate army withdrew during the night
and was not pursued because the roads were in terrible
condition. On May 7 General Franklin's division and part
of Sedgwick's landed on the right bank of the Pamunkey
opposite West Point and were attacked by Confederate
forces but held their own, suffering 194 casualties. General McClellan made his headquarters at White House
on the Pamunkey May 16. General Franklin's Sixth
Corps, and General Fitz John Porter's Fifth Corps, the
latter including the division of Brigadier General George
Sykes, reached Tunstall's Station May 19. The advance

reached Bottom's Bridge on the Chickahominy May 20; that and other bridges had been destroyed. Brigadier General Silas Casey of the Second Division, Fourth Corps, forded the river and was followed by Heintzelman's Third Corps, which pushed a detachment of the Confederates out of Seven Pines. The right of the Union army was at Mechanicsville, while the Confederates were on New Bridge Road. McClellan's army was now straddling the erratic Chickahominy, which was forty feet wide normally and could extend over a wide, swampy area when flooded. The army was put to work building entrenchments and eleven new bridges.

During May the Confederates suffered two setbacks that helped the Union campaign. By withdrawal of the Confederate troops from Portsmouth and Gosport the *Virginia* lost its protective port and was destroyed by the Confederates May 11. On May 8 President Lincoln, Secretary Stanton, and Secretary Chase arrived at Fort Monroe and ordered Major General John E. Wool to capture Norfolk. General Wool landed troops at Ocean View but came too late to stop General Huger from applying the torch to the navy yard and destroying the shipping, preparatory to evacuating the place. The Union troops entered Norfolk without opposition. The officials blamed the escape of the Confederates on lack of promptness by General Wool, and he was relieved of the command at Fort Monroe and succeeded by General John A. Dix.

The Battle of Fair Oaks or Seven Pines

General McClellan was convinced that he was confronting a foe far larger than his own army. His belief that the Confederates might have double his numbers seems to have rested on miscalculations made by Allan Pinkerton's civilian scouts. McClellan repeatedly called for reinforcements, and Washington promised to send General McDowell, who was near Fredericksburg. On May 18 McClellan was ordered to prepare for the coming of McDowell by extending the right of his army north of Richmond in order to establish communication with him; also to supply McDowell from White House.

The Army of the Potomac was continually receiving recruits and accessions, and although the government and McClellan never agreed on figures it had become a formidable body by the end of May. The official report said it had 127,166, of which 98,008 were present for duty. To this was added the force of General Wool, 14,007, with 11,514 ready for duty. General Wool had succeeded General Benjamin F. Butler in command of the Middle Department, but was under McClellan's orders.

Brigadier General J. R. Anderson, who had cavalry scouts watching McDowell near Fredericksburg, reported to General Johnston on May 24 that McDowell was starting to march south. But on that day General Banks was beaten at Front Royal and Winchester, and the retention of McDowell's force became necessary. President Lincoln explained this in detail to General McClellan. Jackson's movement in the Shenandoah Valley was making it impossible for Lincoln to send reinforcements to McClellan, but also leading the President to advise him: "I think the time is near when you must either attack Richmond or give up the job and come to the defense of Washington." McClellan surmised that Jackson's movement probably was meant to prevent reinforcements being sent him. "The time is very near when I shall attack Richmond." He was waiting for the bridges to be completed.

In the meantime McClellan sent General Stoneman with cavalry to cut the Virginia Central Railroad between the Chickahominy and Hanover Court House. This was one of the two Richmond lines; the other went north to Fredericksburg and Aquia Creek, both crossing the South Anna. The President wanted to know why the Aquia railroad was not cut. McClellan replied that he had cut the Virginia Central in three places and would try to cut the other likewise.

General L. O'B. Branch's division of about 9,000 men was located four miles south of Hanover Court House, protecting the Virginia Central Railroad and the communications with Anderson. General Fitz John Porter with the Fifth Corps attacked Branch on May 27 and drove him back. Porter had more than a division of infantry, three regiments of cavalry, and two batteries; he reported 355 killed and wounded, captured 730, and buried about 200 Confederates. McClellan called this a glorious victory; always partial to Porter, who remained a strong partisan of McClellan, he declared "too much credit can not be given to this magnificent division and its accomplished leader." But President Lincoln asked: "If this was a total rout of the enemy, I am puzzled to know why the Richmond and Fredericksburg Railroad was not seized again. . . . The scrap of the Virginia Central from Richmond to Hanover Junction without more is simply nothing." General Marcy, McClellan's chief of staff, reported May 29 that the South Anna railroad bridges had been destroyed, Lincoln sent his congratulations. McClellan countered with the remark that burning the South Anna bridges was the least important result of Porter's movement; "I do not think you at all appreciate the value and magnitude of Porter's victory."

When Johnston learned that McDowell was not coming, he decided to concentrate his attack on the two Federal corps of Heintzelman and Keyes, who were entrenched on the Williamsburg Road south of the Chickahominy. Longstreet was to lead the attack with his own and A. P. Hill's divisions in two lines; Major General Benjamin Huger, who had commanded at Norfolk but never taken part in a battle, was to move by the Charles City Road and hit the left flank of the two corps, and Major General G. W. Smith was to intercept any Federals that crossed the Chickahominy to support Heintzelman and Keyes.

Heavy rains on the day and night before brought flood water down the Chickahominy, and although this would deter McClellan it also was an obstacle for the Confederates. It delayed the attack two hours on May 31 because one division could not get across a creek. At 3 P.M. D. H. Hill attacked Keyes, with the brigades of Brigadier General Samuel Garland and Brigadier General George B. Anderson fighting the division of Major General Silas Casey, which had dug rifle pits and built Casey's Redoubt, with a battery of six guns, about one mile west of Seven Pines. After severe fighting the Federals were pushed back to the line manned by General Darius

Couch's division at Seven Pines. Major General Philip Kearny's division of Heintzelman's corps joined Keyes's defense but was also repulsed.

In the meantime Brigadier General Robert Rodes of D. H. Hill's division had run into fierce resistance in the rear of Casey's Redoubt and was saved from one onslaught by the timely arrival of a battery of the King William Artillery. When he resumed the attack he found himself unsupported in a swampy terrain where the Federal infantry swept the field. Men fought in water up to their knees and some wounded men were drowned before they could be pulled out. Rodes himself was wounded and a number of regimental officers were killed. Going in with about 2,000 men, Rodes had 1,094 killed or wounded, and Colonel John B. Gordon's Sixth Alabama lost 60 per cent of its effectives. During this battle the Federals used the observation balloon of Prof. T. S. C. Lowe.

The fighting at Seven Pines dwarfed the battle at Fair Oaks Station, but there the Confederates had worse luck. Major General William H. C. Whiting of Smith's division led the attack and was badly used. General R. H. Anderson's troops and Hood's Fifth Brigade were moved up to help. The right of General Couch's division, extending to Fair Oaks, was cut off and four regiments, two companies of infantry, and a six-gun battery isolated at the railroad, but the battery opened a flanking fire on G. W. Smith's division. General McClellan ordered Major General E. V. Sumner into the battle. He had been in reserve north of the river and now advanced with the divisions of Sedgwick and Richardson. Crossing was difficult because the bridges were partly submerged; Sedgwick was able to cross, but Richardson's bridge was several feet under water, and after one brigade had waded across Richardson sent the rest around to Sedgwick's bridge. This consumed so much time that they arrived too late to take part in the fighting.

Sumner with Sedgwick's three brigades and Kirby's battery reached the position of Couch near the Adams house at 2:30 P.M. Confederate General Smith took the offensive and attacked Sumner with the brigades of Generals Wade Hampton, James Johnston Pettigrew, and Robert Hatton. The fighting became so intense that Sumner lined up five New York, Massachusetts, and Michigan regiments to charge with the bayonet. He reported: "There were two fences between us and the enemy, but our men gallantly rushed over them, and the enemy broke and fled, and this closed the battle of Saturday."

General Johnston ordered his troops to rest on the field and to be ready to renew the battle the next morning. This proved, he said, that the Confederates were in control of the battleground. At 7 P.M. he was hit by a bullet in the right shoulder and struck in the chest by a piece of shell that knocked him off his horse. He was removed in an ambulance and command devolved on Major General G. W. Smith.

But Smith, who was near a nervous breakdown, made a poor start, and Longstreet later blamed him for losing a fine opportunity to trounce McClellan next day. On this Sunday morning, June 1, Brigadier General George Pickett, supported by some of D. H. Hill's troops, tangled with a large body of Federals, but the action was indecisive.

At noon President Davis appointed General Robert E. Lee to the command of Johnston's army. Johnston was condemned to a period of convalescence that lasted the summer. When he reported back for action on November 12, 1862, the military scene had changed; his army had been reorganized and was firmly in the hands of General Lee. Johnston was given an assignment in the West.

General Lee inspected the positions of the troops on June 1 and ordered them to withdraw to their original camps that night. The army was now augmented by 8,000 or more North Carolina troops under General Theophilus H. Holmes and by a brigade of 2,356 under Brigadier General Roswell S. Ripley.

Both sides claimed a victory, and the Union army cited as proof that it had reoccupied its old positions. The Confederates had taken 10 guns and picked up 7,500 small arms abandoned by fleeing Federals. But the Confederates likewise had reason to complain of their recruits; General Huger's troops did not arrive where ordered and a number of them broke and ran. These were the "Norfolk men" accused by General Longstreet of being halted in their march by a "rivulet." What Freeman calls "the butcher's bill" was not only high but included numerous officers. On the Confederate side Brigadier General Robert Hatton was killed and Brigadier General Pettigrew, who was captured, was so wounded that he was close to death. General Wade Hampton was wounded in the foot and had the bullet extracted astride his horse. While the South was told the Confederates had gained a great victory, President Davis and his commanders were not fooled. They knew that Johnston's plans had failed. Longstreet placed the blame on Huger, but later historians have found that Longstreet also was not free from error.

When General Lee was President Davis' adviser in Richmond he was unable to influence the headstrong General Joseph E. Johnston. Immediately upon assuming command of the army defending Richmond, Lee began to consider ways of forcing McClellan back. "Richmond must not be given up," he declared in one of his rare outbursts; "It shall not be given up!" He had written to his daughter, in a letter quoted by Freeman, that he wanted "to drive our enemies back to their homes. I have no ambition and no desire but the attainment of this object, and therefore only wait for its accomplishment by him that can do it most speedily and thoroughly." This task had now fallen to him and he took it up resolutely.

At an informal conference with his commanders he heard General Longstreet urge an attack on McClellan's right flank; later Longstreet came to him and argued for this action in a private interview, saying it would dislodge the Federal force posted behind Beaver Dam Creek.

On June 11 Lee wrote General Jackson a warm letter of congratulation for his successes in the Valley and informed him he was giving him six Georgia regiments under Brigadier General A. R. Lawton and eight veteran regiments under Brigadier General Whiting at the expense of weakening his own army. He instructed Jackson to keep the passes covered with cavalry and artillery and then bring his main body, including Ewell's, Lawton's, and Whiting's commands, to Ashland, and "sweep down between the Chickahominy and the Pamunkey, cutting up the enemy's communications, etc., while this army attacks General McClellan in front. He will thus, I think, be forced to come out of his intrenchments, where he is strongly posted on the Chickahominy and apparently pre-

paring to move by gradual approaches on Richmond."
He wanted Jackson to precede his troops so that they
could confer and arrange for a simultaneous attack.

At the same time General Lee ordered Jeb Stuart to
make a reconnaissance on the right flank of the Federal
position; this became the famous ride of Stuart around
McClellan. Lee called in his commanding generals for
a meeting at his headquarters June 23. When A. P. Hill,
D. H. Hill, and Longstreet arrived they found Jackson already there; he had ridden fifty miles since midnight,
using horses in relays. Lee explained his plan: Jackson
to march by the heights between the Chickahominy and
the Pamunkey to dislodge the Federal right; A. P. Hill
to cross the upper Chickahominy and march for Mechanicsville in echelon to Jackson; D. H. Hill and Longstreet
to cross the Mechanicsville Bridge, and Longstreet to
move to the right and march down the river in echelon
to A. P. Hill, who would march through Mechanicsville
to Gaines' Mill. At that time General Jackson asserted he
could have his army ready by the morning of June 26,
which was chosen as the day for the advance.

Reinforcement of the Confederates at Richmond was
exactly what General McClellan had been worrying about
for weeks.

Stuart's Ride Around McClellan

In June General Jeb Stuart had carried out the first of
the daring rides that he led into the enemy's country—the
ride around McClellan's army on the Chickahominy.
This was prompted by Lee's desire to get information
about the extent and movement of the Federal right.
General Lee gave the order to Stuart on June 10. It said
nothing about riding around McClellan—that was Stuart's
idea, also brought on partly because Stuart decided it
was easier to continue where he was not expected than
to double back on a road where the Federals were building up interference.

In his instructions General Lee explained that Stuart
was not only to get intelligence about operations and
communications, but to drive in foraging parties, secure
as much grain, cattle, and other provender as he could

manage, and destroy wagon trains said to be passing on
the Piping Tree road. Vigilance and caution were strongly
recommended and reliable scouts were to operate on
front and flanks. Lee wanted Stuart to "save and cherish"
the men and horses he took with him. The order is an
instance of the courtesy Lee exercised in giving a command, especially when he says: "You must bear constantly in mind, while endeavoring to execute the general purpose of your mission, not to hazard unnecessarily your
command, or to attempt what your judgment may not
approve, but be content to accomplish all the good you
can, without feeling it necessary to obtain all that might
be desired." Lee already knew the impetuosity of his energetic cavalry leader.

The raid was undertaken with a great deal of gusto, and
there is no doubt that the lively attitude of the leader was
communicated to the men. A number of observers have
described the "careless gaiety" of the men and called
Stuart "the gayest of the gay," frequently singing his
favorite song: "If you want to have a good time jine
the cavalry." When he called out to his men after
midnight on the moonlit morning of June 12 that
they would move in ten minutes, every man responded
with alacrity. With three days' rations in their pack and
sixty rounds of ammunition they knew that they were
going on some independent adventure. John Esten Cooke,
a member of his staff, wrote almost romantically of
Stuart and the great ride, and his portrait in *Wearing
of the Gray* is famous:

As the young cavalier mounted his horse on that moonlight night he was a gallant figure to look at. The gray coat
buttoned to the chin; the light French sabre balanced by
the pistol in its black holster; the cavalry boots above the
knee, and the brown hat with its black plume floating above
the bearded features; the brilliant eyes, and the huge
moustache, which curled with laughter at the slightest
provocation.

Cooke, carried away by memories of a great past, is
ready to testify that "the glance of the blue eyes of
Stuart at that moment was as brilliant as the lightning
itself."

Stuart started June 12 with 1,200 cavalry and a battery of horse artillery with two pieces. The horsemen included part of the First Virginia Cavalry under Colonel Fitzhugh Lee, part of the Ninth Virginia Cavalry under Colonel W. H. F. Lee, two squadrons from the Jeff Davis Legion under Lieutenant Colonel W. T. Martin, and units from the Fourth Virginia Cavalry riding with Fitzhugh Lee and W. H. F. Lee. Lieutenant James Breathed commanded the artillery.

Riding out of Richmond on the Brock Road, going north as if to mislead the Federals, Stuart headed for the South Anna. There were to be no bugle calls or bivouac fires. After a short rest near Taylorsville the column proceeded southeast to old Hanover Court House, which once resounded with Patrick Henry's legal eloquence. Here stood a scouting party of 150 horsemen of the Sixth United States Cavalry; when they saw what appeared to be an army charging down on them they mounted quickly and were off toward Mechanicsville. A little farther along, at Hawe's Shop, a Federal officer blundered into Stuart's advance, turned hurriedly and led his small detachment out of danger, but Colonel Fitzhugh Lee pursued and discovered the troops belonged to a unit of which Lee had been a lieutenant. According to Cooke what followed smacked of a class reunion.

A company of the Fifth U.S. Cavalry prepared to make a stand at a bridge across Totopotomoy Creek, but when its officer saw the size of Stuart's advance units he fell back to where Captain Royall of the Fifth was drawn up with 100 men. A quick dash by the Ninth Virginia under Captain Latané with drawn sabers routed the Federals after they had discharged their pistols; Latané wounded Captain Royall with his sword and was killed by a pistol shot. The Federals tried to make a stand at Old Church, but here again the Confederate numbers were too large for them. There was a cavalry camp nearby; as the Confederates approached the Federals left it, and Colonel Fitzhugh Lee's men demolished it.

By mid-afternoon the Federals were well aware that a considerable force of Confederate cavalry was operating on their right. They put several hundred infantry and some squadrons of cavalry on Stuart's trail, but their scouts so overestimated Stuart's strength that they remained overly cautious. One officer reported the Confederates had five regiments of infantry, and in repetition this number grew to seven. Thus Stuart's luck in avoiding pursuit was due in part to the inefficiency of the Federal scouts.

His troops had little interference as they continued on the outskirts of the Federal right in a southeasterly direction. At one point they encountered an ordnance wagon mired in the road; the driver cut the horses loose and escaped. The wagon was loaded with canteens and Colt revolvers, and the cavalrymen helped themselves to the firearms. At Putney's Ferry they burned two large transports and the supply train of two New York regiments. At Tunstall's Station on the York River Railroad they captured a guard of fifteen. They cut the wires and felled a large tree to obstruct the tracks. Just then a train approached and the engineer, recognizing a raid, put on full speed and rushed through the station. Bullets from Stuart's guns killed two and wounded eight on the train. Here also Stuart destroyed a wagon train and a freight car loaded with supplies. A little farther on his men burned a railroad bridge over Black Creek.

Brigadier General John F. Reynolds of the Pennsylvania Reserves had been on duty at Fredericksburg under General Irvin McDowell and was one of three generals who arrived at White House Landing with their forces to reinforce McClellan, the others being McCall and Meade. General Reynolds with two brigades marched through Tunstall's Station and made camp at Dispatch, eight miles away. When word came that Stuart and his horsemen were tearing up Tunstall's, General Reynolds was ordered to take after him. He reached Tunstall's with a squadron of cavalry at midnight after Stuart had gone on his way. A car loaded with corn and a bridge beyond the depot were on fire, and Reynolds' men extinguished the flames. They found the telegraph poles at the crossroads cut down. The body of a laborer had been run over by the train. A little later Reynolds was joined by the troops of Upton Emory and General Philip St. George Cooke, and all three failed to catch Stuart. There was some criticism later of their failure, especially that of

Cooke, who in addition to being a Virginian was Stuart's father-in-law.

When Stuart was at Tunstall's he was only four miles from White House, the Federal supply depot on the Pamunkey. This farm had been the home, since 1857, of General Lee's son, Colonel W. H. L. Lee, who had acquired it as a descendant of Martha Custis Washington, who had married George Washington in this house. Stuart had flushed a number of cavalry scouts, who retired toward White House. But Stuart did not follow them, for the base was strongly guarded. Instead he moved on to Talleysville, and as if contemptuous of any pursuit, gave his men three and a half hours for rest. The Federals were still looking for him, but they were hours behind and did not catch up with him.

Colonel Lee, who knew these New Kent roads intimately, was in the van and Lieutenant Jones Christian was to guide the troops to a ford on his farm, Sycamore Springs, which bordered on the Chickahominy. But the river was too swollen to make the ford accessible. Farther down were remains of the burned Forge bridge on a road that ran from Providence Forge to Charles City Court House. Using the surviving timbers and stripping others from an abandoned barn, Stuart's men had a bridge ready in three hours. Half of the men crossed on foot while it was being built, holding the bridles of their horses as the latter swam across; the rest, including the artillery, were able to use the completed bridge. After crossing they burned the bridge. They were on an island between two branches of the Chickahominy and were able to ford the next stream.

It was now 1 P.M. on June 14, the second day out, and Stuart still had to reach Charles City Court House, where he would turn northwest toward Richmond. Ordering his men to rest at the Wilcox Plantation, he turned the command over to Colonel Fitzhugh Lee and ordered him to start the return ride by the River Road at 11 P.M. Then with a courier and a guide he left for Richmond, and early next morning made a report to General Lee. The cavalrymen had no interference on the way back. At night they were able to see Federal gunboats on the James as they rode along, but the Federals did not spot the cavalcade. Stuart returned with 165 prisoners and 260 captured horses and mules. A number of his men had been wounded, but only one man was killed. The Union army reported four killed. General Lee praised the "courage and skill" of officers and men in a general order to the army. The ride caused great enthusiasm in the Confederate ranks and increased Stuart's prestige among his comrades and enemies, adding to the bafflement felt in the Federal capital.

The Seven Days' Battles and McClellan's Change of Base

The Seven Days' Battles took place when General Lee attacked McClellan and McClellan began his retreat to a new base at Harrison's Landing. They were delaying actions, developed by McClellan when he became convinced that he was unable to take Richmond and believed the Confederates to have the larger army. He also was afraid defeat might mean the loss of the whole Union army and thus endanger Washington and the North. On the part of the Confederates these were battles of frontal assaults and flank attacks, of desperate blows against hastily shoveled trenches, of attempts to dislodge enemies protected by woods and swamps. Both armies fought desperately, with violent artillery duels and cavalry charges with saber and carbine, and both commanders made plans that were not carried out by their subordinates.

These battles lasted from Thursday, June 26, through Tuesday, July 1, 1862. They were extremely costly to both sides, but they accomplished McClellan's object, a change of base with the army intact. Confederates and Federals were handicapped alike by the swamps of the Chickahominy and the heavy woods and underbrush. Lee had hoped to catch the long lines of the Federal retreat in the flanks, but the terrain and poor communications worked against him. McClellan not only moved his men and batteries, but a train of more than 5,000 supply wagons, although he had to destroy many tons of food and clothing.

As he withdrew he fought at Mechanicsville, June 26; Gaines' Mill, June 27; Peach Orchard and Savage's Station, June 29; Frayser's Farm or Glendale, June 30; and Malvern Hill, July 1. Thomas L. Livermore, who made a careful analysis of the results, estimated that the Seven Days' Battles saw 91,169 Union forces engaged, with losses of 1,734 killed, 8,062 wounded, and 6,053 missing. The Confederate commanders reported 75,769 engaged, but Livermore estimated that some units were overlooked in their summaries and the total was actually 95,481, with 3,478 killed, 16,261 wounded, and 875 missing. Precise numbers were never verified, but all reports indicated much heavier losses sustained by the Confederate than the Union army, which Lee blamed partly on lack of coordination among his divisions.

On June 25 General McClellan reported home that Jackson's advance was at or near Hanover Court House and that this meant increased danger to the Federal left. Expecting the Confederates to attack him in superior numbers, he sent Washington an excuse: "I regret my great inferiority in numbers, but feel that I am in no way responsible for it, as I have not failed to represent repeatedly the necessity of reinforcements, that this was the decisive point and that all available means of the Government should be concentrated here. . . . If the result of the action, which will probably occur tomorrow or within a short time, is a disaster, the responsibility can not be thrown on my shoulders; it must rest where it belongs." Both President Lincoln and Secretary Stanton rejected his attempt to shelve blame prematurely, and the President told him to consult General Pope, now in command of Washington, who preferred the York River to the James as a base.

If General McClellan was disturbed by the prospect of having to fight superior numbers, General Lee was not. Now in command of the army defending Richmond, his immediate response was to plan a campaign that would push McClellan beyond the Chickahominy and destroy his army. He had sent for General Jackson's army and expected it to arrive in time for his first battle. He would open his campaign at Mechanicsville on June 26. But Jackson encountered various obstacles and had a hard time moving his army. By the night of the 25th he had not yet reached Ashland, and at the rate he was moving he could hardly be expected to arrive at the battlefield in time.

The Confederate troops under D. H. Hill, A. P. Hill, and Longstreet crossed the Chickahominy at 3 P.M. on June 26, driving back outposts of the Federals, who would not make a stand until they reached a point one mile east of Mechanicsville, at Beaver Dam Creek. Here Brigadier General George A. McCall of the Third Division of Fitz John Porter's Fifth Corps had established his troops in an excellent position to repel an attack. Half of the Confederate columns went to Ellerson's Mill, on their extreme right, where Brigadier General Truman Seymour was posted. In both places the Confederates met volleys from guns and muskets so severe that they were thrown into confusion. The Confederates were without proper protection; some found thickets along the stream, others were ordered to lie down and wait until the Confederate batteries had cleared a way. Here Lee had planned a flank attack on the Union lines to be delivered by Jackson, but Jackson had not arrived. Some Confederate units moved down the slope to the creek and thus became targets for the Federals across the stream. Two strong assaults were made at Ellerson's Mill, where Generals Pender and Ripley were sent to turn the Federal position, but the latter was well protected by rifle pits and obstructions, and the flank attack failed.

Lee's first effort was a disaster. Although he had 56,000 men available, only about 16,000 were engaged and casualties ran to around 1,400. The Forty-fourth Georgia Infantry had 335 killed and wounded out of 514 in the regiment. The Federals had an estimated 15,000 engaged and lost 49 killed, 207 wounded.

General McClellan was jubilant; he wired Washington: "Victory today complete and against great odds; I almost begin to think we are invincible." But the danger to his left flank remained, and he decided to abandon the base at White House on the Pamunkey and move to the James. During the night he ordered the Fifth Corps under General Fitz John Porter to withdraw to a new position east of Powhite Creek six miles away.

The repulse did not stop Lee. He ordered batteries up to shell the Federal position on the morning of June 27, thereby expediting the rather hurried withdrawal of Gen-

eral McCall, who had been ordered to move to Gaines'
Mill that night. The Confederates quickly repaired the
bridge at Ellerson's Mill and found another usable structure across the creek. Lee started his troops along the
roads leading to Cold Harbor and Gaines' Mill. Jackson
had finally reached the area with a column of 18,500,
which reportedly was spread out fifteen miles on the
march. But during the crucial days to come he was not
the resourceful Stonewall Jackson. His footsore army
moved slowly, and when it finally reached the Chickahominy it encountered burned bridges and had to rebuild them to get access to the battlefields.

Action at Gaines' Mill

Jackson crossed Beaver Dam Creek that morning, advanced to Walnut Grove Church and then, turning toward Cold Harbor, made a wide detour to get behind
D. H. Hill. Hill started his attack at Gaines' Mill at
2:30 P.M. on June 27, but Jackson's guns were not there
to help him. But Jackson did manage to get some guns
forward to reinforce Captain John Pelham of Stuart's
Horse Artillery. Stuart had observed Federal artillery
moving on the road from Grapevine Bridge and sent
Pelham with two guns to harass them. One gun was
disabled early, but Pelham was not to be thwarted and
pounded away with one napoleon until Jackson's help
came. Numbers never stopped John Pelham; he was to
make a fine reputation for audacity at Fredericksburg.

The battle of Gaines' Mill, with most of the Federals
behind Powhite Creek, was Fitz John Porter's finest defensive operation, for with about 36,790 troops he held
off a force of over 57,000. It was the last of the battles
on the north side of the Chickahominy. The principal
attack was delivered by divisions of Generals Longstreet
and A. P. Hill, with the brigades of R. H. Anderson
and George E. Pickett leading. Porter saw early in the
morning that he did not have enough troops and called
for reinforcements, but the message did not reach
McClellan and he did not get help until afternoon. When
McClellan received word that Porter was in trouble he
sent Major General Henry W. Slocum with 9,000 and

told Porter: "You must hold on till dark." The avalanche of infantry hitting Porter caved in his center and caused much confusion, but Meagher's Irish brigade and French's brigade helped materially to bring about an orderly withdrawal.

But the Federals lost practically the bulk of two regiments, the Eleventh Pennsylvania Reserve and the Fourth New Jersey, which were captured. Also taken was Major General John F. Reynolds of McCall's division, when he lost his way in the swamp country. He was sent to Richmond and later exchanged. Longstreet said the Confederates took 52 guns and thousands of stands of arms. The Union loss was reported as 894 killed, 3,107 wounded, 2,836 missing, the last figure including the captured regiments. The Confederate returns were not complete, but were believed considerably higher.

General McClellan already had ordered the removal of the Army's supplies from White House Landing on the Pamunkey and the destruction of what could not be carried away. Generals Stoneman and Emory retired with infantry and cavalry to Tunstall's Station on the evening of June 27. On the 28th Lee ordered Stuart to follow and ascertain what direction McClellan was taking. Stuart discovered that the Federals had built some fortifications at the Station since his raid there earlier in the month, but they had destroyed the bridge across Black Creek and posted cavalry and artillery behind it. Stuart attacked with his guns and the Federal cavalry withdrew, giving Stuart's troops opportunity to repair the bridge for a crossing. Stoneman's infantry had moved on to White House, where with units of General Silas Casey's command it boarded transports.

When Stuart's advance reached White House after dark it found the depot evacuated and many supplies destroyed. However, there had not been time to complete the destruction, so that Stuart's men were able to pick up many necessities. The only Federal power left was the gunboat *Marblehead,* lying in the river opposite the landing. Stuart had never tackled a gunboat before, but he was not to be deterred from trying. He had seventy-five men dismount and with their rifled carbines deploy on the bank in pairs forty paces apart. The officers on the *Marblehead,* observing some movement on the shore, sent sharpshooters ashore. The two groups fired at each other without results until Stuart ordered up a howitzer from Pelham's battery and began shelling the *Marblehead*. The gunboat was unable to depress its guns sufficiently to hit the bank and thereupon called in its sharpshooters and moved down the river. Stuart was now able to report to Lee that White House Landing was abandoned and McClellan was headed for the James.

On the night of June 28 McClellan announced to his generals that he intended next day to begin moving the army to the James River. This meant that the troops from this point on would use roads leading to Harrison's Landing rather than White House. The army now faced the crossing of the formidable barrier of White Oak Swamp. General Fitz John Porter's troops were among the first to cross, followed by those of Keyes and Slocum. The other divisions were protecting the movement a mile or more in advance of White Oak Bridge.

General John B. Magruder on June 29 attacked units of General Sumner's Second Corps, which had just left entrenchments at Fair Oaks and now were at Peach Orchard (Allen's Farm). The fighting continued until 11 A.M. when Sumner retired in good order and joined the units of Franklin and W. F. Smith, which were based on Savage's Station. This location on the Richmond & York River Railroad and the Williamsburg Road had been used as a supply station and still had some Federal stores, which the army was in process. of destroying. There were 2,500 Union sick and wounded in hospital tents there, most of them from the battle at Gaines' Mill. At 5 P.M. General Magruder led the Confederate attack with Semmes', Kershaw's, and Barksdale's brigades and Kemper's and Hart's batteries. The Confederates drove in the center of General William W. Burns's line, but this was quickly rectified with the help of Sumner and General Brooks' brigade of Smith's division, Sixth Corps. Magruder was driven back but as the Federals moved on they left their wounded behind.

Here the Confederates made use of the railroad to bring forward a flatcar battery, consisting of a thirty-two pounder rifled gun, which fired through a slanting shield covered with iron plates. The Federals turned a heavy fire on it and it was withdrawn. Later the Union army used a number of flatcars carrying guns and howitzers.

The Confederates did not get General Jackson's help here because he was delayed by having to rebuild the bridges destroyed by Fitz John Porter. The Union loss at Savage's Station was heavy, but the fight gave the army time to get its troops and wagons across the White Oak Bridge. General I. B. Richardson's division of Sumner's corps was the last to cross at 10 A.M. the next day, June 30, and the destruction of that bridge gave added time for McClellan's withdrawal.

General D. H. Hill's division then reached White Oak Swamp at noon June 30 and, observing a body of Federal infantry and artillerymen at rest on the farther side of White Oak Creek, he brought up thirty-one guns and opened a concentrated fire upon them. Some units of the Federal wagon train also were standing there and the drivers ran off without their teams. About fifty wagons were destroyed. Federal guns replied quickly and silenced some of the Confederate guns. The firing alarmed mules belonging to a pontoon train that were being watered; they stampeded and were not caught again. Late in the day volunteers brought off one of the wagons and set fire to the rest. In the meantime there was the fighting that Jackson was unable to reach because he had not been informed that Brackett's Ford, one mile above the broken White Oak Bridge, would have provided a crossing for his troops.

At midnight after the battle at Savage's Station, General McClellan sent the Secretary of War a dispatch apparently dictated by his emotional reactions and not by a study of the facts. He attempted to obscure the heavy losses by praise for the men's bravery and blame for the government. He speaks of being

overwhelmed by vastly superior numbers, even after I put my last reserves into action. The loss on both sides is terrible. Had I 20,000 or even 10,000 fresh troops to use tomorrow I could take Richmond, but I have not a man in reserve, and shall be glad to cover my retreat and save the material and personnel of the army. . . . I have lost this battle because my force was too small. . . . I again repeat that I am not responsible for this. . . . You must send me very large reinforcements and send them at once. If I save this army now, I tell you plainly that I owe no thanks to you, or to any other person in Washington. You have done your best to sacrifice this army.

McClellan's dispatch shocked President Lincoln and Secretary Stanton. In the light of later disclosures it seems even more inexcusable than it did in 1862. Evidently his misapprehensions about the strength of the Confederates and his determination not to wreck the army led him to withhold help when it was most needed. In addition to inordinate caution he now exhibited a readiness to shift the blame for a disaster. The dispatch was written under stress of emotion, but McClellan proved that he meant what he wrote by incorporating it later in his final report. The President, torn by worry that he could hardly disguise, took several days to reply, and then wrote with patience and consideration:

It is impossible to reinforce you for your present emergency. If we had a million of men, we could not get them to you in time. We have not the men to send. If you are not strong enough to face the enemy, you must find a place of security, and wait, rest, and repair. Maintain your ground if you can, but save the army at all events, even if you fall back to Fort Monroe. We still have strength enough in the country, and will bring it out.

Frayser's Farm and Malvern

One of the hottest fights of the Seven Days took place at Frayser's Farm, or Glendale, on June 30. General Lee made an elaborate plan to intercept and destroy the rear of the Federal army. Longstreet was to march fifteen miles and take a position below Frayser's Farm with A. P. Hill. Holmes was to be below Longstreet on the River Road. Jackson was to keep close to the Federal rear, crossing at the Grapevine Bridge. Huger was to be posted on the Charles City Road to attack the Federal right flank, held by Franklin's corps.

On the morning of June 30 Longstreet and A. P. Hill were several miles from Frayser's Farm facing the Federals, who were in front of the Charles City Road and the Quaker Road. Hooker was at the Federal left to the south; McCall and Kearny were at the center with Sedgwick behind them; Slocum was at the Federal right to the north. Over by the White Oak Bridge, Jackson and D. H. Hill were north of White Oak Swamp Creek. Huger was some distance to the left of Longstreet and across the Charles City Road, where Slocum engaged in an artillery duel with him. Jackson found the Grapevine Bridge destroyed and made no crossing; D. H. Hill had an idea that he was trying to spare his tired troops.

The hardest fighting took place in front of McCall's, Kearny's, and Seymour's brigades, with McCall losing and retaking ground. Huger was unable to join the fighting because his road was obstructed by fallen timbers. By dark the Confederates had occupied most of the Federal positions of the morning, but McClellan had saved his trains and was able to draw back to the strong defensive position at Malvern. Longstreet said that at least 50,000 Confederates did not get into the battle and Lee's plan for intercepting McClellan went awry. General George A. McCall, riding out with his staff to locate his division, approached a road in a dense pine wood and blundered into the Confederates. The Federals turned their horses quickly about, but the Confederates fired, killing one of the staff, and McCall was taken prisoner by the Forty-seventh Virginia regiment.

A short distance beyond White Oak Swamp the Long Bridge Road led to the Charles City Road and the Willis Church Road, which for part of its length was known as the Quaker Road. The latter was a narrow thoroughfare lined with tangled brush and matted trees, with a few open spaces where the Willis Methodist Church and the parsonage stood. The Union army had passed down this road, leaving the church packed with wounded men, attended by a Pennsylvania surgeon. At the end of the Willis Road and north of Turkey Creek, lay Malvern Hill. Undulating farm land extended to Crew's Hill, about one mile north. The flat terrain to the west of Malvern was mostly wooded and swampy on both sides of the road. The smaller hilly country had been cleared and there were two structures, the farmhouses of Crew and West. The whole place was suited by nature for defense.

D. H. Hill appreciated the strength of Malvern for defense against assaults and was willing to let McClellan alone there, but Longstreet insisted the Confederates had the Union army on the run. Jackson came up from White Oak Swamp about noon and posted his troops along the Methodist Church areas on the Quaker Road. He was ordered to follow the Federals with Huger and Magruder at his right and Longstreet and A. P. Hill in reserve.

McClellan had ridden over Malvern Hill and indicated positions for the troops "in a general way," and Generals Barnard and Humphreys also had inspected the field. But the principal locations of units were determined by corps commanders. During the battle McClellan was at Haxall's, nearly three miles distant. On Malvern, Fitz John Porter had lined up the divisions of Sykes, Morell, and Truman Seymour, who was now commanding the division of the Fifth Corps formerly headed by McCall. To their right were the troops of Kearny, Hooker, and Sickles of Heintzelman's corps, Couch's division of Keyes's corps, and in reserve most of Sumner's troops.

Colonel Henry J. Hunt had found the elevations excellent for placing about a hundred pieces of the artillery reserve, and with the field of assault narrowed the guns had perfect range. These were all pretty well placed by the afternoon of Monday, June 30, when infantry units of General Holmes's division, with a six-gun battery, attacked at 4 P.M. along the River Road near Turkey Bridge, south of the main Federal position on Malvern. The attack was repulsed by General Warren's troops and Hunt's guns, and the Confederates not only received blasts from thirty pieces but also shelling from three gunboats in the James River. The latter, however, fired far beyond the targets and added confusion to the fighting. General Magruder was ordered to support Holmes but could not move his troops in time.

The Confederates were aware that they faced the hardest task of the whole campaign at Malvern. Lee was ready to throw powerful forces against the Union position, but access to it was impeded. After a number of light assaults on July 1 that were in the nature of feeling out Federal strength, the battlefield fell silent for about an hour. At 5:30 P.M. their line erupted with fire from massed artillery, followed by infantry. The command had decided that the Federal position could not be turned and must be rushed; the attacks were made in the open with great impetuosity. The heaviest assaults were against the positions of Couch and Morell. The Confederates came forward in regimental order with colors flying as if at a review; "the woods swarmed with butternut coats and gray." As they advanced to higher ground the Confederates received the full blast of the Union batteries. As some artillerymen fell, others rushed forward to man the guns. The Federals were so excited by the way the attackers were repulsed that the men of several regiments rushed out of the ranks to pursue the melting lines of the Confederates down the hills. When Porter's troops were hard-pressed at the height of the fighting, Sumner sent Meagher's brigade and Heintzelman sent Sickles' The battle lasted about two hours; by dusk the Confederates were back in their former positions, leaving behind fields blotted out by heaps of their dead.

Malvern was fought by infantry against artillery. It was General Lee's great error to order his infantry against many batteries. It was the old tactic of frontal assault, against a fortified position, which he tried once again, to his defeat, at Gettysburg.

Lee had sent each division commander an order to charge the Federal positions when General Armistead's men charged "with a yell." D. H. Hill, who had sized up Malvern Hill as insurmountable under the conditions, wrote a vivid account of the fighting and the losses sustained by the Confederates. He noted that as each Confederate battery came up and took its place fifty Federal pieces were turned on it and it was "crushed in a minute." When Hill advanced on hearing the shouting, his troops fought fiercely for an hour and a half without being supported; finally, as the Comte de Paris expressed it, he "reorganized the debris of his corps in the woods." General Magruder advanced after sunset with nine brigades —those of Mahone, Wright, Barksdale, Ransom, Cobb, Semmes, Kershaw, Armistead, and G. T. Anderson, and

parts of the divisions of Huger and McLaws. Hill wrote:
"Unfortunately they did not move together and were
beaten in detail. As each brigade emerged from the woods
from fifty to one hundred guns opened upon it, tearing
great gaps in its ranks, but the heroes reeled on and
were shot down by the reserves at the guns, which a few
squads reached. It was not war—it was murder. More
than half the casualties were from field pieces—an unprecedented thing in warfare."

Colonel William W. Averell (later Major General),
who covered the Union rear and was present on the
field the next day, July 2, wrote that the morning began
with fog. "Our ears had been filled with agonizing cries
from thousands before the fog was lifted, but now our
eyes saw an appalling spectacle upon the slopes down
to the woodlands half a mile away. Over 5,000 dead and
wounded were on the ground, in every attitude of distress.
A third of them were dead or dying, but enough were alive
and moving to give the field a singular crawling effect."

That night the Federals were weary from their long at-
tendance at the guns and their battling with the oncoming
Confederates, and the rain was falling heavily again, but
their spirits were high. They had proved their ability to
stand their ground and more than one officer declared
Malvern Hill was impregnable. Yet they had hardly had an
hour's rest when orders to withdraw came from headquarters. This surprised the men in the ranks, but they
shouldered their packs and started down the roads. It
was for headquarters to tell them where to go. But to
withdraw from a beaten enemy after such a powerful
demonstration of fighting power was a great blow to
morale. General Hooker expressed it later: "It was like
the retreat of a whipped army. We retreated like a parcel
of sheep; everybody on the road at the same time, and
a few shots from the Rebels would have panic-stricken
the whole command."

By daybreak July 2 the trains had gone ahead unmolested and the troops were moving toward a new camp
ground at Harrison's Landing. It was near the James River;
the land was low and the fields were sodden with the rains.
McClellan had preferred it over City Point because the
channel at the Point was too narrow for supply boats.

There would be plenty of rations, and for the present, no more fighting. The campaign against Richmond was ended, and 15,249 men who had been whole when the Army of the Potomac left Yorktown now were either suffering from wounds or dead. General Lee reported that the Confederates had taken more than 10,000 prisoners, 52 guns, and 35,000 stand of small arms.

In the opinion of the authorities in Washington and of the country General McClellan had proved unequal to a great opportunity. He had sacrificed many months of preparatory work and had embarked on a campaign that his superiors considered doubtful. Now, apparently, he wanted to build up another army for a new campaign. Washington was disturbed. President Lincoln was anxious that McClellan should consolidate his new position and be ready to defend it against possible danger. On July 4 he informed his general that he would be unable to reinforce him sufficiently to mount a new expedition in a month or six weeks, but he would do the best he could; he was sending 10,000 from the Potomac, 10,000 from Burnside, and later on 5,000 would come from Hunter. "Save the army first, where you are, if you can, and secondly by removal, if you must."

Considering what McClellan had just done with the army, the President was puzzled to find him writing on July 7: "My position is very strong, and daily becoming more so. If not attacked today, I shall laugh at them. . . . Alarm yourself as little as possible about me, and don't lose confidence in this army."

Evidently McClellan now had time to reflect, so he turned his attention to the political problems of the government. He wrote the President an extraordinary letter of advice, one that discloses how much he felt himself superior to the man in the White House. He declared the Constitution and the Union must be preserved:

Let neither military disaster, political faction, nor foreign war shake your settled purpose to enforce the equal operation of the laws of the United States upon the people of every state. The time has come when the Government must determine upon a civil and military policy, covering the whole ground of our national trouble.

This rebellion . . . should not be a war looking to the sub-

jugation of the people of any state, in any event. It should
not be at all a war upon population, but against armed
forces and political organizations. Neither confiscation of
property, political executions of persons, territorial organization of states, or forcible abolition of slavery should be contemplated for a moment. . . .

Unless the principles governing the future conduct of our
struggle shall be made known and approved, the effort to
obtain requisite forces will be almost hopeless. A declaration of radical views, especially upon slavery, will rapidly
disintegrate our present armies. The policy of the Government
must be supported by concentrations of military power. The
national forces should not be dispersed in expeditions, posts
of occupation, and numerous armies, but should be mainly
collected into masses, and brought to bear upon the armies
of the Confederate States. Those armies thoroughly defeated,
the political structure which they support would soon cease
to exist.

President Lincoln visited Harrison's Landing July 8 in
an effort to find out what was to be done with the Army
of the Potomac. He asked the commanding general and
the corps commanders if it could be removed from the
Peninsula. His own notes disclose that McClellan thought
this would be very difficult; Fitz John Porter agreed with
McClellan and said it would ruin the country. Generals
Sumner and Heintzelman thought it could be done, though
it might mean "abandoning our cause." Generals Franklin and Keyes approved removal and said it should be
done. General Keyes had been opposed to McClellan's
military strategy for some time. McClellan said the President should appoint a general in chief in whom he had
confidence. He then handed the President his letter on
the policies he thought should be pursued by the Government. Nothing could have been more tactless or more
likely to make the President lose confidence in McClellan.

Late in June the President had made a trip to West
Point, New York, to consult General Winfield Scott, who
had retired there. The subject was appointment of a new
general in chief. On July 11 the President, disregarding
the protests of Secretary Stanton, ordered Major General
Henry W. Halleck to Washington "to command the
whole land forces of the United States as General in
Chief." Halleck, who previously had demonstrated his

unwillingness to go to Washington, now had to obey his superior officer. His first task was to proceed to Harrison's Landing to confer personally with McClellan.

McClellan outlined his new plan—to cross the James River, cut the communications of Richmond with the South, and move to occupy Petersburg. He wanted 30,000 more troops; Halleck talked about 20,000 for a new campaign against Richmond. McClellan said he was willing to make the attempt and he protested against recalling the troops; this, he said, would demoralize the army. But Washington was skeptical, and indeed McClellan did raise his request to 35,000 troops soon after. After a week the cabinet decided to recall the army from the Peninsula.

On August 3 Halleck telegraphed McClellan to take immediate steps to withdraw the army to Aquia Creek. Halleck explained that he could not send the reinforcements asked; that keeping the army on the Peninsula in August and September would mean many more cases of illness and might also lead the Confederates to attack Pope with large forces. McClellan asked that the order be rescinded. He made an eloquent defense of his policies. He cited the good condition and discipline, the security of the command, aided by gunboats. "Here, directly in front of this army, is the heart of the rebellion. All points of secondary importance elsewhere should be abandoned and every available man brought here; a decided victory and the military strength of the rebellion is crushed. It matters not what partial reverses we may meet with elsewhere. Here is the true defense of Washington." But now Halleck had orders and had to carry them out. He replied brusquely: "The order will not be rescinded and you will be expected to execute it with all necessary promptness."

Halleck previously had asked McClellan to feel out the enemy at his front. The day after getting the order to withdraw McClellan attacked the Confederates posted at Malvern Hill, causing them to make a hurried withdrawal. He sent Colonel Averell's cavalry on a reconnaissance as far as Savage's Station. "Our troops have advanced twelve miles in one direction and seventeen in another toward Richmond today," he wired.

During the month of August the Army of the Potomac was placed on transports. General Keyes' corps was left to occupy Yorktown. General McClellan reached Aquia Creek August 24 and on August 27 reported for orders at Alexandria.

15

GENERAL POPE AND
SECOND BULL RUN (MANASSAS)

The success achieved by Major General John Pope at New Madrid and Island No. 10 brought him national attention and made the President and his advisers consider him the most likely officer to rectify a confusing situation among commands in the East. The indecisive results of the various campaigns in Virginia had spread discontent in the nation and dismay in Washington. After the President had given specific orders to Generals Frémont and Banks to trap Stonewall Jackson, and had asked General McDowell to cooperate with them, Jackson successfully evaded them all. On June 24 President Lincoln had journeyed to West Point to consult General Winfield S. Scott on plans for reorganizing the eastern departments under a single commander. On June 26 he issued an order creating the Army of Virginia, and named Major General Pope to the command.

The First Army Corps would be composed of the troops under General Frémont, who had commanded the Mountain Department; the Second would be those of General Banks, who had held the Department of the Shenandoah, and the Third those of General McDowell, who had held the Department of the Rappahannock. Frémont regarded the order to serve under Pope as insulting and unendurable. He detested Pope for the contemptuous manner in which he had disregarded Frémont's specific orders in Missouri, and blamed him for failing to save Colonel James A. Mulligan from de-

feat at Lexington, Missouri. The day after Lincoln's order
Frémont asked to be relieved from his post. His desire
was granted and the command was given to Major General Franz Sigel. By a series of circumstances not wholly
the fault of Lincoln, Frémont was detached from active
service for the rest of the war.

General Pope was not pleased with the prospect before him; he looked on his task as a forlorn hope. He
did not want to command an army in which the corps
commanders were his seniors in rank, and he asked to
be allowed to return to the West, where he had been
successful. But the government wanted him East, and
he was compelled to organize the Army of Virginia, draw
together the scattered units, and begin demonstrations
in the direction of Gordonsville and Charlottesville, in
order to draw the bulk of Lee's army from in front of
McClellan on the Chickahominy. The new army, according to the *Official Records,* had the following strength:
First Army Corps, Major General Franz Sigel, 13,200;
Second Army Corps, Major General Nathaniel P. Banks,
12,100; Third Army Corps, Major General Irvin Mc-
Dowell, 19,300; cavalry brigades, 5,800. General Pope
took command on June 27. After observing the difficulty
of cooperating with General McClellan on an equal basis,
General Pope proposed that some officer superior to
both himself and McClellan get top authority over military action in Virginia. The appointment of "Old Brains"
Henry W. Halleck as general in chief followed on July 11.

When General Pope assumed command of the Army
of Virginia he issued an address to the troops that was
much criticized for its boastfulness and which caused
resentment among the officers of the Confederate army.
In it recurred such phrases as "Let us understand each
other. I have come to you from the West, where we
have always seen the backs of our enemies; from an
army whose business it has been to seek the adversary,
and to beat him when he was found; whose policy has
been attack and not defense. . . . I desire you to dismiss
from your minds certain phrases, which I am sorry to
find so much in vogue amongst you. I hear constantly
of 'taking strong positions and holding them,' of 'lines
of retreat,' and of 'bases of supplies.' Let us discard

such ideas. The strongest position a soldier should desire to occupy is one from which he can most easily
advance against the enemy. Let us study the probable
lines of retreat of our opponents, and leave our own to
take care of themselves. . . ."

General Pope's first dispositions were to order cavalry
units at Fredericksburg to cut the Virginia Central Railroad, which was done. He ordered General Banks to
take cavalry and some infantry, occupy Culpeper Court
House, proceed to Gordonsville, and destroy the railroad running out of that place. Banks got as far as Madison Court House and did not carry out the rest of the
assignment. When Lee had ascertained that McClellan
at Harrison's Landing was not likely to menace Richmond he ordered General Jackson with his own and
General Ewell's divisions to proceed toward Gordonsville on July 13. Jackson learned that Pope's force was
superior to his own and waited for reinforcements. When
Lee became certain that McClellan's force was to remain
at Harrison's Landing and Pope was at the Rapidan he
ordered General A. P. Hill to join Jackson, while General Jeb Stuart's cavalry remained on watch near
Fredericksburg.

To watch the Confederate army and be ready to intercept an advance General Pope placed strong detachments along the turnpike from Sperryville to Culpeper.
The line of the Rapidan was patrolled by cavalry units
under Brigadier Generals John Buford and George D.
Bayard all the way to where it flows into the Rappahannock. Brigadier General Rufus King's infantry division
was kept at Falmouth, opposite Fredericksburg, to guard
stores. When General Bayard became aware of a forward movement by the Confederates on August 8 he
fell back slowly as planned and Brigadier General Samuel W. Crawford's brigade of Banks's Second Corps was
ordered to Cedar Mountain to support Bayard. A little
later General Pope ordered Banks to move with the rest
of his corps to join Crawford, but no battle was intended. General Buford reported a heavy force moving
from Madison Court House to Culpeper and withdrew
toward Sperryville.

Banks had 8,030 men in two divisions under Brigadier

Generals A. S. Williams and Christopher C. Augur, with the Second Division of McDowell's corps under Brigadier General James B. Ricketts, which was ordered up for support but did not fight. General Stonewall Jackson had about 20,000 troops available in brigades from the divisions of Brigadier General Charles S. Winder, Major General A. P. Hill, and Major General R. S. Ewell. Late on August 9, 1862, General Banks moved his corps forward about two miles at Cedar Mountain, also called Slaughter Mountain and Southwest Mountain. Here he clashed with units of Stonewall Jackson's corps. Jackson sent the brigades of Generals William B. Taliaferro and Jubal Early against Banks's line at Cedar Run, where they were met by the brigades of Generals George H. Gordon, Crawford, and Geary. At first the Federals pushed the Confederates back, and Brigadier General L. O'B. Branch of Hill's division reported that General Jackson complained his left was beaten and broken when he ordered Branch to advance. The latter pushed through "the celebrated Stonewall Brigade, utterly routed and fleeing as fast as they could run." Yet the Confederates were able to silence Banks's guns and repulse Bayard's cavalry, and when Ricketts failed to arrive the Federals fell back before the larger forces. Banks's losses were 314 killed, 1,445 wounded, and 622 captured or missing, and among the Federal wounded were Generals Augur, Carroll, and Geary; the Confederate loss was 229 killed and 1,047 wounded and among their dead was General Winder.

When Sigel arrived with 12,000 men his corps took the place of Banks's, which was sent back to be reorganized. Brigadier General Rufus King was ordered up from Fredericksburg on August 11. This gave Pope a force larger than Jackson's, and caused Jackson to withdraw across the Rapidan. On August 14 Major General Jesse L. Reno with the Ninth Corps of 8,000 also joined Pope from Fredericksburg. The next day Longstreet joined Jackson at Gordonsville.

Pope's Army of Virginia was now based on Cedar Mountain. General Irvin McDowell had the center, on both flanks of the mountain; the left under Reno was near Raccoon Ford and commanding the road to Ste-

vensburg and Culpeper Court House. Opposite Pope's
left was Clark's Mountain, on the top of which the Confederates had a signal station, from which they were
able to view the encampments of Pope's army. The hills
nearby ran along the Rapidan to Raccoon Ford, two
miles away, and provided a screen behind which General
Lee could move his troops to attack Pope's left at Somer-
ville Ford and cut his communications with Washington.

Lee determined to put this plan into execution August
18, before Pope could be further reinforced. But on the
16th Pope made a cavalry raid toward Louisa Court
House and captured General Jeb Stuart's adjutant general with his papers. One was a letter from Lee to Stuart
explaining his project of falling upon Pope before divisions of the Army of the Potomac could reach him. Thus
alerted to his danger, Pope ordered his army to withdraw to the north side of the Rappahannock, which he
completed successfully by August 19.

In quick retaliation Stuart raided Pope's camp and
captured his uniform and papers. From these Lee
learned that Pope was to be reinforced by units of the
Army of the Potomac, including its Third Army Corps
under Major General S. P. Heintzelman and its Fifth
under Major General Fitz John Porter. The Third, with
divisions commanded by Generals Philip Kearny and
Joseph Hooker, would add nearly 15,000 men to Pope's
army. Actually Pope would have about 75,000 men to
Lee's 50,000. This prospect led Lee to adopt one of
those audacious moves by which he often overcame superior numbers. He ordered General Jackson, with
Stuart's cavalry, about 24,000 troops, to move around
Pope's right flank in order to cut his communications
with Washington. Lee could depend on Jackson to execute his orders without the slightest delay. Jackson
started from Jeffersonton on August 25, marched northeast through Amissville and Orlean to Salem, where he
turned east to move through Thoroughfare Gap, passed
through Gainesville, and reached Bristoe Station on August 27, covering fifty-one miles in two days with his
"foot cavalry."

Knowing that many tons of supplies were piled
up at the Federal quartermaster's depot at Manassas

Junction, Jackson accepted the offer of Brigadier General Isaac R. Trimble to take his brigade and capture the stores. He added a detachment of Stuart's cavalry. When Trimble arrived he was met by artillery fire, but he overwhelmed the defenders, took 8 guns and 300 prisoners. Next morning Jackson moved the divisions of Taliaferro and A. P. Hill up to the Junction, leaving General Ewell's division at Bristoe. The army was then turned loose on the spoils and the men had an orgy of feasting. Since they could not preserve more than they could eat and carry, the immense stores were destroyed and burned.

Jackson's movement was detected by Pope, but Pope was unable to counteract it immediately because his reinforcements had not all arrived. From August 18 until August 26 his troops had been engaged in daily skirmishes with the Confederates, often in several places at once; thus on August 20 there were skirmishes at Raccoon Ford, Stevensburg, Brandy Station, Rappahannock Station, and near Kelly's Ford. This meant continuous alertness and movement, and there were always some casualties. By August 25 Pope had received only General Kearny's division of 4,500 and Brigadier General John F. Reynolds' Pennsylvania Reserves, 2,500, which came on August 22 and were attached to the corps of General McDowell. The advance of General Fitz John Porter's Fifth Army Corps of the Army of the Potomac had reached Warrenton Junction on the morning of August 27, where General Heintzelman also arrived, but Pope was expecting the corps of both Generals Franklin and Sumner of the Army of the Potomac, and other troops under General Jacob D. Cox from western Virginia. At this time McDowell's and Sigel's corps were at Warrenton; Banks was at Fayetteville in reserve; Reno was on the Turnpike three miles east of Warrenton. Pope felt that if the reinforcements had reached him quickly he could halt Jackson's movement around his right.

General Pope was badly in need of rations and forage. On August 28 he made an urgent appeal for such supplies. In reply he received a formal note from Major General W. B. Franklin, commanding the Sixth Corps, which read: "I have been instructed by General Mc-

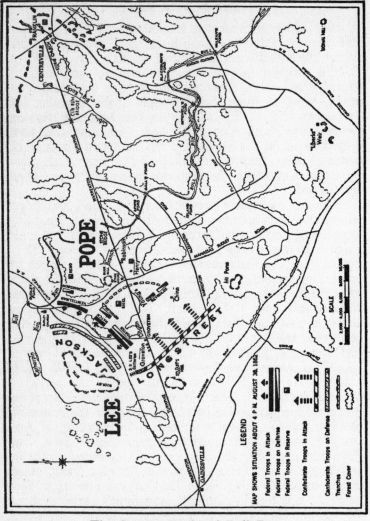

The Second Battle of Bull Run
(Manassas)

Clellan to inform you that he will have all the available
wagons at Alexandria loaded with rations for your troops
and all the cars also, as soon as you will send a cavalry
escort to Alexandria as a guard to the train." General
Pope considered this reply an affront and declared: "Such
a letter when we were fighting the enemy and Alexandria
was swarming with troops, needs no comment."

He felt himself handicapped because the troops did
not move with the celerity he demanded and because
General McClellan, out of sorts because his troops had
been ordered up from the Peninsula, was extremely
dilatory in getting them to the front. At this time Mc-
Clellan was suggesting to the President that one of two
courses ought to be adopted: either "to concentrate all
our available forces to open communications with Pope"
or "to leave Pope to get out of his scrape and at once
use all our means to make the Capital perfectly safe."
President Lincoln, replying on August 29, pointed out
that the first alternative was the right one in his opinion,
but he was offended by the letter and said McClellan
had acted badly toward Pope; "he really wanted him to
fail." McClellan bestirred himself to send the corps of
Franklin and Sumner to Pope, for they reached Centreville on August 30 with 19,000 troops, and Franklin
actually reached the battlefield, although too late to fight.

General Pope thought the Confederate movement
around his right gave him the choice of either abandoning the Rappahannock line and communications with
his superiors or risking the loss of the army and of Washington. This made it necessary for him to stop the Confederates if he could. On the morning of August 27 he
decided to abandon the Rappahannock line, even though
this cut him off from Washington and left the capital
without news of his location for several days. He then
would move toward Gainesville and Manassas Junction,
crush the forces that had marched through Thoroughfare
Gap and get between Lee's army and Bull Run. The
Confederates had left General R. H. Anderson's division of about 6,000 at Waterloo Bridge while their main
body marched along the Upper Rappahannock toward
the Union right. On August 27 Pope ordered McDowell
toward Gainesville by the Warrenton Pike, with his own

and Sigel's corps and Reynolds' division. He ordered
Reno to march on Greenwich and connect with Mc-
Dowell and support him at operations near Gainesville.
He also ordered Kearny's division to follow Reno and
Hooker's division of Heintzelman's corps to Manassas
Junction.

On the afternoon of August 27 Hooker's division attacked Ewell's division at Kettle Run near Bristoe Station. The Confederates had Early's brigade, four other
regiments, and two batteries. Hooker drove them back
along the railroad, but they halted beside Broad Run.
Each side had about 300 casualties. On the way to
Manassas Jackson's troops had skirmished with several
Federal units. The most severe clash near Bull Run developed with a Federal brigade of New Jersey and Ohio
regiments under Brigadier General G. W. Taylor, which
had misjudged the size of the Confederate troops. Taylor
was mortally wounded.

On the night of August 27 McDowell, Reno, and
Kearny had reached their assigned places and therefore
were between the main Confederate army and the forces
of Jackson, who was at Manassas Junction. To strengthen
his right wing, now moving to Manassas Junction, Pope
ordered General Porter to move from Warrenton Junction at 1 A.M. and report to him at Bristoe Station at
daylight on August 28. This was a distance of only nine
miles, but Porter did not arrive there until 10:30 A.M.
Porter had started at 3 A.M. on a night so dark that the
men had to light candles to find the road. (This total
blackness was also experienced by Confederate commanders, and caused General McDowell to lose his way
on the next night.) But Pope was not sympathetic to
Porter's explanation, for he observed that other units
had been able to march despite the darkness, and when
Porter asked permission to rest his men because they
were fatigued, Pope considered his request ridiculous.
This was the beginning of the grievances complained of
later by Pope.

Pope now determined to center his army on Manassas. He ordered McDowell, at Gainesville, to move at
dawn, rest his right on the Manassas Gap railroad and
his left to the east. He ordered Reno to move from

Greenwich to the Junction and Kearny from Greenwich to Bristoe. Kearny would unite with Hooker's division, both belonging to Heintzelman's corps.

Pope now thought he had Stonewall Jackson cornered. But that resourceful commander rarely acted according to the expectations of his enemy. Ewell joined him during the night and at 3 A.M. on August 28 Jackson withdrew from Manassas by way of New Market to Groveton, a cluster of houses on the Warrenton Turnpike. A. P. Hill marched there via Centreville, and Ewell came over the Stone Bridge. He encamped at the cut and embankment of an unfinished railroad, with the Bull Run Mountains at his back and easy access to Thoroughfare Gap and another way via Aldie in the event he had to retreat.

These movements were meant to confuse Pope, and did. Pope's means of observation were bad, and those of communication were even worse, for this campaign was full of orders not delivered, misdirected, and misunderstood. When Pope arrived at Manassas with General Kearny's division the Confederates were not in sight. Assuming from vague reports that Jackson was retreating to Centreville, Pope started his divisions in pursuit. Hooker, Kearny, and Reno were sent toward Centreville. Porter was ordered to come to Manassas. McDowell was diverted to proceed along the Warrenton Pike toward Centreville.

The First Division of McDowell's corps was commanded by Brigadier General Rufus King. King's first brigade was under Brigadier General John P. Hatch; his second under Brigadier General Abner Doubleday; his third under Brigadier General M. R. Patrick; his fourth under Brigadier General John Gibbon. King marched his division east on the pike toward Centreville on the afternoon of August 28, completely ignorant of the fact that the main body of Jackson's army was close at hand, camped along the railroad cut. General Hatch had passed the point where Jackson's troops were concentrated and had not observed them.

When General King's troops came down the pike, Jackson saw an opportunity to strike them in the flank. He designated Generals Taliaferro and Ewell to the task, using

5 brigades of about 8,000 men and 3 batteries. Taliaferro's division and the brigades of Lawton and Trimble
of Ewell's division fell upon Gibbon's brigade late in the
afternoon. Gibbon and Doubleday fought back with energy, but they had no idea of the reserves the Confederates could bring up. The Federal troops fought
until about 9 P.M. They had neither support nor orders
from the top command. McDowell was absent; he had
left just before the Confederates attacked to consult
Pope at Manassas Junction. King and the brigade commanders finally decided that they were in too dangerous
a position to remain and at 1 A.M. exercised their own
discretion and withdrew toward Manassas. Their casualties were severe; Gibbon's brigade alone had 133
killed, 539 wounded, and 70 missing. On the Confederate
side both Ewell and Taliaferro were wounded, Ewell losing a leg.

So bad was the liaison that General Pope, who was near
Centreville, did not get word of the Groveton engagement until 10 P.M. He blamed General McDowell's absence for the lack of reinforcement by Reynolds and
Sigel, which he called "inexcusable." McDowell had heard
the gunfire, and had started back, but added to the mishaps by losing his way.

Pope reported that he had sent orders to McDowell
and King several times during the night to "hold his
ground at all hazards, to prevent the retreat of Jackson
to Lee," so that Pope's whole army might be ready to
attack Jackson at daybreak August 29. King said he
never received the order. Pope also sent orders to Porter, who was supposed to be at Manassas that afternoon,
to move on Centreville at dawn, and similar orders went
to Reno. These units started to carry out the orders.
When Pope learned how King had fared at Groveton, he
changed orders so that King and Porter should move to
Gainesville. When McDowell objected because this would
place King under Porter's orders, Pope modified the order
so that McDowell's corps would move jointly with
Porter's.

While this was taking place Lee was leading his army
along the route that had been followed by Jackson. Longstreet had reached White Plains (now The Plains, Va.)

and General McDowell sent James B. Ricketts' division to delay Longstreet at Thoroughfare Gap. This order was unknown to Pope, but Pope had given McDowell the right to exercise his own discretion. Brigadier General David R. Jones's division was the first to clash with Ricketts. The Federals opened with their batteries and the shells crashed against the rocky walls of the Gap and the thunder echoed through the defile. Longstreet sent General John B. Hood over a cattle trail on the north end of the Gap and ordered Brigadier General Cadmus M. Wilcox with three brigades to march through Hopewell Pass. The pressure on Ricketts at the main Gap became so strong that he broke off the action and withdrew to Bristoe.

The Second Battle of Bull Run, or Manassas, opened early on Friday morning, August 29, 1862, when Major General Franz Sigel, supported by Reynolds' division, attacked the position of Jackson north of the Warrenton Pike about one mile northwest of Groveton. Jackson's troops were extended along the railroad cut from the pike toward Sudley's Mill. General Starke, commanding Jackson's old division, was on the right; Ewell's division held the center under Brigadier General A. R. Lawton, now that Ewell was hospitalized; Hill was at the left. There were long exchanges of gunfire before the troops got into action. At about noon Longstreet moved to the right of Jackson, Hood's two brigades crossing the turnpike, with D. R. Jones to the right of Hood.

On the Federal side the divisions of Generals Hooker and Kearny of Heintzelman's corps were at the Union right, toward Sudley Springs; Sigel was at the Union left, extending south of the Warrenton Pike; Reno was near the center. The fighting was severe and prolonged. Pope expected the corps of McDowell and Porter to move up from Manassas toward Gainesville early in the afternoon. McDowell arrived about 4 P.M. and was sent against the Confederate right, with Reynolds in support. Pope said that at 4:30 P.M. he had sent a "peremptory" order to General Porter, who was presumably at Dawkins' Branch, four or five miles from Pope's headquarters, to get into the action against the Confederate right, while Heintzelman and Reno attacked the left.

Porter did not arrive, and King's division of McDowell's corps was stopped by Longstreet.

Kearny made better progress against the Confederate left. He cut off a brigade and gained a hold on the rail-road cut. Grover's brigade of Hooker's division made a charge that overran the Confederate line, using bayonets and clubbed muskets. Jackson said the Federals penetrated his line for about 175 yards and for a time cut Brigadier General Maxcy Gregg's brigade off from the main Confederate body. But the Fourteenth South Carolina and the Forty-ninth Georgia regiments restored the Confederate line, driving the Federals across the railroad cut "with great slaughter." All of Gregg's field officers but two were killed or wounded, and after several hours of fighting Early's brigade and the Eighth Louisiana regiment moved in and pushed the Federals back about 200 yards from the battle line. At the Confederate right Longstreet ordered Hood and Evans to attack, with the aid of Wilcox, who was recalled from the right. The vigor of the attack pushed the Federal line back until 9 P.M. The Union troops fought desperately every step of the way and when darkness stopped the action their line was at the Chinn house, on the battlefield of First Bull Run.

On the morning of August 30 General Pope believed he had defeated Lee, and that the Confederates were retreating. This also was the impression of Generals McDowell, Heintzelman, and Sigel. The commander who disagreed was Fitz John Porter, and his view was distasteful to Pope. Pope thought he must attack before Lee could retreat too far, whereas the Confederates were afraid Pope might get away. Had Pope been better informed, he would have waited until Generals Franklin and Sumner could join him.

Lee obtained the addition of General R. H. Anderson's division, which he had ordered up from the Rappahannock. When Generals Hood and Wilcox told Lee that they had found the Federal position too strong to be attacked on August 30 Lee withdrew his troops to their original lines. He was convinced that he could repulse the Federals if they attacked him, but he did not wish to bring on a general engagement. He informed President

Davis that his maneuver had drawn the enemy from the Rappahannock and relieved that part of Virginia. Pope had quite other views. He reported to General in Chief Halleck that he had lost at least 8,000 men, killed and wounded, but that the enemy's losses were twice as large and Lee was retreating toward the mountains, which was quite inaccurate.

If the Federals did not attack during the night, Lee proposed to attempt a new movement. He would make diversions on the front in the afternoon and at night march across Bull Run near Sudley Springs and try to get around Pope's rear. But this plan had to be shelved when the Federals attacked. General Pope had ordered the corps of McDowell, Heintzelman, and Porter to "move forward in pursuit of the enemy," and to "press him vigorously all day," and McDowell had been put in command of the pursuit. King's division led, with Sigel and Reynolds in support on the left. The Confederate response was powerful and especially effective against the Federal left. Jackson, being hard-pressed, appealed to Lee for reinforcements and Lee ordered Longstreet to send a division. But Longstreet decided he could immediately do great damage with his guns, whereas it would take an hour to move a division to Jackson's help. When General Stephen D. Lee's eighteen guns were turned loose enfilading the Federal right flank, Jackson had no need for another division. It was during this fighting that the Confederate left ran out of ammunition and fought back with stones, which were plentiful near the railroad cut.

When the Federals began to fall back Lee ordered an advance all along the line. It ran into stiff resistance. If the Federals had had trouble getting their units up on time, so did the Confederates on this late afternoon of August 30. Especial leadership was shown by Brigadier General Robert C. Schenck, commander of the first division of Sigel's corps, who led the troops in person and was wounded, and Brigadier General Zealous B. Tower, commander of the second brigade of Ricketts' division, who also was wounded. Desperate resistance was made by Porter's second division, commanded by Brigadier General George Sykes. As darkness fell Pope decided that it was time to withdraw to his base. The Federals held the Henry House plateau, over which the First Battle of Bull Run had been fought, and were able to make an orderly retreat. There was no rout such as took place after the first battle, but the withdrawal showed the results of hard fighting by weary men. It had begun to rain and there was no rest on the sodden ground. Some men had their guns, others were without them. Different regimental units mingled and stragglers were everywhere. A soldier wrote home: "Everyone you met had an unwashed, sleepy, downcast aspect, and looked as if he would like to hide his head somewhere from all the world."

Franklin's corps reached Bull Run as the Union army was withdrawing over the Stone Bridge and fords. Sumner reached Centreville. Pope's army moved by way of Fairfax Court House and Chantilly toward Washington in a driving rain. At Chantilly the Confederates attempted to harry the Union rear guard but were repulsed in a desperate fight during a thunderstorm late in the afternoon on September 1. The Union lost two able generals, Major General Philip Kearny, who rode into a group of Confederates and was shot down while trying to escape, and Major General Isaac I. Stevens.

The number of Union troops engaged from August 27 to September 2, 1862, including Bull Run and Chantilly, has been placed at over 75,000; the Confederate strength was nearly 50,000. Union reports gave these losses: 14,462 casualties, with 1,747 killed, 8,452 wounded, and 4,263 captured or missing. The reports of Longstreet, Jackson, and Stuart gave Confederate casualties as 9,474, with 1,553 killed, 7,812 wounded, the rest missing.

The result of Pope's campaign was a blow for Lincoln's Administration. By replacing McClellan, Pope became unpopular with the troops, but the basic difficulty was his own inability to handle numerous major units and conduct a cohesive movement. His inability to size up a situation, his contradictory orders, which sent army corps chasing over terrain, his distance from the field the first day, were handicaps, but his presence at the battle later did not help matters. Pope undoubtedly had the

ill will of McClellan and some of the corps commanders, notably McClellan's favorite general, Fitz John
Porter. The absence of Porter from the field on August 29
has been explained in great detail by his supporters and attacked by his opponents. Even if it was unavoidable and
unintentional, an alert commanding officer would have
moved heaven and earth to get accurate information to
his subordinate and provided means for that subordinate
to get similar reports to him. This applied also to
McDowell, whose military acumen had been found want-
ing on this very field a year before.

There are enough orders on record to convict Pope
of inefficiency and bungling. He was induced to resign
his command when McClellan was quietly eased into his
place. Pope was sent to the Department of the Northwest, which he considered "banishment," but where he
made a good record looking after Indian troubles. In
1882 he was named major general in the regular United
States Army (at Bull Run he was a major general of
volunteers, a temporary grade). He died at Sandusky,
Ohio, in 1892, aged seventy.

Removal of Fitz John Porter

The Second Battle of Bull Run left dispirited troops
and bickering generals in its wake. Although the Antietam
campaign, immediately following, changed the feeling of
the troops, it did not obliterate the Fitz John Porter
dispute. General Pope blamed a large part of his defeat
on the failure of subordinate officers to carry out his
orders. He had complained about Major General Porter,
Major General Franklin, and Brigadier General Charles
Griffin, but through a series of maneuvers in Washington
only Porter became the principal target. President Lincoln, on September 5, 1862, relieved Pope of his command and also ordered the three generals to be relieved
until a court of inquiry could investigate them. When
General McCellan returned to reorganize the army the
order was held in abeyance; McClellan kept the officers
at their respective posts through the Antietam campaign.
When McClellan was relieved after Antietam, President
Lincoln directed that Porter be removed from command

of the Fifth Corps, as of September 12.

A military commission met and dissolved, and the matter was placed before a court-martial November 25. The court comprised Major Generals David Hunter and E. A. Hitchcock and Brigadier Generals Rufus King, B. M. Prentiss, James B. Ricketts, Silas Casey, James A. Garfield, N. B. Buford, and J. B. Slough, with Colonel Joseph Holt as judge advocate. The court decided General Porter had disobeyed three of Pope's orders: one of August 27, directing Porter to march on Bristoe at 1 A.M.; the "joint order" of August 29, which asked McDowell and Porter to move with their commands toward Gainesville, to be in a position to reach Bull Run that night or next morning; and the order of 4:30 P.M. of the same date, "to push forward into action at once on the enemy's right flank." It also accused Porter of having retreated without attempting to engage the enemy.

The testimony showed that Porter had delayed only two hours on the 28th on account of darkness and had marched at 3 A.M., and that his experience did not differ from that of Generals McDowell, Kearny, and Reno. General John F. Reynolds testified to the difficult character of the terrain over which Porter had been expected to march. It was also shown that the "joint order" of Pope contained the sentence: "If any considerable advantages are to be gained by departing from this order it will not be strictly carried out." However, the court-martial on January 10, 1863, decided Porter should be dropped from the service ("cashiered") and forever disqualified from holding public office under the government. The decision was approved by President Lincoln, and Porter did not serve again in the war.

Porter sought to have the case reviewed, but that was not done until after General Grant, in 1878, called the decision "an undeserved stigma." On April 12, 1878, President R. B. Hayes appointed a board to hear the evidence. It was composed of Major General John M. Schofield, Brigadier General Alfred H. Terry, and Colonel George W. Getty. This body found that General Pope's orders on August 29 were based on erroneous assumptions of the Confederate position and strength, and that Porter did what any intelligent soldier would do; his conduct was "obedient, subordinate, faithful, and judicious," and "it saved the Union army from disaster on the 29th of August." The board recommended that the earlier decision be set aside and Porter be reinstated in his proper rank. President Hayes submitted this decision to Congress, but obtained no action. On May 4, 1882, President Chester A. Arthur remitted part of the sentence by voiding Porter's disqualification from holding office, but it was not until August 5, 1886, after an act of Congress had been approved by President Cleveland, that Porter was given the rank of colonel in the regular army as of May 14, 1861, but without back pay; on August 7 he was placed on the retired list. Porter served in various municipal offices in New York and died in 1901, aged seventy-eight.

16

McCLELLAN HALTS LEE
AT ANTIETAM

The Return of Little Mac

After the Second Battle of Bull Run (Second Manassas) the morale of the North was down in its shoes. Its spirits were as dark and despondent as those of the South were confident and elated. Washington faced the bitter truth that neither its generals in the East nor the prideful and self-assured War Department could stop Generals Lee and Jackson from wrecking the best of Federal plans.

The panic in Washington was startling. Department clerks were being organized into militia for defense; stragglers, wagons, and ambulances from the front impeded the streets. The government ordered the money at the Treasury Department to be shipped to New York, and the banks did likewise. A gunboat with steam up lay in the Potomac off the White House, suggesting preparations for flight. Yet Lieutenant Colonel Richard B. Irwin pointed out that not less than 110,000 men were available for defense, including Pope's army, "beaten certainly, but by no means destroyed," 40,000 veterans who had taken no part in the campaign, and 30,000 in the garrisons and reserves.

President Lincoln, disgusted with McClellan's delays, his endless calls for more arms and more men, had pulled him out of the Peninsula. General in Chief Halleck was engaged daily in clipping off bits of his authority, withdrawing troops, batteries, even headquarters wagons. "You now have every man of the Army of the Potomac who is within my reach," McClellan told him in desperation. Why weren't his abilities of some use? He addressed a fervent plea to the stony-faced Halleck. "If it is not deemed best to entrust me with the command even of my own army, I simply ask to be permitted to share their fate in the field of battle." It was a heroic speech, but there was no questioning his sincerity. He had taken the men as raw recruits and trained them into a military machine. He was proud of the army; he loved his countrymen even if he didn't tolerate martinets in the War Department.

General Halleck, prompted by Lincoln, was asking McClellan to take charge of Washington, but warned that he was to assume no authority over "the active troops of General Pope." McClellan was startled by what he saw and by the reports friends brought to him from the front; he learned how shattered in spirit the army was. If Halleck would only judge for himself, at first hand—but Halleck was an armchair general now; he had not disclosed any brilliant military talents himself during the days after Shiloh when he presumed to run Grant's business. McClellan was insistent, and finally Halleck acquiesced sufficiently to send his adjutant general, Colonel Kelton, to the front. The result was an explosion.

It seems incredible that Washington should have been so badly informed about what went on half a day's ride from the capital—or so obtuse as not to admit it. But Kelton saw enough in one afternoon to hurry back with bad news, and the next morning both President Lincoln and General Halleck were at McClellan's door before he had finished breakfast.

President Lincoln was shocked at the demoralization

reported by Colonel Kelton. Things were actually worse than McClellan had described them; there were 30,000 stragglers on the roads; the army was entirely defeated. As McClellan reported: "He then said he regarded Washington as lost and asked me if I would consent to accept command of all the forces. I at once said that I would accept the command and would stake my life that I would save the city." McClellan insisted that both the President and Halleck asserted it was impossible to save the city. But McClellan could and would save it.

That is the way McClellan interpreted his command, but during the next few days he was to learn that there were limits to his authority. There was, as he said later, a halter around his neck, and Halleck had hold of it. Washington was angry with McClellan; the President was still offended with him and blamed the failure of Pope on the antagonism of Pope's subordinate commander, Fitz John Porter—McClellan's general. But the President knew that whatever the political game, McClellan was the man to draw the disparate units together. Secretary Gideon Welles reported in his *Diary* a talk with Lincoln on September 7: "I must have McClellan to reorganize the army and bring it out of chaos," said Lincoln. "But there has been a design—a purpose in breaking down Pope, without regard of consequence to the country. It is shocking to see and know this, but there is no remedy at present—McClellan has the army with him." Members of the cabinet also had strongly adverse feelings about McClellan; Stanton, Chase, Welles, and Caleb Smith didn't like him; Chase wrote with bitterness in his diary that giving the command of Washington to McClellan was equivalent to giving Washington to the rebels.

During those first days of September there was a tug for power between General McClellan and General Halleck. McClellan knew the army needed him; Halleck was determined McClellan never again should be able to disregard his authority. He told McClellan that it was "the President's order" that he was not to assume command until the troops had reached "the immediate vicinity of the fortifications."

When Generals Pope and McDowell reached the environs of Washington, McClellan went out to interview them; hearing guns in the distance, he asked the meaning. The two generals implied it was an attack on the Federal rear guard. Then they asked whether McClellan would object if they proceeded on to Washington. No, he wouldn't object, but so far as he was concerned, he was going to wherever the firing was. And so, with a single aide and three orderlies, he started a dash across country, guided by the guns, expecting to intercept the columns.

When he reached the troops it was already dark, but the effect of his arrival was electric. The little general with the porkpie hat, who used to dash about on a black horse with a yellow sash tied about his waist, was immediately recognized. The yell "Little Mac is back on the road, boys!" ran down the columns like a brush fire. Men shouted, threw their caps into the air, yelled after him to come and lead them. There was no doubting what commander held the loyalty of the army.

By September 3 McClellan knew that Lee intended to invade Maryland and Pennsylvania via the upper Potomac; hurriedly he ordered the Second, Ninth, and Twelfth Army Corps to the other side of the Potomac. When he reported this to General Halleck, the chief wanted to know what general he proposed to place in command over these corps. McClellan said he intended to command. Halleck again reminded McClellan of the halter; McClellan had no authority beyond Washington. Actually the only order ever published at this time announced that besides the fortifications of Washington McClellan had command "of all the troops for the defense of the capital." It was under a loose interpretation of this order that McClellan took command of the Army of the Potomac and fought the Confederates to a standstill at South Mountain and Antietam.

He still had several hurdles to overcome. One was similar to what had happened to General Grant, when the latter first proposed to Halleck, then in St. Louis, to move against Forts Henry and Donelson. Secretary Seward came to McClellan to inquire about conditions at Harpers Ferry. McClellan replied that the garrison was useless; it should be withdrawn and added to the main army; the troops at the Ferry could not stop the Confederates from crossing the Potomac, and if the Federals lost their next battle the garrison would be lost, too. Secretary Seward asked McClellan to tell this to Halleck, and the two men went to Halleck's quarters, got him out of bed, and told their story. McClellan wrote later: "Halleck received my statement with ill-concealed contempt . . . and soon bowed us out." Whatever other criticism may be made of McClellan's use of troops, he was right in this instance; before Antietam was fought nearly 12,000 Federals at Harpers Ferry had to surrender to General Stonewall Jackson, when they might have given substantial support to the Union troops in two important battles.

Lee Appeals to Maryland

The Confederate plan to invade Maryland and possibly Pennsylvania was proposed by General Lee almost immediately after Second Manassas and approved by President Jefferson Davis. Lee's decision was the result of both opportunity and necessity. A promising opening for effective action had come to him by the defeat of General Pope and the subsequent break in discipline and demoralization suffered by the Federal armies, partly because McClellan's troops had been added without proper leadership. The withdrawal of McClellan's army from the Peninsula had freed Richmond, temporarily at least, of the need of detaching large units to maintain a vigilant defense. As Lee expressed it to President Davis: "The great advantage of the advance of the army is the withdrawal of the enemy from our territory and the hurling back upon their capital of their two great armies from the banks of the James and Rappahannock Rivers." The Confederate leadership also harbored the hope that a bold stroke might finally convince the foreign nations that the South could not be beaten and must be recognized as a nation.

But Lee was also cautious. He knew the North had the advantage of numbers and had masses of recruits pouring into training camps. This meant that the Confederate army had to strike quickly. He appreciated the fighting spirit of the Southern soldiers, but he saw that they needed proper food and clothing. He had worried about their subsistence on the campaign, but General Longstreet reminded him that in Mexico the troops sometimes lived two or three days on green corn and that no one would starve while the fields were loaded with "roasting ears." The Confederates had not been eating well; the men were famished and their apparel was in a miserable state. A Shepherdstown housewife saw them as "haggard apparitions"; never in the war years did she see such want and exhaustion, and she wondered how men in this condition could fight. Lee had said to General John G. Walker: "Hundreds of them are barefooted and nearly all of them are ragged. I hope to get shoes and clothing for the most needy." This had prompted an earlier order excusing barefoot men from marching into Maryland. General D. H. Hill complained later that this order had sent thousands to the rear and thus had cut the numbers in the regiments.

The situation seemed so favorable to the Confederacy that General Lee, for the first and only time during his command of the Army of Northern Virginia, made a direct appeal to the people, in the tone of a man bringing relief. From his headquarters at Frederick, Lee on September 8 issued a proclamation to the people of Maryland with the object of bringing the state over to the Confederate side. He appealed to their pride and concern for their rights; they were being treated, he said, like a conquered province, arrested and imprisoned contrary to all forms of law; the government "of your chief city" was "usurped by armed strangers"; freedom of speech and of the press had been suppressed. His army had come to restore independence and sovereignty to the state and give its people their "inalienable rights of freedom." He appealed to them to choose sides freely and without constraint—"this army will respect your choice"—and the Southern people would welcome them, but only if they came of their own free will.

It was a temperate appeal, reflecting the attitude of the man who made it, but it was hard to see how it could lead to action. The former governor of Maryland, Enoch L. Lowe, was supposed to lend his influence, but he did not come to greet Lee as expected. Lee left military planning long enough to suggest to President

Davis that, with the Confederates in a strong position, the Confederacy might well propose negotiations for peace; if they were rejected the blame for prolonging the war would fall on the Federals. His project received no official sanction; as Richmond well knew, negotiators were not wanted by President Lincoln, only repentant rebels ready to resume their former loyalties. Before the Marylanders had time to debate Lee's invitation the situation changed; the military prestige that the Confederates had gained by routing Pope at Second Manassas was lost at South Mountain and Antietam; and there was no rising in Maryland, where the Unionists were strong enough to keep the state out of the Confederacy.

Brigadier General John G. Walker, who was chosen by Lee to occupy Loudoun Heights in the effort to capture Harpers Ferry, has reported Lee's comment on General McClellan. Lee was explaining to Walker how he intended to march from Hagerstown to Harrisburg, and run the risk of having McClellan on his line of communication. "Are you acquainted with General McClellan?" asked Lee. "He is an able general, but a very cautious one. His enemies among his own people think him too much so. His army is in a very demoralized and chaotic condition, and will not be prepared for offensive operations, or he will not think it so, for three or four weeks. Before that time I hope to be on the Susquehanna."

Lost Order of General Lee

"Nothing but sheer necessity," said General McClellan of the Antietam campaign, "justified the advance of the Army of the Potomac to South Mountain and Antietam in its then condition. . . . It must then be borne constantly in mind that the purpose of advancing from Washington was simply to meet the necessities of the moment by frustrating Lee's invasion of the Northern states."

The Confederate army, with its purpose of proceeding toward Hagerstown, left Frederick, Maryland, by early morning of September 12 and moved toward the passes in the low mountain ranges that lay east of the Potomac

and were part of the Blue Ridge system. General Mc-
Clellan was moving his army at a very slow pace, for one
reason to keep the protection of the capital in view, for
another to spare the men, who had just been through a
fatiguing campaign and were still in the process of reorganizing their units. At Urbana on September 12 he
learned from President Lincoln that Jackson was crossing the Potomac at Williamsport and that the whole Confederate army probably would be withdrawn from Maryland. "Please do not let him [the enemy] get off without being hurt," Lincoln pleaded. The news meant that
Washington and Baltimore would not be threatened by Lee.

The cavalry under Brigadier General Alfred Pleasonton and part of the Ninth Corps under Major General
Jesse L. Reno entered Frederick soon after the last cavalry rear guard under Brigadier General Wade Hampton
had left on the road that leads to Middletown and the
low Catoctin Mountains. Major General Ambrose E.
Burnside had command of the right wing to which belonged the First and Ninth Corps and the Kanawha
(Western Virginia) Division of Brigadier General Jacob
D. Cox, now associated with the Ninth Corps. General
Jeb Stuart ordered General Fitzhugh Lee to reconnoiter
around the right wing of McClellan's army. General
Pleasonton sent his Fourth Brigade, under Colonel Andrew T. McReynolds, with a battery of guns, to track
Fitzhugh Lee, while with his principal regiments he followed the Confederate main body on the road to Middletown. General Pleasonton had several clashes with Stuart
and pushed him back. He asked for a brigade of infantry
to help him watch Turner's Gap, and General Cox sent
the First Brigade, commanded by Colonel E. P. Scammon, and some guns.

The road from Frederick to Middletown, known as the
National Road, passed through the Catoctin Mountains
and South Mountain and on to Boonsboro', with Hagerstown some distance beyond. The Middletown Valley lies
between the two mountains. Both heights are long and
narrow and run southwest, with the taller South Mountain rising to 1,200 feet. The Valley extends down to the
Potomac River. The Middletown-Boonsboro' road runs
through Turner's Gap in South Mountain; one mile south

is the smaller Fox's Gap, through which passed the old
Sharpsburg Road, along which the British General Brad-
dock marched toward Pennsylvania in the French and
Indian War. About seven miles south of Turner's is
Crampton's Gap, another major path through the mountain,
and one mile south of Crampton's is the Brownsville Gap.

When General Stuart met determined opposition at
South Mountain he reported the presence of the Federal
forces to General D. H. Hill. Hill, with five brigades, had
reached Boonsboro', west of South Mountain, where he
was to guard wagons and guns and watch the roads
leading from Harpers Ferry, in order to intercept any
Federal troops that escaped from Jackson's attack there.
Hill ordered Brigadier General Samuel Garland, Jr., and
Colonel A. H. Colquitt with two batteries to report to
Stuart at Turner's Gap.

General Lee was at Hagerstown with Longstreet on the
evening of September 13 when he learned that the Union
army in considerable strength was moving to the foot of
South Mountain. The speed of this advance was unexpected and made Lee anxious for the safety of his army.
At this time it was split into three parts, which could not
be easily brought together. General Jackson was investing
Harpers Ferry and should have reported taking it by the
12th; General Longstreet was at Hagerstown, thirteen
miles from Boonsboro', where Hill was posted; other units
were separated by the mountain. General Lee called for
Longstreet and asked his views. Longstreet told Lee that
it was too late to attempt to man Turner's Gap the following morning and advised placing his own and D. H. Hill's
corps behind Antietam Creek at Sharpsburg, across one
of McClellan's possible routes to Harpers Ferry. Lee
thought otherwise. Longstreet was so disturbed at the pre-
carious situation of the Confederate army that he was
unable to sleep that night; he arose and repeated his suggestion to Lee in writing. But Lee was determined to support
Hill at South Mountain the next morning, September 14,
in order to remove a threat to McLaws at Maryland Heights.

The reason for the unexpected advance of the Federal
army under McClellan was an incident that affected the
military history of the United States and the outcome of

the war. It was the discovery by McClellan's men of the order in which Lee gave the disposition of his troops for the present movement westward, and thus disclosed what the Federals could not have known in any other way before the plan developed.

At about noon on September 13, 1862, the First Division of the Twelfth Army Corps, General Alpheus S. Williams commanding, stacked arms at Frederick, Maryland, on ground that had been occupied the previous evening by General D. H. Hill. Here a private of the Twenty-seventh Indiana Volunteer Infantry picked up an envelope with three cigars wrapped in a piece of paper. Examination of the paper showed it to be an order to the Confederate troops addressed to Major General D. H. Hill and signed by R. H. Chilton, assistant adjutant general of the Army of Northern Virginia. The soldier who found it and his first sergeant brought the order to Colonel Silas Colgrove, who turned it over to Colonel S. E. Pittman, adjutant general to General Williams. Colonel Pittman recognized the signature of Chilton, with whom he had served before the war, and carried the paper personally to General McClellan.

This document, known as General Order 191, was issued September 9 and communicated to the division commanders of the Confederate army. It gave the following instructions for the march of the army on the Hagerstown road beginning September 10:

General Jackson's command will form the advance, and, after passing Middletown, with such portion as he may select, take the route toward Sharpsburg, cross the Potomac at the most convenient point, and, by Friday night, take possession of the Baltimore & Ohio Railroad, capture such of the enemy as may be at Martinsburg, and intercept such as may attempt to escape from Harper's Ferry.

General Longstreet's command will pursue the same road as far as Boonsborough where it will halt with the reserve, supply, and baggage trains of the army.

General McLaws, with his own division and that of General R. H. Anderson, will follow General Longstreet. On reaching Middletown he will take the route to Harper's Ferry, and by Friday morning possess himself of the Maryland Heights, and endeavor to capture the enemy at Harper's Ferry and vicinity.

General Walker, with his division, after accomplishing the object in which he is now engaged, will cross the Potomac at Cheek's Ford, ascend its right bank to Lovettsville, take possession of Loudoun Heights, if practicable by Friday morning, Key's Ford on his left and the road between the end of the mountain and the Potomac on his right. He will, as far as practicable, cooperate with General McLaws and General Jackson in intercepting the retreat of the enemy.

General D. H. Hill's division will form the rearguard of the army, pursuing the road taken by the main body. The reserve artillery, ordnance, supply trains, etc., will precede General Hill.

General Stuart will detach a squadron of cavalry to accompany the commands of Generals Longstreet, Jackson and McLaws, and with the main body of the cavalry will cover the route of the army and bring up all stragglers that may have been left behind.

The commands of Generals Jackson, McLaws and Walker, after accomplishing the objects for which they have been detached, will join the main body of the army at Boonsborough or Hagerstown.

Each regiment on the march will habitually carry its axes in the regimental ordnance wagons, for use of the men at their encampments to procure wood, etc.

By command of General R. E. Lee.

R. H. CHILTON, Assistant Adjutant General.

The order was addressed: "Maj. Gen. D. H. Hill, commanding division."

Here was an official outline of the routes to be followed by the major units of the Confederate army. General McClellan seems to have accepted it as authentic at once, for on September 13 he sent a message to President Lincoln reflecting the confidence that possession of Lee's order had inspired in him, but not telling how he acquired it. He wired:

I have the whole rebel force in front of me but am confident, and no time shall be lost. . . . I think Lee has made a gross mistake, and that he will be severely punished for it. The army is in motion as rapidly as possible. I hope for a great success if the plans of the rebels remain unchanged. We have possession of Catoctin. I have all the plans of the rebels, and will catch them in their own trap if my men are equal to the emergency. I now feel that I can count on them as of old. All forces of Pennsylvania should be placed to cooperate at Chambersburg. . . .

That morning McClellan had received another warning from General Halleck, in which he said: "The capture of this place [Washington] will throw us back six months, if it should not destroy us." At 11 P.M. McClellan finally told Halleck about the special order of Lee. He also told him that the army would make forced marches in an endeavor to relieve Colonel Miles at Harpers Ferry: "I shall do everything in my power to save Miles if he still holds out." This move was forced on McClellan, who had pointed to the danger of holding Harpers Ferry and had been overruled by Halleck. "I do not by any means wish to be understood as undervaluing the importance of holding Washington. It is of great consequence, but upon the success of this army the fate of the nation depends. . . . Unless General Lee has changed his plans I expect a severe general engagement tomorrow."

The responsibility for losing Lee's order was never placed on any individual. General D. H. Hill emphatically denied ever seeing it, and his adjutant general made an affidavit, swearing that it never had been received in the office of the corps. "Did the courier lose it? Did Lee's own staff officers lose it?" asked Hill. "I do not know." The order received by Hill was a copy made for him by Jackson before he was detached from Jackson's corps; this he carefully preserved.

Hill discounted the value of the order to McClellan, saying it provided the Federals with two facts, one useless and the other misleading. But that the order was considered of the utmost importance was asserted by Generals Walker and Longstreet: Walker was so afraid of losing it that he pinned it securely in an inside pocket. Longstreet explained in *From Manassas to Appomattox*: "The copy sent me was carefully read, then used as some persons use a little cut of tobacco, to be assured that others could not have the benefit of its contents." Or briefly, he chewed it to a pulp. With a bit of nostalgia Longstreet thirty years later said the order had been used as a wrapper for "three fragrant Confederate cigars."

Douglas Southall Freeman wrote in 1914: "There is

little reason to believe that McClellan would have moved
against the passes in South Mountain with even the tardiness he displayed had he not had General Lee's own
statement as to the position of his forces. But for this
accident it is not improbable that Jackson would have
joined Lee after the capture of Harpers Ferry and would
have united with him in an offensive movement."

Lee did not refer to the lost order at this time, and did
not mention it until he made a report of the Sharpsburg
campaign to General Samuel Cooper at Richmond nearly
a year later—August 19, 1863. This was not published
until after the war. Likewise nothing was said at the time
by Longstreet and Stuart. But when, in February, 1868,
General D. H. Hill published an article in which he asserted he was not responsible for the loss, Lee broke his
silence on war experiences to tell two of his associates
about the incident. The men were Colonel William Allan
and E. C. Gordon, the latter clerk of the faculty at Washington College, Lexington, where Lee was President. Lee,
angered at Hill's excuses, told the men individually that a
citizen of Frederick was present when McClellan received
the copy of the order and became jubilant over it. This
citizen sent word to Stuart, who immediately sent a message by courier to Lee at Hagerstown. Lee told Gordon
that although Harpers Ferry did not fall as soon as he had
hoped, he was sure he could have crushed McClellan's
army if McClellan could have been kept in ignorance of
Lee's plans two or three days longer.

Lee's order was modified in only one major particular.
He received a report that a Federal force was moving
from Pennsylvania to Hagerstown and therefore changed
Longstreet's destination from Boonsboro' to Hagerstown,
eleven miles farther northwest. When Longstreet marched
up the pike to Hagerstown, Lee rode with him.

The Battle of South Mountain

The battle of South Mountain was fought on September 14 and was a series of engagements in which the
Union army was thrust against the Confederate defenders
of the mountain passes. The gaps in the mountain were
not always single routes as in the case of Crampton's

but sometimes had multiple roads. Turner's Gap had a main turnpike and several lateral roads in adjacent openings in the hilly country.

Both Turner's Gap and Crampton's are famous for their vistas of wide rolling valleys extending to the Catoctin seen from their crests. General D. H. Hill, clinging to the crest at Turner's Gap, did not let the hazards of the day blind him to the extraordinary spectacle visible from the Confederate lookout near Mountain House. In the plain below, the approaching army of McClellan was spread before him in a vast panorama, some troops already in double lines for giving battle, others coming up to take their positions. Although the coming horde outnumbered his own troops, he gazed at the spectacle with admiration and recalled later that it so satisfied his senses that it caused him no anxiety. But he did not forget to add that he had a full view of four army corps that could brush aside his five brigades "as a strong man brushes off a wasp." A private of the Ninth New York, who obtained a similar view during the ascent of the mountain, remarked that the canvas-covered baggage wagons approaching in the distance seemed like white beads on a string. The enchantment and associations of Crampton's Gap so impressed the correspondent of the New York *Herald*, George A. Townsend, that after the war he returned to build a substantial house at the peak of the pass over which Franklin's division had fought. He also erected a tall arch of brick and stone on which he placed the names of the correspondents and artists of the press who served during the war.

On the night of September 13 General Lee sent a message to General McLaws, telling him of the threat to his rear and urging him to hurry the occupation of Harpers Ferry. He told him that if General Jackson had no other orders for him after that action he was to march north rapidly to Sharpsburg. On the morning of September 14 Lee again sent word to McLaws, indicating his great anxiety over the turn of events. He told McLaws that Stuart and Hill were at Turner's Gap and Munford and Hampton at Crampton's. Lee and Longstreet then rode toward Turner's Gap. After passing Boonsboro', Lee stood at a side of the road and watched Hood's brigade, chiefly Texan regiments, march past toward the mountain. When the Texans saw Lee they began shouting: "Give us Hood!" and the cry went right along the ranks. Lee said: "You shall have him!"

This referred to an incident at the close of the Second Battle of Bull Run (Manassas) when these Texans captured a number of new Federal ambulances and Hood decided to use them for the sick and wounded of his division. A few days later Hood received instructions from Brigadier General Nathan G. Evans, who outranked him, to turn the ambulances over to his brigade of South Carolina troops. Hood refused to yield them to Evans. General Longstreet, feeling that Evans ought to be obeyed in that situation, placed Hood under arrest and ordered him to Culpeper to appear before a court-martial. General Lee canceled the court-martial so that Hood could remain with his troops, but did not release him from technical arrest.

Hood was riding at the rear of the column and when he reached the spot where General Lee stood he was accosted by Lee's adjutant, Colonel Chilton, and called over to Lee. Hood dismounted and Lee said: "General, here I am just upon the eve of entering into battle, and with one of my best officers under arrest. If you will merely say that you regret this occurrence, I will release you and restore you to the command of your division." Hood replied, according to his own version: "I am unable to do so, since I cannot admit or see the justness of General Evans' demand for the ambulances my men have captured. Had I been ordered to turn them over for the general use of the army, I would cheerfully have acquiesced." Lee urged Hood to express regret, but without success. Lee then said he would suspend Hood's arrest "until the impending battle is decided." Hood galloped to the head of his column amid the cheers of his regiments.

The approach to South Mountain was guarded by General Pleasonton's cavalry with the help of several batteries. The first clash took place at 9 A.M. about half a mile below the summit of Fox's Gap, part of the system of roads through Turner's Gap. Here Colonel E. P. Scammons led a brigade of Major General Jacob D. Cox's

Kanawha Division of the Ninth Corps up the mountain road, followed by a brigade commanded by Colonel George Crook. The latter unit had been commanded until that morning by Colonel Augustus Moor. Moor had engaged in an incautious charge in the outlying streets of Frederick and had been captured by General Wade Hampton's rear guard. He was paroled and could take no further part in the fighting.

These brigades were composed of Ohio regiments and numbered about 3,000 men. They were opposed by units from General D. H. Hill's division—the brigade of North Carolina regiments commanded by Brigadier General Samuel Garland, Jr., supported by Colonel A. H. Colquitt's Georgians, who had come over from the Turner's Gap side. One North Carolina regiment was posted behind a stone wall, which the Federals attacked with their batteries. Finding a breach, the Thirtieth Ohio charged the Confederates and fought with bayonets and clubbed muskets. In the course of the fighting for the crest the North Carolinians were driven back and their commander, General Garland, was killed.

General Cox directed a movement along the crest toward the Confederate position near Mountain House, but General D. H. Hill's troops managed to hold off the Federals there. Both commanders called for reinforcements; Cox asked help from Major General Jesse L. Reno of the Ninth Corps. During the afternoon Reno sent the divisions of Brigadier Generals O. B. Willcox, Samuel D. Sturgis, and Isaac P. Rodman to the Gap, but there was no general advance until General Reno ordered it at 5 P.M. Colonel George T. Anderson and Brigadier General Thomas F. Drayton, both of Brigadier General D. R. Jones's division of Longstreet's corps, made a strong attack on Willcox's division.

General Hooker arrived at the base of the mountain with the First Corps early in the afternoon and was ordered to attack north of the Boonsboro' Turnpike. His corps was led by the divisions of Brigadier General George G. Meade, with three brigades; followed by Brigadier General John P. Hatch, with Brigadier General James B. Ricketts in reserve. Brigadier General John Gibbon's fourth brigade of the First Division was ordered to take the direct route up the mountain. The Confederate left opposing them comprised the troops of Brigadier General R. E. Rodes, supported on his right by Brigadier General Nathan G. Evans, and they were gradually forced back. At dark the brigades of Kemper, Garnett, and Joseph Walker, which had been sent down the mountain on a useless errand, returned to the crest to help Rodes and Evans, but they were so exhausted by having to climb up in double quick time that they made no difficulties for the strongly placed Federal brigades. It became evident to the Confederate command that the Federals were strong enough to force the Confederates off the west side of the mountain the next morning.

General Reno rode forward to the skirmish line to determine the prospect at the crest. The Confederates were hidden from sight in the underbrush and woods and the Fifty-first Pennsylvania regiment, which had fought its way up to this point, thought it had routed them. Reno assented to a brief rest period with stacked arms and moved along the front of the line on his horse. A volley came suddenly from the farther wood and Reno fell dead. The Pennsylvanians recovered their weapons amid confusion and cleared the Confederates out of the wood.

Major General W. B. Franklin and the Sixth Corps were responsible for thrusting the Confederates out of Crampton's Gap and winning a clear-cut victory there on September 14. Franklin was at Buckeystown, about six miles southwest of Frederick, with 12,300 men when he received orders from McClellan on the evening of the 13th to move at daybreak. He was to cut through South Mountain by Crampton's Gap; the area east of it, called Pleasant Valley, was to have been cleared of Stuart's cavalry by General Pleasonton. Franklin was to seize Crampton's Gap if not strongly guarded, march to Rohrersville in the Valley, cut off the Confederate forces of McLaws and R. H. Anderson at Maryland Heights, capture them, and relieve Harpers Ferry. General Couch's division of the Fourth Corps was to join him. McClellan told Franklin: "My general idea is to cut the enemy in two and beat him in detail. . . . I ask of you, at this important moment, all your intellect and the utmost activity that a general can exercise."

It took from daybreak to noon for Franklin's troops to get into action and then General Henry W. Slocum's division, advancing through Burkittsville, found the Confederates strongly posted on the side of the road at the base of the Gap and particularly behind a stone wall at the right. They had a battery of eight guns. Slocum came first on Munford's cavalry brigade; beyond were two infantry regiments of Mahone's brigade of General R. H. Anderson's division, and supporting units were those of Brigadier Generals Paul J. Semmes and Howell Cobb, the latter in command of the pass. Batteries were moved up and when Slocum had the support of regiments under Colonel A. T. A. Torbert, Brigadier General John Newton, and Colonel Joseph J. Bartlett the whole line charged the Confederates, went over the stone wall, and pursued them to the crest of the Gap and down the opposite slope. General Brooks' brigade of Major General William F. Smith's division cleared the woods at the left of defenders.

General Cobb, commanding Georgia regiments, and later General Semmes, with Georgia and Virginia troops, tried vigorously to rally their troops, but the superior numbers of the Federals had thrown them into confusion and the men could not be brought back into the fight. Three brigades to support Cobb were ordered up by General McLaws, but arrived too late to be of use. Similarly, on the Union side, Couch's division of the Fourth Corps did not report to Franklin until nightfall and was detached the next day. Franklin estimated that he had 6,500 engaged and that Cobb had 2,200 in the fight, and while he realized that his men had outnumbered the Confederates he added that stone walls and a steep mountain pass were also heavy odds. He had 533 casualties; Cobb and Semmes had 749; others did not report their losses. The Federals captured 400 prisoners, 700 stands of arms, and one gun.

That night Slocum's division was "astride of the mountain," Brooks and Irwin of Smith's division were on the mountain, and Hancock, in reserve, was at the eastern base. Smith's division was ordered into Pleasant Valley, Slocum was to support Smith, and Couch was ordered to Rohrersville. Everything was ready for driving home the attack on McLaws, who, presumably, was bottled up on Maryland Heights with his road to the north blocked. But when Generals Franklin and Smith surveyed the scene before them on the morning of September 15 they hesitated. McLaws had placed the brigades that had fought the day before across the Valley, with those of Brigadier Generals Joseph B. Kershaw and William Barksdale, who came up too late to join in the fight, at their head. The Federals decided that the only unit prepared to attack was General Smith's division of 4,500, and this did not seem enough. They thought the Confederate force quite as large as their own and thus justified their disinclination to follow through. As it turned out, Harpers Ferry surrendered that morning, but of this they had no knowledge at the time.

The number of men engaged at South Mountain was placed at over 28,000 on the Union side and over 18,000 on the Confederate. The official Federal report had 325 killed, 1,403 wounded, and about 1,500 prisoners captured. The latter number may have included wounded Confederates left behind. Of the 889 casualties in the Ninth Corps, 356 occurred in the Kanawha Division. The Confederate casualties were about the same as those of the Union army, but because reports include totals for the whole campaign it has been harder to determine their losses at South Mountain. Generals Reno and Garland were the principal officers killed; among the wounded was Lieutenant Colonel Rutherford B. Hayes of the Twenty-third Ohio Volunteers, later President of the United States.

When the battle of South Mountain ended the Confederate command was convinced that the proposed expedition into Pennsylvania via Hagerstown was at an end. The Federals had the advantage of numbers and position and the Confederates were divided. At 8 P.M. Lee sent a message to McLaws telling him the day was lost and that the army would go to Sharpsburg and then across the Potomac. It would be necessary for McLaws to abandon his position that night. Lee told him to send across the river the trains not required and to unite with the army at Sharpsburg, bringing Major General Richard H. Anderson's division with him. He wanted McLaws to find a suitable crossing of the Potomac and report on it, leaving that at Shepherdstown to Lee.

After conferring with Longstreet, Hill, and Hood, General Lee, who did not immediately disclose his intention to return to Virginia, showed anxiety over the dangerous position of McLaws. He then decided to concentrate the army around Keedysville (called Centreville in some despatches), located halfway between Boonsboro' and the Antietam. He was in such a hurry that the dead and severely wounded would have to be left behind. McLaws was to go to Virginia if necessary, but if he could march on Sharpsburg he was to send word to Lee at Keedysville. Generals Jackson and Walker also were to rejoin the army from Harpers Ferry. Upon further thought Lee decided that Keedysville was not the most suitable place and changed headquarters and rendezvous to Sharpsburg. This would put the army on the west side of Antietam Creek and give it the advantage of the higher ridge above the creek east of the town. The army was there next morning, September 15, when Lee received word from Jackson that "through God's blessing" Harpers Ferry would be surrendered. Since Lee figured that he had only 18,000 with him at that time he greatly needed the troops of Jackson, Walker, and McLaws.

Jackson Takes Harpers Ferry

The Federal disaster at Harpers Ferry, which might have been avoided by the timely withdrawal of the garrison, cost the Union army 44 killed, 173 wounded, and 12,520 surrendered. Among those mortally wounded was the commander, Colonel Dixon S. Miles. The captured troops belonged chiefly to New York militia regiments and volunteer units from Illinois, Indiana, and Ohio, as well as a Maryland Home Brigade.

Harpers Ferry itself was incapable of being defended if hostile troops were posted on the heights above the confluence of the Shenandoah and the Potomac Rivers. The lowest hills, Bolivar Heights, rise behind the town for 300 feet; Loudoun Heights, across the Shenandoah in Virginia, rise to a maximum of 954 feet; Maryland Heights, across the Potomac in Maryland, rise steeply with usable levels at about 600 feet up and maximum height 1,060 feet. The Federal troops had been divided; about 7,000 were on Bolivar Heights, manning rifle pits and fieldpieces; a sizable force had been sent to Maryland Heights and others were posted to guard railroad tracks, bridge approaches, and roads.

General in Chief Halleck was determined to hold Harpers Ferry and had instructed Colonel Miles on September 7: "Our army is in motion; it is important that Harpers Ferry be held to the latest moment. The Government has the utmost confidence in you and is ready to give you full credit for the defense it expects you to make." The authority given Colonel Miles was so precise that when Brigadier General Julius White with 2,500 men withdrew from Martinsburg in the face of superior numbers of advancing Confederates and joined the garrison at Harpers Ferry, he deferred to Colonel Miles as the officer in command, although White outranked him.

The movement to surround Harpers Ferry began September 10, when General Stonewall Jackson crossed the Potomac at Williamsport, moved by way of Martinsburg on the Charlestown (now Charles Town) road and reached the outskirts of Bolivar Heights. The troops of Major General Lafayette McLaws and Major General R. H. Anderson moved up Maryland Heights, where Brigadier General Joseph B. Kershaw said he met "a most obstinate resistance." The Federals withdrew to Bolivar Heights. Using the pulling power of hundreds of men, McLaws was able to get his batteries up the mountainside and place them at about a 600-foot level, dominating Bolivar. Brigadier General John G. Walker sent two regiments under Colonel J. R. Cooke and a unit of the Signal Corps up Loudoun Heights, placing his other troops around the base of the mountain. General Walker asserted later that he had been alarmed by the sound of heavy gunfire coming from South Mountain, and had warned General Jackson that McClellan's whole army was probably attacking there. Jackson surmised it was only a cavalry encounter, but Walker was unconvinced and urged haste. He testified later that by exposing some of his troops he drew the fire of Federal batteries and thus was able to precipitate a reply by all the Confederate batteries and bring on the attack, but several of his fellow officers called him mistaken and said firing was begun by signal from General Jackson. This was one of those controversies over details that agitated commanders who wrote memoirs after the war, and it remained unsettled because the top commander, General Jackson, did not survive to judge the evidence.

The reduction of Harpers Ferry was principally an artillery battle. The shells of the Confederates fell on all parts of Bolivar Heights, and the Federals were hard put to it to get guns at an angle that would reach up the heights. General Jackson had said to his officers: "Fire at such positions of the enemy as will be most effective." When Jackson's troops moved to a ridge south of the Charlestown road Colonel Miles sent troops to oppose him, but Jackson's force was easily the stronger and the Federals were withdrawn.

On the evening of the first day's fighting, September 13, Colonel Benjamin F. Davis of the Eighth New York Cavalry, joined by Lieutenant Colonel Hasbrouck Davis of the Twelfth Illinois, proposed to move the cavalry out of the post on the night of September 14, to evade the surrounding Confederates. Colonel Miles was urged to have his infantry and artillery make a break likewise, but argued that they could not move fast enough, and that he had no authority to evacuate the place. After much persuasion he did finally give the order for the cavalry to leave. With the two Davises in the lead the cavalry, including also Rhode Island and Maryland units, moved out at night, crossed on a pontoon bridge to a narrow road under the cliffs of Maryland Heights. They were several miles along before they met Confederate pickets. They rode across fields and on the Hagerstown Pike north of Sharpsburg they ran into a Confederate ammunition train of over 40 wagons, scattered the cavalry escort and sent the wagons north, capturing about 200 prisoners and taking them into Greencastle, Pennsylvania.

Although fighting was resumed on the morning of September 15, the Federal commander realized that it could lead only to further loss of life and after consulting other officers agreed to capitulation. Brigadier General White was empowered to treat for the Federals and General

A. P. Hill for the Confederates. By the terms individuals were permitted to retain private possessions and the officers were given their sidearms. The men were paroled with the understanding that they would not fight again until exchanged.

One indirect gain was chalked up in favor of the defenders of Harpers Ferry—they kept about 20,000 Confederate troops from the fighting at South Mountain.

The Battle of Antietam

When the Union troops marched through South Mountain and across the valley to the high ground that lies east of Antietam Creek, they beheld a stream flowing slightly southwesterly, crossed by three stone-arched bridges and a number of fords. A fourth stone bridge was near the mouth and out of sight. The national road that ran west from Frederick through the mountain range by way of Turner's Gap crossed the Antietam on the middle or Boonsboro'–Sharpsburg bridge. The Antietam flowed into the Potomac below Shepherdstown, some distance north of Harpers Ferry. The national road forked before reaching Sharpsburg and sent a branch northwest to the Hagerstown Turnpike, which ran straight north from Sharpsburg.

The whole country was rolling and cut up into farms, which contained fields of grain, pastures, and woods. In some places there were ledges and outcroppings of rock. The Potomac River flowed west of this area in such wide swings that toward the north of the terrain, where the battle began, it was less than half a mile from the Hagerstown Pike, while at the center of the field, farther south, it was more than a mile west of the road.

With Sharpsburg as the focal point where Lee had placed his headquarters, the Confederate army faced the Antietam from the west side of the Hagerstown Turnpike, in a general north-south direction. The right (south) end of the line stood in front of Sharpsburg and was held chiefly by Brigadier General David R. Jones's division of Longstreet's command, and the troops of General J. G. Walker, extending down past the hill on which the National Cemetery now stands, to cover the big bend of

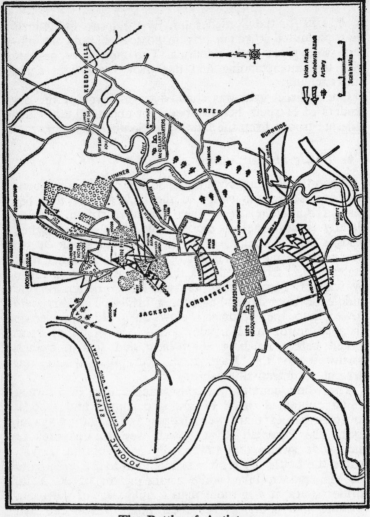

The Battle of Antietam
September 15, 1862

the Antietam and its fords there. To the left (north) of
Jones were the divisions of Major General D. H. Hill and
Brigadier General John B. Hood, and later Brigadier
General Nathan G. Evans occupied a position in the center, north of the Boonsboro' road. Hood's troops extended part of the way up to where General Jeb Stuart's
cavalry was placed at the extreme Confederate left, with
Stuart's horse artillery on a rise of ground over that area.
In the center of the Confederate line stood a conspicuous
white landmark, the one-story Dunker Church; behind
it was what became known as the West Wood, to distinguish it from a smaller East Wood on the east side of
the pike farther north. This terrain was largely assigned
to General Jackson, whose troops with those of General
Walker had reached this field from Harpers Ferry on
the afternoon of September 16.

When it became evident that the Confederate army
would make a determined stand west of the Antietam
and in front of Sharpsburg, General McClellan prepared
his plan of battle. He proposed to make the main attack
on the Confederate left, to the north of the field, using
Major General Hooker's First Corps and Major General
Joseph K. F. Mansfield's Twelfth Corps to start the battle,
with Major General Edwin V. Sumner's Second Corps in
support. Then he expected to use Major General Burnside's Ninth Corps against the Confederate right on the
ridge running southeast of Sharpsburg, and as soon as one
or both of the flank attacks were successful he would
have all the forces available attack the Confederate center. On the evening of September 16 Burnside, who had
been in command of the right wing at South Mountain,
held command of the left wing, and his corps was placed
at the left center of the Union line to guard the third
stone bridge, which ever after has been called Burnside's
Bridge. Here Brigadier General Samuel Sturgis' Second
Division of the Ninth was posted on both sides of the
road leading to the bridge, Brigadier General Orlando
Willcox's First Division was on the ground higher up,
and Brigadier General Isaac P. Rodman's Third Division
was sent farther to the left along the creek with batteries of howitzers. Major General Sumner commanded the
center, comprising his Second Corps and Mansfield's

Twelfth. Major General Fitz John Porter's Fifth Corps was posted in reserve behind the center of the Union line, straddling the national road. Fitz John Porter's infantry was not called on to fight as a whole, and his Third Division, under Brigadier General A. A. Humphreys, did not reach the field until the day after the battle.

General McClellan ordered Hooker's corps to cross Antietam Creek by two fords and the upper stone bridge near Keedysville on the afternoon of September 16. His divisions were commanded by Brigadier Generals Abner Doubleday, James B. Ricketts, and George G. Meade. Over toward the Hagerstown Pike, Meade's Third Division of Pennsylvania Reserves began a lively skirmish with the Confederate left under Brigadier General John B. Hood, who was supported by Colonel S. D. Lee's battalion of artillery. General Truman Seymour's brigade bore the brunt of the fighting, and remained in front of the army. General Hooker made his headquarters at the J. Poffenberger farm east of the road. Half a mile south the house of D. R. Miller was east of the road and his barn was west of it. In the evening General McClellan ordered General Sumner to send Major General Joseph K. F. Mansfield's Twelfth Corps in support of Hooker. The corps did not move until nearly midnight and reached its destination at 2 A.M. on September 17, resting a mile and a half in the rear of Hooker.

During the night Hood's troops, which were exhausted and unfed, were withdrawn and the Lawton and Trimble brigades from Ewell's division from General Jackson's command sent to replace them. Jackson was on hand but Lee still needed three divisions coming up from Harpers Ferry, those of Generals A. P. Hill, R. H. Anderson, and Lafayette McLaws, reported to be on the Sharpsburg road.

This engagement of Hooker's corps on the late afternoon of September 16 was a small skirmish compared with the terrible slaughter that was to make September 17 the bloodiest single day's fighting in the war. The second day's battle was fought with the Union army practically twice the size of the Confederate army, and while it is commonly considered a Union victory because it

forced Lee out of Maryland, it turned out to be more of
a draw because McClellan did not follow up his advantages. McClellan said he had available 87,164; and it
is estimated by some authorities that 23,000 of that
number did not get into the fighting. Lee is estimated to
have had over 59,000 available, but his report said
that fewer than 40,000 fought on his side.

The costly battle of Antietam on September 17 was
fought with great energy by both sides, the Confederates
battling desperately against the superior manpower of
the Union army. It developed in three phases; during
the first the Federals attempted to turn the Confederate
left and penetrated the latter's positions on the west side
of the Hagerstown Pike and into the West Wood behind
the Dunker Church, with heavy losses on both sides;
the second was fought more against the Confederate
center, when Lee was able to make use of some of the
troops that had arrived from Harpers Ferry; and the third
was the Union attack on the Confederate right, during
which Burnside's corps successfully crossed the famous
bridge and fought its way over the hills to the outskirts of
Sharpsburg, where the Confederate line held and the battle closed.

The battle opened at the first streaks of dawn with a
tremendous artillery bombardment from the high hills
west of the creek to those east of it, and the shells
passed over the valley as the opposing batteries tried to
find the strongpoints of the enemy. General Hooker
started the battle by sending Doubleday's division forward against the Confederate left, leading with the
brigades of Gibbon and Phelps, supported by those of
Patrick and Hofmann. Gibbon advanced along the turnpike and his battery, the Fourth U.S. Artillery, took its
position at Miller's barn. The Union line advanced
through a wood and across a cornfield, where the stalks
were as tall as the men. The Confederate brigades of
Lawton, Trimble, and Hays were hardest hit, and General
Jackson ordered up the units of Hood's division that had
fought the night before. Three of D. H. Hill's brigades,
those of Ripley, Colquitt, and McRae, were pushed forward to support Hood. The Confederates regained the cornfield, which changed hands several times during the day.

General Mansfield's corps marched into the battle line at 7 A.M. and with the cooperation of Hartsuff's brigade of Hooker's corps charged through the cornfield into the wood behind the Dunker Church. Soon after the Tenth Maine regiment of Mansfield's corps began firing, General Mansfield protested that they were attacking Union troops. The opposing troops showed no flags, but the officers of the regiment convinced General Mansfield that they wore gray uniforms. Too late, however, for Mansfield, who was on horseback, had exposed himself unduly and was quickly shot down and mortally wounded. The command devolved on Brigadier General Alpheus S. Williams.

About the same time General Hooker was wounded and taken from the field, and General Meade took charge. He withdrew the First Corps from the front and sent it back for reorganization; the fact that it already had 2,470 casualties proved the intensity of the fighting. On the Confederate side Brigadier General William E. Starke was killed, Brigadier Generals John R. Jones and Lawton were wounded. The Confederate line had suffered severely around the Dunker Church, and the principal defense came from Ewell's division, now commanded by General Early, whose troops made use of the protection of ledges of rock, and who had at their left the strong support of Stuart's horse artillery. The Confederate division of General J. G. Walker was brought up from the extreme right to support Hood.

The next vital action came when Major General Sumner's Second Corps was sent across the creek a little below where Hooker had crossed. This was a powerful corps under excellent leadership, but it suffered disastrously because Lee was able to reinforce his troops with McLaw's division of Longstreet's corps, just arrived from Harpers Ferry. The Federal fighting was led by the divisions of Generals John Sedgwick, Israel B. Richardson, and William H. French. Moving up from the creek to the higher land, Sedgwick once again passed through the East Wood and the sanguinary cornfield, where the dead of both sides were piled in heaps. In the wood behind the Dunker Church, Sedgwick met charges by Mc-Laws and Walker and was thrust back to the Hagerstown

Road in disorder. French and Richardson had better fortune; they knocked Hill out of his protected position at the Roulette farmhouse, which stood between the Hagerstown Pike and the Antietam. This brought Hill to a sunken road, which he used as a trench and where he reformed his troops and fought doggedly against the Union waves. His dead and wounded piled up in the road, since designated Bloody Lane. In the adjoining cornfield General Richardson was mortally wounded. He was carried to McClellan's headquarters in the Pry house, east of the Antietam, and remained there six weeks, dying November 3. In the same action Brigadier General Thomas F. Meagher, commanding the Second Brigade of Richardson's division, and Colonel Francis C. Barlow, leading the Sixty-first New York, were severely wounded. General McClellan then gave command of the division to Major General Winfield S. Hancock. Two brigades from Major General Franklin's Sixth Corps were sent at 10 A.M. to reinforce him. Major General Darius N. Couch's First Division of the Fourth Corps also supported Hancock.

The Confederates were holding their line, but they had no luck with assaults. A violent battle developed around the Piper farmhouse, with no advantages to either side. General Stuart, whose artillery had been pounding the Federals from the northwest, started his troops down the Hagerstown Turnpike, but Doubleday's thirty guns were in fine working order and stopped Stuart's raid before it neared the Dunker Church.

General Pleasonton's cavalry was sent across the Boonsboro' bridge to support the Federal line in the center. Several battalions of Brigadier General George Sykes's division of Fitz John Porter's corps also came on the field, but contributed little to the fighting. Most of Porter's corps remained on the east side of the Antietam, in reserve. It was the opinion of some Federal commanders that the Confederates could have been driven off the field on the morning of September 17 with a little more support from the nearly 12,000 troops in Porter's corps that McClellan kept inactive during the hottest part of the battle.

When McClellan saw that the Union army had failed

to rout the Confederates he turned to the third phase of his plan, the attack by General Burnside.

The Crossing of Burnside's Bridge

One of the great dramatic incidents of Antietam was the crossing of the stone bridge that ever since has been called Burnside's Bridge. This substantial structure of stone piers and three arches stands a short distance south of the Sharpsburg–Boonsboro' bridge, where the banks of the Antietam are rather high, especially on the western, or Confederate, side. The bridge dates back to the decade of 1830–1840, when several other stone bridges were erected. Since early morning of September 17 it had been the special concern of Burnside's Ninth Corps, which protected the extreme Union left. Brigadier General Isaac P. Rodman's division held most of the terrain running south of the bridge and covered a ford, while on the opposite bank the Confederates belonged to Brigadier General Robert Toombs' brigade of Longstreet's command. The location of the bridge at a bend in the creek made possible its enfilading by two Confederate batteries located on the high ground near Sharpsburg, where the National Cemetery now stands.

While the battle was raging on the Federal right, Brigadier General Jacob D. Cox was in immediate command at General Burnside's headquarters on the hill east of the bridge. Action around the bridge was limited to artillery duels. The Confederates guarding the opposite area were four brigades of Brigadier General D. R. Jones' division, of which Toombs' brigade was the spearhead. The Confederates occupied several hundred yards above and below the bridge. To reach the bridge the Federals would have to move along a river road with Toombs' sharpshooters only 150 feet away on the other side of the creek. The bridge had room only for eight men marching abreast.

General McClellan sent the order to force passage of the bridge to Burnside at 10 A.M. Three efforts were made to carry it. Brigadier General Samuel D. Sturgis was in command at the center of the Federal line and the brigade of Colonel George Crook was to have the distinction of leading the assault, approaching the bridge from the north. Skirmishers, who were able to find cover among trees growing along the banks of the creek, came from the Eleventh Connecticut Regiment of Rodman's division under Colonel Henry W. Kingsbury, who was killed during the action. When Crook's troops appeared over the crest of the hill the fire of the Confederate batteries and muskets concentrated on them. Crook attempted to find cover for his men, but the place proved too hot for them and they were unable to come up to the bridge. The next effort was made by Brigadier General James Nagle supported by troops of Brigadier General Edward Ferrero, but even with strong artillery fire engaging the Confederate batteries the Federal attack fell apart. In the meantime events on the Federal right were so full of dangers that McClellan reiterated his order to Burnside that the bridge must be forced and the Confederate left engaged. In his report General Sturgis thus described the third assault:

Orders arrived from General Burnside to carry the bridge at all hazards. I then selected the Fifty-first New York, Colonel Robert B. Potter, and the Fifty-first Pennsylvania, Colonel John F. Hartranft, from the Second Brigade, and directed them to charge with the bayonet. They started on their mission of death full of enthusiasm, and taking a route less exposed than the regiments (Second Maryland and Sixth New Hampshire) which had made the effort before them, rushed at a double quick over the slope leading to the bridge and over the bridge itself, with an impetuosity which the enemy could not resist; and the Stars and Stripes were planted on the opposite bank at 1 P.M. amid the most enthusiastic cheering from every part of the field where they could be seen.

The Second Brigade had 95 killed, 368 wounded at Antietam, most of them in this assault. At the same time Scammon's brigade of Rodman's division, supported by Dahlgren howitzers, crossed the ford below the bridge and Crook found a ford above the bridge. The Union troops stampeded Toombs's lines, forcing them over toward Sharpsburg.

At this stage, when Willcox had broken Jones's formations and reached the high ground on which the Na-

tional Cemetery stands, Rodman, coming up to the left of
Willcox, found his forces losing contact with Willcox
and becoming imperiled by new Confederate troops moving toward them from Sharpsburg. When the van of Scammon's brigade first saw these troops emerge from a cornfield the latter were wearing Union-blue uniforms. They
turned out to be three brigades of General A. P. Hill's
division, up from Harpers Ferry, where they had found
the Federal uniforms in better condition than their own
and donned them. Lee supported them with batteries
hurried to their position. As Rodman attempted to direct
the closing of his lines he was hit and mortally wounded.
General Cox ordered Willcox and Sturgis to retire to the
left of their line and Sturgis to close the break. Hill's men
tried hard to enlarge their advantage, but the Federal
line stiffened. The fighting died down. Burnside's
troops had won their hold on the west heights, but the
Confederates regained some of their ground and a lost
battery. While there was sporadic firing until dark both
forces were exhausted by the day's terrible struggles and
groups from both armies began carrying off the wounded.

General Longstreet in his reminiscences, *From Manassas to Appomattox,* relates a "peculiarly painful personal
experience" in connection with Burnside's assault. Colonel
Kingsbury, killed near the bridge, was a brother-in-law
of General D. R. Jones, who commanded the Confederate troops opposite to him. Jones, whose health
was not strong, was greatly affected by Kingsbury's
death and soon afterward asked for a leave of absence.
"Gradually but hopelessly sinking," in the words of Longstreet, Jones died a few months later.

When Longstreet completed his orders along the line
for the night he rode up to Lee's headquarters. Lee
walked up to him as he dismounted and placing his hands
on Longstreet's shoulders exclaimed: "Here is my old
warhorse at last!"

After the Battle

Major General Jacob D. Cox, who was not an unfriendly critic of McClellan, said the crisis of Antietam
came at 10 A.M. The sudden and complete rout of Sedg-

wick's division supported McClellan's belief that Lee had superior numbers and had massed overwhelming forces on the Federal right. General Sumner, having no contact with Hooker's corps under Meade, thought it "utterly dispersed," which was inaccurate. A controversy developed over Porter's inactivity. That a Federal assault could have driven a line between Lee's left and center at a loosely held position in front of Sharpsburg was information sent to General Sykes at a critical moment, and the proposal to advance was put before McClellan. No order was given. After the war General Sykes said he thought "McClellan was inclined to order in the Fifth Corps, but that when he spoke of doing so, Fitz John Porter said: 'Remember, General, I command the last reserve of the last Army of the Potomac.' " When General Porter's attention was called to this evidence, he denied that there ever was such a discussion and said that nearly all of his Fifth Corps was sent to the right and left wings and he actually had less than 4,000 in reserve. The subject then became one of veracity between generals.

The earliest government reports of casualties, which were quoted for at least fifty years, or until newer historians began searching the archives for verification, said that the Union army at Antietam lost 2,010 killed, 9,416 wounded, and 1,034 missing. The Confederates were said to have had 3,500 killed, 16,399 wounded, and 6,000 missing. These figures obviously were compiled by an intense partisan. When Thomas L. Livermore began studying the reports he did not make many changes in the Union totals, but he brought the Confederate casualties within reason; the Union army had lost 2,108 killed and 9,549 wounded, a total of 11,657, and the Confederates had lost approximately 2,700 dead and 9,024 wounded, a total of 11,724. The Confederates left 2,500 dead at South Mountain and Antietam. Apparently the Union army had taken 6,000 prisoners while Lee was in Maryland.

In addition to the other high Union officers who were killed and wounded, Sedgwick, Weber, Hartsuff, and Dane were wounded. On the Confederate side Branch, G. B.

Anderson, and Starke were killed and R. H. Anderson, Toombs, Lawton, Ripley, Rodes, Gregg, Armistead, and Ransom were wounded.

General Lee was ready to take his army out of Maryland, but he did not leave the morning after the battle. Despite his heavy losses he believed he could repulse McClellan. But the Union men on the field were chiefly burial squads. McClellan did not attack Lee, to the disgust of Washington and the wonder of the Confederates. On the night of September 18 Lee moved his army across the Potomac to Virginia.

McClellan engaged in reorganizing and replenishing equipment. He informed the War Department that the infantry was short of shoes and the cavalry of horses. Some of the reports from the front said the Union soldiers demanded only the right-sized shoes, something that would not have occurred to Lee's soldiers, many of whom had to return home barefoot. When McClellan complained the horses were sore-tongued and fatigued, Lincoln lost his customary patience. "Will you pardon me for asking what the horses of your army have done since the battle of Antietam that fatigues anything?" he demanded.

Disturbed by McClellan's failure to press the pursuit of Lee despite instructions from Washington, President Lincoln on October 1 went to headquarters to size up the situation. General McClellan guided him over the battlefields of Antietam and South Mountain, and together they posed for photographs by Mathew Brady. McClellan wrote years later that Lincoln had approved his methods and had said "that he was entirely satisfied with me; that I should be let alone; that he would stand by me." The two men never met again.

After President Lincoln had returned to Washington and had consulted with his staff General Halleck sent the following message to General McClellan under date of October 6:

I am instructed to telegraph you as follows: The President directs that you cross the Potomac and give battle to the enemy, or drive him South. Your army must move now, while the roads are good. If you cross the river between the enemy and Washington, and cover the latter by your operation, you can be reinforced with 30,000 men. If you move up the valley of the Shenandoah, not more than 12,000 or 15,000 can be sent you. The President advises the interior line between Washington and the enemy, but does not order it. He is very desirous that your army move as soon as possible. You will immediately report what line you adopt, and when you intend to cross the river; also to what point the reinforcements are to be sent. It is necessary that the plan of your operations be positively determined on, before orders are given for building bridges and repairing railroads. I am directed to add, that the Secretary of War and the General-in-Chief fully concur with the President in these instructions.

General McClellan delayed carrying out the order on various pretexts. On October 21 McClellan sent General Halleck a message saying he was short of horses and begged leave to ask whether the President wanted him to march at once or to await the reception of new horses, "every possible step having been taken to insure their prompt arrival." Halleck replied that the President "directs me to say that he has no change to make in his order of the 6th inst. The President does not expect impossibilities, but he is very anxious that all this good weather should not be wasted in inactivity." General Halleck was skeptical of the excuse that proper supplies had not been forthcoming. During the final week of October McClellan started moving his army along the Blue Ridge by Lovettsville, Snicker's Gap, and Rectortown and concentrated it at Warrenton. Heavy rains now set in.

President Lincoln told John Hay that after he had "peremptorily" ordered McClellan to advance, nineteen days passed before McClellan put a man across the river and nine more before the army was across. Lincoln began to fear that McClellan "did not want to hurt the enemy." He believed McClellan able to intercept Lee on the way to Richmond and determined to make that the test. When McClellan permitted the Confederates to get away the President decided to relieve him.

The President and his advisers were confident that another great opportunity to deal a knockout blow had been lost by the overly cautious attitude of the commanding general. On November 5 President Lincoln prepared an order to General McClellan, relieving him of the command of the Army of the Potomac and ordering him to turn it over to Major General Ambrose E. Burnside. This was done on the evening of November 7, 1862. Meantime, the Confederacy promoted Longstreet and Jackson to lieutenant generals.

While the Union army had completely knocked out Lee's Maryland campaign and canceled any advantages gained at Second Manassas, it could not claim a clean victory at Antietam. At best the result was a draw. It did not end with the destruction of the Confederate army but enabled Lee to recoup his losses and fight again. The great Union error was ignorance of Confederate strength. As in the Peninsular campaign General McClellan greatly overestimated the Confederate forces, clinging to the conviction that Lee had between 100,000 and 120,000. In this he was not alone; the authorities in Washington were similarly misled, and their anxiety over the defense of the capital was communicated to the commanding general, who actually fought the battle of Antietam without having been specifically appointed to the command. When the lapses of General McClellan are weighed, consideration must be given to the mishandling of the Union armies by Secretary of War Stanton and General Halleck, who had the approval of Lincoln.

McClellan's chief trait, caution, was a handicap when opportunities had to be grasped quickly and situations improvised. In this General Lee was a master. Moreover Lee was a psychologist, the only commander who carefully estimated the traits of his opponents and profited by his past experiences with them.

McClellan did not think he could be blamed for the result or that anyone else could have done better. His big error was in seeking vindication by joining the opposition to the Administration, although he was opposed to both secession and slavery. The elevation of Lincoln's fame as the savior of the Union proportionately lowered the prestige of McClellan. But one of the kindest estimates was made by General Grant after the war. Grant expressed confidence in McClellan's loyalty and patriotism and pointed to the terrible load he had to carry when, as a young major general, he had to form a new army. Grant thought that if McClellan had made his way up he would have succeeded as well as any other general.

An estimate of Lee at Antietam by a modern Southern historian is that of Douglas Southall Freeman. He said Antietam remains a model in the full employment of a small force for a defensive battle on the inner line.

17

JEB STUART'S CHAMBERSBURG RAID

While General McClellan was at Warrenton, Virginia, polishing up the Army of the Potomac, to the dismay of President Lincoln and the War Department in Washington, General Lee was at Culpeper Court House biding his time. The plan he had discussed before the reverse at Antietam, of driving into Pennsylvania as far as Harrisburg and disrupting Federal communications, was still fresh in his mind. His particular animus was against the Baltimore & Ohio Railroad because it hauled supplies from the Middle West directly to Federal military depots. On Monday, October 6, 1862, he summoned Major General J. E. B. Stuart to headquarters, and in the presence of General Jackson unfolded plans for a cavalry raid by Stuart into the heart of the "enemy's country," with the object of carrying out his favorite project.

Lee asked Stuart to take 1,200 to 1,500 horsemen, ride to the vicinity of Chambersburg, Pennsylvania, destroy the railroad bridge over the Conococheague, collect horses, and take into custody state and Federal government officials and bring them back as hostages, to be exchanged for Confederate leaders now in Federal hands. Lee knew he could depend on Stuart to carry out his mission, for Jeb Stuart was the most daring and resourceful cavalry leader the South had produced, whose ability to get out of a dangerous situation victoriously had given him immense prestige. He was now several months short of being thirty years old, but the sandy-colored beard that he allowed to grow profusely made him look older. He already had carried off another brilliant cavalry raid around McClellan when, just before the Seven Days' battles, he rode around the right and rear of the Army of the Potomac and reached Richmond.

Stuart took 1,800 horsemen, divided them into three groups of 600 each, and gave command of these groups to Generals Wade Hampton, W. H. F. (Rooney) Lee, and W. E. Jones. He also took Major John Pelham and four guns of the horse artillery. They started from Darkesville, October 9, and crossed the Potomac at Old Fort Frederick early next morning. Here they brushed past Captain Thomas Logan and a small unit from the Twelfth Illinois Cavalry. Logan could do little but observe the Confederate horsemen ride past, but he was able to send a courier with the information and thus the Federals learned that a raid was on.

At the Pennsylvania line Stuart had an order read to the troops. They were to take the horses they needed but to indulge in no personal pillage. "We are now in enemy country," announced Stuart. "Hold yourselves ready for attack or defense, and behave with no other thought than victory." At Mercersburg the men picked up shoes and clothing and paid in Confederate scrip. By the time they reached Chambersburg at dark they had taken many horses from the farmers and had managed to pick up plenty of fresh food on the way. It rained intermittently. Many of the troopers now wore blue capes and coats that they had taken from shops, and some citizens mistook them for Union cavalry. At Chambersburg the town officials were just able to send an alarm to Governor Curtin at Harrisburg before the Confederates cut the wires. Governor Curtin wired Secretary of War Stanton: "The people have surrendered Chambersburg."

Stuart called for the cash in the vaults of the town's bank, but a zealous banker had removed the funds in time. A group was sent to destroy the Cumberland Valley Railroad bridge over the Conococheague River, but found the bridge to be made of iron and returned baffled. General Lee's favorite project would have to wait. Colonel

A. K. McClure, who represented Chambersburg in negotiations with Stuart, was impressed because Stuart's troopers spoke politely even when they lifted what they wanted. The raiders burned the railroad depot, several trains, machine shops, and warehouses with military supplies, including rifles and ammunition.

Stuart was a daring raider, but a careful leader. Throughout the raid he kept close watch on possible pursuit, for he was aware that the Federals must be converging on him. He did not know the discomfiture in Washington, where Halleck was urging McClellan to close all the roads for Stuart's return, saying: "No man should be permitted to return to Virginia." In this circumscribed area, alive with Federal horsemen, Jeb Stuart was moving steadily along, from Cashtown toward Hagerstown, then to Emmitsburg, a column five miles long, encumbered with extra horses and supplies. McClellan wired Halleck: "I have made such disposition of troops along the river that I think we will intercept the Rebels in their return. All of my available cavalry was ordered in pursuit last night. . . ." There was infantry at or near the fords. McClellan hoped to teach the arrogant Rebels "a lesson they will not soon forget."

From a captured courier Stuart learned that Colonel Richard Rush had a large force at Frederick and General Alfred Pleasonton was leading a cavalry unit toward Mechanicsville. Stuart changed his route, going via Woodsboro. Here a group of the Sixth Pennsylvania Cavalry saw Stuart's column but was too weak to intercept it. On the morning of Sunday, October 12, General Alfred Pleasonton met Stuart's advance at the mouth of the Monocacy River. He was confused because the troopers wore Union blue; the riders approached and when a short distance from the Federals, Stuart gave the order to charge with their sabers. The Federals fired a volley from their carbines and retreated. In the engagement that followed, Major Pelham's guns helped keep the Federals back while Stuart's horsemen, with 1,200 captured horses and 30 hostages, crossed the Potomac over White's Ford to Virginia. General Pleasonton did not consider it useful to pursue.

General Reynolds said: "I must say that their escape

has given me quite a shock—I did not expect they could perform such a feat in our own country. On the Chicka-hominy it was different."

Lieutenant Colonel Richard B. Irwin, on duty in Wash-ington as assistant adjutant general to General Nathaniel Banks in the defense of Washington, wrote in his remi-niscences (in *Battles and Leaders of the Civil War*):

One day in October, shortly after Stuart's raid into Mary-land and Pennsylvania, on returning on board the *Martha Washington* from a review near Alexandria, when the Presi-dent seemed in unusually high spirits and was conversing freely some one suddenly asked: "Mr. President, how about McClellan?" Without looking at his questioner the President drew a ring on the deck with a stick or umbrella and said quietly: "When I was a boy we used to play a game, three times round and out. Stuart has been round him twice; if he goes round him once more, gentlemen, McClellan will be out!"

18

THE ROAD TO EMANCIPATION

The Confiscation Act

If the government of the United States was opposed to slavery, why didn't it free the slaves? This question was asked with increasing irritation by citizens in the North, whether they were abolitionists, radicals, or voters who endorsed the platform of the Republican Party. President Lincoln delayed action during the first half of 1862 for several reasons. One was political: he did not want to confiscate the property of slaveholders in the border states, for Washington still feared this might swing those states into the Confederate column. He had an informal and unreported conference with members of Congress from the border states on the subject of compensating owners, possibly by a bond issue. But no practical method emerged.

As Union reverses multiplied, anxiety increased in

Congress and the conviction grew that freeing of the slaves would be strategically valuable to the North. Congress in July passed the Confiscation Act, and barely avoided a veto from the President. The act made death the penalty for treason, but gave the courts power to commute the sentence to a fine and imprisonment; it directed the President to cause the seizure of all estates, property, and possessions of military and civil officers of the Confederacy or of any of its states, and, after a sixty-day notice, to confiscate the property of all engaged "in armed rebellion" or abetting it. It freed the slaves of those convicted, as well as the slaves of "rebel owners" who took refuge within the lines of the army, and denied protection of the Fugitive Slave Law to any owners of slaves except those who were loyal to the Union. It forbade military and naval officers to surrender fugitives to claimants and authorized colonization and the use of Negroes as soldiers. It gave power to grant amnesty to rebels and to make exceptions to a general pardon.

Senator Charles Sumner of Massachusetts called it "a practical act of emancipation." Five days after Congress adjourned President Lincoln called his cabinet and read a draft of his act of emancipation. The cabinet was not wholly in favor of issuing it while the Union army was losing battles. The subject weighed heavily on Lincoln's mind all during that summer. In speaking on September 13 to a group of clergymen who had come to urge freeing the slaves, he pointed to the difficulties of enforcing such an act, when he could not even enforce the Constitution in the seceded states. He referred to the Confiscation Act, which offered protection to slaves, saying "I cannot learn that that law has caused a single slave to come over to us."

But a few days later the whole atmosphere changed. The Federal army stopped General Lee at Antietam, and an opportunity to announce emancipation of a kind came to Lincoln. He served notice on September 22 that he meant to issue on January 1, 1863, a proclamation that all persons held as slaves in any state or part of a state at that time "in rebellion against the United States," would be forever free, and that he would recommend that owners who had remained loyal to the United States should be compensated for any losses, including loss of slaves.

Lincoln's Proposal for Compensation

When Congress convened on December 1, 1862, President Lincoln had reached the conclusion that the time had come to formulate legislation on slavery. He already had announced on September 22 that he meant to make emancipation effective, for specific categories and places, on the first day of the next year, and he now took the opportunity presented by his annual message to spell out a proposal for action by Congress. Thus the message of December 1, 1862, famous for its invocation of "the last best hope of earth," devotes much of its space to outlining a way of freeing the slave and letting him enter into the duties of a free citizen in a democracy.

The President said that the treaty with Great Britain for the suppression of the slave trade had been put into operation with prospect of complete success. He reported that "free Americans of African descent" had asked to be included in plans for colonizing Negroes abroad, but that several Spanish-American republics had protested against receiving such emigrants "in all the rights as freemen." Only Liberia and Haiti had offered them citizenship, but the emigrants were reluctant to go there. He then took up the subject of "compensated emancipation" mentioned in his proclamation of September 22, 1862.

President Lincoln proposed that Congress draft amendments to the Constitution, to be submitted to the states for ratification, to this effect: (1) Any state that abolished slavery before January 1, 1900, to be compensated by U.S. bonds delivered at the completion of abolition, and to forfeit these bonds if it reintroduced slavery at a later date; (2) slaves freed by the war to be forever free, but owners to be compensated at the same rate as the states if proved not to have been disloyal; (3) Congress to provide with money or otherwise for colonizing abroad free colored persons with their own consent.

The President admitted that emancipation would be unsatisfactory to advocates of perpetual slavery, but he thought the length of time for abolition, thirty-seven years, should mitigate their dissatisfaction. Liberation of slaves was, "in a certain sense," destruction of property; the people of the South, he felt, were not responsible for the original introduction of this property, while the North by using cotton and sugar shared the profits of dealing in them. While the sum required would be large, he thought it smaller than the cost of continued warfare; the ample room for expansion of population and development of natural advantages would make the postponed cost less burdensome than the immediate outlay. The President said he strongly favored colonization, but not for the reason some critics gave, that free Negroes would displace white labor and white laborers. He estimated there would be one colored person to seven whites, if evenly distributed, and he did not believe "that the freed people will swarm forth and cover the whole land." He closed this message with a famous peroration, frequently quoted, but rarely in context with the rest of his annual message. It is as follows:

Fellow citizens, *we* can not escape history. We, of this Congress and this Administration, will be remembered in spite of ourselves. No personal significance, or insignificance, can spare one or another of us. The fiery trial through which we pass, will light us down, in honor or dishonor, to the latest generation. We *say* we are for the Union. The world will not forget that we say this. We know how to save the Union. The world knows we do know how to save it. We— even *we here*—hold the power and bear the responsibility. In *giving* freedom to the *slave*, we assure freedom to the free —honorable alike in what we give and in what we preserve. We shall nobly save, or meanly lose, the last best hope of earth. Other means may succeed; this could not fail. The way is plain, peaceful, generous, just—a way which, if followed, the world will forever applaud, and God must forever bless.

Hunter's Premature Order

Like Major General John C. Frémont before him, Major General David Hunter undertook to free the slaves in his military department without notice to the Executive. On May 9, 1862, he issued an order from Hilton Head,

South Carolina, headquarters of the Department of the South, announcing that since Georgia, Florida, and South Carolina, three states in his department, had taken up arms against the United States, it had become necessary to place them under martial law. "Slavery and martial law in a free country are altogether incompatible. The persons in these states heretofore held as slaves, are therefore declared forever free."

President Lincoln declared the order void and unauthorized; such a decision was a prerogative of the President and could not be left to commanders in the field. He pointed to the joint resolution of Congress, adopted on his recommendation, which said the United States should cooperate with any state that adopted a gradual abolishment of slavery and should compensate for public and private inconveniences. He appealed to the states to make this possible.

The government, in recommending that military and naval commanders employ Negroes, demanded reasonable wages for them and records showing whence they had come, as a basis for possible compensation.

The military enrollment of Negroes in 1862 gave the North the use of 130,000 soldiers, seamen, and laborers, according to President Lincoln. The Confederate government announced that neither Negro soldiers nor their white officers would be granted immunities recognized under the laws of war. President Lincoln replied at once with a general order, dated April 24, 1863, advising the Army that if an enemy did enslave or sell any captured soldier such action would call for retaliation by death. On July 30 he issued a specific order that "for every soldier of the United States killed in violation of the laws of war, a Rebel soldier shall be executed; and for every one enslaved by the enemy or sold into slavery, a Rebel soldier shall be placed at hard labor on the public works, and continued at such hard labor until the other shall be released and receive the treatment due to a prisoner of war."

Payments to Slave Owners

Slave owners were actually paid for their slaves by

Congress. That they were compensated for the loss of their slaves in the District of Columbia has been generally obscured by the greater emphasis given to national emancipation. In December, 1861, Senator Henry Wilson of Massachusetts introduced a bill providing for emancipation of slaves in the District of Columbia and for the payment of compensation to loyal slave owners, the exact amount to be determined by a board of commissioners out of $1,000,000 appropriated for that purpose. The bill passed the Senate but was fought hard in the House. It was opposed by Senator John J. Crittenden of Kentucky and by Representative Clement Vallandigham of Ohio. It was passed by a vote of 92 to 38 and received President Lincoln's signature on April 16, 1862. Payment was made to owners by the United States Treasury of sums not exceeding $300, and the total was slightly under the amount appropriated by Congress.

Negroes Become Contraband

As soon as Virginia ratified its ordinance of secession slaves began to appear at military depots of the United States to ask protection. One of the places easy of access was Fortress Monroe, where General Benjamin F. Butler was in command. On May 24, 1861, a Virginia owner demanded of Butler that he hand over three Negroes who had sought refuge at Fortress Monroe. Butler refused on the ground that the Negroes were "contraband of war," since they had worked on construction of a battery directed against the Union and were owned by the citizen of a state that had declared itself out of the United States.

This was the first time the term "contraband" was applied to refugee slaves, and it became so general that slaves who left their masters and came north were referred to as contraband. Butler notified the War Department that he intended to feed all refugees and employ the able-bodied, keeping an account of the cost. His action was approved by Secretary of War Cameron.

When Butler reported on July 30, 1861, that he now had 900 Negroes to provide for, Secretary Cameron replied: "It is the desire of the President that all existing rights in all the states be fully respected and maintained; in cases of fugitives from the loyal slave states, the enforcement of the Fugitive Slave law by the ordinary forms of judicial proceedings must be respected by the military authorities; in the disloyal states the Confiscation Act of Congress must be your guide."

A Great Song for Freedom

Julia Ward Howe, keeper of the Puritan conscience, believed that works must go with faith, and in her long humanitarian career rose above sectarian limitations. She was born in 1819 near the Battery in lower Manhattan, New York City, when that was still a place for fashionable residence, and was the daughter of an affluent and cultured family that cherished memories of the founders of the Republic. Her father, an investment banker, was a leader in education, a strong advocate of temperance, and active in extending churches into the West. Julia Ward had a bent for writing and persuasion; in maturity she shared Boston's intellectual life, became an abolitionist, and was active in prison reform. In marrying Dr. Samuel Gridley Howe she joined hands with another rabid abolitionist, a supporter of the Free Soil party, and friend of John Brown. He had fought for the liberation of Greece and Poland and became an eminent pioneer in educating the feeble-minded and the blind.

Summing up her career when eighty, Julia Ward Howe said proudly that she had founded a club for young girls, which became a model for similar organizations; that she had pleaded the cause "of oppressed Greece and murdered Armenia"; that she had spoken at both the Boston Radical Club and the Concord School of Philosophy and had occupied the pulpit of her own church and that of others, "without regard to denominational limits"; had pleaded for the slave when he was still a slave and helped initiate the movement for woman suffrage, "when to do so was a thankless office, involving public ridicule and private avoidance." She was respected for her courage, her energy, and her tact.

Yet the one act by which her name became ineradicably linked with the history of the American people was summed up thus: "I have written one poem which, although composed in the stress and strain of the Civil War, is now sung South and North by the champions of a free government."

This was the "Battle Hymn of the Republic."

In the fall of 1861 Mrs. Howe visited Washington, where she found the morale low because of military setbacks and administrative inefficiency. The capital was surrounded by armed camps and it was customary for visitors to hire a carriage and make a tour of the environs. On one such excursion a body of Confederates suddenly menaced an outpost, alarms were sounded, and reinforcements were hurried to the point of attack. Mrs. Howe thus described the effect of the incident on herself and, indirectly, on the country's songs, in her *Reminiscences, 1819-1899*:

We returned to the city very slowly, of necessity, for the troops nearly filled the road. My dear minister was in the carriage with me, as were several other friends. To beguile the rather tedious drive, we sang from time to time snatches of the army songs so popular at the time, concluding, I think, with *John Brown's body lies a-mouldering in the ground; His soul is marching on.* The soldiers seemed to like this, and answered back, "Good for you!" Mr. Clarke [the Rev. James Freeman Clarke] said: "Mrs. Howe, why do you not write some good words for that stirring tune?" I replied that I had often wished to do this, but had not as yet found in my mind any leaning toward it.

I went to bed that night as usual and slept quite soundly. I awoke in the gray of the morning twilight, and as I lay waiting for the dawn, the long lines of the desired poem began to twine themselves in my mind. Having thought out all the stanzas, I said to myself, I must get up and write these verses down, lest I fall asleep again and forget them. So with a sudden effort, I sprang out of bed, and found in the dimness an old stump of a pen which I remembered to have used the day before. I scrawled the verses almost without looking at the paper. I had learned to do this when, on previous occasions, attacks of versification had visited me in the night, and I feared to have recourse to a light lest I should wake the baby, who slept near me. I was always obliged to decipher my scrawl before another night should intervene, as it was only legible while the matter was fresh in my mind. At this time, having completed my writing, I returned to bed and fell asleep, saying to myself: "I like this better than most things that I have written."

The poem, which was soon after published in the Atlantic Monthly, was somewhat praised on its appearance, but the vicissitudes of the war so engrossed public attention that small heed was taken of literary matters. I knew, and was content to know, that the poem soon found its way to the camps, as I heard from time to time of its being sung in chorus by the soldiers.

When everyone was singing it, a friend remarked: "Mrs. Howe ought to die now, for she has done the best that she will ever do."

This judgment was sustained. Mrs. Howe wrote tuneful verses, after the manner of the nineteenth century, but she had no illusions about their permanence. She delighted in being a part of the brilliant circles that included Oliver Wendell Holmes, Longfellow, Emerson, Bryant, Irving, and other major authors.

The "Battle Hymn of the Republic" is not only a poem, but a historic document. It is an inspiring act of dedication, joining high patriotic ideals with religious fervor. It belongs in the category of such rousing hymns as "Onward Christian Soldiers." It owes not a little of its timelessness to the stirring march tempo of the song the soldiers called "John Brown's Body."

Lincoln's Reply to Greeley

Horace Greeley's criticism of Lincoln for failure to make slavery the paramount issue early in the war found expression in a bitter editorial entitled "Prayer of Twenty Millions," which he published in the New York *Tribune* in August, 1862. Lincoln had been racking his brain for months to find a reasonable and just way to end slavery and was now about ready to announce his formula when Greeley's editorial appeared. It stung him to reply in one of the most precise and emphatic statements of policy he ever made. On August 22, 1862, he wrote Greeley:

As to the policy I "seem to be pursuing," as you say, I have not meant to leave anyone in doubt.

I would save the Union. I would save it the shortest way

under the Constitution. The sooner the national authority can be restored, the nearer the Union will be "the Union as it was." If there be those who would not save the Union unless they could at the same time *save* slavery, I do not agree with them. If there be those who would not save the Union unless they could at the same time *destroy* slavery, I do not agree with them. My paramount object in this struggle is to save the Union, and it is *not* either to save or destroy slavery. If I could save the Union without freeing *any* slave, I would do it; and if I could save it by freeing *all* the slaves, I would do it; and if I could do it by freeing some and leaving others alone, I would also do that. What I do about slavery and the colored race I do because I believe it helps to save this Union; and what I forbear, I forbear because I do *not* believe it would help to save the Union. I shall do *less* whenever I shall believe what I am doing hurts the cause, and I shall do *more* whenever I believe doing more will help the cause. I shall try to correct errors when shown to be errors; and I shall adopt new views so fast as they appear to be true views. I have here stated my purpose according to my view of *official* duty, and I intend no modification of my oft-expressed *personal* wish that all men everywhere could be free.

The Emancipation Proclamation

On January 1, 1863, President Lincoln issued the Emancipation Proclamation, as he had promised one hundred days before.

This is generally considered the act that finally freed the slaves in the United States. It did not do so; that was done by the Thirteenth Amendment to the Constitution. The Emancipation Proclamation is "a fit and necessary war measure for suppressing rebellion" and applies only to the seceded states that are not under the control of the United States armies. It makes specific exception of areas so controlled, and makes no mention of the Border States, where citizens loyal to the United States still held slaves.

The Emancipation Proclamation proclaims free all persons held as slaves in the seceded states of the Confederacy, excepting certain parishes in Louisiana and the city of New Orleans, West Virginia, and specified counties of Virginia. It asks the people who are declared free to abstain from violence except in self-defense and to work faithfully for reasonable wages, and declares that they will be accepted in the armed service of the United States. The President characterized the act as "sincerely believed to be an act of justice, warranted by the Constitution upon military necessity."

Major General Carl Schurz, who marched through the South with Sherman, wrote in his *Reminiscences*:

One of the most remarkable features of the history of those times is the fact that most of the slaves stayed on the plantations or farms and did the accustomed work with quiet and, in the case of house servants, not seldom even with affectionate fidelity, while in their hearts they yearned for freedom and prayed for its speedy coming. Only as our armies penetrated the South, and especially when Negroes were enlisted as soldiers, did they leave their former masters in large numbers, and even then there was scarcely any instance of violent revenge on their part for any wrong or cruelty any of them may have suffered in slavery.

The Thirteenth Amendment

The Thirteenth Amendment to the Constitution of the United States was first proposed as a resolution in Congress and passed by the Senate, April 8, 1864, by a vote of 38 to 6. It failed to receive a two-thirds vote in the House and was called up for reconsideration there on January 6, 1865. It was passed January 31, 1865, by a vote of 119 to 56. Every Republican member of the House voted for it; ten Democrats supported it and eight were absent. Delegates from the seven territories, who did not have the right to vote, were given leave to have their approval entered in the minutes.

The adoption of the amendment created great enthusiasm in the halls of Congress and was announced to Washington by a salute from cannon outside the Capitol. It had been ratified by thirty-three of the thirty-six states of the Union when the Secretary of State proclaimed it in effect, December 18, 1865. It reads:

Neither slavery nor involuntary servitude, except as a punishment for crime whereof the party shall have been duly convicted, shall exist within the United States, or any place subject to their jurisdiction.

Congress shall have power, by appropriate legislation, to enforce the provisions of this article.

The second clause removes from the states the power to legislate on slavery. Numerous states had previously abolished slavery within their borders.

State Action Against Slavery

Maryland voters adopted a new state constitution on October 12, 1864, which provided for immediate and unconditional emancipation. On the evening of October 19 a group of loyal Maryland men living in the District of Columbia serenaded the President. He congratulated them on the results of the vote and referred to reports that if defeated in the forthcoming election he would attempt to "ruin the government." He assured them that he was struggling to maintain the government, not to overthrow it, and to prevent others from overthrowing it; if not elected he would do his utmost "that whoever is to take the helm for the next voyage shall start with the best possible chance to save the ship."

The strongly pro-Union areas of western Virginia were powerful enough to detach themselves from the secessionist state government. A conference of leaders met in Wheeling June 11-25, 1862, organized a state government, and elected Francis H. Pierpont provisional governor. Thus West Virginia applied for statehood and on December 10, 1862, Congress passed a bill admitting it to the Union as the thirty-fifth state, which President Lincoln signed into law on December 31, 1862. The President said the action was expedient because it made slave soil free and extended the national authority; if it could be called secession [from the state of Virginia], it was secession in favor of the Constitution.

19

BURNSIDE AND THE BATTLE OF FREDERICKSBURG

Major General Ambrose E. Burnside took command of the Army of the Potomac at Warrenton, Virginia, November 7, 1862. General Lee was at Culpeper and his comment, quoted by General Longstreet, was that he regretted parting with McClellan, for "we always understood each other so well. I fear they may continue to make changes till they find someone whom I don't understand."

General Burnside did not seek command of the Army of the Potomac and was reluctant to accept it. He told some of his officers that he was unfit for the command, which did not lead them to have confidence in him. He was a West Point man (1847) and thirty-eight years old when appointed to the top command of the Army of the Potomac. In 1853 he had left the army in order to manufacture a breechloading rifle of his own invention. When President Lincoln made his first call for troops in April, 1861, Burnside was among the first to volunteer and because of his experience he was made colonel of a Rhode Island volunteer regiment. Before Fredericksburg he fought at Bull Run and Roanoke. A strict disciplinarian, he was not easy to get along with. His individualism extended to his attire and appearance. He wore his own choice of military hat—a black felt with a round dome and a brim turned down all around, like an old-fashioned policeman's helmet, but what especially distinguished his features were the mutton-chop whiskers that since have been called burnsides. There were some remarkable beards among generals in the Civil War but Burnside is the only man who involuntarily named one.

General Burnside had completely changed the organization of McClellan's army. He had divided it into what he termed "grand divisions." The Right Grand Division, under Major General Edwin V. Sumner, had the Second Army Corps, with divisions headed by Brigadier Generals

Hancock, Howard, and French; the Ninth Army Corps of Brigadier General Orlando B. Willcox, with divisions commanded by Brigadier Generals Burns, Sturgis, and Getty, and Pleasonton's cavalry division. The Center Grand Division, under Major General Joseph Hooker, had the Third Army Corps of Brigadier General George Stoneman, with divisions commanded by Brigadier Generals Birney, Sickles, and Whipple; the Fifth Army Corps of Brigadier General Daniel Butterfield, with divisions commanded by Brigadier Generals Griffin, Sykes, and Humphreys, and William M. Averell's cavalry. The Left Grand Division, under Major General William B. French, had the First Army Corps of Major General John F. Reynolds and divisions commanded by Brigadier Generals Abner Doubleday and John Gibbon and Major General Meade; the Sixth Army Corps of Major General William F. Smith, with divisions under Brigadier Generals Brooks, Pratt, and Newton, and the cavalry division of Brigadier General George D. Bayard, who was killed at Fredericksburg and succeeded by Colonel David M. Gregg.

When General Burnside started the Army of the Potomac toward Fredericksburg the Confederate forces extended from Culpeper Court House to Winchester. The First Corps was commanded by Lieutenant General Longstreet, the Second by General Thomas J. Jackson. Jackson had one division at Chester Gap, the rest of his troops at Winchester. The Confederates were not certain of Burnside's destination but had an outpost of infantry, cavalry, and a battery in Fredericksburg under Colonel Ball and on November 15 sent a regiment of infantry and another battery to reinforce it. Generals Lee and Jackson were not satisfied with having to oppose the Federals at Fredericksburg; Lee had hopes of occupying a better position at the North Anna.

Burnside's Right Grand Division under Major General E. V. Sumner reached Falmouth, opposite Fredericksburg, November 17, and Lee had most of his troops moving to heights beyond the town by November 19. On November 21 General Sumner addressed a demand for the surrender of Fredericksburg to the mayor and common council, declaring that its houses were being used for shooting at his troops and its factories and railroads were supplying the enemy. If the place were not given up by 5

P.M. he would allot sixteen hours for the removal of women, children, and disabled, after which he would shell it.

M. Slaughter, the mayor, showed considerable courage. With the consent of the Federal officer who delivered the ultimatum he consulted the Confederates, who assured him that they would not infringe on the town provided it were not occupied by the Federals. In a spirited reply the mayor told Sumner that troops would not be fired on from the town, nor would it furnish provisions or goods for the Confederate troops. Under these conditions Sumner agreed to respect the town. Some of the townspeople became panicky and tried to get out with a few possessions, and one train was thrown into confusion when a few shells were sent toward it by mistake but did no material damage.

Burnside's army made camp on Stafford Heights and beyond, remaining on the northern bank of the Rappahannock. The Confederate army occupied the heights to the south of Fredericksburg, all strongly wooded. Taylor's Hill was nearest the river and was occupied by Major General Richard H. Anderson's division. Just south of it was Marye's Hill, the focal point of the battle, occupied by Brigadier General Robert Ransom and North Carolina regiments and by units of Major General Lafayette McLaws' division, both of Longstreet's corps. This hill was well fortified with rifle pits and batteries, including the Washington Artillery. Beyond Marye's Hill came Telegraph Hill, Brigadier General George T. Anderson's Georgia regiments of Major General George E. Pickett's division; this is now known as Willis' Hill and is the site of the National Cemetery. Beyond it is a taller height known as Lee's Hill because it was used by General Lee for observation. It extends to Deep Run, a creek, around which were placed units of Major General John B. Hood's division. Some distance beyond Hood, General Jackson had 30,000 troops centered at Hamilton's Crossing, and on the hill above them were Major General A. P. Hill, Brigadier General Jubal A. Early, and Brigadier General William B. Taliaferro.

The picket lines toward Fredericksburg were manned by men of Brigadier General William Barksdale's Mississippi regiments, and when the Union engineers began constructing pontoons Barksdale's sharpshooters moved into Fredericksburg and began to fire on the opposite bank. Thus the hope of the people of Fredericksburg to remain outside military action was dashed after Federals and Confederates had agreed to shun it.

Twenty days ensued before the great Federal attack developed; during that time the Confederates had full opportunity to build emplacements for their guns and provide protective cover and locate reserve artillery at best available posts. They had 306 guns including two 30-pound Parrotts. The Federals had 325 to 329 guns under the general command of Brigadier General Henry J. Hunt. The Confederates made good use of their time; Lee caused the railroad from Fredericksburg to Hamilton's Crossing to be torn up; he sent D. H. Hill down the Rappahannock to Port Royal to deter Federal gunboats from proceeding farther; he placed General Early at Snicker's Neck, a possible crossing, and he had General Jackson make his base at Guiney's Station. Thus the watchful Confederate line extended for about twenty miles, ready to concentrate at any point chosen by General Burnside for a movement toward Richmond.

This, one of the most costly and sanguinary battles of the war, was distinguished by a succession of frontal attacks ordered by General Burnside against the wholly prepared and strongly entrenched Confederates. To reach the Confederate positions the Union troops had to cross an open area within easy range of the hostile batteries on the heights. Marye's hill, the objective of the movement, was slightly lower than the hills adjoining. On its crest stood the Marye mansion, a brick building in the southern Federal style, having a central section with a porch and four white pillars, and two one-story wings, making it a landmark visible from the town. At the base of the hill ran an old road somewhat sunken below the stone walls that had been erected on both sides; the wall toward the plain was about three to four feet high and with the deepening of the ditch behind it provided complete protection for troops. At the north end the sunken road led to the Plank Road that extended west from Hanover Street of Fredericksburg. At the south end it met the Telegraph Road.

By December 10 the preparations of the Union Army for an attack were in full swing and carefully watched by the Confederates on the hills. At 3 A.M. on December 11 two signal guns were fired by the Washington Artillery; the Confederate troops moved to the positions assigned them and teams were harnessed for use of the reserve artillery. A mist covered the river and hid the Federals from view of Barksdale's sharpshooters in Fredericksburg, but they recognized the noise associated with building pontoons and as soon as they could distinguish figures on the opposite bank they opened fire. The bridge builders stopped; when they resumed the sharpshooters were again on the job. The Federals withdrew their men, the firing stopped, and again they resumed work, with similar results.

After the third attempt the Federals concentrated their artillery on the town and subjected it to a concentration of shells that sent walls crumbling and started fires. This did not completely dislodge the sharpshooters, so the Federals tried a new tactic. They filled the pontoons with infantry and rushed them across the river, which was about 400 yards wide, expecting by force of numbers to hold the opposite bank even with the certainty that some of their men would be killed before reaching it. This succeeded, but as the Federal infantry began to pour into the streets its progress was hotly contested by the retreating Mississippians, who had built barriers and made such good use of all available cover that the colonel of the Seventh Michigan Regiment reported ninety-seven casualties within fifty yards.

The next day the Federal army moved its Right Grand Division into the town and Burnside sent General Franklin's Left Grand Division across the river over pontoons laid near the point where Deep Run enters the Rappahannock, one and a half miles below Fredericksburg. The Sixth Corps actually had crossed these bridges late on the afternoon of December 11, but all but one brigade had been pulled back because the bridges at the town were not fully completed for Sumner's crossing. On the morning of December 12 the Sixth Corps was ordered to resume crossing and marched about a mile with its right across Deep Run and the Confederates on the hills half a mile away. It was followed by the cavalry brigade under Brigadier General George D. Bayard and the First Corps under Major General John F. Reynolds.

There were approximately 40,000 men in Franklin's Grand Division. Stretched southeast beyond Deep Run were the divisions of Generals Meade, Gibbon, and Doubleday, facing the hills where Taliaferro and Early were stationed. J. E. B. Stuart's horse artillery and D. H. Hill's troops were located on the low ground beyond Doubleday's position. Two divisions from General Hooker's Center Grand Division, the First of the Third Army Corps under Brigadier General David B. Birney, and the Second under Brigadier General Daniel E. Sickles, had been added to Franklin's command.

The battle at this point opened on December 13, at 10 A.M. when Meade's troops advanced under the cover of strong artillery fire. There followed a hard-fought contest in which Meade broke A. P. Hill's line, but was forced back by Early's division. Gibbon and Doubleday also came into the fight, in the course of which Brigadier General Maxcy Gregg of Hill's division was mortally wounded. Hill's division alone had 2,122 casualties, of whom 231 were killed. After several hours of fighting, the Federals were back to their reserve line and the battle died down as the huge Federal attack in front of the Confederate left and center got under way. Meade had lost about 40 per cent of his effectives, and General Bayard was one of those killed.

Lee and Longstreet, standing on the high ground now called Lee's Hill, were watching the onrush of the Federals near Deep Run against the brigades of Lane, Archer, and Pender, massed in the woods, and their rebuff by the North Carolinians, who pursued the bluecoats into the open. Lee turned to Longstreet and remarked: "It is well that war is so terrible—we should grow too fond of it."

An incident of this day's fighting near Hamilton's Crossing became famous in the annals of the war. It was an act of individual enterprise and courage performed by a young Alabaman, Major John Pelham of Stuart's horse artillery, which had been placed to the right of D. H. Hill's division and at the extreme right of the Confederate position, overlooking the fields where Meade and Doubleday lined up their troops to attack the Confederates this side of Deep Run. Young Pelham was both a social lion and an impetuous fighter, always in the lead, eager for battle. On this occasion he was again beforehand. The Confederates had orders to hold their fire and their guns had not yet opened, when Pelham dashed forward with one napoleon and one Blakely, and began firing solid shot into the ranks of the Federal infantry. As this was coming at their flank it created a great deal of confusion in the ranks; also one of his shots struck a caisson and blew it up. As a result the Federal guns were turned on his position and the Blakely was quickly disposed of, but the napoleon, a captured piece from Virginia, kept firing at a rapid rate for an hour. Five Federal batteries turned their guns on Pelham and eventually he was ordered to stop firing and was put in charge of another battery.

Generals Lee and Jackson had observed Pelham's private war, and although Lee remarked that "the young general," meaning Stuart, had started his fire too soon, he praised the major and called him "the gallant Pelham," a name by which Pelham became known throughout the army. Stonewall Jackson is supposed to have said to Stuart the day after the battle: "Have you another Pelham, General? If so, I wish you would give him to me."

Assaults on the Stone Wall

Never was the barrier of stones raised for peaceful uses so valuable to men needing protection for their bodies in warfare as the wall that ran alongside the road at the base of Marye's Hill. The stone bulwark, with the road behind it deepened and earth thrown over the front, was an ideal fortification. Behind it Lee placed Brigadier General Thomas R. R. Cobb's brigade, comprising three Georgia regiments and the Phillips Legion. At the start about 2,500 men stood behind this wall and an extension of it that had been hastily thrown up for about 100 yards at the right. At this end were placed units of the brigades of Generals Kershaw and Barksdale. Late in the afternoon, when the sixth major assault was being made against the stone wall, there stood behind it three brigades and one regiment of Ransom's brigade. The ranks were three and four deep, with those in the rear loading and passing the guns to those in front, providing almost continuous fire.

The night of the 12th, when thousands of Union and Confederate troops rested on the ground, was both damp and cold, with a biting wind numbing the soldiers of both sides impartially.

Major General Couch commanded the Federal advance of Sumner's Right Grand Division in the field, on orders of Sumner, who did not cross the Rappahannock during the battle. Orders were to seize the heights in the rear of Fredericksburg by pushing in the direction of the Plank and Telegraph Roads. General French's division led in three brigade lines about 200 yards apart, followed by General Hancock's division. At eleven o'clock the brigades moved out of the town by Hanover Street and another parallel to it toward Marye's Hill. The troops were temporarily halted by the small canal that runs into Fredericksburg, where a bridge was partly destroyed. A small cluster of houses and a large square brick house, about 150 yards from the stone wall in front of Marye's Hill, were about the only cover that the men could use.

The full account of the six desperate assaults delivered against the stone wall at the foot of Marye's Hill is one of the most heroic in the annals of American warfare, as it is also a demonstration of the most misguided action. Dashing forward in full view of the Confederate batteries, the blue-clad troops rushed forward with hardly a sound. The Confederate guns opened upon them and men dropped right and left from shellfire and musketry. As one attack succeeded another, the men in the following lines moved past hundreds of their fallen comrades, tried desperately to reach the wall and either fell in their tracks or ran wildly to get out of the deadly hail. The first lines broke for the old railroad cut just beyond the Telegraph Road, but the Confederate guns had the range and the result was terrible. As one artillery officer said, a chicken would not have been able to live on that field.

The brigades of Kimball, Andrews, and Palmer of French's division were the first to charge, and some of

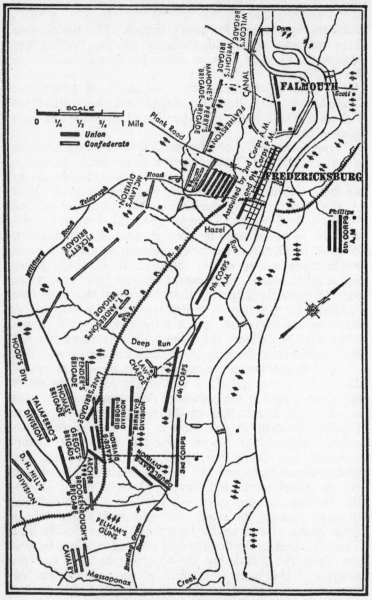

The Battle of Fredericksburg
December 13, 1862

Kimball's men reached a small group of houses near a fork in the Telegraph Road about 150 yards from the stone wall. General Couch was carrying out Burnside's wishes when he sent orders to Generals French and Hancock to storm the Confederate position. "Then I climbed the steeple of the Court House," he wrote later, "and got a clear view of the field. Howard, who was with me, says I exclaimed: 'Oh, great God! See how our poor men, our poor fellows, are falling!' I never had seen fighting like that, nothing approaching it in terrible uproar and destruction." Couch ordered Howard to attack the defenders of the stone wall in the flank. When Hancock and French called for support Howard sent in two of his brigades. After 2 P.M. Sumner, safe on the far side of the Rappahannock, ordered Hooker "to put in everything." The word was that the Confederate position must be taken, no matter how strongly fortified. Hooker was cautious; he consulted Couch and Hancock, and from them learned the desperate character of the onslaught. The plain was already filled with prostrate dead and wounded. Burnside should know about that, so Hooker rode two miles to Burnside's headquarters to tell him "it was no use to try to carry that line." But Burnside was obdurate. Couch, thinking a movement among the Confederates forecasted a withdrawal, told Hooker: "Now is the time to go in!" Hooker sent his two brigades over the ground already covered with the fallen, and added to the heaps of dead.

The Confederates had mastery over the field. They could withhold their fire when an attack began, and then sweep the area with musketry and canister. They had losses, too, but far fewer than the Federals. Brigadier General Thomas Cobb was mortally wounded and died close by; his command was taken over immediately by Brigadier General Joseph B. Kershaw. At the foot of the stone wall stood the little brick house of Mrs. Martha Stevens; in it she worked frantically to provide bandages for the wounded, tearing up her garments for this purpose; she survived the battle twenty years and her house became a shrine for visiting Confederate veterans.

Brigadier General Samuel D. Sturgis' division of the Ninth U.S. Army Corps made the second major assault, during which General Lee thought his line would be broken. But it held. The Federals came within 100 feet of the stone wall before they fell back. The fifth large assault was led by Brigadier General Charles Griffin's division. During these strong assaults there would be smaller ones by units in various parts of the line, so that actually the defenders were kept busy loading and firing.

The sixth and final major assault was made by Brigadier General Andrew A. Humphreys. General Burnside had given specific orders that the Confederate position must be carried before nightfall. To this end Humphreys made the last desperate effort. As his ranks marched to the field, soldiers who had survived earlier attacks tried to deter them from going in. But the ranks obeyed orders until they came close to the stone wall. This time "the stone wall was a sheet of flame that enveloped the head and flanks of the column." Officers and men in the van went down. Humphreys said: "It lasted about a minute, when, in spite of all our efforts, the column turned and began to retire slowly. I attempted to rally the brigade behind the natural embankment . . . but the united efforts of General Tyler, myself, our staff and other officers could not arrest the retiring mass."

The attacks ceased; the guns stopped firing; night fell on that bloody field. The fine-disciplined Federal army lay broken; its young men had been sent against sure death. Well could Couch exclaim: "It is only murder now," and yet go on giving orders to attack, because a commanding officer's word is law, above the dictates of humanity. Safe at his headquarters Burnside exclaimed: "Oh those men. Those men over there. I am thinking of them all the time." Yet at that moment he was planning to resume similar thrusts next day. But his corps and division commanders were satiated. Willcox, Humphreys, Getty, Butterfield, Meade could see that another attack would end as did the first. Colonel Rush C. Hawkins, who said later that he had told Burnside the night before the battle that "it will be the greatest slaughter of the war," was asked to become the spokesman in a protest against renewing the attack. He went to Burnside's headquarters in the Phillips house, where Generals Sumner, Hooker, Franklin, Hardee, and Colonel J. H. Taylor, assistant adjutant general of Sumner's division, were assembled. When Burnside announced that he would attack the next day there was silence, and then Colonel Hawkins was asked by Sumner to speak. He reported the comment of the divisional commanders; Sumner and Hooker backed it up. As a result Burnside countermanded his order for the attack. But he took his revenge later by filing complaints against his officers.

Major W. Roy Mason of the Confederate army, who acted as Lee's emissary in granting Burnside's request for a truce to bury the dead and remove the wounded, described the battlefield the day after the battle (in *Battles and Leaders of the Civil War, Vol. III*):

That day I witnessed with pain the burial of many thousands of Federal dead that had fallen at Fredericksburg. The night before the thermometer must have fallen to zero, and the bodies of the slain had frozen to the ground. The ground was frozen nearly a foot deep, and it was necessary to use pickaxes. Trenches were dug on the battlefield and the dead collected and laid in line for burial. It was a sad sight to see these brave soldiers thrown into the trenches, without even a blanket or a word of prayer, and the heavy clods thrown upon them; but the most sickening sight of all was when they threw the dead, some 400 or 500 in all, into Wallace's empty ice house, where they were found, a hecatomb of skeletons, after the war. In 1865–66 some shrewd Yankee contractors obtained government sanction to disinter all the Federal dead on the battlefields of Fredericksburg, Chancellorsville, the Wilderness, and Spotsylvania Court House. They were to be paid per capita. When I went out to see the skeletons taken from the ice house, I found the contractor provided with unpainted boxes of common pine about six feet long and twelve inches wide; but I soon saw that this scoundrel was dividing the remains so as to make as much by his contract as possible.

It was said that the day of the battle the field in front of the Confederate entrenchments was blue; the next day it was white. The Confederates during the night had helped themselves to the better clothing of the dead Union soldiers.

The numbers engaged at Fredericksburg vary. Burnside's report before the battle had 116,683 available; the

number actually available on December 13 has been
placed at 113,000. Livermore has 113,987 engaged and
106,007 effectives. The Union losses were: 1,284 killed,
9,600 wounded, 1,769 missing; a total of 12,653 casualties.

The Confederate Army had 78,513 troops available;
Livermore estimated 72,497 engaged. Losses were 595
killed, 4,074 wounded, 653 missing; a total of 5,322
casualties. General Longstreet declared about 50,000 Federals and fewer than 20,000 Confederates actually fought
the battle.

Burnside wished to make another attempt to defeat
Lee. He put his plan before President Lincoln, but the
President ordered him to desist. But he was insistent, and
again argued for it, this time without any frontal attack
on Marye's Hill. Lincoln gave a qualified assent. But now
nature became the ally of the men. After weeks of preparation Burnside ordered the army on January 20, 1863,
to march up the north bank of the Rappahannock for
Bank's Ford, where he intended to cross and attack Lee's
left. Again heavy rains began on the eve of the march;
the men and teams started only to find the roads so mired
that passage was impossible. Wagons sank up to the wagon boxes, horses had to be cut loose and in numerous
cases were so deep in the mud that they could not be
saved and had to be shot. This became known as the
Mud March. For a day and a half the troops struggled,
most of the time trying to get back to the camps they
had just left.

Burnside had a long list of grievances that he put before President Lincoln. He told him that Secretary Stanton
and General Halleck ought to be removed from their
offices because they did not have the confidence of the
military. He expressed the opinion that he himself should
retire to private life and tendered his resignation. President Lincoln did not accept it; he did not see how he
could profit by changing the command of the army at that
time.

General Burnside's wrath at officers he considered disloyal to him and remiss in their duties led him to draw
up General Order No. 8, on January 23, 1863, recommending their dismissal or relief "subject to the approval
of the President." His principal anger was directed at

Hooker, whom he accused of criticizing his superiors, creating distrust, giving incorrect impressions, and being unfit to hold an important commission when "patience, charity, confidence, consideration and patriotism" were due from every soldier. He wanted Hooker dismissed. He also asked dismissal of Brigadier General W. T. H. Brooks and Brigadier General John Newton. He asked the relief from duty with his army of Major Generals W. B. Franklin and W. F. Smith, Brigadier Generals Samuel D. Sturgis, Edward Ferrero, and John Cochrane, and Lieutenant Colonel J. H. Taylor.

The President did not act on Burnside's order. Instead, he removed Burnside from the top command three days later and gave it to the chief target of Burnside's attack, Joseph Hooker, now become major general of volunteers. In March, Burnside was placed in command of the Department of the Ohio, and subsequently again served in the field.

Walt Whitman at Fredericksburg

A week after the terrible repulse of the Army of the Potomac at Fredericksburg, Walt Whitman began his visit to camp hospitals at Falmouth. He was already the most dynamic poet in America, but this was known to few outside himself. He had edited the Brooklyn *Eagle* and the Brooklyn *Times* and written for various periodicals, and in 1855 he had published *Leaves of Grass* and won a hearing in a small circle dominated by Emerson, Thoreau, and Bronson Alcott, who recognized him as an innovator but were puzzled by his personality. In December of 1862 he had gone to the front to find his brother, a Union officer, and had remained in Washington as a volunteer nurse, talking with the wounded and writing letters for them. In the period when Henry Wadsworth Longfellow was the dominant American poet and Tennyson the leading English poet, few had heard of Walt Whitman, nor did anyone realize what a challenge to literary creation his work would have to new generations in decades to come.

Walt was facile with the pencil; he took notes and transcribed easily. He found the worst cases of the wounded in a large brick mansion on the banks of the Rappahannock, used as a hospital. He wrote in *Specimen Days*: "Outdoors, at the foot of a tree, within ten yards of the front of the house, I notice a heap of amputated feet, legs, arms, hands, etc., a full load for a one-horse cart." He observed the cases in camp, brigade and division hospitals.

These are merely tents, and sometimes very poor ones, the wounded lying on the ground, lucky if their blankets are spread on layers of pine or hemlock twigs, or small leaves. No cots, not even a mattress. It is pretty cold. The ground is frozen hard and there is occasional snow. I do not see that I can do much good to these wounded and dying; but I cannot leave them. Once in a while some youngster holds on to me convulsively, and I do what I can for him; at any rate stop with him and sit with him for hours, if he wishes it.

Cavalry at Kelly's Ford

Fitzhugh Lee's Brigade was keeping a close watch on the Federals on the upper Rappahannock during February of 1863. On February 24 Lee crossed the river at Kelly's Ford with 400 cavalry to reconnoiter on the Falmouth Road. At Hartwood Church the Confederates met a troop of Federal cavalry and drove them toward the camp of the Fifth U.S. Army Corps, taking 150 prisoners with their horses at a cost of 14 men killed and wounded.

The Federals resented these audacious forays and planned a raid in force to stop them. Brigadier General W. W. Averell received orders on March 16 "to attack and rout or destroy" Fitzhugh Lee's brigade at its base, Culpeper. Leaving 900 men to guard his rear at Morrisville, Averell moved to Kelly's Ford with 2,100 and a battery of guns. The Confederates had posted pickets at the ford and Averell had to cross in the face of a hot fire, but the First Rhode Island Cavalry accomplished this and captured 25 of Stuart's dismounted troopers, losing one officer and two privates. Stuart, re-forming his men on Kelly's Ford Road, ordered the Third Virginia Cavalry to charge the Federals. The latter had taken positions behind stone fences and the Virginians charged with pistols and drawn sabers.

Dashing madly ahead of them was Major John Pelham, the "gallant Pelham" praised by General Lee for his work with the guns at Deep Run, Fredericksburg. He had won the hearts of officers and men by his impetuosity, his cheerfulness, and his reckless courage. Once again Pelham was in perfect form, rising up in his stirrups with his sword held high, shouting "Forward!" A shell exploded near him and a fragment hit the base of his skull; he fell on his back and lay motionless. A trooper, assuming he was dead, lifted him on his horse and rode back to Culpeper. But the lad's heart was still beating and he was taken to a house in Culpeper, where he died at 1 P.M. The brigade held off the Federals and the latter withdrew, but the Confederates had the larger losses, and above all they mourned for Pelham. Jeb Stuart wept; "our loss is irreparable," said he. Surrounded daily by the phenomena of sudden death, he nevertheless ordered observance of thirty days of mourning by the horse artillery, whose tasks Pelham had performed with such earnestness. Pelham's body was taken to Richmond to lie in state in the capitol; then it was taken to his home in Alabama.

20

CHANCELLORSVILLE

General Hooker Takes Command

They called the new commanding general Fighting Joe Hooker. He had won the name at Williamsburg, and whether or not he deserved it more than other men, the public liked it. He was West Point, class of 1837; had been an officer during the Mexican War with brevet rank of lieutenant colonel. On May 17, 1861, he was commissioned brigadier general of volunteers, and on May 5, 1862, major general. He had commanded in all the major

actions in the East, and before the scroll of the Civil War
was finally rolled up he would have put a lot of his fin-
gerprints on it.

Carl Schurz recalled him as a strikingly handsome man.
He was tall and erect, and sat well on his horse, and
among so many generals who cultivated hair on the face
he was unique in being smooth-shaven. Lincoln had inquired about him of his cabinet, and the secretaries had
held differing opinions. It was reported that he was in-
temperate, and Secretary Welles, who approved of Hooker,
said that if this were the case he was not fit to command
an army. Lincoln appointed him to succeed Burnside
without conferring with his advisors; then, in an extraor-
dinarily frank letter, he put some of the strictures to him,
and told what he expected of him. It was a desperate moment in United States history and Lincoln was worn
down with exasperation at the generals he had appointed to win the war.

President Lincoln wrote Hooker on January 28:

I have placed you at the head of the Army of the Potomac.
Of course I have done this upon what appears to me to be
sufficient reasons, and yet I think it best for you to know
that there are some things in regard to which I am not quite
satisfied with you. I believe you to be a brave and skillful
soldier, which, of course, I like. I also believe you do not mix
politics with your profession, in which you are right. You
have confidence in yourself, which is valuable, if not an
indispensable quality. You are ambitious, which, within
reasonable bounds, does good rather than harm; but I think
that during General Burnside's command of the army you have
taken counsel of your ambition and thwarted him as much
as you could, in which you did a great wrong to the country
and to a most meritorious and honorable brother officer.

I have heard, in such a way as to believe it, of your
saying recently that both the army and the Government
needed a dictator. Of course it was not for this, but in spite
of it, that I have given you the command. Only those
generals who gain successes can set up dictators. What I now
ask of you is military success, and I will risk the dictator-
ship. The Government will support you to the utmost of its
ability, which is neither more nor less than it has done
and will do for all commanders. I much fear that the spirit
which you have aided to infuse into the army, of criticising

their commander and withholding confidence from him, will now turn upon you. I shall assist you as far as I can to put it down. Neither you nor Napoleon, if he were alive again, could get any good out of an army while such a spirit prevails in it. And now beware of rashness. Beware of rashness, but with energy and sleepless vigilance go forward, and give us victories.

Major General Hooker took over the Army of the Potomac January 25, 1863. Major General Daniel Butterfield became his chief of staff. The Burnside plan of three grand divisions was dropped and the corps were restored as major units. Hooker was an able administrator, and as his reorganization proceeded the troops regained the hopeful spirit they had lost under Burnside. President Lincoln visited Hooker's headquarters the first week in April and in conversing with Hooker and General Couch said: "I want to impress upon you two gentlemen; in your next fight, put in all your men."

But West Point would never have taught an army commander to put in all his men, even if he arrived on the field with overwhelming numbers. An army such as Hooker's did not act as one unit but as a series of segments, in which the fortunes of left, right, and center depended on the dispositions and strength of the enemy. Yet there was reason for President Lincoln's emphatic advice, for he felt that for once a commander had more than enough men to meet the forces of an army that was inferior in numbers and equipment. According to the *Official Records* of April 30, 1863, Hooker had 130,000 troops, of which 111,000 were infantry. Cavalry was placed at 11,000, and was actually near 12,000. According to Brigadier General Henry J. Hunt, chief of artillery, the artillery had over 400 guns (John Bigelow said 412) with 9,543 officers and men and 8,500 horses. The guns were divided into 74 batteries. No such comparable force could be mustered by the Confederates. As near as anyone could count, General Lee had 65,000 troops and 220 guns. If numbers bred confidence, Hooker was justified in declaring that now he would obliterate Lee.

Design for a Battle

During the last week in April, 1863, General Hooker ordered the division commanders of the Army of the Potomac to be ready to march. Never was a word more welcome to fighting men. Since the terrible ordeal at Fredericksburg in December, 1862, the army had rebuilt its shattered units, added new troops and equipment, and raised its morale under the firm discipline of a commander who was an excellent organizer. Major General Darius N. Couch, who did not wholly approve of Hooker's appointment to the top command, wrote after the war: "Under his administration the army assumed wonderful vigor. I have never known men to change from a condition of the lowest depression to that of a healthy fighting state in so short a time."

Hooker did not intend to make Burnside's mistake of ordering a frontal attack with infantry on Lee's fortified positions in order to drive the Confederates out of Fredericksburg. His plan was to leave some units undisturbed in camp on the east bank of the Rappahannock, where the Confederates would be able to observe the Federals going about their routine chores, send a sizable force (actually three corps) down the Rappahannock opposite Hamilton's Crossing to mislead Lee, and send the bulk of his army up the Rappahannock River and, after crossing, place them at the left flank and rear of the Confederate position. The Confederates occupied Marye's Heights, Willis' Hill adjoining, and a large area of hilly country all the way south to Hamilton's Crossing, much of it heavily wooded. Thus Hooker's army, when placed according to plan, would face south toward Lee's army, and would be located on a wide terrain, intermittently cleared and wooded, and would command the Orange Turnpike, which, running west from Fredericksburg to Orange Court House, passed through Lee's position at the east. The Federal troops were to extend along about three miles of this line, and the central point was to be the house called Chancellorsville, the term also including the fields immediately in front and around it, thus giving its name to the battle. At the back of the Union line was the Rappahannock, which could be crossed by fords and pontoons.

Chancellorsville, the house, was a large two-story brick structure with dormers, with a recessed two-story porch in the central portion, standing at the corner of the Turnpike and the Ely's Ford Road. The land toward Fred-

ericksburg was rolling, and to the south it was hilly. There
were clearings at intervals, where farms had been developed, but much of the terrain was covered with a heavy
growth of scrub oak, pine, and underbrush, so tangled
that it impeded passage.

Hooker's plan to move the army across the Rappahannock to the area of Chancellorsville was ready by April
12. On April 13 he sent Major General George Stoneman
up the river to cross and engage Confederate cavalry
and cut Lee's communications with Richmond. But in the
course of two days Stoneman was unable to cross because
the river had been swollen by heavy spring rains, so he
was called back.

Hooker now set April 27 as the date for starting the
movement of the army. To get on the flank of the Confederate position he had to march his troops along the
meandering Rappahannock, which curved northwest by
west beyond Fredericksburg. Chief of its fords were
Bank's Ford, four miles upstream, United States Ford,
and Kelly's Ford, the latter twenty-five miles upstream.
The Rapidan, flowing south of the Rappahannock for
some distance and emptying into it, also was crossed by
fords, of which Ely's Ford was nearest to Chancellorsville
and Germanna Ford was the farthest upstream. Some of
the troops had to cross two rivers.

Beginning April 27, 1863, the following movements
took place:

The Fifth Corps, Major General George G. Meade; the
Eleventh Corps, Major General O. O. Howard, and the
Twelfth Corps, Major General Henry W. Slocum, crossed
the Rappahannock at Kelly's Ford. The Eleventh and
Twelfth then crossed the Rapidan at Germanna Ford and
the Eleventh by April 30 took a position at the extreme
right of Hooker's line, straddling the Orange County
Turnpike.

Two divisions of the Second Corps, those of Major
General W. S. Hancock and Major General William H.
French, crossed at Bank's Ford April 28, and United
States Ford April 29, pushing aside Confederate pickets
and crossing on pontoons to reach Chancellorsville April
30. One division under Brigadier General John Gibbon
remained in camp at Falmouth.

The Third Corps, Major General Daniel E. Sickles, joined the right wing April 30 by way of Kelly's Ford and Ely's Ford.

Two regiments of the cavalry corps under Brigadier General Alfred Pleasonton clashed with riders of Stuart's cavalry at Germanna Ford April 29 and captured fifty of Stuart's pickets.

The First Corps, Major General Reynolds, the Third, Major General Sickles, and the Sixth, Major General Sedgwick, were ordered in the opposite direction, down the north bank of the Rappahannock, to draw Lee's army to Deep Run and Hamilton's Crossing. The three corps moved separately to the battlefield of Chancellorsville and Marye's Heights, as will appear later.

After Hooker had his army across the Rappahannock he issued a boastful order that seemed more like a burst of oratory than a military document. "The operations of the last three days have determined that our enemy must either ingloriously fly or come out from behind his defences and give us battle on our own ground, where certain destruction awaits him," said he.

Hooker had established his headquarters at Chancellorsville, the house, on the morning of May 1. Behind him was French's division of the Second Army Corps; in front were Hancock's division of the Second and units of Slocum's Twelfth. At the right of Slocum stood Sickles' Third, and at the extreme right was Howard's Eleventh. At the extreme left of Hooker's line, nearest Fredericksburg, was Meade's Fifth Army Corps.

Raids by Stoneman's Cavalry

Before Hooker moved the army to Chancellorsville he made plans to send Major General George Stoneman and the cavalry corps behind Lee's lines to cut his communications with Richmond. Stoneman was to destroy commissary stores along the Virginia Central Railroad, supplies at Gordonsville, and raid the heart of the state. Orders went to Stoneman April 12; Hooker cautioned: "Bear in mind that celerity, audacity and resolution are everything in war and especially is it the case with the

command you have and the enterprise upon which you
are about to embark." But the enterprise was slow in
getting started; heavy rains, flooded rivers, muddy roads
interfered, and the Confederates had outposts at a number of fords, watching for any movement.

A certain gentleman in Washington was waiting for the
start of Stoneman's raid with apprehension. On April
15 President Lincoln wrote Hooker of the uneasiness
caused him by the general's report of delays by Stoneman. "The rain and mud, of course, were to be calcu-
lated upon," wrote Lincoln; "General Stoneman is not
moving rapidly enough to make the expedition come to
anything. He has now been out three days, two of which
were unusually fair weather, and all three without hindrance from the enemy, and yet he is not twenty-five
miles from where he started. To reach his point he still
has sixty to do, another river [the Rapidan] to cross,
and will be hindered by the enemy. By arithmetic, how
many days will it take him to do it? I do not know that
any better can be done, but I greatly fear it is another
failure already."

Stoneman did not actually get started until April 28,
and his departure interfered with Hooker's plans for
Chancellorsville. General Hooker detached Brigadier
General Alfred Pleasonton of the First Division of cavalry from Stoneman's command and gave him the horse
artillery; he also kept three regiments of the cavalry corps
near him. Thus Stoneman's command had about 9,000
men out of nearly 12,000 in the corps.

Stoneman crossed the Raccoon ford of the Rapidan
April 29 and moved in two columns along the lines of the
Orange & Alexandria and Richmond & Petersburg railroads, with Brigadier General William W. Averell of
the Second Division leading one of the columns. For several days Stoneman operated in the vicinity of Louisa
Court House. The corps, working in separate units, destroyed rails, bridges, and telegraph wires along the
North Anna, South Anna, Chickahominy, and James, operating in rain and dense fog and penetrating far into
Confederate country.

General Averell's brigade clashed with 2,000 Confederate cavalry under General W. H. F. Lee, drove them

through Culpeper and to within three miles of Orange Court House. On May 2 Averell received an order to return and rejoin the Army of the Potomac at United States Ford, and on May 3 his command joined in defense of the army's right wing. No order reached Stoneman, and after most of his roving units had returned he recrossed the Rapidan and joined Hooker on May 7. Although he had only 4 men killed and 7 wounded, 139 were reported missing.

First Attack on Turnpike

Hooker was poorly informed about the disposition of the Confederate troops because of the numerous bodies of thick woods that were scattered over the terrain. Brigadier General Alfred Pleasonton, commanding the First Division of the cavalry corps, wanted Hooker to send the Eleventh Corps to Spotsylvania Court House and thus make the Federal line run from Chancellorsville to that point, eight miles away. Hooker rejected this, but agreed to send cavalry on a reconnoitering ride to Spotsylvania that night, April 30. General Pleasonton dispatched the Sixth New York Cavalry under Lieutenant Colonel Duncan McVicar. It reached the Court House without incident but on its return was intercepted in the dark by the Fifth Virginia Cavalry with Jeb Stuart and his staff on hand. The Federal cavalry attacked with carbines and sabers and scattered the Confederates, but the Second Virginia Cavalry came to their support and the Federals, being outnumbered, had to withdraw. Colonel McVicar was killed in the action.

Pleasonton previously had obtained evidence from the diary of a Confederate engineer attached to Stuart's cavalry that Stuart, A. P. Hill, Jackson, and Ewell had decided at a meeting that Chancellorsville was the next Federal objective. He also had intercepted a courier with a message from Lee to General McLaws showing that Lee had been surprised by Hooker's movement but now was on the alert. At this time, on April 30, Pleasonton was convinced Hooker had "ninety chances in his favor to ten against him."

The Orange Turnpike ran in nearly a straight line from

Fredericksburg through the whole Chancellorsville field. The right wing of the army was ready to advance up the turnpike toward Fredericksburg early on the morning of May 1, but Hooker did not give the order until the day was well advanced. Then General Meade's Fifth Army Corps was ordered to march to the left on the turnpike and the Bank's Ford road. The leading division was commanded by Major General George Sykes. When he had moved several miles east toward the Tabernacle Church he met with determined resistance from Confederate units that engaged both his troops and General Slocum's. Opposing them were Confederates from the divisions of Major General McLaws and Major General Richard H. Anderson. The Federals drew back to high ground better suited to defense and to action by their batteries.

The firing was heard clearly at Chancellorsville and at once made Hooker apprehensive. He ordered Major General Darius N. Couch to take Hancock's First Division of his Second Corps to the support of Sykes. After these troops had arrived there and the Federals were in good position to hold their own and possibly advance, General Couch received an order from Hooker to withdraw the divisions and return to Chancellorsville.

Couch and the other commanding generals were amazed and agreed the order must be an error. They hurried a message to this effect to Hooker and in reply received a reiteration of the order. General Warren advised Couch to disobey it. He himself rode back to argue with Hooker.

General Slocum also had been ordered in and when he moved back gave the Confederates an advantage against Couch. Sykes and Hancock started to withdraw; when all but two of Hancock's regiments had given up their position Couch received a third order from Hooker: "Hold on until 5 o'clock." Couch in exasperation sent back the reply: "Tell General Hooker he is too late, the enemy are already on my right and rear. I am in full retreat."

As the Confederates moved forward to take advantage of the Federal retreat several of Hancock's regiments took a defensive position at Mott's Run, under Colonel Nelson A. Miles, and others were ordered to entrench.

The positions could be held, but were definitely defensive. Thus the initiative at Chancellorsville was lost the first day by the apprehensions of Hooker. He was worried by lack of knowledge of the size of Confederate forces in the thickets, and by his need to keep the roads to the fords open behind him. To Couch, who protested, Hooker said: "It is all right, Couch, I have got Lee just where I want him; he must fight me on my own ground." But Couch was skeptical and worried.

When the Federals had assumed their defensive position they were quite able to hold their ground against attack. The Confederates soon found out where Hooker's line was strong. When Brigadier General Henry Heth and three divisions of Major General A. P. Hill's division were effectively stopped during one of their testing operations, Lee and Jackson became convinced that a flank attack, rather than an attempt against Hooker's front, might bring better results. At the crossing of the Plank Road with the Catharine Furnace Road, Lee and Jackson dismounted and went into the pine woods to get away from Federal sharpshooters and compare notes.

Much significance has been given this meeting by historians, for it was here that the vital decision to give up a front attack and find a way of hitting Hooker's troops in the flank was worked out. Jackson was convinced something had happened to Hooker and that he was about ready to pull out. Lee was not so certain. The two commanders called on staff members to study the front for evidence of Hooker's strength. Lee sent Major T. M. R. Talcott and Jackson sent Captain James Boswell, both engineers. They returned within an hour with word that Hooker was so strongly placed in front that an attack would be out of the question there.

Then General Stuart arrived with word that Hooker's right flank was "in the air," meaning not properly anchored against attack. It was then that the two commanders agreed that the time had come for a flank attack. Admirers of Stonewall Jackson have contended that the attack on Hooker's right was Jackson's idea, but members of Lee's staff were convinced that it originated with Lee. Douglas Southall Freeman, who weighed all the evidence impartially, came to the conclusion in his biography *R. E. Lee* that Lee originated the attack and, in his usual manner, turned to Jackson to carry out the details.

Jackson would take his whole corps of 28,000 troops for the movement, leaving Lee only 14,000 standing against the Federal front, but so well screened by forests that Hooker did not know precisely how many they were and where. Jackson obtained a guide who knew the back roads in the person of the son of the owner of Catharine Furnace, Colonel Charles C. Wellford. Jackson was ready to start at 4 A.M., which meant brisk marching. Leading were Brigadier General R. E. Rodes and the Alabamans. Next came Brigadier General R. E. Colston, commanding Trimble's division, mostly Virginia and Georgia regiments, followed by Major General A. P. Hill's division. Jackson and his staff and couriers took a place near the front; Jackson's forage cap covered his forehead, and his tall figure was slumped over on Little Sorrel. As the command filed past where Lee sat on his horse, Jackson stopped briefly and they exchanged a few words; it was the last time Lee saw Jackson alive.

At about 3 P.M. on May 2, Jackson sent a hurriedly scrawled note to Lee: "The enemy has made a stand at Chancellor's, which is about 2 miles from Chancellorsville. I hope as soon as practicable to attack. I trust that an ever kind Providence will bless us with great success."

This reference was to Melzi Chancellor's place, also called Dowdall's Tavern, which had become the headquarters of Major General O. O. Howard and center of the Eleventh Corps.

Jackson's Surprise Attack

On the Federal side, the Eleventh Army Corps was based on the old turnpike that runs west from Chancellorsville to Orange Court House. Talley's Farm lay at the extreme end of the Federal position; Hawkins' Farm adjoined it farther east; a short distance from the pike stood a frame church in a grove, and on the pike stood Melzi Chancellor's. Clearings alternated with woods, which obscured a clear view and reduced the positions available for the guns. Strung out along the turnpike in rather close formation, the troops all faced south, as did the whole Federal line.

The First Division, commanded by Brigadier General Charles Devens, Jr., held the pike. The First Brigade, Colonel Leopold von Gilsa, stood west of the clearing surrounded by dense woods. Two of his regiments were placed at right angles to the pike, and two guns stood in the road itself. The Second Brigade, Brigadier General Nathaniel C. McLean, came next, with Dieckmann's New York battery of four guns facing south. Brigadier General Carl Schurz's Third Division covered much of Hawkins' Farm in the region of Dowdall's Tavern. At the clearing near the tavern the Plank Road joined the pike from the southwest at a sharp angle. Here stood Dilger's Ohio battery, facing south. Next came Colonel Adolphus Buschbeck's brigade of the Second Division of Brigadier General Adolphus von Steinwehr and Brigadier General Francis C. Barlow's Second Brigade, with Wiedrich's New York battery. East of this was a piece of dense woods, then came the Third Army Corps under Major General Daniel E. Sickles and the Twelfth Army Corps under Major General Henry W. Slocum.

General Schurz not only saw the hazards of the Eleventh's position but repeatedly warned General Howard of the lack of proper precautions against an attack from the west. He wrote in his official report: "Our right wing stood completely in the air, with nothing to lean upon, and that, too, in a forest thick enough to obstruct any view to the front, flanks or rear, but not thick enough to prevent the approach of the enemy's troops. Our rear was at the mercy of the enemy, who was at perfect liberty to walk around us through the large gap between Col. Gilsa's right and the cavalry force stationed at Ely's Ford." Schurz realized that an attack from the northwest or west could not be resisted without change of front. He saw that some of the regiments were packed so closely together, with only room for stacks of arms and a narrow passage between the long lines, that maneuvering would be extremely difficult.

Stonewall Jackson's corps, proceeding along small dirt roads behind a thick screen of woods, moved a considerable distance undetected by Federal observers, although clashes with Confederate pickets and cavalry made the brigade commanders apprehensive. But there was one small clearing on a ridge a little over a mile from the Federal position where Jackson's troops had to cross in plain view of the Federal field glasses. They were spotted quickly from General Devens' position, and General Howard sent word to Hooker that a column of infantry was moving westward on a ridge one and a half to two miles south of him, and added: "I am taking measures to resist an attack from the West." This message was dated ten to eleven o'clock (about 11 A.M.). According to the *Official Records,* Hooker at 9:30 A.M. had addressed instructions "To Major Generals Slocum and Howard" signed by his aide Brigadier General J. H. Van Alen. The message, not received until noon, reminded the generals that their corps had been placed to receive a front attack by the enemy:

if he should throw himself upon your flank he [Hooker] wished you to examine the ground and determine upon the position you will take in that event, in order that you may be prepared for him in whatever direction he advances. He suggests that you have heavy reserves well in hand to meet this contingency. The right of your line does not appear to be strong enough. No artificial defenses worth naming have been thrown up and there appears to be a scarcity of troops at that point and not, in the general's opinion, as favorably posted as might be. We have good reason to suppose that the enemy is moving to our right. Please advance your pickets for purposes of observation as far as may be safe, in order to obtain timely information of their approach.

General Howard twenty years later declared he never received this message, and that to his knowledge it did not come to the attention of his adjutant general. To this General Schurz replied that he had personally read the message to General Howard about noon, after Howard, desiring to take a nap, had turned headquarters over to Schurz. A second courier brought a repetition of the message. If Schurz had not reported that an animated discussion followed on the porch, historians might have surmised that Howard was half asleep when the message was read to him.

When Howard expressed the view that the Confederates were headed for Gordonsville, Schurz was "amazed at this belief." Schurz ordered Dilger to find battery positions facing west and faced three regiments about behind Gilsa's position. But he could get no orders from Howard covering other divisions. After 3 P.M. new reports arrived that pickets of General Devens' division had spotted Confederates on the right flank. Confident that he had read the portents rightly, Schurz begged Devens to ride with him to Howard to persuade the commanding general to change the front around. But Devens, too, was not alarmed; he told Schurz that headquarters knew best. Then Howard told Schurz that Hooker had ordered him to send Brigadier General Barlow's Second Brigade to support Major General Sickles' foray against Jackson's troops on the Catharine Furnace Road, and that he intended to ride with Barlow.

Although no one could tell exactly where the moving Confederate column was headed, enough reports came in to Hooker to have kept the whole right wing on the alert. The column was spotted from Hazel Grove by observers from Brigadier General David B. Birney's division of Sickles' Third Corps, as a result of which Birney ordered Lieutenant Robert Sims to turn the guns of his Second New Jersey battery on the Catharine Furnace Road. This alerted Sickles, who asked Hooker for orders to attack the Confederates, and received that order an hour or two later. Sickles took two divisions and attacked Jackson's column; this turned out to be the rear guard, which put up such a hard fight that Sickles had to send for reinforcements. Hooker then moved Barlow's brigade to his support. The shift deprived the Eleventh Corps of its strongest brigade, taking 3,000 troops and leaving 9,000 in the corps.

It was about this time that Major General Couch went to Chancellor House and was greeted by Hooker with the exclamation: "Lee is in full retreat toward Gordonsville and I have sent out Sickles to capture his artillery." Yet even then Hooker accepted the possibility of an attack on his right and ordered the First Division of General Slocum's Twelfth Corps, Brigadier General Alpheus S. Williams commanding, to fortify a line against an attack which might come against them from the west.

Lee had reason for apprehension while Stonewall Jackson was moving his thousands over narrow dirt roads around the end of the Union lines. He had split his army and was taking a chance on Stonewall Jackson's enterprise. The night before Lee had carried on a rolling reconnaissance, meaning that skirmishers and guns probed here and there along the Union line to determine positions and strength, for Chancellorsville was being fought amid tall, compact growths of trees and interlaced underbrush. And now he had kept up skirmishing and a continual fire by heavy guns from various positions, keeping the Federals guessing and on edge.

General Fitzhugh Lee had ridden forward with his cavalry scouts and observed General Howard's corps from a distance. His report was that the Federals clearly were not expecting an attack. General Jackson, who always sized a situation up for himself, went back with Lee and also reconnoitered the area. He then placed the Stonewall Brigade under Brigadier General Paxton at the point where the Germanna Road enters Orange Plank Road. He led his column along the Brock Road to the turnpike and turned east toward Chancellorsville. After advancing about one mile he halted to form the lines of attack. Brigadier General Rodes's division was at the front, with Brigadier General George Doles in command and located at the right of the turnpike. At Doles's right was Brigadier General A H. Colquitt's brigade. Brigadier General R. E. Colston, commanding Trimble's division, formed the second line; behind him were the troops of Major General A. P. Hill's Light Division. Stapleton Crutchfield's artillery unlimbered in a field to the right of the turnpike. The order of battle was completed a little after 5 P.M. Stonewall Jackson, on his horse beside Rodes, said: "Are you ready, General Rodes?" "Yes sir," replied Rodes. "You can go forward then," said Jackson.

It reads like a tame performance when put on paper many years after the action, but it must record a tense and exhilarating hour. But it also indicates the calm deliberation that attended preparations for a battle on which Lee and Jackson were staking the welfare of their army. Rodes nodded to Major Henry Blackford and immediately one bugle call sounded the advance; it was repeated by other bugles far afield; the skirmish line sprang forward, and then the long lines moved, some down the open road, others into the dark underbrush. Minutes would be used up before the line would strike the Federal position. The men of the Eleventh Corps were mostly at ease, preparing their meal. Their first warning came not from the general onslaught, but when, in the words of General Howard, "like a cloud of dust driven before a spring shower appeared the startled rabbits, squirrels, quail and other game flying wildly hither and thither in evident terror." Then the gray coats came out of the woods everywhere and with that wild screech known as the rebel yell fell upon the extended lines of General Devens. As men described it later, the Federal units lost cohesion, the defense that should have been ready fell apart, even the low embankments that had been built up were mostly useless because the foe came from the west and the trenches had been dug with an attack from the opposite angle in view. Some troops did jump to the other side of the breastworks and try to stem the gray tide, but they were as isolated individuals. Many of the Federals ran back and collided with others who were still unsuspecting; the Confederates were firing and loading as they advanced. General Steinwehr held his own for about an hour before retiring; Schurz and Howard and many brigade commanders tried to rally the troops, but some kept running all the way to Chancellorsville. It took an hour before the guns at Hazel Grove could be informed, turned about, and used against the attackers, and then their shells had no precise target but fell into the woods where the Confederates were supposed to be. General Howard, making his report to Hooker, mentioned the density of the woods as the principal reason why Jackson managed to get so close to his position, but General Devens said his skirmishers had found cavalry and some guns in front of his First Brigade as early as 4 P.M. Howard also said that the absence of General Barlow's brigade, which had been sent to help Sickles on the Catharine Furnace Road, deprived him of his only reserve for covering his right flank.

On the evening of May 2, when darkness made further

action against the Eleventh Corps hazardous, partly because the wooded terrain made it difficult to distinguish friend from foe, the Confederate attack stopped. The brigades of General Rodes, which had been the first to overrun Howard's position, were now as badly mixed up as the Federals and needed time to reorganize. Jackson authorized Rodes to move back and the third and reserve line commanded by General A. P. Hill to move up front, some units getting so close that they could hear the Federals felling trees and building up embankments just beyond them.

This was the opportunity, historians have contended, for Hooker to rush in troops to be ready to slam back at Jackson's forces with augmented infantry and artillery, and they have pointed out that Jackson's men could not have stood up against such a determined Union assault. But Hooker was now definitely on the defensive, misjudging his foe and concerned with keeping his roads to the fords at his rear open for withdrawal. At this hour, when audacity was so greatly needed by the Federals, fate handed them another undeserved advantage. General Stonewall Jackson, the best strategist of the Confederacy next to Lee, was shot down by his own troops and so dangerously wounded that he was out of the battle from then on, and, as it proved eight days later, out of all fighting forever.

Wounding of Stonewall Jackson

About 9 P.M., when General R. E. Rodes was moving back and General A. P. Hill was moving up, Jackson rode forward on Little Sorrel to make his own reconnaissance, as was his custom. With him were several members of his staff. He rode east on the Orange Plank Road, then followed another smaller road until his group distinctly heard Federal activities in front of them. They were already beyond the Confederate picket line, and Jackson turned around and trotted back to the Plank Road. As they approached the road there was a shot on Jackson's left, then a volley. General A. P. Hill shouted: "Cease firing!" Little Sorrel bolted, ran north into the woods; other horses reared in fright. As the officers tried to control their mounts and yelled out that the soldiers were firing on their own men, someone on the right, where a North Carolina regiment of Pender's brigade had just taken position, yelled: "It's a lie; pour it into them, boys!" and a full volley struck the group. Two men were killed; Captain Boswell of the engineers and Sergeant Cunliffe of the signal corps. Jackson's horse carried him against the branches; his cap was raked off and his head struck. Captain Wilbourn of the signal corps and other officers caught the horse and lifted Jackson down. He had been hit in several places. His left arm hung limp, the upper arm bone had been splintered. A. P. Hill asked: "Is the wound painful?" "Very painful, my arm is broken," replied Jackson. He was also hit in the right hand, and called the wound "a mere trifle." A short time later shells dropped on the road, and Hill was so bruised by a piece of shell that cut off his boottops that he could not walk, and had to turn his division over to General Rodes.

Jackson was in a dangerous spot; at intervals the Federals shelled the road. Jackson's men tried to carry him, then found a litter; as they walked cautiously along the road one of the litter bearers was hit in both arms and dropped his burden; another took off. The staff men and A. P. Hill decided to withhold the news of Jackson's injury from the soldiers. Jackson had said: "Just say it is a Confederate officer." But some penetrated the secret in the dark. General Pender stepped up to the litter and said: "Ah, General, I am sorry to see you have been wounded. The lines here are so much broken that I fear we will have to fall back." Jackson answered: "You must hold your ground, General Pender! You must hold your ground, sir!"

Eventually they picked up an ambulance; there were two wounded officers inside; the lesser-wounded man gave up his place to the general. The other was Colonel Stapleton Crutchfield, artillery chief of the Second Corps. When they reached the house of the Rev. Melzi Chancellor they obtained some whisky, and here came Dr. Hugh McGuire, surgeon of the corps. He gave Jackson morphine for his pain and observed that the general had lost a great deal of blood. He entered the ambulance, and kept a finger on Jackson's artery. The wagon moved slowly over four miles of bumpy road to the field hospital that had just been erected behind the Wilderness Tavern on the Turnpike, arriving there at 11 P.M. The tavern is gone now, but a frame house of the period stands on the opposite side of the road; it was once a dependency of the tavern. General Jackson was put into a special tent and an examination showed that his left arm was shattered and several bones of his right hand had been fractured by a bullet that lay just under the skin. The bullet was removed. After Jackson had been given chloroform his arm was amputated about two inches below the shoulder.

Jackson revived and remained at the field hospital Sunday and Monday, May 3 and 4. On Monday morning a courier arrived from General Lee with the following message:

GENERAL: I have just received your note, informing me that you were wounded. I cannot express my regret at the occurrence. Could I have directed events, I should have chosen for the good of the country to be disabled in your stead. I congratulate you upon the victory, which is due to your skill and energy. Very respectfully, your obedient servant, R. E. LEE, General.

Jackson's comment was: "General Lee is very kind, but he should give the praise to God."

One of Jackson's visitors was the chaplain, the Rev. B. T. Lacy, brother of Major Lacy, whose plantation, Elwood, was nearby. Later Major Lacy retrieved Jackson's amputated arm, placed it in a box and buried it in the family burying ground, where a small stone marks the site today. The historic Lacy house, standing on a wooded knoll within sight of the Turnpike, sheltered officers of the American Revolution as well as of the Civil War, and was used during the battles of Chancellorsville and the Wilderness, when wounded lay in rows on its grounds. Under its roof Light-Horse Harry Lee, father of Robert E. Lee, wrote his *History of the Revolution in the South*, and Lafayette had been there. The Lacys also were the first to place a marker at the spot where Jackson was shot.

Jackson was placed in an ambulance on Monday, May 4, and carried by way of Spotsylvania Court House to

Guinea's Station, usually called Guiney's, on the Richmond, Fredericksburg & Potomac Railroad. He had expressed the wish to stay at the plantation of Thomas Chandler, whom he knew. Adjoining the main house was a small office building with three rooms, one of which became Jackson's bedroom.

After Jackson and A. P. Hill had been wounded and left the front the Confederate lines were still in a state of confusion. New regiments had been moved up as the brigades of General Rodes and Colston, which had become greatly entangled in their attack on the Eleventh Army Corps, went back to reform. Thousands of men were packed together in the thickets where the moonlight failed to penetrate. They could hear movements on the front opposite them and could not determine whether they came from friend or foe. The Federal artillery had the range and swept the Plank road with canister, which emitted flinty sparks as it struck.

Command of Jackson's corps was to devolve on Major General J. E. B. Stuart, but it was nearly midnight before he reached the front line. In the meantime General Rodes had exercised command. General Stuart had attempted to get from Jackson some idea of his plans for the next day, but Jackson, in the hands of his surgeon, Dr. McGuire, had nothing to give him. "Tell General Stuart to act upon his own judgment and do what he thinks best," came the word from the stricken commander; "I have implicit confidence in him." Thus no one knew what dispositions Jackson had intended to make, nor was anyone familiar with the topography ahead.

On May 7 the Rev. B. T. Lacy, Jackson's chaplain, came from Guiney's Station with sober countenance to ask Early's surgeon to go there for consultation with Dr. Hunter McGuire. Lee asked him to speak to Jackson: "Give my affectionate regards and tell him to make haste and get well and come back to me as soon as he can. He has lost his left arm, but I have lost my right." As word of Jackson's delirium reached him, he protested "God will not take him from us, now that we need him so much." That Sunday, May 10, he told Chaplain Lacy: "Tell him that I wrestled in prayer for him last night, as I never prayed, I believe, for myself."

During Jackson's convalescence pleural pneumonia set in and carried him off at 3:15 P.M. on May 10. His last words, spoken in delirium, were: "No, no, let us pass over the river and rest under the shade of the trees." He was buried in Lexington, Virginia. His horse, which survived twenty or more years after the battle, became an object of interest at veterans' reunions and state fairs.

General Jackson has been described numerous times, but no one drew his portrait so well as did John Esten Cooke, the Southern author who became a lieutenant on the staff of General J. E. B. Stuart and later a captain of artillery. In *Wearing of the Gray* he described Jackson as he saw him at Cold Harbor in June, 1862, soon after A. P. Hill had been repulsed and when Cooke was sent by General Stuart

to ascertain if Jackson's corps had gone in and what were his dispositions for battle. A group near a log cabin twenty paces from Old Cold Harbor House, was pointed out to me and going there, I asked for the General. Some one pointed to a figure seated on a log dingy, bending over, and writing on his knees. A faded, yellow cap of the cadet pattern was drawn over his eyes; his fingers, holding a pencil, trembled. His voice, in addressing me, was brief, curt, but not uncourteous; and then, his despatch having been sent, he mounted and rode slowly across the field.

A more curious figure I never saw. He sat his rawboned sorrel—not the "old sorrel" however—like an automaton. Knees drawn up, body leaning forward, the whole figure stiff, angular, unbending. His coat was the dingiest of the dingy; originally gray, it seemed to have brought away some of the dust and dirt of every region in which he had bivouacked. His faded cap was pulled down so low upon the forehead that he was compelled to raise his chin into the air to look from beneath the rim. Under that rim flashed two keen and piercing eyes—dark, with a strange brilliancy, and full of "fight." The nose was prominent, the mustache heavy upon the firm lip, close set beneath: the rough, brown beard did not conceal the heavy fighting jaw. All but the eye was in apparent repose; there was no longer any tremor of anxiety. . . . There was something absent and abstracted in his manner as he rode slowly to and fro, sucking a lemon, and looking keenly at you when he spoke, answering briefly when necessary.

Lieutenant Cooke saw him that midnight in 1862, "when, as I slept in a fence corner, I felt a hand upon my shoulder, and a voice said: 'Where is the General?' It was Jackson, riding about by himself, and he tied his horse, lay down beside General Stuart and began with, 'Well yesterday's was the most terrific fire of musketry I ever heard!' Words of unwonted animation coming from Jackson. . . ."

So often was Jackson cheered by his troops that when his men heard a distant yell they would exclaim: "That's Jackson or a rabbit!"

In a letter written from Fredericksburg, May 21, 1863, Lee expressed to General Hood his grief at the loss of Stonewall Jackson. "I grieve much over the death of General Jackson—for our sakes, not for his. He is happy and at peace. But his spirit lives with us, and I hope it will raise up many Jacksons in our ranks. We must all do more than formerly. We must endeavor to follow the unselfish, devoted, intrepid course he pursued, and we shall be strengthened rather than weakened by his loss."

General Longstreet was not on hand to fight at Chancellorsville. Several weeks before he had been ordered to Petersburg and thence to Suffolk to collect supplies. When Hooker's movement developed, both General Lee and the War Office in Richmond sent Longstreet orders to proceed at once to Chancellorsville. He replied that his troops could not march until his wagons were back. The orders became more urgent and frequent, until Longstreet finally asked whether he was to march and abandon his wagons. Receiving no reply, he waited until the wagons returned, then started back.

Before he reached Richmond en route he received news of the South's "brilliant victory" at Chancellorsville. He considered it Lee's "most brilliant achievement." He rejoined Lee at Fredericksburg and found him in grief over Jackson. Lee told General Hood, who was with Longstreet, that he believed that if he had had his whole army with him Hooker would have been demolished. "But God ordered otherwise."

Cavalry Action at Hazel Grove

When Sickles moved his brigades to attack Jackson's rear guard on the Catharine Furnace Road he created a gap about a mile long from Hazel Grove to the right of the Twelfth Corps. Hazel Grove was a clearing on high ground, and if the Confederates had possessed it they would have cut off Sickles' corps. Brigadier General Alfred Pleasonton had charge of Martin's New York horse artillery and several regiments of Pennsylvania cavalry standing near the Grove. The Eighth Pennsylvania was ordered to report to General Howard, and upon reaching the Plank Road three quarters of a mile away came unexpectedly upon Stonewall Jackson's column, which had just attacked the Eleventh Corps. Drawing sabers, the cavalry regiment dashed at full speed through the column to save itself, surprising the enemy but losing three of its principal officers. At Hazel Grove, Pleasonton collected a formidable battery of twenty-four guns, loaded double canister and aimed so that their shot would strike the ground halfway between the guns and the woods. At dusk Stonewall Jackson's men came on in five to six lines and carrying a Union flag, but the deception was quickly seen and as they charged with the rebel yell Pleasonton's guns fired with terrible effect. A second attempt to charge likewise failed. An aide on Pleasonton's staff said: "The roar was a continuous one and the execution terrific." General Pleasonton reported that "suspecting the Confederates might play the trick of having their men lie down, draw the fire of the artillery, then jump up and charge before the pieces could be reloaded, I poured in the canister for about twenty minutes and the affair was over."

Although the repulse of the Confederates at Hazel Grove saved the Federals from a disaster greater than the one that struck the Eleventh Corps, the grove was occupied on Sunday, May 3, by General J. E. B. Stuart after General Sickles' Third Corps had been pulled back to connect with the Twelfth Corps. Placing thirty guns there, Stuart used the day to shell the Third and the Twelfth Corps.

To mislead Lee, Hooker planned to send a sizable force down the bank of the Rappahannock for several miles to the locality where General Franklin had crossed with his Left Grand Division during the battle of Fredericksburg. Hooker ordered Major General John Sedgwick to move there with his Left Wing, which comprised the First Corps, under Major General John F. Reynolds, the Third Corps under Major General Daniel E. Sickles, and Sedgwick's own Sixth Corps, in all about 55,000 men. The troops began their march about noon of April 28. Sedgwick took a position at what was already alluded to as Franklin's Crossing; Sickles went beyond him and Reynolds' corps was the farthest downstream. Reynolds occupied almost the same place he had occupied before crossing during the December battle.

Pontoons for five bridges were placed that night under the direction of General Henry Benham, but being behind schedule the work had to continue in daylight next morning. Fortunately there was a fog, but this also protected sharpshooters on the south bank, who harassed the engineers. When the fog lifted Reynolds ordered Brigadier General James S. Wadsworth to clean out the rifle pits. Wadsworth called two regiments from the Iron Brigade to cross over in boats that had been brought along. He went with them in a boat and made his horse swim across by holding the bridle. The riflemen, chiefly members of Georgia regiments, were overpowered and some farther down the bank were captured by surprise; about ninety were taken, but at the cost of sixty Union casualties.

When the bridges were completed two divisions were marched across on April 29, one from the First and one from the Sixth Corps. The area on the south side of the Rappahannock was under the immediate command of Major General Jubal A. Early, whose division belonged to Stonewall Jackson's corps. Early moved his division to the front along the line of the railroad, his right near Hamilton's Crossing and his left near Deep Run. He had admitted that the Confederates did not know what Hooker meant to do with his army; when the fog lifted he saw that "the slopes of the opposite hills were semi-covered with troops the whole distance from opposite Fredericksburg to a point nearly opposite the mouth of the Mattaponix." They might have been massed as a feint, he surmised, or for a crossing, and he could not find out the strength of the force already across because some were obscured by the river's deep banks. Thus Hooker's demonstration had the Confederates guessing. Early sent word of the crossing to General Jackson, and more troops of Jackson's corps were brought up, including the commands of Brigadier General R. E. Rodes, who had D. H. Hill's division, Brigadier General Colston's, who had Trimble's, and A. P. Hill. The Confederates also brought up guns and there was some firing at Union troops engaged in entrenching.

Hooker asked Sedgwick whether any troops had been drawn off by the Confederates, and Sedgwick replied all were still there; he might have added that many more had been added, had he known. General Jackson conferred with Lee about the possibility of attacking the Federals. Lee reminded him how difficult the fighting had been in this very area during the battle of Fredericksburg, but told Jackson to inspect the position; if he thought he could succeed, Lee would give him the order to go ahead. Jackson studied the Union position as Early had done and concluded not to attack. Later came his conference with Lee, during which they made plans for Jackson's strategic march around the left flank of Hooker's army, which turned out so disastrously for the Eleventh Corps.

By April 30 Early was convinced that the Federal army on the Rappahannock was making a mere demonstration to cover a serious move elsewhere. Lee likewise had discovered that Hooker's main body was at Chancellorsville and in the afternoon drew three divisions from this front. About this time Lee sent the first of his dispatches to President Jefferson Davis urging that Longstreet be called back from his foraging trip in southeastern Virginia. On the same day Hooker ordered Sickles to leave the field, march back on the north bank, and cross the Rappahannock at Bank's Ford above Fredericksburg. It was a long and tiring march.

On May 1 Hooker turned to the defensive at Chancellorsville, but he still nursed the hope that something might be done by Sedgwick. He sent word: "Tell Sedgwick to keep a sharp lookout and attack if he can succeed." Sedgwick and Reynolds concluded that if they attacked a major engagement might result, and they were not ready to fight alone. The corps commanders waited for further orders. They came on May 2 when Hooker wired: "Direct all bridges taken up at Franklin's Crossing and below before daylight, and for Reynolds Corps to march at once, with pack train, to report to headquarters." The recrossing of Wadsworth's troops from the south bank was done under artillery fire from the Confederates, who achieved a direct hit on one bridge. Reynolds' corps had to march twenty-three miles; finding no pontoons at Bank's Ford they had to go to the United States Ford before they could cross the Rappahannock above Fredericksburg. Reynolds reached Hooker's headquarters just as the bad news about the Eleventh Corps broke, and he was ordered down the Turnpike to help stop the rush of Howard's men from the battlefield.

General Sedgwick, with nearly 23,000 in his division, marked time until 11 P.M. on the night of May 2, when he received Hooker's order, issued at 4 P.M. and relayed by General Butterfield, "to take up his line on the Chancellorsville Road and attack and destroy any forces he might meet." He added that Sedgwick "would probably fall upon the rear of Lee's force and between them they would use Lee up." That day Sedgwick had brought the rest of his troops across the river to the south bank and moved up to the River Road, or Bowling Green Road, forcing the Seventy-seventh Louisiana Infantry to fall back to the Confederate line along the railroad. It happened that strong units of Early's forces had been marched out that morning in pursuance of an order by Lee that had been misinterpreted by his adjutant, Colonel R. H. Chilton. Lee wanted Early to head for the Plank Road if in his discretion he thought he was not holding in check any large force. But the order first came to Early as a direct command to move, and he did so. When he learned from a courier the details of the order, and also received an alarm from the troops he had left behind as reserve, he turned his forces around and reoccupied his former positions.

By dawn Sedgwick's troops, taking the Bowling Green Road, had reached the rear and left of Fredericksburg. Units from the Second Corps crossed the river from Falmouth and obtained a footing in Fredericksburg. As the Federal skirmishers advanced Brigadier General William Barksdale, whose brigade had been posted near the town, retired before superior numbers. Early posted Barksdale's regiments, mostly Mississippi men, in the trenches on Marye's Hill between the Marye House and the Plank Road, behind the stone wall that had been so stoutly defended in December, and on the slopes of the hill to the southeast known as Lee's Hill, because Lee had watched the battle of Fredericksburg from that spot. Grimes's battery of the Washington Artillery was placed on Marye's Hill, and Brigadier General William N. Pendleton's reserve battery was posted on Lee's Hill. In all about 10,000 Confederates were manning the defenses.

Brigadier General John Gibbon's Second Division of the Second Corps, which had been awaiting orders on the Falmouth side of the river, crossed into Fredericksburg and moved up Hanover Street to turn the Confederate left, but he was stopped by the canal, which had one bridge that had been torn up. Repairs were practically impossible as the open ground was swept by artillery, especially by a battery of Brigadier General C. M. Wilcox's brigade of Anderson's division, which had been unable to get to Marye's Hill in time. Another attempt to turn the Confederate right was made at Hazel Run by Sedgwick's Second Division, commanded by Brigadier General Albion P. Howe.

But by 11 A.M. the Federals had made no progress and Sedgwick realized that a frontal assault would have to be made. Two columns were directed to attack at the same time, one at Lee's Hill, the other against Marye's Hill and the formidable stone wall and sunken road behind it. Major General John Newton of the Third Division led the advance, with Brigadier General William T. H. Brooks's division following. Newton concentrated his guns—twelve rifled cannon and six napoleons—on this area. The Confederate infantry was two lines deep behind the stone wall.

The Union troops advanced in the face of a terrible artillery fire, but the Confederates at the wall withheld their fire until the men were about twenty-five yards away. Then "a blinding rain of shot pierced the air." The effect was terrible; many men fell and others tried to find shelter, but most of the troops pressed forward.

One of the privates of Company F, Seventh Massachusetts Infantry, which was in the lead, said the officers yelled "Retreat! Retreat!" but the men, eager to get at the enemy, shouted back: "Forward! Don't go back! We shan't get so close up again!" Their recoil was only a matter of minutes; they pushed forward a second time and went over the wall with fixed bayonets. One unit found the flank of the defenders and enfiladed them, and started a panic in the Confederate ranks. This time they did not hold out. Many of the defenders surrendered and Newton's men took up to 1,000 prisoners. The rest hurried over the rolling hills behind Marye's and Lee's Hills.

Sedgwick testified later: "I lost 1,000 men in less than 10 minutes in taking the heights of Fredericksburg."

The land is undulating and by rallying the men as they reached each ridge Early's brigade commanders managed to make a stand. They moved back nearly three miles, within sight of Salem Church, an oblong brick structure used by the Baptist denomination. Here were units of Mahone's brigade and other elements of McLaws' division, moving forward to reinforce them. The attack by Sedgwick had caught Lee unawares, and he had hurriedly withdrawn forces from his Chancellorsville line and sent them to reinforce Early as soon as word of the retreat reached him. The Confederates made a determined stand and by nightfall had stopped Sedgwick, whose casualties for the day reached about 1,500 killed and wounded.

Sedgwick had reason to expect help from Hooker, but none came, and the prospect of crushing Lee's army between two Federal pincers faded away. During that Sunday night the Confederates threw up trenches east of Salem Church and early on Monday morning, May 4, struck at Sedgwick's troops with a large force and pushed them back and recovered Marye's Heights. At 1 A.M. on May 5 Sedgwick received Hooker's instructions to guard

the safety of his corps and if necessary withdraw by way
of Banks' Ford, where General Henry W. Bentham had
constructed pontoons. This indicated to Sedgwick that
he could expect no reinforcements from Hooker, and he
began withdrawing across the river. At 3:30 A.M. Sedgwick received an order that Hooker had issued at 1:30
A.M., countermanding the order to withdraw, but Sedgwick's troops were already across. Thus Hooker had repeated his earlier vacillation, when he first ordered withdrawal and then countermanded the order when the
troops had given up a promising position. The incident
also disclosed the time lost in communication by couriers.

General Hooker had expected Sedgwick's Sixth Corps
to appear at daylight, being unaware of the obstacles in
the way; later on he complained that Sedgwick had been
dilatory in executing his orders. By 8:30 A.M. it was evident from Chancellorsville that the Twelfth Corps and
part of the Second also were being pushed back and
that Geary's right was being turned.

At about 9:15 A.M. General Hooker was standing on
the porch of Chancellor House leaning against a pillar
when a cannon shot hit the pillar, demolishing it and
knocking Hooker down. He was stunned, but was able to
get on his horse. It was the testimony of General Couch
that Hooker gave practically no orders for some hours
after this and that the fighting was carried on by each
division commander doing what the situation called for.
Hooker sent for Couch, and the latter found him lying on
a camp bed. Hooker said: "I turn command of the army
over to you. You will withdraw it and place it in the position designated on this map."

At midnight Hooker called a council of his corps commanders, which Couch, Howard, Meade, Reynolds, and
Sickles attended. Hooker explained that he could not
jeopardize the army because he must protect Washington. Howard, Meade, and Reynolds voted to attack;
Sickles and Couch voted against the proposal, Couch
making the reservation that he would advance if he could
designate the point of attack. Hooker thereupon announced that he would assume the responsibility of taking the army back across the Rappahannock. Although
the bridges were endangered by the rising waters the

army was safely transferred across during the night of May 6 and resumed its former camp at Falmouth.

Casualties incurred during the Chancellorsville campaign, May 1–4, were huge. The *Official Records* placed them at 12,145 for the Union Army, with 1,082 killed, 6,849 wounded, 4,214 missing. Another early military record placed the Union total at over 16,000, with 1,512 killed. Livermore's analysis did not differ a great deal, with 1,575 killed. The first report of Confederate casualties was in proportion: 1,581 killed, 8,700 wounded, 2,000 missing; Livermore, using the *War Records,* placed the Confederate casualties higher with 1,665 killed, 9,081 wounded, 2,081 missing, a total of 12,827. The missing list was usually rectified later, as stragglers reported belatedly at roll call, but in many instances men simply quit. Among the dead and wounded were many officers. Generals Berry and Whiple were killed on the Union side and Devens and Kirby wounded. General Paxton was killed on the Confederate side and Stonewall Jackson grievously wounded; his death resulted later from complications. The wounded included Generals A. P. Hill, Nichols, Ramseur, McGowan, Heth, and Pender. The true number of losses of a great battle could never be obtained because the final disposition of the wounded was not available. Many wounded died weeks after a battle because medical science could apply only limited knowledge.

Corps and division commanders made futile attempts to determine why General Hooker had "lost his nerve." No one could find a convincing reason for his indecision at Chancellorsville. He had a good military record, although some doubted his ability to hold a top command. Therefore some credence was given to the possibility that he was stunned when a shot struck the porch pillar against which he was leaning. But that occurred several days after his vacillation had begun. None of his early mistakes, however, would necessarily have lost the battle. His first blunder, recalling the troops of Hancock and Sykes when they had just taken a fine defensive position on high ground, was damaging, but could have been retrieved. It was even contended by corps commanders that a massed attack on Jackson's position immediately after the Eleventh had been routed, done with superior numbers and guns, would have achieved results. There were other mistakes—the failure to rush adequate ammunition to fighting units, and the idleness of large bodies of troops and guns in reserve. Apparently Hooker had no sooner occupied the field according to his plan when he became worried about the possibility of losing the fords, which meant a safe route to cover if a retreat were necessary. To fight with a river at one's back was considered a major risk in all army manuals; it was the specific criticism Buell had made of Grant's disposition of troops at Shilohl.

Major General Couch, who withdrew from the Army of the Potomac after Chancellorsville, denied the insinuations that Hooker might have been drinking. Hooker had given up liquor when he started the campaign; thus the lack of stimulant, rather than its presence, might be blamed. At this distance from the catastrophe it appears that, like many others, Hooker was an efficient subordinate, but unable to make the hard decisions that fall upon the top command.

Lincoln's Hunt for a General

Hooker's defeat at Chancellorsville caused an emotional crisis in Lincoln's life. The lanky President could put on an air of unconcern when others were disturbed, and was able to cushion bad news with an anecdote, but the first week in May, 1863, his behavior was different. Lincoln had seen the magnificent organization of the Army of the Potomac in camp; he had watched the troops in review, and although he had reservations about Hooker's temper and appetites, he could appreciate his administrative work. He had looked to Hooker to do what McClellan was incapable of doing—throw in all the forces he had, see the fight through to the end.

During the unfolding of events at Chancellorsville Lincoln was eager and anxious; when good news failed to come he became nervous, paced the floor, expressed his concern in his features. Secretary of the Navy Welles spoke of Lincoln's "feverish anxiety to get facts"; and when the facts did not come he could only be hopeful.

It was the afternoon of May 5 before the War Department received a wire from Major General Daniel Butterfield, chief of staff of the Army of the Potomac, saying the army had withdrawn to the north bank of the Rappahannock and now was "safely encamped" on its former ground. No word could have been more disheartening to the watchers in Washington. With hands clasped behind his back Lincoln paced the room muttering "My God! My God! What will the country say!"

Lincoln was in no mood to wait for the telegraph instrument to tick out in code what everybody already knew. Summoning General Halleck to accompany him, he was off for the railroad station and General Hooker's headquarters. There he quickly heard all that Hooker could tell him, but although commanders like Meade could tell him much else, he did not interrogate them. In the evening he rode back to Washington, leaving Halleck to stay overnight and find out "everything." When Halleck returned the next day Lincoln went with him to Secretary Stanton's office and the three men agreed that Hooker must not have the command of another battle. Hooker had assured Halleck he had not wanted the top command and was quite willing to give it up, but he did wish to remain in the service and if possible command his former division. Secretary Chase and his supporters, who had backed Hooker, had suffered a severe blow, but Lincoln was not yet ready to antagonize them openly. He was letting Hooker continue his work of reorganizing the army, a task of which Hooker was capable.

In the next few weeks Lincoln was courteous to Hooker, who lost some of his despondency. Hooker had told Meade "he had had enough of it and almost wished he had never been born." Meade knew Hooker had "failed to show his fighting qualities in a pinch," but he put most of his doubts into letters to his wife and the public did not get to share his views. In the meantime Lincoln was collecting opinions. On May 22 Lincoln asked General Couch about the Army of the Potomac. Couch had been the frankest critic of Hooker ever since the first order to withdraw from in front of the Confederate advance demoralized the army on the first day at Chancellorsville. From that moment he knew Hooker was a "whipped man," and when Hooker finally asked his corps commanders whether he should withdraw across the river—already having made his decision to do so—Couch voted for withdrawal because he had lost confidence in Hooker's ability to bring a victory out of defeat. Now Lincoln was asking him, would he accept the top command if it were offered him? Decidedly no, said Couch, nor would he fight longer under Hooker; he asked to be relieved. Who then would be eligible? Meade, said Couch. The President pondered the matter. Couch stepped out of the Second Army Corps, Major General Winfield S. Hancock took over. When Lee, a few weeks later, was moving north and sending Pennsylvania farmers scurrying for the far hills, Governor Curtin had need of a general and obtained the loan of Couch to organize the resistance.

Lincoln kept on making inquiries. On May 31 Major General John F. Reynolds took temporary leave from his command to go to Washington; Major General Abner Doubleday took his place. The story was that Reynolds had heard he was being considered for the top command. On June 2 Reynolds had an interview with the President. Later he told Meade that Lincoln had offered him command of the Army of the Potomac and that he had refused it. He told his family that he had a reservation—he wanted freedom from control, but there were three men in command in Washington, and a general in the field was not free. Reynolds had a fine upstanding record; he had commanded ably whenever ordered, at Mechanicsville, Gaines' Mill, Second Bull Run, Fredericksburg; it was not his fault that he had been kept on the sidelines at Chancellorsville. He had been outspoken to Lincoln, telling him Hooker would no longer do, but Lincoln had rebuked him mildly, saying he was not disposed to throw away a gun because it missed fire once; he would pick the lock and try it again. The crucial decision was yet to be made.

21

THE VICKSBURG CAMPAIGN

Corinth and Iuka

Major General Henry W. Halleck transferred his headquarters from St. Louis to Pittsburg Landing on April 11, 1862, and took personal command of the armies as Grant's superior. Grant remained second in command, but it was a post without duties, for Halleck simply ignored him. He was unable to remove Grant—Washington could stop that—but he could put him on the shelf, which he now proceeded to do. Important reports of the subordinate commanders, which were to pass through Grant's hand, never reached him, and General Buell went over his head and gave his report directly to Halleck, so that Grant did not see it until it was published by the War Department. Consequently Grant never filed a report on Shiloh.

Grant smarted under the treatment, and several times was ready to quit the Department, but he had a firm supporter in Sherman, who, recalling how he was called insane by his enemies, urged Grant to bide his time, despite indignities and insults. Grant was a patient man; he did not talk much about his difficulties and his reports were always respectful. Eventually Halleck learned to work with him and even to favor him, and Grant survived all his opponents and detractors, including Halleck, because he had the confidence of President Lincoln.

General Halleck reorganized the armies. After the taking of the Confederate fortifications at Island No. 10 the Army of the Mississippi, under the command of Brigadier General John Pope, joined Halleck with 21,510 men at Hamburg Landing. This command Halleck placed at the left of the armies. The Army of the Ohio, under General Buell, occupied the center; Grant's Army of the Tennessee was on the right, but command of the right wing was given to Brigadier General George H. Thomas, up to this time with Major General Buell, and under him were the divisions of W. T. Sherman, who had been made a major general of volunteers, and Brigadier General Stephen A. Hurlbut and two new divisions made from the former units of Brigadier General B. M. Prentiss, who had been captured, and Major General C. F. Smith, who was fatally ill. These commands went to Brigadier General Thomas West Sherman, who had commanded at Port Royal, South Carolina, in 1861, and Colonel T. A. Davies. Major General McClernand had the reserve, comprising his division and that of Major General Lew Wallace. These additions and changes gave Halleck over 100,000 men.

Halleck followed the Confederates cautiously, whereas Grant was certain the Confederates could have been wiped out by a swift pursuit. Halleck took one month to cover the thirty miles to Corinth, and with his belief in fortification had the troops throwing up entrenchments every night. General Pope had two clashes with the Confederates at Farmington, four miles east of Corinth, but was unable to press his advantages because Halleck pulled him back.

Beauregard now had about 50,000 men, half the number in Halleck's army. By May 19 he was ready to abandon Corinth; he so advised the Confederate Adjutant General, General Cooper, and outlined the path of his retreat; his plan was approved by President Davis' military adviser in Richmond, General Robert E. Lee. On May 30 Beauregard withdrew, marching first to Baldwin and thence to Tupelo. To confuse Halleck he staged one of the best hoaxes of the war. To give the impression that he was receiving reinforcements he caused a train of cars to shuttle back and forth amid the cheers of his soldiers, and kept campfires burning and had reveille sounded when most of his men were already out of the town. The bluster misled Halleck, who told his commanders to prepare to be attacked the next day. Then it turned out that Beauregard had removed everything of value and all the sick and wounded had been evacuated. Generals Pope and Buell were sent in pursuit for about thirty miles, with no effect.

When Halleck began moving his armies without consulting Grant the latter made several requests to be relieved, but Halleck refused this until he reached Corinth.

Then General Sherman prevailed on Grant to stay with the command. After the fall of Island No. 10, Fort Pillow and Memphis had been taken with the help of the Navy, and Grant asked that he be given the command of West Tennessee at Memphis. This was approved and Grant plunged into administrative work, but not for long. On July 11 General Halleck was ordered to Washington, to assume direction of all Federal armies, so he ordered his next in command, General Grant, to Corinth, without telling him why. Although the responsibility for the whole Department of the Mississippi now fell upon Grant, Halleck remained "very uncommunicative" and it was not until October that Grant was actually recognized as commander of the Department.

Although there had been over 100,000 troops in this area, their power had been dissipated, presumably by Halleck. General Sherman believed Halleck had meant to make a unified move south and thus "solve the whole Mississippi problem," but had been overruled by Washington. General Pope had been called to take a command in the East and his divisions had been divided among the others at Corinth; General Thomas, relieved from command of the right wing, had resumed command of his division under Buell, and Buell's Army of the Ohio had been started toward Chattanooga. McClernand's command had gone to Bolivar and Memphis. In a few weeks McClernand went to Washington in order, as it turned out, to get a bigger position for himself, and Major General E. O. C. Ord took the command in his absence. Added to Grant's jurisdiction at Corinth was the army unit of General W. S. Rosecrans, with divisions under Colonels C. S. Hamilton and T. A. Davies, who became brigadier generals in October.

After Memphis came into Federal hands on July 21, 1862, navigation on the Mississippi was open as far as Vicksburg. The removal of this obstacle to the free use of the river became a necessity for the Union armies. This also would isolate Confederate troops still operating in Louisiana and Arkansas and stop supplies from the West to their armies east of the Mississippi. When Halleck was called to Washington to take the top command and Grant succeeded as commander of the Army of the

Tennessee at Corinth, General Sherman followed Grant as commander of the District of West Tennessee with headquarters at Memphis, with the division of General Hurlbut added to his jurisdiction.

On September 13 General Sterling Price with about 8,000 men seized Iuka, Mississippi, which was abandoned without a fight by a garrison of Wisconsin troops under Colonel R. C. Murphy. Price was thought to be headed east to join Bragg in eastern Kentucky. Grant ordered General Ord to move on Iuka via Burnsville, going with him, and sent General Rosecrans via Jacinto to approach Iuka from the south by two roads to take Price in the flank. The leading division, Hamilton's, was attacked by Price out of sight and hearing of Ord's columns, and the onslaught was so severe that the Federals had 148 killed and 570 wounded. The Eleventh Ohio Battery, which lost 72 killed and wounded in half an hour, was taken twice by the Confederates and retaken at the point of the bayonet. Price withdrew quickly before he could be engaged by the rest of the troops and joined Van Dorn at Dumas, Mississippi.

Grant proceeded to Jackson, leaving Rosecrans in command at Corinth. His army was now strung out over 150 miles with Ord at Bolivar, north of Grand Junction, and Sherman at Memphis. Sherman made a strong point of Fort Pickering there and sent detachments to threaten Van Dorn's supply base at Holly Springs, and had Colonel Benjamin H. Grierson raid as far as the Coldwater with his Sixth Illinois Cavalry. On October 3 Van Dorn with about 40,000, including Price's troops, moved on Corinth in two columns and pushed Rosecrans' divisions back to the line of redoubts that had been started by Halleck. Price's column penetrated the strong point held by Colonel Davies, but was beaten back by musket fire and bayonet charges. As Price's column wilted, Hamilton's regiments turned with fierce energy on Van Dorn's, and the whole Confederate line broke. The Confederates reportedly had 1,423 killed, thousands wounded, and lost 2,265 prisoners. Rosecrans had 315 killed, 1,812 wounded. General Ord took up the pursuit and at the Hatchie River inflicted more damage on Van Dorn's army, causing it to make a wide detour, but it regained Holly Springs. Lieu-

tenant General J. C. Pemberton then took top Confederate command, with his line on the Tallahatchie River below Holly Springs, an advance unit on the Coldwater
and others at Grand Junction and Hernando.

By November, Grant had prepared plans to proceed
against Pemberton in a major move to take Vicksburg
from the northeast. He would go from Grand Junction to
Holly Springs and Abbeville, have McPherson come from
Corinth to join him at Holly Springs and Sherman to
reach the Tallahatchie on his right. He was authorized to
draw on the Department of Arkansas, commanded by
General S. R. Curtis and temporarily by Brigadier General Frederick Steele, and thence obtained a force under
Brigadier General A. P. Hovey, which was intended to
strike near the Tallahatchie at Grenada to cause Pemberton concern for his communications. This was done by
December. Grant reached Oxford, Mississippi, and Sherman located at College Hill, ten miles from Oxford.
Hovey's thrust worked better than expected. When his
cavalry reached the railroad near Coffeeville, Pemberton
took alarm, called in his line from the Tallahatchie, and
fell back to the Yallabusha near Grenada.

Attack at Chickasaw Bluff

Grant, who had suffered plenty of slights from General
Halleck, now had Halleck's confidence, or at least his cooperation, but trouble was coming from another quarter.
Major General John A. McClernand, a former Illinois
representative, was a stubborn, politically ambitious man,
who had been useful to Lincoln as a Democrat supporting the war effort. To get himself placed in a special military category, McClernand had gone to Washington in
October and placed before the War Department a scheme
of his own to capture Vicksburg. He urged that he be
given authority to raise troops, organize them, and lead
them down the river in association with the Navy. Rear
Admiral David D. Porter met McClernand and heard
his plans for the expedition. With President Lincoln inclined to favor a political supporter, Secretary of War
Stanton on October 21, 1862, gave McClernand authority
to make his headquarters in Springfield, Illinois, and

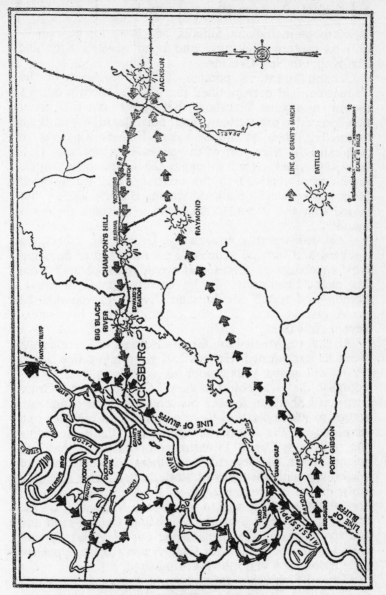

Grant's Vicksburg Campaign
March 29-May 18, 1863

raise troops in Indiana, Illinois, and Iowa for an expedition to capture Vicksburg and open navigation on the Mississippi to New Orleans.

General Grant, as commander of the Army of the Tennessee, had been notified that the President wanted a movement against Vicksburg, but he was not told about McClernand's instructions, and only heard about them indirectly. When he did he asked Halleck who was to command the river part of the projected expedition. Halleck authorized Grant to name the commander, unless orders were received to the contrary, and when Grant indicated he would name Sherman, Halleck agreed, but added that the President might wish to name the commander.

This was warning enough for Grant; like others, he doubted McClernand's fitness; he wanted a man he could trust in charge of forces that would be separated from his direct supervision. So he quickly named Sherman, hoping to forestall McClernand. Events proved that he acted just in time. But the expedition ran into unexpected difficulties.

At Oxford, Mississippi, Grant disclosed to Sherman the plans he had formed. Halleck had given him a free hand: "You will move your troops as you deem best to accomplish the great object in view." On December 8 Grant instructed Sherman to take one division of his command, return to Memphis, and there organize into brigades and divisions all the troops he would find there, including the unit from Curtis' Department of Arkansas that had joined Grant. He was to move them to the vicinity of Vicksburg with the help of Porter's fleet, and he could draw on the quartermaster at St. Louis for transportation for 30,000 men. He was to land above Vicksburg, on the Yazoo if practicable, cut the Mississippi Central road and the road crossing the Black River out of Vicksburg and be ready to cooperate with Grant when the latter pushed Pemberton back in northwest Mississippi.

General Sherman's action became known as the battle of Chickasaw Bayou, or Chickasaw Bluffs. The bluffs were part of the Walnut Hills and were the high land dominating a wide area of swampy terrain where the Yazoo River turned and twisted, forming bayous, and entering the

Mississippi above the Tuscumbia Bend above Vicksburg.
The hills began immediately north of Vicksburg and extended north by east about fifteen miles. At the northern end, projecting over the Yazoo, was Haines' Bluff; adjoining it on the south was Drumgould's. Both were strongly fortified; there also were rifle pits covering all the usable landing places and sharpshooters concealed in the heavy wooded growth and on the County Road that ran along and over the hills.

Grant's plan was to proceed from Oxford and draw Pemberton from Vicksburg while Sherman effected a footing north of the town. Sherman in Memphis formed the First Division under Brigadier General A. J. Smith, took the Second Division under Brigadier General Morgan L. Smith and the Third Division under Brigadier General George W. Morgan. As the Arkansas troops that had been east had returned to their base at Helena, Arkansas, Sherman drew on that department for his Fourth Division under Brigadier General Frederick Steele. The Memphis contingent of about 20,000 embarked on about forty steamers, and Steele with 13,000 joined at Helena on twenty more. It was a strangely assorted collection of boats, river craft with paddle boxes and walking beams, and with bales of hay, cotton, and even rails built up to protect the boilers, which ordinarily were open to the winds.

They made their first stop on December 25, Christmas Day, at Milliken's Bend on the Mississippi, some miles above the spot where the Yazoo enters the former. Here Brigadier General Stephen G. Burbridge of General A. J. Smith's division moved inland with about 6,000 infantry and some cavalry to destroy the Vicksburg & Texas Railroad that runs to Monroe, Louisiana, from Vicksburg, and after a foray covering about 75 miles Burbridge returned with a herd of 196 beef cattle.

The Federals learned that the Confederates had been sinking barges and planting torpedoes (now called mines) in the Yazoo long before. Weeks ago the *Marmora* and the *Signal* had been taking torpedoes out of the Yazoo but had been handicapped by sharpshooters; Porter then sent up the *Baron de Kalb*, the *Pittsburg*, the *Queen of the West*, and the *Cairo* to shell the nests of sharpshooters, with the unfortunate result that the *Cairo* touched off a torpedo with its bottom and sank, but with no lives lost. Similar bad luck pursued Porter when he sent gunboats up the Yazoo on December 28 to shell Confederate batteries on Drumgould's Bluff. The ironclad *Benton* led the boats, but its officer, Lieutenant Commander William Gwin, received a mortal wound because he insisted that a captain's place was on the quarterdeck and refused to use the protected pilothouse.

Sherman moved his troops ten miles up the Yazoo and landed them on the plantation of Albert Sidney Johnston, who had died at Shiloh. Sharpshooters had taken cover there and the Federals made short work of the plantation buildings. The divisions were to seize the County Road and attempt to pass beyond it to the bluffs, while General A. J. Smith was to move to the extreme left and clear the road leading to Vicksburg. During reconnaissance on December 28 General Morgan L. Smith was severely wounded in the hip and had to turn his command over to Brigadier General David Stuart.

On the 29th Sherman ordered a general assault, but the troops encountered a severe fire from artillery and rifles and lost heavily. Sherman recalled later that General Morgan, who had boasted: "General, in ten minutes after you give the signal I'll be on those hills," was responsible for the failure of the attack because he had not obeyed orders or even crossed the bayou in person. The Sixth Missouri Infantry was unable to ascend a bank; Sherman reported that the men "actually scooped out with their hands caves in the bank, which sheltered them against the fire of the enemy who, right over their heads, held their muskets outside the parapet vertically and fired down."

Sherman had considered his dispositions favorable for a renewal of the attack on December 30, but an impenetrable fog settled down on the lowland and the plan had to be abandoned. Sherman could hear the whistles of trains arriving in Vicksburg and assumed that the place was getting reinforcements, but the Confederates showed no inclination to start an offensive. He was also waiting to hear the sound of Grant's guns from Yazoo City, but in vain. He broke off the attack and by January 2, 1863, had his whole force and supplies back on the transports. The expedition had been costly. The Federals lost 208 killed and 1,005 wounded; the Confederate Brigadier General Stephen D. Lee reported 63 killed and 134 wounded. Lee also claimed the capture of 332 Federals and 500 stand of arms.

Grant had issued an order to Sherman on December 23 to delay his expedition, but the order did not reach Sherman because General Nathan Bedford Forrest had broken Grant's communications by one of those raids that combined recklessness with daring and made havoc behind the lines. In this mid-December raid Forrest crossed the Tennessee from the east into Federal-occupied territory.

At the same time General Earl Van Dorn dealt Grant a powerful blow when he raided Holly Springs. Here he captured Colonel R. C. Murphy of the Eighth Wisconsin Volunteer Infantry and 1,500 men of this unit and Illinois troops. He destroyed stores that would have supplied the army for weeks. The disaster was laid at the door of Colonel Murphy, who had evacuated Iuka two months before, and who had known in advance of Van Dorn's approach and made no preparations to meet him. Grant called Murphy's failure either disloyalty or gross cowardice. The loss of the supplies compelled Grant to send men to scour the countryside for fifteen miles around for food and forage.

Arkansas Post

On December 18 Grant had received orders from Washington to divide his command into four army corps. He was to give command to General McClernand of the one that would operate down the Mississippi. Although McClernand remained subordinate to Grant, this was hardly satisfactory to either. Grant obeyed the order and sent word to McClernand at Springfield, Illinois, but the message did not arrive in time to affect Sherman's expedition.

McClernand, who had expected to operate independently, called his the Army of the Mississippi and divided it into two corps: the first of Morgan's and A. J. Smith's divisions, to be commanded by Morgan; and the second of Steele's and Stuart's, to be commanded by Sherman. He arrived at Sherman's headquarters January 3, 1863. When he took command General Sherman pointed out to him that for some time Federal convoys using the river had been endangered by Confederates manning Fort Hindman, at the Post of Arkansas, commonly called Arkansas Post, over forty miles above the confluence of the Arkansas and the Mississippi. With their commands fully equipped, here was an opportunity to reduce it. General McClernand, eager for action, agreed. Cooperation by the gunboats was necessary, but Admiral Porter disliked McClernand and did not wish to deal with him. But the matter was urgent, so General Sherman took McClernand with him to call on Porter, who was stationed at the mouth of the Yazoo on the *Black Hawk*. They arrived at midnight and Sherman, outlining the opportunity, begged Porter to put aside his antipathy for the sake of this expedition, and won his agreement.

McClernand decided to lead the troops and Porter came to lead the gunboats in person. They reached their landing place below Fort Hindman on January 10. Sherman's divisions were commanded by General Steele, with brigades under Blair, Hovey, and Thayer, and by General Stuart, with brigades under G. A. Smith and T. Kilby Smith. General Morgan commanded the Second Corps. The naval section included the ironclads *Baron de Kalb, Louisville, Cincinnati;* the gunboats *Black Hawk* and *Tyler;* the ram *Monarch;* and the tinclads *Rattler* and *Glide.*

Fort Hindman was a bastion on the classical plan of four angled corners and casemates. It had eighteen guns of various calibers, several outlying works on the levee, and a parapet extending about one mile from the fort to a swamp. It was defended by nearly 5,000 troops under General T. J. Churchill. The gunboats raked the works on January 10 with shrapnel and rifle shells, and the *Rattler* enfiladed the fort and had its cabin knocked off. On the next day the troops moved up to the fort from two directions and began the attack after the gunboats had started firing. After some hours a white flag was displayed on the parapet. General Sherman and an aide went up to the fort, and General Steele brought his troops close to the parapet. Porter's gunboats were so close that they were practically against the fort, with their bows on shore. Colonel Garland took responsibility for the white flag, but a brigade commanded by General Deshler refused to stack arms. Whereupon Sherman went to the commanding officer, General Churchill, and warned him to order Deshler to give up, because a single shot might land the whole of Steele's division on Deshler's brigade. General Churchill demanded of Garland: "Why did you display the white flag?" Garland replied: "I received orders to do so from one of your staff." Churchill denied giving such an order. Deshler, a West Point man, said he had received no orders to surrender, whereupon Churchill said: "You see, sir, that we are in their power and you may surrender." The number of prisoners taken was 4,791.

General McClernand was still on board the *Tigress,* giving contradictory orders, so Sherman went to see him. McClernand was in high spirits. Sherman found him saying: "Glorious! Glorious! My star is ever in the ascendant! I'll make a splendid report. I had a man up a tree," referring to a man who had watched the surrender from a tree in order to report to McClernand. When McClernand made his report he omitted mention of the part played by the gunboats.

There was much feeling against Colonel Garland among the Confederate officers and he asked leave to stay with Sherman that night. Sherman wrote in his memoirs: "I had a [hospital] room cleaned out and occupied it that night. A cavalry-soldier lent me his battered coffee-pot with some coffee and scraps of hard bread out of his nosebag; Garland and I made some coffee, ate our bread together and talked politics by the fire till quite late at night, when we lay down on straw that was saturated with the blood of dead or wounded men."

Grant wrote McClernand that he disapproved of the expedition against Hindman, but when he learned how completely successful it had been he had to stifle his objections. Here McClernand had scored, although he now had to forget his Army of the Mississippi and become commander of one of the four army corps subordinate to Grant. In the ensuing weeks he gave as little attention to

Grant's orders as he could and thus widened the breach between them, which could end only with his own discomfiture.

Naval Operations

The United States Navy first called on Vicksburg to surrender on May 10, 1862, after Farragut's squadron had obtained the surrender of the principal towns upriver from New Orleans and silenced most of the Confederate batteries. Those at Grand Gulf still held out. Commander Lee of the *Oneida* made the demand for surrender and was refused. Concurring was Brigadier General Thomas Williams, who had with him about 1,500 troops provided by General Butler. Farragut had the *Hartford, Brooklyn,* and *Richmond,* and eight gunboats. The *Hartford* ran aground 200 miles north of New Orleans and lost two days there.

Farragut reached Vicksburg on May 23. He sized up the situation as unfavorable for an attack. Bluffs that rose up to 190 feet were topped by batteries armed with columbiads. They could drop shells on the fleet, but gunners on the ships would have to tilt their guns at a difficult angle in order to heave shells on the bluffs. Farragut decided the time had not come to engage the batteries. He left the gunboats to patrol the river below Vicksburg under Commander James S. Palmer and returned to New Orleans.

President Lincoln and the Navy Department had no true knowledge of the difficulties of navigation and attack from the water. They were determined Farragut should proceed up the river and if possible meet Flag Officer Charles Henry Davis and his gunboats coming down from Cairo. Farragut started up again, taking Porter's mortar boats and General Williams' troops, now increased to 3,200 men. The *Hartford* grounded once more, but was pulled loose in seven hours. Farragut now had the *Hartford, Brooklyn,* and *Richmond,* six gunboats, six steamers of Porter's mortar flotilla, and sixteen mortar boats.

At 2 A.M. on June 28 Farragut signaled the fleet to start past Vicksburg. The ships moved in two columns, with

the eight gunboats on the port (left) side and the three
battleships on the starboard (right) side, the latter steaming some distance apart from one another. The mortar
boats, located at both banks of the river, opened the bombardment. General Williams had placed a battery on a
neck of land and joined in the firing. The large ships managed, much to the surprise of the gunners, to land shells
on top of the targets. But the Confederate batteries
were able to strike the ships in many places. Porter's
mortar steamboats suffered; the boiler of the *Clifton*
was hit, scalding members of the crew; the *Jackson* lost
its steering wheel and the *Westfield* its engine frame. The
Hartford was hit in a number of places. Farragut reported the forts could be passed, but no advantage was
gained as long as the Confederates had forces large
enough to prevent landings. Flag Officer Davis joined
him July 1 with gunboats and mortar boats of the Mississippi squadron that had been lying at Memphis.

The Yazoo River, which enters the Mississippi about
twelve miles above Vicksburg, was a base for Confederate
vessels. The Federals knew that an armored gunboat, the
Arkansas, was being converted into a formidable fighting
craft at Yazoo City. A preliminary expedition upstream
had been undertaken by Lieutenant Colonel Alfred W.
Ellet with the rams *Monarch* and *Lancaster,* the latter
commanded by the nineteen-year-old Charles Rivers Ellet, nephew of Alfred and son of Charles Ellet, Jr., de-
signer of the fleet. They moved fifty miles up the Yazoo,
and their mere appearance so affrighted the Confederate
officer at Liverpool Landing that he set fire to three gunboats, the *Polk,* the *Livingston,* and the *Van Dorn.* The
Ellets rejoined their fleet, and soon thereafter Lieutenant
Colonel Ellet was made a brigadier general in charge of the
Mississippi Marine Brigade, to do patrol work on the
river, and young Ellet became a colonel and commander
of the ram fleet.

A new reconnaissance was planned for the Yazoo, to
include the partly armored *Carondelet,* Commander
Henry Walke; the wooden Gunboat *Tyler,* Lieutenant
William Gwin; and a ram, *Queen of the West,* Lieutenant James M. Hunter. They had proceeded hardly six miles
up the stream on July 15, 1862, when the *Arkansas* sud-

denly appeared coming toward them. The insufficient armor of the three was well known to their officers, so they turned about and only the *Carondelet* took the *Arkansas* under fire. The *Tyler* steamed close to the *Carondelet;* the latter was able to use only its two stern thirty-two-pounder guns and finally, with disabled steering gear, ran into shoal water, where it drew only six feet, against the thirteen needed by the *Arkansas*. The shots of the gunboats were not without effect; the conduit between boiler and smokestack of the *Arkansas* was smashed and the stack riddled; the pilot was fatally wounded. The heat in the fire room went up to 130°, and the firemen had to be relieved every 15 minutes.

The commander of the *Arkansas,* Captain Isaac N. Brown, was determined to take his vessel to Vicksburg. Nothing daunted, he steamed straight for the United States fleet of about twenty vessels, only one of which had steam up. Every vessel tried to blast the *Arkansas* with broadsides, but Captain Brown maneuvered so well that no Federal craft was certain where the ram might strike. Captain Brown wrote later: "As we advanced the line of fire seemed to grow into a circle constantly closing. The shock of missiles striking our sides was literally continuous . . . shrapnel shot were coming on our shield deck 12 pounds at a time. . . . [A] ram was across our way ahead. As I gave the order, 'Go through him, Brady!' his steam went into the air and his crew into the river." The stricken ship was the *Lancaster* and many of its crew were scalded.

With help from Porter's mortarboats and Davis' gunboats, which shelled Vicksburg batteries, Rear Admiral Farragut took his major ships past the town on the night of July 15, his fleet including the *Hartford, Richmond, Oneida, Iroquois, Sumter,* and four gunboats. The United States ships were especially eager to eliminate the *Arkansas* in passing the Vicksburg bluffs, but in the darkness of the night they could locate it only by the flashes of its guns and thus it became a difficult target. So it came about that only one shot actually struck the *Arkansas,* but this was an 11-inch 160-pound missile that did the damage of ten minor projectiles. The shot penetrated its armor, disabled its engine, destroyed its dispensary, and knocked overboard the pilot Brady, who earlier that day had steered the craft through the United States fleet. On July 22 the Federals made one more attempt to destroy the *Arkansas;* the *Essex* and the *Queen of the West* were sent to ram it, but both failed. After this engagement the United States fleets left north and south on different errands, giving the Vicksburg batteries a respite of four months.

The naval vessels under Rear Admiral Porter's jurisdiction had plenty of occasions for daring exploits. They were shallow craft, many converted from river steamboats, and when not properly armored were protected by bales of cotton piled high on their decks. To the hazards of gunfire must be added the danger of striking snags— huge logs and trees that drifted downstream—as well as getting stranded on sandbars that were continually shifting with the current. Few of the vessels taken on isolated raids by impetuous captains escaped damage, and a number were totally destroyed.

The *Queen of the West* had once carried excursionists on happy voyages; now it was equipped with a powerful ram and guns. It took part in the reconnaissance up the Yazoo that spotted the *Arkansas,* but was of little help there. In a foray with the *Essex* against the *Arkansas* on July 22, 1862, Colonel A. W. Ellet on the *Queen* tried to ram the *Arkansas,* but failed. On December 12 the *Queen* went up the Yazoo on an expedition in which the ironclad *Cairo* hit torpedoes and sank. On February 2, 1863, Colonel Charles R. Ellet took the *Queen* past the Vicksburg batteries in daylight, a bit of bravado that startled both friend and foe; on the way he saw the Confederate *Vicksburg* at a dock and stopped to ram it, while projectiles fell like rain around him. His boat was hit several times, but not dangerously. Steaming to the Red River, Ellet burned three craft heavily laden with stores, picked up a small ferryboat, the *De Soto,* for use as a tender, and raided the Red River and the Atchafalaya. On February 14 the *Queen* captured a transport, *Era No. 5,* left it at the mouth of the Red River and ran upstream with the *De Soto,* looking for prizes. In passing a battery the *Queen* ran aground and the crew had to jump for it. Some got aboard the *De Soto,* others including Ellet floated downstream on cotton bales, landing safely on their prize, the *Era*. Because the *De Soto* had lost its rudder they burned it and started upstream in the *Era*.

The *Queen of the West* was now in the hands of the Confederates, who repaired and floated it and gave it a new flag. Porter, knowing what Ellet was up to, dispatched the gunboat *Indianola* past Vicksburg to give Ellet support if he needed it. When the *Indianola*'s commander met the *Era* coming upstream, he continued to the Red River on an errand of his own. Nothing happened, so the *Indianola* returned upstream, dragging two coal barges. These cut its speed and gave the Confederates a chance to overtake it, which they did with four armed vessels, one of them the reconstructed *Queen*. They rammed the *Indianola,* which ran ashore and surrendered. The *Queen* now stood guard over the *Indianola,* which the Confederates expected to refloat. At this point Admiral Porter sent a barge disguised as a gunboat downstream with the current. When the officer on the *Queen* saw this gunboat coming he left a guard on the *Indianola* and hurried out of danger down the river. The guard in turn set the *Indianola* on fire.

Finally the *Queen* reappeared as one of a Confederate flotilla on the Atchafalaya, during the Confederate defense of Port Hudson, and in March was destroyed in attacks by Federal vessels under Lieutenant Commander A. P. Cooke.

Capture of Baton Rouge

Baton Rouge, Louisiana, was captured by the Union army without opposition on May 12, 1862, when Brigadier General Thomas Williams landed 1,400 men and two sections of a battery. The troops, augmented by others, were used on varying errands upriver, such as reducing hostile batteries along the banks. Later in the year General Earl Van Dorn planned to drive the Federals out of Baton Rouge, possibly as a preliminary to an action to recover New Orleans. He placed Major General John C. Breckinridge in command of two divisions, the first under Brigadier General Charles Clark, the second under Brigadier General Daniel Ruggles; three batteries and two companies of cavalry. Also present, but taking no part in the action, were 250 Louisiana Partisan Rangers under Colonel Francis Pond, Jr. Breckinridge said he had not more than 2,600 men; the Federals had fewer than 2,500. The initial attack at dawn, October 24, threw back Williams' line, but the Federals rallied and by 10 A.M. had driven the Confederates from the field. Brigadier General Williams and Colonel George T. Roberts of the Seventh Vermont were killed, and the Union troops lost 84 killed, 266 wounded. Of the Confederates, Brigadier General Clark was wounded and captured and three brigade commanders were wounded; they also lost 84 killed and had 315 wounded.

A number of war vessels attempted to help in the defense: the *Essex, Cayuga, Sumter, Kineo,* and *Katahdin.* Here occurred the final event in the history of the embattled *Arkansas.* Captain Brown had turned his command over to Lieutenant Stevens in order to visit in Grenada, Mississippi. There he was taken ill, and while sick in bed he received word from Stevens that General Van Dorn had ordered the *Arkansas* to Baton Rouge to join in the attack. Captain Brown ordered Stevens to remain at Vicksburg until he could join him, then hurried by train to Vicksburg only to discover that the *Arkansas* had left four hours before. Again he entrained, worrying about engines not properly repaired. Stevens, crowding on steam, came within sight of Baton Rouge when one engine broke down and the vessel was thrown ashore. In this situation the *Essex* approached for the kill. Stevens ordered his crew ashore and lingered only long enough to set the *Arkansas* on fire. Thus, Captain Brown wrote, "the great *Arkansas,* whose decks had never been pressed by the feet of an enemy, was blown into the air."

To Vicksburg from the South

The failure of the first expedition against Vicksburg from the north caused Grant to devise an entirely different plan—to attack from the south and east. This meant moving over 40,000 troops by the land route west of the Mississippi River and crossing the river below the forts; also the use of the naval vessels to carry provisions down the river under the fire of the batteries. Some of Grant's best friends were skeptical of results. Rear Admiral Porter would have the Navy cooperate in every way, but he doubted seriously that the plan would succeed; so too did General Sherman, whose apprehensions were not lifted until the campaign was well under way.

Grant had been alarmed by the destruction of his supplies at Holly Springs by Van Dorn; for his new expedition he worked out a plan by which the army could move without a train of supplies or a depot; he had learned how much to carry and how much the countryside could provide. He told Sherman that had he possessed, in December, 1862, the experience of marching and maintaining armies without a regular base, he would have gone forward from Oxford as originally planned. Sherman remained confident that Grant might have taken Vicksburg from the direction of Oxford in January, and that he lost six months of hard work by the change.

Running past the Vicksburg batteries was a dangerous and spectacular business. When Grant proposed to carry his army to a point below Vicksburg by a route west of the Mississippi it also became necessary to send transports and barges loaded with hay and provisions past Vicksburg. The barges, floated with the current, kept to the west bank, while the gunboats engaged the batteries.

On the night of April 16 seven ironclads led by Rear Admiral Porter, three transports, and ten barges slipped past the bluffs and on April 27 six transports and many barges followed the same route. The batteries on the bluffs opened one after another and sent a rain of shells down on the vessels; the gunboats replied; houses on both sides of the river caught fire and lighted up the night. General Sherman described the scene as both sublime and terrible. Many of the vessels were hit; the *Henry Clay* was set on fire by shells and burned, and the *Tigress* sank. General Sherman had dragged yawl boats across the swamp and had them waiting below the batteries to pick up men from disabled boats. All these craft were ready to carry Grant's army across the river to the east bank.

To begin operations against Vicksburg from the south and east Grant concentrated his troops at Hard Times, Arkansas, and waited for transports to take them across the Mississippi below the heavily fortified Confederate post at Grand Gulf. Admiral Porter took twenty barges and transports past the Vicksburg batteries during the night of April 16, and subsequent nights, suffering some losses and damage. On April 29 he shelled Grand Gulf without reducing it. Grant's army then marched six miles south and crossed at Bruinsburg on April 30. As four divisions of McClernand's corps proceeded inland to Port Gibson they were attacked by the commander of Grand Gulf, Brigadier General John S. Bowen, with two brigades. Bowen was repulsed and one of the Confederate commanders, Brigadier General E. D. Tracy, was killed. Seeing his position turned, Bowen on May 3 evacuated Grand Gulf and marched to join Pemberton's army.

While this was going on Grant asked Sherman if he would pretend to make an attack at Haines' Bluff, on the Yazoo, to divert Pemberton's attention from the lower landings. He did not like to give an order, for the feint would have the appearance of a repulse for Sherman, and would result in the usual criticism in the North. Sherman, who was always willing to cooperate with Grant, entered into the spirit of the ruse. While Porter's eight gunboats bombarded the forts as if in preparation for an attack, Sherman landed eight regiments and made an ostentatious show of action. As a result Pemberton withdrew troops from the south and rushed them north sixty miles in a hurried march. On orders from Grant, Sherman withdrew and joined the main forces below Vicksburg at Willow Springs on May 3.

Early in May the Richmond authorities suggested to General Lee that Major General George Pickett's division should be sent to Vicksburg to reinforce Pemberton. Lee responded that if his army were thus weakened he might have to fall back on the defenses of Richmond. Pickett was not sent.

General Joseph E. Johnston, who had been kept at Tullahoma, Tennessee, by his superiors in Richmond when his coordination of troops in Mississippi was urgently needed, now received orders to assume the chief command in person at once, and to take with him 3,000 troops from Bragg's army, who would be replaced by Confederates taken by the Federals at Arkansas Post and later released. Richmond promised him reinforcements from Beauregard's troops. Johnston, who was still ill, arrived to find direction of Pemberton's forces extremely difficult. He also received word that General Earl Van Dorn had been assassinated. He was positive that Pemberton would have to unite all his forces and defeat Grant outside of Vicksburg at once, and warned emphatically that if Pemberton retired to Vicksburg he would have no alternative but surrender.

The Federal divisions marched rapidly northeast. Pemberton had ordered Brigadier General Gregg to bring his brigade up from Port Hudson, and when Gregg reached Raymond he was met by General McPherson's Seventeenth Corps and driven out of the place to Jackson. Here he found Brigadier General W. H. T. Walker's brigade from Beauregard's eastern department. General Johnston, still a sick man, arrived that night; he expected to collect 12,000 reinforcements in a few days but he had warned Richmond that if troops were drawn from Tennessee that state would have to be given up. Pemberton's main army was at Edwards' Station (or Depot). Under the impression that McPherson's corps, which had marched to Clinton, was detached to prevent the junction of Johnston's reinforcements with Pemberton, Johnston ordered Pemberton "if practicable" to attack McPherson with all the force he could assemble. But Sherman was also marching toward Jackson, which the Federals occupied by force on May 14, raising the Stars and Stripes to the top of the state capitol of Mississippi. Casualties ran to several hundred on both sides, and the Confederates lost seventeen guns and burned their stores.

Both Grant's quick decisions and the disposition of his forces brought disaster to the Confederates in the next few days. Pemberton decided, after consultation with his officers, to move south from Edwards' Station to cut Grant's communications on the road from Port Gibson to Raymond, but Grant had cut them himself and was not dependent on them. When Pemberton found

Baker's Creek too swollen to ford he decided to follow an earlier order from General Johnston to join him at Clinton, but circumstances already had changed the situation. Grant, expecting this move, had centered his forces on Bolton's Station, halfway between Clinton and Edwards'. Making a long detour to find a usable bridge over Baker's Creek, Pemberton reached Champion Hill (also called Champion's). Upon getting specific reports on May 16 about the direction of Pemberton's army, Grant hurried his troops forward on roads converging on Edwards' Station.

Fighting near Champion Hill

Brigadier General Alvin P. Hovey, commanding the Twelfth Division of McClernand's corps, struck Pemberton's troops on the northern road between Jackson and Vicksburg, and reinforced by two brigades from McPherson's corps joined battle on the Confederate left. The brunt of the day's fighting fell on Hovey, Brigadier General John A. Logan, Brigadier General Marcellus Crocker, and generally on McPherson's corps. General McClernand with two divisions put in the day watching Major General W. W. Loring's division, and although both commanders were importuned by their superiors to get into the battle they ignored orders while neutralizing each other. Grant blamed Pemberton's escape partly on McClernand's lack of "reasonable promptness," but admitted that he had himself unwittingly opened the road to retreat for Pemberton when he removed units to reinforce Hovey, nobody being aware that these units had blocked a retreat. Grant characterized the fighting as two or three hours of skirmishing and four hours of hard fighting. Only about 15,000 Federals were engaged; Hovey had 1,200 casualties, more than one-third of his division, but captured 1,200, while Logan captured 1,300. The Federals lost 410 killed, 1,844 wounded, and 187 missing. Brigadier General Lloyd Tilghman of the First Brigade of Loring's division was killed.

In order to get his army safely back to Vicksburg, Pemberton had to cross the Big Black River. To cover the withdrawal of the troops he used General Loring's division, and then halted Major General John S. Bowen's troops at rifle pits to get Loring's troops across. But owing to harassment by Federal troops Loring turned south, moved entirely around Grant's left, turned east, and led his division into Jackson. Thus he was enabled to join Johnston and escape the capitulation of Vicksburg. The final Confederate troops crossed the river on the morning of May 17, when Grant's troops were again attacking, leaving their fieldpieces behind. They crossed on a railroad bridge and another temporary bridge near it, and destroyed them on Pemberton's orders. Such destruction could retard but not stop the Federals. They crossed on May 18th on floating bridges and pontoons.

General Pemberton, in his report to Johnston, said he had 17,500 effectives in his movement. He reported that he had available sixty days' rations in Vicksburg and Snyder's Mill. When Johnston learned that Pemberton had fallen back to Vicksburg he was exasperated. He blamed himself for not having taken command of Pemberton's army in person, though he admitted he was not strong enough for the ride. His order to Pemberton reflects his chagrin: "If Haines' Bluff is untenable, Vicksburg is of no value and cannot be held; if, therefore, you are invested in Vicksburg you must ultimately surrender. Under such circumstances, instead of losing both troops and place, we must, if possible, save the troops. If it is not too late, evacuate Vicksburg and its dependencies, and march to the Northeast."

But once in, Pemberton did not know how to get out. Building up his own forces, Johnston clung to the hope of relieving Pemberton, but he realized his forces were inadequate in comparison with the growing numbers of Grant's army. In the letters that the two Confederate commanders managed to get through the Federal lines there are suggestions of marching out northward or across the river, but Pemberton reports the bombardment getting stronger, trenches coming closer, and messengers from Johnston failing to get through with badly needed percussion caps.

When Grant ordered his second and last major assault on the heavily defended parapets, May 22, the defenders again demonstrated their ability to stand off the severest onslaught. The attack was delivered at 10 A.M. by troops of Sherman, McPherson, and McClernand, accompanied by heavy shelling. The strongest defenses consisted of a huge redoubt dominating the Jackson Road and held by the Third Louisiana, and this became the objective of regiments of McPherson's corps. The attack was delivered with great energy and at times the Federals planted their flags on the Confederate parapets, but the defenders used musket fire and grenades so effectively that after two hours of incessant struggling the Federals had to withdraw to their trenches without gains.

General Grant had come forward on foot with Sherman to survey the assault and while there received a message by courier from General McClernand to the effect that his troops had captured the parapet in front of his section and "the flag of the Union waves over the stronghold of Vicksburg." He asked Grant to renew orders to McPherson and Sherman to press attacks on their fronts so that the enemy would not concentrate on him. General Grant said: "I don't believe a word of it." Sherman protested that this was official and he was ready to do his share. Grant then started for McClernand's front, giving Sherman a tentative order to try another assault if by 3 P.M. he had sent no other word.

Sherman brought up Brigadier General Joseph A. Mower's brigade from Brigadier General James M. Tuttle's division and made a second assault at 3 P.M., with similar results. It turned out that McClernand's men had taken two small lunettes that were open to the rear, so that once the troops had overrun them they were at the mercy of the Confederates farther back and were captured. The casualties this day were the heaviest of the campaign—3,199, of which number 502 were killed and 2,550 wounded.

Secretary Stanton gave Grant authority to remove McClernand, but Grant delayed action, and General Rawlins, his aide, ascribed his lethargy to a bout with the wine bottle. Rawlins could talk up to Grant and urged him to let drinking alone in the interests of his clear mind and the safety of the army. Another provocation by McClernand was the publication, in the *Missouri Democrat* of St. Louis, of an order in which he congratulated his troops, spoke favorably of his own generalship, suggested that McPherson and Sherman had failed to support him, and that Grant had lost a likely victory by failing to reinforce him. When Sherman read this he exploded in anger, broke into Grant's headquarters, and demanded that McClernand be removed from the command.

Grant called for a copy of the order and upon reading it removed McClernand, ordering him to Springfield for violating War Department orders against unauthorized publication. Major General Edward O. C. Ord succeeded to command of the Thirteenth Army Corps. When Colonel Wilson delivered Grant's order McClernand exclaimed: "I am relieved. By God, sir, we are both relieved!" McClernand, who owed his command to Lincoln, protested to the President, but again Lincoln was not willing to interfere with Grant, who was doing the job he wanted done, so he regretfully told McClernand: "I cannot give you a new command, because we have no forces but that already have commanders."

McClernand's writing was looked upon as a political document and praised by those who opposed Grant. He was later assigned to an army command in Texas, but failing to win the Administration's approval he resigned from the Army in November, 1864.

Grant now decided that frontal attacks against fortified positions were useless and that complete investment of Vicksburg was indicated. Troops were moved up close, and trenches covered with logs and large enough for a man to stand up in them were constructed. Rifle pits were dug and batteries placed in favorable positions. The army finally had 220 guns in position and a battery of heavy naval guns manned by sailors. The troops were within 600 yards of the opposing trenches and the distance was being continually shortened. The Federal line extended fifteen miles north and south from Haines' Bluff to Warrenton, effectively cutting Vicksburg off from the country. In the town itself June was a month of short rations and the simplest kind of food.

But the strong redoubt on the Jackson Road challenged the Federals to make one final attempt to reduce it, and this time they determined to mine the position. This was Grant's first attempt to use a mine, and the operation and results were similar to Burnside's attempt at Petersburg, Virginia, over a year later. The First Brigade of Brigadier General Mortimer D. Leggett of Major General John A. Logan's First Division of McPherson's corps, chiefly Illinois regiments, was called on to do most of the pioneer work, preparing gabions and fascines for galleries to be mined.

When the Confederates on May 25 offered the Federals a truce to bury the dead still lying about from the assault of May 22, the chief engineer of the Army was able to make a close inspection of the area to be mined. Soldiers who had been coal miners were used to drive a gallery four feet wide, five feet high, toward the parapet of the fort, and then build lateral galleries.

A total of 2,200 pounds of powder was exploded on the afternoon of June 25. The Confederates, in anticipation of the attack, had moved back their line so that only a few men were affected by the explosion. They also had been countermining, without effect. The Federals captured the crater made by the explosion but suffered much from grenades rolled down on them by the defenders. A Negro who had been employed on the Confederate side was thrown into the air and landed in the Federal lines; he was then given a job in General John A. Logan's headquarters. A second mine destroyed a Confederate redan July 1. Both sides were busy digging tunnels for mines when hostilities closed.

Pemberton Yields Vicksburg

Pemberton notified his four division commanders on July 1 that "unless the siege of Vicksburg is raised, or supplies are thrown in, it will become necessary very shortly to evacuate this place." He asked about the ability of the troops to make the march necessary for a successful evacuation. The commanders had doubts and two of them, Major Generals Smith and Bowen, advocated surrender. General Johnston, when consulted, refused to carry on negotiations, telling Pemberton: "It would be a confession of weakness on my part, which I ought not to make, to propose them." As early as June 15 he had told Secretary of War Seddon: "I consider saving Vicksburg hopeless."

At 10 A.M. on July 3 white flags were raised on part of the Confederate lines and fighting stopped there. Major General John S. Bowen and Colonel L. M. Montgomery, Pemberton's aide, brought the commander's written request for an armistice to arrange terms. Pemberton asked that three commissioners represent him and three act for Grant, "to save further effusion of blood, which must otherwise be shed to a frightful extent, feeling myself able to maintain my position for a yet indefinite period." Grant was there to dictate terms, not to arrange a bargain through commissioners; he refused to meet Bowen, whom he had known in St. Louis before the war, but said he would meet Pemberton in front of McPherson's corps at 3 P.M. He sent Pemberton word that "the useless effusion of blood you propose stopping by this course can be ended at any time you may choose by the unconditional surrender of the city and garrison." He praised the courage and endurance of his opponents and said they would be treated "with all the respect due to prisoners of war."

There followed at three o'clock the famous hillside chat between the commanding generals. They met near an oak tree that soon afterward disappeared under the knives of those who had an insatiable appetite for souvenirs. Grant knew Pemberton; they had served in the same division during part of the Mexican War. When Grant, in reply to Pemberton, reiterated that he had no other terms than unconditional surrender Pemberton, according to his own account, declared: "I can assure you, sir, you will bury many more of your men before you enter Vicksburg."

Grant did not reply. Confederate General Bowen took Brigadier General Andrew J. Smith aside and they conferred separately. Bowen asked that the Confederate army be permitted to march out with its small arms and field artillery. This was rejected. Grant then agreed to send his final terms at 10 P.M. He talked matters over with his generals and sent word to Pemberton that he wanted paroles signed by officers and men; officers could take side arms and clothing, and the field, staff, and cavalry officers could take one horse each. The privates could take their clothing but no other property. Cooking utensils and rations could be removed, and thirty wagons would be set aside to carry heavy articles.

Pemberton had no choice. He considered Grant's final terms a modification of unconditional surrender, which would have meant making everyone a prisoner of war. Grant had learned from Admiral Porter that there was no transport available to carry a huge number of prisoners to Cairo and thence to points to be exchanged. It would be easier to parole them. He judged that many of the Confederates had homes in the Southwest, were tired of fighting, and probably would go home and spread word of the hardships they had suffered.

The Vicksburg newspaper that was printed on wallpaper and has since become a museum piece advised the Federals that if they wished to eat their dinner in Vicksburg on July 4 they had better first "ketch your rabbit." In its last issue on July 4 the newspaper announced the rabbit had been caught. The people of Vicksburg had suffered many privations. The siege had lasted forty-seven days.

The Vicksburg garrison marched out on July 4, stacked arms, and marched back in again. The Union army was led into Vicksburg by General John A. Logan's Third Division of McPherson's army corps, and the United States flag was raised over the courthouse, which is today a war museum. Grant rode down to the riverbank to congratulate the fleet on the "joint victory." He saw that many citizens had carved holes out of the firm yellow clay of the banks of the Mississippi and the Big Black Rivers, and even had rooms with clay walls separating them. In these quarters they were safe from shelling from the fleet.

Grant had judged the temper of the troops and the situation rightly. The Confederates still had rations for about two weeks and thus drew on their own supplies. Grant kept their whole army in Vicksburg until paroles were signed. The commanders signed in duplicate, one copy for the Federal records and one for their own. Every private signed individually, keeping one copy for himself. The total number paroled was 29,491. Grant believed many were tired of fighting, and this was verified when some refused to sign, preferring to be Union prisoners until the end of the war, whereas others absented themselves entirely. Pemberton asked Grant to let him arm a battalion, so that he could keep the troops in line, but Grant refused this request, for he was quite willing to see men desert the Confederate ranks, which many did after they had marched out.

There was no direct wire to Washington, so Grant had to report his victory by sending Captain Dunn of his staff to Cairo with this message for General Halleck:

The enemy surrendered this morning. The only terms allowed is their parole as prisoners of war. This I regard as a great advantage to us at this moment. It saves, probably, several days in the capture, and leaves troops and transports ready for immediate service. Sherman, with a large force, moves immediately on Johnston, to drive him from the state. I will send troops to the relief of Banks and return the Ninth Army Corps to Burnside.

Grant reported that the surrender included 31,600 men, 172 cannon, and 60,000 muskets. Many of the small arms were better than some of those carried by Union troops; therefore the latter took the better Confederate arms and placed their own in the stacks of captured guns. The Confederates reported they had 6,000 in their hospitals.

The principal land actions under Major General U. S. Grant in 1863 covered about 180 miles of fighting and skirmishing after May 1. The Union army had 43,000 men during most of the campaign and was swelled to around 75,000 at the end.

General Grant estimated the total Confederate forces operating against him at 60,000; Johnston reported he had 24,000 and Pemberton around 30,000. The Union army had 9,362 casualties in the eight weeks, May 1 to July 4, when the principal fighting took place; this comprised 1,514 killed, 7,395 wounded, 453 captured or missing. Incomplete Confederate reports for the same period indicated about 9,000 casualties, with 1,200 killed, 3,572 wounded, and 4,227 captured or missing. Grant said he was fortunate in fighting the Confederates in detail, in units of 5,000, 8,000, and 11,000 except at Champion Hill, where he met 25,000. His chief battles were: near Port Gibson, May 1; Raymond, May 12; Jackson, the state capital, May 14; Champion Hill, May 16; Big Black River crossing, May 17. At Champion Hill the Federals had 410 killed, 844 wounded.

After Vicksburg, President Lincoln made Grant a major general in the regular army, the highest rank then available; Sherman and McPherson were made brigadier generals in the regular army.

The Union generals had frequent access to dispatches that passed between Pemberton and General Joseph E. Johnston and knew that General Johnston had been collecting a big force near the Big Black River with the intention of attacking the rear of Grant's army. They estimated Johnston's force at 30,000 to 40,000 men; actually Johnston had about 20,000 effective infantry and artillery and 2,000 cavalry. Grant drew on several corps to give General Sherman command of an army large enough to operate against Johnston. Immediately after Vicksburg surrendered, the troops were put in motion toward Bolton; they included the Thirteenth Corps under General Edward O. C. Ord, the Ninth under Major General John G. Parke, and Sherman's own Fifteenth. Near Clinton, Sherman discovered that Johnston in withdrawing "had caused cattle, hogs and sheep to be driven into the ponds and there shot down, so that we had to haul their dead and stinking carcasses out to use the water."

On July 9 Sherman reached Jackson, where Johnston's army had halted behind light entrenchments and rifle pits. Johnston was determined to repel assaults, and ordered Brigadier General W. H. Jackson's cavalry to guard the fords of the Pearl River. The Federal artillery reached every part of the town. An assault by Brigadier General Jacob G. Lauman's division of Ord's corps on July 12 was repulsed by Major General John C. Breckinridge. Lauman's Illinois regiments had 533 casualties, and the total for all Federal units ran close to 1,000. Despite this Johnston realized that his troops could not resist a siege. On the night of July 16 he left by way of bridges over the Pearl and established camp at Morton. The Union divisions, after burning Jackson, were called back to Vicksburg, while General Sherman's corps went into camp near the Big Black River.

After the Union army occupied New Orleans and Baton Rouge, the Confederates strongly fortified Port Hudson, Louisiana, 135 miles upriver from New Orleans. They placed 21 heavy guns there, built up their garrison to 16,000 men, and extended trenches and rifle pits for three miles. In December, 1862, Major General Nathaniel P. Banks succeeded Major General Butler at New Orleans as commander of the Department of the Gulf, and his major objective was to clear the Mississippi River valley of opposition all the way to Vicksburg, cooperating in this with the fleet. He promptly reoccupied Baton Rouge, which had been relinquished by Butler when troops were needed elsewhere, and planned a major expedition against Port Hudson. For this purpose he ferried nearly 20,000 men to the country around Port Hudson, an area of swollen bayous, flooded roads, thickly interlaced trees and semitropical jungle, and miasmic swamps and ooze. For seven weeks the troops were engaged in actions around Port Hudson, placing it in state of siege.

The Confederate garrison under Major General Frank Gardner had been reduced to about 7,000 defenders because troops had been sent to aid Vicksburg, but their defense was exceedingly capable, and in two unsuccessful assaults Banks's troops had 4,000 casualties. The Federals also had clashed in a number of engagements with a Confederate force of about 5,000 under General Taylor, who received reinforcements from Texas and began to menace the west bank of the Mississippi near New Orleans, threatening Banks's communications to such an extent that General William C. Emory warned him that he would have to choose between Port Hudson and New Orleans. The Federals prepared two mines and had 1,000 volunteers ready to charge into the works as soon as the mines were sprung, when word came of the surrender of Vicksburg.

Grant had written General Banks describing the terms enforced at Vicksburg and promising him "all the troops he wanted" to capture Port Hudson, the only river stronghold still in the hands of the Confederates. Banks published the contents of the letter and a copy was tossed over the parapet and found its way to General Gardner, commander at Port Hudson. Gardner told Banks that if the news were true he could not hold out longer. He surrendered unconditionally on July 9, turning over 6,223 men, 51 guns, and 5,000 small arms. His men were famished. The Federals took 6,340 prisoners, and liberated about 500 of their own men. They had 707 killed, 3,336 wounded, 319 missing, but this did not count the thousands who were stricken by pestilential fevers. This was the first appearance in battle of colored troops—the Corps d'Afrique, which had fifteen men killed.

Grant and Cotton Speculators

During this period Grant was harassed endlessly by administrative duties and had to deal with countless civilian matters in his department. His most questionable order, No. 11, curtailing the activities of speculators who attempted to profit by shortages induced by the war, was issued at this time. What makes it a blot on Grant's record is that he characterized all venal operators as Jews and directed that all Jewish traders be kept out of his Department. Bruce Catton, who examines all facets of this controversial order in *Grant Moves South* (1960) proves that Grant was not anti-Semitic by nature but that the bias against Jewish traders was characteristic of this period. Grant's indignation was fanned when his father, Jesse Grant, arrived with a plea for special treatment. He had formed a partnership with two Cincinnati Jews named Mack to obtain a permit from his son to buy and ship cotton. Traders frequently came into the Southern areas occupied by Union troops by means of special permits and bought cotton, for which they paid in gold, a violation, until then, of the Treasury act against using specie. Grant, who saw himself being used, promptly had both his father and associates escorted out of his Department. When Washington learned of Grant's order General Halleck informed Grant that President Lincoln wanted the order revoked because it reflected on the religion of citizens loyal in their support of the North, and so Grant withdrew it.

While Grant thus received the President's reproof because he had expressed himself forcibly in an order, General Sherman escaped censure when he wrote similar opinions to Secretary Chase of the Treasury in a letter, which did not see the light until Sherman's *Memoirs* appeared in 1875. Sherman therein explained how United States gold currency was being abused. In the early part of the war Southern sympathizers in Tennessee destroyed their cotton with the approval of the Confederate government whenever Federal armies approached, because they expected it to be seized. When speculators discovered "that ten cents would buy a pound of cotton behind our army; that four cents would take it to Boston, where they could receive thirty cents in gold," and that salt, bacon, powder, firearms, percussion caps were worth as much as gold to the South, a brisk traffic resulted. At Memphis, Sherman ordered that gold, silver, and Treasury notes of the United States were contraband of war in his area, and should not go into the hostile interior of Tennessee. But Secretary Chase wanted to promote the purchase of cotton, which was worth about $300 a bale and usable in foreign exchange. He encouraged the movement of cotton out of the Southern states and thus, according to Sherman, started hundreds of greedy speculators down the Mississippi, often paying gold for cotton to enemies of the Union, who had stores of cotton hidden and used the proceeds to the detriment of the United States.

22

THE GETTYSBURG CAMPAIGN

Lee Begins His March North

In the spring of 1863 the fighting spirit of the Confederate army in Virginia was at its peak. Despite its inferiority in men, ordnance, and supplies, it had proved more than equal to the challenge of the Federals. The Confederate government at Richmond was heartened by

the great successes at Fredericksburg and Chancellorsville, but the President, Jefferson Davis, was disturbed
because these victories had brought no change in the
Federal determination to fight rather than compromise,
and had not won national recognition for the Confederacy
from European governments. Also, the position of the
South had not materially improved. The land that was
being ravaged belonged to the South. The Federal army
was intact and being reinforced. In the West, General
Pemberton's defense of Vicksburg was not promising.
New Orleans and the Mississippi River were controlled
by the Federals.

During the second week of May, 1863, President Davis
called General Lee from his headquarters near Hamilton's Crossing on the Rappahannock and held a conference at Richmond. The Secretary of War, Seddon, and
other members of the cabinet were present. General Lee
said he was ready to lead a new expedition into the lush
Pennsylvania farmland, which was filled with livestock and supplies badly needed by the Confederate army.
There were indications that General Hooker, then at Stafford Heights opposite Fredericksburg, was preparing for
a new campaign, and the prospect of more fighting along
the Rappahannock did not please the Confederate leaders.
Lee had hopes of drawing the Army of the Potomac from
its base and defeating it on Northern territory, without
placing Richmond in any danger. As he said after Chancellorsville, he had considered his army invincible. Despite its lack of clothing, ordnance, food, and horses it
was a powerful fighting machine.

Before the new campaign started, Lee reorganized his
army. His hardest task was to replace Stonewall Jackson.
Jackson, better than any other commander, suited Lee's
manner of delegating authority; if Lee had a general plan,
Jackson knew how to carry out the details. To the com-
mand of Jackson's Second Army Corps, Lee appointed
Richard S. Ewell, who was promoted to lieutenant general.
Longstreet remained in charge of the First Corps, but
Lee took General Richard H. Anderson's division from
this corps to begin to form a new one, the Third, with A. P.
Hill, also promoted to lieutenant general, in command.

At first Lee was not certain that Richmond might not

be threatened by a new movement of the Federal forces. He recommended bringing up General Beauregard and troops from the Carolinas and placing his headquarters at Culpeper, to worry Washington. The Federal army was being reinforced, but Lee's scouts had been unable to ascertain Hooker's plans. Within a few weeks withdrawals of small Federal forces from the Tidewater suggested that Richmond would not be threatened. Lee, who was still at Hamilton's Crossing, ordered the advance to begin June 3, when a number of divisions left the Fredericksburg encampments and took the direction of Culpeper Court House. General Hill and the Third Corps were left behind to watch Hooker. When Hooker saw that Confederate troops were leaving he placed pontoons across the Rappahannock at Deep Run and sent over a force of infantry with artillery support. Lee retarded the advance of the Second Corps pending developments. When he had Hill make demonstrations farther down the river Hooker withdrew and recrossed the Rappahannock.

Hooker knew what would happen if Lee moved his army and he was prepared for action, but he had to ask Washington about every important step. On June 5 he wrote to President Lincoln for specific instructions. He reminded Lincoln that the "major general commanding the army," meaning General Halleck, had ordered him to "keep in view the importance of covering Washington and Harpers Ferry, either directly or by so operating as to be able to punish any force of the enemy sent against them." Then, continued Hooker, "in the event the enemy should move, as I almost anticipate he will, the head of his column will probably be headed toward the Potomac, via Gordonsville or Culpeper, while the rear will rest on Fredericksburg." He believed it his duty to "pitch into his rear, although in doing so the head of his column may reach Warrenton before I can return. Will it be within the spirit of my instructions to do so?" Then he added a strong appeal for "one commander for all of the troops whose operations can have an influence on those of Lee's army. Under the present system, all independent commanders are in ignorance of the movements of the others; at least such is my situation." Lincoln replied the same day. He said he had turned over to General Halleck the task of replying concerning military matters. He warned that if Lee came to the north of the Rappahannock, Hooker ought not cross to the south of it. If Lee should leave a rear force at Fredericksburg and Hooker was tempted to fall upon it, it would fight in entrenchments and worst him, while Lee's main force would be getting the advantage of Hooker northward. "In one word, I would not take any risk of being entangled upon the river, like an ox jumped half over a fence, and liable to be torn by dogs front and rear without a fair chance to gore one way or kick the other." This was bitter advice to Hooker, since the President showed he had no confidence whatever in any fighting Hooker might do.

Despite restrictions on his actions, General Hooker was alert and conscientiously trying to find out what Lee was doing. He had his reorganized cavalry corps and now ordered General Pleasonton to raid General Stuart's camp at Culpeper and get information about the whereabouts and movements of the Confederate forces. During this first week in June, 1863, Stuart's cavalry was strung out between Brandy Station and Culpeper. Stuart's headquarters were in a house on Fleetwood Hill, north of Brandy Station and about four miles from Beverly Ford on the Rappahannock. Since camping there he had been staging reviews of his troops, which satisfied his love of pageantry. The fields in this area were the scene of a review of 4,000 horsemen on May 22. By June 5 the brigades of Generals Beverly H. Robertson and William E. Jones had been added, almost doubling his numbers, so another review was called for. This was quite elaborate, with a cavalry charge accompanied by artillery fire as part of the program. Following this General Lee sent word that he would like to review the cavalry, so another program was given June 8, slightly subdued because Lee would not permit charges or gunfire. On the next day Stuart was to pack up and march north.

This was the time when General Pleasonton chose to intervene. On the night of June 8 he reached the northern bank of the Rappahannock. He had three divisions of cavalry and two brigades of infantry, in all 10,981 men. He divided them into two columns and at daybreak on June 9 Brigadier General John Buford, with infantry under

General Ames, crossed at Beverly Ford, while Brigadier Generals David McM. Gregg and Duffié, and infantry under General Russell, crossed at Kelly's Ford. Buford crossed first and drove in Stuart's pickets toward the main body at St. James' Church. Stuart sent Robertson to Kelly's Ford and Colonel M. C. Butler's Second South Carolina Cavalry to Brandy Station. Gregg crossed at Kelly's Ford and headed for Brandy Station and sent Duffié to Stevensburg. In the clash at Brandy Station, Brigadier General W. H. F. Lee was wounded. At Stevensburg, Duffié was attacked by Colonel Butler's South Carolinians and Colonel W. C. Wickham's Fourth Virginia Cavalry, and after some fighting retained a hold on the village. During the battle Colonel Butler lost a leg. Moving up from Brandy Station, Gregg found Buford hotly engaged, and charged Fleetwood Hill. The hill changed hands several times and when Duffié failed to arrive to help, Gregg had to give it up, losing three out of four guns. Finally Duffié arrived with word that Confederate infantry was moving up from Culpeper, whereupon General Pleasonton ordered his brigades to withdraw the way they had come. This was considered one of the first engagements in which protracted cavalry fighting took place, although there had been numerous skirmishes before. The Federals lost 421 killed and wounded, the Confederates 301.

Colonel Butler lost his leg under unusual circumstances. He had stopped in the road to talk with Captain W. D. Farley, Stuart's aide, and their horses' heads were facing opposite directions. A shell struck the ground, bounced up and cut off Butler's right leg above the ankle, passed through his horse and Farley's horse and carried away Farley's leg at the knee. Farley died but Butler survived and later became a U.S. Senator.

Pleasonton's raid uncovered a large body of Confederate infantry around Culpeper. Hooker moved his right up the Rappahannock and on June 13 occupied Thoroughfare Gap. Pleasonton and Kilpatrick had a number of brushes with Stuart, one at Aldie, Virginia, June 17, another at Uppersville, Virginia, June 21, after which Stuart withdrew through Ashby's Gap.

General Hooker had good reason to be irritated with

the Administration. It kept him at the head of the Army of the Potomac when a crisis was impending, but it tied his hands. His orders were contradictory. Even after Chancellorsville, Lincoln had asked Hooker to assume the offensive. And what was Hooker to make of the dispatch he received from Lincoln on June 14: "If the head of Lee's army is at Martinsburg and the tail of it on the Plank Road between Fredericksburg and Chancellorsville, the animal must be very slim somewhere. Could you not break him?" Then there was the attitude of Lincoln's reluctance to remove Hooker after Chancellorsville, reported by Major General John F. Reynolds to General Meade and not known to Hooker.

Early in June, when no one knew for certain which way Lee meant to march, the presence of large masses of Confederate infantry moving up the Shenandoah Valley alarmed Governor Andrew G. Curtin of Pennsylvania. He warned the citizens of the impending invasion and announced organization of departments of defense in Harrisburg and Pittsburg (the city did not officially spell it "Pittsburgh" until years later). In command of home defense was Major General Darius N. Couch, who had been so disgusted with Hooker that he had left the Army of the Potomac. Unfortunately, he had no dependable troops in Pennsylvania; the state's generals and enlisted men were at the front, and the stolid farmers of southern Pennsylvania did not seem eager to rush to arms. Among the Pennsylvania leaders in the Union army were Generals Hancock, Meade, Reynolds, and Pleasonton. By mid-June Curtin could point to evidence that the Confederates were coming, for Brigadier General Albert G. Jenkins arrived with cavalry to levy on Chambersburg for supplies.

General Lee had great difficulty screening his movement into Pennsylvania from General Hooker's Army of the Potomac. This difficulty increased after he had given General Stuart discretionary orders to detach himself from the Confederate army with the major part of his brigades and move independently. In his report after the battle General Lee attributed part of his failure to ignorance of the movements of the enemy, and some of his officers as well as later historians blamed the absence of

General Stuart for this. There is no doubt that had Stuart been acting in close cooperation with Lee or Longstreet as the eyes of the army Lee would have been better informed. Longstreet, in trying to establish why the Confederates failed, wrote with bitterness of Stuart's absence, which he thought due either to "a misapprehension of orders or love of the éclat of a bold raid." Lee's orders, however, did give Stuart considerable range of action, so that the blame must rest in part on Lee.

On June 22 Lee sent a letter to Longstreet enclosing an open letter to Stuart, then acting in cooperation with Longstreet. In this Lee asked concerning the enemy:

Do you know where he is and what he is doing? I fear he will steal a march on us and get across the Potomac before we are aware. If you find that he is moving northward and that two brigades can guard the Blue Ridge and take care of your rear, you can move with the other three into Maryland and take position on General Ewell's right, place yourself in communication with him, guard his flank and keep him informed of the enemy's movements, and collect all the supplies you can for the use of the army. One column of General Ewell's army will probably move toward the Susquehanna by the Emmitsburg route, another by Chambersburg. Accounts from him last night state that there was no enemy west of Fredericktown. A cavalry force (about one hundred) guarded the Monocacy Bridge, which was barricaded. You will, of course, take charge of Jenkins' Brigade and give him necessary instructions. . . .

On the next day, June 23, Lee replied to notes from Stuart, saying:

If Hooker's army remains inactive you can leave two brigades to watch him and withdraw with the three others, but should he not appear to be moving northward, I think you had better withdraw this side of the mountain tomorrow night, cross at Shepherdstown next day, and move over to Fredericktown. You will, however, be able to judge whether you can pass around their army without hindrance, doing them all the damage you can, and cross the river east of the mountains. In either case, after crossing the river, you must move on and feel the right of Ewell's troops, collecting information, provisions, etc. Give instructions to the commander of the brigades left behind to watch the flank and rear of the army and (in the event of the enemy leaving their front) retire from the mountains west of the Shenandoah, leaving sufficient pickets to guard the passes, and bringing everything clean along the valley, closing upon the rear of the army. As regards the movement of the two brigades of the enemy moving toward Warrenton, the commander of the brigades to be left in the mountains must do what he can to counteract them; but I think the sooner you cross into Maryland, after tomorrow, the better. . . . Hill's first division will reach the Potomac today and Longstreet will follow tomorrow. Be watchful and circumspect in all your movements.

When Lee gave his instructions to Stuart he told Longstreet that Stuart might go by way of Hopewell Gap and pass by the rear of the enemy. Longstreet also thought that a better route than bypassing the Potomac by the Confederate rear, which might disclose Lee's plans to the enemy. "You had better not leave us unless you can take the proposed route in rear of the enemy," said Longstreet. In later writings Longstreet gave the impression that he had been opposed to Stuart's leaving his army, but it is evident that he placed no obstacle in the way of Stuart's going.

Longstreet did expect the cavalry that remained behind to keep in touch with his First Corps, and he asked Stuart to instruct the commanding officer, who he supposed would be General Wade Hampton, to connect with him at Millwood. This request Stuart disregarded. He named Brigadier General B. H. Robertson to remain behind with his own brigade and that of Brigadier General William E. Jones, and two batteries of horse artillery. Robertson was to cover Ashby's and Snicker's gaps, and to prevent the enemy from obtaining possession of them. He was to watch at Harpers Ferry and, if the enemy moved beyond his reach, he was to cross the Potomac and follow, keeping on his right and rear, offer what resistance was necessary, and counteract any movement on Warrenton. Stuart ordered Robertson to report anything of importance to Longstreet.

While Robertson carried out orders to watch the gaps and carry out other picket duty, he seems to have been unable to give Lee any precise information about Hooker's movements. The contention of Stuart's defenders that Lee was not deprived wholly of the cavalry because of the brigades left behind would seem to be offset by the fact that Lee gained nothing important from the latter.

Meade Takes Command

Major General George Gordon Meade, commander of the Fifth Army Corps, was appointed commander of the Army of the Potomac on June 28, when the President accepted General Hooker's resignation. Hooker virtually had been forced to resign when his superiors in Washington refused to let him start military action that he considered highly necessary. They conceded that he had built a fine organization after the defeat at Chancellorsville, that he was personally eager to fight, and that many of his subordinates were loyal to him. But ever since Lee started north they had checked Hooker. He had been warned against attacking Lee's rear at Fredericksburg. When, on June 10, he suggested an immediate march on Richmond, he was told that Lee's army and not Richmond was his objective. On June 28 Hooker ordered the Twelfth Corps to Harpers Ferry, to be joined by the troops on Maryland Heights and to work with General Reynolds in destroying Lee's communications. This was countermanded by General Halleck. Hooker then resigned, with the statement that he was not allowed to maneuver his own army in the presence of the enemy.

The reason for the Administration's lack of confidence in Hooker was his conduct of Chancellorsville and his retreat there. When President Lincoln and General Halleck had investigated that battle they agreed with Secretary Stanton that Hooker's action was inexcusable. They then determined that he should not command during another major battle. When Lee's march north showed that a battle was imminent, Stanton urged the appointment of a new commander. Major General John F. Reynolds evidently had been considered, but had refused. Hooker's resignation was at hand, and was accepted, and Meade was named. It was considered likely that Meade would object, so any protest was denied him at the start. General James A. Hardie, chief of staff of the Secretary of War, was sent to order both Hooker and Meade to make the transfer of command immediately. When Hardie was leaving and Meade was bidding him farewell, Meade said: "Well, I've been tried and condemned without a hearing, and I suppose I shall have to go to execution." Meade's Fifth Corps was given to Major General George Sykes, who had commanded its Second Division at Chancellorsville. Meade later made General Reynolds commander of his left wing.

General Meade was forty-eight, and a graduate of West Point, class of 1835. He had served in the Seminole War, worked as a civil engineer on railroads, and in 1842 returned to the military service as a topographical engineer. He served in the Mexican War and afterward was employed on lighthouses as captain of topographical engineers, and on the Great Lakes. In 1861 he was made brigadier general of volunteers and commanded the Second Brigade of the Pennsylvania Reserves. He was wounded at Frayser's Farm and out of the fighting until Second Bull Run, where he commanded a division. At Chancellorsville, he was a major general of volunteers and in command of the Fifth Corps.

First Day at Gettysburg

On the night of June 28 Longstreet from Chambersburg gave General Lee information that vitally affected his campaign into Pennsylvania. Longstreet had a scout named Harrison, whom he provided with gold to pay for visits to Washington, Frederick, and other places to get information about the Union Army. On June 28, Harrison arrived with important news. He disclosed that Hooker had crossed the Potomac on June 25 and 26 and had two army corps at Frederick, one near Frederick, and two near South Mountain. When Longstreet informed Lee the latter was inclined to be skeptical and was said to have regretted that he was not hearing from General Stuart. Eventually he decided to question the scout.

The scout was also credited with bringing information that Hooker had been replaced by Meade. Inasmuch as the appointment of Meade was not announced to the army until June 28, the day Harrison reached Longstreet, there is some doubt that Harrison, who had a difficult and long road to travel, actually conveyed that news, or that Lee reversed his orders solely on this man's report. On June 28 Lee still had his army facing north. General Ewell was headed for Harrisburg. He had reached Carlisle on June 27 and had sent back 3,000 head of beef cattle, taken from Pennsylvania farmers, and word where 5,000 barrels of flour were stored. Longstreet was to follow Ewell on June 29. General John D. Imboden's cavalry brigade had been ordered to guard Ewell's left, but had been diverted to Hanover. Brigadier General John B. Gordon of Early's division had moved through Gettysburg to York; after he had crossed the Susquehanna River at Wrightsville the bridge had been set on fire by Pennsylvania militia. Stuart's troops had tried to help the citizens put out the fire, but could not save the bridge. Part of Early's division was at York on June 28.

General Lee acted quickly to fend off the threat from the Union army. He now realized that he could not afford to have the Union army endanger his rear while his units were scattered. He immediately countermanded the march to Harrisburg and reversed the direction of the army. He ordered a concentration at Carlisle. Ewell being already there, he ordered him to move to Cashtown or Gettysburg. Lacking the help of cavalry scouts, General Lee called in the cavalry command of General Imboden, which was at Hanover, two days' ride away, and those of Generals Beverly H. Robertson and William E. Jones, still in Virginia. He ordered Longstreet to follow Ewell, both going by way of Chambersburg. General Pickett's division of Longstreet's corps was to remain in Chambersburg to protect trains and the rear. General Heth's division of Hill's corps was ordered to Cashtown, to be followed by Pender's division on June 30, and R. H. Anderson's on July 1.

General Lee had been disturbed by a report that suggested a large body of Federal troops was near Gettysburg. This was relayed by General Hill, who said that Brigadier General J. J. Pettigrew's brigade of Heth's division had started for Gettysburg the day before to obtain shoes and turned back after seeing Federal cavalry and hearing infantry drums outside the town.

Lee's headquarters had been at Greenwood, sixteen miles from Gettysburg. Early on the morning of July 1

he started riding down the Chambersburg Pike, in company with Longstreet. As they rode along they heard the
distant rumble of artillery fire. Eager to find out what it
meant Lee hurried ahead alone. At Cashtown he found
General R. H. Anderson and asked him for news, but
Anderson had none. Anderson quoted Lee as saying: "I
cannot think what has become of Stuart. . . . I am in
ignorance as to what we have in front of us here. . . . If
it is the whole Federal force, we must fight a battle here."

The Chambersburg Pike led in a southeasterly direction to Gettysburg. This country town in the rolling hills
east of the low Green Ridge mountains was a place where
all roads converged like spokes of a wheel. Running
northeasterly from Gettysburg was the road to Philadelphia. Due north went a road to Carlisle, twenty-seven
miles away. To the southwest ran the road to Hagerstown, thirty-six miles away. The Harrisburg road, northeast by north, was between the Carlisle and Philadelphia
roads, and Harrisburg was only thirty-six miles distant.
South of Gettysburg there were three important thoroughfares that would have important roles in the battle: the
Emmitsburg Road, going southwest and passing between
two ridges that were to become historic; Seminary and
Cemetery ridges; Taneytown Road, running south and east
of Cemetery Ridge; and the Baltimore Pike, going southeast. One other road out of the town was the Hanover
Road, east by south.

General Meade gave Major General John F. Reynolds
field command over the First, Third, and Eleventh
Corps and over the movements of Brigadier General John
Buford's two cavalry brigades. This made Reynolds the
highest ranking officer in contact with the enemy on the
eve of the battle and the man who had the greatest influence on the first day's fighting. With this Reynolds
turned the command of his First Corps over to Major
General Abner Doubleday. On June 30 General Sykes,
who commanded the Fifth Corps, was still ten miles east
of Taneytown, while General O. O. Howard with the
Eleventh Corps was at Emmitsburg. In a late dispatch
Meade told Reynolds that he must fall back on Emmitsburg if opposed by any force and added: "Your present

position was given more with a view to an advance on Gettysburg than on a defensive point."

Reynolds made his headquarters in a tavern on the Emmitsburg Road near Marsh Creek. He not only expected a battle but thought it might take place just north of Emmitsburg covering the road to Taneytown. When he urged commanders of his two left corps to move up he added: "Face towards Gettysburg." Buford had similar views. It was Buford's cavalry that had kept General Pettigrew's footsore men from requisitioning new shoes on June 30. Buford had his two brigades watching two approaches to Gettysburg from the north.

The Confederate advance came down the Cashtown Road early on July 1, 1863. This was General Heth's division of Hill's Third Corps. Brigadier General James J. Archer's brigade was at the right of the pike, and Brigadier General Joseph R. Davis' at the left. Skirmishers were well out in front and were exchanging shots with Union men at Willoughby's Run. The first Federals to challenge them were dismounted cavalrymen of Colonel Thomas C. Devin's brigade, comprising one Pennsylvania and three New York regiments. All were equipped with new Spencer repeating carbines. Working with them was young Lieutenant John Haskell Calef, only five years out of West Point, now commanding Battery A, Second U.S. Artillery, his six guns holding the center of Devin's line, blasting away until overcome by Colonel W. J. Pegram's nineteen.

Buford and Reynolds had climbed to the cupola of the Seminary and sized up the situation as dangerous. Reynolds hurried General Wadsworth's division and Captain James Hall's Second Maine Battery to the spot where the guns gave evidence that the battle was on, and ordered Generals Doubleday and Howard to follow at once. Wadsworth had been posted at the Codori Farm on the Emmitsburg Road and to reach the fighting Reynolds led the way through fences and across farmland. The battling was at Willoughby's Run, Seminary Ridge, and in the cut of the unfinished railroad. Buford had about 2,500 men, and the First Corps would supply 8,200. Wadsworth's division comprised two brigades, the Iron Brigade of Brigadier General Solomon Meredith, chiefly

Wisconsin regiments and some Michigan and Indiana men, and Brigadier General Lysander Cutler's brigade of New York and Pennsylvania troops. Cutler was first in battle, crossing the Chambersburg Pike and the unfinished railroad bed to engage Davis. The Iron Brigade moved west of the Pike to the McPherson farm, over the ridge. Just beyond, Tennessee and Alabama troops of Archer's brigade were moving from the north into McPherson's wood, 200 yards from the stone barn, General Reynolds urged the approaching Federals to seize it before the Confederates could make it a base for enfilading. As he rode toward the wood he shouted: "Forward, for God's sake, forward!" An instant later he pitched off his horse and on his face. A bullet had entered his skull and General Reynolds was dead.

From now on the battle increased in intensity and in the number of combatants. General Howard stepped into General Reynolds' authority, and General Carl Schurz took over command of the Eleventh Corps. If that corps had been censurable for being surprised by Stonewall Jackson at Chancellorsville, it redeemed itself nobly by its fighting ardor. No less resolute was the First Corps; these two, with their 18,000 men, stood off the Confederate army as it grew with the arrival of new divisions. Ewell's corps arrived with General Rodes' division in the van, taking position on Seminary Ridge. Ewell saw the strategic advantage of Oak Hill and placed Carter's artillery on it, enabling it to catch Doubleday's troops in the flank. At 3 P.M. General Early's division moved up. As the whole Confederate line advanced under the eyes of Lee the Federal line began to withdraw, some of the troops moving through Gettysburg to the east. The Federal artillery tore great gaps in the Confederate ranks, but the numbers were unequal. As the Federals fell back to Cemetery Hill they found the defense line strong both in batteries and entrenchments. Late in the afternoon General Hancock arrived with orders from Meade to take command of the left wing.

Many of the Federal batteries had suffered severely, but none had experiences as fantastic as those of Colonel Charles S. Wainwright of the First Corps Artillery. Hearing the order that the troops were going to hold Cemetery Hill at all costs and never having heard of any other hill than Seminary, Colonel Wainwright assumed that the defense of his position on Seminary was meant. The dispositions of his batteries were excellent and his fire did great damage to the Confederates, but as their numbers increased he became practically isolated. Only after he saw the blue lines moving steadily away from him did it occur to him to follow, and then he attempted to avoid alarming the enemy by a quick withdrawal and took his time. But as he proceeded along the Cashtown Road at a walk the Confederates spotted him and raced down the ridge with their muskets. They shot down horses; three caissons had to be abandoned and one blew up, and one gun was left behind. The brigade lost eighty men and as many horses.

During the fighting on the McPherson farm, John L. Burns of Gettysburg, "a little old man in a swallowtail coat with brass buttons," joined the Wisconsin troops with his rifle. He was three times wounded, but survived to become a local hero.

The advantage of occupying Cemetery Hill and the high ground around it was immediately clear to General Lee, and also to Generals Early, Rodes, and Trimble of Ewell's corps, but Ewell was quite guarded in his views about it. Because the generals were so insistent, Ewell sent Lee word that Rodes and Early said they could take Cemetery Hill if supported on the right, and Ewell added that it might be well to occupy the higher ground that seemed to command Cemetery Hill. Lee observed through his field glasses that "some of those people" were there now—his usual way of referring to the enemy. He said he was not able to give them troops. The higher ground was Culp's Hill, which was directly east of the end of Cemetery Ridge and dominated it. This had been quickly seen by the Federals, and one of the first acts of General Hancock when he arrived on the field was to order General Wadsworth's division to secure it.

General Lee decided to approve an attack but to leave its execution to General Ewell's discretion, and this inhibited Ewell from decisive action. As Lee phrased it in his report, "General Ewell was instructed to carry the hill occupied by the enemy, if he found it practicable, but to avoid a general engagement until the arrival of the other divisions of the army, which were ordered to hasten forward. He decided to await Johnson's Division . . . which did not reach Gettysburg until a late hour."

Ewell has been made the subject of attack by commentators seeking a reason for Lee's defeat at Gettysburg, and his delay in attacking Culp's Hill has been called catastrophic. Several Federal officers have testified that before the Federal defenses on the hill were consolidated and strengthened, they could not have withstood a strong attack, but Brigadier General Hunt pointed out that Ewell's men were in no condition for an assault after the day's fighting, Rodes alone having 3,000 casualties out of 8,000.

Second Day: Battle for the Round Tops

On July 2, 1863, the second day at Gettysburg, two great armies faced each other and fought a terrible battle with artillery and infantry amid the rocky defiles of Devil's Den and the stone-filled slopes of Little Round Top. It was fought under extraordinary circumstances: the top generals in the field on both sides disagreed with their superiors on how and where the combat should take place; the commanding general of the Union army was carrying his heavy responsibility for only the fourth day. Both armies suffered the largest losses of any single action during the Gettysburg campaign; the Union commander in the field was censured for disregarding his orders, and his Confederate opposite ended the day with the conviction that the only chance for final victory had been thrown away.

Before Little Round Top is reached Cemetery Ridge is lost in sloping country heavily loaded with rocks and boulders. Some distance west there is a wood, then comes a cleared space about 300 yards wide, leading up to Plum Run. This run stretches east toward Little Round Top, then turns southwest and meets a branch flowing from Seminary Ridge. Between the two lies Devil's Den, so packed with great stones and boulders that it might have been a place where giants of old hurled huge rocks at one another.

Although it is customary to call Gettysburg a three-day battle, the Union army was not present in full until late in the afternoon of the second day, July 2. When General Meade took over command from General Hooker, he expressed surprise, much to the annoyance of Hooker, at the scattered condition of the army. He managed, however, to bring the various units together quickly enough to meet the separate attacks by the Confederates, though it took most of the day. Several brigades of the Third Corps came from Emmitsburg at 9 A.M. The Artillery Reserve was up by 10 A.M. Brigadier General Samuel W. Crawford's Third Division of the Fifth Corps arrived at noon. But Major General Sedgwick's Sixth Corps did not reach Rock Creek until 4 P.M., when it completed a march of thirty-four miles from Manchester.

The absence from the field of a large segment of the army made an offensive on the second day impossible. As General Meade and his engineers studied the topography, they found Gettysburg much less favorably situated than the line of Pipe Creek, and believed that the Union army was best placed to fight on the defensive. Meade took cognizance of the danger of the Confederates' turning his flank and threatening his communications; before Longstreet's attack opened he had wired General Halleck: "If satisfied the enemy is endeavoring to move to my rear, I shall fall back to my supplies at Westminster."

At that time he had asked his chief of staff, Major General Daniel Butterfield, to prepare a plan for the withdrawal of the army; this was not issued as an order but was shown to several commanding officers, including General John Gibbon and General Seth Williams, the latter assistant adjutant general; both approved the arrangements. The order was regarded as provision for a contingency, and was so described by General Meade and General Butterfield in testimony before the Committee on the Conduct of the War, but years later Generals Butterfield and Sickles said it showed Meade's intention to retreat and thus acquired a derogatory meaning.

On July 2 Culp's Hill, on the extreme Federal right, the north end of the line, was occupied by the Twelfth Corps, with Brigadier General A. S. Williams in com-

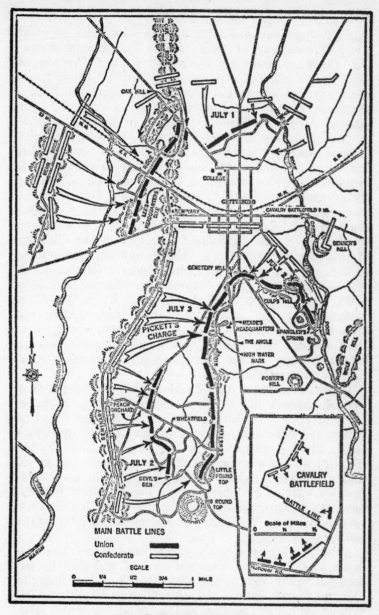

The Battle of Gettysburg
July 1-3, 1863

mand, Major General Slocum having taken over the right wing. This was east of the Baltimore Turnpike and Brigadier General James S. Wadsworth's First Division of Doubleday's First Corps was located at its left. At Cemetery Hill and in the general area where the Taneytown and Emmitsburg Roads meet stood units of Major General Howard's Eleventh Corps, including the divisions of Brigadier General Francis C. Barlow, Brigadier General Adolphus von Steinwehr, and Major General Carl Schurz, which had borne the fierce impact of Stonewall Jackson's surprise attack at Chancellorsville. Cemetery Ridge continued south through Ziegler's Grove to the clump of trees that became a famous landmark, thence south to Little Round Top. Most of this terrain was given to General Hancock's Second Corps, with the divisions of Brigadier Generals John Gibbon and Alexander Hays to the fore and that of Brigadier General John C. Caldwell to their left and rear. Major General Daniel E. Sickles' Third Corps was located slightly west by north of the Little Round Top area. The Sixth Corps, needing rest after its long march, was placed in reserve about where the Baltimore Pike crosses Rock Creek. General Henry J. Hunt's artillery reserve was east of the Taneytown Road near the George Weikert farm.

On the morning of July 2 General Meade made a number of changes in the disposition of troops. Brigadier General John W. Geary's division of Slocum's Twelfth Corps had been stationed during the night at the Union left, with two regiments at the base of Little Round Top. It was now ordered back to Slocum's line at the Union right and Sickles' Third Corps was to assume the position vacated by Geary. Major General John Buford's cavalry division also had been at the Union left, but was now ordered to Westminster, leaving no cavalry at the left for the afternoon.

General Sickles thought there were many disadvantages to the location assigned to him and said he had found a better one farther afield; Meade asked Brigadier General Henry Hunt, chief of artillery, to look over the ground with him. Sickles had in mind two bold ridges of rock that formed an angle near the Peach Orchard, about 600 yards from the woods on Seminary Hill, where the Confederates were posted. Hunt saw that this position offered excellent opportunities for artillery action, but it would extend Sickles' line greatly, since it would have to connect with the left of the Second Corps on the ridge north of Little Round Top, and would have to be strongly occupied, with more troops than Meade had available. Apparently Meade never gave his consent for Sickles to take this position, but Sickles was a headstrong man, not easily diverted from his aims, and soon he was occupying most of the terrain he had indicated.

When Hunt returned with guns from the artillery reserve, Sickles had placed General Birney's division on the crest from Devil's Den to the Peach Orchard and along the Emmitsburg Road, Brigadier General J. H. Hobart Ward's brigade on the left, Brigadier General Charles K. Graham's brigade at the angle, with Brigadier General A. A. Humphreys' division on Graham's right. Hunt saw that Sickles' corps was entirely too weak to cover the area he had chosen. Meade now called a conference at headquarters. Sickles was late in arriving, and just as he rode up a volley of gunfire hit the Federal left. Meade met Sickles and told him not to dismount, but to go back to his corps, and he, Meade, would follow and inspect the position. When he saw Sickles' thin line he was alarmed and Sickles considered pulling back some of the troops, but just then Longstreet's guns opened and Meade told Sickles he would have to fight where he was. He ordered Major General George Sykes' Fifth Corps to fill the gap, and progressively added Brigadier General John C. Caldwell's division of Hancock's corps, which was posted on Cemetery Ridge, and detachments from the Twelfth and Sixth Corps. These latter troops would have remained in reserve if Sickles had not taken the extension of the front line into his own hands.

General Meade sent General Warren up Little Round Top to inspect the Union line. Warren discovered to his amazement that there were no Union troops there. The Signal Corps men were still there, but the officer was about to fold up his flags and leave. Looking toward the Confederate position, Warren saw a wood that might make excellent cover for troops. To determine whether it was occupied he ordered a battery in Sickles' line to send a shot into the woods; this caused an agitation among men concealed there and the glint of sunlight on bayonets and rifle barrels betrayed to Warren that the wood was occupied. This was a threat to the unprotected Union left. Warren hurried calls to Meade for a division and asked Sickles for a brigade. Sickles couldn't spare it.

Warren Saves Little Round Top

General Warren was still alone with the signal officer. Said Warren: "He was about to fold up his flags and withdraw, but remained at my request, and kept waving them in defiance. Seeing troops going out on the Peach Orchard Road" (they were part of Sykes' corps) "I rode down the hill and fortunately met my old brigade. General [Stephen H.] Weed, commanding it, had already passed the point and I took the responsibility to detach Colonel [Patrick H.] O'Rorke, who, on hearing my few words of explanation about the position, moved at once to the hilltop. About this time First Lieut. Charles E. Hazlett of the Fifth Artillery, with his battery of rifled cannon, arrived. He comprehended the situation instantly and planted a gun on the summit of the hill. He stayed there until he was killed."

Thus, as subsequent events proved, General Warren became the man who saved the Union army from losing control of the Round Tops. Once in the possession of the Confederates, they would have provided heights from which hostile artillery could enfilade the Union left. In retrospect it could be said that disaster would have hit the Union army if Warren had not been there. To this should be added honors for the brigade that Warren persuaded to come to Little Round Top. Colonel Strong Vincent, who was to lose his life that day, marched up the hill with regiments that were to prove their mettle in the ensuing conflict. They included the Twentieth Maine, Colonel Joshua L. Chamberlain; the Sixteenth Michigan, Lieutenant Colonel Norman E. Welch; the Forty-fourth New York, Colonel James C. Rice; and the Eighty-third Pennsylvania, Captain Orpheus S. Woodward.

The Twentieth Maine had been leading, and when the brigade went up the hill in reverse it was at the rear. It

is related that three Chamberlain brothers were riding
abreast as shells from Longstreet's guns began crashing
among the boulders. With Colonel Chamberlain was
Lieutenant Tom, acting as his adjutant, and John, a
member of the Christian Commission. As a shell whistled by the colonel said: "Boys, I don't like this. Another
such shot might make it hard for mother. Tom, go to the
rear of the regiment and see that it is well closed up.
John, pass up ahead and look out a place for our
wounded."

General Lee became convinced on the morning of
July 2 that he would have to attack the Union army in
force. It was no longer possible to avoid a general engagement. He also decided, after a reconnaissance, to attack with his right. This meant that General Longstreet's
corps would be used, and Longstreet had lost his argument that it would be better to move around the Federals. As he phrased it in the first of several versions of
his recommendation to Lee, he had said: "All we have
to do is to throw our army around by their left and we
shall interpose between the Federal army and Washington. We can get a strong position and wait. . . . Finding
our object is Washington the Federals will be sure to
attack us. When they attack we shall beat them."

"No," said Lee, "the enemy is there, and I am going
to attack him there."

It was part of Longstreet's cherished plan that the
campaign into Pennsylvania be offensive in strategy and
defensive in tactics. Because Lee was opposed to his
views he was to come out of the Gettysburg campaign a
disgruntled man, blaming the result on Lee's disregard
of his advice. In later years he became the chief critic of
Lee's failures, and entered into bitter arguments with
Lee's defenders, especially General Jubal A. Early.

On the morning of July 2 McLaws' and Hood's divisions of the First Corps had reached Marsh Creek,
four miles from Gettysburg, with the Washington Artillery. At about 9 A.M. Colonel E. Arthur Alexander's artillery battalion reached Willoughby's Run. Two units of
the First Corps were still on the way: Pickett's division
was at Chambersburg and Law's brigade of Hood's division at New Guilford, both with over twenty miles to cover.

Longstreet considered the Federal position "a field of tremendous power upon a convex curve," which permitted concentration at threatened points and had natural strength improved by defenses. General Lee did not intend these concentrations to be made against one wing of his army. He therefore ordered General Richard S. Ewell to prepare an assault on the Federal position at Culp's Hill, which dominated the Federal right, to start when he heard Longstreet's guns against the Federal left, and he ordered General A. P. Hill at the center to be prepared to make a demonstration with the Third Corps and to watch for an opportunity to attack. Thus, with proper coordination, Meade's forces would be challenged at pivotal points and the whole Confederate line would have a chance to take advantage of a break in the Union defense.

So far no large Confederate forces had been placed at the right, opposite the Federal left at Little Round Top. As the First Corps came up it was ordered to the right of the Third Corps, with Kershaw's brigade in the lead. General McLaws' division was ordered to the far side of the Seminary Ridge and to move along Marsh Creek, behind the woods, keeping out of sight of the Federal signal station on Little Round Top. McLaws passed Black Horse Tavern and then headed for the Emmitsburg Pike, but as he went over a hill his troops came into clear view from Little Round Top. General Longstreet immediately ordered a countermarch; the troops doubled back, went farther west to the dry bed of Willoughby Run and again turned south, and thus moved toward the Federal position screened by heavy woods.

When the Confederate generals took stock of the terrain over which they were to fight they didn't like it. Not only Longstreet but General E. M. Law held a frontal attack objectionable. Law took his objections to his commander, General Hood. He informed him that the right flank of the Federal line was vulnerable; that the Federals were strong in front and the issue of a frontal attack was doubtful; that even if the attack were successful, it would be so costly that the troops would be unable to follow it up: finally, it was unnecessary. General Law convinced himself there was an easier way: move the troops up on Round Top from the south during the night; this would force the Federal army to change its front and attack. The protest went to General Longstreet, but he was in no mood to convey it to General Lee. He already had lost his argument, and he was not disposed to send again to Lee, who was five miles away. Hood, Law, and General W. N. Pendleton thought the imminent attack would rob the Confederates of ultimate victory. Longstreet agreed with them, but he replied that General Lee's orders were to guide the left by the Emmitsburg Road and go forward.

Peach Orchard and Devil's Den

The Confederate attack opened with a terrific artillery battle. For more than an hour the two armies hurled shells and canister. The Confederate batteries under Colonel E. Porter Alexander of the artillery reserve, Colonel Henry C. Cabell of McLaws' division, and Major M. W. Henry of Hood's plastered every sign of Federal activity for hours. The Federal artillery drew upon its reserves. The duel had many unusual aspects. It was fought at fairly close range, 500 to 800 yards; sometimes, in a desperate stand, closer. Some guns occupied terrain so difficult that only manual strength could get them over the huge crags. The most damaging action against Sickles' extended line came from Alexander's fifty-four guns west of the Peach Orchard.

Remarkable experiences were recorded. There was Charlie Smith's back-breaking effort to place six Parrott rifles up Little Round Top, just ahead of the panting Confederates eager to capture them. The Confederates overran the battery as one gunner spiked a gun, then the Federals recaptured them. There was Captain James E. Smith and his six Parrotts of the Fourth New York Battery on a slab in Devil's Den, blazing canister at oncoming waves of gray at 300 yards. In the steaming air the cannoneers worked like madmen. Battery B of the First New Jersey Artillery fired 1,342 rounds that day. The most extraordinary experiences were lived through by the men of the Ninth Massachusetts—those that survived. They were set down by Captain John Bigelow in

his reminiscences, *The Peach Orchard, Gettysburg, July
2, 1863*. His men worked tirelessly and hit their targets
—Bigelow says a Confederate told him after the war
that one shell accounted for thirty casualties out of
thirty-five men in one company, but it may have taken
more than one shell.

After two hours of fighting Sickles' lines were caving
in; Kershaw was threatening Bigelow's battery from one
point, Barksdale from another. When the batteries were
ordered out of the Wheat Field, Bigelow's was the last
to stand off the advancing Confederate infantry. Behind
him, about 400 yards, was the Trostle house, and in a
stone wall was the gate through which he hoped to pull
his guns. The sharpshooters were getting his men. Just
as a cannoneer was about to pull the lanyard of a gun
he was shot down; a second man rushed forward, and he,
too, went down; so did a third. The fourth man made it.
Before Bigelow could get his guns back to the stone wall
the colonel of his outfit ordered him to stand where he
was because there were no troops behind him and some
would have to be brought up. As four of Bigelow's napoleons continued to pour canister into the advancing
Confederates, Bigelow ordered one section of two guns
to get away. One gun got through the gate and turned
over; the crew put it back on its wheels and sped on.
The second drove headlong against the stone wall; the
wall shattered, the horses went over, the gun followed.
Bigelow, who had survived a splintered arm, was hit by
two bullets. As the Confederates rushed at the guns the
gunners put one man out of action with a handspike,
brained another with a rammer staff. Yet Bigelow and
his survivors got away. The battery lost four guns;
twenty-eight out of sixty gunners were killed or wounded.

When the fighting was at its height the brigade of
Brigadier General E. M. Law of Hood's division was ordered to take the rocky fastness of Little Round Top
from the southwest. As its regiments struggled up the
craggy slopes, dodging among the boulders, they were
subjected to the deadly fire of sharpshooters who felled
dozens of their men. Foremost in the assault was the Fifteenth Alabama under Colonel William C. Oates, who ordered his regiment to move to the right and climb the

less exposed sides of Big Round Top. It was an arduous climb, but once on top Colonel Oates had before him the whole panorama of the Union line and recognized the possibility of enfilading it with guns from a height dominating the whole Federal left. This was a great opportunity, but the guns were far away; instead a courier arrived with orders from General Law for immediate action against the left of the Union line. The Fifteenth Alabama and the Forty-seventh moved down again and prepared to take the Union defenders in the flank.

The Confederate onslaught was developing rapidly; Sickles was badly hit and Law's remaining troops, five Alabama and two Texas regiments, were moving against the defense that Colonel Vincent had organized at General Warren's call. At the extreme left of the Union line stood the Twentieth Maine and its resourceful officer, Colonel Joshua L. Chamberlain. Observing Colonel Oates' Alabamans about to turn his flank he maneuvered the left half of his regiment into a position at a right angle with the rest and facing the direction from which Oates's infantry was advancing. This change was made while the troops continued their defense in front. When the Alabama troops finally emerged on the Federal flank they encountered volleys from behind rocks and trees by their fully prepared opponents. The fighting became man to man; breaking ranks, both sides fought like Indians, shooting from behind boulders, clubbing their enemies with rifle butts. Colonel Oates thought he had driven the Federals from their position for good after five assaults, but each time they were back, fighting as hard as ever. The Union troops had carried sixty rounds per man; when these gave out Colonel Chamberlain, in a desperate effort, ordered a bayonet charge against the Alabamans. It surprised the Confederates and threw them back. At the bottom of the slope they were suddenly taken in the flank by a company of Chamberlain's sharpshooters who had become detached from the regiment. The Confederates thought they were surrounded. An orderly retreat was impossible; Colonel Oates told the men to get back as best they could, and said later: "When the signal was given we ran like a herd of wild cattle, right through the line of dismounted cavalrymen."

Because of its exposed position General Sickles' Third Corps bore the brunt of the fighting on July 2. Its right rested on the Peach Orchard and extended toward Little Round Top. The extreme left of its line was held by Major General David B. Birney's division, which had to accommodate itself to the protruding masses of rock. Birney's picket line reached the Emmitsburg Road, and his sharpshooters were able to proceed as far as 300 yards in advance by dodging among the boulders.

General Humphreys' division east of the Emmitsburg Road was hard-pressed and had to call on General Hancock for reinforcements. On July 2 Hancock was ordered to command both his own corps and the Third, after General Sickles had a leg taken off by a shell fragment late in the afternoon. General John Gibbon's brigade went in to support Humphreys'. When General Hancock sent Brigadier General Caldwell's division into the battle Father William Corby, chaplain of the Irish Brigade of that division, mounted a rock and pronounced absolution as the men knelt; the next instant they rushed into the battle. Father Corby's effigy in bronze stands today on the spot where this incident took place.

The Federals paid a terrible price for their unlucky foray into the Peach Orchard and the Devil's Den.

After the battle, when the broken bodies of Sickles' men lay scattered about the Wheat Field and the rocks of Little Round Top, and Sickles himself had lost a leg, an acrimonious controversy developed between Meade and Sickles. Meade asserted that Sickles not only had failed to carry out his orders but had placed his troops in an untenable position without authority. When the artillery firing commenced on the afternoon of July 2 and Meade cast his eyes over the field beyond Little Round Top, he was angered by Sickles' extended lines. But it was too late to rectify them, and he told Sickles: "Stay where you are and fight it out." He had intended, he said, that after General Geary had withdrawn from the Federal left and rejoined his corps on Culp's Hill, Sickles was to occupy Geary's position, which he failed to do. Meade said he told Sickles that Sickles' right was to be Hancock's left, and Sickles' left was to be on Round Top. "Now his right was three-quarters of a mile in front of

Hancock's left and his left one-quarter of a mile in front of the base of Round Top leaving that key point unoccupied. . . . Sickles' movement practically destroyed his own corps, the Third, causing a loss of 50 per cent in the Fifth Corps and very heavily damaged the Second Corps . . . producing 66 per cent of the loss of the whole battle, and with what result? Driving us back to the position he was ordered to hold originally."

Sickles rejected every one of Meade's accusations. He said he did not have orders to occupy Round Top, and had he done so his lines would have been as thin as those of skirmishers. He blamed much of his loss on the circumstance that Meade had ordered General John Buford's cavalry from the left, leaving Sickles without ability to get information.

Ewell Repulsed at Culp's Hill

The fighting at Culp's Hill on the right of the Federal lines developed after 6 P.M., when Longstreet's troops were threatening the Federal left. Lee had ordered Ewell to begin his attack when he heard Longstreet's guns on the left, but Ewell was several hours late. General Meade had taken the Twelfth Corps from its position on Culp's Hill and moved it to the other end of the line, to help the threatened left. When Meade's order arrived Major General Henry W. Slocum ordered the Third Brigade of Geary's division to remain behind to man the breastworks that the corps had erected the day before. This brigade was commanded by Brigadier General George S. Greene and comprised five New York regiments. The breastworks had been strongly built with trees felled by men used to cutting timber and provided excellent protection. Ewell's attack was led by Major General Edward Johnson's division. Greene's brigade had been strung along the breastworks and managed, with the help of about 1,000 men from other corps, to throw back Johnson's attacks. The Confederates were able, however, to occupy the trenches that had been vacated by the divisions of Geary and Ruger when they were sent to the Federal left.

During the night these two divisions returned and

next morning, July 3, pushed Johnson's men out of their trenches and down Culp's Hill. Another attack by Ewell was delivered by the brigades of Hoke and Avery of Early's division against the Eleventh Corps at Cemetery Hill, but was repulsed with well-directed artillery fire and reinforcements from Hancock's corps. It is believed that Ewell's tardiness was one of the factors that Lee considered responsible for the defeat at Gettysburg, where he had looked for a coordination of all efforts and failed to get it.

After the fighting had ceased on July 2 General Meade called a council of his corps commanders in the little one-story cottage on the Taneytown Road that he had made his headquarters. General Meade wanted to know what action the generals proposed for the following day. Major General Daniel Butterfield, chief of staff, proposed the questions and the officers gave their views. The questions were: (1) Should the army remain in its present position or retire to another nearer its base of supplies? (2) If the army remained, should it attack or await attack by the enemy? (3) How long should the army wait for an attack?

The consensus was to correct the position of the army but to remain where it was; also, not to attack. Most of the generals thought the army should wait one day for Lee to attack. General Howard wanted to wait until 4 P.M. the next day and if Lee did not attack by then, to attack him. General Hancock did not wish to attack unless the army's communications were cut. General Sedgwick wanted the army to wait at least one day. General Slocum wanted to "stay and fight it out." General Meade also told Major General John Gibbon of Hancock's corps, who was not a corps commander but had been asked to attend, that he expected Lee to attack on Gibbon's front, because he had failed on both flanks and would next try the center.

Third Day at Gettysburg: Pickett's Charge

It was now Friday, July 3, 1863, and two days of desperate fighting at Gettysburg had not produced a decision. The Confederate army, on the offensive, had reached far toward the Federal lines and inflicted grievous hurt, but had been hurt itself. Yet both armies were in strong positions now. General Lee had said, after the fighting had stopped on the day before: "We have not been so successful as we wished." General Ewell had a hold on Culp's Hill, but he had not been able to push the Federals off. Longstreet's corps had pushed the Federals out of Devil's Den and up to Little Round Top, but the strongly entrenched Union line still held. Both sides had taken a measure of the opponent's power, and waited. Lee was stronger now—General George E. Pickett had arrived with three brigades and General Jeb Stuart finally had reached Gettysburg with two brigades of cavalry. But Lee had lost veterans—Barksdale had been killed; Pender and Semmes had been mortally wounded; Hood, J. M. Jones, and G. T. Anderson had suffered wounds that would temporarily incapacitate them.

Both sides were strong enough to fight again; neither side had been hit hard enough to wish to withdraw to a new line. The second day almost had brought success to Lee; he would strike again on the third. He stated his intentions in his report: "The general plan was unchanged. Longstreet, reinforced by Pickett's three brigades, which arrived near the battlefield on the afternoon of the 2nd, was ordered to attack the next morning, and General Ewell was ordered to attack the enemy's right at the same time. The latter during the night reinforced General Johnson with two brigades from Rodes' and one from Early's division."

Longstreet, to whom this was to be a day of anguish, contended, many years later, that Lee had not given him such orders on the night of the second day. Instead, he said, he first heard the orders from Lee the morning of July 3. Historians said Longstreet did not challenge Lee's report until many years after Lee's death. It is certain that Longstreet looked upon Lee's plan to make another frontal attack on the Union position with disfavor and even alarm. Longstreet's cherished plan of getting around the Union left had been rejected by Lee, and the assault of July 2 against the Federals in front of Little Round Top had failed to break their line. Now Longstreet was expected to attack again, against a strong position that had been reinforced. It is difficult to tell, at this distance from the event, how many of the objections Longstreet mentions in his reminiscences were actually put to Lee, but they were present in Longstreet's mind and accounted for the way he conducted his part of the enterprise.

That morning General Ewell, another reluctant commander, was expected to renew the attack on Culp's Hill that had been broken off the night before. But Generals Ruger and Geary were there ahead of him; before Ewell was under way the Federals opened up on his troops with twenty guns, whereas the Confederates were not properly supplied with artillery. The result already has been mentioned; Edward Johnson's troops were repulsed and the Federals held on to the crest that dominated Cemetery Hill.

General Lee planned the great attack with scrupulous care. At first he wished to use the divisions of McLaws, Hood, and Pickett against the Federal center, but because of objections from Longstreet he shifted to the left center and replaced McLaws with the division of General Henry Heth of A. P. Hill's corps, and Hood with two brigades from General Pender's command. Heth had been wounded and his place was taken by Brigadier General J. Johnston Pettigrew, whose brigade in turn was led by Colonel James K. Marshall. Pender also had been hit, and General Lee appointed General Isaac Trimble to lead this section. The third would be Pickett's division, with General Pickett in command of the assault.

As the forces now lined up for the assault, Pettigrew was at the right (north) and his brigades were those of Colonel J. M. Brockenbrough (Virginia), Brigadier General Joseph B. Davis (Mississippi and North Carolina), Colonel James K. Marshall (North Carolina), and Brigadier General James J. Archer (Alabama and Tennessee). Archer had been captured by General Doubleday on July 1 and Colonel B. D. Fry was in command. Next to Pettigrew would come Trimble, with a brigade of North Carolinians under Brigadier General James H. Lane and Brigadier General Alfred M. Scales's brigade under Colonel L. J. Lowrance. At the right of the line stood Pickett's three brigades of Virginia regiments, led by Brigadier Generals Richard B. Garnett, Lewis A. Armistead, and James L. Kemper. Two brigades from Hill's corps were kept in reserve—Brigadier General Cadmus M. Wilcox's and Perry's under Colonel David Lang.

How many men took part in Pickett's charge? The convenient number, reported by Longstreet in his memoirs and repeated by historians, is 15,000. More precise numbers are believed to have been: Pickett's command, 4,900; Pettigrew's, 5,000; Trimble's, 2,500, a total of 12,400 fighting men. The addition of the two brigades kept in reserve would raise the total nearer to the 15,000.

Of the leaders, the greatest interest has attached to Pickett, whose name takes precedence over all others in the historic annals. He was a thirty-eight-year-old Virginian who belonged to the West Point class of 1846. He had seen service in Mexico and in the Northwest boundary dispute. Casting his lot with the Confederacy, he served with distinction on the Peninsula, especially at Gaines' Mill, and became a major general in 1862. He wore his hair long, and when some admiring women asked Lee for a lock of his hair, he suggested that they turn to Pickett. The charge of July 3 was the peak of Pickett's career. At first he was pleased by the prospect of success, but later he looked on it as a mistake of judgment, and a coldness developed between him and General Lee.

The Confederate chief of artillery was Brigadier General William N. Pendleton, but the direction of the batteries for the charge had been given by Longstreet to Colonel E. Porter Alexander. Pendleton was a clergyman and after the war was rector of the Grace Episcopal Church in Lexington, Virginia, which was attended by General Lee. Colonel Alexander had lined up seventy-five fieldpieces on his front and Pendleton first sent him seven 12-pounder howitzers, but recalled them later when fire from the Federal batteries threatened to destroy them. There were approximately 63 pieces on General Hill's front, so that the Confederates could concentrate the fire of 138 guns against Cemetery Ridge. They also had two Whitworth rifles, English 10-pounder breechloading guns with the longest range on the field—5,000 yards. Hill had located these near the railroad cut, and they could attack from the flank.

Longstreet had the responsibility for ordering both the artillery attack and the charge, and he faced it with depressed spirits. He told Colonel Alexander to advise Pickett when the guns had done enough damage to make the charge possible. This alarmed Alexander, who did not want the burden of the decision. Longstreet explained that he wanted Alexander to determine when the guns had silenced those of the enemy. If the artillery fire did not drive off the enemy or greatly demoralize him, "I would prefer that you should not advise General Pickett to make the charge." Alexander retorted that since the field would be obscured by smoke he could tell the effect only by the enemy's return fire. If there was an alternative to the attack, it ought to be considered carefully before the ammunition was used up; in case of an unfavorable result there would not be enough left for another effort. "And even if this is entirely successful it can only be so at a very bloody cost." He finally agreed: "When our artillery fire is doing its best I shall advise General Pickett to advance."

When the time came for the bombardment, Longstreet sent word to Colonel J. P. Walton, commander of the artillery reserve: "Let the batteries open; order great care and precision in firing." Colonel Walton gave the order and two signal guns from the Washington Artillery exploded. A second later the whole Confederate line on Seminary Ridge burst into flame. It was 1:07 P.M.

On the forenoon of July 3 the Federal army was binding up its wounds of the day before, replenishing its ammunition chests and increasing its defenses. There were two interruptions to the calm of the day; the repulse of the Confederates at Culp's Hill and the destruction of the Bliss barn. The barn was located in the low part of the swale between the Confederate and Federal positions, west of the Emmitsburg Road and somewhat closer to the Union line at Ziegler's Grove than to the Confederate. It was being used by Confederate sharpshooters, who were picking off officers of Hays's division. The Federals sent infantry to take the barn and after several assaults and some losses held it and set it afire. A. P. Hill's batteries opposite then opened up and expended ammunition that brought no advantages.

When the firing stopped about 11 A.M. the whole battle-field acquired the peaceful air of a rural countryside, steaming in the hot July sun. Sometimes the trees stirred in a brief westerly breeze. The powder smoke drifted away; the sky was clear. Behind the Federal lines some regiments opened rations and brewed coffee.

In the center of the Federal line stood Brigadier General John Gibbon's division of Hancock's Second Corps. The clump of trees that the Confederates had singled out as the objective of Pickett's attack had Colonel Norman J. Hall's brigade to the South and Brigadier General Alexander S. Webb's brigade to the north. To the left of Hall was Brigadier General William Harrow's brigade. Lined up near the clump of trees were the Sixty-ninth Pennsylvania, the Fifty-ninth New York, and the Seventh Michigan regiments. To the north of the trees the low stone wall turned east for a few yards, creating an angle. Here were the Seventy-second Pennsylvania and the 106th Pennsylvania. At the east point of the angle stood the Seventy-first Pennsylvania. Farther to the Federal right were regiments of Brigadier General Alexander Hays's Third Division, with batteries under Captain John G. Hazard. Between the clump of trees and the angle stood a battery that was to win renown, Lieutenant Alonzo H. Cushing's Battery A of the Fourth U.S. Artillery, which belonged to Hazard's artillery unit.

The Federal guns were under the excellent supervision of the chief of artillery, Brigadier General Henry J. Hunt. He had not only seen to it that sufficient ammunition was in reserve, but his instructions for care in firing had conserved it and lightened the burdens of the supply trains. His expertness was recognized by practically every commander except General Hooker, who hobbled Hunt's usefulness at Chancellorsville, to his own cost. Both Hunt's father and grandfather had served in American forces, as far back as the Revolution. He was forty-two when the Civil War broke out. A West Point man of the class of 1839, he had served with a distinguished battery in the Mexican War, where he was twice wounded and twice cited for gallantry. Just before the Civil War he had collaborated on a manual of field-artillery tactics. He had served as an artillery officer in the major campaigns in the East.

That morning General Hunt, after ascertaining that "everything looked favorable at Culp's Hill," moved along Cemetery Ridge to inspect the batteries. Suddenly "a magnificent display" greeted his eyes. On Seminary Ridge, extending for about two miles, he could discern batteries already posted or wheeling into a long, unbroken mass, from opposite Gettysburg to the Peach Orchard. Such a sight, he reflected, had never been seen on this continent, and rarely, if ever, abroad. He reasoned that this might be a defensive measure, but more likely it might mean a cannonade preparatory to an infantry assault on the Federal center, with the object of crushing batteries and infantry. As an artillerist he thought also that this might cause the Union cannoneers to exhaust their ammunition. He felt that the batteries on the Federal front, whether of the army corps or of the reserve, must act as a unit in defense under the chief of artillery. For this reason he instructed artillery and battery commanders to withhold their fire fifteen or twenty minutes after the cannonading began, then to concentrate on the Confederate batteries most damaging to them, firing slowly, so as not to run out of ammunition when the Confederate infantry charge reached Cemetery Ridge.

Hunt managed to pass the word around and had just arrived at the last battery stationed on Little Round Top when he heard the Confederate signal guns. In an instant the huge bombardment rolled over the valley with a crash of thunder. Seminary Ridge, its guns and its green forest background, began to disappear behind great billows of powder smoke, through which the explosions of the guns showed like jets of bright flame. A rain of solid shot and iron particles began to fall on the infantry and the artillerists waiting on Cemetery Ridge. A shell from the first signal gun was said to have killed a man—Lieutenant S. S. Robinson of the Nineteenth Massachusetts Infantry. The Confederates killed and wounded many of the waiting infantry, but much of the projectile storm went over the crest and dropped behind it, where it damaged wagons and killed horses, but was less hard on the infantry.

General Gibbon, whose division was behind the low stone walls at the front, had taken the opportunity during

the lull before the cannonading began to enjoy a cooked
meal on the far side of the Ridge. According to Lieutenant
Frank A. Haskell, Gibbon's aide, who described it in a
famous letter to his brother, which has been published as
The Battle of Gettysburg (1958) the meal included
stewed chicken, boiled potatoes, toast, bread, butter, tea,
and coffee. General Hancock partook of it; Meade
came by and was invited in, so were Newton and Pleasonton. After dining the officers lighted cigars and talked
about the military situation. Then all went about their
business except Hancock and Gibbon and his staff. Hancock was dictating a letter when suddenly the Confederate
bombardment exploded. Servants disappeared, horses
tore loose, two mules were knocked to pieces, a mess-
wagon horse was torn by a shell, Gibbon's groom was
knocked off his horse, dead. Hancock made a pretense
of continuing to dictate, then gave it up. Only Gibbon's
horse, tied to a tree and munching oats, was undisturbed.

The Confederate gunners could not rectify their aim,
because they could not see through the clouds of smoke
where their shells fell, but they sprayed the whole Federal
area so thoroughly that they created terrible havoc. Guns
and carriages were struck; caissons blew up; gunners fell
in mangled heaps beside their pieces. Lieutenant Haskell
drew on a rich vocabulary to describe the noise of the
projectiles; he heard them shriek, hiss, growl, and sputter;
he saw missiles that seemed to hang suspended in air
before they disappeared in fire and smoke, and that hit the
ground with a thud and plowed the soil.

General Hunt knew that gunners hardly could stand
silent under such punishment. Soon Federal batteries were
responding, but some of those he had warned did not start
firing until General Hancock rode up and ordered them to
reply. This started a minor controversy between General
Hancock and General Hunt, and after the war Hunt vigorously defended the right of the chief of artillery to
instruct the batteries, even in the face of the superior
corps commander. One of the officers, Lieutenant Colonel Freeman McGilvery of the First Volunteer Battery of
the artillery reserve, posted on the Federal left, held
his guns silent until ordered by Hancock to open up;
then he shot a few rounds until Hancock had departed,

when he again obeyed Hunt, confident that an infantry commander did not know how to deal with artillery. As a result McGilvery was able later to confront the Confederate infantry with bursts of gunfire that effectively stopped them in front of his sector.

Greatest Spectacle of the War

Then the Confederate guns stopped firing after two hours of bombardment, the smoke lifted, and the regiments and brigades came forward to take part in the most thrilling and tragic spectacle ever seen on the American continent.

Over on Seminary Ridge the Confederate officers had been watching for indications of the effectiveness of their bombardment. Occasionally they could see the flash of an explosion as a Federal caisson blew up, but for the most part Cemetery Ridge was shrouded in gunsmoke.

One of the anxious watchers was Colonel Alexander, who saw his supply of ammunition diminishing with every volley from his batteries and was afraid he would run out before the big charge was on. He sent a note to Pickett: "General: If you are coming at all you must come immediately or I cannot give you proper support; but the enemy's fire has not slackened materially, and at least eighteen guns are still firing from the cemetery itself." He meant Cemetery Ridge. After the courier had left with the note Alexander observed that the Federal fire began to die down. He rushed off another note to Pickett: "For God's sake come quick. The eighteen guns have gone. Come quick or my ammunition will not let me support you properly." Actually the eighteen guns were not removed, although Alexander may have observed some change of batteries.

Pickett received the first note while Longstreet was near him. He handed it to Longstreet and asked: "General, shall I advance?" Longstreet looked away, then nodded slowly. Pickett saluted and said: "I am going to move forward, sir."

He galloped off with alacrity, but Longstreet was depressed. A few minutes later Longstreet was conferring with Alexander, and when Alexander told him how low the ammunition was, he was half inclined to stop Pickett. But Alexander explained that the present opportunity would be lost, because it took too long to bring up more ammunition. And Longstreet said: "I don't want to make this charge. I don't believe it can succeed. I would stop Pickett now, but that General Lee has ordered it and expects it." He was to repeat substantially the same remarks in his memoirs, and to regret the charge the rest of his life.

What the Confederate officers said as they started on their fatal mile has been garnered from letters and reminiscences. General James L. Kemper's brigade was in Pickett's first line and Kemper was on horseback. He rode back to the third brigade, where General Lewis A. Armistead was coming forward with the men on foot. "Look at my line," called out Armistead; "it never looked better on dress parade!"

State pride was in evidence, too. Pickett shouted a number of words that the men could not hear, but he did say: "Up men and to your posts! Don't forget that you are from old Virginia!"

"Now, Colonel," Pettigrew cried to Colonel Marshall; "for the honor of the good old North State, forward!"

One veteran's remark has been perpetuated by historians; it is ascribed also to other battles, and may well have been spoken numerous times under similar circumstances. As the troops rose up a rabbit jumped out of the brush and raced to the rear. "Run, ole har'," said a voice. "If I was a har' I'd run too."

The men manning the stone walls and batteries of the Union line were aroused by the spectacle of the advancing Confederate host. "Here they come!" they cried, almost in relief because the tension of waiting was over. Men who had been clinging to every stone and bit of raised earth for shelter now stood up to see what was taking place; some climbed on boulders or convenient walls. They saw a line of skirmishers emerge from the woods of Seminary Hill, and then another; their formation was open, their movements were free. Then came the troops, first one line and after an interval a second, then a third, and a few officers on horseback, and well spaced among the ranks were nineteen colors—the blue flag of Virginia and the red battle flag with the blue cross and thirteen white stars.

They were human beings with guns, marching straight against massed infantry and batteries, in an open field, because one man had ordered them to go in a final desperate effort to turn the tide of battle. They would march into the dip of the swale, come up toward the Emmitsburg Road that ran across their path like a danger line, thrust aside the rails of the fences along that road, and climb the gentle slope toward the low stone walls where the Federal soldiers waited with loaded muskets—if they could.

Before they were halfway across the field the iron shot of Federal batteries fell upon their ranks; gaps appeared in the marching lines; men fell dead or writhing with pain. Flags sank and were raised again; sank again and were raised many times, for there was a military tradition that men fought to keep a flag flying as the symbol of their cause, although in the heat of battle they thought of nothing but killing or keeping from being killed. There were Federal skirmishers to meet now, coming down the slope to the Emmitsburg Road, delaying the advance where possible, and taking the severest punishment when the Confederates finally fired. And the Confederate batteries were firing at intervals over the heads of their own men.

Pickett, at the extreme Confederate right, had to turn his command to the left just before reaching the Emmitsburg Road, in order to move toward that clump of trees in the center of the Union line that was the Confederate objective. This was done in the swale, where the terrain enabled them to halt briefly and re-form lines already shaken by Federal firing, some of which had come from McGilvery's and Rittenhouse's batteries. McGilvery had thirty-three guns stationed halfway between Cemetery Ridge and Little Round Top, while Rittenhouse had six Parrott guns on Little Round Top.

These guns had another important role in the battle. As Pickett's men moved forward Colonel Alexander attempted to place some of his batteries at Pickett's right flank. He managed to line up eighteen guns, but they proved of little use. McGilvery's men spotted them at once and deluged them with shells.

As the gray line climbed the slope in front of the Union position all semblance of regimental formation was lost. The Confederates were now facing volleys of musketry from massed troops just above them, and worse yet, they were in direct line of blasts of canister from the batteries. Under such conditions men could only run forward singly or in groups to fire, then kneel down while loading to fire again. Behind the low wall and along the rough ground covered with slashings that constituted the Union front were packed the regiments of the divisions of Brigadier Generals Hays and Gibbon. The defense at the clump of trees that was the focal point of Pickett's attack was shared by the Nineteenth Massachusetts of Colonel Arthur F. Devereaux, belonging to Colonel Norman Hall's brigade; and Colonel Dewitt C. Baxter's Seventy-second Pennsylvania, of Brigadier General Alexander S. Webb's brigade. Stretched along the front were the brigades of Colonel Thomas A. Smyth (New York, Connecticut, New Jersey, and Delaware regiments), and of Colonel George L. Willard (four New York regiments). In the second line were four regiments of Colonel George L. Willard's brigade of Hays's division. So close were the men packed that some were lying on the east slope of the high ground, in danger from flying shrapnel. The skirmishers in this area came from the Eighth Ohio of Colonel Samuel S. Carroll's brigade, with Lieutenant Colonel Franklin Sawyer directing the men.

The low wall of stone and rubble that extended southward from Ziegler's Grove turned west for over 200 feet and then south again. The latter point became famous as the angle at which blue and gray fought in a terrible man-to-man encounter, with clubbed muskets and stones, before the force of onrushing men pushed the vanguard over. Inside the angle and between that and the clump of trees stood the guns of Battery A of the Fourth U.S. Artillery, commanded by Lieutenant Alonzo H. Cushing, brother of W. B. Cushing, who was to win fame by destroying the Confederate ram *Albemarle.* Cushing's doom had been sealed before the Confederates reached his battery, for he had been disastrously hit during the cannonade; three of his caissons had been blown up and replaced, wheels had been shot off; one cannoneer

after another had fallen beside the guns; Cushing himself
had been hit and finally fatally wounded in the groin, but
he had served the guns with canister in the face of the
advancing troops until his collapse.

When the Seventy-second Pennsylvania was drawn
back by General Webb, Colonel Hall brought up the
Seventh Michigan and the Twentieth Massachusetts and
ordered them to fire on the Confederates at 200 yards,
and gave the second line orders to fire at 100 yards. The
effect was deadly and the attacking lines wavered and
fell back. But the fire of the Confederates took its toll,
too, and one regiment at the angle could not withstand
it and left a gap that the Confederates hurried to seize.
Colonel Hall urged other regiments to move forward to
stem the tide, but commands could not be heard, and "a
disposition on the part of the men to fall back a pace or
two to load gave the line a retiring direction." After ten
minutes the impulse to drive forward had been built
up by the example of the officers and the advancing
colors; the troops rushed upon the crowd of Confederates
in desperate hand-to-hand fighting; the intruders were
overwhelmed and either threw down their arms or fled
back over the wall.

Brigadier General Alexander S. Webb, who was wounded, gave the following dramatic description of the Confederate irruption at the angle:

The 71st Pennsylvania Volunteers were advanced to the
wall on the right of the 69th Pennsylvania Volunteers.
Three of Cushing's guns were run down to the fence, carrying with them their canister. The 72nd Pennsylvania volunteers were held in reserve under the crest of the hill. The
enemy advanced steadily to the fence, driving out a portion
of the 71st Pennsylvania Volunteers. General Armistead
passed over the fence with probably over one hundred of
his command, and with several battle flags. The 72nd Pennsylvania Volunteers were ordered up to hold the crest,
and advanced to within forty paces of the enemy's line.
Colonel R. P. Smith, commanding the 71st Pennsylvania,
threw two companies of his command behind the stone wall
on the right of Cushing's battery, fifty paces retired from
the point of attack. . . . The 69th Pennsylvania and most of
the 71st Pennsylvania, even after the enemy were in their

rear, held their position. The 72nd fought steadily and persistently, but the enemy would probably have succeeded in piercing our lines had not Colonel Hall advanced with several of his regiments to my support. Defeated, routed, the enemy fled in disorder. General Armistead was left, mortally wounded, within my lines, and forty-two of the enemy who crossed the fence lay dead. This brigade captured nearly 1,000 prisoners, six battle flags and picked up 1,400 stands of arms and 903 sets of accoutrements.

General Armistead was a spectacular figure as he marched at the head of his brigade. He had drawn his sword and carried his black felt hat on the tip of the blade. The point pierced the hat and the hat slipped down, and Armistead put it back up. He reached the stone wall with a crowd of yelling men behind him, pulled himself over the low wall and ran up to Cushing's guns, now silent. A volley from the 72nd Pennsylvania hit him and he went down. Union soldiers picked him up and carried him to the rear. The surgeon saw that he was mortally wounded and asked if he had any messages. The surgeon quoted him as saying: "Say to General Hancock for me that I have done him and you all a grievous injury, which I shall always regret." He died soon after. Some Southern writers have challenged the accuracy of the surgeon's report, but there it is. Armistead had been with Hancock when he made his decision to side with the state of Virginia in the war; he had been emotionally moved, and his last words were believed to have a reference to that meeting.

General Hancock was riding up and down the line, giving orders. Colonel Devereaux of the Nineteenth Massachusetts spotted him and shouted: "They have broken through; shall I go in?" "Go in there pretty damn quick!" yelled Hancock. Some time later a bullet hit the pommel of his saddle, drove a tenpenny nail from the saddle into his flesh and wounded him painfully. Hancock insisted on remaining in the battle, remarking contemptuously later that the enemy was running out of ammunition and resorting to tenpenny nails.

There were many minutes in this tense and crowded half hour when the Federal troops feared they might be overwhelmed. But after the Confederate brigades became confused, there was no leadership that could make itself heard, and there was no support. Confederate Brigadier General Cadmus Wilcox, whose brigade had been kept in reserve, started up with his Alabama regiments near the Codori House, but by that time the Confederates were moving back to the rear; the great attack had failed.

Numerous regiments and batteries contributed to the repulse of the Confederates. The accomplishments of the Second Vermont Brigade of Brigadier General G. J. Stannard brought honor to that New England state. General Hancock had observed an opportunity to attack Pickett's brigade in its right flank as it wheeled and headed for the clump of trees. The Thirteenth and Fourteenth Vermont delivered the blow and the demoralization of Kemper's brigade was complete. The Vermonters acquired a special reputation because they had enlisted for nine months, put in most of their time drilling, and were within a few days of the end of their terms.

There was a patch of rough, rocky ground a short distance south of the clump of trees that was the Confederate target, and here existed a gap between the Sixty-ninth Pennsylvania and the Fifty-ninth New York regiments. A little to the rear and the left of the Sixty-ninth Pennsylvania, Captain Andrew Cowan's First New York Battery was working five guns. On came a group of determined Confederates led by a young major waving his sword; as they reached the rough spot the major climbed up ahead of them yelling: "Take the guns!" Cowan called for double canister. His lieutenant was hit; two of the gun crew fell as they were serving the guns; a third toppled just as he gave the signal to pull a lanyard. The guns blasted their terrible charge into the faces of the Confederates; they crumbled, with the young major dead among them. The monument marking the spot where Cowan's battery stood bears the legend: "Double canister, at ten paces."

The brigades of Pettigrew and Trimble, coming under fire later than Pickett's, suffered considerably less, but as the casualties of the attacking divisions ran from 50 to nearly 70 per cent, they did not go unscathed. In front of them were the 108th and the 126th New York regiments of Hays's division, with considerably more firepower than at the angle. As Pettigrew's troops recoiled from the volleys of the massed Federal infantry the brigade of Colonel J. M. Brockenbrough, made up of Virginia regiments and at the left of the Confederate line, was taken in the flank by the Eighth Ohio, which rushed forward at the command of Lieutenant Colonel Franklin Sawyer with such impetuosity that the Confederates turned for the rear, thus helping to demoralize the brigade of General James J. Archer, which followed.

The Confederate batteries could no longer fire without hitting their own men. And Pickett's calls for support remained unanswered. The brigades of Wright and Posey were supposed to have been alerted to support Wilcox, but were held back by Longstreet when the issue of the charge was evident. The wave that had broken over the Union walls receded. The men in gray and butternut brown had done all that human beings could do against greater numbers. Some walked slowly back, turning around every few paces to fire once more. Others, having thrown aside their arms, were standing with upraised arms or waving handkerchiefs in pleas for surrender. On the crest of the Federal position the horde of prisoners was so large that the officers of batteries being brought up recoiled, thinking the Confederates had overrun their lines. On the slope in front of the wall great numbers of dead and wounded had changed the color of the greensward to gray.

On Seminary Ridge, General Lee had ridden back and forth, observing the issue of the struggle. Now as the men came back, he spoke consolingly to them. There is testimony that he took the blame upon himself. When Pickett told him: "I have no division now. Armistead is down, Garnett is down, and Kemper is mortally wounded," Lee replied: "Come, General Pickett, this has been my fight and upon my shoulders rests the blame." To Lieutenant Colonel A. J. L. Fremantle, British observer who watched Pickett's charge, he said: "This has been a sad day for us, Colonel, a sad day, but we can't always expect to win victories." In his official report Lee blamed the exhaustion of ammunition for the guns, saying he had not known this.

The Union command attempted briefly to anticipate a

possible attempt by Hood's division to support the retreating Confederates. Colonel William McCandless's brigade was ordered forward and went as far as the
sanguinary Wheat Field. Here it clashed with troops of
Brigadier General Henry L. Benning's command and discovered there was still plenty of fight in that unit. General Hunt said later: "An advance from Cemetery Ridge
in the face of the 140 guns then in position would have
been stark madness."

Two cavalry actions took place late on the afternoon
of July 3 at the extreme right and left of the Federal line.
At the right, beyond Round Top, Brigadier General Judson Kilpatrick sent three cavalry charges against the
Confederates defending the end of their line. All were
repulsed with loss and in the third a most promising
young officer, Brigadier General Elon J. Farnsworth, who
had received his star just before the battle, was killed.
He had protested to Kilpatrick that "these men are too
good to kill," but Kilpatrick was obdurate and the charge
was made.

At the extreme right of the Federal line General Stuart
crossed the Hanover Pike to the Rummel farm, which
he held with three brigades, with batteries posted near
Cross's Ridge. The Federal brigades in the action were
those of Colonel John B. McIntosh and Brigadier General
George A. Custer, which drove Stuart's troops out of
the Rummel farm. A charge was led by Generals Wade
Hampton and Fitzhugh Lee and repulsed by Federal batteries, in the course of which Hampton was wounded.
The Federals effectively stopped the Confederates from
proceeding farther around the Union right.

The Cost of Gettysburg

Brigadier General John D. Imboden was called to
General Lee's headquarters that night of July 3, after the
Confederate hopes were wrecked. He has left an unfor-
gettable picture of Lee riding up from a session with
General A. P. Hill, a weary man on a jaded horse, so
tired that he could hardly dismount. The roar of the
guns had ceased and moonlight flooded the battlefield.
Imboden said: "General, this has been a hard day on

you." Lee replied: "Yes, it has been a sad, sad day to us." After a pause he commented on the magnificent behavior of Pickett's troops and then said: "If they had been supported as they were to have been—but, for some reason not yet fully explained to me, were not —we would have held the position and the day would have been ours." Then "in a tone almost of agony," he added: "Too bad! Too bad! Oh, too bad!"

Lee then instructed Imboden on the "arduous, responsible and dangerous" duty of taking charge of the transfer of wounded to Virginia. Imboden had 2,100 men ready for duty, and McClanahan's 6-gun battery; Lee could not provide more men, but promised more artillery. He directed Imboden to take the Chambersburg road over the mountain, then any other route to Williamsport; to stop there to feed the horses, then ford the river and march without a halt to Winchester.

The next day, July 4, General Imboden organized the wagon and ambulance train for the wounded and Lee sent him eight guns of the Washington Artillery and several others, so that Imboden had twenty-three guns for defense and part of General Wade Hampton's cavalry for a rear guard. After noon of July 4 a blinding rainstorm with high winds erupted and lasted the rest of the day and all night. Imboden began moving at 4 P.M. and when his advance started to descend the mountain at Cashtown his column was seventeen miles long. The column was well under way before Imboden was able to take charge; he had to ride from the rear to the front in the blinding rain, all along the route hearing the unending wails and groans of the wounded. He changed the route of the column to go to Greencastle; here on July 5 a crowd of men, angered at the Confederate invasion, began breaking the spokes of wagons with axes. When the cavalry was ordered to arrest the attackers as prisoners of war the sabotage stopped. Small bands of Union cavalry also appeared to harass the train.

At Williamsport the Confederate wagons halted and housewives were impressed into service to prepare food for the sick and wounded. The surgeons now had their first opportunity to ameliorate the suffering. A new obstacle was the flooded river, too high for fording. Here

Imboden received word that a Federal force of 7,000, in 23 regiments of cavalry with 18 guns, was on the way to attack him. He posted guns on the hills outside of Williamsport and organized the teamsters into companies to augment his troops. The Federals belonged to the forces of Brigadier Generals John Buford and Judson Kilpatrick, plus Colonel Pennock Huey's brigade of General Gregg's division. They attacked first with artillery and then sent dismounted men on a charge, but the Confederate guns were well handled and held them off. General Fitzhugh Lee came in time up the Hagerstown Road with 3,000 cavalry, and the Federals withdrew. The Confederates had about 125 casualties and captured 125 Federals.

The First, Second, and Third Corps of the Confederate army crossed at Falling Waters, Maryland, July 13 and 14, during torrents of rain. The bridge, which had been partially destroyed by the Federals, was repaired and a ford was also used. Major General Henry Heth's corps had supervision over this part of the passage. The wheels of the many wagons and batteries cut the approach to the bridge into deep ruts and puddles and men waded in mud up to their knees. Longstreet described how a wagon loaded with wounded missed the end of the bridge and fell into the torrent, but troops on the bank rushed forward, righted the wagon, and saved everyone in it.

Brigadier General J. J. Pettigrew's division of the Third Corps formed the rear of the infantry. Major General Fitzhugh Lee's cavalry had been assigned to protect the rear, but departed for the Virginia side, leaving only a small squadron, which left soon after. On July 14 General Kilpatrick's Third United States Cavalry fell upon the North Carolina infantry of Pettigrew's command. Pettigrew mistook the approaching horsemen for Confederate cavalry. Kilpatrick charged and cut off 1,500 Confederate soldiers, several guns, and 3 standards. The Union troops lost 29 killed, while the Confederates had 125 killed and wounded. Among those mortally hit was General Pettigrew, who had invoked the honor of "good old North State" when he led the Carolinians in the great charge at Gettysburg. General Lee, who described Kil-

patrick's raid as "a feeble attack," said "the army has
lost a brave soldier and the Confederacy an accomplished
officer."

Independence Day, July 4, 1863, became a day of patriotic fervor such as the United States had not known for
decades. At 10:30 A.M. President Lincoln addressed the
nation as follows:

The President announces to the country that news from
the Army of the Potomac, up to 10 P.M. of the 3d, is such as
to cover that army with the highest honor; to promise a
great success to the cause of the Union, and to claim the
condolence of all for the many gallant fallen, and that for
this he especially desires that on this day He, whose will, not
ours, should ever be done, be everywhere remembered and
reverenced with profoundest gratitude.

The war correspondents had kept the telegraph operators busy after the battle of Friday, July 3, describing
the repulse of the great Confederate charge. That night
the Associated Press reported from Meade's headquarters that a decisive battle had been fought and won; it
gave great credit to the Federal artillerists and said of
the infantry: "The enemy today at their hands has received the greatest disaster ever administered by the
Union forces."

Two days later the nation learned that Vicksburg, too,
had fallen. The news came in a dispatch sent by boat
up the Mississippi to Cairo and in it Acting Rear Admiral David D. Porter told Secretary Welles of the
Navy: "I have the honor to inform you that Vicksburg
surrendered to the United States forces on the 4th of July."

Pemberton and his army were prisoners, but what
about Lee? For the next few days Washington officials
were frantic. Would Meade bag the beaten Confederate
army? Meade's first dispatches were inconclusive; it was
not clear whether Lee was pulling out of Pennsylvania
completely or consolidating for a new stand. But when
Washington realized that he was escaping across the Potomac the exasperation was tremendous. Noah Brooks,
correspondent for the *Sacramento Union,* who had access to Lincoln several times a week, recorded the President's "grief and anger," and John Hay saw "hope struggling with fear" in the President's demeanor. When it

became obvious that the Confederates were getting away Lincoln burst out: "We had them within our grasp. We had only to stretch forth our hands and they were ours. And nothing I could say or do could make the army move." In his despair he expressed the view that the war might go on indefinitely.

For once General in Chief Halleck was not among the harsh critics of the Union commander. He seems to have understood that an army that had just lost one-fourth of its effectives could not sally forth to attack another army at bay without considerable hazard. But the generals were not agreed on what to do next. At Meade's headquarters Noah Brooks found General James S. Wadsworth so affected by inaction that he was almost in tears. Meade was deliberate. A whole week went by before he called a council of corps commanders on July 12. Meade proposed to send three columns of 20,000 men each against Lee. Warren and Pleasonton favored renewing the fighting; Sedgwick, Slocum and French were opposed. Howard was noncommittal and later wrote Lincoln that Meade's whole action was justifiable. Lincoln replied that he was grateful to Meade for Gettysburg and considered him a brave and skillful officer and a true man, but felt he and the army had let the ripe harvest go to waste.

Congress, which often tendered thanks for great military services, was unjustifiably slow in recognizing such accomplishments at Gettysburg. Not until January 28, 1864, did it pass a formal resolution, and then it led with commending Hooker and the Army of the Potomac for covering Washington and Baltimore, and then cited Generals Meade and Howard "and the officers and soldiers of that army" for their skill and heroic valor at Gettysburg. Over two years later, on May 30, 1866, Congress thanked General Hancock "for his gallant, meritorious and conspicuous share in that great and decisive victory." Politics, obviously, had interfered with gratitude.

The enormity of the disaster to the Confederate cause at Gettysburg was not lost on the South and in the subsequent attempts to find the reason even the respected commander, Robert E. Lee, came under fire. Criticism of Lee's strategy by Southern journals caused him concern, but only one attack, in the Charleston *Mercury*, moved him to defend his position on Gettysburg in a letter to President Jefferson Davis. In it he expressed his conviction that the army had achieved "a general success, though it did not win a victory. I thought at the time that the latter was practicable. I still think if all things could have worked together it would have been accomplished." Given the knowledge he then had, he explained, he did not know what better course to pursue; had he foreseen that the last attack would fail to drive the enemy from his position he would have tried some other course. He took comfort in the fact that the crippled condition of the Federal army enabled the Confederates to retire "comparatively unmolested," and added: "The unexpected state of the Potomac was our only embarrassment." True to his nature of not blaming individuals, he did not mention any lapses or omissions by subordinates.

But nine days after writing thus the continued hunt in the South for a scapegoat got under his skin. He wrote again to President Davis, mentioning that the blame was centered on him and remarking that the general remedy for want of success in a military commander was his removal. He therefore requested Davis "to take measures to supply his place." He cited his inability to accomplish his own desires or meet the expectations of others and mentioned "the growing failure of my bodily strength." He had not yet recovered from the effect of the attack of the spring. "I am so dull in making use of the eyes of others I am frequently misled." Therefore, he suggested that the President look for "a younger and abler man."

Some of his comments suggest that he was not free from the human trait of humbling himself unduly, especially when he wrote that it "would be the happiest day of my life to see at its [the army's] head a worthy leader—one that would accomplish more than I could perform and all that I have wished. I hope your excellency will attribute my request to my true reason, the desire to serve my country, and to do all in my power to insure the success of her righteous cause. I have no complaints to make of anyone but myself. I have received nothing but kindness from those above me. . . ."

Thus he did not actually resign, and if his integrity

were not so thoroughly a part of his character, one might attribute the tone of the letter to a desire for a vote of confidence. This he certainly received from Davis, who had no intentions of replacing Lee. Though several officers would have liked to possess Lee's authority, the South never had an anti-Lee party, in the same sense that the North was divided over McClellan and Grant.

For generations Gettysburg was the biggest and most costly battle in American history. It gained prominence not only because of its size, but because it foreshadowed the doom of the Confederacy. It has been the subject of numerous studies; its strategy and tactics have been analyzed and commendation and blame have been fixed, according to the measure applied to the evidence. The tons of metal thrown into these fields during three days have been weighed and nearly all of the Minié balls and scraps of shrapnel have been picked up. The numbers that fought and the numbers killed and injured are still matters of analysis and conjecture, for the records of 100 years ago were not precise.

The official count says that the Union army had 3,072 killed, 14,497 wounded, 5,434 captured or missing, a total of 23,003 casualties. The same source, U.S.A., says the Confederates lost 2,592 killed, 12,709 wounded, 5,150 captured or missing, a total of 20,451 casualties.

But there are strange discrepancies. The Confederate army reported that it left 770 wounded men behind. But the medical director of the United States Army reported that 6,802 wounded Confederates from the battle of Gettysburg were on his rolls. The U.S. Adjutant General's Office reported that for July 1 through July 5 there were 12,227 captured Confederates, wounded and unwounded, on the rolls.

One count finds that on June 30, 1863, the Army of the Potomac had 97,368 on its lists, to which were added 4,310, making a total of 101,678. But of these the actual numbers ready for duty were 93,500. Whereas Thomas L. Livermore, in his analysis, finds the Federal army had 83,289 effectives on July 1. In similar fashion he gives the Confederates 75,054. Another report gives the Confederates a net of 77,518 on May 31. There are no complete and final figures.

23

TWO MINUTES TO IMMORTALITY

On November 19, 1863, there took place at Gettysburg, Pennsylvania, an event that made an indelible impression on American history. It was the dedication of the National Cemetery, at which President Lincoln made a two-minute address that has become the peak expression of pure democracy. On that day it comprised "the dedicatory remarks by the President of the United States." Today it is known and loved the world over as the Gettysburg Address.

The cemetery grew out of necessity. In the farmland south of Gettysburg, where the battle had raged in July, lay the bodies of thousands of hurriedly buried men, some so lightly covered with earth that the rains had washed the soil off their bones. The state of Pennsylvania, urged by the citizens of Gettysburg, invited eighteen states to help provide a suitable burial spot on Cemetery Hill, close by the graveyard where the town of Gettysburg buried its dead. A plot of ground was bought and paid for by the states, and while several thousand bodies were being transferred to the new site, the formal dedication of the cemetery was set for November 19, 1863.

Oratory was a cultivated art in those days, growing out of the need of a man to project his voice as far as possible to be understood by a crowd. One of the great orators was Edward Everett, who had been Secretary of State under President Fillmore, president of Harvard College, governor of Massachusetts, United States senator, and minister to England. He had been a candidate for Vice President of the United States on a ticket opposed to that of Lincoln in 1860. To gain him as orator the Gettysburg committee shifted the date for his convenience. It then invited other distinguished guests by means of a printed circular, which went to the President, members of his cabinet, state governors, and other officials.

President Lincoln's acceptance surprised the committee, and its member from Illinois, Clark E. Carr, suggested belatedly that he be invited to speak. So the committee asked the President to "set apart formally these grounds to their sacred use by a few appropriate remarks," six weeks after Everett had been asked to give the oration.

President Lincoln asked Secretary Stanton to provide a special train for the trip to Gettysburg, and it moved from Washington via Baltimore and Hanover, Penna., on the afternoon of Wednesday, November 18. Of the cabinet only Secretary of State Seward, Secretary of the Interior John P. Usher, and Postmaster General Montgomery Blair joined the party. The President's secretaries, John G. Nicolay and John Hay, were there, but they were not yet as prominent as they were to become later. At Gettysburg the President was accommodated in the house of Judge David Wills, who had helped promote the cemetery; Edward Everett also was a guest there. The Wills House was located on a corner of the public square, and although it survives, its first floor has been altered and houses a drugstore.

That evening a crowd collected in front of the residence and Lincoln came out and spoke briefly, saying he did not have any speech to make then. After that he went to his room and put in some more time on his address. Actually he already had written some of it in Washington and carried it with him. After breakfast on the morning of November 19 he made a new draft.

The exercises began with a procession to the cemetery, led by Major General Darius N. Couch. Generals Meade, Stewart, and Scott had been invited, but did not appear; neither did the justices of the United States Supreme Court nor the Vice President. Seven governors and one former governor were present. There were four bands, including the Marine band of Washington. The President and cabinet members were on horseback; the President's horse was a small one and Lincoln's feet nearly touched the ground. He wore a tall hat, a formal frock coat, and white gloves. The news reports said 15,000 people came for the ceremonies.

Edward Everett began speaking a little after noon and

spoke for two hours less three minutes. Lincoln had read the address, which had been made available in proof-sheets. It filled two newspaper pages. Everett favored the classic attitudes of oratory; he had memorized his speech and moved across the platform in a studied manner. When he closed his address a song written for the occasion was sung, and then Ward H. Lamon, former Illinois law partner of Lincoln and now marshal of the District of Columbia, introduced the President.

The scene has been described vividly by Dr. William E. Barton, Lincoln biographer, who made a study of original reports for his book, *Lincoln at Gettysburg*. He pictured the throng on the platform, the crowd listening attentively to Everett, the soldiers in orderly array, and the lone photographer, who failed to get his camera ready for operation before Lincoln finished. It was said that Lincoln began in a high, thin voice, but that it carried. The correspondent of the Cincinnati *Commercial* reported: "The President rises slowly, draws from his pocket a paper, and when commotion subsides, in a sharp, unmusical treble voice, reads the following brief and pithy remarks. . . ."

Of the "brief and pithy remarks," the following is the version approved by Lincoln:

Fourscore and seven years ago our fathers brought forth on this continent a new nation, conceived in liberty and dedicated to the proposition that all men are created equal.

Now we are engaged in a great civil war, testing whether that nation or any nation so conceived and so dedicated can long endure. We are met on a great battlefield of that war. We have come to dedicate a portion of that field, as a final resting-place for those who here gave their lives that that nation might live. It is altogether fitting and proper that we should do this.

But, in a larger sense, we cannot dedicate—we cannot consecrate—we cannot hallow—this ground. The brave men, living and dead, who struggled here, have consecrated it, far above our poor power to add or detract. The world will little note, nor long remember, what we say here, but it can never forget what they did here. It is for us the living, rather, to be dedicated here to the unfinished work which they who fought here have thus far so nobly advanced. It is rather for us to be here dedicated to the great task remaining before us—that from these honored dead we take increased devotion to that cause for which they gave the last full measure of devotion —that we here highly resolve that these dead shall not have died in vain—that this nation, under God, shall have a new birth of freedom—and that government of the people, by the people, for the people, shall not perish from the earth.

The legend arose that the President's address had been ignored by the newspapers of the day. This was not exactly true. Actually it was overshadowed by the space given to Everett's address. Some opposition newspapers ridiculed it as a political speech. But practically all the major newspapers mentioned it, many using the report of the Associated Press.

Dr. Barton was especially interested in discovering who really appreciated the greatness of the address. Everett congratulated Lincoln on the stand, but this was to be expected as an act of politeness. But evidently Everett meant what he said, for the next day he wrote Lincoln a memorable letter in which occurs the line: "I should be glad if I could flatter myself that I came as near to the central idea of the occasion in two hours, as you did in two minutes." Lincoln, who had recognized the solemnity of the ceremonies, and had worked hard on his address, was said to have considered his talk a failure, but Everett's letter made him think better of it. Appreciation of the quality of the address grew slowly. Dr. Barton discovered no word from Horace Greeley of the New York *Tribune,* James Gordon Bennett of the New York *Herald,* or Henry J. Raymond of the New York *Times.* An anonymous reporter for Joseph Medill's paper, the Chicago *Tribune,* wired his newspaper the next day: "The dedicatory remarks by President Lincoln will live among the annals of man." But the *Tribune* did not elaborate editorially on his prediction.

In the course of months various journals discovered eloquence, beauty, and power in the President's words. Today, five copies of the Gettysburg Address in Lincoln's hand are extant. The first and second draft, prepared in Washington and Gettysburg, are in the Library of Congress. The third copy was written out by Lincoln at the request of Edward Everett, to be sold at a fair in New York for the benefit of soldiers. In recent years it was bought by popular subscription for the Illinois State Historical Library in Springfield, Illinois. Lincoln wrote two copies for George Bancroft, the historian, the second for facsimile reproduction in a book sold for the benefit of soldiers and sailors in Baltimore. Of these the first is now in the Library of Cornell University, Ithaca, New York. The second was bought by a former Cuban ambassador to the United States, Oscar B. Cintas, and presented in his will to the White House, where it now hangs in the Lincoln Room.

The Amnesty Proclamation of 1863

Congress, by an act of July 7, 1862, had authorized the President to extend pardon and amnesty to persons who participated in the rebellion in any state, with such exceptions as he might consider expedient. On December 3, 1863, President Lincoln proclaimed a full pardon and restoration of all property rights except those in slavery to all who conformed to certain conditions. They must take an oath to support the Constitution, and abide by the laws of the nation and the President's policy regarding slaves. Excepted from the pardon were Confederate government officials and agents; military and naval officers above the rank of colonel or naval lieutenant; all who had given up seats in Congress and on the bench and left the United States army and navy to join the Confederacy. Also excepted were all who in a position of authority in any way had treated colored or white persons who were in the service of the United States otherwise than lawfully as prisoners of war.

By the same proclamation, those who took the oath were authorized to form a loyal state government on republican lines in ten southern states, Virginia excepted, provided they numbered not less than one-tenth of the total votes cast in the 1860 national election and had been qualified voters under the election law existing before secession. The United States would protect them against invasion or domestic violence, if this was desired by the governor.

24

THE NATIONAL ELECTION
OF 1864

In 1864 the national election came around again and
President Lincoln and the Republican administration
faced a test of their leadership at the polls. When the
two major parties prepared to nominate candidates in
the spring, the strength of the Administration was not
fully evident. There was great dissatisfaction with the
conduct of the war. Despite immense sacrifices and heavy
losses the Union had not been able to defeat the Confederate States. Grant's army was still inching along in
front of Petersburg. Sherman was meeting tough resistance while hewing his way through the South. In the
North practically every city, town, and hamlet had tragic
reminders of the cost of the war in sons lost in battle,
maimed men walking the streets, and wounded languish-
ing in hospitals. No one knew exactly what inroads the
advocates of an immediate peace had made into the public whose support Lincoln needed for his program of
holding the Union together.

Opposition to Lincoln's policies had grown in his own
party to such an extent that in the spring of 1864 his
close advisors doubted they could get a majority in Congress for important Administration measures. Much criticism grew out of the prolongation of the war and the suppression of certain constitutional liberties. The principal
opposition to Lincoln's renomination came from groups
supporting his own Secretary of the Treasury, Salmon
P. Chase, and from followers of Major General John C.
Frémont, who advocated even stronger efforts against
the Confederacy. Lincoln highly valued Chase's financial
ability and called his tenure in the Treasury a "national
necessity," but he considered Chase's ambition to be
President a "bad habit," and preferred to see him on
the bench. Later he named him Chief Justice of the United States to succeed Roger B. Taney. Major General
Frémont, who had been the first nominee for President

of the new Republican party in 1856, sought vindication for what he considered unjust treatment by the President. His premature emancipation of slaves in the Western Department in October, 1861, had forced Lincoln to repudiate it, and a few months later Lincoln had removed him from the command after an investigation disclosed inefficiency and confusion in his affairs. Frémont's followers met in Cleveland and nominated him for President; he withdrew during the campaign.

Supporters of Lincoln, while recognizing these adverse portents, took comfort from the elections of the fall of 1863, in which the Republicans had made gains. The Vallandigham Democrats in Ohio suffered a serious defeat at the hands of John Brough, who was elected Republican governor by 100,000 plurality. In Pennsylvania, where the Democrats also made immediate peace an issue, the Republican governor, Andrew G. Curtin, was re-elected. In New Jersey the Republicans gained, although they did not command a majority. In New York the upstate counties overcame whatever disaffection remained in New York City, where the bloody draft riots of July, 1863, had left ill feeling, and the Republicans elected a number of state officers. In the spring of 1864 New Hampshire, Connecticut, and Rhode Island endorsed Lincoln, and fourteen states had declared for him by the time the convention opened.

The National Union convention of the Republican party met in Baltimore, June 7, 1864, with a Kentuckian as temporary chairman and William Dennison, former governor of Ohio, permanent president. Delegates were admitted from Tennessee, Louisiana, and Arkansas. Virginia was excluded, but delegates were admitted from West Virginia, which had organized as a state and would legally become a member of the Union on June 20. The radical delegation from Missouri was seated. Lincoln received every vote for the nomination except that of Missouri, which then moved to make the nomination unanimous. For the Vice Presidency the Republicans wanted a man from a Southern state and passed up Hannibal Hamlin of Maine, the incumbent, and Benjamin F. Butler of Massachusetts, to name Andrew Johnson, a Democrat of Tennessee, who, as senator, had remained loyal to the Union and had been appointed military governor of Tennessee by Lincoln in 1862. This became known as the National Union ticket.

The convention backed President Lincoln and the conduct of the war, and its platform demanded no compromise with the South, but unconditional surrender and a return to "just allegiance to the Constitution and the laws of the United States." It declared slavery hostile to the principles of republican government and said "justice and the national safety demanded its utter and complete extirpation from the soil of the Republic." It endorsed the Emancipation Proclamation and the employment of former slaves as Union soldiers, which had been opposed by some Republicans; supported the government's acts against slavery, and favored an amendment to the Constitution terminating it forever. It called for "ample and permanent provision" for those who had been wounded in defense of the country. The threat of the South not to recognize Negroes in uniform led the platform to recommend "prompt redress for any violation by the enemy of the uses of civilized nations in times of war." It also asked a liberal and just policy of foreign immigration; favored speedy extension of the railroad to the Pacific; recommended economy and rigid responsibility in expenditures and a vigorous and just system of taxation, so that the national credit might be inviolate and able to redeem the public debt. Finally it took notice of the expedition of the French against Mexico by supporting the government's stand against encroachment of any monarchical government sustained by foreign military power on the Western continent and in close proximity to the United States. It was a platform that expressed the convictions of the majority, not concessions to special groups with no object of carrying out the recommendations.

In thanking the convention Lincoln gave special approval to the recommendation for amending the Constitution to abolish slavery, calling it a fitting and necessary conclusion to the final success of the Union cause. He also promised that the State Department and the Executive would continue to maintain the position they had taken toward France and Mexico.

The Democratic party had issued a call for its nominating convention to meet July 4, 1864, but postponed it to August 26. By that time Clement L. Vallandigham, the Ohio peace advocate who had been convicted of interfering with the army by the military court and "exiled" to the Confederacy when Lincoln commuted the sentence, had returned from Canada to take part in the convention. Vallandigham and his followers represented the extreme opposition to the war and were known as Copperheads. Many other conflicting opinions were represented in the convention, but all members were united in their bitter antagonism to Lincoln and his administration.

Some Democrats wished the war to be carried to a conclusion under new management; others wanted to wipe out the past by cessation of fighting and a convention of all the states to reconcile differences. The "War Democrats" favored men of military experience, foremost of whom was Major General George B. McClellan. Although he had been removed by Lincoln for failing to follow up military advantages, many considered his tardiness caution and conservation of human life. McClellan had not been reappointed to a command and was bitter toward his former superior, who, in his opinion, had hampered him. There was support also for John A. Dix, major general of volunteers, who was one of the so-called Albany Regency that had controlled Democratic politics in New York State for many years, and who had been given a military department after serving briefly as Secretary of the Treasury under Buchanan. There also was minor mention of Major General John C. Frémont. Some of the Peace Democrats, notably from Maryland, were opposed to McClellan because he had made arbitrary arrests in their state, but the belief that he would get many Army votes helped his candidacy and he was nominated. For Vice President the Democrats named George H. Pendleton, a representative from Ohio known as a Peace Democrat and Administration opponent.

Vallandigham, who had a hand in writing the Democratic party platform, was head of the Knights of the Golden Circle, a secret society with lodges and passwords, also affiliated with the Order of American Knights. In the spring of 1864 Major General William S. Rosecrans, then in Missouri, informed Washington that his agents had joined the American Knights and obtained their secrets, which he wished to disclose to the President. Lincoln sent his secretary, John Hay, to see Rosecrans, and Hay reported that the Knights planned to bring Vallandigham back from Canada to the Democratic convention, and that if Vallandigham were rearrested they would "unite to resist the officers and protect him at all hazards." Lincoln, who had treated the earlier secret organization with "good-humored contempt," refused to become alarmed by the present disclosure.

The Democratic platform was devoted entirely to denouncing the war and the Administration, and was so extreme in its denunciation of acts of the government, some of which McClellan had made effective as a military commander. Grant, in a scathing letter, asked whether McClellan could "lower his sword before the enemy." McClellan accepted the nomination, but insisted the Union must be maintained; it was "the one condition of peace; we ask no more." Senator Charles Sumner retorted, "if we do not obtain more the Union then becomes an empty name." The platform set forth that the Democratic party wanted to preserve the Union "and the rights of the states unimpaired." It asserted that since

under the pretence of a military necessity higher than the Constitution, the Constitution itself has been disregarded in every part, and public liberty and private right alike trodden down, and the material prosperity of the country essentially impaired, justice, humanity, liberty and the public welfare demand that immediate efforts be made for a cessation of hostilities, with a view to an ultimate convention of all the states, or other peaceable means to the end that at the earliest practicable moment peace may be restored on the basis of the Federal Union of the States.

The platform alleged interference by the military authority in elections in Maryland, Kentucky, Missouri, and Delaware; subversion of civil by military law in states not in insurrection; arbitrary military arrest, imprisonment, trial, and sentence of American citizens in states where civil law existed in full force; suppression of freedom of speech and of the press; denial of the right of asylum; open and avowed disregard of state rights; the employment of unusual test-oaths; and interference with and the denial of the right of the people to bear arms. It condemned the "shameful disregard" by the Administration of the suffering of prisoners of war. The platform also promised the soldiers "care and protection, regard and kindness" from the party, "in the event of our attaining power."

What one soldier in the field thought of the issues of the campaign is disclosed in the letters of James A. Connolly, major in the 123rd Illinois Infantry, published as *Three Years in the Army of the Cumberland.* Connolly told his wife that he considered McClellan a man of straw doing the bidding of the Peace Democrats and the Fernando Wood crowd, so that they could patch up a dishonorable peace and pocket the spoils. He was pleased that McClellan was not a peace man, and felt this stand would help the war sentiment in the North and lessen opposition to the drafts. Connolly recorded that October 11 was election day in Ohio, and his division halted by the roadside from 12 noon to 3 P.M. to allow Ohio soldiers to vote. He said that very few Copperhead (antiwar) votes were cast.

On August 23, six days before the Democratic convention met, President Lincoln wrote a brief note on how he expected the election to go; without disclosing its contents he asked the cabinet members to sign it. It showed how anxious he was about the outcome. Lincoln had written: "This morning, as for some days past, it seems exceedingly probable that this administration will not be re-elected. Then it will be my duty to so co-operate with the President-elect as to save the Union between the election and the inauguration; as he will have secured his election on such ground that he cannot possibly save it afterward."

President Lincoln was re-elected, but the voting showed a big division of opinion among the citizens of the North. Out of over 4,000,000 votes cast, Lincoln's plurality was one-tenth of the total. The revised total gave Lincoln 2,216,067 popular votes, against 1,808,725 for McClellan, and 212 electoral votes against 21. Three states not represented in 1860 voted strongly for Lincoln; they were Kansas, admitted in 1861; Nevada, admitted in 1864, just eight days before the balloting; and West Virginia, admitted June 20, 1863. No votes from Louisiana, Tennessee, and Arkansas were canvassed by Congress. The states that gave a majority to McClellan were New Jersey, Delaware, and Kentucky. The vote was close in the large states. New York, where the draft riots had disclosed bitter antagonism to the war by the immigrant population, gave Lincoln only 6,749 more votes than McClellan out of over 730,000 cast for both parties. Ohio, the hotbed of Vallandigham's pacifism, gave Lincoln 59,438 more votes than McClellan. Kentucky showed considerable opposition to Lincoln, for McClellan received more than double the votes cast for Lincoln. In analyzing the election for Congress, President Lincoln said that the total showed an increase of 145,551 voters over the 1860 election, this in spite of the fact that the soldiers of 7 states—Massachusetts, Rhode Island, New Jersey, Delaware, Indiana, Illinois, and California—to the number of about 90,000 were not permitted by the states to vote away from home. Men who lived in the territories, or served in the Army from those areas, also had no voice in the voting.

On November 10 a procession with bands and transparencies marched to the White House in Washington to serenade the President. He spoke through an open window. He said the country had proved its ability to sustain a national election in the midst of a civil war.

The strife of the election is but human nature applied to the facts of the case. Human nature will not change. In any future great national trial, compared with the men of this, we shall have as weak and as strong, as silly and as wise, as bad and as good. . . . It [the election] shows that, even among candidates of the same party, he who is most devoted to the Union, and most opposed to treason, can receive most of the people's votes. It shows also that we have more men now than we had when the war began. Gold is good in its place, but living, brave, patriotic men, are better than gold.

Lincoln then asked all who had a common interest in the country to unite to save it.

For my part I have striven, and will strive, to avoid placing
any obstacle in the way. So long as I have been here I have
not willingly planted a thorn in any man's bosom. . . . May
I ask those who have not differed with me to join with me
in the same spirit toward those who have?

General Grant at City Point asked Secretary Stanton
to congratulate the President, saying in his message:
"The election having passed off quietly, no bloodshed or
riot throughout the land, is a victory worth more to the
country than a battle won."

When the second session of the Thirty-eighth Congress
convened on December 5, 1864, President Lincoln made
a favorable report on the national housekeeping. He said
the Treasury had a balance of nearly $19,000,000 despite
the payment of interest of $53,685,421 on the public
debt of $1,740,690,489. The United States Navy, built
and building, comprised 671 vessels, with 4,610 guns and
510,396 tons, marking an increase during the year of 83
vessels over losses by shipwreck and battle. There were
51,000 men in the naval service. The Navy had captured 324 vessels during the year, making the total for
the war years 1,379.

Pensions already were being paid to invalid soldiers
and sailors and to widows, orphans, and dependent moth-
ers of veterans. The President reported 22,767 Army
and 712 Navy pensioners, as well as over 26,000 de-
pendents of all classes. He noted that the country was
paying pensions to 1,430 persons because of the American Revolution, only twelve of whom were ex-soldiers;
seven died during the year. The rest received pensions
because of relationship.

It was at this time that President Lincoln appealed to
Congress to pass the Constitutional amendment abolishing slavery. As narrated before, it had passed the Senate
in the first session, but failed to get the two-thirds vote
of the House. He respected the opposition, but believed
the election showed the strong feeling of the people, and
while this was not a mandate he thought the House might
reconsider, since the measure would "most certainly" pass
in the next Congress. The House did reconsider in January, 1865, and after three weeks' debate passed the

resolution by 119 to 56, thus preparing it for ratification
by the states.

25

GENERAL SHERMAN'S
CAMPAIGNS IN GEORGIA

During the winter of 1863–64 General Sherman, in
command of the Department of the Tennessee, was frequently annoyed by the depredations of roving bodies of
Confederate cavalry, notably the "critter company" of
General Nathan Bedford Forrest. He also observed that
the Confederates had enough infantry and cavalry in
Mississippi to create hazards for navigation of the Mississippi River. The main body of Confederates was commanded by the late bishop of Louisiana, Lieutenant General Leonidas Polk, who made his headquarters at Meridian, Mississippi. This was a railway center with a network of roads penetrating to all parts of the South, so
that its warehouses were filled with supplies for the army.
Polk had a division of infantry under General W. W. Loring posted at Canton, Mississippi, and another under
General S. G. French at Brandon. He had two divisions
of cavalry, one holding the terrain from the vicinity of
Yazoo City to Jackson and the other Forrest's, which
was supposed to be posted at Como but invariably was on
the loose.

General Sherman had Meridian well canvassed by a spy
and came to the conclusion that a quick stroke might un-
settle the complacent Polk and yield results. He drew on
General Hurlbut at Memphis for two divisions and on
General McPherson for another, putting about 20,000
men on the alert. To build a cavalry force of about
10,000 Sherman expected Hurlbut to provide 7,500, and
he wanted Brigadier General W. Sooy Smith to add his
2,500 and to lead them against Forrest, whose numbers
changed but who was understood to have about 4,000
men at this time.

The Meridian expedition got under way February 3, 1864, in two columns, one commanded by General McPherson and the other by General Hurlbut, with an advance unit of cavalry under Colonel E. F. Winslow. The troops covered 150 miles in 11 days. Sherman rode with them and narrowly escaped capture from Confederate horsemen while staying overnight in a Decatur house. Word had gone out among the Confederates that Sherman was headed for Mobile, and this confused them. General Polk withdrew hurriedly from Meridian for Demopolis, Alabama, and for five days Sherman's troops destroyed everything of use to the Confederate army. This included food and munitions. The Confederates complained that the troops burned 10,000 bales of cotton and 2,000,000 bushels of corn and carried off 8,000 slaves. Two hotels and various gristmills were burned and Sherman did a thorough job of destroying rail connections, tearing up the rails of the Mobile & Ohio and the Selma & Jackson. Sherman reported that he captured 500 prisoners and had ten miles of Negroes. While some of the latter joined the army en route, others probably had been employed by the Confederate army.

General W. Sooy Smith never did arrive. General McPherson went back to Canton, and General Sherman made a vain effort with Winslow's cavalry and Hurlbut's infantry to locate Smith, after which they, too, returned to Canton. This raid was described by General Joseph E. Johnston as a repulse for Sherman. Smith, it turned out, had waited for an ice-bound brigade and consequently had not started until February 11. Then Forrest had stopped him near West Point on the Mobile & Ohio and defeated him with an inferior force. Sherman reported Smith's derelictions to Grant, and although Smith later on asked Sherman to erase the censure from the record, Sherman's disappointment was so great that he refused to do so. Smith's failure deepened Sherman's contempt for the cavalry. Lloyd Lewis, in writing *Sherman, Fighting Prophet,* devoted a whole chapter to Sherman's appraisal of cavalry as inefficient, badly disciplined, unruly, and wasteful especially of men and horses. Describing his attitude toward cavalrymen, Lewis wrote: "They were romantic, he was practical; they were reckless, he was efficient; they were dramatic, he was realistic." Their best work was done as scouts. Sherman held that a cavalry command of 1,000 was afraid of the sight of a dozen infantry bayonets. His principal criticism was that they were not useful for tearing up railroad tracks, work they preferred to leave to infantrymen. When Sherman developed this point of view on the basis of his own observation he had no direct knowledge of the part played in the Shenandoah Valley by the cavalry of Sheridan and Jeb Stuart.

Grant Takes Top Command

On March 1, 1864, President Lincoln signed an act of Congress reviving the military grade of lieutenant general. On the same day he sent Congress his nomination of Ulysses S. Grant for this rank, and it was confirmed March 2. Grant was ordered to appear in Washington, and on March 9 the President gave him his commission in the Executive Mansion, in the presence of the cabinet, several members of Grant's staff, and Grant's eldest son, Frederick Dent Grant, who had been with him during the siege of Vicksburg. The President made a brief address of presentation and Grant made a suitable reply, having been handed a copy of the address before the meeting so that he could draft his own.

Grant had intended to remain in the West, but when he inspected the system prevailing in Washington, and had visited the Army of the Potomac, he decided that the man in command of all the armies ought to work in the East. He was impressed with the efficiency of Major General Meade, and was touched when the latter invited Grant to replace him, in the event it was good for the country; Grant determined to be with the Army of the Potomac in the field, but to give his orders through Meade, so that the services of this able commander would not be lost. He decided to place Sherman in his former post as commander of the Military District of the Mississippi, advance McPherson to Sherman's post as head of the Department of the Tennessee, and give command of McPherson's Corps to Major General John A. Logan. Grant had discussed with Lincoln the return to the mili-

tary service of those generals who, for one reason or
another, were now detached—McClellan, Burnside, Frémont, Buell, McCook, Negley, and Crittenden. Lincoln was
anxious that these experienced commanders should be
employed where best fitted, and Grant asked Sherman to
look after the last four. Sherman discovered that rank
was more important to these men than service to the
country, but Crittenden and McCook did return to the
army, although Buell apparently was stopped by Secretary Stanton.

Before the spring campaign could open Grant drafted a
master plan in the hope of coordinating the action of the
various armies. He wanted "to work all parts of the
army together," and for Sherman he proposed the elimina-
tion of General Joseph E. Johnston's army. He had been
eager for some time to confront Johnston, whose headquarters were at Dalton. He had attempted in February
to get General Thomas moving against Dalton, but Thomas
had been unable to press the campaign because he lacked
forage and supplies. To Sherman, Grant wrote: "You I
propose to move against Johnston's army, to break it up
and to get into the interior of the enemy's country as
far as you can, inflicting all the damage you can against
their war resources. I do not propose to lay down for you
a plan of campaign, but simply lay down the work it is
desirable to have done and leave you free to execute it in
your own way. Submit to me, however, as early as you
can, your plan of operations."

Only Washington had held the rank of lieutenant general, and Winfield Scott had held the rank of brevet lieutenant general. (A rank by brevet meant the officer could
use the title as a mark of honor, but could not exercise
the command nor receive the pay that would adhere to a
regular promotion to that rank.) Grant said in his letter
to Sherman that Sherman and McPherson were "the men
to whom, above all others, I feel indebted for whatever I
have had of success." Sherman reciprocated with his
usual effusiveness and with a fervent appeal: "Do not
stay in Washington. Come out West; for God's sake and
for your country's sake, come out of Washington. . . . Here
lies the seat of the coming empire. . . ." Sherman was
confusing his vision of the greatness of the West with

the military necessity; Grant was aware that his major job now was to defeat Lee.

Sherman now had command of military activities in all the territory west of the Alleghenies and north of Natchez. After conferring with the commanding generals of the four departments under him, Sherman consolidated the Eleventh and Twelfth Corps of Generals Howard and Slocum into one called the Twentieth and gave the command to General Hooker. He gave Howard the Fourth Corps, in place of General Gordon Granger, who had a leave of absence and later was active against Mobile in General Canby's Department of the Gulf. He also gave Slocum command of the District of Vicksburg. In order to have sufficient rolling stock to transport supplies, Sherman canceled civilian traffic on the railroads; ordered military posts within thirty miles of Nashville to haul their stores in wagons; required troops going to the front to march on their own legs and livestock to be driven on the roads. He asked the railroad management to obtain locomotives and cars sufficient to haul about 130 carloads of supplies daily.

On May 1, 1864, when Sherman was preparing to move against Johnston, he had available 98,797 men and 254 guns, as follows: General Thomas, head of the Department of the Cumberland, had 60,773, based on Chattanooga; General McPherson, Department of the Tennessee, had 24,465 centered at Huntsville, Alabama; General Schofield, of the Department of the Ohio, at Knoxville, Tennessee, had 13,559. In addition there were a number of cavalry units under Generals Stoneman, Garrard, McCook, and Kilpatrick. General Steele was assigned to the Red River of Arkansas to succeed General Banks, who was moved to New Orleans. On June 9, when the campaign was already under way, Major General Francis P. Blair took command of the Seventeenth Corps, with two new divisions under Generals Leggett and Crocker.

General Johnston, at Dalton, had about 50,000 troops, including Georgia militia under General G. W. Smith.

General Sherman's Georgia campaign began May 5, and by May 9 General McPherson had passed through Snake Creek Gap and surprised Confederate cavalry west of Resaca. He found Resaca too strong to attack and fell back three miles to entrench, a circumstance that amazed Sherman, who declared McPherson had overlooked an opportunity to bag half of Johnston's army. "Strengthen your position, fight anything that comes and threaten the safety of the railroad all the time," wired Sherman, who immediately ordered the rest of the commands to move up. Johnston abandoned his rather extensive defenses at Dalton but fought doggedly on the defensive at Resaca, which was strongly fortified. Hooker and Howard did most of the fighting throughout May 13. On May 15 Johnston left Resaca hurriedly, his dead unburied and his wounded deserted, but the fighting had not been one-sided, for the Federals had Hooker, Manson, and Kilpatrick wounded, none seriously, while Sherman counted his losses for the first ten days in the field at 600 killed and 3,375 wounded. Johnston kept on retreating until he reached Cassville, where he expected to give battle May 19; Sherman ordered his troops concentrated there, but by the 20th Johnston had left and crossed the Etowah River. The Federals attributed his departure to the threat to his left flank by McPherson, but years after the war Johnston explained to Sherman that his corps commanders, Generals Hood and Polk, had contended that they were open to enfilading, and Hood had demanded an offensive against Schofield. Johnston thereupon canceled his plans and withdrew.

During the rest of May heavy fighting took place around New Hope Meeting House, four miles northeast of Dallas. After crossing the Etowah, Hooker moved around the mountains to Allatoona. This brought on a clash with a large force of infantry on the road leading from Allatoona to Dallas. The fighting in this area continued for a week; both sides were entrenched behind logs, and there was sporadic musketry and skirmishing. The cavalry of Stoneman and Garrard entered Allatoona without opposition, making possible rail connections with the rear. When Johnston moved out of the New Hope field, June 4, Sherman's troops had command of the railroad from Allatoona and Acworth to Big Shanty, having penetrated 100 miles "of as difficult country as was ever fought over by civilized armies." During the May fighting Sherman's three armies had 1,863 killed and missing and 7,436 wounded, Sherman explaining that the missing inevitably meant prisoners taken by the enemy. The Confederates, who did not count in this way, reported 721 dead, 4,672 wounded. In the meantime McPherson had entered Rome and destroyed factories there, then moved to the left, passed around Dallas, and headed for the Chattahoochee River. In an engagement that started with a cavalry fight at Powder Springs the Confederates lost a considerable number of prisoners.

General Blair joined the expedition at Acworth on June 8 with his new Seventeenth Corps of 9,000 troops and left a garrison of 1,500 at Allatoona. Sherman estimated his current strength at 100,000 effectives, after making allow- ances for losses by battle and disease. At New Hope, General Johnston was estimated to have over 64,000. On June 10 Sherman's army moved to Big Shanty and next day a supply train arrived, the Federal engineers having rebuilt a railroad bridge over the Etowah, which John- ston had burned. From this point the Federals could ob- serve that the Confederates occupied a line ten miles long on three prominent hills, Kenesaw, Pine Mountain, and Lost Mountain. Sherman's troops moved south on the railroad to Peach Orchard, where they entrenched and advanced gradually with some fighting.

Death of General Polk

While studying the Confederate works on Pine Moun- tain, General Sherman observed a battery about 800 yards from the base of the hill and a group standing near it. He ordered General Howard to fire three volleys at the group. Later he learned that one of the shells had struck General Leonidas Polk and killed him. Polk, the former Bishop of Louisiana, was fifty-eight. His training at West Point overcame his clerical profession; he was made a major general in 1861 and in 1862 a lieutenant general. He commanded a corps at Shiloh. Much of his early career was in education, and he was the principal founder of the University of the South, a Protestant Episcopal institution at Sewanee, Tennessee. In the Confederate army he was succeeded by Lieutenant Gen- eral Alexander P. Stewart.

General Johnston was no Stonewall Jackson. He was unable to outwit the larger army despite its long extended lines and its distance from the base. He now prepared to make a determined stand against Sherman at Kenesaw. For this purpose he drew in his lines from Pine Mountain and Lost Mountain and built up strong, contracted positions. The Federal army moved likewise. Despite the weather—it had rained daily for nineteen days—Sherman kept up the pressure, fighting almost daily and gaining some ground. He wired General Halleck on June 23: "The whole country is one vast fort and Johnston must have at least fifty miles of connected trenches, with abatis and finished batteries." Hooker and Schofield advanced on the Powder Springs Road to within three miles of Marietta. But the generals agreed that it was unwise to keep on extending their lines; an outright assault on the Confederate works was necessary. This began on the morning of June 27, when ten miles of Federal trenches blazed with musketry and artillery fire. The columns moved on up to the parapets, but could not hang on. Both Brigadier General Harker and Brigadier General Daniel McCook were mortally wounded. The assault had not routed the Confederates, but some of the troops were able to dig in close to the parapet. The heaviest Federal losses were in front of the divisions of Cheatham and Cleburne, of Hardee's corps. Sherman said his army lost about 2,500 killed and wounded, McPherson having 500 and Thomas nearly 2,000 casualties. General Johnston admitted 808 casualties in two corps and thought the Federal estimate of its losses too low; he thought there must have been 6,000 casualties.

When General McPherson's army was moved from the base of Kenesaw Mountain (now spelled Kennesaw), to the right and his line extended toward Turner's Ferry on the Chattahoochee, General Johnston withdrew from Kenesaw and Marietta to a point along the Chattahoochee protected by a strong bridgehead and entrenchments that crossed the railroad five miles south of Marietta. In pursuing him General Thomas' advance came in contact with an entrenched rear guard at Smyrna and engaged the troops on July 4. Generals Schofield and McPherson took positions below Thomas; General Stoneman's cavalry went down the Chattahoochee bank until it was opposite Sandtown, where Johnston's cavalry kept it under observation. General Garrard's cavalry division of the Army of the Tennessee was sent eighteen miles up the river to Roswell, to destroy factories that had been making cloth for the Confederates and to take possession of a ford.

Johnston's army and trains were inside the bridgehead, which Sherman described as "one of the strongest pieces of field fortification that I ever saw." Sherman's headquarters now were at Vining's Station and the railroad was being repaired up to that point. From the high ground behind the station Sherman observed that Johnston had sent only his cavalry and trains across the river and was still on the west bank. Sherman reported to Halleck that he had pontoons enough for four bridges and that all the regular crossing places were covered by forts, apparently constructed long ago. Atlanta was only nine miles away and instead of attacking it or its forts direct, Sherman proposed to make a circuit and destroy all its railroads.

Rousseau's Cavalry Raid

Whatever adverse opinions Sherman may have held about the cavalry as a whole, he profited frequently by its aid during this campaign. He now sent General Rousseau at Nashville orders to collect several thousand cavalry out of scattered detachments in Tennessee and bring them to Decatur, Alabama. Thence he was to proceed south to break up the main railroad line serving Johnston from Alabama, running from Opelika to Montgomery. Rousseau started on July 9, destroyed stores encountered on the way, sent cavalrymen after guerrillas, and reached the Coosa River near Ashville on the 13th. His First Brigade remained on one side of the river while the other went across, and the two proceeded down stream on opposite banks. The Second crossed below Horseshoe Bend, where General Andrew Jackson had defeated the Creek Indians in 1814. Here the two brigades were attacked by a force of Confederate dismounted cavalry under Clanton, which they routed. At Talladega they destroyed commissary stores. On the 16th Rousseau crossed the Tallapoosa about thirty-five miles from Montgomery, Alabama. On July 17 they hit the railroad at Loccopaca, 135 miles southwest of Atlanta, and tore up the rails. A Confederate force from Montgomery attacked them at Chewa Station, but was repulsed. Rousseau's troops then destroyed a trestle twelve miles from Montgomery. Turning east, they reached Opelika July 19 and burned army supplies and railroad installations, tearing up the tracks. A larger Confederate force now appeared in pursuit; Rousseau left the railroad and started back to Sherman's lines, which he reached July 22, when Sherman was already engaged in the environs of Atlanta. Rousseau reported the loss of 12 killed, 30 wounded; he brought back 300 horses and 400 mules. Yet in spite of the hard work these cavalrymen had done tearing up railroad tracks in the enemy's country, Sherman found it difficult to concede their effectiveness. He wrote: "As usual, the cavalry did not work hard and their destruction of the railroad was soon repaired." He did not take into account that the Confederates could repair rails in a hurry just as the Federals had done.

Before Johnston moved General Schofield crossed successfully at Soap's Creek; General Garrard's cavalry crossed at Roswell and held its ground until the advance of the Army of the Tennessee was across. Both positions were above the river from Johnston. On the night of July 9 he put his army across the Chattahoochee, burning the railroad bridge, trestle bridges, and pontoons. Sherman was now ready to take the rest of his army across the river north of the railroad bridge, and when General Stoneman returned from his cavalry reconnaissance on July 15 he was sent to Turner's Ferry to replace General Blair's division. On July 17 the general crossing started and the troops were off toward Atlanta. General Thomas went by way of Buckhead, Schofield at his left by Cross Keys; McPherson moved to a point between Stone Mountain and Decatur, breaking up the railroad on the way, and meeting with Schofield's troops at Decatur that night.

As Sherman advanced and Johnston fell back the people of Georgia were terror-stricken. Would Johnston never fight and throw out the invader? Georgia was giving him its best provender, and Sherman was stealing the rest. State and local officials sent delegations to Richmond to demand a new commander and the rescue of Atlanta. Jefferson Davis and his cabinet were badly alarmed. Davis sent General Bragg to Atlanta to size up the situation, and the latter reported, July 15, that he could not find out what plans Johnston had, if any. "Position, numbers and morale are now with the enemy." Two of the Confederate corps commanders, Hood and Stewart, favored an offensive but Hardee favored the present policy of retiring. Bragg thought that if a change in command was to be made Hood would be far better in the emergency than anyone else; he would give "unlimited satisfaction," but he was not a great general.

President Davis naturally consulted General Lee and the latter replied with his usual gravity; obviously he was disturbed at the prospect of a change in command. "It is a grievous thing to change commander of an army situated as is that of the Tennessee." He was afraid they might lose both Atlanta and the army. "Still if necessary it ought to be done. I had hoped that Johnston was strong enough to deliver battle." Lee was guarded in his estimate of Hood's abilities. He considered him a good fighter, earnest and with zeal, industrious on the battlefield and careless off, but he did not know how Hood might act when he had the whole responsibility. He added: "General Hardee has more experience in managing an army. . . . May God give you wisdom to decide in this momentous matter." This was as near as Lee came to saying he preferred Hardee. Hardee had been offered command of the army once before, to succeed Bragg, and had refused it.

Davis was just as reluctant as Lee to see a change in the top command at Atlanta. After getting Bragg's report he made one more effort to get a specific statement of plans direct from Johnston. But Johnston's reply did not satisfy him. Johnston said that since the enemy had double his numbers he would have to remain on the defensive and watch for an opportunity to fight to his advantage. On July 17 Davis ordered Johnston relieved and General John B. Hood placed in command, and it was effected July 18. The telegram to Johnston was sent by Adjutant General Cooper and gave the reason: "I am directed by the Secretary of War to inform you that, as you have failed to arrest the advance of the enemy to the vicinity of Atlanta, far in the interior of Georgia, and express no confidence that you can defeat or repel him, you are hereby relieved from the command of the Army and Department of Tennessee. . . ."

Sherman learned of it when one of his spies came in that morning from Atlanta with a copy of a newspaper containing the orders. He immediately asked General Schofield, who had attended West Point with Hood, about Hood's characteristics. Schofield replied that Hood was bold even to rashness, yet courageous in the extreme. Sherman decided this meant fighting and sent warnings to all his division commanders to be prepared for battle and ready for sallies. "This was just what we wanted, to fight in open ground, on anything like equal terms, instead of being forced to run up against prepared entrenchments. . . ." Later on General McPherson, who also had been a classmate of Hood at West Point, told Sherman that Hood was brave, determined, and a hard fighter, though of no great mental capacity.

When General Hood took over the Confederate army he was bitter about its condition and what had happened to it. He put all the blame on General Johnston's leadership, asserting Johnston had broken the spirit of the army by continually retreating before an inferior foe when he had the men, the arms, and the terrain to defeat the Federals. Hood was convinced the Confederate Army of Tennessee was superior to any force the Federals could bring against it; its defeat was "the inevitable result of strategy adopted." In his report he went back to the time when Johnston commanded it at Dalton. On May 6 the army had 70,000 men at Dalton and orders from Richmond were to assume the offensive. Hood looked on the Federals with contempt; they were "little superior in numbers, none in organization and discipline, inferior in spirit and confidence." The territory to operate in was mountainous, suitable for strong positions of resistance. What happened?

This magnificent army, said Hood, began to retreat.

With each advance of the Federals it fell back. By day it fought, by night it fell back. Daily it threw up earthworks only to abandon them. This lasted seventy-four days and nights. Hood drew a lesson from this experience: if an army fights a battle and holds its position, its loss is less than if it retreats, for in retreat it leaves behind its wounded, men asleep in the trenches, stragglers, and deserters. Hood said Sherman's forces when they entered Atlanta were nearly the same in number as when they left Dalton; although this was not quite true it enabled Hood to drive home his argument. The Confederate Army of Tennessee had lost 22,750, nearly one-third of its strength. When the army was turned over to Hood at Atlanta, July 18, 1864, he found it to have 48,750. Years later Hood was still bitter, but he conceded some qualities to Johnston. His caution exceeded his boldness, Hood said. "He is a man of courage and ability, and a fine organizer of an army for the field, but he lacks the bold genius of Lee. . . . He invariably throws up entrenchments, fortifies his line, and there remains in deliberation upon the best means to defeat an enemy without risking a general engagement, when, suddenly, he finds himself outflanked, and issues the usual order for retreat."

Hood's Defense of Atlanta

After General Thomas' army had crossed Peach Tree Creek it occupied a narrow pocket of land between the creek and the Chattahoochee River, and likewise was some distance from the armies of McPherson and Schofield, who were over toward Decatur. General Hood saw this gap as an opportunity to strike hard at Sherman's right wing and possibly to crush it between the two rivers. Despite the warnings about the unpredictability of Hood the Federal commanders were fairly surprised when the Confederates burst out of their entrenched positions on July 20, 1864, and assaulted Thomas' troops. The Federal reports say the men were just resting after the noonday, but the Confederates said the attack was unavoidably delayed until 4 P.M.

The main assault fell on Brigadier General John Newton's division of the Fourth Corps and Brigadier General R. W. Johnson's division of the Fourteenth, and hit especially hard the troops of Major General Joe Hooker's Twentieth Corps. The Confederate troops were those of Lieutenant General A. P. Stewart, who had taken General Polk's command after the latter's death; Lieutenant General William J. Hardee's, and Major General B. F. Cheatham's, formerly Hood's. Because of the removal of a division between Hardee and Cheatham and misunderstanding about moving their units, a delay resulted. Although the Confederates had been instructed to carry everything in a rush and to stop at nothing, using the bayonet at close quarters, Hardee's men failed to thrust their attack home. When Confederates appeared to turn Newton's exposed flank General Thomas, who was in the rear of that division, brought up field guns and turned them on the attackers. With cohesion lost and a desperate hand-to-hand combat developing, the Hood plan, which he had considered practically perfect if followed, collapsed, and the Confederates went back to their trenches.

Hardee's men had encountered low entrenchments and apparently considered them an obstacle too difficult to surmount in the face of rapid firing. This was General Hood's explanation of the loss of his first battle in defense of Atlanta. To his astonishment Major General P. R. Cleburne told him that prior to the assault General Hardee rode along the line and warned Cleburne to look out for breastworks. This was fatal news to Hood, who was positive that the continual throwing up of breastworks by the Confederates when Johnston was in command had given them a feeling of security behind them and of insecurity in front of them. This was one of the objections Hood had to Johnston's way of fighting, but his principal complaint was against the habit of retiring in the face of the enemy, which, he declared, broke the spirit of the Confederate troops. Hood now wanted to restore their morale by striking out with full force against the Federals, and for a time he did succeed in making considerable trouble for Sherman, but even with the addition of the Georgia state militia and other forces he was not a match for Sherman.

The Federals lost 300 killed, 1,410 wounded, at Peach Tree Creek; the Confederate losses were placed at 1,113 killed, 2,500 wounded, and 1,183 missing.

General Hood did not let the first repulse interfere with his urgent business of saving Atlanta. Learning from his cavalry eyes, General Wheeler, that General McPherson's left flank was exposed and vulnerable near the Georgia Railroad between Decatur and Atlanta, and that a large number of Federal wagons was parked near Decatur, he decided on a maneuver somewhat similar to the one that had served Stonewall Jackson so well at Chancellorsville. He would send troops by night around the Federal positions and attack the extreme left in rear and flank, with all the power at his command. Intermittent stands of forest would help conceal the march.

Hood also had his chief engineer, Colonel Prestman, examine the line of fortifications that Johnston had partially completed. Prestman reported the line was too close to the city and on too low ground. Hood ordered a new line to be constructed on higher ground, and next morning General Sherman, at the Howard House outside of Atlanta, was able to observe through his field glass Confederates at work on entrenchments.

The next day the Federals closed the gaps between their divisions. Bald Hill, an important Confederate outpost, was seized by General Force of Leggett's division, assisted by Brigadier General Giles A. Smith, who had taken command of the Fourth Division of Major General Francis P. Blair's Seventeenth Army Corps when Brigadier General Walter Q. Gresham was wounded at Peach Tree.

The failure of the Confederate army to destroy the right wing of Sherman's army made Hood more determined than ever to strike with a large force without delay. The next day he instructed his generals in the parts they must play in support of General Hardee's movement toward McPherson's flank and rear, which was to be made during the night. Major General Wheeler, who was to furnish cavalry guides, was to take position at Hardee's right with all his cavalry and to attack with Hardee at daylight. General Cheatham was to help on the right, and when McPherson was driven back upon Peach Tree

Creek, General G. W. Smith would come in. General
Stewart would interfere with any aid given by Thomas
to McPherson and join in the fighting when it became general. Thus the Federal army would be thrust "down and
against the muddy stream in their rear," a prospect that
Hood drove home to his generals. It was as good a
plan as any general ever devised, but it seems to have accepted Confederate success from the break of day. Unfortunately the Federals were not willing to play the
game.

McPherson's Last Battle

The next stage can be followed from the vantage point
of the commanders of the opposing armies, both of whom
have left reports of how the sound of firing out Decatur
way affected them. General McPherson did not expect a
general attack on his army, neither did Sherman. The two
were sitting on the steps of the Howard House, Sherman's headquarters, when they heard sounds of gunfire
increasing on the left, in the direction of General G. A.
Smith's division of the Seventeenth Corps, mingled with
the deeper boom of artillery fire coming from the direction of Decatur. Oddly enough McPherson and Sherman
had just been exchanging views on the personality of
Hood, and both agreed to be on their guard against
Hood's impetuosity. Obviously they had been too late
applying this decision. McPherson called his staff together, mounted, and rode away to investigate. Sherman
quickly sent orders to Schofield to send a brigade to
Decatur.

In the meantime, on the other side: General Hood,
who knew what was going to happen, took a position
near Cheatham's right at daybreak and awaited events.
At about 10 or 11 A.M.—that is, the same time when
McPherson and Sherman were discussing Hood on Sherman's front steps—Hood also heard firing that puzzled
him. He knew from the sound that something was not
going according to plan. He did not hear that continuous
roar of musketry and the "genuine Confederate shout"
that would indicate Hardee was carrying the line, so he
sent a staff officer to find out what had happened. He

learned "with astonishment and bitter disappointment" that the attack was only partially successful; Hardee's troops had come up against different lines of entrenchments. Some they had attacked and held. They had failed to turn McPherson's left, which was of vital importance to the whole scheme, and were now engaged against entrenched positions, which Hood had sought to avoid. Hood ordered Cheatham to attack on his front; this succeeded until Sherman's batteries began enfilading and causing Cheatham to abandon his position. General Smith moved his Georgia state militia forward in support of Cheatham, but the numbers against them were too great.

The Federals had supposed the attack to be delivered by a small force that had been able to get around the Seventeenth Corps by using the cover of woods on the Union left flank. When they woke up, Sherman sent orders to General Logan to throw the Army of the Tennessee into the battle. The Federals had been handicapped because Sherman had sent Garrard's cavalry division on a raid of destruction of railroads and bridges east of Atlanta and hence lacked his cavalry reconnaissance. The Confederates had taken Murray's battery, four guns on General Giles A. Smith's left flank, and several hospital corps.

Once alarmed, the Federal support developed quickly. The Confederates had taken only a few wagons of the parked train when they were routed from that place. At 4 P.M. Hood's troops made a sally out of their Atlanta trenches against General Logan at Leggett's Hill, where they were repulsed. They did capture De Gress's battery of four 24-pounder Parrott guns, and a battery of the First Illinois Artillery, turning them against the Federals. General Schofield brought twenty guns near the Howard House to bear on the Confederates. The Federals that had been driven back rallied under General Logan's leadership and regained their lost ground as well as the Parrott guns, although two other 6-pounders were taken away by the Confederates, who then retired behind the trenches at Atlanta. Hood said Hardee carried off eight guns and Cheatham took five. Hood comforted himself with describing the battle as a partial success, which had checked the Federals' "reckless manner of moving" and the danger of leaving gaps between divisions.

The Battle of Atlanta was another costly affair. The Union army reported 500 killed, 2,141 wounded, and 1,000 missing. General Logan estimated the Confederate casualties at not less than 10,000, and although this may have been an extreme guess, he reported burying 3,220 Confederates in front of his lines.

Two major generals died in the battle. On the Union side John B. McPherson was shot and killed soon after leaving Sherman. On his way to the front he had ordered up some reserves of the Fifteenth Corps to the exposed left flank, had urged some troops of Dodge's corps to hurry forward, and then, almost alone, had followed a road behind the Seventeenth Corps and entered a wood, where he was shot down. His body was recovered immediately and taken to Sherman's headquarters at the Howard House.

Who should succeed to McPherson's command? Sherman was aware of the place ambition and personal pride have in the make-up of most men, even military leaders. General Logan might be considered in line; he had taken McPherson's post temporarily. Sherman consulted General Thomas, who warned him not to appoint Logan, reminding Sherman that Logan and Blair were "political generals," who had one eye on public office. Sherman thought Major General O. O. Howard was qualified, and Thomas agreed. When Sherman sent his nomination of Howard to General Halleck he had a quick response. Halleck approved and the President immediately confirmed the appointment. Howard's Fourth Corps then went to Major General David S. Stanley. Sherman regretted the appearance of favoring West Pointers; they just happened to be in line and, after all, he concluded, they did know how to do the job.

The appointment of Howard floored Hooker. The commander who lost Chancellorsville and had been superseded just before Gettysburg, still felt he was in line, and here was a public slight. The Fourth Army Corps led the Army of the Cumberland, of which Major General George H. Thomas was commander. Hooker asked Thomas to be relieved from command of the Twentieth Corps and Thomas, with evident satisfaction, "heartily recommended" this to Sherman. Hooker was a troublemaker; his free opinions were often circulated and created bad feeling. But his bravery was unquestioned; he had done notable work in tight situations in half a dozen major battles—Williamsburg, Fair Oaks, Seven Days, Second Manassas, South Mountain, Antietam, Fredericksburg, Lookout Mountain, Missionary Ridge. Temperament killed his chances, and he resented being ignored. He was just a few weeks short of fifty. He resigned from active service and left the army entirely after the war, taking up residence in New York.

The Fall of Atlanta

General Sherman, in camp twenty miles south of Atlanta, during the night of September 2, 1864, was disturbed by distant explosions. General Slocum was located at Chattahoochee Bridge with the Twentieth Corps and had orders to feel his way toward Atlanta. In the morning of September 3 Hardee had withdrawn his army to Lovejoy's Station, and the opportunity to encircle him was gone. But better news was forthcoming: Atlanta had been evacuated and General Slocum had moved in unopposed. When a courier reached Sherman with the news he first communicated it to General Thomas, and he saw that staid gentleman unbend in an unexpected manner: "he snapped his fingers, whistled, and almost danced." Word went to Washington over the telegraph: "Atlanta is ours and fairly won." Sherman decided to let pursuit of Hood wait, take his army to Atlanta and environs, and give it a few days' rest. Thus the Army of the Cumberland surrounded Atlanta, the Army of the Tennessee went to East Point, and the Army of the Ohio to Decatur.

Atlanta was a fortified place and, in the eyes of Sherman, no longer suitable for residence. If its inhabitants remained he would have to keep a large number of troops, possibly a division, there as a garrison; this had been necessary in New Orleans, Vicksburg, Memphis, and Natchez. He therefore ordered all the people of Atlanta to leave. The people who had remained in Atlanta, many of whom were without means, were appalled. James M. Calhoun, mayor, and two councilmen addressed an impassioned protest to Sherman. They pointed out that some women were pregnant, others had little children; husbands were either in the Confederate army, prisoners, or dead. Houses beyond Atlanta already were crowded with refugees who had retired as the Federal armies advanced. "What has this helpless people done," asked the mayor, "that they should be driven from their homes, to wander strangers and outcasts and exiles, and to subsist on charity?"

Sherman was quick to defend his course. He deluged the mayor and councilmen with a flood of words about the war, the guilt of the South, and his determination to root out the enemy. Atlanta might again become a battleground, said he, so in asking the citizens to leave he was doing them a kindness. Hardships of war? "War is cruelty and you cannot refine it," said the general; "and those who brought war into our country deserve all the curses and maledictions a people can pour out." The Confederates had sent men and munitions to carry the war into Kentucky and Tennessee, and hundreds and thousands of women and children had fled from the Confederate armies and desperadoes, "hungry and with bleeding feet."

To accommodate the exodus a neutral station was established at the next railroad station south of Atlanta, known as Rough and Ready. General Hood had asked for an exchange of Confederate prisoners for Union soldiers held at the stockade of Andersonville, but Sherman already had sent most of his captives north and could only call back 2,000 that had not yet reached Chattanooga. These he offered in exchange for Generals Stoneman, Buell, and others, but he was unwilling to make any general exchange, for he argued that the Federals would be sent to other armies than his own, while the Confederates would return immediately to service under Hood. Hood cooperated at the neutral camp, and citizens from Atlanta went there with whatever household goods they could carry.

As a man of feeling Sherman must have realized the inhumanity of his order, for he again undertook to justify it in a report to the Chief of Staff, Major General Halleck. Several weeks after the order had been issued he

rationalized the whole proceeding. His real reasons, he
told Halleck, were: he wanted the houses of Atlanta for
military storage and occupation. He wanted to contract
the lines of defense, limit the size of the garrison, build
citadels and redoubts, which meant destroying houses.
The poor would either starve or have to be fed by the
army, and a civil population would make possible clan-
destine relations with the enemy. And again he repeated,
Atlanta was a fortified town and as captors "we have a
right to it."

He got into a much more involved argument with
General Hood, in which he recounted all the iniquities of
the Confederacy; Hood in turn rejected his accusations
and retorted that the United States government had invaded his country, insulted his flag, and subverted free
institutions with the bayonet, and he called Sherman's
"kindness to the people of Atlanta" hypocritical. "We
will fight you to the death," he declared. Sherman could
outwrite and outtalk practically everybody, but now he
realized that nothing was to be gained by trading epithets,
and he closed the correspondence with the brief assurance that there were no "Negro allies" in his army, as
Hood had charged.

In Washington, General Halleck applauded. He said
the Confederates had not only burned mills and factories
but had stripped their own people of provisions; "We
have fed this class of people long enough." But General
Halleck did not approve General Hunter's course in burning private houses and uselessly destroying private property. "That is barbarous." Even Halleck drew the line
somewhere.

The capture of Atlanta had one important influence on
the North. The campaign for Lincoln's re-election was on,
and there was much discontent over the length and bloody
character of the war. Maimed and suffering men who returned to their families from the Southern battlefields
talked of horrors rather than glory. The dissidents were
especially active in Ohio and Indiana. Even Lincoln was
worried lest the effect of the draft lose the state of Indiana to the Republicans. Election of its governor was
set for October 11, and it was the only state whose soldiers could not vote in the field. Lincoln appealed to

Sherman to let some of his Indiana soldiers go home to vote in the state election; they need not stay for the Presidential election. Generals Logan and Blair and Colonel Benjamin Harrison already had crossed the Ohio to speak for the ticket. But with Hood still active and threatening, Sherman could not release men of the Indiana regiments because they were needed at the front. The capture of Atlanta, combined with several other successes, restored confidence that the end of the war was near and thus retarded efforts to overturn the Administration.

Hood Starts for Nashville

In September, Sherman heard details about the terrible condition of Union prisoners at Andersonville, Georgia. He sent an appeal to General Hood to permit a trainload of clothing and personal accessories to go through to Andersonville with a disbursing officer. Hood consented, and Sherman enlisted the help of a friend who was vice-president of the Sanitary Commission of St. Louis, asking for underclothing, 400 pairs of scissors, and 1,200 fine-tooth combs, as well as plenty of soap. The train was made ready but before it could move, the Confederates, alarmed by the possibility that Sherman might get there first and release and arm the prisoners, moved them to Florida. Eventually the supplies reached them at Jacksonville, as Sherman said: "before the end of the war."

General Hood was convinced that the Confederate army was dispirited because of its defeats, and that its morale could be raised by offensive operations. After the evacuation of Atlanta, Hood determined to operate in the rear of Sherman's army, draw him back into the mountains, and defeat him there. He blamed the loss of the battles of July 20 and 22 and August 31 on Lieutenant General William J. Hardee, who had failed to carry out Hood's plans. At this time Hood had 40,403 men, hardly enough for his ambitious project. He demanded reinforcements, and when he failed to get them from President Davis he determined to embark on his expedition anyhow. He would move boldly into Tennessee with the cooperation of the cavalry corps of Lieutenant General Nathan Bedford Forrest, who was now in charge of all cavalry in this Department. Then he would take a straight route to Nashville. He explained his plan to General Beauregard, who seemed to favor it, but President Davis was quite reluctant to have him try the adventure. Davis thought Hood ought to fight Sherman when the latter marched north from Atlanta with his army divided. Eventually, however, he gave a reluctant consent.

Hood moved the Confederate army from Lovejoy Station to Palmetto Station on the West Point road, September 21, and ordered his supply depot established at West Point. Sherman suspected that Hood was moving into Alabama and intended to interfere with his railroads. On September 24 he had bad news from Athens, Alabama; General Forrest had arrived with a large force of cavalry and captured the Federal garrison of about 950, including three Negro regiments.

President Davis arrived at Palmetto on September 25 to confer with Hood and his generals and look into the controversy over the fall of Atlanta. Hood had asked that Hardee be relieved of his command and this was eventually done, Hardee going into North Carolina and Major General P. R. Cleburne taking his place. Davis made a speech to the troops in which he forecast that Hood soon would be cooperating with Forrest in Middle Tennessee and that the Yankees would have to retreat or starve. On September 27 he announced the formation of the Military Division of the West, with General Beauregard in command, his authority to extend over Hood and over General Richard Taylor's army in Alabama. This was satisfactory to Hood.

By October 1 Hood had crossed the Chattahoochee and had sent Brigadier General W. H. Jackson's cavalry to operate against Sherman's railroad near Marietta. Sherman was certain Hood meant to destroy his rail communications and had already been in touch with Grant about the defense of Tennessee. Grant was routing all western troops to Nashville. Sherman ordered General Thomas to Nashville and also sent Brigadier General James D. Morgan with part of the Fourteenth Corps, both still making use of rail transportation. Sherman left the Twentieth Corps, under Major General Henry W. Slocum, in Atlanta and started for Marietta. But he still believed that Thomas could take care of Hood, thus giving Sherman an opportunity to go on his favorite expedition, to the sea. "Why will it not do," he asked Grant, "for me to destroy Atlanta and march across Georgia to Savannah or Charleston, breaking roads and doing irreparable damage? We cannot remain on the defensive."

Sherman had guards posted along the railroad, with blockhouses at important bridges and entrenchments at railroad stations. But he was aware that the enemy could raid his lines and that he must keep Hood from interrupting his main route. He left the environs of Atlanta, October 3 and 4, crossed the Chattahoochee, and reached Marietta the next day. He had 5 army corps with a little over 60,000 effectives, as well as two small cavalry divisions under Kilpatrick and Garrard.

Hood in the meantime had ordered General Stewart to occupy Big Shanty and send a detachment to Acworth, destroying rails as far as possible. He found only light resistance at Big Shanty and took 170 prisoners; then General Loring advanced on Acworth and 250 Federals surrendered there. The two forces then joined Hood's main body at Lost Mountain, after destroying ten to fifteen miles of railroad.

The Federal army had over 1,000,000 rations of bread stored in Allatoona. When General Hood was attacking railroad installations from Acworth to Big Shanty he sent Major General S. G. French's division of three brigades, over 4,000 men, to seize the place and destroy the stores. Sherman was told that Confederate troops were moving in the direction of Allatoona and by wigwag system signaled Brigadier General John M. Corse, then at Rome, to proceed at once to Allatoona. The garrison there consisted of a brigade of 890 men commanded by Lieutenant Colonel Tourtelotte, and there were two small redoubts, which had been built during the advance the previous June.

General Sherman, watching on Kenesaw Mountain, on October 6, 1864, had the experience of tracing action in several directions—the campfires of the Confederates, the burning railroad installations, and the progress of General Cox of the Twenty-third Corps, moving to intercept the Confederates. Sherman had ordered Cox to indicate his march by burning "houses and piles of brush as it progressed," a typical piece of ruthlessness, and thus pillars of smoke disclosed his way.

The Confederates had surrounded Allatoona, but the garrison was able to defend itself at the redoubts. Thereupon General French sent an ultimatum to the Federals telling them they were surrounded and had five minutes in which to surrender unconditionally, in order to avoid "needless effusion of blood." General Corse replied "that we are prepared for the 'needless effusion of blood' whenever it is agreeable to you."

The Confederates attacked at once and the fight continued all forenoon. The Federals were driven behind the two redoubts, but were always able to repulse the Confederates, for the redoubts were so built that one was able to enfilade the attackers of the other. After 1 P.M. the Confederates withdrew, leaving their dead and wounded behind. General Hood said they withdrew because General French heeded a false report that a large body of Federals was approaching to cut him off from the rest of his army, but the Federals were certain he had failed.

The Federal casualties included General Corse, who had a cheek and an ear cut by a bullet, Colonel Tourtelotte, who was shot in the hips but continued to command, and Colonel Redfield, of the Thirty-ninth Iowa Infantry, who was killed. The Federals had 142 killed, 858 wounded, 212 missing; they buried 231 Confederates and took 411 prisoners, including Brigadier General Young. General Sherman saw the defense of Allatoona as proof that fortified posts should be defended to the last, regardless of the relative numbers of defenders and opponents; in this instance there were approximately 1,944 defenders and over 4,000 attackers.

This time the railroad was in the hands of the Federal armies, so the Confederates gave Sherman a dose of his own treatment. They burned every tie and bent all the rails for eight miles of track, from Big Shanty to above

Acworth. Sherman had to assign 10,000 men to repair the road, using an estimated 35,000 new ties and 6 miles of new rails. In seven days the railroad was running again. Sherman took great pride in the speed with which repairs of roads and bridges were made from Nashville to Atlanta in 1864, but he knew it was a fruitless task, with "Hood, Forrest, Wheeler, and the whole batch of devils" turned loose. The Federals would lose 1,000 men a month to hold the roads, Sherman told Grant; therefore he proposed to let the rails go and strike out with his wagons. "I can make this march and make Georgia howl!" he declared.

General Sherman was confident now that he could march across Georgia for Savannah and Charleston and bring the war home to everybody en route. He wired Grant: "I would infinitely prefer to make a wreck of the road and most of the country from Chattanooga to Atlanta, including the latter city; send back all my wounded and unserviceable men, and with my effective army move through Georgia, smashing things to the sea." This would put him on the offensive again and Hood would have to follow him. General Grant did not immediately reply, and Sherman gained the impression that neither Grant nor Thomas particularly favored his project. But by October 16 Sherman had a message from General Halleck which "intimated" that Washington was willing he should undertake the march to the sea, and that the fleet would await him at Ossabaw Sound, below Savannah.

General Hood moved quickly out of Sherman's path, crossed the Coosa River, twelve miles below Rome, and reappeared at Resaca. On October 12 he demanded the "immediate and unconditional surrender" of the garrison there, announcing that "all white officers and soldiers" would be paroled, but "if the place is carried by assault no prisoners will be taken." Colonel Clark R. Weaver, the commanding officer, expressed surprise at Hood's threats. "In my opinion I can hold this post," he replied. "If you want it, come and take it."

But Hood was bluffing; there was a bit of skirmishing, but he did not assault Resaca. After tearing up twenty miles of rails up to Tunnel Hill he captured over 400 men of the Forty-fourth U.S. Infantry, all Negro troops, at Dalton. On October 16 General Charles R. Woods of General O. O. Howard's corps took Ship's Gap and soldiers of the Twenty-fourth South Carolina Infantry. Sherman was now telegraphing General Thomas at Nashville to send him reinforcements; Thomas replied that he would order Schofield to join him with two divisions, and also send General Joseph A. Mower and General J. H. Wilson. Grant had sent Wilson from Virginia to take command of Sherman's cavalry; Sherman sent him to Nashville to remain with Thomas, keeping only 4,500 horsemen to add to his own army. Thomas also sent Sherman a bit of advice: "I hope you will adopt Grant's idea of turning Wilson loose, rather than undertake the plan of a march with the whole force through Georgia to the sea, inasmuch as General Grant cannot co-operate with you as first arranged."

But Sherman was not to be diverted from his fixed idea. He told Schofield that he meant to "make the interior of Georgia feel the weight of war. . . . We must follow Hood until he is beyond the reach of mischief, and then resume the offensive." Sherman was now ready to send the Fourth Corps back to Thomas and let him defend the line of the Tennessee; he would push on into Georgia. He wired the acting quartermaster general in Atlanta: "On the first of November I want nothing in Atlanta but what is necessary for war. Send all trash to the rear at once and have on hand thirty days' food and but little forage. I propose to abandon Atlanta and the railroad back to Chattanooga, to sally forth and ruin Georgia and bring up on the seashore."

Sherman thought the Federal gunboats patrolling the Tennessee River would provide an obstacle for Hood when he attempted to cross it, but Hood managed to get his army across at Courtland four miles above Florence and below Muscle Shoals. He occupied Florence and reached Tuscumbia, Alabama, on October 31. By a remarkable piece of ill fortune for the Federals, Forrest on the same day appeared at Johnsonville on the river and with cavalry and fieldpieces crippled and captured two Federal gunboats and five Federal transports, a feat that won Sherman's admiration.

Grant finally gave in to Sherman's persistent arguments for a march to the sea. On November 2 he sent a dispatch agreeing that Thomas should now be able to take care of Hood and destroy him. "I say then, go as you propose." Grant reiterated his approval on November 7: "Great good fortune attend you!" By November 10 Sherman's army had turned its back on Hood and the Tennessee; General Corse, at Rome, had orders to burn all mills and factories and join Sherman; General Thomas had word that General A. J. Smith was at Paducah with two divisions and would soon reach Nashville and "was perfectly satisfied with his share of the army." Sherman appreciated the drama of the situation—"two hostile armies marching in opposite directions," and a thousand miles of hostile country ahead for him.

26

BATTLES IN THE WEST:

CHICKAMAUGA AND MISSIONARY RIDGE

Bragg Versus Buell

On June 9, 1862, General Halleck ordered Major General Don Carlos Buell to take the Army of the Ohio and move against Confederate forces in East Tennessee, his first objective being Chattanooga. Buell was told to put the Memphis & Charleston Railroad into condition for the regular movement of supplies. This was a task that would call for many men and materials because it was being raided continually by General Nathan Bedford Forrest and Colonel John Hunt Morgan and their swift-riding cavalry. Chattanooga was being watched by General Ormsby MacKnight Mitchel, who had only about 9,000 troops and had stationed them at Battle Creek, Tennessee, nine miles above Bridgeport, Alabama, and twenty miles below Chattanooga, and at Stevenson. Buell sent divisions commanded by Major General Alex-

ander McCook and Major General Thomas L. Crittenden
to Stevenson and Battle Creek, and kept forces under
Major General William Nelson and Brigadier General
Thomas J. Wood along the Nashville & Decatur Railroad.
Other troops were put at work cutting lumber and build-
ing pontoons for use in the advance.

Small units of Buell's army guarding bridges and outposts were the special objects of attack by the Confederate cavalry, which frequently surprised and overran
them, carrying off many prisoners. Buell was bitterly
contemptuous of cowardice and insubordination, and he
condemned failures in blistering terms, publishing the
names of commanders and regiments in army orders. But
some of the Federal troops fought back and inflicted
losses on the raiders. At Murfreesboro, Tennessee, Forrest captured 800 Federals; the latter had 33 killed, 62
wounded, while the Confederates had 50 killed. Morgan
raided Cynthiana, Kentucky, but was driven off. At
Courtland Bridge, Alabama, the raiders captured 100
Federals, constituting most of the guard. At Gallatin,
Tennessee, in August the raiders captured 200 Federals,
but when they returned next day they were beaten off.
There were numerous cavalry fights in Kentucky and
Tennessee that kept the Federals on the alert.

Early in 1862, Brigadier General George H. Thomas,
in an action to clear eastern Kentucky of Confederate
forces, moved from his camp at Lebanon with about
4,000, including a battalion of cavalry, to dislodge Brigadier General Felix K. Zollicoffer, who had come from
Cumberland Gap with about 4,000 men and entrenched
on the north bank of the Cumberland, opposite Mill
Springs, Kentucky. Major General George B. Crittenden took command over Zollicoffer's force and ordered an attack on Thomas before he could bring up all
his units. A Confederate, Crittenden was the son of
Senator John J. Crittenden and the brother of Major
General Thomas L. Crittenden of the Union army. The
Confederates attacked at Logan's Cross Roads, January
18, 1862, and gained an initial advantage but were soon
hard-pressed and routed; they escaped across the river,
abandoning 11 pieces of artillery with complete equipment, 150 wagons, more than 1,000 horses and mules,

and many stores. The Union forces lost 40 killed, 207 wounded; the Confederates 125 killed, 309 wounded, 99 missing.

During a lull General Zollicoffer, mounted and covered by a waterproof coat, passed Colonel Speed S. Fry of the Tenth Kentucky regiment unrecognized on the road. A second Confederate fired and wounded Fry's horse. Colonel Fry and his party retaliated at once, and Zollicoffer fell dead.

Jefferson Davis was greatly dissatisfied with General Beauregard's withdrawal to Tupelo. He ordered Colonel W. P. Johnston, son of Albert Sidney Johnston, to interview Beauregard and ferret out details about losses, diseases, defenses, and resources, which Beauregard had not seen fit to report to Richmond. At about the same time Beauregard decided to take sick leave and recuperate at a resort near Mobile, Alabama, leaving General Braxton Bragg temporarily in command at Tupelo. Acting on his own authority, he did not notify the Secretary of War in Richmond of his departure. Colonel Johnston found him at his retreat and was favorably impressed with everything he learned, and so reported to Richmond.

But President Davis, who resented Beauregard's indifference to him, announced that Beauregard had left his post without permission and on June 27 appointed Bragg to the command of the post in the West. Beauregard was surprised and annoyed. He demanded the return of his command, but the Confederate authorities made excuses. After Beauregard's recuperation they appointed him to command of the Department of South Carolina and Georgia, with headquarters in Charleston. Beauregard had influential friends who asked his reinstatement as commander of the Army of the Mississippi, but Davis condemned Beauregard's conduct as unmilitary and stood by his order. Davis was a strong supporter of Bragg, and even after Bragg's bad showing in the field brought him to Richmond as military adviser.

The Confederate reverses in Kentucky and Tennessee made the Confederate war office eager to recover some of the territory before it was irretrievably lost to the growing Federal forces. Bragg decided that the best policy was to consolidate East Tennessee. When he took over the Confederate army at Tupelo he had available 45,080 effectives. This included about 11,000 troops belonging to the units of Generals Price and Van Dorn, which were expected to operate against the communications of Grant in northern Mississippi. Not counted were about 2,000 cavalry of General Forrest and Colonel Morgan.

Major General E. Kirby Smith, who had arrived in Knoxville in March to operate in East Tennessee, had about 13,550, including 1,055 cavalry. In order to support Smith, General Bragg in June sent a division commanded by Major General John P. McCown to Chattanooga, adding about 10,000 men to Smith's army. Bragg also sent Colonel (later General) Joseph Wheeler with a brigade of cavalry into West Tennessee and Brigadier General Frank C. Armstrong with another brigade into northern Alabama.

On the Federal side a number of changes took place in midsummer. General Halleck was ordered to Washington on July 11 to become General in Chief. This placed Grant again in command of the Army of the Tennessee and put the central command in Washington, whence Halleck would send orders to Buell. Buell had organized his Army of the Ohio into three corps, the first under McCook, the second under Crittenden, the third under Major General Charles C. Gilbert, who took over the command formerly held by General Nelson.

The harassment of Federal troops continued throughout the summer. On August 18, 1862, Morgan captured almost 200 men of the Seventy-first Ohio Volunteers, which belonged to Grant's command, at Clarksville, Tennessee. General R. W. Johnson of Buell's army rode in pursuit of Morgan and attacked him near Hartsville. But Morgan had a larger force of tough fighters, who inflicted 80 casualties and captured 75 Federals, including Johnson.

Buell had supplied General William Nelson with field batteries and cavalry to use against Morgan. On August 30, 1862, when the Second Manassas was being fought in Virginia, Nelson found himself matched against a much larger force under General Edmund Kirby Smith at Richmond, Kentucky. The Federal forces consisted of six Indiana, two Kentucky, and one Ohio infantry regiments, two Michigan batteries, and the Seventh Kentucky Cavalry. Many of them were raw recruits, facing their first battle. They lost 206 killed and 844 wounded, and inflicted 450 casualties on the Confederates, but the latter captured 4,303, 9 guns, and all the wagon trains, giving them further confidence that Buell would not be hard to defeat.

A short time later tragedy struck Buell's official family. General Nelson, in command of Louisville, had assigned to Brigadier General Jefferson C. Davis the work of arming the citizens of Louisville. An argument developed and Nelson ordered Davis to report back to General H. C. Wright at Cincinnati, whence he had come. Davis objected that Nelson did not have authority over him, whereupon Nelson told him the provost marshal would put him across the river if he didn't go. Davis went. When Buell reached Louisville, Wright ordered Davis to report to Buell. On September 29 Davis, in company of Governor Oliver P. Morton of Indiana, accosted Nelson in the office of the Galt House, in Louisville, and demanded satisfaction for an insult. Nelson derided him; Davis flipped a crumpled visiting card in his face, whereupon Nelson slapped him, and left. Davis procured a pistol from a friend, and when Nelson reappeared fired point-blank at him, hitting him just above the heart. Nelson died within the hour. Buell did not have time for a court-martial of Davis and asked Halleck to have a military commission try him. No charges were preferred. Later a grand jury indicted Davis for manslaughter, and he was released on bail, but never brought to trial.

Cumberland Gap and Perryville

Because Cumberland Gap was considered a gateway into East Tennessee, General Halleck and Buell planned to check Confederate use of it by placing troops there. They ordered out the Seventh division of Buell's Army of the Ohio, comprising four brigades under Brigadier General George W. Morgan, about 8,500 men equipped with 22 heavy guns. General E. Kirby Smith tried to dislodge Morgan without success. When Buell made a feint of threatening Chattanooga, General Kirby Smith left the Gap and marched his troops back to help Bragg. General Carter L. Stevenson took a turn at cutting off Morgan's supplies and by the end of August, 1862, had acted so effectively that Morgan's battery horses were starving to death. The Federals had built large installations at the Gap and used it as a training post. During the night of September 17 Morgan's troops began evacuating the Gap, destroying buildings and stores of small arms and shells. They were delayed by road obstructions and frequently had to hew fresh paths through forest areas to bypass rock barriers. They also were harassed by Confederate cavalry under Colonel John H. Morgan, but they crossed the mountains successfully and on October 3 reached the Ohio River at Greenup, Kentucky, with a loss of 80 men, but saving all guns and wagons.

General Bragg had conferred with General Kirby Smith in Chattanooga on July 31, and the two had decided to campaign against Buell in middle Tennessee. Bragg started to move units of his army westward. General Buell had concentrated his forces at Nashville, but when he learned that Bragg was likely to endanger Bowling Green, Kentucky, he left General Thomas to hold Nashville and moved the bulk of his army to Bowling Green, arriving there September 15. At the same time Bragg marched on Munfordville and on September 16 attacked the Federal garrison there. Although greatly outnumbered, the Federal troops fought well. They comprised Indiana regiments and artillery and the Nashville Provost Guard. Although they inflicted over 700 casualties on the Confederates, the latter prevailed and captured 3,566 Federal troops. This alarmed citizens of Louisville and Cincinnati and caused exasperation in Washington.

Acting as a victorious general would, Bragg on September 18, 1862, issued a proclamation to the people of Kentucky to rally to his support. A similar appeal was made by General Kirby Smith. A secession party in the state announced support of the Confederacy and, having obtained control of the state capital, Frankfort, inaugurated a provisional governor of Kentucky on October 4, 1862, under protection of Bragg's bayonets.

The growing strength of Bragg and the Confederate

elements in Kentucky together with Buell's inability to stop Bragg caused Washington to send an order relieving Buell of the command and appointing Major General George H. Thomas to the post. Thomas refused to supersede his chief and told Halleck that "General Buell's preparations have been completed to march against the enemy, and I therefore respectfully ask that he be retained in command." Senators Crittenden and Davis and two Kentucky representatives also protested to President Lincoln, and the order was withheld.

But decisive events were in the making. On October 4 General Rosecrans defeated General Van Dorn at Corinth, Mississippi, thereby removing support that was important to Bragg.

When Bragg's army reached Bardstown, Louisville, to which the state government had moved, expected an early attack. Citizens of Louisville and Covington began throwing up earthworks. Buell said the arrival of Bragg at Bardstown gave the Confederates virtual possession of the whole of Kentucky east of the Louisville & Nashville Railroad, with the exception of Louisville and Covington. General Polk's corps was moved to points near Louisville, but the Confederates changed their plans when Buell, satisfied that his army was ready to take the offensive, began marching toward Bardstown on October 1.

During the next week Buell made several feints, helping to confuse Generals Kirby Smith and Polk about his intentions. Polk withdrew from Bardstown, and Buell finally had General McCook's corps crowding Polk until they reached the vicinity of Perryville, where an inconclusive battle was fought by parts of both armies on October 8, 1862.

Kentucky had been suffering from an extended drought, and there was little water available along the route of the armies. The Confederate rear guard held possession of some pools of water in the bed of Doctor's Fork. Colonel Daniel McCook of Sheridan's division attacked the Confederates and obtained possession of the water at dawn. The Confederates attempted to regain the position, but were repulsed by Sheridan's and Mitchell's divisions. There was also water in the bed of the Chaplin River, where the Confederates were stationed. In the afternoon

Bragg ordered an assault and severe fighting developed as Polk's three divisions, supported by cavalry, assaulted Generals McCook and Sheridan. The First Division of the Third Corps, commanded by Brigadier General Albin Schoepf, reinforced McCook, and the battle ended at nightfall, before General Thomas came up with his corps. Buell expected to renew the fighting next morning, but Bragg threw away an advantage and withdrew, on the advice of his corps commanders. The Union army lost 845 killed, 2,851 wounded, 515 missing; the Confederates lost 510 killed, 2,635 wounded, 251 missing. Buell had 54,000 troops, but less than half were engaged.

Rosecrans and Murfreesboro—Stones River

After the battle of Perryville, General Bragg consulted Generals Polk and Hardee on the army's next move and both advised withdrawing to a more favorable position. The army then marched to Harrodsburg, where it was joined by the forces of General Kirby Smith and took steps to counter Buell's pursuit. When this did not come Bragg ordered his army to Murfreesboro, Tennessee, sending General Forrest ahead to protect the advance.

Bragg's movement was virtually a retreat. The Confederates destroyed supplies they could not carry, but they managed to haul a heavy load of provisions and household goods of sympathizers, and thousands of head of livestock. The army followed the train of supplies, with General Joseph Wheeler's cavalry protecting the rear. Buell's horsemen tried to raid the long caravan from the flank and clashed twenty-six times with Wheeler before breaking off the pursuit.

Bragg first made his headquarters at Tullahoma and then moved to Murfreesboro. By order of the Confederate Secretary of War, James A. Seddon, Bragg's army was placed under command of Gen. Joseph E. Johnston, who had recuperated from wounds received at Seven Pines in May. Johnston also had authority over General J. C. Pemberton's army at Vicksburg, but, as it turned out, Pemberton did not always follow Johnston's directions. When President Davis came west in December to inspect the defenses of Vicksburg he ordered Johnston

to detach troops from Bragg's army and send them to
Pemberton under command of Major General C. L. Stevenson. General Johnston did not wish to remove nearly
one-fourth of Bragg's forces when Confederate troops in
Arkansas could be spared more easily, but Davis overruled him. To this weakening of Bragg's army Johnston
ascribed the subsequent disaster at Murfreesboro, or
Stones River, and this widened the breach between Johnston and Davis.

Buell's inactivity after Perryville led Washington to relieve him. William S. Rosecrans, lately made major general of volunteers, was given command of the Army of
the Cumberland on October 20, 1862.

General Buell was respected for his intelligence and
military acumen, but his unbending attitude made him
disliked by officers, while his rigid discipline alienated
the volunteers. He frequently stood up to his superiors
and thus had gained the animosity of Secretary Stanton
and General Halleck. Major General Lew Wallace, who
had himself tangled with Halleck, was surprised when
the Adjutant General of the United States Army conveyed an order from Halleck naming Wallace presiding
officer of a military commission that was to convene
November 20, 1862, at Cincinnati to investigate and
report on the operations of the army under Buell in
Kentucky and Tennessee. Other members of the commission were Generals E. O. C. Ord, Albin Schoepf, N. J.
T. Danna, Daniel Tyler, and Major Don Piatt. Piatt was
judge advocate, and incautiously intimated to Wallace
that Stanton and Halleck wanted to get rid of Buell,
although there was no charge against him. The commission heard Buell, who was rigidly correct, and the generals who had served with him, including McCook, Wood,
Thomas, Rousseau, and Granger. The commission noted
that the Confederates had gained advantages by some
omissions and delays attributable to Buell, but found
extenuating circumstances. The complaint that Buell had
failed to reach Chattanooga in time to check Bragg was
explained by the time needed to repair the Memphis &
Charleston Railroad; since this was done by order of General Halleck, the latter was obviously to blame. The inability of Buell to comprehend what was going on at

Perryville was established, and it was concluded that his delay in ordering support for McCook and his absence from the field had handicapped the Federals.

The report of the commission was duly made to Washington. General Wallace believed that General Halleck suppressed it, because it reflected on Halleck, but Wallace had preserved a copy and later published it.

After marking time at Nashville for weeks, General Rosecrans on December 26 ordered the army to march toward Murfreesboro. He had 56,671 troops, including 51,822 infantry and artillery and 4,849 cavalry; he considered the cavalry entirely inadequate. General McCook commanded the right wing, General Thomas the center, and General Crittenden the left wing.

The army was continually harassed by the Confederate cavalry under General Wheeler. On December 30 Wheeler attacked the wagon train of Colonel John C. Starkweather's brigade of the First Division, Thomas' corps, at Jefferson, and the Federals lost twenty wagons and had 122 casualties in repulsing him. More disastrous was a raid Wheeler made at noon the same day at La Vergne. Here Wheeler captured the supply train of McCook's corps, taking 700 prisoners and destroying an immense amount of supplies. The next day Colonel Moses B. Walker's brigade of Thomas' corps reached La Vergne and recaptured most of the men and animals. Wheeler managed to strike at another point, where he bagged 300 prisoners. These he paroled and sent back to Rosecrans, who could not order them to fight until they had been properly exchanged.

The first clash at Murfreesboro took place on December 30, 1862, and consisted chiefly of an artillery duel lasting several hours and one minor infantry fight. General Bragg decided to attack the next morning, and as a result General Hardee sent Cleburne and McCown against McCook, who held the Federal right. The two Confederate divisions hit those of R. W. Johnson and Davis with such force that they swept over artillery and infantry and in an hour half of Johnson's troops were casualties. General Thomas was holding the Federal center and with Rousseau's division and Shepherd's brigade tried to support McCook, but the fighting went against him. General Rosecrans had ordered the left wing, under Crittenden, to move against the strongly held position of Breckinridge. Crittenden sent Van Cleve's division across Stones River, and it was supposed to gain high ground for artillery and an assault on Breckinridge's position, but it had to cross a mile and a half of terrain and river at a time when McCook was in serious trouble. It was recalled to help build a new front on the turnpike. The most disastrous incident of the day was the rout of the Federal right wing, which was driven back several miles, but General Rosecrans was able to get the center and left to take a firm stand and to place his guns in such a good position that repeated assaults by four to six brigades of the Confederates availed nothing.

The next day, January 1, 1863, was quiet and misled Bragg into believing that Rosecrans was about to retreat. He felicitated President Davis on the auspicious opening of the new year. But on the morning of January 2 he saw that the Federal forces east of Stones River were entrenched and that Colonel Samuel Beatty, who had taken command of Van Cleve's division of Crittenden's corps when Van Cleve was wounded, was in a position to enfilade Polk's line. He thereupon ordered six brigades of Breckinridge's corps to drive the Federals off the summit and occupy it. What resulted was a complete reversal of previous fortune. It is best told in the words of General Crittenden's report:

Van Cleve's Division, under Colonel Beatty, had crossed the river on the 1st and Grose and Hazen had followed with their brigades on the 2nd. The fight opened on Colonel Beatty's line and lasted about twenty minutes. Before this battle I had been inclined to underrate the importance of artillery in our war, but I never knew that arm to render such important service as at this point. The sound judgment, bravery, and skill of Major John Mendenhall, who was my Chief of Artillery, enabled me to open fifty-eight guns almost simultaneously on Breckinridge's men and to turn a dashing charge into a sudden retreat and rout, in which the enemy lost 1,700 or 1,800 men in a few moments. I witnessed the effect of this cannonade upon the Confederate advance. Mendenhall's guns were about 100 yards back from the river. Van Cleve's Division of my command was retiring down the opposite slope, before overwhelming numbers of the enemy, when the guns, the fire of which had been held until our men should no longer be exposed to it, opened upon the swarming enemy. The very forest seemed to fall before our fire and not a Confederate reached the river. . . . The pursuit was made by Negley's men and Morton's Pioneer Corps, with portions of my command under Cruft, Hazen and Grose, and a part of General Jefferson C. Davis' command.

Confederate General Breckinridge testified to the extent of the Federal artillery: "It now appeared that the ground we had won was commanded by the enemy's batteries, within easy range, on better ground, upon the other side of the river. I do not know how many guns he had. He had enough to sweep the whole position from the front, the left, and the right, and to render it wholly untenable by our . . . artillery and infantry."

Those twenty minutes decided the battle. The Confederate army had 10,266 casualties out of about 40,000, with 1,294 killed, 7,945 wounded. The Federal losses in the whole campaign were 13,249 casualties, out of 43,400, with 1,730 killed and 7,802 wounded, the rest captured or missing. After the battle Bragg retreated to Tullahoma, thirty-six miles away, and Rosecrans entered Murfreesboro. A number of Confederate commanders, led by General Polk, expressed their dissatisfaction with Bragg's leadership, and at the request of President Davis, General Johnston was given authority to relieve Bragg from the command, but he did not exercise it at this time.

Chickamauga

After Gettysburg, General James Longstreet urged the Confederate Secretary of War Seddon to consider special efforts for strengthening the army of General Bragg in Tennessee, enabling it to defeat General Rosecrans and thus achieve gains in the West to offset the tightening situation in the East. Longstreet wanted to go there with detachments of the Army of Northern Virginia, but he had not mentioned the subject to his superior officer, General Lee, because Lee "was opposed to having important detachments of his army so far beyond his reach."

Longstreet, who had shown by his reports and inter-

views with Lee that he considered his military ideas better
than those of Lee, had another ambition; he proposed
to supersede Bragg and take the top command in the
West. To this President Jefferson Davis would not agree.
But the Richmond cabinet took up with Lee the subject
of reinforcing Bragg, and all agreed that General Longstreet and his First Corps should be detached from the
Army of Northern Virginia and sent West. This must
have been conceded by Lee with some reluctance, for
on August 31, 1863, he still had hopes of attacking and
defeating Meade. He then wrote to Longstreet asking
him to get the army ready for offensive operations and
said: "I can see nothing better to be done than to endeavor to bring General Meade out and use our efforts
to crush his army while in its present condition."

This was hardly in tune with Longstreet's views of the
desperate condition of the Confederacy. He did not see
any profit in offensive operations unless the Confederates
were strong enough to cross the Potomac, while "on this
side" Meade would probably go into one of his fortified
positions, which Lee could not afford to attack. There
was more to be accomplished in the West than by an advance in Virginia. Lee made no further objection, but insisted on vigorous action and energetic pursuit.

The transport of Longstreet's army from Orange Court
House, Louisa Court House, and other parts of Virginia
called for almost superhuman efforts under the direction
of the Quartermaster General, CSA, Brigadier General A. R. Lawton. The little one-track railroads had different gauges and defective locomotives and rolling stock.
Troops had to move via Richmond, North Carolina, and
South Carolina; they were delayed by welcoming parties
and breakdowns. At Richmond Major General John B.
Hood, not yet fully recovered from his Gettysburg wound,
resumed his command. Brigadier General E. P. Alexander led his six batteries to Petersburg, departed on flat
cars for Wilmington, N.C., was taken across the Cape
Fear River by ferry, and finding no cars available at Augusta, Ga., sent most of his guns west overland. They
failed to reach Bragg in time for the Battle of Chickamauga. Although Longstreet's troops jammed the Southern
railroads and proceeded with great clatter from September

9 on, Washington does not appear to have known what was up until three or four days later.

The battle of Chickamauga was fought September 19 and 20, 1863, in northwestern Georgia, just across the Tennessee border, by the Federal Army of the Cumberland under Major General William S. Rosecrans, and the Confederate Army of Tennessee, under Lieutenant General Braxton Bragg. It was one of the bloodiest battles of the war, fought chiefly in timber along the west bank of Chickamauga Creek, and so badly handled that it broke the commanding officers on both sides. It could be accounted a Confederate victory in that it dislodged the Federals and sent them back to Chattanooga, but every advantage was lost by the dilatory and indecisive attitude of Bragg.

After Bragg had taken his army into Chattanooga to make that his base in July, 1863, General Rosecrans placed the component parts of his army in such strategical positions that Bragg became alarmed for his safety. Thomas, with the Fourteenth Corps, had crossed the Chattanooga River and occupied Wills' Valley, between the Sand and Lookout mountains, the latter screening his troops from Bragg's observation. Major General Alexander D. McCook, with the Twentieth Corps, on September 7 crossed Lookout and occupied Alpine, while Thomas moved over Lookout on September 9 toward McLemore's Cove, a valley between Lookout and Pigeon mountains. Major General Thomas L. Crittenden, with the Twenty-first Corps, was stationed in Wills' Valley. The Reserve Corps was under Major General Gordon Granger and the cavalry under Brigadier General Robert B. Mitchell. The total strength of the Federal army was nearly 57,000.

General Bragg considered his position in Chattanooga dangerous and on September 8 moved out. General Crittenden sent Brigadier General Thomas J. Wood's First Division to occupy the town. Bragg headed for La Fayette, twenty-two miles south of Chattanooga, east of Pigeon Mountain, and placed Major General F. B. Cleburne's division of D. H. Hill's corps on guard at three gaps in the mountain. Nothing of this was known to Rosecrans, who thought Bragg was in full retreat into the heart of Georgia. Yet within the next ten days Bragg was getting reinforcements in response to his appeals to President Davis. Major General Simon B. Buckner's corps of 8,000 had been withdrawn from Knoxville. General Johnston's army had sent the divisions of Major General John C. Breckinridge and Major General W. H. T. Walker, 9,000 men, and later two brigades commanded by Brigadier Generals John Gregg and Evander McNair, of 2,559 men. The units of Longstreet's corps were now arriving and would add 11,716 effectives. The total number of men available to Bragg at this time has been estimated from official returns at 71,551.

Chickamauga Creek flowed north to the Tennessee and was hardly waist deep. Parallel with it to the west ran La Fayette Road. West of the road were Lookout Mountain, Snodgrass Hill, and Horseshoe Ridge. Also west of La Fayette Road was Dry Valley Road, which ran north and at McFarland's Gap in Missionary Ridge hit the road that ran east to Reed's Bridge on the creek. The other roads continued north to Rossville.

On September 9 Thomas ordered Major General James S. Negley's division through Stevens Gap to McLemore's Cove. Negley, with his staff and several brigade officers, rode ahead without adequate precautions. At Dug Gap in Pigeon Mountain they were suddenly fired on by Confederate pickets. When Negley saw that he was facing a large force he called for help. Thomas ordered Absolom Baird's division to the Cove, but Baird did not get there until September 11. Negley was saved when Bragg was unable to get his commanders to attack on September 10. Lieutenant General D. H. Hill considered an attack impracticable, and Major General T. C. Hindman wanted to wait on Hill. Thomas, now aware that Bragg was present in force, recalled Negley. As the latter withdrew through Stevens Gap Bragg sent Cleburne in pursuit, but Negley escaped unscathed.

Bragg then ordered General Leonidas Polk, commander of his right wing, to take Major General W. H. T. Walker's reserve corps and catch one of Crittenden's divisions at Lee and Gordon's Mills, on September 13, but Polk found that the division had crossed Chickamauga Creek, and demanded more men.

Immediately thereafter General Rosecrans, observing the massing of Bragg's troops, brought his own commands closer together. He put all of Crittenden's corps at Lee and Gordon's Mills, and ordered up General McCook's Twentieth Corps to join Thomas and Thomas to move to the left beyond Crittenden. During the night of September 18-19 Thomas marched from Crawfish Springs north past Crittenden's position. General Granger with the Reserve Corps was ordered to remain in Chattanooga.

On the morning of September 19 General Thomas sent Brigadier General Brannan orders to reconnoiter the Confederates on the Chickamauga, and a brigade under Colonel John T. Croxton came upon dismounted troopers of Brigadier General Nathan B. Forrest's cavalry corps near Reed's Bridge. The Confederate cavalry fell back on infantry, and a general engagement developed along the west bank. Units from Brannan's division were supported by Baird's division of Thomas' corps, but the two were harshly handled by Brigadier General St. John Liddell's division of Walker's Confederate reserve corps, and sent back in disorder. The timely arrival of the division of Brigadier General Richard W. Johnson, which had made a hurried march of over five miles from Crawfish Springs checked Liddell, but encountered stubborn opposition from Cheatham's division of 7,000, which in turn had to meet the advancing divisions of Major Generals John M. Palmer and Joseph J. Reynolds.

The fighting at Chickamauga on September 20 turned largely to the advantage of the Confederates because of the experienced tactics of Longstreet and the blunders of Rosecrans. Longstreet reached Bragg's headquarters on the night of September 19, and was given command of the left wing. Several of General J. B. Hood's brigades already had entered the battle lines on the 19th, and the brigades of Generals Kershaw and Humphreys of McLaws' division also were ready to fight.

At a midnight conference Rosecrans and his corps commanders agreed that Thomas should hold a line running from Missionary Ridge to Reed's Bridge Road. To this line were added Johnson's division of McCook's corps and Palmer's of Crittenden's, so that Thomas had eleven brigades in his front line and three in reserve. Granger's Reserve Corps was to take post on the east slope of Missionary Ridge, ready to support McCook or Thomas. At 6 A.M. Thomas became disturbed because the Confederates were moving on his left less than a mile away and asked Rosecrans to send back Negley's division, to augment his left toward Reed's Bridge. Rosecrans ordered Negley to comply and one brigade, Beatty's, reached Thomas in time; two others were delayed.

Polk, commanding Bragg's right wing, was to attack at dawn, September 20, but did not move until nearly 9 A.M. This delayed Longstreet, who had Bragg's left wing. Polk hit Baird's division at Thomas' left and the fighting soon extended to the divisions of Johnson, Palmer, and Reynolds. Baird was in trouble, and Thomas sent urgent messages to Rosecrans for reinforcements. Rosecrans complied, hustling off the rest of Negley's brigades and two brigades of Sheridan's division, those of Laiboldt and Bradley. But although the Federal line was repulsing Polk, Rosecrans, miles away, worried over extricating his army intact. By his orders General James A. Garfield, his Chief of Staff, instructed McCook to get ready to move from the right to Thomas' left, for the left must be held at all hazards, "even if the right is withdrawn wholly to the present left." Rosecrans suggested that Thomas move his reserves north and keep Crittenden and McCook on his right. Thomas replied: "The enemy are pushing me so hard that I cannot make any changes. The troops are posted behind temporary breastworks."

At this point the whole Union army was placed in jeopardy because Rosecrans gave an irresponsible order based on unverified information. A courier from Thomas, arriving with a request for aid, remarked that in passing the rear of the divisions he thought Brannan's out of line and Reynolds' flank exposed. Soon a second courier arrived and said there was a "chasm" between Reynolds and Wood. Immediately Rosecrans turned to an aide and dictated an order to Wood, telling him to "close up on Reynolds as fast as possible and support him."

Wood knew he would have to withdraw from in front of the enemy, but the order was explicit. McCook agreed. Wood pulled back his brigades and marched them around

Brannan to reach Reynolds. On the way he met General Thomas, who said not Reynolds but Baird needed support and diverted Wood to Baird. The damage was done. A wide hole had been opened to the Confederates.

Polk's failure to break the Union line had delayed Longstreet, who was to cooperate with Polk. Longstreet now ordered his left wing, commanded by Hood, to strike Thomas' right at the point where Wood adjoined Brannan. But Wood had moved out and when Bushrod Johnson's division, with the brigades of Gregg and Mc-Nair in the lead, jumped off at Brotherton's Farm, they rushed into a gap. Johnson's men, with brigades from Major General Hindman's division of Polk's Corps close behind, in all had over 20,000 men and 42 guns. They fell on two of Davis' brigades of McCook's Corps and on one of Sheridan's divisions, sliced several regiments off the rear columns of Wood and Van Cleve, and took Brannan in the flank. Their impetus carried them up to the Dry Valley Road, where Sheridan was trying to rush two brigades to Thomas. The Federal left was thrown into confusion. Brigades broke up and men started north to Rossville without waiting for orders. Mc-Cook and Crittenden were swept along; Rosecrans went to Chattanooga at the urging of Garfield, to prepare a new defense.

There Rosecrans paced the floor, giving way almost to hysteria. But on the field Major General George H. Thomas kept control of the situation. Grimly determined, he calmly ordered the consolidation of his divisions, built up his defense, saved the United States army from utter rout. A new name came into popular use when General Garfield remarked to Rosecrans: "Thomas is standing like a rock." From then on he was the Rock of Chickamauga.

Longstreet attempted to attack Thomas' rear, but found the route blocked. Brannan and part of Woods' command formed a new line at right angles with Thomas' position on Horseshoe Ridge. The Federals held the right until Longstreet brought up his reserve division, when the Federal line moved back 200 yards to Snodgrass Hill.

Here Thomas developed a strong defense against Longstreet's onslaughts, taking a heavy toll. Just when he seemed about to be pried loose from his position two brigades of General Gordon Granger's Reserve under Brigadier General James B. Steedman arrived and thrust back the column trying to envelop Brannan's right. Bragg's right wing had been too badly used to enable him to send reinforcements to Longstreet, who made one last desperate effort at dusk to push Steedman back. Near 4 P.M. Rosecrans ordered Thomas to take full command and bring the army back to a new position at Rossville. Thomas L. Livermore in *General Thomas in the Record* (Massachusetts Historical Soc., 1892) wrote:

Late in the afternoon of the second day, when ordered to retire to Rossville, he carried out the hazardous undertaking by a display of audacity. Having given orders how each division was to be withdrawn, he placed himself at the head of one of them, and by a terrific charge in column, broke through the opposing line, and then, sweeping around its rear, gathered in guns and hundreds of prisoners. Under cover of this attack the rest of the army was withdrawn to safety.

Bragg did not pursue. Thomas reorganized the troops at Rossville during the 21st, and withdrew that night to Chattanooga.

The blow to the Union army was severe, for with 58,000 troops available Rosecrans had 16,170 casualties—1,657 killed, 9,756 wounded, 4,757 captured or missing. The Confederates, with 66,000 troops, had 18,454 casualties; 2,312 killed, 14,674 wounded, 1,468 missing. One of the Confederate dead was Brigadier General Benjamin H. Helm, brother-in-law of Abraham Lincoln. Secretary of War Stanton, when he heard of the defeat, said bitterly: "I know the reason well enough. Rosecrans ran away from his fighting men and did not stop for thirteen miles."

Chattanooga and Missionary Ridge

The defeat of Rosecrans at Chickamauga and his retreat to Chattanooga awoke the Washington authorities to the imminent danger of losing Tennessee. On the night of September 23, 1863, Secretary Stanton hurriedly called a meeting of the war council to consider reinforcing Rosecrans. He had to get President Lincoln out of bed for the meeting. Secretaries Stanton, Seward, and Chase, General Halleck, and the superintendent of military transportation, General D. C. McCallum, were among those attending. The council decided to detach from the Army of the Potomac General O. O. Howard's Eleventh Corps, and the Second Division of Major General Henry W. Slocum's Twelfth Corps, under Brigadier General John W. Geary, and rush them to Chattanooga under the command of Major General Hooker. Originally, the entire corps was to have gone, but Slocum refused.

It took only a day to get the troops started at Manassas Junction, Bealeton, and Alexandria, and on September 25 they were on their way, but they had 1,157 miles to travel over seven connecting railroad lines, some with different gauges, which meant transferring from one set of trains to another. The troops started on the Baltimore & Ohio, then proceeded west to Indianapolis, thence south to Louisville, Nashville, and Bridgeport, Alabama. While some of the units arrived at their destination by September 30, others did not get there until October 15. The army had expected to carry its own complement of well-trained horses and mules, but this was ruled out and Hooker was supplied with animals at Nashville, many of them undernourished and too weak for heavy duty.

The Administration in Washington was now convinced that the man to overcome the crisis in Tennessee was the victor of Vicksburg, General Grant. He was ordered to Cairo and thence to Louisville, but stopped en route at Indianapolis, where he found Secretary of War Stanton, who accompanied him to Louisville. On October 15, 1863, Stanton gave Grant command of the new Military Division of the Mississippi, which would include the Departments of the Ohio, the Cumberland, and the Tennessee, and all the territory from the Mississippi to the Alleghenies north of Banks's southwestern area. Stanton gave Grant the choice of leaving department commanders where they were or relieving Rosecrans and putting General George H. Thomas in his place.

Grant chose to appoint Thomas and ordered him to hold Chattanooga at all hazards. Thomas replied: "We will hold the town till we starve." This was not an extravagant statement. The troops already were on half rations of hard bread, and meat came from such emaciated cattle that the soldiers called it "beef dried on the hoof." There was so little forage that nearly 10,000 horses had died during the campaign in eastern Tennessee. The meager supplies for the army came from Nashville over a railroad that was continually being torn up by Confederate raiders; they reached Bridgeport on the Tennessee River, twenty-six miles from Chattanooga, where they were unloaded and taken in wagons over a hilly route sixty miles long.

Grant met Rosecrans at Stevenson, Alabama, October 21, and when he heard the plans Rosecrans had made he thought them excellent and wondered why the general had not been able to put them into effect. He entered Chattanooga on October 23. Messages from General Halleck urging haste in reinforcements and supplies already had reached Grant and Sherman at Vicksburg, and Sherman was on his way with four divisions, going by boat to Memphis and thence eastward on the Memphis & Charleston Railroad, repairing it as he moved along. Fortunately the Union army had available an expert in railroad operation—General G. M. Dodge, who was to become widely known after the war for opening the first transcontinental railroad. Grant had Dodge assigned to rebuilding the Nashville & Chattanooga, a gigantic task. It called for the detachment of 8,000 men, who had to live on the country. Sawmills and blacksmith shops of the region had to be used; bridges had to be rebuilt and rails laid, and even coaches and freight cars had to be reconstructed. Dodge was equal to the job; in forty days he had built 182 bridges and replaced 102 miles of track from Decatur to Nashville. Grant ordered General McPherson at Vicksburg to send eight out of ten of his locomotives and all but ten of his cars. By November 15 Sherman reached Bridgeport, Alabama, with four divisions.

Confederate General Bragg made good use of his natural advantages after Rosecrans withdrew into Chattanooga, a town of 2,500 people located on the south bank of the Tennessee. Four railroad lines met there.

Through a valley five miles wide ran Chattanooga Creek. At the east Missionary Ridge was 500 to 800 feet high; at the west Lookout Mountain rose 2,300 feet. Separated from Lookout by a creek was Raccoon Mountain. Bragg held the three heights and his entrenchments crossed the valley. There were pickets at the foot of the mountains and on the roads, and rifle pits halfway up Missionary Ridge. When President Jefferson Davis surveyed the terrain, Bragg told him the destruction of the Federal army was only a matter of time. When Sherman saw the extent of the Confederate lines he said: "General Grant, you are besieged," and Grant replied: "It is too true."

General Rosecrans had made Brigadier William Farrar Smith chief engineer of the Army of the Cumberland and had planned to use river craft to open a supply line to Bridgeport. Grant was impressed with Smith's ability and extended his command. Several crude stern-wheelers were being built with scows, and enough planks had been cut for two bridges and many pontoon units. Another steamboat was being built at Stevenson.

Grant did not lose any time to get the supply line operating. Brown's Ferry crossed the Tennessee west of Chattanooga and was in Confederate hands. Grant ordered General W. F. Smith to take 4,000 men from Chattanooga, put 1,800 in pontoon boats, float them to Brown's Ferry, and capture the pickets, then march the rest of the men down with materials for a bridge. By daylight October 28 the height above the ferry was seized, and by 10 A.M. a pontoon bridge was laid. General Hooker marched up from Bridgeport and reached Lookout Valley at Wauhatchee in the afternoon. General O. O. Howard moved to Brown's Ferry, and General John W. Geary was three miles below the Ferry. On the night of October 28 Longstreet attacked Geary's division and fighting went on in the dark until about 4 A.M., when Geary's mules stampeded toward the enemy's lines; the troops mistook them in the dark for cavalry and deserted their positions, and the fighting ceased. The Union troops had 77 killed; the Confederates about 300.

The supply line was now properly protected and began service. The steamboat could carry 40,000 rations and 39,000 pounds of forage with the help of scows. Moving

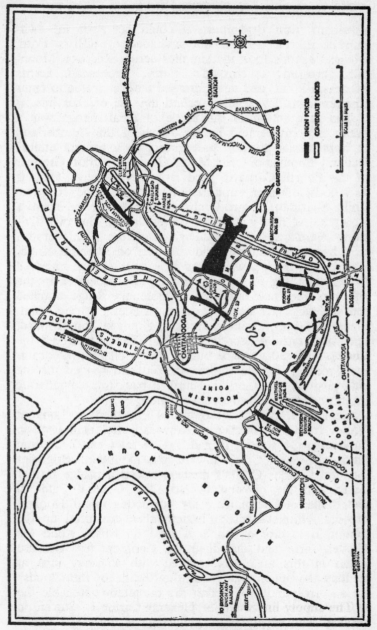

The Battle of Chattanooga
November 23-25, 1863

upstream from Bridgeport, it could not fight the swift current in one section but unloaded at Kelly's Ford, whence wagons took the supplies across Raccoon Mountain, crossed at Brown's Ferry, proceeded across Moccasin Point, and again crossed the Tennessee to enter Chattanooga. The soldiers called this the cracker line.

The first action in the battle of Chattanooga was a preliminary movement by the Army of the Cumberland to improve its position preparatory to a general attack. General Thomas ordered Major General Gordon Granger of the Fourth Corps to send Brigadier General Thomas J. Wood's division, supported by that of Major General Philip Sheridan, toward Orchard Knob to test the enemy's strength. At 12:30 P.M. on November 23 the two divisions marched out in full view of the Confederates, who had their batteries and rifle pits on Orchard Knob. The Union troops, with flags in proper order, appeared to be marching in review, and the Confederates in the rifle pits and their officers on Missionary Ridge watched the spectacle. At Fort Wood, the Federal strong point, Generals Grant, Thomas, Hooker, Granger, and Howard, and the Assistant Secretary of War, Dana, observed the troops. At 1:30 P.M. the bugles blew a charge; the drummers took it up; the troops wheeled and headed for the rifle pits, overran them and pushed back the Confederate infantry, and took over Orchard Knob.

General Hooker, whose troops extended in Lookout Valley from Wauhatchee to Brown's Ferry, at 8 A.M. on November 24 started Brigadier General Geary's division across Lookout Creek toward the mountain. Brigadier General Charles Crufts's division seized a bridge farther north and the division of Brigadier General Peter J. Osterhaus, of Sherman's army but acting under Hooker, crossed. Hooker's three divisions then advanced up the mountain toward a bench of land on which stood the Craven farm and dislodged the Confederates. Because much of this area was covered with a heavy mist at midday the action was called the "Battle of the Clouds" by a correspondent. Finding the mountain untenable the Confederates, under Major General Carter L. Stevenson of Hardee's corps, withdrew during the night and joined Bragg's army on Missionary Ridge. They burned the bridge over Chattanooga Creek and thus obstructed the passage of Hooker, who was to march to Rossville the next morning.

General Sherman's divisions had completed a tough march of 350 miles from Memphis to comply with Grant's orders to get to Chattanooga in a hurry. On November 23, after mishaps with roads and bridges, they were finally stationed behind the hills opposite the mouth of the Chickamauga. Sherman ordered a brigade of the Second Division of his Fifteenth Corps under Brigadier General Giles A. Smith to North Chickamauga Creek to man boats for a pontoon bridge, drop at midnight to a point above the mouth of the South Chickamauga, and land two regiments. After capturing most of the pickets Smith landed the rest below the South Chickamauga.

Next other brigades of Brigadier General Morgan L. Smith's Second Division were rowed down, followed by those of Brigadier General John E. Smith's Second Division of the Fourteenth Corps. By November 24 there were 8,000 men behind the freshly built trenches on the east bank of the Tennessee. Another Smith—this time the engineer William F.—directed placing a pontoon bridge over the Tennessee and a second one over Chickamauga Creek, and the rest of Sherman's command was able to move over 1,300 feet of pontoons that carried horses and artillery as well as infantry. At 1 P.M. the first three Smiths and the division of Brigadier General Jefferson C. Davis, now belonging to the Fourteenth Corps of the Army of the Cumberland, and Brigadier General Hugh Ewing's division of the Fifteenth Corps of Sherman's army, formed columns and with skirmishers going ahead marched to the base of a hill that belonged to the Missionary Ridge sector. They went up a hill and pulled up some guns, and found that they had reached two high points that were lower than Missionary Ridge itself. The main ridge was across a depression and had a wagon road and a railroad tunnel, which the Confederates were occupying. Sherman ordered the hill to be fortified and extended his line across the hill into the plain. In a minor action on his left flank General Giles A. Smith was wounded.

The storming of Missionary Ridge on the afternoon of November 25 was a remarkable feat, accomplished by the troops of the Army of the Cumberland, without specific orders to go the whole route. These troops were located on Orchard Knob and belonged to the divisions of Generals Wood and Sheridan of the Fourth Corps and Generals Baird and Johnson of the Fourteenth Corps. Practically all were Illinois, Indiana, and Ohio regiments. General Sherman had not been able to turn Bragg's right, and there was a lull in the fighting when General Grant determined to get a foothold on the lower part of Missionary Ridge, where Confederate rifle pits still provided an obstacle against a Federal advance. He ordered General Thomas to send the four divisions to take the rifle pits, starting when six signal guns were fired.

At 3:40 P.M. the guns were fired and 24,536 troops rushed forward. The assault was so powerful that the front lines of the Confederates were thrown back in a panic, although their batteries immediately opened up on the Federals. The Confederates deserted the rifle pits and climbed up the ridge, and the Union troops climbed after them. General Grant saw that his orders were being exceeded and the troops might be exposed to a costly repulse. He demanded to know who had given the order for the troops to climb the ridge, but Generals Thomas and Granger replied that they had not done so. "They started without orders," said Granger; "when those fellows get started all hell can't stop them."

At the front both Generals Wood and Sheridan denied having given the orders, but they were confident the men could get to the top, and Granger sent word that if they could take it, to push ahead. Climbing Missionary Ridge was back-breaking; the troops clambered over rocks and up ravines, and fought in groups out of formation, but they kept going up, and their approach was so menacing to General Bragg that he began to call for reinforcements, drawing Cheatham's division from the front where Sherman with nearly 25,000 men had fought well but made little progress. Eventually the Union troops were so far up that the Confederate gunners could not depress their pieces sufficiently to hit them; then the gunners lighted the fuses of shells and rolled them over the crest of the ridge. Despite the advantages of the position, the Confederates could not push back the oncoming Federals; Sheridan's men went over the edge, then Wood's, and then came the task of clearing the summit of the Confederates. They made use of the Confederate artillery with considerable success, and the attempts of Generals Bragg, Hardee, Cleburne, and Bate to rally their men proved useless. The Confederate break could not be repaired. General Bragg said: "A panic which I had never before witnessed seized upon officers and men, and each seemed to be struggling for his personal safety, regardless of his duty or his character." Bragg was unable to explain to himself the reason for the break at his left; this was "shameful conduct," for the position should have been held by a line of skirmishers against any assaulting column. He also deplored the "bad conduct of veteran troops," and he surmised the show of strength of the "immense forces" arrayed against the Confederates may have intimidated them. The Confederates were ordered to fall back to Chickamauga.

The ridge having been taken, General Grant did not attempt to criticize anyone, and the other commanders were openly exultant, Granger remarking jokingly to the troops: "You have disobeyed orders, all of you, and you know you ought to be court-martialed!" General Sheridan followed the retreating Confederates, dislodged them from a second hill, and pressed them so hard that they burned a pontoon bridge at Chickamauga Crossing before all their troops were across. The divisions of Sheridan and Wood captured 3,800 prisoners and 31 guns, and had 2,337 casualties.

Longstreet and Burnside at Knoxville

General Grant learned that on November 4 General Longstreet had left the Chattanooga front to operate against Burnside and Knoxville. Apprehensive over Burnside's situation and urged by Washington to relieve it, Grant ordered General Thomas to attack the Confederate right, in order to force Longstreet's return. But Thomas insisted that he was in such straits that he did not have enough horses to move a gun. Grant could merely acquiesce and hope for the prompt arrival of Sherman. But Sherman was delayed by high water in the Elk River and had to detour thirty miles in order to cross. Though baffled, Grant continued to make plans for an early attack on the Confederate position before Chattanooga.

What had happened was that Bragg, grown over-confident after his victory at Chickamauga, decided to order Longstreet to attack Burnside and take Knoxville. He called Longstreet, Hardee, and Breckinridge to him and announced the order in arbitrary fashion. Long-street, who was already irked because Bragg had not followed up the results of Chickamauga, pointed out that detaching some 20,000 troops from the Confederate army, which was strung out over six miles, invited a mass attack by Grant, and suggested that the Knoxville expedition could succeed only if the Confederate army were concentrated behind the Chickamauga River and Longstreet made a swift march against Burnside, coming back to Bragg before Sherman's reinforcements reached Grant. But Bragg did not listen to him. He estimated Burnside's force south of Knoxville at 15,000; Long-street thought there were 8,000 more Federals north of Knoxville and at Cumberland Gap, and close to 100 guns.

Actually Longstreet would have about 20,000 troops. He had the divisions of McLaws and Hood, the latter commanded by Brigadier General Micah Jenkins; two battalions of artillery under Colonel E. P. Alexander, who had served Longstreet so efficiently at Gettysburg, one under Major A. Leyden and the other under Major Frank Huger; and four brigades of cavalry under Major General Joseph Wheeler. Colonel Alexander's artillery was withdrawn from Lookout Mountain and his and McLaws' commands were expected to entrain at Tyner's Station on November 4, but the lack of sufficient railroad transport caused delays of over a week. Longstreet was reinforced November 22 by two brigades of General Buckner's division, which took no part in the offensive.

General Burnside, with part of Brigadier General Malon D. Manson's Twenty-third Corps, first occupied Knoxville on September 2, 1863. On September 9 Confederate General John W. Fraser surrendered his force at Cumberland Gap. Burnside moved out of Knoxville, but when small units of the Confederate army began testing his resistance at different points, he abandoned the Tennessee valley south of Loudon in order to concentrate on the northern bank. General Wheeler's cavalry tried to cut off the cavalry division of Brigadier General William P. Sanders, but Sanders beat them off and they recrossed the river.

Fortifications had been begun by the Confederates at Knoxville, and General Burnside now decided to take advantage of them and place his army under their protection. He had thirty miles to go, with supply trains, and as he began to withdraw General Longstreet started his troops in two columns to intercept Burnside. This resulted in two actions, one at Lenoir on November 14 and another at Campbell's Station on November 17. The division of Major General Lafayette McLaws was successfully opposed by the Federals of Colonel John F. Hartranft's Second Division of the Ninth Corps. Longstreet attempted to turn the Federal left flank by using three brigades under General Micah Jenkins, but neither this nor subsequent efforts availed to stop Burnside from reaching the protection of Knoxville on November 17. Here the Federals worked hard to complete several forts and throw up a continuous line of earthworks with rifle pits and parapets for infantry.

The Confederates carefully planned attacks on Burnside's fortified positions, of which the strongest was Fort Sanders. Knoxville is on the north bank of the Holston River, and Fort Sanders was at the western end of the town, covering the Kingston road. It had been begun by the Confederates as Fort Loudon and consisted of an earthen bastion, 125 yards wide on the north and 95 yards on the west, protected by a 12-foot ditch. Burnside's engineer officer, Major Orlando M. Poe, had made the works especially hard to scale and placed impedimenta in front of the ditch. The Federals also had a long line of wire entanglements some distance ahead of their entrenchments.

General Bragg had become concerned for his army during Longstreet's absence and now sent his chief engineer, General Leadbetter, to urge an early attack on Knoxville. Longstreet had been promised reinforcements from Chattanooga and Virginia and was awaiting them, but Leadbetter was obdurate. An assault on Fort Sanders, planned for November 28, was postponed because of murky weather and carried out on November 29, when brigades of Generals Bushrod R. Johnson and Gracie added 2,625 troops to Longstreet's army. The lead in the attack at dawn was taken by General McLaws. The Confederates relied on sharpshooters in the rear to pick off any Federals showing their heads above the parapet and ordered the infantry to advance with fixed bayonets, without firing guns or shouting. The Confederates encountered great opposition from Federal artillery, but some of the color bearers managed to plant their flags on the parapet, only to be shot or captured. McLaws sent back word to Longstreet that the fort was protected by wire network, and no ax to cut it could be found. Longstreet thereupon ordered the attack reversed, and the brigades withdrew. Later he decided the wire could have been overcome and blamed himself for his order.

This order proved a calamity for the Confederates, for within half an hour Longstreet, still on the field, received a telegram from President Davis telling him that Bragg had been forced back and ordering him to cooperate. A second message from General Wheeler, who was with Bragg, asked Longstreet to join the army at Ringgold "if practicable." The qualifying words gave Longstreet the excuse for following his own judgment, and when later messages told him that Bragg had retreated as far as Dalton, Longstreet felt that the lack of rails and bridges for 100 miles between them justified him in following his own course. He determined to remain at Knoxville, but an intercepted letter from Grant to Burnside, advising the latter that three columns were marching to his relief, one of them headed by General Sherman, and other difficulties, caused Longstreet to break off the siege on December 4. He had lost 198 killed, 850 wounded, 248 captured or missing, whereas Burnside had lost 92 killed, 394 wounded, 207 captured or missing.

Some minor clashes occurred as Longstreet retreated, Major General John G. Parke attacking the rear with cavalry, and one skirmish of some size took place at Bean's Station on December 14. But Longstreet was now looking for good food and forage and did not want to start a major engagement.

General Grant believed that Longstreet had Knoxville so thoroughly invested that he would starve Burnside out unless help arrived, so he dispatched Major General Gordon Granger with the Fourth Corps to rescue Burnside. Granger moved with such "reluctance" that Grant lost patience with him and directed General Sherman to pick from 3,500 to 5,000 men from the garrison at Kingston and troops moving up the Tennessee, and relieve Burnside. Sherman did not even need to stop for supplies, which would follow him by steamboat. Sherman, as usual, could be depended on to execute an order with speed; taking Granger with him, he entered Knoxville on December 6. Here he had two surprises. Longstreet had raised the siege and started for Virginia, and Burnside not only had a fine lot of cattle but was able to serve Sherman a dinner of roast turkey with trimmings that did not look like starvation rations. Burnside explained that he had been able to keep open a route to the Union sympathizers in the French Broad River country, from whom he obtained provisions. Sherman then returned to Chattanooga with his troops.

General Grant credited the Confederate command with assisting the Federal success by making serious blunders. He cited Bragg's "grave mistakes": first, sending Longstreet, "his ablest corps commander," with 20,000 troops to Knoxville; second, sending Buckner's division after him on the eve of battle; third, placing so many of his troops on the plain in front of his "impregnable position." Grant was inclined to blame Jefferson Davis for Longstreet's journey to Knoxville. Grant said his victory was won under the most trying circumstances of the war.

The estimated effective strength of the Union army at the battle of Chattanooga was 60,000 men. (Livermore made it 57,871.) Losses were 752 killed, 4,713 wounded, 350 captured or missing. The army captured 40 pieces of artillery, 7,000 stand of small arms, and many vehicles. The Confederates had 361 killed, 2,180 wounded, and reported 4,146 captured or missing, but as Grant sent 6,100 prisoners north and there were many stragglers and deserters, the true Confederate loss must have been much larger.

The Confederate command changed after Chattanooga. Longstreet went back to Virginia without fanfare. Bragg was relieved December 2. General Polk was in command until December 27, when General Joseph E. Johnston succeeded. After February 24, 1864, Bragg was in Richmond, and "under the direction of the President was charged with the conduct of military operations in the armies of the Confederacy."

27

THE GREAT LOCOMOTIVE CHASE

One of the most daring and certainly the most spectacular of raids undertaken by a group of soldiers in hostile territory was that which has become known in Civil War history as the great locomotive chase. This was the exploit by which James J. Andrews, a Union spy employed by Headquarters of the Army of the Ohio, in April, 1862, led twenty men into Georgia to burn railroad bridges. The adventure has fired the imagination of young and old alike, and while it has been described in great detail from the Union point of view, it is no less dramatic when viewed from the side of the Confederate pursuers.

The present account rests principally on the memoir that one of the participants, William Pittenger, of the Second Ohio Infantry Regiment, wrote for *Battles and Leaders of the Civil War,* and the comment of Major General Don Carlos Buell.

Andrews was a tall, bearded man of great self-assurance, well fitted by his cool nerve to operate in hostile country. His pose was that of a peddler who sneaked quinine into Confederate lines, a drug needed to combat malaria and other fevers. He had done some work for General Buell, but that exacting officer had no high opinion of Andrews' services. After Buell left Nashville for Savannah in the campaign that led to Shiloh, Brigadier General Ormsby M. Mitchel had the task of holding the Union line in Middle Tennessee and establishing communications along the Memphis & Charleston Railroad. Mitchel decided to occupy Huntsville and possibly advance toward Chattanooga, and for this purpose the interruption of Confederate rail traffic to Chattanooga from Georgia would be useful. This is exactly what Andrews proposed to do, and General Mitchel authorized him to carry out his plan.

Andrews proposed to take twenty-four picked soldiers, put them in civilian clothes, and direct them to make their way in parties of three or four to Marietta, Georgia, where Andrews would take charge. The men were chosen for secret and dangerous duty from three Ohio regiments belonging to the brigade of General J. W. Sill. They changed to civilian clothes, and their only arms were revolvers. Five of the men failed to reach the appointed place, but nineteen met Andrews early on the morning of April 12, 1862, at the hotel in Marietta, having traveled on the Georgia State Railway out of Chattanooga.

The leader had been in Atlanta and over the railroad a few weeks before and his study of timetables and stations had convinced him that he could seize a locomotive and cars at Big Shanty, Georgia, now called Kennesaw, run them in the direction of Chattanooga, and have his men set bridges on fire as they proceeded. On the way down, however, the men had encountered numerous soldiers on the trains and had observed that Big Shanty was now a sizable Confederate camp. To attempt a seizure in the midst of armed men seemed practically impossible to some of the party, but Andrews refused to halt. He asserted that he meant to carry through his scheme or die, and invited any man who wished to withdraw to do so. No one drew back, however, and the big adventure was on.

The men took a train from Marietta to Big Shanty, a distance of eight miles. Big Shanty was a breakfast stop, and as the passengers went inside the station to eat, the engineer and fireman joined them, leaving the train unattended. Andrews' party included two engineers and a fireman; they uncoupled the locomotive, tender, and three baggage and box cars from the rest of the train and jumped aboard the engine, which was named *General;* the rest of the men boosted and pulled each other into a freight car and slammed shut the door. An engineer threw the throttle and the train started. Before guards and spectators could determine what was going on, the train was going at top speed down the track and around the hills.

But the Southern train crew, rushing out of the station, knew that persons unknown had stolen their train. One of them was the conductor, William A. Fuller, whose tenacity and resourcefulness were to give him a brilliant place in Confederate history. With no other locomotive and no telegraph available Fuller and one other man, Anthony Murphy, foreman of the railroad machine shops in Atlanta, started out after the captured train on foot. This would have seemed foolhardy but for the fact that Fuller knew the line ahead was packed with trains coming South and that the fugitive train could not go far without meeting them. Fuller and Murphy found a handcar and started speeding down the track until they hit a break in the rails that Andrews had made and were thrown off the track. They righted the handcar and proceeded to the next station, Etowah.

Andrews had planned his expedition for April 11, to coincide with General Mitchel's attack on Huntsville, but a series of heavy rains had impeded the army's progress and Andrews had postponed his raid to the next day, April 12. He was running the captured train on its original time schedule, which indicated that he would meet two trains at designated points, and one local freight. He stopped the train at intervals to have his men tear up track, cut telegraph wires, take on water, and load on railroad ties for burning. Andrews was a man of extraordinary coolness; at stops he explained his hurry by saying he was rushing a powder train through to Beauregard. Everything worked smoothly at the start, but at Etowah, Andrews in his haste omitted an important precaution. An old locomotive, the *Yonah,* owned by an iron company, was standing at the station with steam up. It could have been put out of commission, but Andrews did not want to arouse the place; nor did he wish to lose time. He hurried on to Kingston.

Here a train occupied a siding, in order to give right of way to an approaching local freight. Andrews also took the siding. When the freight arrived it carried a red flag, which indicated another train was to follow. According to Pittenger, Andrews stepped up to the conductor and demanded: "What does it mean when the road is blocked in this manner, when I have orders to take this powder to Beauregard without a minute's delay?" The reply was: "Mitchel has captured Huntsville and is said to be coming to Chattanooga and we are getting everything out of there."

There was nothing for Andrews to do but wait until the road was clear. When the extra arrived it too bore a red flag, indicating that another train was following. Andrews could only mark time for another hour. He was the only man in contact with the crews of the other trains; the two engineers and firemen were in the cab; the rest were cooped up in the boxcar, listening to outside voices but unable to determine the reason for the long wait. Eventually the third train reached Kingston and passed; Andrews' train then had the right of way and proceeded at full speed.

Four miles out of Kingston Andrews had stopped to cut telegraph wires and tear up a rail, when his men suddenly heard the whistle of a locomotive in the distance behind them. There was but one explanation for this—a Confederate train was on the way and could only have been sent in pursuit. Andrews was in trouble. He already had lost a lot of valuable time because the road was blocked by trains. Now he had to get up speed to keep ahead of pursuers. But Andrews' cool, calculating attitude did not change.

The whistle that had startled the Union raiders came from the locomotive on which rode William A. Fuller, the conductor whose train had been stolen. When he and his companion reached Etowah, they discovered the *Yonah,* the locomotive Andrews had failed to destroy. Fuller raised an alarm, collected a group of soldiers, boarded the *Yonah,* and started down the track. When he reached Kingston he found three trains blocking the road, but he did not stop to move them aside. He and the soldiers took the locomotive and one car of the train at the end of the line and raced anew after Andrews.

In the meantime the Union men had removed a rail and hurried on to Adairsville. Here they found another train on the sidetrack and an express expected from Calhoun, nine miles away. Taking a chance on reaching Calhoun before the express had left there, they hurried on and arrived at the station just as the express was pulling out. The latter backed up, but an end of it obstructed the track, and Andrews had to argue persuasively before the conductor would pull up his train and let the captured train through.

When Fuller and the pursuing Confederates reached the point before Adairsville where Andrews' men had torn up a rail, they reversed the engine in time to avoid wrecking it. They could not repair the damage, but their determination to capture the raiders was as strong as ever. Again they started down the track on foot. Once more they were in luck. The train that had just pulled out of Adairsville came toward them; they hailed it and persuaded the conductor to run it back to the station. At Adairsville they uncoupled the cars; all the soldiers piled on the locomotive, the *Texas,* and its tender and once again started off at full speed, the engine running backwards.

Fuller must have been a pretty angry man when he met the express and learned that Andrews had bullied another conductor into letting him get by. Andrews, on the *General,* was not far ahead, but he was confident that he now had a clear road all the way to Chattanooga. He would pull up another rail, just to be safe, then head for the bridge over the Oostanaula and set it on fire.

His men jumped from the cars and started pulling up a rail, and just when they were hard at it they heard the whistle of a locomotive and saw an engine billowing smoke in the distance. Not equipped with tools for taking up rails, they had to leave the task uncompleted and jump back on board in a hurry.

There were still ways of delaying Fuller, and they worked a number of devices to do so. They dropped a car on the road; Fuller's engine picked it up and pushed it ahead. They dropped another and the same thing happened, and when Fuller reached Resaca he left both cars there. Andrews had time to cut telegraph wires and take on water, but he was running short of fuel and the next woodyard was miles away. The *General* was giving every bit of power of which it was capable, but the two locomotives were pretty evenly matched. They raced around hills and through villages, and all the time the pursuers kept their hands on the whistle cord, tooting a warning of vengeance to come. At one station Fuller dropped a man with a message for the Confederates at Chattanooga announcing the coming of Andrews' raiders and urging their capture. The first half of the message got through and the people at Chattanooga became thoroughly alarmed.

Here are the maneuvers that followed after passing Resaca:

Andrews dropped a rail on a track at a curve. Fuller's engine hit it with a jolt and tossed it aside.

Andrews ran through Dalton and stopped to cut wires and obstruct track within a hundred yards of a Confederate camp.

Andrews' men tore the last boxcar apart, piled up the wood, and started it burning. Rain was falling and a fire was hard to maintain, but it finally got under way. The Union men took the car to the center of a covered bridge, uncoupled it and left it to start the bridge burning. Fuller's engine arrived before the fire was well begun, picked up the burning car, pushed it forward, and dropped it at the next sidetrack.

Now Andrews had no fuel left and no time to stop for any. In a short time all the steam in the *General* would be used up. The men made a number of suggestions. One was to ambush the pursuers and fight them with revolvers against guns. Another was to start walking toward the Union lines in a body. But Andrews did not approve either plan. He ordered the men to drop off the locomotive and separate, going off into the hills.

This they did. The engineer reversed the engine and let it run toward the oncoming Confederates. But its steam was down and it slowed up. Fuller's engine backed away, then picked it up. The Confederates left their train and started out after the Union men over the hills in the drizzling rain.

The Confederates lost no time in pursuing the raiders. Several were caught within a few hours and all but two within a week. These two were caught later. Two men who had reached Marietta too late to take the train with Andrews were also caught. Since the men had conducted the raid in civilian clothes, they were technically spies and not entitled to the consideration shown men in uniform. After a court-martial in Chattanooga, Andrews and six of his men were hanged in Atlanta, and a civilian who had joined them suffered the same fate. Fourteen who were in prison in Atlanta awaiting trial overpowered their guard and escaped, but of these six were recaptured. They were paroled in March, 1863.

The Union survivors received promotions and medals, and the Confederates became heroes in the South. General Buell said Andrews was not in a position to have done any permanent damage to the bridges. But the recklessness and daring of the raiders and the stubbornness of the pursuers stirred great admiration and enthusiasm. The locomotive *General* is preserved at Chattanooga and has been exhibited at world fairs and on other special occasions. The *Texas* is preserved in the Cyclorama Building in Atlanta.

28

THE RAIDS OF MORGAN, DAHLGREN, AND QUANTRILL

One of the most reckless of the Confederate cavalry raiders was John Hunt Morgan, who realized the dream of many a Southern partisan by actually crossing the

Ohio River and making a dash through southern Indiana and Ohio, even clattering at night through the streets of Cincinnati. Morgan operated chiefly in Kentucky and Tennessee and although under orders of army commanders frequently ignored them.

Morgan had served in the cavalry corps during the Mexican War, emerging as a lieutenant. He became a cavalry scout for the Confederate army in Tennessee and took part in the battle of Shiloh, after which he was made a colonel. He raided Federal garrisons and communications and caused the Union commanders much distress. In July, 1862, he rounded up 65 Federals in Lebanon, Kentucky, and in December engaged in a sharp tussle with Ohio, Illinois, and Kentucky cavalry and infantry at Hartsville, Tennessee, killing 55 and capturing 1,800. For this feat he was made brigadier general.

In the summer of 1863 General Bragg wanted to move out of Tullahoma to Chattanooga and ordered Morgan to strike at General W. S. Rosecrans' supply depots, harass Louisville, and tear up the Louisville & Nashville Railroad. Morgan told Bragg that he wanted to cross the Ohio River and raid Ohio, but Bragg did not see any gain in this operation and refused to give the order. Morgan was not to be stopped by a mere command, so he went ahead on his own.

Morgan had 2,460 men and 4 guns when he left Burkesville July 2. He crossed the Cumberland River and clashed with the Twenty-fifth Michigan Volunteers, who were guarding a bridge at Green River. They gave him a hot fight, and he lost 50 killed and many wounded. Back in Lebanon, Kentucky, July 5, he captured the Federal garrison of about 400. He then marched to Brandenburg, Kentucky, on the Ohio River, seized two steamboats, and ferried his troops across to Indiana before a Federal gunboat could find him and the Indiana Home Guards could stop him.

News of Morgan's coming spread quickly through the towns along the Ohio and the governor of Indiana, Oliver P. Morton, called out the mounted militia while the Federal army ordered Brigadier General Henry M. Judah to proceed up the Ohio to Cincinnati to cut Morgan off. But Morgan knew that his safety lay in speed, and he pushed his tired troopers to keep moving night and day. Riding from Indiana into Ohio, he passed through Cincinnati at night. In Ohio cavalrymen were converging on Morgan's route and it was clear that he would have to get back across the river in a hurry with his captured horses. But he already had planned to cross on the upper Ohio. Making a feint as if to ride to Hamilton, Ohio, he turned sharply south, crossed a wide segment of the state, and reached the river at Buffington Bar on July 18. The next day his pursuers caught up with him. Morgan tried to fight his way out and lost about 120 of his men, while 700 were captured. He managed to get his compatriot, Brigadier General A. R. Johnson, across the river to West Virginia with 300, some of whom were drowned in the effort.

With the remnant of his troop Morgan now turned north and again evaded his pursuers as he followed the course of the Ohio River toward Pennsylvania. His object seems to have been to reach a different state, but on July 26 he asked a militia captain near New Lisbon, Ohio, to parole him and his men, and the captain assented. But the captain's superior, Brigadier General J. M. Shackleford, refused to honor any parole and turned Morgan over to the Ohio authorities. These, recalling that an Ohio civilian had been placed in Libby Prison because he was advocating emancipation, promptly locked Morgan and his principal officers in the state prison at Columbus. On November 27, 1863, Morgan escaped with six captains of his cavalry and made his way back to the Confederate lines. His escape caused a great sensation, because collusion was suspected. Apparently he and his men had penetrated the cell walls with two small knives, removing the masonry to enter an air chamber and digging a tunnel under the outer foundation walls. This took them twenty days to complete. Morgan and Captain Thomas H. Hines, a troublesome agitator, crossed the Ohio at Cincinnati and finally came in contact with a detachment of Morgan's cavalry at Burkesville. They had several skirmishes with Union cavalry, in one of which Captain Hines was recaptured.

In April, 1864, Morgan was back in the saddle at the head of 3,000 men, operating in East Tennessee and

Southwestern Virginia. Four hundred of his troop were on foot but eventually were provided with horses taken from the government stables at Lexington, Kentucky. Morgan's assignment was to stop Federal units that were destroying Confederate stores, supplies, and railroads in Virginia and Eastern Tennessee. He clashed with Major General William W. Averell and Major General George Crook when they were raiding salt works and lead works in southwestern Virginia, and fought a day's battle with General S. G. Burbridge at Mt. Sterling, Kentucky, and Cynthiana, Kentucky, June 11, 1864, in which 300 Confederates were killed or wounded and 400 were captured, while the Federals had 150 casualties. In August he was in Jonesboro, Georgia, but soon thereafter was preparing to lead a raid at Bull's Gap, Tennessee. While leaving a house at Greenville, Tennessee, he was shot and killed, reportedly after being betrayed by a personal enemy, September 4, 1864.

The Fatal Raid of Colonel Dahlgren

A daring cavalry raid into the environs of Richmond, planned by General Judson Kilpatrick and carried out with the eager cooperation of Colonel Ulric Dahlgren, who lost his life in it, stirred up considerable excitement on both sides from February 28 to March 4, 1864. Kilpatrick was known as a wild and impetuous rider who was called "Kill-cavalry" by his men. Colonel Dahlgren was a son of Rear Admiral John Dahlgren, inventor of the Dahlgren gun, and was a fanatical fighter in spite of a wooden leg. The raid brought about an exchange of letters between General Robert E. Lee and Major General George G. Meade over incriminating documents said to have been found on Dahlgren's body.

One explanation of the adventure is that General Kilpatrick proposed to make a swift raid into Richmond, liberate Federal prisoners there, and spread word of the amnesty proclamation of President Lincoln. Lincoln is said to have been told about this and to have sent for General Kilpatrick. General Meade doubted that the project was practical and in this was supported by General Pleasonton, but Lincoln is supposed to have approved it. When it was ordered Meade prepared diversions on the Confederate left so that Kilpatrick might find a way of getting around Lee's right. He ordered Brigadier General Custer with 2,000 cavalry to ride through Gordonsville toward Charlottesville and destroy the Lynchburg railroad bridge near that town. He also sent Major General Sedgwick with the Sixth Corps and part of Birney's division of the Third Corps to move toward Madison Court House on Robertson's River.

Although Kilpatrick's project was supposed to be secret, word got around in Washington and Colonel Ulric Dahlgren made a determined plea to join, which General Meade granted. Kilpatrick took 3,500 cavalry from his own Third Division and a battery of horse artillery and crossed the Rapidan at Ely's Ford on the night of February 28, 1864. He moved across the Wilderness and when near Spotsylvania Court House gave Dahlgren a detachment of 500 men and ordered him to make a wide detour, cross the James River to the south bank, liberate the Union prisoners on Belle Isle, and enter Richmond by the Mayo bridge at 10 A.M. on Tuesday, March 1, where they would meet.

Neither of the two groups got as far as Richmond. Kilpatrick crossed the South Anna and proceeded down the Brook Road, where he forced back pickets and a small advance body of Confederates. The defenders called up support and soon Kilpatrick was confronted by an artillery battery under command of Colonel G. W. Custis Lee, son of Robert E. Lee. Failing to hear any firing that might denote the approach of Dahlgren, he fell back and made camp at Atlee's Station. Here he was attacked that night by cavalry led by General Bradley T. Johnson and General Wade Hampton. Kilpatrick considered the advantage of surprise lost and led his force down the peninsula, crossed the Chickahominy and made camp safely at Mechanicsville.

In the meantime Colonel Dahlgren had been destroying property and creating alarm. Near Frederick's Hall Station he captured Maryland artillerymen and about a dozen Confederate officers holding a court-martial. He crossed the South Anna and reached the Kanawha Canal, where he ordered Captain J. F. B. Mitchell to take 100 men and destroy whatever came in his path. Mitchell burned six grist mills, one sawmill, a number of barges laden with grain, and ruined a canal lock. Then he rejoined Dahlgren. The latter had failed to find a good fording place and blamed a Negro lad who had misguided them, presumably out of ignorance, and had him hanged forthwith. It began to rain heavily and Dahlgren realized that he would fail to meet Kilpatrick. He was ready to turn back.

During the night of March 2, Captain Mitchell, with 300 horsemen, became separated from Colonel Dahlgren. He forced his way through skirmish lines near the Pamunkey, and next morning found General Kilpatrick. Dahlgren, with his small force, crossed the Pamunkey and the Mattapony. On the night of March 2 he was suddenly attacked by a sizable force of Confederates near Walkertown, but managed to get away. At midnight he was ambushed near King and Queen Court House and fell at the first fire. The 135 men with him surrendered.

When Dahlgren's body was examined the Confederates asserted they found two papers that interested them profoundly. One was an address signed "Ulric Dahlgren," in which the writer declared: "We hope to release the prisoners from Belle Isle first, and having seen them fairly started, we will cross the James River into Richmond, destroying the bridges after us, and exhorting the released prisoners to destroy and burn the hateful city; and do not allow the Rebel leader, Davis, and his traitorous crew to escape." The second paper purported to be a list of instructions. It was not signed and said that "once in the city it must be destroyed and Jeff Davis and cabinet killed. Pioneers will go along with combustible materials."

These papers were carried by Lieutenant Pollard of the Ninth Virginia, which had fought Dahlgren's men, to General Fitzhugh Lee in Richmond. For authentication Lieutenant Pollard also carried Dahlgren's artificial leg. The Confederates published the two papers in the Richmond newspapers, where they were seen by General Meade. He asked General Kilpatrick about them, and Kilpatrick reported that all officers insisted Colonel Dahlgren had made no address to the troops. But Kilpatrick admitted that he had seen an address by Dahlgren on which he had written "approved" in red ink. This address, he said, was practically that published in the Richmond newspapers, except that it did not carry the instructions to destroy the city and kill President Davis and his cabinet. Oddly, Dahlgren's name was misspelled in one place.

A few weeks later General R. E. Lee sent General Meade photographs of the two papers and asked whether their instructions were authorized by the U.S. government or by Dahlgren's superior officer and approved. General Kilpatrick said the endorsement he had written on one of the papers did not appear on these copies and that no such orders ever had been given. General Meade forwarded Kilpatrick's comment to General Lee with the declaration that "neither the United States Government, nor myself, nor General Kilpatrick authorized, sanctioned, or approved the burning of the city of Richmond and the killing of Mr. Davis and his cabinet, nor any other act not required by military necessity and in accordance with the usages of war."

The diversion by General Custer, which was part of the plan to draw attention from Kilpatrick, alerted General Jeb Stuart and his cavalry and they formed a plan to trap Custer, which almost succeeded. Before Custer reached Charlottesville he learned that the bridge he was to destroy was guarded by cavalry and four batteries, so he turned back. General Stuart lined up his troops along the road Custer would follow on his return, but a guide led Custer down a side road and almost into Lee's lines. Custer discovered his danger in time, made a quick turnabout, and rode back to the main road. In the meantime Stuart, learning that Custer had turned aside, moved down another road to head him off. This left the main road open, and when Custer returned to it he was able to move to his base without opposition. Both Union and Confederate troops reported casualties of about 300.

A confederate guerrilla whose name is a byword for ruthlessness in Kansas was William C. Quantrill, who had the rank of colonel of cavalry but operated independently on the Kansas-Missouri border. He had fought at Wilson's Creek. With a band of 300 horsemen he raided

Lawrence, Kansas, on August 21, 1863, killed and injured about 200 men and boys, and burned down a number of dwellings. His band was said to have included the later outlaws, Cole Younger and Frank James. The cruelty was not all on the Confederate side. Quantrill's raid was in reprisal for excesses committed by Abolitionist bands. The principal antislavery leader was James H. Lane, a former lieutenant governor of Indiana, who made Lawrence his headquarters and raided and burned settlements on the Missouri-Kansas border.

Major General J. M. Schofield, commanding the Department of Missouri, considered the situation so desperate that he thought the only remedy would be to remove from the border counties all slaves entitled to freedom, all families of men known to belong to the bands, and all those known to sympathize with the raiders. General Thomas Ewing, commanding at the border, issued his Order No. Eleven, which became notorious in Missouri history because it ordered all who lived in the border counties that were the scene of guerrilla depredations to be removed out of his jurisdiction. President Lincoln on October 1, 1863, instructed General Schofield to act with calm and forbearance in keeping order, making the military obey orders, letting no one assume authority to confiscate property or entice slaves from their homes, or return fugitive slaves, or interfere with expression of opinion. The matter "of removing the inhabitants of certain counties *en masse*," Lincoln left to Schofield's discretion. When a radical group in Missouri asked Lincoln to remove Schofield, citing among other reasons that he had not allowed the Lawrence murderers to be pursued into Missouri, Lincoln replied that to prevent the "threatened remedial raid" was the only way to forestall an indiscriminate massacre.

Quantrill was mortally wounded by Federal troopers in Kentucky in 1865 and died in Louisville.

29

FARRAGUT IS LASHED TO
THE RIGGING AT MOBILE BAY

Rear Admiral David Farragut had agreed with General
Grant that an attempt to capture Mobile should be made
immediately after Vicksburg and Port Hudson fell. But the
determination of the Administration to divert troops to
General Nathaniel Banks' expedition up the Red River
held up action against Mobile. Here was a key city and
a fortified harbor on the Gulf that had to be blockaded
by the United States Navy in order to keep the Confederate blockade runners away, when the Navy might
have used its ships to greater advantage elsewhere. Moreover, the harbor was well suited to shelter hostile craft,
and the Confederates were taking advantage of their
freedom from attack by building gunboats at Selma on the
Alabama River, with the object of bringing them down
to Mobile Bay.

The channel into the bay wound among sand barriers,
the largest of which was Sand Island. The Confederates
had manufactured many torpedoes (mines) that would
explode on contact, and had planted them along the
channel. There also were two forts at the mouth of
Mobile Bay: Fort Morgan on Mobile Point, east of the
channel, a large brick structure of the kind favored in
the first half of the century, with three tiers of heavy guns
and a water battery of seven guns near the shore line,
and Fort Gaines. This was a smaller structure several
miles across the water to the west, on Dauphin Island.
There also was another small fortification, Fort Powell,
some distance beyond Fort Gaines. Mobile was thirty
miles north of the Gulf.

There was little secrecy about what the Confederates
were about, so the United States Navy knew that they had
been building a formidable ironclad called the *Tennessee*. It had been brought down the river to the lower bay
on May 20, 1864. It was under the command of Admiral

Franklin Buchanan, who had handled the *Virginia* (*Merrimack*) on the day it sank the *Cumberland* and *Congress* at Hampton Roads. He had been wounded in the fighting. The *Tennessee* was 209 feet long, had a beam of 48 feet and a shield of 78 feet, 8 inches, rising 8 feet above the deck. Its plates were 2 inches thick and were used in double and triple applications. It carried 6 rifled guns.

Farragut knew that his wooden vessels were vulnerable to attack by ironclads and had asked Secretary of the Navy Gideon Welles repeatedly to give him ironclads; even one or two would be a protection, but none came. "It appears that it takes us twice as long to build an ironclad as anyone else," he complained. But by July, 1864, views changed in Washington; Farragut received three monitors and the promise of a fourth. Likewise on August 4 a division of troops from General E. R. S. Canby's command, under the actual command of Major General Gordon Granger, formerly of the Fourth Corps, Army of the Cumberland, arrived with 1,800 men from New Orleans and landed on Dauphin Island, in the rear of Fort Gaines, equipped to begin a siege.

Admiral Farragut and staff took the tender *Cowslip* and steamed past Sand Island and into the channel, to determine where the gunboats were located. They were lying farther up in the lower bay beyond Fort Morgan, and the ironclad *Tennessee* was among them. It was also seen that a red buoy marked the eastern point of an area where the Confederates had been planting torpedoes. There were also black buoys between which torpedoes had been placed, blocking the entrance westward, and Farragut warned his commanders that they must steer east of the buoys.

The fourth monitor, *Tecumseh,* arrived from Pensacola on August 4, when Farragut was ready to proceed without it. He called a council on board the flagship *Hartford* and announced the order of battle for the following morning. The ships were stripped for action. The fleet was to be preceded by the four monitors in a single column: *Tecumseh, Manhattan, Winnebago,* and *Chickasaw.* The first pair had two 15-inch guns in one turret each; the second pair had four 11-inch guns in two turrets each. Although Farragut had expected to lead the fleet, his associates persuaded him to give that position to the *Brooklyn,* commanded by Captain James Alden, a descendant of John Alden of Plymouth Plantation. The *Brooklyn* had four bow guns and an apparatus for picking up torpedoes. Each ship was fastened by cables to another vessel. Thus the *Brooklyn* led with the *Octarara,* followed by the *Hartford* and *Metacomet,* the *Richmond* and the *Port Royal,* the *Lackawanna* and the *Seminole,* the *Monongahela* and the *Kennebec,* the *Ossipee* and the *Itasca,* the *Oneida* and the *Galena.* In all, eighteen vessels of war. The admiral's launch, the *Loyall,* steamed on the port side of the flagship, the side away from Fort Morgan.

The fleet started up the channel at 5:45 A.M. on August 5, 1864. The first vessel to fire was the *Tecumseh,* which sent a fifteen-inch shell toward Fort Morgan. The enemy responded, and soon the air was ringing with the thunder of guns from forts and ships. As the view of the bay became obscured by powder smoke Farragut climbed the rigging in order to get a better prospect. He went up the mainmast as far as the shrouds just below the maintop, where the pilot had his perch. When Flag Captain Percival Drayton of the *Hartford* saw Farragut up there he sent the signal quartermaster, Knowles, aloft with a small rope to put around the admiral to keep him from falling in case of a sudden lurch of the ship. Farragut protested at first, then realized the need and helped fasten the rope around himself. This was the origin of the report that Farragut was "lashed to the rigging" during the battle, an incident that gave him a reputation for daring and courage. There was another moment in the battle when a similar precaution was taken. Farragut was greatly amused when this was described in newspapers all over the North and remarked to Captain Drayton: "How curiously some trifling incident catches the popular fancy! My being in the main rigging was a mere accident, owing to the fact that I was driven aloft by the smoke. The lashing was the result of your own fears for my safety." After the war a portrait painter persuaded Farragut to assume the position he had in the rigging, and this became his best-known posture.

Part of the way up the channel the *Brooklyn* halted and signaled that the monitors were right ahead and that it could not proceed without passing them—the monitors having much slower engines. Farragut signaled back: "Order the monitors ahead and go on."

As the *Brooklyn* halted, the *Tecumseh* moved west of the line marked by the red buoy and hit one of the torpedoes. It began to sink almost immediately. Only twenty-one men who managed to jump were saved, and ninety-three went down inside the boat, including the captain, Tunis A. M. Craven. The pilot, John Collins, reported later that when the boat was struck he and the captain met at the foot of the ladder leading to the top of the turret; the captain said: "After you, Pilot," and as Collins raced to the top the vessel seemed to drop from under him and the captain with it. Four of those saved reached Fort Morgan and were made prisoners; several others were picked up in a boat that a courageous ensign rowed under the guns of the fort and brought safely back to shipboard.

When the ships stopped briefly they became targets for all the shot and shell the Confederates could rain on them, and it was during these few minutes that the Federals had their greatest casualties. The *Hartford* was not spared. When the *Brooklyn* failed to advance, Farragut inquired about the depth of water to the left of that ship, and on being informed that it was sufficient ordered the *Hartford* to take the lead. It was at this point, presumably, that someone on the *Brooklyn* shouted to Farragut that there were torpedoes ahead. Farragut's reply was "Damn the torpedoes!" and in some reports this is followed by "Full speed ahead!" This cry was repeated throughout the North with vast relish and was always associated with Farragut.

The ships passed over the torpedoes, which failed to explode. The *Hartford*, with guns blazing, proceeded toward the Confederate gunboats with its chained partner, the *Metacomet*. It received so many direct hits from the Confederate gunboat *Selma* that the *Metacomet*, being the faster vessel, was unchained to make a direct attack on the *Selma*. It came to close quarters, and after its shots had wounded the captain and killed his first lieutenant the *Selma* surrendered. The Confederate gunboat *Gaines* ran aground and took fire, and the third, the *Morgan,* moved into shoal water and escaped during the night.

The *Tennessee* in the meantime steered toward the *Brooklyn* and sent two shots into that vessel, then moved past. Three broadsides from eleven guns on the *Richmond* poured solid shot on the *Tennessee,* without inflicting any visible damage. Some time later the *Monongahela* rammed the *Tennessee* head-on, without knocking it out.

The *Hartford* had anchored four miles above Fort Morgan and the other vessels were following suit when the *Tennessee* appeared again, evidently intending to ram the ships. Farragut thought Admiral Buchanan was foolish to try this alone. The fleet was put on the alert and took up its anchors again. The *Monongahela* once more tried to ram the *Tennessee,* but damaged only itself. The *Lackawanna* likewise failed. The *Tennessee* and the *Hartford* appeared to head for each other bow-on, but actually they only scraped sides. A single gun blast from the ironclad killed five men on the *Hartford.* Farragut had jumped to the rail and held on to the mizzen rigging, and again a rope was fastened around him. In an attempt to run down the *Tennessee* the *Lackawanna* struck the *Hartford* amidships and barely avoided a second collision. The Federal fleet now concentrated its fire on the *Tennessee.* Some shots struck its rudder chains and put it out of control. Admiral Buchanan then surrendered.

The U.S. gunboat *Chickasaw* later shelled Fort Powell, which was evacuated at 10 P.M. On August 6 the *Chickasaw* shelled Fort Gaines, which surrendered next morning to General Granger. Fort Morgan, commanded by Brigadier General Richard L. Page, was better equipped to hold out. General Granger sent to New Orleans for 25 guns, 16 mortars and 3 additional regiments of infantry, and began a bombardment on August 22. The fort raised the white flag on August 23 and surrendered 500 men and 50 guns to General Granger and Admiral Farragut.

The capture of Mobile was not effected until the spring of 1865. On March 17 Major General E. R. S. Canby, commander at New Orleans, began operations ordered by General Grant. The attack was made by two columns, one of 32,000 under General Canby, and the other from Pensacola under Major General Frederick Steele, with 13,000 troops. The reorganized Thirteenth Corps was commanded by Major General Gordon Granger and the reorganized Sixteenth by Major General Andrew J. Smith. The siege train was commanded by Major General Richard Arnold, chief of artillery. The Confederate defenses were manned by 10,000 troops and 300 guns under Major General Dabney H. Maury, and there were five gunboats.

On April 9 an assault by 16,000 captured the works with 3,423 prisoners. Forts Tracy and Huger were blown up by the Confederates on April 11. General Granger crossed the bay and entered the city of Mobile April 12, when General Maury and 4,500 troops retreated to Meridian, Georgia. General Richard Taylor surrendered all forces in this area east of the Mississippi to General Canby May 1. The campaign had cost the Federals 189 killed, 1,201 wounded, 27 captured. General Kirby Smith surrendered the troops west of the Mississippi May 26, and President Johnson declared the amnesty May 29, 1865.

30

BATTLE OF THE *KEARSARGE* AND THE *ALABAMA*

The most famous privateer of the Confederate Navy was the *Alabama,* built at Birkenhead by the Lairds, well-known British shipbuilders. It raided United States commerce for twenty-two months, causing tremendous loss to Northern merchants before it was destroyed.

The *Alabama* was one of a number contracted for in England by J. D. Bulloch, a former captain in the United States Navy, who was serving the Confederacy as an undercover business agent in Europe. The ship was to cost about $250,000, a large sum in those days. After being referred to by the shipbuilders' number, 290, while under construction, it was named the *Enrica*. The United States, through its minister, Charles Francis Adams, had furnished proof that the ship was destined for the Confederacy and Lord John Russell finally had ordered it detained, but Bulloch took possession before the order could reach him. On July 26, 1862, he sailed the completed vessel out of Liverpool on a well-publicized trial trip, with male and female guests on board for the day's ride. The guests were dropped at sea and taken ashore by a tug, and the *Enrica* steamed for the Azores, where a bark, the *Agrippina,* waited with guns and munitions for transfer to the *Enrica*. On August 24, 1862, the *Enrica* became the *Alabama* under the command of Captain Raphael Semmes, who had been raiding United States commerce in a converted passenger steamer called the *Sumter*.

The *Alabama* was a wooden ship of 1,040 tons, 200 feet long, with a 32-foot beam, rigged as a barkentine and propelled by two engines of 300 horsepower each, capable of 12 knots by steam and 15 knots when sail was added. It had 8 guns, 24 officers, and crew of 120. It captured United States merchantmen on the high seas from the Cape of Good Hope to Singapore, Brazil, and Newfoundland. Its first daring exploit was luring the *Hatteras,* a converted river-excursion steamer, from the midst of a fleet in Galveston harbor and sinking it in the Gulf. This was the only "warship" outside of the *Kearsarge* that it tackled. In the course of its depredations on commerce the *Alabama* seized 64 merchantmen and burned 53 of them.

On June 11, 1864, the *Alabama* entered the harbor of Cherbourg and asked permission of the French authorities to refit at one of the national docks. This required reference to Paris and a delay of several days, enabling the United States consul to warn the American minister in Paris, who communicated the news to Captain John A. Winslow of the *Kearsarge,* then at Flushing in the Netherlands. The *Kearsarge* stopped for a day at Dover for dispatches and on June 14 reached Cherbourg, but remained outside the harbor because of a twenty-four-hour limit. When Captain Winslow went ashore in a boat to

call on the French maritime commander and on the
United States consul, he received a declaration that Captain Semmes had given the Confederate commercial agent
to convey to the United States consul. It read:

To A. BONFILS, Esq., Cherbourg: SIR: I hear that you were
informed by the U.S. Consul that the *Kearsarge* was to
come to 'this port solely for the prisoners landed by me and
that she was to depart in 24 hours. I desire you to say to
the U.S. Consul that my intention is to fight the *Kearsarge*
as soon as I can make the necessary arrangements. I hope
these will not detain me more than until tomorrow evening,
or after the morrow morning at furthest. I beg she will not
depart before I am ready to go out.

The decision of Captain Semmes puzzled the men on
the *Kearsarge,* but it was explained later that Captain
Semmes considered the vessels about evenly matched and
wished to be known not as a corsair, but as a fighter.
During the next few days the Federals learned from
French pilots that Semmes had sent ashore chronometers,
specie, and bills of ransomed vessels, and his crew was
sharpening cutlasses and boarding pikes.

The *Kearsarge* also prepared for action. It was 232
feet long with a beam of 33 feet, tonnage of 1,031, and
had two engines of 400 horsepower each. Its wooden
hull was protected with plating of sheet-chains, which
were covered over with deal boards. The ship carried
seven guns—two 11-inch Dahlgrens, which proved most
powerful; a 30-pounder rifle; and four light 32-pounders.

That Captain Semmes's fighting spirit was up was
proved by an address he made to his officers and crew
on the morning before the battle, when he admonished
them that they had another opportunity of meeting the
enemy—the first since they sank the *Hatteras.* "In the
meantime you have been all over the world, and it is not
too much to say that you have destroyed, and driven
under neutral flags, one half of the enemy's commerce.
. . . The name of your ship has become a household
word wherever civilization extends! Shall that name be
tarnished by defeat? The thing is impossible. Remember
that you are in the English Channel, the theater of so
much of the naval glory of our race, and that the eyes

of all Europe are at this moment upon you. . . ."

News of the coming encounter had been published in the newspapers and caused a large crowd to converge on Cherbourg, some coming from Paris to witness a naval battle. About 15,000 persons are believed to have been along the coast on the morning of Sunday, June 19, when the *Alabama* finally steamed out of harbor. It was escorted to the limits of French authority by the French commander of the port and a small steamer, the *Deerhound*, flying the flag of the Royal Mersey Yacht Club. The *Kearsarge* was nearly seven miles from shore, having taken this position to intercept the *Alabama* if it made an attempt to escape by leaving French waters.

The two ships started for each other at high speed, and the *Alabama* fired one broadside at 1,800 yards and two others before the *Kearsarge*, at 900 yards, replied with its starboard guns. The *Alabama* kept its broadside toward the *Kearsarge*, with the result that the two ships began moving in circles with a strong port helm at a distance of about a quarter of a mile. The *Kearsarge* used its 11-inch shells with great effect, and although it was hit a number of times only three men were wounded. The *Alabama* was hit at the water line and began to settle after completing the seventh circle. It set sail and headed for the French coast. The *Kearsarge* stopped its progress with a few more well-placed shots, and the Confederate ship struck its colors. Later a controversy developed over the charge of Captain Semmes that he had been fired on after he had struck his colors; this was denied by Captain Winslow. The *Alabama* then lowered boats and the master's mate rowed over to the *Kearsarge*, admitted the surrender, and asked help, which was given.

The steam yacht *Deerhound* came up and Captain Winslow asked its owner, John Lancaster, to help save the men of the sinking ship. The *Alabama* went down by the stern, assuming a perpendicular position. The yacht lowered boats and picked up Captain Semmes and a number of other officers and men. The *Deerhound* then set course for England, carrying a shipload of Confederates who should have been prisoners of the *Kearsarge*. This action was strongly criticized by the Navy De-

partment as contrary to naval custom, but it had no way
of catching Semmes. In his report to his government
Semmes complained that he had not known that the
Kearsarge was protected by iron chains and therefore
was "ironclad."

The climate of opinion in Europe was strongly affected
by the destruction of the *Alabama*. The French admired
the audacity of the smaller ship challenging the larger.
The crowds that had gathered at Cherbourg cheered when
the *Alabama* left the dock and moved out into the open
sea; they were silent when the victorious *Kearsarge* arrived after the battle. The diplomatic effect, however,
was quite the contrary. The Confederate representative
in Brussels, Colonel A. Dudley Mann, informed Judah
P. Benjamin, the Confederate Secretary of State, that it
was generally believed that Captain Semmes acted most
injudiciously in meeting the *Kearsarge* in open combat,
and most improperly in choosing Sunday as the day for
the engagement. Europe now considered him the aggres-
sor and Mann felt the European friends of the Confederacy "will be disinclined to manifest any regret at
his defeat." Recalling the Yankee assertions that the
Confederacy was not their equal on the sea, Mann said:
"Unfortunately we have exemplified this inequality in a
convincing manner at the very portals of Europe."

The growing coolness of the French government toward the Confederacy was observed by its representatives in the detention of the Confederate frigate *Rappahannock* in the harbor of Calais. The ship had collided
with a French vessel on entering the port, and the court
rendered a judgment for damages against its commander.
There followed many weeks of delay, during which the
French government refused to give the *Rappahannock*
clearing permission on various pretexts, including shortage of crew and coal. While the emperor gave his permission for it to sail, the ministries withheld it. This
gave the United States Navy time to send four cruisers
to watch outside the port, a circumstance the Confederate agents blamed on French hostility. Thus the *Rappahannock* proved useless to them.

The Alabama Claims

During the entire course of the war, the United States government labored through diplomatic channels to persuade the British government to stop British firms from building ships for the Confederacy. Minister Charles Francis Adams was in constant communication on this subject with Lord Palmerston and Lord John Russell. Both professed they were doing what they could under the law to maintain neutrality. Laird, the Liverpool shipbuilder, was a member of the House of Commons, and was cheered when he defended his course.

J. D. Bulloch, the Confederate agent, not only acquired the *Alabama,* but the *Florida* and *Shenandoah* from British owners. Minister Adams said the United States would permit privateering if ships were furnished the Confederacy. Lord Russell on April 5, 1863, ordered the *Alexandra* held, but a British court voided the order. Two formidable rams were being built by the Lairds when the British government finally bought them outright. Before Adams heard this he sent Lord Russell a warning that if the rams sailed it would be considered an act of war.

In 1864 Bulloch bought a ship in Glasgow through intermediaries and it became the *Shenandoah,* 790 tons. It destroyed many Yankee whaling ships in the Pacific, and after Lee surrendered burned or sank twenty-four whalers in the Arctic.

But the Americans had kept a list of losses, and when the war was ended they presented their bill. They asked compensation for damages caused by twelve Confederate cruisers that had been outfitted by the British and had used British ports. Among them were the losses caused by the *Alabama*—$7,050,293. The losses charged against the *Shenandoah* were only $400,000 less.

The British also had claims for damages, and there were disputes, such as the Vancouver-Washington boundary, that remained to be settled. Negotiations dragged for years. The British refused at first to negotiate, because their honor was involved. But a new government eventually discovered that its honor would be strengthened by a settlement of all claims. Eventually a formal commission, sitting at Geneva, worked over the whole mass of charges and countercharges. The tribunal was appointed by the King of Italy, the President of the Swiss Confederation, the Emperor of Brazil, the President of the United States, and the Queen of Great Britain. The American member was Charles Francis Adams, who had tactfully reminded the British of their obligations during the war. American counsel were William. M. Evarts, Caleb Cushing, and Morrison R. Waite.

In September, 1872, the tribunal awarded the United States damages of $15,500,000 in gold for losses sustained from the operations of the *Alabama, Florida,* and *Shenandoah.* Although this was considerably less than the proved losses, the tribunal enabled the United States to make a full statement of the culpability of the British ministers and the aid given the privateers in British ports, including those of the Bahamas and the Caribbean. The British public was outraged when it learned that the Americans blamed them for "prolongation of the war," and Lord Granville estimated that losses might be as high as $3,000,000,000. The British had counterclaims, and eventually the United States had to pay nearly $7,000,000 for these and for the adjudication of the Halifax fisheries dispute.

31

WILDERNESS AND SPOTSYLVANIA

Grant Moves into the Wilderness

The Army of the Potomac, reorganized and strengthened during its winter sojourn, 1863–1864, north of the Rapidan River, began its major campaign May 4 under the direct supervision of General Grant. It was commanded by Major General George C. Meade, and its effective strength was around 100,000, although some reports placed it at 118,000. As now organized the army had three infantry corps, in which the former First and Third Corps had been absorbed. They were the Second, commanded by Major General Winfield S. Hancock, with four divisions under Major General David B. Birney and Brigadier Generals Francis C. Barlow, John Gibbon, and Gresham Mott; the Fifth, under Major General G. K. Warren, with as division commanders Brigadier Generals Charles Griffin, John C. Robinson, Samuel W. Crawford, and James S. Wadsworth; the Sixth, under Major General John Sedgwick, with three divisions under Brigadier Generals H. G. Wright, George W. Getty, and James B. Ricketts. The cavalry corps was under Major General Philip H. Sheridan, and the artillery under Brigadier General Henry J. Hunt. Not subject to Meade but associated with his army was the Ninth Corps, commanded by Major General A. E. Burnside, who outranked Meade and received his orders through Grant. This corps had four divisions, the fourth of which was composed of Negro regiments under Brigadier General Edward Ferrero. There were 19,486 effectives in the Ninth Corps.

The Wilderness already had made a vast amount of trouble for the Federal armies; it was responsible for Hooker's dilemma at Chancellorsville. It was an area of dense forest and heavy undergrowth, with relatively few cleared places where farms were located. The Orange Court House–Fredericksburg Turnpike, which had had more great armies tramp over it than any other road in the country, was fairly straight and usable, and so were one or two other main roads, but others that entered the heart of the forest were narrow and dark. The Wilderness had made possible Stonewall Jackson's long march around the right flank of the Union army and the surprise attack on General Howard's Eleventh Corps. This western end of the Chancellorsville field was now to become the center of Grant's move against Lee. Once more troops were to march past Wilderness Tavern and traverse the terrain where Jackson had been struck down. There were plenty of hillocks throughout the Wilderness where a few feet of dirt covered bodies hastily buried in the spring of 1863, and there were skulls and bones and tatters of old military cloth where wild animals had rooted among the unknown dead.

During this winter General Lee never had been far from the Fredericksburg–Chancellorsville area where he had won two great battles with the help of Federal inefficiency. Headquarters of the Army of Northern Virginia were two miles northeast of Orange Court House. The First Corps, under Lieutenant General James Longstreet, was posted at Gordonsville; the Second, under Lieutenant General Richard S. Ewell, was encamped near the Rapidan above Mine Run; the Third, under Lieutenant General A. P. Hill, often called Powell Hill in his army, was to the left of Ewell upstream. There were about 62,000 men available to Lee.

Lee was not without knowledge of Grant's preparations to move. Major General E. M. Law reported that Lee called his corps and division commanders to the Confederate signal station on Clark's Mountain on May 2 and there viewed Federal troop concentrations north of the Rapidan in Culpeper County. Lee had expressed the opinion that the Federal army meant to cross the river at Germanna Ford or Ely's.

Brigadier General D. McM. Gregg's division of cavalry crossed the Rapidan at Ely's Ford, drove back the Confederate outposts, and laid down pontoons. Hancock's corps began crossing on May 4 and took the familiar road to Chancellorsville. Brigadier General J. H. Wilson's cavalry division followed a similar routine at Germanna Ford, where Warren's Fifth Corps crossed, and then took the road to the Orange Turnpike. Warren was to march to Todd's Tavern, and to be followed across the ford by General Sedgwick and the Sixth Corps. The supply train, carrying three days' forage and ten days' rations, crossed by the Culpeper Mine Ford.

Grant was now coordinating the work of all the Union armies. Before starting with the Army of the Potomac he received a cordial expression of confidence from President Lincoln, who wrote him: "The particulars of your plans I neither know or seek to know. You are vigilant and self-reliant, and, pleased with this, I wish not to obtrude any constraints or restraints upon you. While I am very anxious that any great disaster, or the capture of our men in great numbers, shall be avoided, I know these points are less likely to escape your attention than they would mine." General Grant's reply was a superlative expression of gratitude and esteem. He told President Lincoln that from the first day of his entry into the volunteer service he never had any cause for complaint and had never expressed or implied a complaint against the Administration or the Secretary of War "for throwing any embarrassment in the way of my vigorously prosecuting what appeared to be my duty." This was true so far as it applied to Lincoln, but Grant had suffered numerous slights and impediments from General Halleck, which he may have had in mind when he thanked Lincoln.

Grant's army, as well as his supply train of over 4,000 wagons, was across the river by the morning of May 5. General Meade made his headquarters at the Wilderness Tavern. General Lee was now aware of the concentration of Federal troops and ordered divisions of General Ewell's Second Corps to march on the Orange Turnpike to attack the Federals. Farther south in the Wilderness there was a parallel road, the Orange Plank Road, and Lee ordered General A. P. Hill to move up on that. General Longstreet was ordered up from Gordonsville; he took the Catharpin Road south of Orange Plank Road and then turned into the latter. Lee did not expect to start a general engagement until he had Longstreet's support, and that was expected early on the morning of May 6. He had not expected Grant to move into the Wilderness, where there was so great danger of mishaps, but when he did Lee was ready to check him.

Grant had sent General Wilson's cavalry ahead toward Parker's Store southwest of Todd's Tavern on the morning of May 5. At noon Wilson was fiercely attacked by General Wade Hampton's division of Stuart's cavalry, causing Wilson to fall back on the advancing columns of General Warren. Brigades of General Ewell's Second Confederate Corps rushed to oppose General Griffin's advancing units of Warren's corps. As the Confederates ordered up Generals Wilcox and Heth to support Ewell a furious fight developed along the Orange Plank Road. Grant sent Generals Wright and Getty of Sedgwick's corps, and Hancock was ordered to the support of Getty.

Getty fought with Major General Heth's division of Hill's command. Hancock sent the divisions of Birney and Mott and two brigades to support Getty. They held their line without gaining any advantages. In the fighting Getty was wounded and Brigadier General Alexander Hays of Birney's division was killed. Hays had commanded a division of Hancock's corps in the defense of Cemetery Ridge against Pickett's charge at the battle of Gettysburg and Grant remembered him as his West Point and Mexican War comrade.

Wilson's cavalry was getting the worst of it from Brigadier General Thomas L. Rosser's cavalry brigade when Gregg's division of Sheridan's cavalry corps came up and helped drive Rosser back some distance.

Grant was aware that Longstreet was en route with about 12,000 men. Hancock's position had been considerably strengthened by the arrival of Brigadier General James S. Wadsworth's Fourth Division of Warren's corps, comprising many New York regiments. Grant ordered Hancock to attack Hill's left. Burnside was ordered to take two divisions and get between Wadsworth and Warren's other divisions and attack Hill in the center, with an effort to get on Lee's right.

On the night of May 5-6 General Lee was at his headquarters near the house of the Widow Tapp on the Orange Plank Road. Across the road stood a battalion of artillery under Lieutenant Colonel William T. Poague, and over toward the nearby Brock Road was part of Hill's Third Corps. The divisions of Major Generals Henry Heth and Wilcox were to be relieved at midnight by Longstreet, but the latter did not arrive in time. Major General Charles W. Field of Longstreet's army was not far off, however, and had orders from Longstreet to move up at 1 A.M. Lee sent verbal orders at 10 P.M. for him to move up, but he adhered to his original orders and did not come, with the result that he was not on hand to help when the Federals attacked the next morning.

The Federal attack burst into full fury at 5 A.M. and the spear of the assault fell on General Wilcox's division. The underbrush allowed troops to press forward unseen; no one could tell how many Federals were com-

ing. Wilcox's men fell back and calls for reinforcements
went to Lee. He rode over to rally Wilcox's men, but
they moved back with deliberation. Wilcox ordered
Poague's batteries to fire into the woods. Lee, looking
anxiously for Longstreet, spotted unfamiliar soldiers coming forward in spite of the retreat. They were members
of the Texas regiments of Gregg's brigade and suddenly
Lee became as excited as any raw recruit. "Hurrah for
Texas!" he shouted, waving his hat. He started forward
with the oncoming troops past Poague's guns.

But when the men saw what Lee was doing they began
protesting. "Go back, General Lee, go back!" they yelled,
and one sergeant seized the bridle of his horse and tried
to stop him. Lee disregarded them until Colonel Charles
S. Venable reminded him that Longstreet had come
up and awaited orders. Lee turned back reluctantly.

Longstreet's corps not only stopped the retreat of the
Confederate Third Corps but pushed the Federals back
to their original lines. With General Kershaw in the lead
they fought with new vigor, and many men fell on both
sides. The cost was terrible; Gregg's Texans lost two-
thirds of their number in casualties. But the Federal line
held. There were several other strong assaults; Longstreet, moving through an unfinished railroad right of
way south of the Plank Road, attempted to turn the Federal left, and at the same time another attack was started
on the Plank Road. Both Lee and Longstreet had great
hopes for success of this double maneuver, when tragedy struck the Confederate command. As Longstreet
moved up past Mahone's brigade a volley of musketry
came from the woods at the right; Longstreet was hit
by a bullet that entered near his throat and went into
his shoulder, causing severe bleeding. By the same volley
Brigadier General Micah Jenkins of Field's division was
mortally wounded. Longstreet explained his tactics to
Lee as best he could and Lee took command of the
action, but the impetus was gone.

Longstreet was to be incapacitated for some time. Soon
thereafter General Hill was taken ill and had to give up
his command. General Richard H. Anderson assumed
Longstreet's command, General Jubal A. Early took
Hill's corps, and General John B. Gordon succeeded

Early as commander of his division. The Confederates also lost General J. M. Jones, killed, and General L. A. Stafford, mortally wounded, while the Union army lost General Wadsworth, killed, in the battle of May 6.

That night another great calamity hit the battlefield of the Wilderness as the pine woods caught fire from the shelling. The woods that had been fought over were filled with wounded men, many of whom could not move. During the late afternoon even some of the breastworks, protected by logs, had caught fire and the soldiers had fired through the logs as they burned. The men worked desperately trying to get the wounded out of the brush, but in many cases the flames were too strong to permit access. It was estimated that about 200 Union men were burned to death in the woods. For days the whole area was overlaid with a thick haze of blue smoke from the burning pines.

On the morning of May 7 Grant laid plans to move the army southeast to Spotsylvania Court House. Grant feared that Lee might make a swift move to Richmond to crush Butler, who had landed at City Point on May 5. Grant also wished to get between Lee's army and Richmond, and if that failed, to draw him into the open field. As the segments of Grant's army prepared to follow the roads to Spotsylvania, Grant and Meade with staff officers rode ahead. As they passed Hancock's command on the Brock Road the men cheered, for they saw that the army was not to retreat but to continue south.

Lee had given General Anderson orders to start for Spotsylvania at 3 A.M. on May 8, but Anderson started the night before without resting his men, and explained later that he could not bivouac because the woods were on fire. As he marched he put trees across the road to impede the Union army.

Anderson's unimpeded march to Spotsylvania had another explanation. During May 7 General Sheridan's cavalry had been fighting the Confederates at Todd's Tavern. At nightfall Sheridan had ordered General Wesley Merritt to move up the road to Spotsylvania and guard the bridge that crosses the Po River, where the Confederate army would have to cross. But General Meade changed the orders and removed Merritt from the job of holding the bridge. This gave Anderson an open road to Spotsylvania Court House, where General Wilson was trying to hold fast until the arrival of more Federal regiments. Such is General Grant's explanation. There is another version that says Merritt did not have orders to hold the bridge and therefore received orders from General Meade to go to the Block House, east of the Po bridge.

Whatever the circumstances, Sheridan believed that he had been overruled by General Meade. He told Meade that he could whip Jeb Stuart if given half a chance, but if Meade was going to continue to give orders to the cavalry over his head Meade might as well take command of the cavalry. Meade carried the controversy to Grant, who decided that this was a good time to turn Sheridan loose on Lee's communications. He gave orders to Sheridan verbally and later Meade gave him the orders in writing. Sheridan was to cut railroad and telegraph lines, seize stores for his own use and destroy those not needed, draw the Confederate cavalry after him, and thus relieve pressure on the Union army. If Sheridan needed forage and other supplies he was to procure them at the depot at City Point, where Butler had just arrived. With Sheridan's cavalry away the work of hauling forage from Fredericksburg also would be curtailed.

Stuart's Last Campaign

Meade had a strong sense of duty, which kept him from asserting his self-importance, contrary to Couch and Sickles, but nevertheless he was irked when Grant went over his head. Late in the war, when Grant was giving orders to Sherman, Meade wrote his wife: "I wonder whether he will smother him as he did me."

Sheridan's independent raid toward Richmond began on the morning of May 9, 1864, and he was absent from the Army of the Potomac for sixteen days. Assembling at Fredericksburg, he had three divisions of seven brigades. The first was commanded by Brigadier General Wesley Merritt, who moved up because Brigadier General A. T. A. Torbert had been disabled; under him the brigades were headed by Major General George A. Custer and Colonel Thomas C. Devin. The second division was under Brigadier General David McM. Gregg, with Brigadier General H. E. Davies, Jr., and Colonel J. Irvin Gregg in command of brigades. The third division was under Brigadier General James H. Wilson, with Colonel John McIntosh and Colonel George H. Chapman. With the batteries and supply train for 12,000 troops Sheridan's command extended thirteen miles when it left Hamilton's Crossing and took the Telegraph Road toward Richmond.

When word reached General Stuart that Sheridan was on his way he sent General William C. Wickham with a brigade in pursuit. Wickham tangled with Sheridan's rear guard at several places with minor results; at Mitchell's Shop, Sheridan's troops stopped a squadron of the Third Virginia in a fight in which that regiment's colonel, Matthews, was mortally wounded. Sheridan crossed the North Anna at Davinport's Bridge and then moved to Beaver Dam, Virginia, where he had a stroke of luck.

Two Confederate railroad trains filled with Federal prisoners from Spotsylvania were at the station, about to start for Richmond. Custer's brigade captured the guards, freed 378 Federal soldiers, destroyed the trains and Confederate warehouses containing 1,500,000 rations and medical stores. During the night his men removed the tracks for a long distance. Stuart's main body caught up with the Federals on May 10 and there were some minor skirmishes on the way to the South Anna, but the Federal force was entirely too large to permit Stuart to start a major battle. Near Ashland, Virginia, General Davies was attacked by Colonel Thomas T. Munford's Second Virginia of Wickham's brigade, while Davies was destroying warehouses, tracks, and trestles.

By hard riding Stuart reached Yellow Tavern in advance of Sheridan and prepared to oppose his ride to Richmond. But until he knew what forces Bragg could muster there he did not know whether to attack Sheridan in front or on the flank. He sent his adjutant general, Colonel H. B. McClellan, to find out, and McClellan returned with word that Bragg had about 4,000 irregulars

and expected to be reinforced by three brigades from
Petersburg. Stuart decided to remain on Sheridan's flank.
General Fitzhugh Lee's brigade had fought with part of
Sheridan's force, during which time the Confederates lost
Colonel H. C. Pate of the Fifth Virginia Cavalry.

At Yellow Tavern, Stuart ordered all cavalry except
the First Virginia to dismount and take positions on the
side of the Telegraph Road, while he placed a battery of
two pieces on a rise in the middle of the road. When
Sheridan's squadrons approached at 4 P.M., May 11, they
charged, overran the two guns, and drove back Stuart's
left. Stuart raced to the road to rally his men. The Federal horsemen belonging to General Custer's brigade
dashed down the road past about eighty Confederates, who
fired at them as they passed. The First Virginia counter-
charged, and the Federals wheeled and rode back to their
main body. A Federal trooper who had been unhorsed
was running alongside the cavalry when he turned, saw a
mounted officer, and fired his pistol at him. He hit Stuart.

Stuart's wound was serious. He called to his men: "Go
back! Go back and do your duty as I have done mine,
and our country will be safe. I had rather die than be
whipped." Stuart was conveyed by ambulance to Richmond, where he died the next day, May 12, 1864. He
was thirty-one years old, had been graduated at West
Point in 1854, and was known for his restless energy,
his tendency to work his troopers hard; his social graces,
and flair for dramatic effects.

The Bloody Angle at Spotsylvania

Spotsylvania is located on a ridge about three miles
long between the Po and the Ni rivers in Virginia. As
General Grant recalled in his memoirs, the Mattaponi
(he spelled it Mattapony) is formed by the junction of
the Mat, Ta, Po, and Ni rivers. By reaching the ridge
first, the Confederate army was able to occupy the high
ground inside the rivers and obstruct Grant's free passage toward Richmond. As Grant saw the armies on
May 9, the Confederate line was in a sort of angular semi-
circle, with Spotsylvania Court House, a small village,
inside. General R. H. Anderson's division of Longstreet's

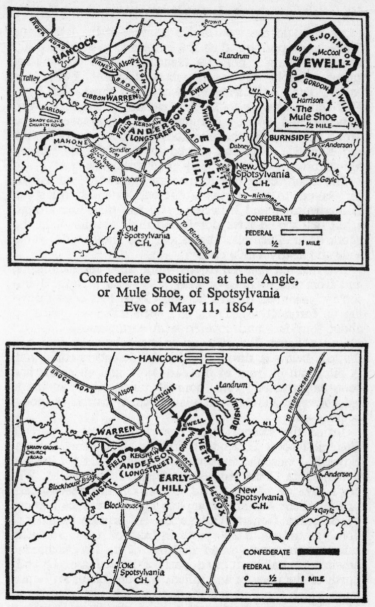

Confederate Positions at the Angle,
or Mule Shoe, of Spotsylvania
Eve of May 11, 1864

Federal attacks at the Bloody Angle, Spotsylvania
May 12, 1864

corps faced to the west and northwest at the left of the Confederate position; then the line came to a sharp peak, almost a triangle, held by General Ewell's corps; then turned sharply southeast, where General Early was posted. The Confederate line was about three miles long. The Union army was at the outside of this line, with Hancock and Warren occupying the right covering the Brock Road; then the line moved around to Sedgwick and Burnside. Hancock moved to the right of Warren, which forced Lee to bring up reinforcements.

The Confederate line formed an "awkward and irregular" salient to the northwest. It was extended when the Confederates found it necessary to run their line around a hill that would have dominated their position if in the hands of the Federals. The salient was about 1,200 yards wide and nearly a mile deep.

Lee realized that the troops would need entrenchments, and from the evening of May 8 General Edward Johnson's division of Ewell's Second Corps had been throwing up fortifications. Trees had been felled and piled up about four feet and covered with earth; above this was placed a heavy log with an aperture between that and the logs below it, through which the defenders could aim. A ditch ran in front of the earthwork and an abatis had been constructed from pointed pines. On the inside ledges were shelves with places where cartridges could be piled up.

Inside the salient, from west to east, stood part of General Robert E. Rodes's division, then came General Edward Johnson's division. At Johnson's right toward Spotsylvania Court House was General Cadmus M. Wilcox's division of the Third Corps. On the western face of the salient was an incomplete line of trenches manned by Brigadier General George Doles's brigade of Rodes's division, and about 200 yards in front of it was a smaller salient with open ground in front of it. The Richmond howitzer battalion formed part of its defense. Directly north of the apex of the salient was the Landrum house, from which the Federals started in their big offensive of May 12; on the northwest a road ran from the Scott house to the salient, a distance of about half a mile. Inside the salient, near where the line of trenches crossed the angle, stood the McCoull house, center of fighting on May 10 and 12; farther south, toward the final line of trenches, stood the Harrison house, near which Lee had his headquarters.

The Sixth Corps under General Sedgwick was sent to Spotsylvania May 8 to take a position at the left of Warren's Fifth Corps and thus near the Federal center. On the morning of May 9 General Sedgwick had supervised the construction of some rifle pits and was warned against exposing himself near a battery of field artillery, because Confederate sharpshooters, some distance away, had been peppering the spot with bullets. When the *zing* of a bullet was heard a soldier threw himself on the ground, and Sedgwick, who was passing by, exclaimed: "Why, my man, I'm ashamed of you, dodging that way. They couldn't hit an elephant at this distance." The soldier replied that he believed in dodging because he had dodged a shell once, and if he had not done so it would have taken his head off. General Sedgwick laughed.

A moment later a sharpshooter's bullet hit Sedgwick in the face and he fell. Blood spurted from the wound, and he died soon after. His body was taken to the headquarters of General Meade, where it rested on a pall of evergreen boughs and was viewed by numerous officers. His military ability was highly esteemed and he was greatly mourned. He was buried at Cornwall Hollow, Connecticut. After the war a monument was erected on the spot where he fell. General Horatio G. Wright of the Third Division was named to the command of the Sixth Corps.

At 6:10 P.M. on May 10 the Second Brigade of Wright's division of the Sixth Corps attacked from the Scott house on the segment of the Confederate line held by General Doles. The onslaught was too powerful to be stopped; Upton's troops pierced the line and overran the position, capturing, they said, up to 1,000 prisoners, including the Richmond howitzers. (The Confederates admitted 300.) General Gershom Mott was to have sent troops in support, but he failed to do so, so that Upton, pushing forward into Gordon's line and finding his flanks in danger of being enveloped, had to withdraw. The action proved to Grant that the Confederate line could be broken. He promoted Upton to brigadier general for his success.

On the morning of May 11, the day after Upton's hard battle, General Grant made a report to Major General Halleck, in the course of which he used the phrase about fighting all summer, which became famous. The dispatch read:

GENERAL: We have now ended the sixth day of very heavy fighting. The result to this time is much in our favor. But our losses have been heavy, as well as those of the enemy. We have lost to this time eleven general officers killed, wounded or missing, and probably twenty thousand men. I think the loss of the enemy must be greater, we having taken over four thousand prisoners in battle, while he has taken but few, except stragglers. I am now sending back to Belle Plain all my wagons for a fresh supply of provisions and ammunition, and propose to fight it out on this line if it takes all summer.

The arrival of reinforcements here will be very encouraging to the men, and I hope they will be sent as fast as possible, and in as great numbers. My object in having them sent to Belle Plain was to use them as an escort to our supply train. If it is more convenient to send them out by train to march from the railroad to Belle Plain or Fredericksburg, send them so.

I am satisfied the enemy are very shaky, and are only kept up to the mark by the greatest exertions on the part of their officers, and by keeping them intrenched in every position they take.

Up to this time there is no indication of any portions of Lee's army being detached for the defense of Richmond.

May 11 was a day of rain and biting winds, adding chilly discomfort to the harassed men manning the lines. The Federals brought no major action, and the Confederates were occupied all day with pick and shovel, adding to their earthworks. In the afternoon the pickets in front of Johnson's lines thought they detected noises that suggested changes in the Union position. As near as they could make out in the commotion raised by the storm the sounds might indicate a withdrawing movement.

General Lee had received reports from another source.

His son W. H. F. Lee, called "Rooney" by his family, had returned to the army after being exchanged. He was a brigadier when captured and on his return was made a major general. He now commanded a division of Stuart's cavalry and reported to his father that Federal wagons had been spotted moving to Fredericksburg, and wounded to Belle Plain. These reports suggested to Lee that the Federals might be withdrawing. If so he intended to be prepared to attack their moving lines. To that end he ordered the withdrawal of advanced batteries from the salient, having them ready for a possible move.

General M. L. Smith of the engineers had decided the salient could be held without artillery. Johnson's troops saw the batteries leaving without knowing the reason. Eventually only eight guns remained in the salient.

General Lee had his headquarters near the Harrison house at the base of the salient. According to a statement by General Heth, which was seen in manuscript by Douglas Southall Freeman, Lee said on the evening of May 11: "This army cannot stand a siege; we must end this business on the battlefield, not in a fortified place."

Not long after the guns were withdrawn General Johnson became disturbed by the movement on the other side of the woods. He decided that a Federal attack was in the making, and his alarm caused the batteries to be ordered back to their former positions.

The noises that Johnson's men had heard were caused by Hancock's massing his brigades to the northwest of the salient. Between 4:30 and 5 A.M., while a chilly fog covered the whole area, brigades from the divisions of General Francis C. Barlow and General David B. Birney, supported by Generals Mott and Gibbon, rushed upon the Confederate entrenchments at the peak of the salient, where stood the brigades of Brigadier General George H. Steuart and Brigadier General John M. Jones. A Virginia battery of Page's battalion had been moved into the apex of the salient, but was able to fire only one round before it was overwhelmed. The Federals found a gap in Jones's brigade and poured in like a torrent; they worked their way behind the Stonewall brigade, commanded by Brigadier General James A. Walker, dis-

arming most of them. By the time they hit the second
Confederate line of resistance they had captured Generals Johnson and Steuart, about 2,000 men and 20 guns,
12 belonging to Page and 8 to Major W. E. Cutshaw.

The new earthwork was located near the McCoull
house and proved a formidable obstacle to the Federal
attack. It was fought over for the rest of the day and
here occurred the greatest loss of life. General John B.
Gordon was in command most of the time. He checked
the Federal advance with three brigades, and while he
was bringing up new troops he observed that General Lee
had ridden up from the Harrison house and was moving
along with the troops. General Gordon stopped to remonstrate with him. "Go back, General, this is no place for
you. We will drive them back," shouted Gordon, and the
men nearby repeated his words. This was another of the
"Lee to the rear!" incidents. A sergeant took hold of
Lee's horse and led it toward the rear.

What happened that day in the salient was the worst
that could come to bodies of frantically fighting men.
Hancock's brigades held on as the troops of the Confederate First Corps tried again and again to dislodge
them. There was dogged fighting by Johnston's North
Carolina and Pegram's Virginia brigades; Rodes and
Ramseur, endeavoring to regain the Confederate breastworks, lost all semblance of organization. The Federals
threw in fresh divisions of Sedgwick's Sixth Corps, now
commanded by General Wright, while General Warren's
troops fought with Anderson's division on the west front,
where Anderson held his ground. Wilcox with the Confederate Third Corps drove the Federals back on the
right. But they could not push the Federal troops out of
the salient. While Gordon moved up some brigades,
others were put to work building a new line of defense
at the base of the salient, about 1,500 feet south of the
McCoull house line. In the meantime the soldiers fighting at the breastworks there had only one order: to hold
on, which for many of them meant a fight to the death.

Nothing in the war equaled the ferocity at the Bloody
Angle of Spotsylvania, not even the peak of Pickett's
charge at Gettysburg.

The fighting at the Angle was frenzied, maniacal. Men

lost all semblance to human beings as they shot, clubbed, and grappled with one another across the breastworks. Guns of the Fifth U. S. Artillery, pushed up to the trench, poured canister into hordes of human bodies, only to lose the cannoneers in the common bloodletting. At times the lines were four deep and every bullet hit a man, no matter how aimed. The area was thick with gunsmoke and soaked by rain. "The mud was halfway to our knees and by our constant movement the fallen were almost buried at our feet." Mortars 800 yards in the rear plumped shells into Confederates crowded behind the breastworks. A group of twenty to thirty Confederates held up cloth torn from tents in a plea of surrender; the Union men yelled for them to come on. They jumped upon the breastworks, hesitated; within a moment they were filled with bullets by their own men behind them. Several oak trees were so thoroughly gnawed by crossfire that at 3 P.M. they toppled inside the Confederate lines.

At midnight on May 12 the firing at the Angle ceased. The Confederates withdrew, leaving the terrain and its heaps of dead to the Union army. The next day, with rain still falling, burial parties attempted to cover the dead. At the fortified line the diggers simply shoveled the breastworks over them.

Of the great army that Grant led into the Wilderness, 26,815 were incapacitated after Spotsylvania, either as killed or wounded, while 4,173 were missing, most of them captured. Only the Union made an official report, which was: Wilderness, 2,246 killed, 12,037 wounded, 3,383 missing; Spotsylvania, 2,725 killed, 13,416 wounded, 2,258 missing. The casualties at Spotsylvania on May 12 were estimated by Major General A. A. Humphreys as 13,268 for the Union army and over 10,000 for the Confederate, but the latter did not make a statement of losses for the whole.

32

FROM SPOTSYLVANIA TO COLD HARBOR

Five days of almost continuous rain at Spotsylvania made Grant tell General Halleck on May 16, 1864: "You can assure the President and Secretary of War that the elements alone have suspended hostilities, and that it is in no manner due to weakness or exhaustion on our part." The roads were so bad that even the ambulances could not carry the wounded to Fredericksburg. And yet Grant could assert that "the army is in the best of spirits."

On May 18 an assault by Generals Hancock and Wright in an attempt to recover their former position was stopped by Lee. Grant noted that all the news was bad; Sigel defeated at New Market, Butler at Drewry's Bluff, Banks in Louisiana. But Grant ordered a movement south on the left flank for May 19, and asked that Port Royal on the Rappahannock be made his new base of supplies.

Lee, finding an opening on the Federal right, attacked May 19 with Ewell's Second Army Corps, with General Early's division in reserve. He hit 6,000 raw troops commanded by Brigadier General Robert O. Taylor that were to join Hancock's corps. Generals David B. Birney and Samuel W. Crawford, the latter with the Pennsylvania Reserves, repulsed Ewell and took a number of prisoners.

At this juncture Grant decided he had more artillery than he could conveniently bring into action at any one time, so he sent over 100 pieces back to the defenses of Washington. This cleared the roads of more than 200 six-horse teams and cut down the hauling of forage. He reduced the artillery again before reaching the James. The disclosure that a large number of guns can handicap an army is remarkable, since Grant started the Wilderness campaign with 274, against Lee's 234, and he would now have fewer than Lee. On May 18 Lee was writing Richmond that he could not attack Grant's strong line without great loss of men, because Grant's artillery was superior in weight of metal and range.

There was one astute Federal officer, Brigadier General Henry J. Hunt, chief of artillery, who had built up the artillery reserve that proved highly useful at Malvern Hill, Chancellorsville, and Gettysburg, who did not think cutting down on guns in order to save transport was an advantage. He wrote later: "When, in 1864, in the Rapidan campaign, it [the artillery reserve] was 'got rid of,' it reconstituted itself, without orders, and in a few weeks, through the necessities of the Army, showing that 'principles vindicate themselves.' "

On May 20 Grant put his army in motion for a left-flank movement toward Richmond, through the lush countryside that had not yet been hit by the fighting. With Hancock's corps in the van, the route led to Guiney's Station on the Richmond & Fredericksburg Railroad, then south to Bowling Green and Milford. General Warren's corps followed, while those of Burnside and Wright were delayed at Spotsylvania to mislead Lee. Grant believed Lee missed a great opportunity by not striking each corps separately, but he was prepared to move the others in support if this had happened. Burnside and Wright moved out on the night of May 21, when Grant had his headquarters with Wright at Guiney's and the Confederates tried a slight probing attack. There were clashes between the troops of Hancock and Ewell as the Union army proceeded to the Mattaponi and the North Anna.

The Confederates already had taken strong positions on the North Anna, with entrenchments on both banks. Hancock drove off the opposition at the North Anna bridge on the evening of May 23, crossing next day. Warren's vanguard waded across at Jericho Ford, several miles upstream, and laid pontoons, and his corps entrenched on the south bank. The Confederates assaulted in force that night but were thrown back with loss. But when Burnside attempted to cross at Ox Ford, he discovered Lee's center strongly posted on the south bank, too strong to attack. Fortunately a usable ford was found between Ox Ford and Jericho, but when Major General Thomas L. Critten-den was sent across he was strongly attacked by units of Lieutenant General A. P. Hill's command and suffered severely, though he held his own.

Lee's withdrawal to the North Anna while interposing strong obstacles between Grant and Richmond provides an excellent example of his military astuteness. Always working with smaller numbers, Lee kept pace with Grant's advance, anticipated his crossings, and finally forced Grant to take a new direction. Lee's dispatches to President Davis at this time show his determination to guard the main route to Richmond and strike Grant while he was moving.

Grant saw the difficulty of dislodging the Confederates in this position and proposed crossing the Pamunkey River, which is formed by the North Anna and the South Anna. He informed Halleck: "Lee is really whipped. The prisoners we now take show it, and the action of his army shows it unmistakably. A battle with them outside of entrenchments cannot be had. . . . I may be mistaken, but I feel that our success over Lee's army is already assured." Grant was mistaken. Despite the attrition that was wearing down the Confederate strength, there was tremendous fighting energy left, which was to cost Grant many men.

On May 26 General Grant informed Halleck:

To make a direct attack from either wing would cause a slaughter of our men that even success would not justify. To turn the enemy by his right, between the two Annas [North and South Anna rivers] is impossible on account of the swamp upon which his right rests. To turn him by the left leaves Little River, New Found River and South Anna River, all of them streams presenting considerable obstacles to the movement of our army, to be crossed. I have determined therefore to turn the enemy's right by crossing at or near Hanover Town. This crosses all three streams at once, and leaves us still where we can draw supplies.

On the night of May 26 Grant took the army back where they came from, to the north side of the North Anna, and placed the Pamunkey between himself and the Confederates. The army marched with Wright in the van, Hancock at the rear, the reverse of the movement from Spotsylvania. Sheridan's cavalry reached Hanover Ferry on the morning of May 27 and Wright's corps arrived soon after. The whole army was across the Pamunkey May 28.

Grant now ordered his supplies to be based at White House Landing on the Pamunkey, where they had been during McClellan's Peninsular campaign. Hanover Town was twenty miles from White House and twelve miles from Mechanicsville and Meadow Bridge over the Chickahominy. Although Grant had left units behind to mask the withdrawal of his army from in front of Lee, the latter reacted early to the change by occupying Hanover Court House, fifteen miles northwest of Hanover Town. In rapid movements Lee placed his forces so that they extended beyond Totopotomoy Creek, with his right on Shady Grove Church, his right center near Atlee's Station on the Gordonsville Railroad, where Lee made his headquarters; his left at Hanover Court House.

While General Lee was contracting his defensive line and keeping Grant from finding an open road to Richmond he spoke hopefully of his ability to defeat Grant. But his dispatches to President Davis at Richmond warned repeatedly that he must have more troops. He wanted greatly to have help from General Beauregard, but the latter was reluctant to yield any troops. On May 23 Lee pointed out to President Davis that if General B. F. Butler was too strongly situated to be attacked, no more Confederate troops would be needed there than were necessary to keep him in the entrenchments. But since Grant's army was to be "strengthened by all available troops from the North," it would be better policy to "unite on it and crush it." "I should be very glad to have the aid of General Beauregard in such a blow," said Lee, believing in the success of a united effort. Lee did not want Grant to approach the Chickahominy and did not see why he and Beauregard could not combine against him after he had crossed the Pamunkey, or fight together on the Chickahominy if they were forced.

Beauregard had a different view; he thought Lee should hold a defensive line on the Chickahominy and send troops to himself, so that he could defeat Butler and prevent the union of Butler and Grant. Lee had fought on the Chickahominy before and did not favor a battle of position there; he preferred to check Grant while Grant had the outer line and was in motion.

Two days later Lee warned President Davis that Grant was getting strong reinforcements. An intercepted dispatch from Grant to Burnside informed Lee that, up to May 15, 24,700 men had sailed from Washington to join Grant. "If General Beauregard is in condition to unite with me in any operation against General Grant I should like to know it and at what point a combination could be made most advantageous to him," wrote Lee. On May 28 Lee, outlining the routes taken by Grant, again suggested a way for Beauregard to unite with him; Lee would deliver battle on a field nearer Richmond if this were more convenient to Beauregard. On May 29 the two generals conferred at Lee's headquarters; Beauregard was convinced that with only 12,000 to bottle up Butler (actually 13,000 infantry, 850 artillery, 680 cavalry, total 14,530) he could spare no troops. Lee therefore told Richmond briefly that he would engage Grant with the force he had. Beauregard had warned Jefferson Davis that Richmond would be endangered if he divided his force to reinforce Lee.

But the next day Lee found out that Butler was about to send troops to Grant; this was the transfer of General W. F. Smith's corps via steamers from Bermuda Hundred down the James River to White House Landing on the Pamunkey. Lee now asked for troops from the Richmond garrison, where Major General Robert Ransom had nearly 7,000 effectives. This time his warning was more emphatic: "If this army is unable to resist Grant the troops under General Beauregard and in the city will be unable to defend it."

That evening he wired that Beauregard had left the decision to the War Department. "The result of this delay will be disaster," said Lee. "Butler's troops will be with Grant tomorrow. Hoke's at least should be with me at 8 tomorrow." That settled the issue for General Bragg and President Davis in Richmond. Beauregard also had a sudden change of view. He informed General Bragg that he felt authorized by an earlier letter of the President's to send reinforcements. He was just a few minutes ahead of Bragg's order, which had been prepared before Beauregard's concession came. Hoke's brigade was put on trains and started for Richmond.

To determine Lee's intentions Grant had Sheridan reconnoiter toward Hanover Court House. At Haw's Shop, Brigadier General David Gregg's Second Division came upon an entrenched position manned by dismounted Confederate cavalry under General Wade Hampton and General Fitzhugh Lee, supported by a brigade of South Carolina infantry. Several hours of severe fighting brought no decision until Gregg was reinforced by a brigade under Brigadier General George A. Custer, which, according to the report, marched up with its band playing. The combined forces of dismounted cavalry fell upon the Confederates and overran their position. Union casualties were put at 228; the Confederates lost about twice that number.

At 5 P.M. on May 30 when Major General Warren's Fifth Corps was marching to the Union left by way of the Mechanicsville Road, Lieutenant General Jubal A. Early, who had succeeded to Ewell's command, attacked with considerable force and pushed back Brigadier General Samuel W. Crawford's Third Division, opening the Union left to the danger of a flank attack. General Meade thereupon ordered an attack by General Hancock's Second Corps, and the troops assaulted the Confederates in their front just before dark. They captured rifle pits and held them through the night, despite a midnight attempt of the Confederates to dislodge them. Warren was thereby enabled to hold his ground, and Burnside was moved up to be ready to support him.

Another cavalry action took place on May 30 when Brigadier General Torbert was attacked at 2 P.M. near Old Church and in a three-hour battle pushed the Confederate cavalry back on Cold Harbor. At about the same time Brigadier General James H. Wilson, sent to cut the Virginia Central Railroad, clashed with Brigadier General P. M. B. Young's brigade of Hampton's cavalry and occupied Hanover Court House.

On May 31 Sheridan attacked two brigades of cavalry under General Fitzhugh Lee near the crossroads of Cold Harbor (sometimes called Old Cold Harbor). Lee also had Clingman's brigade of infantry from General Hoke's division in support. Sheridan pushed them back some distance and was about to retire when he received orders to hold his ground until night.

The Confederates were as determined to dominate Cold Harbor as the Federals were to keep them from it. Cold Harbor was only a tavern, a well, and a crossroads, but the roads made it an important spot. It received its name from the old English practice of calling a tavern that offered lodging but no meals a cold harbor. Control of its roads would interfere with Federal communications with White House. It was only a short distance from Gaines' Mill and Mechanicsville, and the roads had been used often during McClellan's Peninsular campaign in 1862.

When General Fitzhugh Lee reported to General Lee on May 31 that the Federals were advancing toward Cold Harbor, Lee saw an opportunity to turn Grant's flank before his troops were strong enough to make a stand. He moved Anderson's division out of the line between Breckinridge and Early and placed it near Beulah Church, one mile northwest of Cold Harbor. General Hoke's division was to act under Anderson's orders. This would give Lee about 15,000 troops to arrest the Federal line and turn it back in confusion on its marching columns. The attack was to be made at dawn on June 1.

The Confederates were in position by the required time, with Kershaw's brigade in the lead. The road to Cold Harbor was held by General Sheridan's cavalry corps, dismounted, heavily armed with repeating carbines and including horse artillery. They fought behind light entrenchments, but their numbers were far inferior to those Anderson could bring up.

But Anderson's attack foundered on the first move. Leadership in the attack had been given to the Twentieth South Carolina Regiment, which only recently had arrived from garrison duty in that state and had been added to Kershaw's brigade. It was led by a forty-year-old lawyer, Lawrence M. Keitt, who had been a member of the United States Congress before the war. Keitt led the attack against Sheridan's seasoned troopers, riding ahead of his brigade with his sword raised, thus providing a perfect target. He fell almost at the outset, and Sheridan's carbines created so much havoc in the ranks of his regiment that the men broke and ran for cover, thereby exposing the second brigade to similar confusion. General Anderson tried to direct a new attack but had no cooperation from Hoke, and when Wright's Sixth Corps arrived to support Sheridan the day's opportunity was lost.

General W. F. Smith's Eighteenth Corps, coming from Bermuda Hundred to White House, was the victim of mixed orders that caused it to march many miles out of its way over dusty roads under the broiling sun. After posting 2,500 men to guard the base at White House, Smith set out on the afternoon of May 30 with about 10,000 infantry and artillery, but without supply wagons of food or ammunition. That evening General Grant sent specific instructions for him to march up the south bank of the Pamunkey to New Castle. Grant informed Smith that Sheridan was keeping watch on the left flank as far out on the Mechanicsville and Cold Harbor roads as he could go. He assured Smith that any movement of the Confederates toward Smith would be seen and followed up. The position of the Army of the Potomac, Grant explained, was as follows: the left of the Fifth Corps was on the Shady Grove Road, extending to the Mechanicsville Road and about three miles south of Totopotomoy creek. The Ninth Corps was to the right of the Fifth, then came the Second and Sixth, forming a line on the road from Hanover Court House to Cold Harbor, and about six miles south of the Court House.

At daylight on June 1, Smith, then in camp three miles from New Castle, received an order from Grant's headquarters to proceed at once to New Castle Ferry and take a position between the Fifth and Sixth Corps. Thinking this an emergency, he hurried the troops off without breakfast, and on reaching New Castle found no troops there. Then he received word from General Grant that a mistake had been made; the order should have read Cold Harbor instead of New Castle. In the ensuing march many men became exhausted and dropped out of the ranks. While en route Smith received an order from Meade to form at the right of the Sixth Corps, hold a line from

Bethesda Church to Cold Harbor, and join the Sixth in an attack. This line was six miles long, and Smith wondered how he was to hold it with only 10,000 troops and at the same time deliver an assault.

On the night of May 31 Grant had ordered Wright's Sixth Corps to move up from the extreme right, and when Lee learned of this early next morning he had Anderson's division do likewise. As units of Anderson's command passed near Warren's front, Warren was ordered to attack him in the flank while Wright would attack in front. Warren was unable to do more than use his artillery and explained this was because of his extended line. Wright and Smith were not ready to attack until afternoon. When Smith decided that he would join in the attack rather than hold the line—since he couldn't do both—he sent word to Meade that his troops had no ammunition beyond what was in their cartridge boxes.

The terrain in front of Wright and Smith was open for several hundred yards and then came a wood in which the Confederates had dug rifle pits. Directly in front of the Federals were the Confederate divisions of Major General Robert F. Hoke, just arrived from Beauregard's army, Brigadier General Joseph Kershaw, and Major General George E. Pickett. At a little after 4:30 P.M. the Union troops rushed forward across the open space and headed for the Confederate lines. The units of Brigadier General William Brooks and Brigadier General Charles Devens opened the fighting. They were met by a heavy musket fire, but Clingman's brigade of Hoke's division, which lacked the experience of old campaigners, gave way and the Federals bagged about 250 prisoners. It was a different story on the left where Brigadier General David A. Russell attacked. His troops were hard hit by a galling fire both in front and flank, and he was wounded. He ordered the men to lie flat to hold their position and remained with them the rest of the action.

That night General Smith sent headquarters another call for ammunition, and received an order from General Meade to attack next day with his "whole force and as vigorously as possible." Smith's reaction may be deduced from his curt response to his commanding general; any attempt to attack in his present condition was "preposterous," he declared; he would be overrun. He reported that he had called on General Wright for 100,-000 rounds of ammunition. During the night a new order postponed the attack of June 2 to 5 P.M. At 2:30 P.M. next day General Meade issued another order, announcing that the attack would take place at 4:30 A.M. on June 3.

By this time General Lee was recovering from the disability that had tied him to an ambulance cot and was able to make a short stay at headquarters at Gaines' Mill, where the mill, which had survived the rigors of the Peninsular campaign, had been burned down by Sheridan's raiders only a few weeks before. During the night of June 1 and the day of June 2 the opposing forces were occupied in transferring units and strengthening lines in anticipation of harder fighting to come. Lee expected Grant to attack June 2 and was puzzled when he didn't. Grant shifted Hancock to the left of Wright at the right of the Federal line; Burnside was placed at Bethesda Church in reserve and his trenches ran right across the Old Church Road. The Federal line, from northwest to southeast, now comprised Burnside, Warren, Smith, Wright, and Hancock. Opposed in the same order were Heth, the three divisions under Early—Rodes, Gordon, and Ramseur—then three of Richard Anderson's corps—Field, Pickett, and Kershaw—then Hoke, Breckinridge, and Wilcox, the last almost touching Grapevine Bridge on the Chickahominy. A. P. Hill's divisions were moved from the extreme Confederate left to the right beside Wilcox, with Mahone in reserve.

The final assault to dislodge the Confederates from their entrenched positions took place as scheduled on the morning of June 3 and is the principal action of the Battle of Cold Harbor. It proved to be the most costly assault ever delivered by the Union army in a single maneuver, for it left Grant's finest veteran troops in heaps of dead and wounded in front of the Confederate lines. At 4:30 A.M. a signal gun was fired by the Tenth Massachusetts Light Battery of Hancock's corps. The battalions of three corps moved forward through clearings, woods, and swamps. During the night it had rained and dusty areas of the day before were now puddles and mud.

Hancock's Second Corps advanced at the right, opposing the troops of Breckinridge and Wilcox; Wright's Sixth Corps was moving against Kershaw and Hoke, with Smith's Eighteenth Corps at its right. The contours of the terrain made it difficult for one corps to keep track of another's advance. A deadly artillery fire fell upon the advancing troops, augmented by a continuous blaze of musketry, for the Confederates had become proficient in keeping guns loaded for unbroken firing. The First Division of Hancock's corps under Brigadier General Francis C. Barlow drove in the Confederate first line and took three guns, but the fire from the second line sent its men reeling. Eight colonels in Hancock's corps died in the first assault. Smith's brigades cleared out rifle pits at his front but lost heavily.

Men fell so rapidly that the troops were ordered to lie down, where they were often at the mercy of sharpshooters. The separate advance of the corps caused them to move on divergent lines and opened them to enfilading fire. The commanding officers rushed a spate of messages back to Meade demanding that artillery silence the enfilading batteries. An order from headquarters to the corps commanders told each to attack with his entire forces without reference to the movement of troops at left or right. A few units responded, others, unable to advance, merely kept on firing. A third order demanded a general assault along the whole line; to execute it was, in the words of Major General Martin T. McMahon, "a simple and absolute impossibility." The units remained where they lay. Such a tragic episode had not happened in four years of desperate fighting.

In half an hour Grant had 7,000 casualties. By 7:30 A. M. fighting had ceased. Grant thereupon consulted the front-line corps commanders to see what they had gained and what they thought could be won by further fighting. The commanders differed; Burnside was hopeful; Hancock and Warren doubted success could be obtained; Wright thought something might be gained with the help of Hancock and Smith, and Smith thought this possible, but was not "sanguine." At noon Grant called

off the attacks and told Meade reconnaissances should be
made in front of every corps, also "advances to advantageous positions by regular approaches." He warned all to
be ready to resist an assault, especially if the Confederates broke through Smith's lines. But the Confederates
did not attempt one.

Wounded Die While Generals Argue

The wounded from three days' fighting lay strung out on
the terrain over which the Federal assaults had been
made; they lay there in the broiling sun and in the damp
of the night, and their groans dismayed the troops
close at hand that could not reach them. No man dared
go into the open by day to rescue a soldier, for Confederate sharpshooters were all through the opposite
woods. Also, only at night could the troops throw up
entrenchments. Major General William F. Smith of the
Eighteenth Corps wrote: "For three days no cessation of
hostilities was asked for, and common rumor gave as a
reason that there was fear of a refusal, as there were
no dead or wounded of the enemy between the lines to be
cared for. Some of our wounded were brought in by men
who risked their lives in the act, and some were rescued
by digging trenches to them. The groans of such as could
not be reached grew fainter and fainter until they ceased."

General Grant, in his *Personal Memoirs*, explained
the long-drawn-out negotiations with General Lee to rescue the wounded. His account is quite dispassionate, and
it makes a dismal record of the obstacles that military
procedure placed in the way of humane measures. Grant
opened the correspondence on June 5, and, briefly summarized, these wordy documents were: (1) Grant suggested that when no battle was raging, either party be
authorized to send unarmed men bearing litters to pick
up the dead or wounded without being fired on, and he
was willing to accept any other method to this end that
Lee might name; (2) Lee replied saying this might lead
to misunderstanding and proposed a flag of truce; (3)
Grant's rejoinder on June 6 (with wounded still lying
out there) agreed that both sides carry a white flag and
start between the hours of 12 noon and 3 P.M.; (4) Lee

said he could not agree to this method but that when either party wanted such permission they should ask for it by a flag of truce; (5) Grant replied that the wounded needed attention and he asked a cessation of hostilities for this purpose, at whatever hours Lee would fix; (6) Lee agreed, but it had taken forty-eight hours to get this small request finally agreed to. Lee presumably set the hours, for Grant's next letter explains that it took four hours for Lee's message to reach him and then the time to pick up the wounded had passed. He closed his letter with: "Regretting that all my efforts for alleviating the sufferings of wounded men left upon the battlefield have been rendered nugatory, I remain, etc. . . ."

The Federal losses at Cold Harbor were exceptionally large. Grant published a report from the office of the adjutant general, which placed the casualties from May 31 to June 12 at 1,769 killed, 6,752 wounded, and 1,537 missing, a total of 10,058. Many of the missing were obviously dead. Thomas L. Livermore concentrates on June 1 to 3 and has 10,922 killed and wounded, and 1,816 missing. General Humphreys reported that after the fighting of June 1 to 4 the Union field hospitals had 8,913 wounded men, which gives a good idea of the terrible toll taken by the Confederates. The Confederate losses were much lower, but no accurate figure has been preserved. The *Official Records* estimate of 1,200 killed and wounded and 500 missing is probably too low.

General Lee's report of the Union assault of the morning of June 3 was sent to Davis at 1 P.M., when the fighting was over. His expression is as factual as that of Julius Caesar on the Gallic campaigns. "So far every attack of the enemy has been repulsed," he wrote. "The only impression made on our line was at a salient of General Breckinridge's position, where the enemy broke through and captured front of a battalion. He was immediately driven out with severe loss by General Finnegan's brigade & the Md. battalion and the line restored." At 8:45 P.M. he reported to Secretary of War Seddon: "Repeated attacks were made upon General Anderson's position, chiefly against his right, under General Kershaw. They were met with great steadiness and repulsed in every instance. The attack extended to our extreme left,

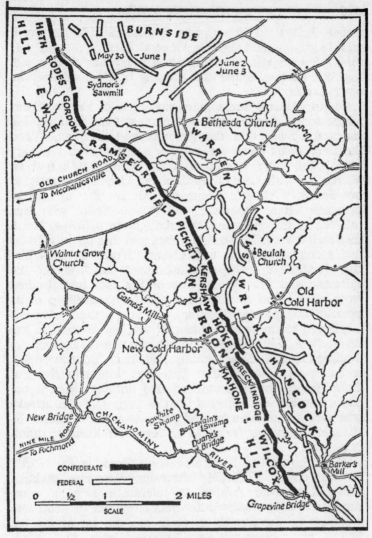

The Battle of Cold Harbor
June 3, 1864

under General Early with like results. Later in the day it
was twice renewed against General Heth . . . but was
repulsed with loss. . . . Our loss today has been small,
and our success, under the blessing of God, all that we
could expect."

Major General Smith made no secret of his utter contempt for General Meade's orders at Cold Harbor. He
asserted openly that the generals had no plan. When
the third order came for another assault on that bloody
field Smith flatly refused to obey. Later Smith had an
altercation with General Butler, and Grant was ready to
put Smith in Butler's command, but Butler was able to
persuade Grant otherwise and it was Smith who was
relieved of his command of the Eighteenth Corps. Smith
disclosed later in his war reminiscences that on July 10 he
had a confidential talk with Grant. "I tried to show him
the blunders of the late campaign of the Army of the
Potomac and the terrible loss of life that had resulted
from what I had considered a want of generalship in its
present commander [Meade]. Among other instances
I referred to the fearful slaughter at Cold Harbor on the
3d of June. General Grant went into the discussion, defending General Meade stoutly, but finally acknowledged,
to use his own words 'that there had been a butchery at
Cold Harbor, but that he had said nothing about it because it could do no good.' " The author of the attacks
was Grant, not Meade, and later Grant told Smith he
thought Smith was trying to hit him over Meade's shoulders.

Great hopes had been pinned on Grant in the North,
but the costly Wilderness campaign dampened enthusiasm. Many who refused to tolerate talk of a com-
promised peace accepted the mounting toll of dead and
wounded as the terrible price to be paid for saving the
Union. No concessions were expected from the Confederates, for although short of provisions and losing manpower their armies still fought with demoniac fury.
Fortunately the North could take some comfort in the
steady progress of General Sherman, who seemed to be
accomplishing his purposes without the heavy grinding
down of human lives that accompanied the slow movements of Grant.

Secretary of the Treasury Chase wrote in May, 1864, that the military successes people talked about evaded him: Grant had achieved very little, and that little at great cost. "Still my hope is with him. He seems the ablest and most persistent man we have. Sherman has done well and apparently more than Grant."

Officially President Lincoln had to express continued confidence to keep up the Northern morale; at the Sanitary Fair in Philadelphia, a few weeks after Cold Harbor, he admitted that the war, in its magnitude and duration, was one of the most terrible, but hoped it would never end without re-establishment of the national authority over the national domain. Turning a phrase of Grant's to his own purposes Lincoln said: "Speaking of the present campaign General Grant is reported to have said: 'I am going through on this line if it takes all summer.'. . . I say we are going through on this line if it takes three years more." Actually Grant had told General Halleck when in the midst of the Spotsylvania battles: "I propose to fight it out on this line if it takes all summer." Lincoln continued: "I have never been in the habit of making predictions in regard to the war, but I am almost tempted to make one . . . that Grant is this evening, with General Meade and General Hancock, and the brave officers and soldiers with him, in a position from which he will never be dislodged until Richmond is taken."

Thus Lincoln tried to keep up the morale in the North and his supporters echoed his confidence, but with heavy hearts and much discouragement. The opposing Democrats and peace advocates were loudly denouncing Grant and his campaign and preparing for the national conventions, hoping to unseat Lincoln in the fall election. The disaster of Cold Harbor was not easily brushed aside. Although there had been greater losses in other attacks, the enormity of the casualties in a brief period of time, the fact that frontal attacks had been made over a widely extended terrain without proper support or adequate artillery protection on the flanks, and the contradictory character of some of the orders, caused general criticism of the commanding general. Grant did not talk much about the battle at the time, but in his *Personal Memoirs* he wrote, twenty years later, that he regretted the last assault at Cold Harbor, and likewise that of May 22, 1863, at Vicksburg. He admitted that no advantage was gained to compensate for the heavy loss.

Grant had become convinced that he would have to adopt a new strategy in order to overcome Lee's resistance and bring the war to an early close. Wearing down Lee by attacking his positions north of Richmond was too slow and demanded too great a sacrifice of life; Grant would augment it by getting across the lines of supply that fed Lee's army. These were south of Richmond, with Petersburg the principal rail center for supplies from the Southern depots and granaries. With Lee's lines only forty yards away he would withdraw his troops, pass on pontoon bridges the unpredictable Chickahominy that had made so much difficulty for McClellan, cross the James River on pontoons, and move around to Petersburg. Adam Badeau, in *A Military History of U. S. Grant*, said this operation "transcended in difficulty and danger any that he had attempted in this campaign." He wrote:

The whole plan of the national commander at this juncture assumed magnificent proportions. Sherman was advancing towards Atlanta and the sea, and General Edward R. S. Canby, commander of the Department of the Gulf, had been ordered to begin the attack against Mobile to meet him, so that the rebel forces west of the mountains were all engaged; Hunter was moving up the Valley of Virginia; Crook and Averell were converging from the West and Southwest, to cut off entirely the supplies reaching Richmond from these directions; Sheridan was advancing to complete the destruction and isolation on the North, while Grant himself moved with the bulk of his forces against Petersburg and the Southern railroads.

33

EARLY THREATENS WASHINGTON

Although the number of troops that Lee had available for the defense of Richmond after Cold Harbor were fewer than the ever-growing army of Grant, he had the audacity to detach some of them for purposes elsewhere if the necessity arose. Even when uncertain of Grant's next move and warned that it might be against Petersburg, Lee on June 12, 1864, ordered Lieutenant General Jubal A. Early to lead the Second Corps from its position at Gaines' Mill to the Shenandoah Valley, with the primary object of stopping the house-burning and pillaging carried on by General David Hunter on the route to Lynchburg. Here Early's corps would combine with the forces of General John C. Breckinridge, who had fought General Sigel at New Market in May and who also was headed for Lynchburg. In the ensuing campaign Early would have the top command.

In addition, Lee also had in mind a diversion that might take some of the Federal pressure from his front. If Early could dispose of Hunter, he was free to move up the Valley, cross the Potomac near Leesburg, in Loudoun County, or at or above Harpers Ferry, and threaten Washington. Lee knew how jealously the Federal government watched over the safety of its capital, and his experience told him that any feint in that direction would call for Federal reinforcement. But apparently Lee did not plan to capture the capital. Early has testified that when he suggested this to Lee, the latter said it would be impossible. But as always Lee expected his generals to profit by changing conditions.

This was especially true after Early had blocked Hunter at Lynchburg and begun the pursuit of the Federals. Lee was now defending a line that included Petersburg, and Grant was actively challenging him. But even in this emergency Lee weighed the possibilities. He asked Early whether he wanted to continue with their plan or rejoin the army at Petersburg. Early decided to carry on. Lee continued to send instructions and suggestions, and again said he would let Early determine whether the condition of his troops would permit a movement across the Potomac.

Breckinridge's infantry division comprised the brigades of Generals John Echols, Gabriel C. Wharton, and John C. Vaughn, the last being dismounted cavalrymen. In order to give Breckinridge a command commensurate with his distinction Early placed General John A. Gordon's division under his orders. The Stonewall brigade was now commanded by Brigadier General William Terry. Other troops in Early's expedition were the divisions of Major Generals R. E. Rodes and S. D. Ramseur. The Cavalry under Major General Robert Ransom had brigades commanded by Generals McCausland, Imboden, W. L. Jackson, and Bradley T. Johnson. The three battalions of artillery were commanded by Lieutenant Colonel J. Floyd King. Early's infantry numbered slightly more than 10,000. They were poorly shod, many of them being barefoot, and they lacked sufficient food. Shoes had been ordered, but did not arrive until after the men had tramped through the mountains and were near Frederick, Maryland.

One of Early's assigned tasks was to destroy bridges and railroads that served the Federals, especially the bridges of the Baltimore & Ohio Railroad and the locks of the Chesapeake & Ohio canal. At Martinsburg the Federals had a big supply depot, and here Major General Franz Sigel had about 5,000 men. The advance of the Confederates, whose numbers were put as high as 20,000 by alarmed country folk, unnerved Sigel. He sent Colonel James Mulligan and the Twenty-third Illinois to reconnoiter. Mulligan clashed with General Johnson's cavalry at Leetown and was driven back at first, but later, with support of a unit from Sigel, he pushed Johnson back and retarded Early's advance sufficiently to enable Sigel to evacuate Martinsburg with a long wagon train and railroad cars filled with supplies. Sigel had to leave behind warehouses filled with food and equipment, as well as heaps of packages intended for individual soldiers. These were plundered by men of Gordon's division, who unexpectedly acquired not only necessities but delicacies such as they had not tasted for years.

Sigel crossed the Potomac at Williamsport and took his troops to Maryland Heights. General Max Weber evacuated Harpers Ferry, destroying some stores but leaving plenty intact for the Confederates. He, too, retreated to Maryland Heights, burning the railroad and pontoon bridges across the Potomac. While the Confederate columns under Generals Gordon and Breckinridge drove the Federals back into their fortifications, the principal aim of Early's divisions was to keep moving on the roads through South Mountain. Only General McCausland went farther afield, for Early sent him to Hagerstown, where he levied on the citizens for $20,000, said to have been a misunderstanding of Early's instruction to get $200,000.

On July 6, when Early was resting at Sharpsburg, Lee sent a courier—none other than his son Robert—to inform Early of a new development that might have farreaching effect. He reported that an attempt was to be made on July 12 to free more than 17,000 Confederate prisoners at Point Lookout, on the tip of Maryland, where the Potomac flows into Chesapeake Bay. Early was to arrange to have a cavalry force in the direction of Baltimore, and apparently merge the Confederates into his army as soon as they were freed. The "threat to Washington" was assuming new proportions.

Early did not describe the plans for seizing the Point Lookout camp, and probably did not know them. The daring scheme was directed by Colonel John Taylor Wood, grandson of President Zachary Taylor and nephew of President Jefferson Davis by his first marriage. Lee commented to Davis: "If any human agency can insure success I think it will be accomplished by Colonel Wood, to whom I would be willing to trust the operations on land as well as sea." This ambitious enterprise was to start from Wilmington, N. C., and use gunboats to attack the camp. Colonel Wood proposed to send a boat to Cherrystone to cut the telegraph wire to Old Point Comfort, and, if possible, the wire that ran from there to Washington. Major General W. H. C. Whiting, at Wilmington, was instructed to provide Wood with two 20-pound Parrott guns.

The greatest caution was observed in discussing the proposed expedition, but Lee's son, Major General W. H. F. Lee, who was acting with Wood, reported that it was gossiped about on the street in Wilmington. General Robert E. Lee said it would not be safe to "throw across the Potomac any party," because the advance to the river would be dangerous. He recommended sending with Colonel Wood some officer known to the prisoners, and to sort them out quickly for military service in cavalry, artillery, and infantry units. The scheme was full of possibilities, for Washington and environs had great stores of small arms, which might be captured. But the hazards were so great that the whole plan was abandoned on order of President Davis before Early was near Washington. The Confederates learned later that on July 10 the Federal government began removing prisoners from Point Lookout.

As soon as Washington learned how Sigel had been pushed out of Martinsburg and Early was marching toward the Potomac, the wildest rumors began to circulate. General Halleck, now Chief of Staff, estimated that a minimum of 20,000 troops were with Early. What alarmed the Federal authorities was the knowledge that, while Washington was ringed with forts, the soldiers were too few to man them, and what men there were had little experience. The Washington commander was Major General Christopher C. Augur, and the garrison of the defenses consisted of 9,643. There were 1,819 infantry, 1,834 artillery, and 63 cavalry north of the Potomac, and 4,064 infantry, 1,772 artillery, and 51 cavalry south of the stream.

Washington was surrounded by forts and would have been a position of great strength if they could have been manned properly. General John G. Barnard, who had laid them out, said there were fifty-three forts and twenty-two batteries within a perimeter of thirty-seven miles. There were 643 guns and 73 mortars. Every prominent point had an enclosed field fort; these forts were 800 to 1,000 yards apart and were connected by rifle trenches with emplacements for two ranks; there were also roads connecting the various works. The guns could sweep all approaches, and had three ways of concentrating crossfire on points where an enemy was likely to make a stand. The forts had abatis and bombproofs. To man the forts called for 25,000 infantrymen, 9,000 gunners, and 3,000 cavalry for outpost duty, a total of 37,000.

A call to Grant to rush reinforcements to Washington caused him to order General Meade, commanding the Army of the Potomac, to send the Third Division of the Sixth Corps, 2,250 men, commanded by Brigadier General James B. Ricketts. As the situation became more alarming Grant ordered two additional divisions of the Sixth under General Horatio G. Wright to proceed from City Point to Washington. Since the Nineteenth Corps under Major General William H. Emory was about to reach Fort Monroe from New Orleans, he prepared to send that, too, if necessary. He asked President Lincoln whether he should put his own troops on the defensive and come himself. Lincoln replied that a vigorous effort might now destroy the enemy's force; there was a "fair chance" of doing so, but he would not give an order. Grant decided that the troops in Washington and at Early's rear should be enough; it would create a bad impression for him to leave the front. "I have great faith that the enemy will never be able to get back with much of his force," he said.

With Sigel and Weber isolated at Maryland Heights and Hunter making a wide detour through the Kanawha Valley, there was no powerful force to interpose between Early and Washington. But there was one energetic officer who rose to the emergency. He was Major General Lew Wallace, who was not in favor with Chief of Staff Halleck and had been occupying the relatively quiet post of commander of the Eighth Corps and the Middle Department, with headquarters in Baltimore. He was impressed with the vital importance of keeping open the railroad lines that served the national capital. He became aware of the dangerous situation that was developing when the president of the Baltimore & Ohio consulted him on July 2 about keeping open the line to Harpers Ferry. Wallace's military jurisdiction extended only as far as the Monocacy River, but that was an important outpost. At Monocacy Junction the Baltimore & Ohio sent a branch line to Frederick. Wallace had a blockhouse with two guns and a 24-pound howitzer at the Junction, covering the iron bridge of the railroad. There were also a stone bridge and a wooden bridge, carrying major highways.

Wallace moved quickly. He was able to bring together upwards of 2,300 men. The units included Maryland militia, but they would serve. The First Separate Brigade of the Eighth Corps, under Brigadier General Erastus B. Tyler, had various Maryland and Ohio regiments lacking their full complement of men, and the Baltimore battery. Wallace sent Tyler with 1,000 men to Frederick. From General Augur in Washington he obtained Lieutenant Colonel D. R. Clendenin and the Eighth Illinois Cavalry, which he sent to the Catoctin Pass to get information about the Confederate advance. Clendenin had about 400 men and a few guns, and he ran into about 1,000 Confederates under General Bradford Johnson near Middletown. After a lively skirmish the Union troops fell back toward Frederick, but Colonel Charles Gilpin and the Third Maryland infantry came to their support with a charge, and Johnson retired.

On that afternoon of July 7 detachments of Brigadier General James B. Ricketts' Third Division of the Sixth Corps began unloading at Baltimore. Ricketts had no knowledge that Early was in Maryland until General Wallace explained the gravity of the situation; then, to Wallace's great satisfaction, he endorsed the stand at the Monocacy and ordered his troops to move there at once. Not all of them reached the battlefield in time; two regiments and part of another of the Second Brigade were delayed, but about 3,350 veterans of the Army of the Potomac joined Wallace and brought the Union strength up to around 6,000.

The battle at the Monocacy on Saturday, July 9, 1864, has a special place in history as a sort of courageous last stand by trained and untrained Union troops against seasoned raiders almost double their number. Early found the Federals "strongly posted" on the east bank of the Monocacy, and his first attempt to dislodge them was a failure. He sent McCausland across the river with a brigade of cavalry; the men dismounted and struck Wallace's left flank and were forced back. Breckinridge then brought Gordon's division to support McCausland, and Gordon made the chief attacks on the Union front. He came up against Ricketts' lines and found the Federal left much stronger than he had expected, but in the end the Confederates prevailed and the Federals had to fall back. Grant praised the "commendable promptitude" with which Wallace had met the challenge and concluded, as did Wallace and other military observers, that the day Early spent fighting this battle lost him the opportunity to enter Washington before it was fully reinforced. Grant wrote in his *Personal Memoirs*:

There is no telling how much this result was contributed to by General Wallace's leading what might well be considered a forlorn hope. If Early had been but one day earlier, he might have entered the capital before the arrival of the reinforcements I had sent . . . General Wallace contributed on this occasion, by the defeat of the troops under him, a greater benefit to the cause than often falls to the lot of a commander of equal force to render by means of a victory.

The Federals reported the loss of 90 killed, 579 wounded, and 1,290 missing. Early said that between 600 and 700 unwounded prisoners were taken by the Confederates. His own loss of killed and wounded was about 700. The road to Washington was now open, and the goal was only thirty-five miles away.

When it became known in Washington that Early had levied on Frederick for $20,000, and that no sizable troops stood in his way to Washington, the capital really became agitated. Families living on the outskirts in Maryland crowded down the Seventh Street road bringing their household goods. Noah Brooks, journalist, described the city in "ferment," as the mail, telegraph, railway travel, and New York newspapers were cut off. Not only the able-bodied citizens but refugees and "contraband" Negroes were pressed into the militia. General Christopher C. Augur was in command of the Department of Washington, and General Alexander McD. McCook had command of the forts.

President Lincoln and his family were living at the Soldiers' Home, not far from Fort Stevens, for the summer. When Early was nearing the capital on Sunday, July 10, Secretary Stanton sent a carriage with orders to bring Lincoln back to the White House. Noah Brooks reported that this irritated the President greatly, as also did the act of the Assistant Secretary of the Navy, Gustavus V. Fox, in ordering a vessel to stand by on the Potomac to take on the President if he had to flee the capital.

At daybreak on July 11 Early's legion was up and ready to start the great adventure of marching on Washington. Many Confederate commanders had dreamed of getting there, and Lee had fought costly battles with this object in view. Early ordered McCausland to go down the Georgetown Pike and then led his main body from Rockville toward Silver Spring. A brigade of General Imboden's cavalry under Colonel Smith was in the van. The road led to the Seventh Street Pike, one of the main thoroughfares into Washington from the North.

Near Silver Spring a small detachment of Federal cavalry barred the way, but they drew back when Smith attacked. He then dismounted his troopers and sent them ahead as skirmishers. Here were the country houses of Francis P. Blair, Sr., who called his place Silver Spring, and of his son, Montgomery Blair, the Federal Postmaster General. When Major Henry Kyd Douglas reached the house of the elder Blair he placed a guard over the property to prevent pillaging. Generals Early and Breckinridge later used it as their headquarters and enjoyed Blair's well-stocked wine cellar.

A little after noon Early came within sight of Fort Stevens and ordered his army to rest. Here was the first obstacle to be overcome in his progress toward the national capital. Early observed that the works were but "feebly manned." He ordered General R. E. Rodes to send out skirmishers and move his division into the works if he could. But before Rodes could carry out the order the Confederate officers discerned a cloud of dust on the road behind the fort and a column of Federals entered the works. A number of batteries began to fire at the Confederates and Early saw that he could not take the post by surprise. "It became necessary to reconnoiter," he said.

Early now sized up the prospect before him. The plan to enter Washington was his, not Lee's, and he studied it calmly. When Rodes' skirmishers had driven the Federals—chiefly Home Guards and militia—back to their works Early and his staff examined the fortifications to determine whether they could be carried by assault. He thought them "exceedingly strong" and noted that there appeared to be enclosed forts for heavy artillery, with a tier of lower works in front of each, "pierced for an immense number of guns," the whole connected by curtains with ditches in front, strengthened by palisades

and abatis. Timber had been felled and left on the ground
as an obstacle. He observed that Rock Creek ran through
a deep ravine on the right and had the works on the
Georgetown Pike beyond it, and that the works on the
left, "as far as the eye could reach," seemed to have the
same "impregnable" character. Early recalled that out of
a force of not over 10,000 at the outset he had lost men
in the skirmishes, and in the fighting at Monocacy, and a
lot of exhausted and shoeless men had fallen out on the
line of march, so that his infantry now had only about
8,000 muskets. He had about forty pieces of artillery
and a few pieces of horse artillery. Further, McCausland reported that the works on the Georgetown Pike
were too strongly manned to assault.

That night Early called a conference of Major Generals
Breckinridge, Rodes, Gordon, and Ramseur at the Blair
house. There was urgent need for action, especially when
Early reminded them that the passes of South Mountain
and the fords of the Upper Potomac would soon be
closed against them. They evidently were not willing to
turn back without a fight, so Early determined to assault
the Federals at daylight.

Time was working against the Confederates. They had
gained by Hunter's absence and Sigel's withdrawal, and
had been stronger than the Federal units encountered in
Maryland. But now Grant's veteran troops were arriving to displace the young and old groups that had rallied
to the defense of the capital under General Augur. On
the afternoon of July 11, the day Early sized up Fort
Stevens, the Washington waterfront came alive with
troops leaving the steamers. General Horatio Wright's
two divisions arrived, and before 2 P.M. there came the
first steamerload of 800 men of General Emory's division of the Nineteenth Corps, fresh from the ill-fated
Red River expedition, by way of Fort Monroe. At 4 P.M.
Wright's troops displaced the Home Guards at Fort
Stevens, and by nightfall General Ricketts' division of
the Sixth Corps, which had helped Wallace at Monocacy,
took over the picket line. The capital was ready for the
Confederates, but it had been a close race.

Early heard about their arrival. General Bradley T.
Johnson, who had been detached to be ready for the

prison break at Point Lookout, sent a message late that night that two corps had arrived and that Grant's whole army was probably in motion. That was the way Early put it, but his military experience must have told him that Grant was hardly likely to leave the James River. The news, however, decided Early. As soon as it was dawn on July 12, Early rode to the front to verify the report with his own eyes, and saw the parapet of Fort Stevens lined with troops. He decided to remain that day and retire at night. The dream of capturing Washington was ended.

In his memoirs years later Early wrote that he had "reluctantly to give up all hopes of capturing Washington, after I had arrived in sight of the dome of the Capitol, and given the Federal authorities a terrible fright." The fright was true, and the dome had been completed six months before Early stood before Washington.

Early decided to remain in front of the Federal fortifications all day on July 12, and to march away at night. For most of the day Confederate skirmishers were active in front of Fort Stevens, and sharpshooters in two houses across the ravine were proving dangerous. President Lincoln, eager to survey the scene, came in the afternoon and stood on the parapet, a fine target for sharpshooters in his tall form and high hat. General Wright was urging the President to get down, when a man standing nearby was hit by a bullet. Then—so goes the legend—a young soldier yelled "Get down, you fool!" The speaker, whom Lincoln heeded, has been identified as Captain Oliver Wendell Holmes, Jr., who later wrote his name indelibly into his country's judicial history.

Though the Federal troops were now strong enough to challenge Early, they remained inside their fortifications, satisfied with keeping Rodes' and McCausland's skirmishers at a distance. Late in the afternoon, however, the Confederates had become so troublesome that General Wright demanded authority to attack them. Both General Halleck and General Augur were reluctant to hazard an offensive, but when the Confederates' creeping tactics brought them near the fort they consented. General Wright ordered Brigadier General Frank Wheaton out with a detachment of the First Brigade of the Second Division. At about 6 P.M. guns from Fort

Stevens opened the attack before an audience of official spectators watching from the ramparts, and Wheaton's men sprang forward. But instead of encountering a weak skirmish line they were confronted by well-posted infantry under Rodes, who called for reinforcements. The Confederate soldiers did not look confidently on fighting here, but they stood their ground, and the Federals, not eager to continue, withdrew with about 280 casualties.

Early now made preparations to retire. He sent for Major Henry Kyd Douglas, who was acting as adjutant, and told him he was to take charge of a detail of 200 men whom Early had ordered up for picket duty. He was to hold the line until after midnight, unless driven in or ordered away, and then march them as a rear guard until cavalry fell in behind them. Early also placed Breckinridge in the van, with Rodes and Ramseur following. He had word that General Bradford Johnson had burned the bridges on the Gunpowder River that served the Philadelphia and Harrisburg roads, and Early ordered him back from his march to Point Lookout, where the prison delivery would not take place. Johnson's men captured Major General William B. Franklin on a train, but Franklin eluded his guard and escaped.

When Major Douglas rode away with the rear guard he observed behind him the red light of a house in flames. It was Falkland, the home of Postmaster General Montgomery Blair, probably fired by a retreating soldier, to Douglas' regret. Although Early felt that retaliation was justified for Hunter's acts in Virginia, he disclaimed knowledge of this incident and said it served to notify the Federals of the Confederate retreat.

Early's escape, when so many Federal divisions had been brought together, was again cause for much criticism. General Wright attempted to organize pursuit, but Early turned southwest from Rockville to Poolesville, crossed the Potomac at White's Ford on July 14, and rested his army at Leesburg. His troops managed to salvage all the livestock they had collected, and carried off all the Federal prisoners they had taken at Monocacy. The Confederates moved through Snicker's Gap to the Shenandoah, and their route was contested by small bodies of Federals at Snicker's Gap, Island Ford, Darksville, Stevenson's Depot, and Winchester. Major General George Crook of the Army of West Virginia and General William Averell commanded some of the pursuing forces; Averell, on July 20, inflicted a serious defeat on Ramseur's division on the way to Winchester. But nobody bagged Early.

Conscription and Draft Riots

The Confederate government adopted conscription on April 16, 1862, after the loss of Forts Henry and Donelson showed the need for more trained troops. It called up whites between the ages of eighteen and thirty-five, but exempted numerous officials and civilians in so-called essential occupations. By September 27, 1862, the Confederates extended conscription to all between thirty-five and forty-five as well. At first only men forty and under were taken, but after the defeats at Gettysburg and Vicksburg men of forty to forty-five were included. On Feb. 17, 1864, conscription was extended to all whites between seventeen and fifty. Those seventeen and eighteen years old, and those forty-five to fifty, were allocated to state defense and were not to serve beyond the limits of their states.

The United States government had made good use of state militia, but its need dictated Federal conscription, which was approved March 3, 1863. The U. S. Provost Marshal was placed at the head of a bureau of the War Department to administer it. Substitutes were accepted, and a drafted man could pay $300 for an exemption. Eventually local municipalities, counties and states added to the bounty money and offered as high as $677 to induce men to volunteer. This started the practice of "bounty jumping" by means of which a man would collect a bounty and disappear. However, many payments were made to the wives of recruits.

The draft was conducted by provost marshals in cities. On Saturday, July 11, 1863, a drawing began in the provost marshal's office in New York, N. Y. When the names were published on Sunday angry crowds gathered. They resented the fact that most of the drafted men were mechanics and laborers, who were expected to serve three years. The next day, July 12, a mob formed outside the office of the provost marshal at Third Avenue and Forty-sixth Street, New York, and when the drawing proceeded windows were smashed, the office was wrecked and the building was set on fire. When the police were overpowered soldiers fired on the mob. As rioting spread the militia was called out. Before order was restored over 10,000 infantry, the Seventh New York regiment, the First Division of the New York State National Guard, United States cavalry and three batteries of artillery from the Army of the Potomac, patrolled the streets of New York. Estimates of the number of dead and injured ran as high as 1,000.

The draft was temporarily suspended. On August 10 it was resumed and continued in orderly fashion.

On July 18, 1864, President Lincoln, acting under authority of a recruiting law passed a few weeks earlier, called for 500,000 volunteers for military service, for one, two, or three years, as they might elect, and if the numbers needed were not obtained by September 5 a draft for troops to serve one year was to be instituted. Areas that had furnished more than their quotas would receive credit against the numbers now needed.

34

FIGHTING IN THE SHENANDOAH VALLEY

Stonewall Jackson's First Campaign

Thomas J. Jackson's military fame began at the First Battle of Bull Run (Manassas) and resulted in his being named major general. He was now known throughout the command as Stonewall Jackson. When General Joseph E. Johnston took command of the Department of Northern Virginia in October, 1861, he gave Jackson command of the District of the Shenandoah, with headquarters at Winchester. The ordeal of the inhabitants of the Valley was now about to begin and would be intensified during the rest of the war, as the opposing armies ravaged this productive and beautiful land.

Some of Jackson's troops were badly trained militia, but he also received the brigades of Generals R. B. Garnett, William B. Taliaferro, William Gilham, and S. R. Anderson, and the Seventh Virginia Cavalry under Colonel Turner Ashby. He was supposed to have 6,000 troops available, but the number was often less. During the winter of 1861–1862 Jackson attempted to damage Federal communications. His men made a breach in a dam of the Chesapeake & Ohio Canal near Hancock, Maryland, occupied the town of Bath on January 4, 1862, bombarded Union troops at Hancock, and occupied Romney when it was evacuated January 10.

When Jackson learned that Federal troops were leaving western Virginia in order to join McClellan in the Peninsular campaign he began a series of actions intended to keep the Federals from moving. When he marched to Kernstown he was attacked March 23 by Brigadier General James Shields, who had 6,000 infantry and 750 cavalry against Jackson's 3,000 infantry and 200 cavalry, although not all were engaged on either side. Jackson retreated to Swift Gap Run. The Federals had 118 killed, 450 wounded; the Confederates 80 killed, 375 wounded.

In May, Jackson was reinforced by a division under Major General Richard S. Ewell, so that he now had available over 13,000 men. Ewell did not take part in the next action, near McDowell. Here Jackson engaged the troops of Brigadier General Robert H. Milroy and those of Brigadier General Robert C. Schenck, who had about 2,300 engaged. It consisted of Schenck's extricating Milroy from a difficult position under a height held by the Confederates. The Federals reported 26 killed, 227 wounded, whereas Jackson had 75 killed, 424 wounded. The Federals retreated to Franklin, where General Frémont arrived May 13.

The next engagement was a surprise attack at Front Royal against part of the army of Major General Nathaniel P. Banks and was much more serious for the Federals. Jackson attacked on May 23, drove the Federals out, and they retreated as far as Winchester, twenty miles away, where General Banks made a stand. This time Jackson had the benefit of Ewell's division, and the action, which included skirmishes at Middletown and Newtown, was so menacing that Banks retreated across the Potomac, spreading consternation among the Union command in Washington. Jackson announced that he had captured 3,050 prisoners, 750 of whom were sick and wounded in Winchester and Strasburg hospitals. Banks reported 62 killed, 243 wounded, 1,714 captured or missing. Jackson had about 16,000 men. Banks on June 16 reported 7,113 in his ranks. The Union command ordered General Shields to cross the Blue Ridge and join General Frémont's forces in the Valley.

At Cross Keys, Jackson fought Frémont, the latter with 10,500 men sustaining losses of 114 killed, 443 wounded. At Port Republic, Jackson encountered Brigadier General Erastus B. Tyler with about 2,500 men from Shields's division and routed them; by the time General Frémont arrived with reinforcements Jackson had burned the bridge across the Shenandoah and Frémont was unable to cross. The Federals lost 67 killed, 393 wounded, 558 missing. Jackson's total loss for the campaign was placed at 230 killed, 1,373 wounded.

Jackson now prepared to move his troops to the Peninsula to fight with Lee against McClellan.

Sheridan in the Shenandoah

The activities of Federal troops in the Shenandoah Valley in the spring of 1864 had been a source of trouble for General Lee, calling for the detachment of sizable bodies of Confederate troops to checkmate the Union army. One of the Federal units was commanded by Major General Franz Sigel, whose headquarters were at Winchester. When Sigel moved up the Valley he encountered a Confederate force at New Market, comprised of a brigade of cavalry and a battery under Brigadier General John Imboden, and two brigades of infantry and a battalion of artillery under Major General John C. Breckinridge. On May 15, 1864, they drove Sigel back to Winchester with a loss of 120 killed and 560 wounded, while the Confederates lost 85 killed and 320 wounded.

Confederate General Jubal A. Early by the summer of 1864 was so exasperated by the destruction of mills, factories, and residences that he saw in the Shenandoah Valley and other parts of Virginia that he decided on retaliation in kind. He ordered Brigadier General John McCausland to take his brigade and that of General Johnson and a battery of artillery and proceed to Chambersburg, Pennsylvania, to collect $100,000 in gold or $500,000 in currency for damages done by Federal troops in the South. Early had especially in mind fine Southern homes that had been put to the torch by General David Hunter, and he considered the sum asked just compensation. When McCausland crossed the Potomac on July 29 and moved north Early made a number of diversionary movements toward Harpers Ferry, Hagerstown, and other places to draw attention from McCausland. When the officials of Chambersburg refused to pay the levy "the greater part of the town was laid in ashes" according to Early, who wrote long after the war that he alone was responsible for this act and did not regret it.

McCausland did not return to Virginia unscathed, although the Federal units sent out to intercept him did not bag him. General William Averell caught up with him at Moorfield, West Virginia, August 7, and had a sharp altercation in which the Confederates lost 100 killed and wounded and 400 captured and missing, while the Union troops had 9 killed, 22 wounded. The Federal cavalry included the Fourteenth Pennsylvania, Eighth Ohio, First and Third West Virginia, and First New York. The raid did cause a wave of anger and exasperation in the North, which had not known or cared much about Hunter's ravages in Virginia. Even President Lincoln was aroused, and on August 14 he wrote General Grant: "The Secretary of War and I concur that you had better confer with General Lee and stipulate for a mutual discontinuance of house burning and other destruction of private property."

Major General Philip H. Sheridan conferred with General Grant in Washington on August 5 and on August 7, 1864, took command of the Middle Military Division, which included the Middle Department, the Department of the Susquehanna, and the Department of West Virginia. Two divisions of cavalry, one commanded by Brigadier General Alfred Torbert, the other by Brigadier General James H. Wilson, which had been active in the Petersburg-Richmond area, were included, as well as the brigades of Colonel Charles R. Lowell, Jr., and Colonel Thomas C. Devin. The infantry under Brigadier General George Crook consisted of the Sixth and Eighth Army Corps and part of the Nineteenth. The original base of the Middle Division was at Harpers Ferry. This became known as the Army of the Shenandoah.

When General Jubal A. Early's forces moved out of Martinsburg and up the Shenandoah Valley, Sheridan sent troops in pursuit. They harassed Early's rear guard ten miles from Winchester. On August 11 General George A. Custer's cavalry brigade discovered a large part of Early's troops at Sulphur Springs Bridge, three miles from Winchester, and attacked with one battery. After a fight of two hours Custer was forced back.

Devin's brigade, moving toward Newtown in an attempt to flank Early, who was proceeding toward Strasburg, became engaged with Early's column at White Post. After fighting for three hours Early's troops withdrew to Newtown. General Crook's infantry, which had camped during the night at Berryville, arrived in time to join in harassing the Confederates, who consolidated their forces in front of Newtown, while the Federals camped six miles southwest of Winchester.

The Federals, keeping in contact with the rear guard of Early's forces, clashed with the latter August 12 on a hill near Strasburg on which the Confederates had placed a battery. As the Federal infantry came up it skirmished with the Confederates at Cedar Creek, three miles north of Strasburg. Here the Federals camped for several days while the Confederates, first evacuating Strasburg and then re-entering it, fortified Fisher's Hill, above the town. About this time General Fitzhugh Lee's cavalry and Major General John B. Kershaw's division joined Early.

On August 13 Colonel John S. Mosby perpetrated one of his quick raids from the other side of the mountain range. A long supply train belonging to Sheridan's army had been slowly making its way up the Valley and had reached Berryville, where it stopped to feed and water the horses. A large number of livestock were in the train. Without warning Mosby and his partisan troopers, whose ride through Snicker's Gap had not been reported, appeared in the midst of the supply train and sent a great many of the drivers and military escort flying. The Confederates cut out 500 horses, 200 beeves, and 200 prisoners, and destroyed 75 wagons. These and other difficulties caused the Federal forces to be ordered back to Charlestown.

The setback was only temporary. General Sheridan refused to move forward without proper support and as a consequence the next Federal attempt in the Valley was better organized. The army was ordered to march up the same roads as before, and on September 3 part of the Nineteenth Corps reached Berryville and entrenched. General Early's command also was on the alert and attacked the vanguard of General Crook's infantry, but no general engagement resulted. On September 18 General William Averell had driven a unit of Early's cavalry out of Martinsburg. On September 19 Crook's army resumed its advance and when within a short distance of Winchester came upon strong forces of Early's army and attacked. The fighting lasted from noon to 5 P.M., when Early's forces rushed off the field, closely pursued by Sheridan.

This part of Sheridan's campaign had been costly. At Fisher's Hill the Federals lost 52 killed and 457 wounded, but at Winchester they lost 697 killed, 3,083 wounded, and 338 captured or missing. The Confederate losses were reported to be much higher, but exact figures are unknown. The Federal forces had 37,711 men and the Confederates 17,103.

By the 20th of September the Union troops had advanced to their former lines along Cedar Creek beyond Strasburg and the Confederates held their fortified post on Fisher's Hill. General Crook prepared for a surprise attack on the Confederate position before dawn on September 22, making a direct charge on the camp while a flanking column assailed the rear. The Confederates were driven from their position with heavy losses and retired to Mount Jackson. As Sheridan's forces moved toward Harrisonburg, Early retired by Cross Keys and Port Republic toward Charlottesville, moving through Brown's Gap. Here the Confederate rear guard made a determined stand and stopped pursuit by General Wesley Merritt.

Devastation of the area so that it could no longer support Confederate troops was part of Sheridan's plan to make the Shenandoah untenable for future raids. On the ground of military necessity Sheridan burned and wrecked the principal economic facilities of the region, destroying mills and granaries and railroad connections. The Union commanders attempted to justify the general destruction on the ground that the Valley harbored guerrillas and ruffians; also the burnings were in reprisal for others committed by the Confederates. However, it is incontestable that the destruction began in Southern territory. General Wesley Merritt said: "The Valley from Staunton to Winchester was completely devastated and the armies thereafter occupying that country had to look elsewhere for their supplies."

General Wilson's cavalry raided Staunton September 27, destroying the railroad station, and Waynesboro on September 28, wrecking a railroad bridge. Other forces operated from Harrisonburg to Mount Crawford. The whole countryside was turned into an arid region at a time when the fields were rich with crops.

By October the army returned and entrenched on the northeast bank of Cedar Creek, near Middletown. Generals Custer, Merritt, and Torbert on October 8 encountered the cavalry of Confederate Generals Rosser and Lomax at Thom's Brook and after hard battling drove them back twenty miles and captured prisoners and guns.

General Sheridan was greatly pleased because he had brought the war home to the people of the Valley. Heretofore, said he, they had no reason to complain, for they had been living in abundance; now they were getting sick of the war. He wrote General Grant from Woodstock, October 7, 1864, describing his methods. With satisfaction he mentioned one act that would place him beside the most ruthless of commanders. "Lieutenant John R. Meigs, my engineer officer, was murdered beyond Harrisonburg, near Dayton. For this atrocious act all the houses within five miles were burned."

He also itemized: "In moving back to this point the whole country from the Blue Ridge to the North Mountains has been made untenable for a rebel army. I have destroyed over 2,000 barns filled with wheat, hay, and farming implements; over seventy mills filled with flour and wheat; have driven in front of the army over 4,000 head of stock, and have killed and issued to the troops not less than 3,000 sheep." However, he also had provocation, for he said that since he came into the Valley every train, every small party, and every straggler had been bushwacked by the people, many of whom had protective papers from commanders, and he had turned back to Martinsburg over 400 wagonloads of refugees, mostly Dunkers, who had been conscripted by the Confederates. General Merritt destroyed only 630 barns and 47 mills. Colonel Henry Kyd Douglas, staff officer with Early, wrote years later of the terrified women and children and of the clergyman's daughter, standing in front of her home while the stables were burning, tearing her hair and repeating the oaths of the skirmishers and shrieking with wild laughter, for the horrors of the night had driven her mad.

Of the Confederate guerrillas who operated outside of army organizations Colonel John Singleton Mosby was the most resourceful and most feared by the Federals. Riding chiefly at night with bands of supporters numbering from fifteen to two hundred, Mosby created great havoc among Federal communications in the Virginia counties of Fairfax, Loudon, and Fauquier, and in the Shenandoah Valley. He was born December 6, 1833, and received a law degree from the University of Virginia in 1852. He joined J. E. B. Stuart's First Virginia Cavalry and took part in Stuart's ride around McClellan and in numerous raids. In January, 1863, when Mosby was a captain, Stuart authorized him to take a number of men and operate independently. He began by raiding Federal camps for information, capturing officers and horses. His exploit in pulling Brigadier General Edwin H. Stoughton out of bed, and seizing him and thirty-two others in the middle of Federal headquarters, made him widely known. Mosby had a slight, wiry figure, wore two pistols in place of a saber, and had a hat with gold cord and ostrich plume and a cloak lined in scarlet. His troop derailed trains, raided supply columns, robbed army paymasters, and attacked cavalry units. His men were adept at fighting at close quarters with Colt revolvers.

When reprisals between Federal and Confederate armies became the method used to suppress harassment of troops, guerrilla warfare in the Valley became ruthless and costly. The Federals began destroying all means of subsistence in the Valley and burning the houses of noncombatants, sometimes merely because houses had been burned by the Confederates in other parts of Virginia. In 1864 the situation became so desperate that Grant recommended to Sheridan that families of Mosby's men be sent to Fort McHenry or some other places as hostages. At the same time he advised that "when any of Mosby's men are caught hang them without trial." While such orders have been known to overawe civilians, they have no effect on armed bands. On September 23, 1864, United States cavalrymen belonging to Brigadier General George A. Custer's command shot four and hanged two of Mosby's men at Front Royal. Shortly thereafter Mosby caught some men of Custer's command; he hanged three and shot three, but one of the men shot feigned death and survived. Mosby professed disgust at this sort of retaliation, saying later: "I felt in doing it all the pangs of the Athenian jailer when he handed the cup of hemlock to the great Athenian martyr." He sent his scout John Russell to Sheridan's headquarters with a report of the executions and the promise: "Hereafter any prisoners falling into my hands will be treated with the kindness due to their condition, unless some new act of barbarity shall compel me reluctantly to adopt a course of policy repulsive to humanity."

So great was the feeling against Mosby that Secretary of War Stanton ordered him to be excepted from parole at the end of the war, but General Grant obtained his parole. A great admirer of Grant, Mosby became a Republican and campaigned for Grant for the Presidency in 1872. President R. B. Hayes named him U.S. consul in Hong Kong, where he served from 1878 to 1885. Later he was employed as an attorney in the Department of Justice, but his last years were darkened by poverty. He died May 30, 1916.

General Sheridan was called to Washington for consultation October 13, 1864, and on October 15 started out with General Torbert and part of the cavalry, with the intention of operating against Gordonsville. He was hardly on his way when he received word at Front Royal that the Confederate signal station on Three Top Mountain had relayed a message from Longstreet to Early saying: "Be ready to move as soon as my forces join you and we will crush Sheridan." This was an example of how well armies were able to read wigwag messages sent in code by opposing forces. Sheridan immediately ordered the cavalry back to camp.

General Early had been faced with the necessity of either withdrawing to obtain supplies and forage, or of dislodging the Union forces. He chose the latter and laid his plans so carefully that the Federal cavalry failed by reconnoiter to discover any concentration of forces. Yet before dawn on October 19 the Confederate troops under Kershaw, Ramseur, Gordon, and Pegram hit General Crook's camp with such an impact that the men could hardly get into their clothes, much less prepare a defense. These troops, and to some extent Emory's, were overwhelmed, and rushed back in panic. General Wright's troops, farther back, tried to make a stand, but had to retire, fighting. A cavalry brigade on the right stood its ground for a time. The Federal units rallied, but the pressure was so great that they had to retire until they had reached a line some distance north of Middletown. They suffered especially from Confederate artillery.

Sheridan's Ride to Cedar Creek

General Sheridan, returning from Washington, had stopped for the night in Winchester. He received word at 6 A.M. on October 19 that there was gunfire in the direction of the army and started for the front. Soon he found the road so blocked with wagons and wounded men that he had to take to the fields to make any progress. His ride, which resulted in turning defeat into victory, became legendary, especially after Thomas Buchanan Read wrote his poem "Sheridan's Ride," which was recited by schoolboys for generations. In it Sheridan's onrush was practically breathless, but according to his own account he had a great deal of hard work to do to renew the battle. In his memoirs (1888), Sheridan wrote:

My first halt was made just north of Newtown, where I met a chaplain digging his heels into the sides of his jaded horse, and making for the rear with all possible speed. I drew up for an instant and inquired of him how matters were going at the front. He replied: "Everything is lost; but all will be right when you get there"; yet, notwithstanding this expression of confidence in me, the parson at once resumed his breathless pace to the rear. At Newtown I was obliged to make a circuit to the left to get around the village. I could not pass through it, the streets were so crowded, but meeting on this detour Major McKinley of Crook's staff, he spread the news of my return through the motley throng there.

When nearing the Valley Pike, just north of Newtown, I saw about three-fourths of a mile west of the pike a body of troops, which proved to be Ricketts' and Wheaton's divisions of the Sixth Corps, and then learned that the Nineteenth Corps had halted a little to the right and rear of these; but I did not stop, desiring to get to the extreme front. Continuing on parallel with the pike about midway between Newtown and Middletown, I crossed to the west of it and a little later came up in rear of Getty's division of the Sixth Corps. When I arrived this division and the cavalry were the only troops resisting the enemy; they were apparently acting as a rearguard at a point about three miles north of the line we held at Cedar Creek when the battle began. General Torbert was the first officer to meet me, saying as he rode up: "My God! I am glad you've come!"

Jumping my horse over the line of rails, I rode to the crest of the elevation, and there, taking off my hat, the men rose up behind their barricade with cheers of recognition. I then turned back to the rear of Getty's division, and as I came behind it a line of regimental flags rose up out of the ground, as it seemed, to welcome me. They were mostly the colors of Crook's troops, who had been stampeded and scattered. . . . The line with the colors was largely composed of officers, among whom I recognized Colonel R. B. Hayes, since President of the United States. . . . Returning to the place where my headquarters had been established, I met near them

Ricketts' division under General Kiefer, and General
Frank Wheaton's division, both marching to the front. When
the men of these divisions saw me they began cheering and
took up the double-quick to the front.

All this consumed a great deal of time and I concluded to
visit again the point to the east of the Valley Pike, from where
I had first observed the enemy, to see what he was doing.
Arrived there, I could plainly see him getting ready for
attack, and Major Forsyth now suggested that it would be
well to ride along the line of battle before the enemy assailed
us, for although the troops had learned of my return, but
few of them had seen me. Following his suggestion I started
in behind the men, but when a few paces had been taken I
crossed to the front, hat in hand, passed along the entire
length of the infantry line; and it is from this circumstance
that many of the officers and men who then received me
with such heartiness have since supposed that that was my
first appearance on the field. But at least two hours had
elapsed since I reached the ground, for it was after midday
when this incident of riding down the front took place, and I
arrived not later, certainly, than half-past ten o'clock.

The presence of Sheridan reassured the troops, and
they regained confidence in their own powers to recover
what they had lost. Early's commands had become scattered and were difficult to bring together. Moreover, the
Confederate soldiers, deprived of many necessities, were
overcome by the quantity of goods in the Federal camp
and broke ranks to plunder it. General Early assigned
troops of Wharton's Brigade to clear the camp, but as
soon as this had been done a new crowd of stragglers fell
upon the booty. The Federal cavalry now began to harass
Early's flanks, and in the afternoon the whole Federal line
advanced with artillery. The Confederates made a brave
defense and held their line until the Federals found an
opening between brigades and pushed through. The ensuing retreat soon affected all units and the officers
could not stop them. Early tried to carry with him a large
amount of captured artillery and wagons filled with
medical and other supplies, but a bridge broke down
just above Strasburg, the road became clogged, and the
whole heap was cut off by a small band of Federal cavalry.
Thus, said Early, a "glorious victory" was turned into a
complete debacle. The Confederate line finally solidi-

fied itself some seven miles below Mount Jackson.

General Early explained: "There was an individuality about the Confederate soldier which caused him to act often in battle according to his own opinions, and thereby impair his own efficiency, and the tempting bait offered by the rich plunder of the camps of the enemy's well-fed and well-clothed troops was frequently too great for our destitute troops."

Several small actions took place in the next few weeks, but for major movements Cedar Creek closed the 1864 campaign in the Shenandoah.

Both sides lost heavily in the campaign, and many valuable officers were killed or wounded. The total number of wounded was unusually large and was attributed to artillery fire. The Union troops placed their casualties at 16,952, of which number 1,938 were killed, 11,893 wounded, and 3,121 captured or missing. At Cedar Creek the Federals lost 644 killed, 3,480 wounded, 1,591 missing. The Confederates were supposed to have had 3,000 killed and wounded there, but General Early said the number was 1,860, and that 1,000 of his men were taken prisoner. The Federals lost Generals Russell and Mulligan killed, and Generals McIntosh, Upton, and Chapman wounded. The Confederates lost Major Generals Rodes, Gordon, Goodwin, and Ramseur killed, and Fitzhugh Lee, Johnson, Wharton, and Battle wounded.

35

THOMAS VERSUS HOOD
IN TENNESSEE

When General Sherman on November 15, 1864, started on his cherished plan of making Georgia howl and marching to the sea, Major General George H. Thomas had approximately 59,534 troops under his command. But his garrison at Nashville had only 10,-

000 infantry, and 10,000 cavalry of Major General J. H. Wilson's command, many of them unmounted. The rest of the army was miles from Nashville. The Fourth Corps of about 12,000 men under Major General D. S. Stanley, and the Twenty-third of 10,000 under Major General John M. Schofield, were at Pulaski, Tennessee. Major General Gordon Granger's division was at Decatur, Major General Lovell H. Rousseau's at Murfreesboro, and Major General James B. Steedman's at Chattanooga. The cavalry division of Hatch and the brigades of Croxton and Capron with about 7,700 men, were in the vicinity of Florence, Alabama, keeping watch over the movements of General J. B. Hood. Major General A. J. Smith's two divisions of the Sixteenth Corps, comprising 14,000 troops, which Sherman had ordered General Rosecrans to send from Missouri to Nashville, had reached Paducah and were eagerly awaited by Thomas.

Hood, with the Confederate troops based on Florence and Tuscumbia, was now ready to jump off on his big gamble—to bag Thomas and win all of Tennessee. As the intentions of Sherman to strike south into Georgia became clear, Hood had been arguing with his superior officer, General Beauregard, for independent action in Tennessee. The Confederate top command still had hopes of following Sherman and making things hot for him in Georgia, but Hood presented strong arguments against being given this task. He convinced Beauregard, who explained to President Davis that the roads and waterways in Tennessee had been rendered almost impassable by the rains, and for Hood to move artillery and wagons to catch up with Sherman, who had a head start of 250 miles, with bridges gone and forage destroyed, was practically hopeless. Taking Hood out of Tennessee would turn over to Thomas the richest part of Alabama and its key cities.

General Hood started his Tennessee campaign November 19 and reached Columbia on Duck River November 27. This alarmed Schofield at Pulaski and caused him to take his troops on a quick night march to get the road to Nashville before Hood could interpose his army. Schofield had reached Columbia and thrown up entrenchments before Hood got there. Hood then decided to put his troops at Schofield's rear by a roundabout maneuver and attack when Schofield retreated. He laid pontoons three miles above Columbia on November 29, sent General Nathan Bedford Forrest's cavalry and General Cleburne's division across, and ordered Lieut. General S. D. F. Lee to feint with artillery at Schofield's front to hold his attention. Hood reached a spot where he observed the Federal troops marching on the pike from Columbia to Spring Hill, twelve miles distant. He saw a splendid opportunity to attack the marching column in the flank, break it up and destroy it, and his imagination raced ahead to visualize the complete rout of Thomas as a result. He ordered General Cheatham to take the pike near Spring Hill and Cleburne to support Cheatham. He also ordered up Stewart and Johnston of Lee's corps.

Although his orders were definite, nothing happened. Hood discovered to his dismay that he was not being obeyed. The reasons given by Cheatham, who waited for Stewart to protect his right, did not satisfy him. He ordered Stewart to form on the right so as to extend across the pike. Stewart moved up in the dark, went into bivouac, but did not touch the pike. Because he did not do so the Federal troops marched practically unmolested down the pike past Hood's big army, "almost under the light of its campfires." The Federals expected Hood to attack them, and Colonel Henry Stone of Thomas' staff agreed later that a single Confederate brigade planted across the pike would have prevented Schofield's retreat and cut him off from every avenue of escape. Hood was frantic. He had recommended Cheatham for promotion; now he wrote Richmond, withdrawing the recommendation; Cheatham apologized, and Hood reinstated the recommendation. But his great opportunity was gone.

In the meantime Schofield was trying to get his troops to Nashville and warding off persistent attacks by Forrest's cavalry. He had a wagon train five miles long, which General Wood's division was protecting. During the night he moved his troops from Spring Hill to Franklin, with Major General Jacob D. Cox in the advance. Here the terrain was better suited for defense, but Hood was jubilant again. He decided he would attack in force and have

General Forrest ready to envelop both flanks of the Federals and "complete the ruin of the enemy by capturing those who attempt to escape in the direction of Nashville." The Federals had dug a fine line of trenches. Hood ordered an assault by Cheatham, Stewart, and Cleburne, in order to "drive the Federals into the river." They pushed the Federals out of the first line, but met with stubborn resistance behind it, and when Colonel Emerson Opdyke of General Stanley's corps charged he recaptured the trenches and about 1,000 Confederates inside them. A fierce contest ensued; men fought at close quarters and were dragged from one side of the breastworks to the other by their coat collars and their hair. At dusk Johnston's division of Lee's corps joined, but the rest of Lee's troops did not come up in time.

The battle at Franklin was costly to the Confederates and must have shaken Hood's dream of conquest considerably. Counting the minor action at Spring Hill the day before, where two brigades of Schofield's army were attacked by Forrest and some infantry, the losses were: Union, 189 killed, 1,030 wounded, 1,104 missing; Confederate, 1,750 killed, 3,800 wounded, 702 missing. In no other single action did the Confederates lose so many major officers. Major General Cleburne was killed. Brigadier General John Adams, of Mississippi, rode over the ditch of the trench to seize the colors; he and his horse were shot and killed by the color guard as the horse had its forelegs over the earthworks. Four other Confederate brigadiers were killed; Major General Brown and five brigadiers were wounded. On the Union side, Generals Stanley and Bradley were wounded.

Hood's army was now weakened and dispirited, while Thomas' army was stronger than ever. General A. J. Smith's corps had come up, and some of his troops were present at the battle of Franklin. In the opinion of President Lincoln and Generals Grant and Halleck now was the time for Thomas to wipe out the threat of the Confederate Army of Tennessee. But all that Washington heard was that Thomas was not ready. Among other excuses, he was waiting for his cavalry to be fully provided with horses; of 12,000 men only 6,600 were mounted. Grant exploded: "Attack Hood at once and wait no longer for a remount for your cavalry. There is great danger in delay resulting in a campaign back to the Ohio River."

The dispatches that Grant sent to Thomas urging him to fight are evidence that, despite West Point emphasis on strict obedience, a general in a democratic army could exercise considerable individuality. The tables were turned on Grant; just as Halleck in 1862 had become exasperated because execution of his orders was delayed, so Grant was practically helpless in trying to move the imperturbable Rock of Chickamauga.

On December 2 Grant was urging Thomas to attack Hood. "If Hood is permitted to remain quietly about Nashville, you will lose all the road back to Chattanooga and possibly have to abandon the line of the Tennessee." On the same day Grant had another thought; Thomas' citizen employees were armed for the defense of Nashville (the Quartermaster Corps accounted for over 10,-000); he could open an offensive. "You will now suffer incalculable injury upon your railroads if Hood is not speedily disposed of." On December 5 Grant was warning Thomas to look after Forrest and attack Hood. "Time strengthens him in all possibility as much as it does you." On December 8 Grant told Thomas to avoid a foot race with Hood to see who "can beat to the Ohio." "Now is one of the finest opportunities ever presented of destroying one of the three armies of the enemy." On December 11 Grant advised Thomas to "accept such weather as you will find."

Thomas was replying patiently. "As soon as I get up a respectable force of cavalry I will march against Hood." . . . "I will make the necessary disposition and attack Hood at once." . . . "I will obey the order as promptly as possible, however much I may regret it." Halleck was more brusque than Grant: "If you wait till General Wilson mounts all his cavalry, you will wait till doomsday." General Thomas was undisturbed; Grant called him "slow and deliberate, sensible, honest and brave." However, Thomas' assistant adjutant, Colonel Henry Stone, twenty-three years later admitted: "From December 2 until the battle [Nashville] was fought on the 15th, the General in Chief did not cease, day and night, to send him from the headquarters at City Point, Va., the most urgent and often the most uncalled-for orders in regard to his operations, culminating in an order on the 9th relieving him. . . ."

Grant had decided on December 9 to relieve Thomas and put Schofield in his place. When he learned that the roads were covered with a sheet of ice he held up the order. By December 13 Grant had lost all patience. Major General John A. Logan was at headquarters at City Point; Grant authorized him to proceed to Nashville to take over Thomas' command, if Thomas had not moved by that time. Becoming "restless," he determined to go himself and started for Washington. Here he learned from Thomas that the battle was to be fought the next day. Logan had reached Louisville and waited, for the same reason. The result was everything Grant could have hoped; the general whom he had characterized as "not so good in pursuit as in action" had delivered a victory.

The battle of Nashville was fought December 15 and 16, 1864. It was opened by Major General James B. Steedman, who pinned down two divisions of Cheatham's corps on the Confederate right, attacking with two brigades of Negro troops. Most of the corps of General S. D. Lee was also held by General Wood's threat against Montgomery Hill. The Confederates were strongly entrenched, and the Federals delivered a series of assaults against the Confederate left. The latter were pushed out of five strong redoubts on the Hillsboro Pike, Wood's and A. J. Smith's troops pursuing the Confederates two miles beyond their positions of the morning.

For the next day's fighting Hood reorganized along the base of a line of hills on which his troops had thrown up earthworks, securing also their flanks and creating a salient on Overton's Hill. Hood's line also had the protection of stone walls, felled trees, and woods behind it. Colonel P. Sidney Post, whose brigade had been active at Montgomery Hill, attempted a direct assault on a strong point, but the defense was so effective that Post's brigade lost 300 and his supporting brigade 250 in a few minutes. Colonel Charles R. Thompson, leading Negro troops against another strong point east of the Franklin pike, lost 467 killed and wounded. Such direct assaults were too costly, but Brigadier General John McArthur of the First Division of General A. J. Smith's corps was determined to rush a fortified post held by Major General William B. Bate of Cheatham's corps. He did so with fixed bayonets at the same time that Hatch's cavarly took two other hills nearby, and pulling two guns to the top of one, opened on Bate. A second brigade attacked with repeating rifles. The onslaught proved too much for the defenders. Their line broke and the Federal troops now rushed forward over Hood's positions. They captured General Edward Johnson and most of his division and fourteen guns.

The battle of Nashville completed the disorganization of Hood's Army of Tennessee. The Federals pursued it, but with many handicaps. The cavalry had fought dismounted, and had to send back to Nashville for the horses that were available. The Confederates destroyed most of the bridges and pontoons; the Union army had pontoons of its own, but by a confusion of orders they were sent to Chattanooga instead of the front.

The Union army reported that Thomas had 55,000 troops available at Nashville and that 43,260 were actually engaged. Casualties in the battle were 387 killed, 2,558 wounded, 112 captured or missing. Union sources estimated Hood's strength at 37,937, not counting detached cavalry units. He placed his casualties at the battle of Franklin at 4,500. He reported 21,000 at Tupelo and said his casualties for the campaign did not exceed 10,000, but General Thomas reported 13,189 Confederate prisoners and 2,000 deserters. General Forrest's cavalry command was assigned to service in Mississippi and other troops went to General Maury defending Mobile. Hood resigned his command and left the Army of Tennessee on January 23, 1865. He was then ordered to Texas to organize troops willing to come to the support of General Robert E. Lee in Virginia, but before he could do effective work Lee had surrendered. Hood remained in Mississippi and on May 31, 1865, surrendered to the United States Army in Natchez, and was paroled and left free to go to New Orleans and Texas.

36

CUSHING DESTROYS THE
ALBEMARLE

In an act of personal daring that stirred widespread admiration in the North, Navy Lieutenant William B. Cushing destroyed the Confederate ram *Albemarle* at its dock at Plymouth, North Carolina, on October 27, 1864. The resourcefulness and hardihood displayed by Cushing brought him national fame and eventually the rank of commander. The *Albemarle* was an ironclad steamship built by the Confederates on the Roanoke River in North Carolina, and it was capable of doing considerable damage. Designed by John C. Porter of the Confederate Navy, the ship was 152 feet long, with a beam of 45 feet and an 8-foot draft. It had a prow or ram of solid oak plated with 2-inch iron and was driven by two engines of 200 horsepower each.

The small Federal force at Plymouth was unable to make much resistance when the *Albemarle* appeared in front of it on April 19 and bombarded the fortifications while General Hoke attacked with infantry on the land side. The Confederates occupied the post, and the *Albemarle* sank a Union steamboat, the *Southfield,* not far from Plymouth and chased another, the *Miami,* down the river. On May 5 the *Albemarle* appeared at the mouth of the Roanoke prepared to challenge the Union fleet on blockade duty there. The latter had four double-enders, two gunboats, and a ferryboat, all commanded by Captain Melancton Smith. In the encounter the *Albemarle* rammed the U.S. *Sassacus,* and the Federal ship's boilers burst, scalding part of the crew. But the *Albemarle* evidently did not want to fight the Union fleet as a whole and headed back up the river to its berth at Plymouth.

The Federal command considered the *Albemarle* a potential troublemaker and decided that it ought to be destroyed. The Confederates also were wary of Federal forays up the river and protected the vessel against surprise attacks. Sentinels were posted along the river, to protect not only the ship but Plymouth, eight miles from the mouth of the Roanoke. When the Navy studied the problem Lieutenant Cushing was at hand, with a reputation for daring established by earlier exploits. Admiral S. P. Lee of the North Atlantic squadron thereupon asked him to prepare a plan for either capturing or destroying the *Albemarle*.

Cushing was a sort of rebel against discipline, to such an extent that he had been dropped by the Naval Academy at Annapolis in his senior year. This happened before the war broke out, but after hostilities began he managed to become an acting master's mate and prove his mettle, on one occasion sailing a prize ship from Philadelphia to New York with its captured crew. The Navy needed a Cushing; by July, 1862, when he was only nineteen, he had become a naval lieutenant.

In this capacity he became engaged in naval exploits that demanded quick action. When his ship, the *Commodore Perry*, became stuck on a bank of the Blackwater River and was about to be rushed by Confederates from the landside, Cushing pushed a field gun up to the forecastle and with the help of volunteers beat back the attack by firing point-blank at the foe. On another raid up the Onslow River in North Carolina he captured two prizes; then his ship, the *Onslow*, ran aground, and he defended it with a single pivot gun. When the attack became too dangerous he piled his men into a boat, set fire to the ship, and escaped. On another occasion he led two boats and twenty men up the Cape Fear River and captured a number of Confederate officers.

Thus Cushing was the logical choice to put the *Albemarle* out of action. He accepted the job with alacrity and set about making elaborate preparations. Only a night raid would enable him to get close to the port and the ship. With the remark "Another stripe or a coffin" he obtained fifteen volunteers and arranged to use a launch. A cutter with five men was to follow him at a distance to give help when needed.

Ironclads were notoriously unprotected below the water line and this Cushing determined to exploit. He had a torpedo device prepared, which would enable him to extend a boom with a torpedo at one end of it, and detonate the torpedo by means of a lanyard device. For this purpose he had to guide the boom and pull the lanyard at the same time. It was difficult to operate under ordinary conditions; how to manage it in a hostile area, possibly after being detected, was a great feat.

Cushing's party moved noiselessly up the Roanoke River on the night of October 27, 1864. There were guards along the river, and there was a sentinel posted on the sunken *Southfield,* yet Cushing crept by them undetected. He was opposite Plymouth and near the *Albemarle* before the watch on the ship became suspicious, challenged him, and shot off a gun. Cushing put on power and headed straight for the ram, when he suddenly saw that the Confederates had built a barrier by connecting a series of logs some distance from the ship. Cushing sheered off, turned around, and then with full power drove squarely at the log barrier. His propulsion carried him across. By this time the Confederates were fully alert; shots were hitting the boat and a bonfire was started on the land to illuminate the area. Cushing coolly lowered his boom, put the torpedo under the overhang, and pulled the trigger. The torpedo exploded under the hull at the same time as a shell from a gun hit the water beside the boat; the men were thrown out and Cushing dived and swam, telling the men to save themselves. He got rid of his sword and worked off his shoes and coat, swimming for the opposite bank. The Confederates were soon putting out a boat of their own; Cushing swam downstream until out of sight of Plymouth, then he headed for the bank. He was so exhausted that he fell in his tracks, sprawling half in mud and half in water, and there he lay until daylight.

To get back to the mouth of the Roanoke, Cushing had to make his way through the jungle of matted underbrush, mostly swamp. At one time he was within inches of being stepped on by passing soldiers. He reached a Confederate outpost on the bank, waited until the men were busy elsewhere, then unloosened their boat and let himself down the stream. It was dark when he reached the bay. He rowed toward a light and found that it was on the U.S. picket ship *Valley City,* which picked him up.

He had accomplished his mission. His men were prisoners, but the *Albemarle* was destroyed for further use. The Navy made Cushing a lieutenant commander, and Congress, at the request of President Lincoln, voted a resolution of thanks.

37

NEGRO TROOPS IN THE UNION ARMY

Negroes in the blue uniforms of the United States Army played important roles in the Civil War. According to the *Statistical Record of the Armies of the United States,* by Frederick Phisterer, the number enrolled was 186,097, including 7,122 white officers. Deaths amounted to 36,847; of these diseases took 29,658. The mortality rate was larger than that of white troops. Not all fought in battles. President Lincoln said, in his annual message to Congress dated December 8, 1863: "Of those who were slaves at the beginning of the rebellion, fully 100,000 are now in the United States military service, about one-half of which number actually bear arms in the ranks. . . . So far as tested, it is difficult to say they are not as good soldiers as any."

Frederick Douglass, whose mother was a Negro slave, already had twenty years of writing and speaking against slavery behind him when the Civil War broke out. He saw it as a war of liberation and wrote: "Never since the world began was a better chance offered to a long-enslaved and oppressed people. The opportunity is given us to be men." In August, 1862, when General David Hunter had been authorized to use Negro troops, Douglass came to the White House to confer with President

Lincoln on recruiting Negroes. Douglass had disapproved of the methods of John Brown and had become a strong supporter of the Administration's efforts to improve the situation of the Negroes who fled the South and came into the North without subsistence.

An example of the complicated situation in the North was the confusion resulting from the Fugitive Slave law, which was still in effect when the war broke out. The early policy of the Administration, to keep the support of Union sympathizers in the border states who held slaves, sometimes caused the authorities to return fugitive slaves to their masters. General Grant stopped this by an order effective in his department in 1862.

The commanding generals had varying opinions on the military capacities of Negro troops, but none doubted their courage. General William T. Sherman was the most critical, but his army was impeded during his march to the sea by large bands of men, women, and children, who had left the plantations and were hailing the Federal troops as deliverers. Sherman was unable to make provision for their care. One of his generals, Brigadier General Jefferson C. Davis, was accused of deliberately cutting off bands of Negroes from his corps and leaving them where they would be captured by the Confederates. His conduct was investigated, and although nothing came of the inquiry, he was passed over for promotion by Secretary of War Stanton.

When the President first considered the enlistment of Negroes, he favored, in such a volatile state as Maryland, that enlistment be voluntary, with the consent of the masters or payment of their price. This, however, did not last long. The War Department quickly heard that forcible enlistment was being practiced in Maryland by recruiting commissioners. This was similar to the old method of impressment of seamen; the recruiting officer would take a file of soldiers into a neighborhood and carry off Negroes without anybody's consent.

General Grant gave the strongest endorsement of the Negro soldiers. John Hay reported Grant as saying that they were admirable soldiers in many respects; quick and docile in instruction and very subordinate; good in a charge; excellent in fatigue duty. But he added his doubts that any of them could have stood the week's pounding at the Wilderness and Spotsylvania as his men did; "no other troops in the world could have done it."

Negro soldiers did not at first receive as much pay as white troops. But the agitation led by Thomas Wentworth Higginson of Boston and others brought their pay up as of January 1, 1864. John M. Langston of Ohio said: "Pay or no pay, let us volunteer."

A desperate attempt of Union troops to get a foothold in Charleston harbor as part of action to reduce the forts took place on July 18, 1863. It was the assault on Fort Wagner at the northern end of Morris Island, which became memorable for the part played by the famous Fifty-fourth Massachusetts Regiment of Volunteers, Negro troops under the command of Colonel Robert Gould Shaw, who died in the battle.

Before this effort Rear Admiral S. F. Du Pont, commanding the South Atlantic Blockading Squadron, had attacked Fort Sumter with nine ironclads on April 7, 1863, in the course of which the *Keokuk* was sunk.

General Quincy A. Gillmore landed 6,500 men with 51 guns on Folly Island, July 10. Troops sent to Morris Island overran a battery on July 11 but the Federals lost 49 killed and 123 wounded, against 12 casualties reported by the Confederates. On July 18 the major attack was made against Fort Wagner, a long earthwork that crossed the end of the island. Here was an assault in the open against a garrison well equipped and protected behind parapets. General G. C. Strong's brigade of six regiments was supported by Colonel H. S. Putnam's of four, which cost the attackers dearly. The total number of Federals killed was 246; wounded, 880; captured or missing, 389. They lost their principal commanders: Brigadier General Strong and Colonels John L. Chatfield, Robert Gould Shaw, and H. S. Putnam. The 100th New York Colored Volunteers fought in Putnam's brigade. The Confederate defense was led by Brigadier General William B. Taliaferro.

Robert Gould Shaw, Boston-born, was a young Harvard graduate, aged twenty-four, when the war broke out. He served in the Seventh New York Volunteer regiment, becoming captain in 1862, and was made colonel of the Fifty-fourth Massachusetts when it was organized, leading it to the front in May, 1863. A memorial by Augustus St. Gaudens was erected on Boston Common in 1897.

An action that for its size was unusually bloody was the capture by the Confederates under Major General Nathan Bedford Forrest of Fort Pillow on April 12, 1864. This post was located on the Mississippi River 40 miles above Memphis and was garrisoned by 557 troops (295 white, 262 Negro) that were units of the Second U. S. Light Artillery, Sixth U. S. Heavy Artillery, and Thirteenth Tennessee Cavalry. The fort had six field pieces; Major Lionel F. Booth of the Sixth commanded. A detachment of Forrest's Cavalry, dismounted, under Brigadier General James R. Chalmers, drove the Federals inside the works. Forrest, arriving late, demanded unconditional surrender. Booth had been killed, but the defenders asked a delay of one hour in his name. The gunboat *New Era* had been shelling the Confederates. Forrest observed that a steamboat loaded with bluecoats was approaching and reduced the truce to twenty minutes. The Federals replied: "We will not surrender."

Forrest then ordered a charge. In the course of the action the Federal troops were routed and sent flying toward the river to escape. The Federal report said that Forrest's men yelled: "Forrest's orders," which was taken to mean "no quarter." The Confederates denied that they were bent on massacre because many of the defenders were Negroes, and pointed out that they took as prisoners 164 whites, 75 Negroes, and 40 Negro women and children. The Federals had 400 casualties, Confederates, 80.

The report spread through the North that Forrest, a former plantation owner, had ordered the "Fort Pillow Massacre," by which name the action became known. An inquiry was made by the Committee on the Conduct of the War in Washington and General C. C. Washburn, of the District of Western Tennessee, asked General S. D. Lee, of the Confederate Department of Alabama, Mississippi and East Louisiana what attitude the Confederate army intended to take toward Negro troops in the Federal service. General Lee denied that there had been any excesses at Fort Pillow, outside of the natural resentment of the soldiers against a "servile race armed against their masters and in a country which had been desolated by almost unprecedented outrages." He said that the garrison had never surrendered, and had fought back in retreating.

Negro troops also fought in actions described elsewhere in this history. They repulsed the Confederates at Ship Island in August, 1863, when seven Negro companies fought beside three white companies. They took part in battles at Petersburg, Olustee (Florida), Bermuda Hundred, Nashville, Fort Powhatan, Milliken's Bend, and Port Hudson.

Repeal of the Fugitive Slave Act

It took Congress a long time to repeal the Fugitive Slave Act, which had been abhorrent to many Northern communities for years and which no longer could be enforced there. Although repeated efforts were made to get Congress to recognize its obsolescence, the attempts failed at several sessions. Finally in June, 1864, the Committee on the Judiciary reported an act repealing the Fugitive Slave Law of 1850 and the third and fourth sections of the original law of 1793. It passed the House by a party vote of 86 to 60, all Administration men but one voting for it. It passed the Senate June 22 and was approved by the President on June 28, 1864.

The Man Who Opposed Dred Scott

Roger B. Taney, Chief Justice of the United States, died October 12, 1864. A native of Maryland, he was appointed to the high office in 1836 and served twenty-eight years, during which his strong convictions in favor of slavery were not without influence on his decisions. Most famous of these was the Dred Scott decision, in which he and the majority of the Court decided that the Negro was property and not a citizen under the Constitution. This decision of 1857 helped bring about the secession of the South and also helped elect Lincoln, who opposed it. The Chief Justice, however, was not a secessionist, and did not leave the Union. He gave the oath of office to nine Presidents, beginning with Martin Van Buren, and twice to Abraham Lincoln, who had been his most outspoken opponent. Despite the controversy over his views, Taney was respected as an honest, sincere jurist of irreproachable character. He was eighty-seven years old when he died.

President Lincoln appointed Salmon P. Chase Chief Justice, and Chase took office December 15. He served eight years, until his death in 1873. He had favored emancipation for years and his views were in tune with those of the advancing Republic.

38

SHERMAN'S MARCH
TO THE SEA

Major General William T. Sherman's March to the Sea was an extraordinary expedition through the heart of Georgia, from Atlanta to Savannah, carried out in the fall of 1864, intended to break the supply system of the Confederacy and hasten the end of the war. With the determination to destroy all factories, mills, and stores that could help the Confederate armies General Sherman led over 60,000 troops from Kingston to Savannah, November 12 to December 22, cutting a swathe of devastation from 20 to 25 miles wide for over 300 miles, destroying not only military but industrial enterprises and creating resentments so deep that, after nearly a century, his march is still execrated in the area he traversed.

The expedition is remarkable in that it would never have been tried but for the enthusiasm and insistence of its commander. When General Hood still had a sizable army in Tennessee and the roving cavalry units under Confederate Generals Forrest and Wheeler were included by Sherman in "the whole batch of devils turned loose," Sherman was confident that Major General George H.

Thomas, with proper support, could hold Hood and dominate the western situation. When he argued that the only way to break the backbone of the Confederacy was to destroy the support of its armies in the heart of the South, he had to convince both General Grant and the military administration in Washington. Grant had unbounded confidence in Sherman, but he had himself faced unexpected difficulties that had wrecked some of his best plans. When he suggested that he might send troops to Wilmington, North Carolina, to await Sherman's coming, Sherman declared that nothing less than the subjugation of Savannah would impress the Confederacy: "They may stand the fall of Richmond, but not of all Georgia." After Hood's campaign got under way Grant became doubtful that General Thomas would have enough men to withstand him. But Sherman was sending him reinforcements: Stanley's Fourth Corps, 15,000 men; Schofield's Twenty-third, 10,000; A. J. Smith's division in Missouri, 14,000; also 5,000 cavalry under General Wilson. Sherman argued: "Unless we can depopulate Georgia it is useless to occupy it, but the utter destruction of its roads, houses, and people will cripple their military resources. I can make the march and make Georgia howl!" He did not want to act on the defensive but on the offensive; it would cost the lives of 1,000 men a month to patrol the roads.

After giving a qualified assent General Grant had doubts and opposed the plan in a letter to President Lincoln. This unsettled Lincoln, who replied that a misstep by Sherman might be fatal to his army. The next day Grant reversed himself; he now thought better of the plan. This decided the government; Secretary Stanton and Chief of Staff Halleck told Sherman to go ahead; he could march to Savannah, where the fleet would meet him. This was good news to Sherman; he would break communications and go where no wire could reach him.

General Sherman's army was organized in two wings of two corps each. The right wing, from the Army of the Tennessee, was placed under Major General O. O. Howard and comprised the Fifteenth Corps under Major General P. J. Osterhaus and later Major General John A. Logan, and the Seventeenth Corps under Major General

Francis P. Blair, Jr. The left wing, the Army of Georgia, was under Major General Henry W. Slocum and comprised the Fourteenth Corps under Brigadier General Jefferson C. Davis and the Twentieth Corps under Brigadier General Alpheus S. Williams. The cavalry division under Brigadier General Judson Kilpatrick was under direct orders of Sherman. These troops marched in four parallel columns on different roads and covered the 300 miles to the sea. They comprised about 60,000 men, including 53,923 infantry, 4,438 cavalry, and 1,718 artillery. They occupied Savannah on December 22, 1864. After that Sherman's army was augmented for the final stages of the campaign against General Johnston. At Goldsboro, North Carolina, the army was joined March 21 by elements of the Army of the Ohio under Major General John M. Schofield, comprising the Tenth Corps, under Major General Alfred H. Terry; the Twenty-third Corps, under Major General Jacob D. Cox; two additional regiments of cavalry; and, after April 5, 1865, the reserve artillery under Captain William E. Mercer. By April 10, 1865, Sherman had 88,948 on his rolls.

As General Sherman left Kingston, Georgia, for Atlanta on November 12, he reflected on this "strange event"—two hostile armies marching in opposite directions, each believing it was going to wind up the war. He now announced the marching routine. The guns would be reduced to 65. There would be about 2,500 wagons with six mules to each, and 600 ambulances with 2 horses to each. Each soldier carried 40 rounds of ammunition. Each corps would have its own train of about 800 wagons, making a line five miles long; they took the road, while the men used the bypaths. Behind each regiment would be one wagon and one ambulance. The men could forage liberally, but not enter dwellings; corps commanders would decide what mills, houses, and cotton gins were to be destroyed; in general, where the army was unmolested, no destruction would take place, but where there were hostile acts there would be devastation, "more or less relentless," according to the measure of hostility. Horses, mules, and wagons might be appropriated freely, but the poor were to be favored. Families were to retain "a reasonable portion for their maintenance." Negroes might be carried along if of service, organized as pioneers and used on road work. The army had rations for twenty days, plenty of beef cattle, and forage for five days, after which it would live on the country.

On November 14 the United States engineers, under Colonel O. M. Poe, destroyed the depot, roundhouse, and shops of the Georgia Railroad in Atlanta and set them on fire; the flames ignited other buildings and a large part of the city was destroyed. The army left on November 15 and 16, and as one band struck up "John Brown's Body" the troops shouted the chorus, "Glory, glory, hallelujah!" The Atlantans never forgot the burning of their city, although more than half had been saved by the efforts of the troops to confine the fire.

The general with the reddish beard, who could outwrite and outtalk any officer in the army, was "Uncle Billy" to his troops. He liked to remember that as he rode among them a soldier would call out: "Uncle Billy, I guess Grant is waiting for us at Richmond!" He responded to the exuberance of the men, the feeling of exhilaration in the air. He noted that officers and men had a "devil may care" attitude; the responsibility for getting this army safely to its destination was his. Sherman was always aware of what was going on around him; how the people acted, what they said; he noted that the Negroes at Covington were "simply frantic with joy." The army quickly acquired a lot of camp followers, but Sherman asked an old Negro to explain to his people that if they came with the army they would merely hinder the work of freeing them and eat up the food needed for the fighting men. Sometimes "Uncle Billy" got off his horse and instructed the men how to make rails unusable; heat the middle of a rail red hot and then twist it around a telegraph pole or trunk of a sapling; "I gave it my personal attention," said he.

His instructions read well, but how was he to regulate thousands of young men given a free hand to collect provisions? The countryside was so well stocked that the soldiers came back loaded with food of all kinds; the wagons bulged with corn and oats. Dwelling houses were not to be entered, but how did Uncle Billy account for the soldiers who dressed up in the costumes of the past—uniforms of Revolutionary soldiers, formal attire of the early days of the Republic, even women's gowns? Then there were the slave women who wanted most of all to cook and wash for the troops and the girls who loved to dance with the men in blue when the corps went in bivouac. The men were to march fifteen miles a day, but considering all the raids on corn cribs and cold cellars and other distractions, they had trouble making ten.

Macon was fortified by state militia, but Sherman's army tore the railroad apart and bypassed the town. General Howard entered Milledgeville on November 20; the legislature had been in session but fled at his approach. There were a few minor clashes with local militia. The Confederate cavalry leader General Wheeler made a stand December 4 at the Oconee River and was attacked by Kilpatrick. Wheeler, according to Major James A. Connolly, had to run "at an ingloriously rapid rate through the streets of Waynesboro," to the satisfaction of Kilpatrick, who had known him at West Point. Kilpatrick had 50 casualties but captured 300 men. Connolly thought Kilpatrick an egotistical little popinjay who looked like a monkey on horseback.

General Beauregard had been commander of the Confederate Military Division of the West since President Jefferson Davis appointed him at Augusta, Georgia, on October 2. His command extended from the Mississippi River to Georgia. Davis now asked Beauregard to take over the defense as far as the seacoast. Beauregard, as well as the Confederate command in Richmond, did not know where Sherman would strike next. Sherman, with his extended columns, practiced the trick of misleading the enemy by sending troops in one direction and then making a quick change to another. Beauregard sent part of the Macon garrison to reinforce Lieutenant General William J. Hardee at Savannah. Davis informed Beauregard that he expected him to stop Sherman, and Beauregard replied on December 6 that Sherman could be kept out of Augusta, Savannah, and Charleston. Yet he instructed General Hardee to hold Savannah as long as possible but not to let the garrison be captured, which indicated that he had little confidence in holding out. There were then about 10,000 troops in Savannah.

The Federals did not meet with determined opposition until they were within thirteen miles of Savannah, where the Confederates had drawn up several lines of fortifications, one, four miles from the city, being helped by a swamp and a deepened canal. On December 13 the Second Division of the Fifteenth Corps under Major General William B. Hazen attacked Fort McAllister and carried it at the point of the bayonet. It was located four miles from the Ogeechee River, where Admiral Dahlgren and the fleet were awaiting Sherman. The fort had held about 230 men, and Hazen lost 24 killed and 110 wounded.

Sherman's army was fortunate in being able to connect with Rear Admiral John A. Dahlgren's fleet, for in the vicinity of Savannah there were no provisions to be had. A great part of the terrain was under water. The pickets floated around in boats, and one trooper returning to his regiment reported that he had waded a mile and a half in knee-deep water.

General Sherman now prepared to occupy Savannah, but not knowing the size of the Confederate army or its capacity for defense, he addressed a demand for its surrender to General Hardee, saying he had guns that could cast "heavy and destructive shot" as far as the city, and that if his demand were not met he could use "the slower and surer process of starvation." General Beauregard was in the city and dictated a reply in which Hardee refused to surrender, denied he was isolated, and said he had conducted his operations according to the rules of civilized warfare. Beauregard then directed a quick evacuation of the city. Hardee rushed completion of a pontoon bridge over the Savannah River. The Confederates began marching out December 20, leaving behind heavy guns and stores and blowing up their ironclads and the navy yard. Beauregard warned Davis that they would now lose the railroad from Augusta to Charleston, and Charleston also, and asked for reinforcements from Lee in Virginia. Davis replied that Lee could spare no troops, and in writing Lee he expressed his amazement at the news. He wanted a concentration of troops in order that he should be able to oppose Sherman.

While General Sherman was making preparations to attack he received word that the city had been found evacuated. Sherman, deciding that President Lincoln would enjoy his "pleasantry," on December 22 dispatched a note to the telegraph office at Fort Monroe for transmission to Lincoln: "I beg to present you as a Christmas gift the city of Savannah, with 150 heavy guns and plenty of ammunition, also about 25,000 bales of cotton." It reached the President on Christmas Eve. Lincoln, in his reply, graciously admitted that all honor belonged to Sherman, since "none of us went further than to acquiesce" in the project. Then Lincoln added that, considered with the work of General Thomas, it was indeed a great success.

Sherman also took the opportunity to make a report of progress to General Grant, who was at City Point, Virginia. He told Grant that his army started from Atlanta with 5,000 head of cattle and reached Savannah with 10,000, after consuming mostly turkeys, chickens, sheep, hogs, and the cattle of the country. Mules that drew the wagons included many "not recovered from the Chattanooga starvation"; they were replaced and the poor ones shot. The state of Georgia lost 15,000 first-rate mules by his operations. Horses were plentiful; every officer had three or four led horses, and each regiment seemed to be followed by at least fifty Negroes and footsore soldiers riding on horses and mules. He ordered "great numbers" of these horses shot, because it disorganized the infantry to have too many idlers mounted. Other surplus horses would be sent to the Quartermaster's Department.

The army now turned north, with the object of occupying the principal cities of South and North Carolina and stopping a junction between the Confederate troops in these areas and Lee's Army of Northern Virginia. A number of changes took place. General Benjamin F. Butler made a failure of his attack on Fort Fisher, North Carolina, on December 25, but Major General A. H. Terry succeeded there on January 15, 1865. As Sherman's army began its march February 1 other changes were brewing. On February 6 General Robert E. Lee became commander in chief of all the Confederate armies, yielding rather reluctantly. On the same day John C. Breckinridge succeeded James A. Seddon as Secretary of War of the Confederacy. The heavy rains continued; the rivers were swollen and the bridge over the Congaree was destroyed by retreating Confederates. "The roads were infamous," wrote Sherman.

Burning of Columbia

General Sherman entered Columbia, the capital of South Carolina, on February 17 and put General O. O. Howard in charge of the city. He found that a long pile of cotton bales had been set afire when General Wade Hampton's cavalry left the city, but it was impossible to place the blame. The railroad depot and a warehouse had been burned to the ground and bags filled with corn and meal were partially burned. During the night a greater tragedy occurred. Several houses began to burn, possibly started by the fire in the cotton bales; a high wind carried the flames farther and by next morning the heart of Columbia had been destroyed. The old state house, the institution of the Sisters of Charity, a hotel, several churches, and possibly 1,300 dwellings were burned. Troops were put to work to stop the flames, with small success. The charge was openly made that soldiers participated in setting fire to buildings, on the ground that they were paying South Carolina back for its leading part in secession. Sherman at first thought drunkenness was to blame and later accused General Wade Hampton of causing it, not from malicious intent but by filling the city with lint, cotton, and tinder. But he admitted that some soldiers, including officers who had been imprisoned by the Confederates and rescued by Sherman, might have had a hand in spreading it. Later on the foragers were accused of setting fire to the pitch-pine forests. General Sherman ordered the Methodist College of Columbia to be turned over to the Sisters of Charity and gave the mayor 500 beef cattle, and 100 muskets to keep order in the streets.

The U.S. engineers dismantled the state arsenal and removed a large quantity of munitions, which they dumped into the Saluda River. One percussion shell exploded as it hit another near the water; the flame followed a train of spilled powder to the wagons and exploded them, killing sixteen men and destroying wagons and mules. The troops also demolished the mint where Confederate money had been printed, and the soldiers gambled among themselves with the banknotes. The troops marched on, February 20, "having utterly ruined Columbia," as Sherman put it.

The Confederate leaders had been losing confidence in Beauregard as the campaign proceeded. Neither General Lee nor President Davis expected him to give up Columbia so easily. They were shocked when Beauregard, after telling them that the army would move to Chesterville, suddenly announced that he would have to retire to Greensboro, North Carolina. Then came the evacuation of Charleston by Beauregard's orders. Actually Charleston was outflanked and Beauregard knew he could not hold it, but Davis was sending General Hardee orders to stay. Thereupon Beauregard gave Hardee peremptory orders to evacuate Charleston. He did so on February 17-18, and on the 18th a Federal brigade under General Schimmelpfennig moved in. On February 22 the Confederates had worse news—Wilmington, North Carolina, had fallen. On that day Major General A. H. Terry and the Tenth Corps of Major General John M. Schofield's Army of the Ohio occupied it.

General Lee tactfully suggested to the Confederate Secretary of War Breckinridge that he had heard that Beauregard's health was feeble. It was evident that Beauregard had no new military ideas to offer, now that he had been crowded out of the citadel where he had opened the war. Lee suggested that General Joseph E. Johnston take over the command. On February 23 Lee directed Johnston to take command of the Army of Tennessee and all troops in the Department of South Carolina, Georgia, and Florida and to "concentrate all available forces and drive back Sherman." Lee said he would assign Beauregard to duty as Johnston might select. Beauregard was willing to go along with Johnston, who had sized up the Southern cause as hopeless and had no other object in continuing the war than to obtain terms of peace that would satisfy the South.

Marching in the most miserable weather, Sherman's army reached Cheraw on March 3. The rains continued and the roads were so miry that the troops had to stop to corduroy them by cutting saplings and laying them down. Cheraw had extensive Confederate stores as well as property of Charleston citizens, sent there for safety. The Federals found 24 guns, 2,000 muskets, and 3,600 barrels of gunpowder. There also were eight wagonloads of fine wines, which General Blair distributed equitably among the divisions.

The principal military activities of this period were cavalry encounters and rear-guard skirmishing. On March 10 Confederate General Wade Hampton surprised Kilpatrick's camp and for a short time had possession of his artillery and numerous horses, but the Federals rallied and Hampton had to withdraw and leave the booty, although his men broke the spokes of the artillery wheels. The Confederates asserted they had taken 500 Union prisoners and liberated 173 of their own men. The Federals admitted 600 were missing; they also lost 80 killed and 421 wounded, but asserted the Confederates had 1,500 casualties.

Kilpatrick's cavalry, scouting on March 15, came upon and captured Colonel Alfred Rhett and a few aides. Rhett had been in command of the Charleston garrison and had been a confirmed secessionist editor on the Charleston *Mercury*. A day later Kilpatrick captured 217 men of Colonel Rhett's Charleston troops. This was during an action at Averasboro, North Carolina, which lasted all day. Here the divisions of Brigadier General Nathaniel J. Jackson and Brigadier General William T. Ward of the Twentieth Corps were sent against an entrenched position of Hardee's troops. Hardee retreated about 400 yards to a new line and held it until dark, when he left. The Federals lost 77 killed and 477 wounded, and said the Confederates left 108 dead on the field.

General Slocum and the Fourteenth Corps moved on to Fayetteville, North Carolina, arriving there March 10. Sherman arrived a day later and established communication with the Federal army in Wilmington, which sent a

steamboat laden with mail and clothing. Sherman asked
Major General Terry at Wilmington to send by boats
all the shoes, stockings, drawers, sugar, coffee, and flour
he could spare, as well as oats and corn. He said he
had to get rid of 20,000 to 30,000 useless mouths and
wanted to send them down the Cape Fear River, and in
vehicles and on captured horses, to Wilmington. Then he
outlined his next move.

We must not give time for Jos. Johnston to concentrate at
Goldsboro. We cannot prevent his concentrating at Raleigh,
but he shall have no rest. I want General Schofield to go on
with his railroad from Newbern [now New Bern] as far
as he can, and you should do the same from Wilmington. If
we can get the roads to and secure Goldsboro by April 10, it
will be soon enough, but every day now is worth a million
of dollars. I can whip Jos. Johnston provided he does not
catch one of my corps in flank, and I will see that the army
marches hence in compact form.

Once connected with Schofield, Sherman would be
ready for "the next and last stage of the war." He respected Johnston as a military man; knew he would not
be misled "by feints and false reports," as Beauregard
and Hardee had been. He also admitted he would have
to exercise more caution than formerly. Sherman overestimated the size of Johnston's army, figuring that he
had 45,000, including 37,000 infantry and 8,000 cavalry. But there is a great discrepancy between the numbers computed by Sherman and those admitted by Johnston. Sherman thought that Major General Robert F.
Hoke's division, which belonged now to General Bragg's
Department of North Carolina, had 8,000, but actually
it had about 4,500. Other Confederate units were similarly reduced.

Before leaving Fayetteville, General Sherman destroyed
the arsenal, foundries, and machine shops. General
Johnston commented later that a quantity of valuable
machinery had been brought to the arsenal from Harpers
Ferry and was destroyed with the buildings. "As it was impossible that the Confederacy could ever recover it, its
destruction was, at the least, injudicious," said General
Johnston. But Sherman felt the Federal government

should never again trust the state with an arsenal. He was committed to the "utter demolition" of the railroads and the "utter destruction" of the enemy's arsenals. Much of the destruction, in South Carolina especially, was practically total warfare on the population. Major James A. Connolly, whose letters were published as *Three Years in the Army of the Cumberland* (1959), said he was "perfectly sickened" by the devastation spread by the Federal army; that every house except the church and the Negro cabin was burned down and women, children, and old men were turned out homeless into the mud and rain.

When Sherman's army advanced as usual in parallel columns some distance apart, Johnston saw an opportunity to strike one of the sections. General Wade Hampton had determined that the Federal army was headed for Goldsboro; the right wing was across the Black River, about half a day ahead of the left wing, which had not reached it. Hampton found a likely battlefield on the road four miles from Bentonville, and Johnston prepared to strike the left column March 19. Hampton threw some light entrenchments across the road, and General Hoke's troops were placed with their center on the road and the rest at right angles to the road. When General Slocum's column reached the place he deployed several brigades and attacked, and was repulsed. He moved up two divisions of General Jefferson C. Davis' corps and formed a new defensive position with two divisions of the Twentieth Corps.

According to General Johnston's report, the Confederates charged with General Hardee leading the right wing, with the support of General Bragg; they passed over the first Federal line in double-quick time and at the second line, now manned by both lines of Federal troops, "General Hardee led the charge and, with his knightly gallantry, dashed over the enemy's breastworks on horseback, in front of his men." The Confederates said they pursued the Federals into a thick wood of young pines, so dense that the movements of the troops could not be controlled, so that after some more fighting, the Confederates withdrew. On the other side, General Sherman reported that although General Hardee attacked from 3 P.M. until dark on March 19, he was everywhere repulsed. Sherman, marching with the Fifteenth Corps some distance away, answered Slocum's call for aid by rushing General Blair's corps to the Bentonville road. General Johnston was departing, so the Federals began harassing his rear, and the 20th was devoted to skirmishing and cavalry attacks. Sherman was wary of consequences and started his trains back to Kinston for provisions. The next day, March 21, it rained again and the army was inactive until noon. Then General J. A. Mower, "ever rash" as Sherman described him, discovered a weak spot in the Confederate extreme left flank, and leading the Twentieth Corps, broke through the line and began pushing the Confederates back toward Bentonville and Mill Creek, which threatened to cut off their only line of retreat. The Confederates immediately began calling up nearby cavalry and infantry units, and according to Johnston they managed to push Mower back. But actually, Sherman, alarmed because a major engagement might develop, ordered Mower back and tried to check the Confederate concentration on Mower by skirmish fire along the whole line.

Here, Sherman admits, he made a great mistake, for he should have followed Mower's lead and started a general battle, which would have resulted in a Federal victory. "With the knowledge now possessed of his small force," wrote Sherman years later, "I committed an error in not overwhelming Johnston's army." Johnston said later that he had only 14,000 infantry and artillery, not counting cavalry. Sherman reported that in the action at Bentonville his army lost 191 killed, 1,168 wounded, 287 missing; the Confederates reported 228 killed, 1,467 wounded, 658 missing. The Federals said they took 625 prisoners.

On March 22 Sherman met General Terry at Cox's Bridge and on March 23 they rode together into Goldsboro and found that General Schofield had already arrived. Thus the whole army was assembled. Sherman had marched 425 miles from Savannah to Goldsboro, crossing five large rivers and a terrain largely inundated, but as he said, "with the army in superb order."

39

BEAUREGARD AND BUTLER
AT DREWRY'S

Early in 1864 the Confederate government at Richmond was studying its military dispositions, its expectations from conscription, and its resources with the object of meeting the massive thrusts that were bound to come from the Federals early in spring. Federal strength was growing daily and there was no longer any hope of an invasion far into Federal territory; at best the high command looked for a break in the ring and the possibility of separating the Federal strength and defeating it piecemeal. Fighting defensive actions on interior lines had one advantage—it gave easy access to supply depots. General Lee's line was strong, but it ran to the north of Richmond; the south side of the James was more vulnerable.

In April, General Grant stopped the exchange of prisoners, a war measure prompted by his conviction that he could thus curtail Confederate manpower, but an act that could hardly be called humane. For thousands of Union men, racked by disease, ill fed and ill clothed, lay wasting away at Andersonville, Georgia, Libby Prison in Richmond, and Salisbury, North Carolina. These were wrecks of men who could be saved only by their return to their homes in the North, whereas the Confederates from Northern prisons, fed with army rations and receiving medical care, returned home healthy and were immediately put back in the ranks.

General Pierre G. T. Beauregard, the most volatile and imaginative of the Southern commanders, and often considered unreliable, had become dissatisfied because his work on the defenses of Charleston brought him no field action. He asked for leave to retire to his Alabama retreat at about the same time that General Lee suggested to the Richmond government that Beauregard be moved to North Carolina or the south side of the James. Gen-

eral Braxton Bragg, now military adviser to President
Jefferson Davis, had a higher opinion of Beauregard's
ability than did Davis. He ordered him to assume command of the Department of North Carolina and Cape
Fear, with headquarters at Weldon, North Carolina.
When Beauregard learned its extent he promptly called
it the Department of North Carolina and Southern Virginia, and within a few days he would have charge all
the way from Wilmington, North Carolina, to Petersburg,
Virginia.

Thus Beauregard was just in time to play a major part
in confronting Major General Benjamin F. Butler's expedition up the James. This appears to have been Butler's own project, proposed by him to Grant when the
latter was inspecting the Federal troops at Norfolk and
Fort Monroe, April 1 and 2. Grant went there from
Washington to meet Butler and determine for himself
whether Butler ought to command on the Peninsula in the
forthcoming operations against Richmond, and he had
satisfied his curiosity and decided in Butler's favor. Butler
then proposed to move up the James and land on the
area between the James and the Appomattox Rivers, the
area of Bermuda Hundred, which Butler thought would
make possible operations against Richmond from the
South.

Grant approved the operation, but he specified that
the concentration of troops was to be at City Point. He
pointed out that Richmond was the objective, and cooperation between Butler's force and the Army of the Potomac was necessary. "When you are notified to move,
take City Point with as much force as possible," wrote
Grant in his instructions. "Fortify, or rather intrench, at
once, and concentrate all your troops for the field there
as rapidly as you can." The difference between City
Point and Bermuda Hundred was that City Point af-
forded a base for moving directly on Petersburg, whereas
Bermuda Hundred left little room for offensive action if
the Confederates could place a force between the James
and Appomattox Rivers.

On May 5, the day Grant's great offensive began in the
Wilderness, Butler moved up the James River. He had
about 36,000 troops comprising the Tenth Army Corps

under Major General Quincy A. Gillmore and the Eighteenth Army Corps under Major General William Farrar Smith. The unit moved upstream on every conceivable kind of transport, including ferryboats, canal boats, tugs, sloops, schooners, and side-wheelers. Butler left Brigadier General Edward W. Hinks's Third Division of Negro troops at City Point and then moved on to land the bulk of his troops at Bermuda Hundred. On May 6 they began digging entrenchments on a line three and one-half miles long from Walthall's Landing on the Appomattox to the James River. The objective was Richmond, about twelve miles away, but between Richmond and Butler was the strongly built Fort Darling and the entrenchments and rifle pits of Drewry's Bluff on the James, about four miles distant, the principal point of defense for Richmond.

On May 9 General Butler ordered the Tenth and the Eighteenth Corps to move toward Petersburg. They marched over four miles to Swift Creek, which they found impassable. The bridges were held by Confederate troops armed with artillery, and the railroad bridge did not provide proper footing. Generals Gillmore and Smith gave General Butler their opinion that if Petersburg was to be taken he must place a bridge over the Appomattox behind the line and attack it from the east. To this Butler replied tartly that he "was not going to build a bridge for West Point men to retreat over."

Butler ordered an operation toward Richmond on May 12. Gillmore was to hold the Petersburg Road, and when the Eighteenth Corps had passed Chester Station on the railroad General Kautz was to destroy as much as possible of the Danville Railroad. General Hinks was to move the Negro division from City Point to Point of Rocks on the Appomattox. Brigadier General Godfrey Weitzel, who commanded the Second Division of the Eighteenth, pushed forward in the van with skirmishers and encountered a hot fire from the Confederate defense points. On May 13 Brigadier General W. T. H. Brooks' First Division reached the strong defense line of Drewry's Bluff. The Confederates had prepared for attacks by building trenches and numerous rifle pits, and the Federals made little progress from this point. The only incident worth noting was the instruction of General Smith to Generals Brooks and Weitzel to defend their positions in the dense fog against surprise by stretching telegraph wires along the stumps of trees. This was to have considerable repercussion.

General Beauregard, who was responsible for the defense of Drewry's Bluff, had plans of his own for wiping out Butler. When he submitted his project to his superiors, General Bragg and President Davis, they were not enthusiastic, but they realized that Butler was a threat and would have to be faced. The Confederate Secretary of War, Seddon, was worried; he warned Beauregard that Richmond must be protected at Drewry's, especially when some Federal cavalry penetrated the outer defenses of Richmond. Beauregard made plans to fight Butler on May 16. General Ransom was to move against the Federal right and cut Butler off from Bermuda Hundred. General Hoke was to attack the Federal left, with General Colquitt's brigade in reserve. Beauregard ordered General W. H. C. Whiting to be ready to move into the fighting on the Federal left from Port Walthall Junction.

The start of Beauregard's strategy was confused because the troops had to operate in a dense fog. Ransom drove into Butler's front lines and took some prisoners, but some of his units became separated in the fog. When Ransom halted and asked for help Beauregard sent one of Colquitt's units. Hoke made a similar advance, then met with stout opposition, whereupon Beauregard had Ransom send him troops, which failed to find him. The Federals were subject to heavy artillery fire, and despite the confusion caused by the fog the Confederates managed so to threaten the right flank of the Federal advance that General Smith, following the orders of Butler, ordered his corps to retire across Proctor's Creek to the safety of the entrenchments. The four regiments of Brigadier General Charles A. Heckman's brigade of Weitzel's division, chiefly Massachusetts troops, were badly mauled, but the Confederate losses also were high, especially in front of the telegraph wires, where they were "slaughtered like partridges." General Heckman was captured. The Richmond newspapers spoke of the

wires as a devilish contrivance which none but a Yankee
could devise. Beauregard's greatest disappointment was
the failure of General Whiting to play a major role in
finishing Butler off. Late in the day Beauregard was still
sending messages to Whiting reminding him of Blücher
at Waterloo. As usual, losses were reported variously for
the actions of May 12–16, 1864. Butler estimated that
he had 4,500 casualties, of which number 1,478 were
missing. Other figures place his dead at 390, wounded
at 2,380. Beauregard had approximately 355 dead, 2,000
wounded. General Grant saw that Butler's position at
Bermuda Hundred was excellent for defense, but Beauregard had effectively corked his bottle and the Army
of the James lost much of its usefulness when it did not
follow Grant's instructions to make City Point the base.

40

GRANT MOVES SOUTH
OF THE JAMES

The Civil War moved into its final phase in Virginia
when General Grant gave up his attempt to dislodge Lee
from his entrenchments north of the James River and determined to strike in the rear and get between him and
his supplies. Cold Harbor had taught Grant finally that
nothing was to be gained by frontal attacks on a well-
entrenched army that refused to take risks. Moreover, as
Lee fell back on his strong interior lines near Richmond, Grant had to cross the unbridged Chickahominy
and guard the Fredericksburg Railroad as a supply line.
    Under date of June 5, 1864, Grant wrote to Major
General Halleck from Cold Harbor that he proposed to
move to the south side of the James. He had learned
"after thirty days of trial" that the enemy proposed to
act on the defensive behind breastworks, or "feebly on
the offensive immediately in front of them," and he was

unwilling to pay the price in lives that assaults demanded. He explained that he would hold the ground now occupied until the cavalry could be sent west to destroy the Virginia Central Railroad from about twenty-five or thirty miles west of Beaver Dam. This done, he would move the army to the south side of the James either by crossing the Chickahominy and going to City Point, or crossing at the mouth of the Chickahominy, for which he would need large-sized ferries. "Once on the south side of the James River I can cut off all sources of supply . . . except what is furnished by the canal."

Destruction of the canal was of the utmost importance, because it helped supply both Lee's army and Richmond. Grant sent orders to Major General David Hunter to start this destruction at Lynchburg; if Hunter did not succeed Grant would send cavalry up the south side of the river to cross on pontoons and accomplish it. He reiterated in his instructions to Hunter: "Lose no opportunity to destroy the canal." He ordered General Sheridan to take two divisions and start the destruction of the Virginia Central at Charlottesville and then join Hunter's force on the return.

General Sheridan started on his assignment by crossing the Pamunkey at New Castle on June 7 and on the 9th Lee was reporting to President Davis his guess that Sheridan was out to join Hunter to demolish railroads. Lee sent General Wade Hampton and General Fitzhugh Lee to move alongside with their cavalry, keeping Sheridan on their right. General Hunter tangled with a Confederate force at Piedmont near Staunton June 5 and reported 130 Union dead and 650 wounded, but he estimated Confederate losses at 460 dead, including the commander, General W. E. Jones.

Hunter then proceeded to Lynchburg. Here Hunter, with the divisions of Sullivan and Crook and the cavalry of Averell and Duffie, was turned back by a strong detachment from Lee's army June 17–18. The Federals lost 100 killed, 500 wounded; the Confederates had 200 casualties. Hunter began a retreat northwest in West Virginia, and Sheridan did not find him.

General Hunter blamed his inability to take Lynchburg on lack of ammunition, but the Confederate General Jubal A. Early, who was sent in pursuit of Hunter, blamed his failure on time lost in pillaging and dilatory movement. As Early followed Hunter's trail he encountered "heart-rending" evidence of depredations on unarmed inhabitants of Virginia, especially at Lexington. Early set down in his memoirs that Hunter's route from Lynchburg was lined with tragedy; houses had been burned, families had been left without a morsel to eat; old men, women, and children had been robbed of all clothing except what they wore; furniture and bedding had been cut to pieces; women's trunks had been rifled and their dresses torn to pieces—even Negro girls had "lost their little finery."

In Lexington, Hunter burned Virginia Military Institute, with its library and appliances, sacked Washington College, and destroyed the house of former Governor Letcher of Virginia. In the same county Hunter's troops, according to Early, hanged "a Christian gentleman who had killed a marauding Federal soldier who was insulting and outraging the ladies of his family." There is no reason to doubt Early's report, although he wrote freely of Yankee depredations and once admitted that his own troops also got out of hand.

The change of base of a huge army from carefully held positions to an area where natural barriers had to be overcome and new lines of supply established was a hazardous undertaking. Grant estimated that he had 115,000 men, with hospital orderlies, cooks, and other noncombatants included in the count, when he crossed the James, June 14 and 15. To withdraw while facing the enemy meant placing units in position for flank and rear-guard defense in case of pursuit, creating diversions in other directions to confuse the enemy and draw off some of his troops; moving supplies to have them available for troops on the march. In this case it also meant providing for protection against hostile gunboats and river craft and having on hand enough vessels to ferry the troops.

Meade was in immediate command, but Grant planned the strategy. The army, with its artillery and supplies, moved across the Chickahominy and the James without Lee's being aware for several days exactly where Grant was and what he was doing. With all marching units carefully protected, the main body of Grant's army headed for Wilcox's Landing, where the engineers in 10 hours laid down a bridge 13 feet wide resting on 92 boats across a river 2,100 feet wide at that point. The bridge was supported against the current by three schooners anchored at the center. Troops began to cross early on June 14, and half of the infantry, 4,000 cavalry, 3,500 beef cattle, and an artillery and wagon train thirty-five miles long was across by midnight of the 16th, a stupendous operation in hostile country, with a Confederate army of nearly 80,000 only thirty-five miles away.

Major General J. F. C. Fuller, British authority on military campaigns, decided that Lee's inaction for three days when Grant was moving across the James meant that Lee was completely outgeneraled. His views were not welcome to Southern historians, but one, the Confederate artillery commander General E. Porter Alexander, wrote that here Lee lost "the last, and perhaps the best chances of Confederate success," calling the outcome more damaging than Gettysburg. Although such opinions, voiced in retrospect, are often fallible, General Alexander thus contributed to admiration for Grant's strategy.

General Grant went to Bermuda Hundred on June 14 to confer with General Butler on an immediate advance against Petersburg and then returned to the place of embarkation to have General Meade speed crossing by General Hancock's corps, also ordered to Petersburg.

General Beauregard, who was watching Butler's forces at Bermuda Hundred and trying desperately to hold his command together in the face of requests for reinforcement by Lee, as early as June 7 told General Bragg, President Davis' military adviser in Richmond, that he believed Grant was about to move south of the James. This may have been a good guess, but on June 9 he amplified it, telling Bragg that Grant would go around Lee's flank and either advance on both banks of the James or go below the James and operate from the fortified position at Bermuda Hundred.

On June 10 a number of Federal units actually did strike out from Bermuda Hundred to test the defenses at Petersburg; they comprised cavalry from General Butler's army under the command of Brigadier General August V. Kautz and Colonel Samuel P. Spear. The Confederate defenses were hastily manned by General H. A. Wise from Home Guards and civilians, and the Union cavalry withdrew after losing 20 killed and 67 wounded.

All this time General Beauregard, who was in command of the Petersburg sector, was pleading with Richmond for the return of troops that had been removed to support Lee, especially those under command of Major General Robert F. Hoke. Beauregard warned that he would either have to leave the entrenchments he had built to keep Butler immobilized at Bermuda Hundred or he would have to abandon Petersburg. The Confederate military authorities were slow to act on Beauregard's requests. On June 14 General Lee told President Davis "I think the enemy must be preparing to move south of James River," but his subsequent dispatches show that he was not positive exactly what Grant's objective would be. Beauregard had described Petersburg as "nearly defenseless." By the night of June 14 the advance of Grant's army had reached Bermuda Hundred and Lee ordered Hoke's division to Drewry's Bluff.

The Siege of Petersburg Begins

Next to Richmond, Petersburg was the most important military center in Virginia. Actually it was of greater usefulness to the Confederacy than Richmond itself, for the latter was defended primarily because of its prestige as the capital, whereas Petersburg was the center of supply. Into it ran five railroads that carried provisions from the productive interior for transshipment to the Confederate armies. The Richmond & Petersburg ran north; the Norfolk & Petersburg ran southeast to Norfolk; the Southside ran west to Lynchburg; the Petersburg & Weldon tapped North Carolina; and the Petersburg & City Point had its terminus at City Point.

Many tons of provisions were brought to the city over a network of roads, some of which were covered with strips of wood and known as plank roads. To control a highway was almost as useful as controlling a railroad, and the Jerusalem Plank Road, which ran to Jerusalem,

Virginia, now called Courtland, was one of those fought over in the campaign.

Petersburg was a city of 18,000 people, situated on the south bank of the Appomattox River, twenty-three miles south of the Confederate capital, and only eight miles from the Federal base at City Point, which was located where the Appomattox flows into the James. Before the safety of the city was ever threatened by the expeditions of Generals Butler and Grant, the Confederates had begun to fortify the environs. The campaign of General McClellan in 1862 directed attention to the vulnerability of Petersburg, and Captain Charles H. Dimmock, Confederate engineer, was ordered to construct a line of trenches and artillery emplacements, which became known as the Dimmock line. This line ran around the city's southern limits for ten miles with both ends curving up to the Appomattox River. It had provision for fifty-five batteries, more than the Confederate army would have available for such an extended front.

The Confederate command obviously did not intend to keep troops encamped at Petersburg while Grant's major forces were north of the James. Beauregard was the only commander who was greatly concerned. When he asked Bragg on June 7 to return to his forces the divisions of Hoke and Ransom he said: "Should Grant have left Lee's front, he doubtless intends operations along James River, probably on south side. Petersburg being nearly defenseless would be captured before it could be reinforced." On June 9 Beauregard told Bragg that Grant probably would use Bermuda Hundred as a base for attacking Richmond. That day the first Federal reconnoiter of Petersburg's defenses took place, with General Wise's brigade of 2,200, including hastily armed civilians, manning the defense line. This still further alarmed Beauregard. It was not until June 15 that Lee ordered Hoke, who had 7,656 men, to report to Beauregard, and told Bragg that Ransom also should be sent.

Lee's reluctance to transfer troops from north of the James until he was absolutely sure where Grant was headed has been interpreted as lack of knowledge of Grant's operations, as against the apparent certainty of Beauregard. On June 14 Lee informed President Davis

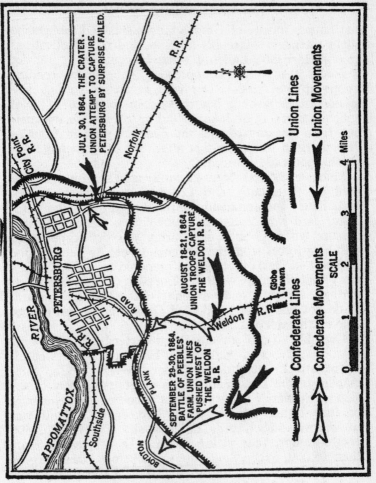

The Petersburg Campaign
Summer, 1864

that he was unsure of Grant's movements and thought he might intend to place his army behind the fortifications around Harrison's Landing, where he could easily transfer it across the river. "I apprehend he may be sending troops up the James River with a view of getting possession of Petersburg before we can reinforce it." Not until the morning of June 15 did he get precise information from Beauregard that the Federals were in front of Petersburg in force. On that afternoon Lee ordered Ransom to report to Beauregard.

Much credit has been given Beauregard for guessing right on Petersburg, and Lee has been criticized proportionately for apparently misreading the situation. But Beauregard was dealing in probabilities, and Lee had to be sure where Grant's main army was before he could withdraw forces from the Richmond line. As late as June 14 Lee told Davis that he had prepared to attack Grant's army that morning, "but it disappeared from before us during the night," and on June 16 Lee told Beauregard, "I do not know the position of Grant's army and cannot strip north bank of James River."

General Grant assumed that Petersburg was only sparsely garrisoned and could be taken by a well-directed attack. He ordered General W. F. Smith, commander of the Eighteenth Corps of Butler's Army of the James, to march from Bermuda Hundred to Petersburg on June 15 and take the place "immediately." Smith was to take with him Kautz's 2,500 cavalry and Hinks' 3,500 Negro troops, thus giving Smith a total force of more than 16,000. When Smith appeared before Petersburg on June 15, 1864, Beauregard had only 5,400 men to defend it. These included 3,200 still on the Howlett line and Wise's 2,200. Grant was right in thinking Petersburg could be taken easily. Only one man stood in the way—General Smith, who, for some inexplicable reason, threw away the opportunity and condemned Grant to a siege of Petersburg that lasted from June, 1864, to April, 1865, and cost thousands of casualties.

Smith arrived at 10 A.M. and spent until 5 P.M. in reconnoitering. When he ordered up his artillery he learned that the horses were being watered, so he delayed the attack until 7 P.M. His troops carried Confederate battery No. 5 and nearly a mile of the outer line, but in the gathering dusk of the June evening Smith stopped the assault at 9 P.M. He explained later that it was wiser to hold what he had than to risk losing it. General Grant did not agree. Years later he blamed the failure of his plans in part on the deliberate movements of Smith. The British commentator Major General J. F. C. Fuller decided that "Smith's lack of energy may well be considered one of the most serious errors of the entire campaign."

Beauregard lost no time in demanding reinforcements, and Bragg ordered Hoke to join him. Beauregard also directed General Bushrod R. Johnson to leave the lines at Bermuda Hundred and come to Petersburg. He informed General Lee of this and also threatened to withdraw his skirmishers and pickets, which would take the cork out of the bottle that held General Butler. Lee received this dispatch at 2 A.M. on June 16 and became alarmed; he asked Beauregard not to withdraw the pickets and skirmishers, and Beauregard consented. Lee now began making new dispositions of troops, but he still had to tell Davis that he did not know what force was opposing Beauregard nor whether any part of Grant's army was there.

This ignorance was to be cleared up within hours. Grant had ordered Hancock's Second Corps to follow Smith to Petersburg, but Hancock was in a dilemma. He had been told to wait for rations ordered by Grant and did so, although not in actual need of them. Grant blamed Meade for not urging Hancock forward, and Meade explained that Grant's orders did not reach him. However, Hancock was able to reach the outskirts of Petersburg the night of June 15. The next day the roads were full of marching men and rolling caissons as Meade's army started: units of the Second, Fifth, Sixth, and Ninth Corps were headed for Petersburg.

On the morning of June 16 Hancock's troops entered the battle. The Confederates manned guns behind redans, and the Federal advance was costly. On June 17 the Federal attack began at 3 A.M. and continued after nightfall; it broke the Confederate line, but the Union troops could not follow through. That night Beauregard left campfires burning while he withdrew his troops silently to an inner line, where new trenches were prepared before dawn—axes, bayonets, knives, "every utensil that could be found"—being employed.

On June 18 Lee ordered his troops to Petersburg. He told General Hampton to watch Sheridan, who was headed for White House, but if Sheridan boarded transports there, Hampden was to hurry to Petersburg. General Kershaw's division, vanguard of Lee's army, arrived early that morning; Field's division followed. Livermore estimates that they added 25,000 men to Beauregard's defenders. At 11:30 A.M. Lee was on the ground, and Beauregard could say jubilantly that "for the present at least, Richmond and Petersburg were safe."

The fighting was severe, and the Federals gained little. General David B. Birney was temporarily in command of the Second Corps, after Hancock's Gettysburg wound had incapacitated him. Colonel Joshua L. Chamberlain of the Twentieth Maine was wounded, and Grant made him a brigadier general.

The honors for the stubborn defense went to Beauregard, but Richmond distrusted his independence. The argument over Lee's strategy continues. Lee now had the task of protecting Richmond and Petersburg on a line twenty-five miles long, from White Oak Swamp across the James River to Jerusalem Plank Road. Official returns showed that he had 54,751 men available in June, 1864, whereas Grant had 90,000 by midsummer. The Federal losses at Petersburg, from June 15 through June 18, were over 10,000 casualties, including 1,298 killed, 7,474 wounded, 1,814 missing.

President Lincoln made a personal visit to Grant's headquarters June 21, 1864, starting from City Point on the James River. The President, wearing as usual his high silk hat and frock coat, rode past the troops accompanied by Grant, having, in the words of Horace Porter, "the appearance of a country farmer riding into town, wearing his Sunday clothes." He was cheered by the troops and especially by the Negro regiments that were to be so severely used in the assault at the Crater. When Lincoln returned to Washington he quoted Grant, according to Charles Sumner: "I am as far off from Richmond now as I shall ever be. I shall take the place; but as the rebel papers say, it may require a long summer's day."

Battle of the Petersburg Crater

The most spectacular incident in the siege of Petersburg was the explosion of the Federal mine that produced the Battle of the Crater. This was the most disastrous mining operation of the whole war, resulting in gross mismanagement of troops after the explosion and causing many casualties. Its principal predecessor was the explosion of the large mine at Vicksburg, where the results were similarly indecisive.

In assaults on the Confederate lines June 17 and 18, 1864, by the Ninth Corps under General Burnside, the Union troops crossed a ravine in which ran the Norfolk & Petersburg Railroad and on reaching its crest faced a fortified outpost of the Confederates near Cemetery Hill called Elliott's Salient. The ground sloped gently from the Confederate position to the Union line, a distance of about 130 yards. One of the units holding this front was the Forty-eighth Pennsylvania Volunteer Regiment of about 400 men, many of whom were miners from the upper Schuylkill coal region. When its commander, Lieutenant Colonel Henry Pleasants, mining engineer, heard his men speculating on the ease with which they could build a tunnel and blow up the Confederates, he proposed this operation to General Burnside. Burnside favored it, but both General Meade and the chief engineer of the Army, Major Duane, said the tunnel could not be built because it would be too long and lack ventilation. Grant approved, however, and Burnside ordered the work started June 25.

Colonel Pleasants had to improvise tools and materials, which made the feat all the more remarkable. He could get no supplies of boards or lumber to use in supporting the roof of the shaft, so he tore down an old bridge and sent two companies to sawmills outside the lines to cut the timbers. Ordinary picks had to be bent straight for mining. Colonel Pleasants was unable to get an accurate instrument for triangulation and had to be satisfied with an old-fashioned theodolite that General Burnside procured from Washington. Dirt had to be removed in cracker boxes, strengthed with hoops from beef barrels.

The hill behind the Union front sloped steeply to the ravine and thus enabled the miners to start their tunnel some distance down the hillside. They dug a tunnel 510-8/10 feet long. To avoid heavy clay encountered less than halfway in, the tunnel had to be sloped upward slightly. Two lateral galleries were then extended directly under the Confederate fortifications, one 37 feet long, the other 38 feet. The dirt was carried out and covered with bushes so that Confederate observers in trees could not identify it. An air tube was constructed in the shape of a long wooden box running the length of the tunnel; its mouth was at the opening; the tunnel was closed by a door and just inside the door was a fireplace with a chimney rising to the surface of the hill. When the fire was lighted fresh air was drawn into the tunnel through the tube and thus reached the miners where they were working.

No mine can be kept wholly secret from the enemy because sounds of digging can be detected through the earth, but the exact location is not easily determined. The Confederates began to countermine feverishly, and exaggerated fears spread through Petersburg that the whole place might be blown up. The Confederates did not strike the Union tunnel, which was only twenty feet below their fort when completed.

In order to draw troops from the Confederate lines Grant sent General Hancock with his corps and Sheridan with two cavalry divisions to Deep Bottom to threaten Richmond. Lee detached troops for its defense until he had only about 18,000 facing the Federals in the trenches at Petersburg. Grant ordered his troops back in time to be at hand for the explosion of the mine. He then made careful preparations for the assault. Major General Gouverneur K. Warren of the Fifth Corps was to hold his entrenchments and place extra troops on the right next to Burnside: Ord was to be ready to support Burnside. The front of the parapets was to be cleared of abatis so that the troops met no obstructions. Burnside was to push his troops past the hole that the mine would make and go over the top of the hill.

In spite of months of work and the most careful timing, the mine incident became a series of the most inexcusable blunders. Burnside had given front place in the assault to a new division, Brigadier General Edward Ferrero's Fourth Division of the Ninth Corps, comprising about 4,300 Negro troops. They were eager to lead, but never having been under fire they were displaced by General Meade, who ordered up Major General James F. Ledlie's First Division. The first brigade was to be led by Colonel E. G. Marshall. Burnside had planned to move troops to the right and left of the big hole after the explosion, but Meade again interfered and ordered a direct attack to the crest of Cemetery Hill.

Colonel Pleasants had demanded 14,000 pounds of powder for the mine, but General Meade reduced the amount to 8,000. Pleasants lighted the fuse to detonate the mine at 3:15 A.M. on July 30, 1864, expecting an explosion in fifteen minutes. When nothing had happened by 4:15 A.M., two volunteers crawled into the tunnel and discovered that the fuse had burned out at a place where it was spliced. They made a new splice, relighted it, and hurried back to safety, and at 4:45 A.M. there was a tremendous blast. The earth shook, an immense mass of dirt, guns, men, and timbers rose into the air, and a huge cloud of dust spread over the area.

Thinking the debris was about to fall upon them, the Union troops in the front line rushed to the rear and ten minutes were lost getting them back into line. The troops were then ordered forward and had to climb over the abatis that they had built to obstruct Confederate assaults because, as Grant said later, Burnside had disregarded his instructions to have it removed. As the leading units pushed forward some rushed into the crater and others around it; troops coming up pushed from behind and soon formed a dense mass. Major William H. Powell, aide-de-camp to General Ledlie, wrote later that the sight was so extraordinary that the men halted at the rim of the crater to stare down at it. The hole was 30 feet deep, 60 feet wide, and 170 feet long, filled with broken gun carriages and men buried in the debris, some up to the waist, others up to the neck, still others upside down with legs protruding. Major Powell wrote, in *Battles and Leaders of the Civil War*:

Colonel Marshall yelled to the Second Brigade to move forward and the men did so, jumping, sliding and tumbling into the hole over the debris of material and dead and dying men, and huge blocks of solid clay. They were followed by General Bartlett's brigade. Up on the other side of the crater they climbed, and while a detachment stopped to place two of the dismounted guns of the battery in position on the enemy side of the crest of the crater a portion of the leading brigade passed over the crest and attempted to reform. In doing so members of these regiments were killed by musket shots from the rear, fired by Confederates who were still occupying the traverses and entrenchments to the right and left of the crater. . . . Owing to the precipitous walls the [Union] men could find no footing except by facing inward, digging their heels into the earth and throwing their backs against the side of the crater or squatting in a half-sitting, half-standing posture.

The Confederates were recovering from their early demoralization and within an hour began sweeping the crater with canister, doing frightful injury. A Negro brigade under Colonel Joshua K. Siegfried was sent in when the crater was "crowded to suffocation." Officers were being killed everywhere. Major Charles H. Houghton of the Fourteenth New York Artillery reported the field

was swept by both artillery and infantry fire of the enemy from both directions and was so thickly strewn with killed and wounded, both white and black, that one disposed to be so inhuman might have reached the works without stepping on the ground. The sun was pouring its fiercest heat down upon us and our suffering wounded. No air was stirring within the crater. It was a sickening sight; men were dead and dying all around us; blood was streaming down the sides of the crater to the bottom, where it gathered in pools for a time before being absorbed by the hard red clay.

An attempt was made to advance a brigade to the right of the crater, without success. The Fourteenth New York Heavy Artillery captured both prisoners and field guns, and repulsed a countercharge with a Confederate fieldpiece, but was unable to hold its ground for lack of support.

The principal Confederate defense was under the command of Major General William Mahone, who brought up two brigades, chiefly North and South Carolina troops, and drove the Federals from their advanced position. Generals Lee and Beauregard had taken their post in the Gee house, 500 yards behind the action. Another unit of Mahone's division charged at 10:30 A.M. and was repulsed. At 1 P.M. Mahone pushed a large force over the rim of the crater and a hand-to-hand fight ensued, in which the Confederates also lost heavily. But the situation was hopeless for the Federals, and many surrendered.

The Union loss at the Battle of the Crater, on June 30, 1864, was 3,798 casualties, of whom 504 were killed, 1,881 wounded, and 1,413 captured or missing. Elliott's brigade on the Confederate side was estimated to have had 677 casualties, more than half of the Confederate total. General Mahone placed the number of Federal prisoners at 1,100. General Lee reported 929 prisoners and estimated 700 Federals had been killed.

The Petersburg Crater was a most glaring example of inefficiency and mismanagement. It indicated a complete lack of coordination among units and a startling disregard of responsibility among the top commanders. The Joint Committee on the Conduct of the War held an inquiry and interviewed the officers. The principal blame fell on General Burnside, whose inability to safeguard human life already had been abundantly shown at Fredericksburg, and whose procrastination when he should have ordered the troops in the Crater to withdraw was without excuse. He was removed from the command and resigned from the Army a few weeks later. Testimony also found General Ledlie at fault; he had sat in a bombproof during most of the action, apparently drunk. He was permitted to resign. Grant, writing twenty years later, was still bitter about Ledlie's conduct. Although General Meade escaped censure, it was obvious to many that his lack of confidence in the project from the start was reflected in his orders.

General Meade on August 18, 1864, ordered General Warren to get a hold on the Weldon railroad as near the Confederate fortifications as he could and to destroy the road. Warren advanced with his Fifth Corps and a brigade of General Kautz's cavalry under Colonel Samuel P. Spear. When the Confederates discovered the movement they sent General Heth's division to stop Warren, but the Federal troops drove Heth back after severe fighting. Meade sent reinforcements from the Ninth Corps as well as General McGregg's cavalry and a railroad-demolition contingent of 200 men.

Warren established his headquarters at the Globe Tavern. On August 19 the Confederates attacked again, having been reinforced by three brigades under Mahone, Pegram's artillery and W. H. F. Lee's cavalry. The brunt of the attack fell on General R. B. Ayres' Second Division of Warren's corps. The Confederates were repulsed and Warren consolidated his position at the Globe. He drew back to give his guns an open field and entrenched, and when the Confederates advanced next morning he used his artillery to great advantage and smashed the assaults. But the three-day fighting was costly; the Federals listed 4,278 casualties, of which number 251 were killed, 1,148 wounded, and 2,879 captured or missing.

Quickly grasping the advantage for once, Meade ordered General Hancock to withdraw two divisions from Deep Bottom and hurry to the Weldon railroad line at Reams' Station, to continue the demolition. Hancock's troops tore up large segments of the line August 22-24, with Spear's and McGregg's cavalry doing picket duty. On August 25 Hancock was attacked by a large body that included nine brigades of Wilcox's, Heth's, and Field's Divisions, supported by Pegram's artillery. Meade, who was at Warren's headquarters, ordered up brigades of Brigadier General Gershom Mott's Third Division of the Second Corps, as well as Brigadier General Orlando B. Willcox's Third Division of the Ninth Corps. By misdirection Willcox failed to reach the battlefield in time. There the heaviest attacks were sustained by Brigadier General Nelson A. Miles' First Division of the Second Corps. The Confederates were stopped, but the Federals were unable to gain because several regiments of Miles' division, made up of recent recruits, failed to obey orders. The Federals lost 140 killed, 529 wounded, and 2,073 captured or missing, the high number of the missing again testifying to a breakdown of discipline. The Confederates had 720 dead and wounded.

For some time the Confederate government had been anxious to have General Lee control all its military movements, but he had felt that his duties as commander of the Army of Northern Virginia and of Virginia and North Carolina did not permit him to extend his supervision. Davis wanted him to have charge of the South Atlantic states and all forces east of the Mississippi River. The Confederate Congress created the rank of general in chief, and on February 6, 1865, Davis appointed Lee to this post, which he accepted February 9. His connection with armies not directly under his eye was largely advisory.

Assault on Fort Stedman

The final offensive of the Confederates at Petersburg came on March 25, 1865, when Major General John G. Parke was in command of the Union Army, General Meade being on furlough. General Lee ordered a surprise attack on Fort Stedman. This was a fortified post on Hare's Hill, named for a colonel of the Eleventh Connecticut who had been killed at Petersburg during the previous August. It was a unit in a series of batteries protecting a station on the supply railroad, where General Willcox's Ninth Corps had its depot. Although Lee had come to the conclusion that assaults on fortified works were too costly for his army, he decided to make one more effort, hoping that by seizing redoubts in the rear of the Federal main line he might cause Grant to curtail his lines. He explained to President Davis that if successful he might be able on the approach of General Sherman's army, "to hold our position with a portion of the troops and with a select body unite with General Johnston and give him [Sherman] battle."

Confederate Major General John B. Gordon attacked with over 10,000 men and overran the fort and several batteries, capturing Colonel Napoleon B. McLaughlen, who commanded. The next strong point, Fort Haskell, repulsed the attackers and the supply railroad was saved from destruction. The Confederates turned Fort Stedman's guns on the Federals and the latter immediately massed troops to retake the position. This task fell principally on the 200th Pennsylvania under Lieutenant

Colonel W. H. H. McCall and other Pennsylvanians, all belonging to Brigadier General John F. Hartranft's division. McCall's regiment took Fort Stedman in twenty minutes, but lost 122 men, out of the total of 260 lost by the division as a whole. The 208th Pennsylvania retook the battery and the 211th Pennsylvania, under Colonel James H. Trimble, charged the Confederates and routed them. They left 1,600 prisoners in the hands of the Federals.

General Lee reported to Richmond that when he found the works could be held only at a great sacrifice he withdrew the troops, but admitted that in the withdrawal they had suffered their greatest losses. He thereupon informed President Davis: "I fear now it will be impossible to prevent a junction between Grant and Sherman, nor do I deem it prudent that this army should maintain its position until the latter shall approach too near." He surmised that General Joseph E. Johnston's army had been reduced by desertions, so that the united armies of Grant and Sherman would exceed those of the Confederates by nearly 100,000. He was intimating that he might have to retreat, and this, to the leaders in Richmond, meant a withdrawal from the capital itself.

One more disaster was in the making—the battle of Five Forks, Virginia, on April 1, in which General Sheridan defeated the Confederates under Major General George Pickett. After destroying the railroad around Charlottesville, and burning mills and factories, Sheridan had led his 10,000 cavalry to White House, where his supplies were held for him. On the way he was attacked by Confederate cavalry at Ashland, but continued on to White House, and rejoined Grant at City Point March 26.

On March 30 Sheridan proceeded from Dinwiddie Court House to Five Forks, at the extreme right of Lee's line. Grant expected an attack there would weaken the Confederate center and enable him to send Wright's corps against it. Lee sent Pickett with five brigades to reinforce the threatened flank at Five Forks, and Sheridan was forced to fall back. Grant sent General Warren and the Fifth Corps in support, but only one division, that of General Romeyn B. Ayres, got into the fighting. Warren used a day in moving, halting at Gravelly Run, which was in flood. When Sheridan could not locate Warren the next day he removed him and placed Brigadier General Charles Griffen in command. Sheridan carried Five Forks, and the Confederates were demoralized. The Federals took 4,500 prisoners by nightfall of April 1.

Grant, who knew that Warren was likely to prove too cautious in an emergency, had given Sheridan authority to displace him if this were necessary for success. In his memoirs Grant explained that he respected Warren's ability, but should have transferred him to other duties before the battle. This makes Grant culpable of administrative error. Warren demanded a trial but did not obtain one until 1879. Then the court exonerated him of blame and criticized Sheridan's action, but the report did not appear until three months after Warren's death.

Grant followed up the victory of Five Forks by a general attack on the Confederate positions early on the morning of Sunday, April 2, 1865. The most important gain was made by General Horatio G. Wright's Sixth Corps, which broke through the Confederate line, reached Hatcher's Run, and moved on to destroy the South Side Railroad, taking several thousand prisoners on the way. On this day Lieutenant General A. P. Hill, who led the Confederate Third Corps, was killed near the Boydton Plank Road.

Lee now prepared to abandon Petersburg. At about 10 A.M. he sent word to President Davis: "I advise that all preparations be made for leaving Richmond tonight." Davis was in his pew in St. Paul's Episcopal church when the message was brought to him. He left quietly and prepared to take a special train southward, on the final journey of the Confederate government.

The last resistance at Petersburg was at two defense posts, Fort Gregg and Fort Baldwin. In the face of imminent defeat the Confederates fought desperately, and Fort Gregg was taken only after a hand-to-hand fight.

41

THE RED RIVER EXPEDITION
OF BANKS AND PORTER

After the victory at Vicksburg Grant was in command of a fine fighting machine that could be used with telling effect against Confederate bodies east of the Mississippi and, in the opinion of Grant, accomplish its object without bloodshed. He therefore suggested to General Halleck a campaign against Mobile, to start at Lake Pontchartrain. Using Mobile as a base troops could operate against Bragg and, by threatening to cut off supplies that he and General Lee received from the Deep South, compel him to turn aside to meet this danger. But General Halleck refused to consider the project, even when Grant repeated his request in July and again in August. All Grant wished was help from the Navy to protect the debarkation of troops and leave to visit New Orleans if the project was approved.

Grant realized that the refusal was based on the Administration's desire to get a foothold in Texas, which it felt might be made a base by a foreign government to interfere in the war. Grant thought Texas could have been made secure by sending a garrison to Brownsville, so that there would be no wasting of troops in Western Louisiana and Eastern Texas. But Washington thought otherwise, and an order to Grant to send 4,000 troops to General Banks in Louisiana was followed soon after by an order to send the Thirteenth Corps, General E. O. C. Ord commanding, to Banks, and to cooperate with Banks on movements west of the Mississippi.

Grant now saw that what had happened at Corinth, where a fine army was broken up and another had to be reassembled, was being repeated at Vicksburg. Washington began to order segments of Grant's veteran army to different locations. The Ninth Corps was sent back to Kentucky; 5,000 men went to General Schofield in Missouri; a brigade under Brigadier General T. E. G.

Ransom went to Natchez. The latter move paid off, for Ransom arrived in time to intercept 5,000 head of beef cattle and munitions that the Confederates were sending East.

When Grant went to New Orleans to confer with Banks a horse he was riding shied at a locomotive in the street and threw him, knocking him unconscious and causing a painful swelling of one side of his body. He was taken to Vicksburg on a litter by steamboat, and it was weeks before he could attend to his duties. In September Halleck ordered Grant to send forces via Memphis and Tuscumbia to help Rosecrans in the relief of Chattanooga, and Grant responded with divisions drawn from Sherman, McPherson, and Hurlbut, placing Sherman in command.

Banks was a more astute politician than experienced soldier. Born in Massachusetts, he was forty-eight years old in 1864. He had already been a member and speaker of the Massachusetts House, Representative in Congress and Speaker of the House, and governor of Massachusetts. Known as the "Bobbin Boy" in politics, he was at different times a member of the Free Soil, American (Know Nothing), Republican, Liberal Republican, and Democratic parties; before the end of his life he had been elected to Congress nine times.

The first attempt to carry out the wishes of the Administration and plant the United States flag on Texas was made by General Banks in September, 1863. At that time part of the Nineteenth Corps, under the command of Major General William B. Franklin, was sent by sea to Sabine Pass with four gunboats under Lieutenant Crocker. They moved up the Pass to attack the fort. The gunboats *Clifton* and *Sachem* were disabled by shots in their boilers and had to surrender. The others, the *Granite City* and *Arizona*, withdrew.

A new expedition was started by Banks from New Orleans on October 26, 1863, with a detachment of the Thirteenth Corps under Major General C. C. Washburn, comprising about 5,000 effectives. The *Monon, Owasco,* and *Virginia* accompanied the troops. Major General N. J. T. Dana landed at Brazos Santiago, at the mouth of the Rio Grande, on November 2, drove back the Confederates on the mainland, and occupied Brownsville on

November 6 and Point Isabel on November 8. Another detachment under Brigadier General Ransom landed at Corpus Christi and took Fort Esperanza at Matagorda Bay December 30.

While this operation was going on General in Chief Halleck sent word on January 4, 1864, that the government wished the expedition to proceed up the Red River; that Major General Frederick Steele, commanding the Department of Arkansas, was to cooperate, and that General Grant should send troops from the Department of the Mississippi. Neither Banks nor Grant favored the expedition. Banks had his chief engineer present a review of the conditions necessary for success, all of which were difficult and time-consuming, but Halleck persisted and Banks went ahead.

General Banks planned to march north to Alexandria, Louisiana, by the route of the Teche, making Alexandria his base and then proceeding to Shreveport, where he expected to be joined by Major General Frederick Steele, who was to come down from Arkansas. This took for granted that Steele would be able to dispose of the opposition, which he had been unable to do in Arkansas. There were 500 miles between Banks and Steele, and in between were the undefeated Confederate forces of General Edmund Kirby Smith.

Banks had available in the Department of the Gulf two divisions of the Thirteenth Corps under Brigadier General Thomas E. G. Ransom, 4,773 men, and two infantry divisions of the Nineteenth Corps under Major General William B. Franklin, 10,699 men, and the cavalry division of the Nineteenth under Brigadier General Albert L. Lee, 4,653 men. He also had the Corps d'Afrique of Negro soldiers under Colonel William H. Dickey, 1,535 men. This gave the Army of the Gulf, with minor additions, 22,368 troops. General Steele would add at least 10,000 effectives.

The orders from General Halleck said a body of troops could be drawn from Vicksburg. Grant authorized Sherman to send Brigadier General Andrew J. Smith, with detachments of the Sixteenth and Seventeenth Corps. These comprised the first and third divisions under Brigadier General Joseph A. Mower and three brigades of infantry and two batteries under Brigadier General T. Kilby Smith—in all 8,935 men. Thus the total available to Banks, without counting Steele's possible contribution, was reported to be 31,303.

Banks was delayed in New Orleans, where he was supervising the installation of the new "free" state government on March 4. He ordered his second in command, General Franklin, to start the campaign by marching up the Teche, by way of Opelousas and Bayou Boeuf, to Alexandria. Rear Admiral David D. Porter, who had taken Smith's troops on transports, on March 12 landed them at Simsport, whence they marched to attack Fort de Russy, a Confederate outpost at the mouth of the Red River. Porter's squadron of eighteen gunboats, twelve of them ironclad, reached that point March 14, 1864. The fort was vulnerable from the land side, and before Porter could get into action Smith captured it, bagging 260 Confederates and losing only seven men of his own.

Porter picked up cotton and loaded it on barges on the way up, and at Alexandria he found much of it in warehouses. He put his men at work baling and loading, and had them scour the plantations for more cotton. Over 3,000 bales were said to have been sent to Cairo. The Confederates had begun to set fire to cotton as soon as they learned of the expedition, and some reports say they destroyed 100,000 bales, depriving their own planters of their means of subsistence. When Banks finally arrived at Alexandria on March 24, his headquarters boat had on board a number of speculators who had government permits to travel with the army, and who expected to profit by shipping cotton. As Banks resented their presence they later accused him of mismanagement and contributed to ill feeling.

In the meantime Grant had been made general in chief and in this capacity he sent word to Banks that if the taking of Shreveport took ten or fifteen days more than the time allotted for Smith's stay by Sherman, Banks was to send Smith's troops back, at the specified time, "even if it should lead to the abandonment of the main object of the expedition." Banks therefore could count on Smith's help for only twenty-six more days.

Above Alexandria the Red River flows over rapids, with

small falls above and below them. The low water greatly handicapped Porter's fleet in trying to pass the rapids; the *Eastport* was stuck on the rocks for three days, and the hospital ship *Woodford* was wrecked. Supplies had to be transferred to wagons and hauled around the rapids, and then put back on the boats. Finally Porter was able to move his boats upstream to Grand Encore, while Banks marched toward Natchitoches.

Lieutenant General Richard Taylor, commanding the Confederate district of West Louisiana, had retired to a point on the river thirty-six miles above Alexandria. On the night of March 21 General Mower with two divisions and the First Brigade of cavalry under Colonel Thomas J. Lucas surprised the Second Louisiana Cavalry of Colonel William G. Vincent at Henderson's Hill, twenty-three miles above Alexandria, and captured 250 men, 200 horses, and four guns. He then returned to Alexandria while Taylor withdrew to Natchitoches.

Between March 27 and April 5 the Federals advanced their columns and boats, and General Taylor withdrew his Confederate army farther into Northwestern Louisiana. On April 7 General Lee's Federal cavalry skirmished with a Confederate brigade belonging to the Texas division of General Jack Green, who had just arrived. Taylor also had received reinforcements from Arkansas and from General Sterling Price's Missouri army. He had more than 11,000 fighting men available and determined to make a stand near Mansfield, forty-two miles from Shreveport. At Sabine Crossroads Taylor deployed his troops at a clearing 1,200 yards long, 900 yards wide, with a ravine running through the middle.

The Federal column was strung along through a wooded area for twenty miles, led by General Lee's cavalry. There were only about 4,500 Union troops with four batteries ready at the clearing when Taylor threw his whole force at them. The Federals were driven back; they struck their own advancing column, and when they hit the cavalry train the teamsters stampeded. But there were other Federal troops ready to dispute Taylor's assault, and the bulk of the army was saved by the firm stand of the First Division of the Nineteenth Corps under Brigadier General William H. Emory, ably supported by the Second Brigade of Brigadier General James W. McMillan.

Banks' expedition now faced the prospect of harassment along wooded roads with no opportunity for maneuvering, with supplies endangered and Porter's boats running the risk of being isolated by low water. Steele's troops had not arrived and Smith's were about to be withdrawn. On April 9 Banks ordered a return to Grand Encore and the end of the expedition. There was a major clash with the Confederates that day at Pleasant Hill, in which the latter were completely repulsed and scattered. The Federals recovered all their lost artillery and captured two guns. General Kirby Smith reported to President Jefferson Davis: "Our troops were completely paralyzed by the repulse at Pleasant Hill." But Banks was not encouraged to resume the offensive. The Union troops concentrated at Grand Encore April 11 and entrenched.

On April 12 the fleet and transports carrying Kilby Smith's command were ambushed near Blair's landing by Confederate cavalry under General Jack Green, which was posted on bluffs. But the Federals took up the challenge. Kilby Smith's men, firing from behind cotton bales, picked off horsemen while the gunboats *Lexington* and *Osage* poured their shot into the Confederate regiments. One cannonball decapitated General Green, and the attack collapsed.

When Admiral Porter reached the rapids above Alexandria he faced a serious problem. The low level of the water had exposed many rocks. How to save the flotilla was a point that worried the leaders until an experienced engineer, Lieutenant Colonel Joseph Bailey of the Fourth Wisconsin Cavalry, took charge. The only way to raise the water in the channel was to store it behind a dam and release it when a vessel had to pass. Colonel Bailey's method became one of the great feats of the war. He found lumberjacks in the Wisconsin regiments and put them at work felling trees. He brought stone down the river on barges from quarries. Wing dams and cribs were built with the labor of 3,000 men and the use of many vehicles. After a series of mishaps, such as the premature opening of the channel, when water pressure pushed aside some of the obstructions, both light and heavy craft were guided over the mile of dangerous rapids. In order to lighten the craft some of the armor and guns were removed and transported around the rapids by land. Bailey was made a brigadier general and given the thanks of Congress.

Banks' troops delayed their return until Porter's boats were out of danger. Banks testified that up to April 26 his own command had 3,980 casualties, of which 289 were killed, 1,541 wounded, and 2,150 missing. On the return march from Alexandria the army lost 165 killed, 650 wounded, and 450 captured or missing.

The fleet had a number of encounters with the enemy and suffered losses. The largest ironclad, *Eastport,* had the worst misfortune. It struck a torpedo, which made a hole that was repaired after considerable effort. On the way down it grounded several times and was refloated, until finally it could not be dislodged and had to be destroyed. At one point the Confederates awaited the approach of some of Porter's light-draught tinclads with twenty guns. The flagship *Cricket* was hit thirty-eight times and had nineteen shells pass through it. Twelve men were killed and nineteen wounded out of a crew of fifty. When the pilot was wounded Admiral Porter took the helm. A pump-boat was hit in the boiler, and captain and crew, as well as 200 Negroes who were on board, were scalded to death.

The Confederates continued to mass guns along the river to attack the boats as they appeared. A disastrous action took place below Alexandria when the gunboats *Signal* and *Covington* were escorting the quartermaster's boat, *Warner.* The Confederates had twenty-five pieces of artillery and reportedly 6,000 men ready for the attack. The gunboats fought back with spirit for five hours, but were so badly damaged that they could not be saved. One was set on fire by its commander; the other had to be abandoned, and its crew was captured. During the Red River campaign the United States Navy had 120 casualties, and more than 200 others not in the Navy were lost on the boats.

Grant's plan of campaign for the spring of 1864 contemplated Banks turning the Red River area over to General Steele, giving up all of Texas except the Rio Grande, and concentrating Banks' forces against Mobile. But the time lost on the Red River expedition spoiled this plan; in the words of Grant, it "eliminated the use of 40,000 veterans, whose cooperation with the great campaign had been expected—10,000 with Sherman and 30,000 against Mobile."

Banks was relieved of a command in the field, but not at Grant's suggestion. Major General Edward R. S. Canby became commander of the Department of the Gulf and as such took Mobile on April 12, 1865. He also received the surrender of the last Confederate major officer to give up, General Kirby Smith, on May 26, 1865.

42

THE BOMBARDMENT AND CAPTURE OF FORT FISHER

Fort Fisher, located on the peninsula between the Atlantic Ocean and the mouth of the Cape Fear River in North Carolina, was a formidable Confederate earthwork not captured by the Federal forces until January 15, 1865. It was the principal sea defense of Wilmington, North Carolina, a port favored by blockade runners during most of the four years that it was accessible. The fort had forty-four guns mounted in barbette. Connected with the main work were batteries located along the ocean front, connected by galleries and leading up to the larger Mound Battery. On the southern side of the point was an isolated work, Fort Buchanan, with four guns.

The first Federal attack, on December 20–25, 1864, was a cooperative effort between the fleet and the army, which failed. The fleet was under the command of Rear Admiral David D. Porter, and the army under that of General Benjamin F. Butler. It used sixty vessels, including five ironclads, among them *New Ironsides*. The naval bombardment was led December 24 by Admiral Porter's flagship, the *Malvern,* with heavy firing by the steam frigates *Minnesota, Colorado,* and *Wabash,* each carrying twenty-five 9-inch guns. The Federals decided that they silenced numerous pieces of the fort, but Colonel William Lamb, the Confederate commander, said the guns were ordered to reply at intervals of thirty minutes because they were short of ammunition. A powder boat was brought close to the fort during the night of December 23 and exploded there, but the fort suffered no serious damage.

The troops were to make an assault on the land side of the fort. When General Godfrey Weitzel inspected the approaches he decided the attack could not be made without great loss of life and so reported to General Butler. The Federals had received a report that the Confederate General Hoke was marching toward Wilmington with a division of Lee's army. They captured some North Carolina reserves, who were based at a camp located behind the sand hills on the riverbank north of the fort, but called off the assault. The naval command was greatly incensed at this and blamed General Butler for the failure of the expedition.

Secretary of the Navy Welles asked General Grant to cooperate in a second effort forthwith and he consented. This time command of the troops was given Major General Alfred H. Terry. The units assigned were the Second Division of the Twenty-fourth Army Corps under Brigadier General Adelbert Ames and the Third Division of the Twenty-fifth Corps (Negro) under Brigadier General Charles J. Paine, in all about 8,000. Not quite confident that the army would do its job, Admiral Porter arranged for an independent assault from the ocean side by a contingent of sailors and marines recruited from the ships.

The ships came from Beaufort and began bombarding the fort on the afternoon of January 13, 1865. The firing continued the next day and night. About noon of January 15, Porter landed 1,600 sailors and 400 marines from 35 of the ships. They were armed only with cutlasses and pistols and were expected to rush the parapet and fight at close quarters. The first line advanced too rapidly for those coming later and was ordered to lie down and await the coming of the other ranks. When the latter came up they also lay down, and soon the whole beach from the water's edge to the batteries was crowded with men and the momentum of the assault was lost. The Confederates harried them with musket fire and the sailors had nothing with which to retaliate. They fell back and the whole assault failed.

This time, however, the army was ready to rush the fort from the land side and carry the fight into the traverses. After hard fighting the fort surrendered to the army at 8 P.M. The army lost 184 killed, 749 wounded, 23 missing, or 956 casualties. The fleet lost 82 killed, 269 wounded, and 35 missing, or 386 casualties. General Terry captured 112 officers and 1,971 men. The next day a mine exploded and the army lost 25 killed, 66 wounded.

43

THE LONG ROAD TO APPOMATTOX

Lincoln and the Confederate Commissioners

As the war dragged on, many influential persons spoke out for peace, but ways of obtaining it were lacking. Late in December, 1864, Francis P. Blair, Sr., individually made an attempt to find an opening for negotiations leading to peace and precipitated an inquiry by Congress. A full account of what took place was prepared by Secretary of State Seward and included the following steps:

Blair, who was a friend of the President, asked for simple permission to cross the lines and go to Richmond. He was well acquainted with men there, and while he intended to sound them out, there was no commitment by the Federal government and everything he did was on his own responsibility. Blair had an interview with

Jefferson Davis, who gave him a letter saying he would be willing to enter into negotiations for the restoration of peace and that if he could be assured that a commission would be received, he would name one. When this letter was shown to President Lincoln he wrote Blair saying he might tell Davis that he, Lincoln, was ready to receive any agent that he or any other influential person "now resisting the national authority" might informally send with the object of securing peace to the people of "our one common country."

Blair gave this letter to Davis, remarking that Lincoln's reference to "our one common country" related to Davis' "two countries," and Davis replied that he so understood it. The proceedings then changed to the military when Major General O. B. Willcox, commander of the Ninth Corps of the Army of the Potomac, sent word that Alexander H. Stephens, R. M. T. Hunter, and J. A. Campbell wished to cross the lines at Petersburg and go to City Point as peace commissioners. It appeared that they had sent a letter to General Grant saying they came in following the conditions laid down by Lincoln in his letter to Francis P. Blair. After more sparring President Lincoln asked Secretary Seward to go to Fortress Monroe and meet the three men informally and give them his three indispensable conditions, which were:

1. The restoration of the national authority throughout all the states.

2. No receding by the Executive of the United States on the slavery question from the position assumed thereon in the last annual message to Congress and in preceding documents.

3. No cessation of hostilities short of an end of the war, and the disbanding of all forces hostile to the government.

Lincoln told Seward that he was willing to hear anything they had to say not inconsistent with these conditions and added: "You will not assume to definitely consummate anything."

On the same day Lincoln wired Grant: "Let nothing which is transpiring change, hinder, or delay your military movements or plans." Grant replied there would be no armistice. The Confederate commissioners sent word that they wished to go to Washington. Evidently the

negotiations were going to break down before they had
started, because under date of February 1, 1865, Grant
sent Secretary Stanton an unprecedented message saying:

I will state confidentially, but not officially, that I am convinced upon conversations with Messrs. Stephens and Hunter,
that their intentions are good and their desire sincere to
restore peace and Union. I have not felt myself at liberty
to express even views of my own or to account for my
reticency. This has placed me in an awkward position,
which I could have avoided by not seeing them in the first
instance. I fear now their going back without any expression from anyone in authority will have a bad influence. . . .
I am sorry that Mr. Lincoln can not have an interview with
the two named in this dispatch, if not with all three now
within our lines.

General Grant's message changed Lincoln's purpose
and he agreed to meet the men at Fortress Monroe. He
reached there on the night of February 2 and found
Secretary Seward on one steamer and the Confederates
on another. The three commissioners came aboard the
President's steamer next morning and conferred for several hours with President Lincoln and Secretary Seward.
No one else was present and no record was made of the
talk, which was quite informal. President Lincoln described it thus:

On our part the whole substance of the instruction to the
Secretary of State . . . was stated and insisted upon, while
nothing was said inconsistent therewith; while by the other
party it was not said that, in any event, or on any condition,
they ever would consent to re-union, and yet they equally
omitted to declare that they would never consent. They
seemed to desire a postponement of that question, and the
adoption of some other course first, which, as some of them
seemed to argue, might not lead to re-union, but which
course, we thought would amount to an indefinite postponement. The conference ended without result.

The commissioners returned to Richmond and reported
the terms Lincoln had made a condition of peace, and
Jefferson Davis summarized them for the Confederate
Congress. "The enemy," he said, "refused to negotiate
with the Confederate States or any state separately be-

cause that would be recognizing them as separate powers and the United States would grant an armistice only on assurance that the authority of the Constitution would be re-established, with especial acceptance of the amendment recently voted by Congress abolishing slavery. They also reported that Lincoln would make a very liberal use of his authority over penalties in dealing with individuals." The *Richmond Sentinel,* expressive of Davis' views, commented: "Our advance, though invited, has been met with the most intolerable of insults. We have been fairly forced to the wall. . . ."

Although the Confederate government refused to accept Lincoln's terms, it recognized the necessity of ending the war before all was lost. Jefferson Davis and his cabinet were well informed about the attrition that was wearing down their armies. A month after Gettysburg, Lee was telling President Davis that "the number of desertions is so great and still continues to such an extent that unless some cessation of them can be caused I fear success in the field will be seriously endangered. . . . The Virginians go off in many cases to join the various partisan corps in the state. . . . Many cross the James River near Balcony Falls en route for the South along the mountain ridges."

Only a week before General Lee had published an amnesty order giving a pardon to all officers and men who were absent and who should return within twenty days, as well as to all punished or under sentence for absence without leave or desertion, but not for those twice convicted. Lee said this caused many to give the pardon "a wrong interpretation" and leave as a result.

Grant and Lee

Both General Lee and General Longstreet investigated the possibilities of beginning negotiations for peace while they were defending Petersburg. Longstreet had talked the matter over with his Union friend, General E. O. C. Ord. When Lee made a report on this subject to President Davis in a dispatch dated March 3, 1865, he undoubtedly had acted after a previous understanding with Davis. He wrote:

I have proposed to General Grant an interview, in the hope that some good may result, but I must confess that I am not sanguine. My belief is that he will consent to no terms unless coupled with the condition of our return to the Union. Whether this will be acceptable to our people yet awhile I cannot say. I shall go to Richmond tomorrow or next day to see you, and hope you will grant me an hour's conversation on the subject. Gen. Longstreet proposed that I should meet Gen. Grant at the point where he met Gen. Ord, and desired to have two or three days' notice. I have therefore appointed Monday next for the interview with Gen. Grant.

Lee thereupon wrote Grant: "Sincerely desiring to leave nothing untried which may put an end to the calamities of war I propose to meet you . . . with the hope that an interchange of views may be found practicable to submit the subjects of controversy between the belligerents to a convention for settlement."

Grant sensed that Lee's proposal was based on political rather than military issues. With this he could have nothing to do, so he replied briefly that he had no authority to meet Lee "for a conference on the subject proposed. Such authority is vested in the President of the United States alone."

On the afternoon of April 7, 1865, General Grant made a direct attempt to invite the surrender of General Lee's Army of Northern Virginia. He had reached the village of Farmville at noon and made his headquarters in the village hotel. He had word from General Sheridan saying he had started from Prince Edward Court House for Appomattox Station, because he had learned that seven trains of provisions and forage for the Confederate army were there and he intended to capture them.

Grant had been thinking over what he had heard from a Dr. Smith, a Virginian who was an officer in the regular army and also related to the Confederate General Ewell, now a prisoner. Ewell had said that he considered the Southern cause lost when Grant's troops got across the James River and that it was the duty of the Confederate authorities to make the best terms they could when they still had a right to claim concessions. He felt that for every man killed after that someone was

responsible, and that this would be but little better than
murder. He was not sure Lee would consent to surrender without consulting the President of the Confederacy, but hoped he would. This evidently made an impression on Grant, for it is one of the reasons he gives
for opening the correspondence with Lee. Under date of
April 7, 1865, 5 P.M., he addressed Lee:

The result of the last week must convince you of the
hopelessness of further resistance on the part of the Army of
Northern Virginia in this struggle. I feel that it is so, and
regard it as my duty to shift from myself the responsibility
of any further effusion of blood, by asking of you the surrender of that portion of the Confederate army known as
the Army of Northern Virginia.

Grant gave the note to General Seth Williams, his adjutant general, with instructions to have it sent into Lee's
lines by way of General Humphreys' front, which was
near Lee's rear guard. After midnight Grant's headquarters received the following reply from Lee:

I have received your note of this date. Though not entirely of the opinion you express of the hopelessness of
further resistance on the part of the Army of Northern Virginia, I reciprocate your desire to avoid useless effusion
of blood and therefore, before considering your proposition, ask the terms you will offer on condition of its surrender.

To Grant this was not a satisfactory reply. So he wrote
again, the next day, April 8:

Your note of last evening in reply to mine of same date,
asking conditions on which I will accept the surrender of the
Army of Northern Virginia, is just received. In reply I would
say that peace being my first desire, there is but one condition I insist upon, viz.:
That the men surrendered shall be disqualified for taking
up arms against the Government of the United States until
properly exchanged. I will meet you, or will designate officers to meet any officers you may name for the same purpose, at any point agreeable to you, for the purpose of
arranging definitely the terms upon which the surrender of
the Army of Northern Virginia will be received.

Lee found it hard to think of surrender. He must have been hoping to gain some concessions when next he wrote. Grant did not receive his reply until midnight of April 8. It read:

I received at a late hour your note of today in answer to mine of yesterday. I did not intend to propose the surrender of the Army of Northern Virginia, but to ask the terms of your proposition. To be frank, I do not think the emergency has arisen to call for the surrender of this army, but as the restoration of peace should be the sole object of all, I desired to know whether your proposals would lead to that end. I can not, therefore, meet you with a view to surrender the Army of Northern Virginia; but as far as your proposition may affect the Confederate States forces under my command and tend to the restoration of peace, I should be pleased to meet you at 10 A.M. tomorrow on the old stage road to Richmond, between the picket lines of the two armies.

Lee knew how desperate his situation was. There was no food; the rations were down to gruel in a tin cup. The commands were melting away; men were simply walking off, to get food for themselves and to be done with fighting. Lee's army was now down to a hard core of officers and men who had fought for years without the thought of giving up. On this night Lee's army rested a few miles east of Appomattox Court House. Calling a number of his commanders to report at his campfire, Lee consulted them about the situation. Lieutenant General Longstreet came; so did Major General John B. Gordon, Major General Fitzhugh Lee, and a number of division commanders and staff officers. The consensus was that if Fitzhugh Lee's cavalry went forward and encountered only cavalry, it would attempt to break through and clear the road for the infantry, but if Grant's infantry was blocking the road there was no way out but surrender. The test was to start at 1 A.M., when the troops would be aroused again and Fitzhugh Lee would start west. It was the last campfire conference of Lee's army.

That night General Custer's division of Sheridan's cavalry made a quick dash to destroy the railroad west of Appomattox Station. There he found seven Confederate supply trains. Three were run off by the trainmen when they saw the riders coming. Four were taken by Custer. At dawn Fitzhugh Lee's Confederate cavalry followed by Gordon's infantry came, found Custer and attacked him. Then Confederates burned one of the trains; Custer sent the remaining three off to Farmville. The cavalry tangled in a general melee, and the Federals lost two guns and were coming off second best when they gave way and disclosed the massed infantry of Griffin's and Ord's commands closing in on Gordon's flanks and behind him. Lee had heard the firing and sent his aide, Colonel Venable, to Gordon to find out what was taking place. Gordon, faced by superior numbers, was unable to move. Venable returned with this message from Gordon: "Tell General Lee I have fought my corps to a frazzle, and I fear I can do nothing unless I am heavily supported by Longstreet's corps."

According to Venable, Lee then said: "Then there is nothing left for me to do but to go and see General Grant, and I would rather die a thousand deaths."

Colonel Venable described the scene, as quoted by Brigadier General Armistead L. Long in his *Memoirs of Robert E. Lee*:

Convulsed with passionate grief, many were the wild words which we spoke as we stood around him. Said one: "Oh general, what will history say of the surrender of the army in the field?"

He replied: "Yes, I know they will say hard things of us; they will not understand how we are overwhelmed by numbers. But that is not the question, Colonel; the question is, is it right to surrender this army? If it is right, then I will take all the responsibility."

Lee still wanted more opinions from his officers. He called Lieutenant General Longstreet and Major General William Mahone to come up, and Longstreet found him wearing his finest uniform: a new one with sword and sash, a handsomely embroidered belt, fine boots, and gold spurs. "The handsome apparel and the brave bearing failed to conceal his profound depression," wrote Longstreet. Lee's splendid attire, which he wore later when meeting Grant, was the result of necessity. The

Confederate army was so hard-pressed that Lee's head-quarters baggage had to be destroyed. Lee and his staff thereupon saved their best clothes and gave up nearly all others.

Lee talked over the situation. Gordon's advance was facing a formidable barrier that he could not break; Meade was closing in on the rear. What was Longstreet's view? Longstreet asked if the bloody sacrifice of the army would help the cause in other quarters. Lee thought not. "Then your situation speaks for itself," was Longstreet's reply. Apparently General Mahone had similar views. Lee once more asked Longstreet to endorse that opinion, which he did.

General Lee confided to Brigadier General E. Porter Alexander, chief of artillery of the First Corps, that he did not expect Grant to demand an unconditional surrender. Lee would surrender the army on condition that it would not fight again until exchanged. With his adjutant, Colonel Walter H. Taylor and Colonel Charles C. Marshall to accompany him, Lee mounted his good horse, Traveller, and started for the place on the road that he had named in his last note to Grant. Preceding the party was a sergeant carrying a white flag. When they reached the designated spot they did not find Grant but an officer with a flag, Lieutenant Colonel Charles R. Whittier of Major General Humphreys' staff, who had a letter for General Lee. He said he would wait for an answer.

Grant had been suffering from a neuralgic headache, and had been able to get little sleep. He went with members of his staff to Meade's headquarters and took some coffee. He had been willing to meet Lee, but some of his staff thought Lee's reply did not indicate an outright surrender and convinced Grant he should not attempt to consider terms. Grant, however, did not want to break off the talk entirely, so he wrote a new note and sent it by Colonel Whittier. It read:

Your note of yesterday is received. As I have no authority to treat on the subject of peace, the meeting proposed for 10 A.M. today could lead to no good. I will state, however, General, that I am equally anxious for peace with yourself, and the whole North entertains the same feeling. The terms upon which peace can be had are well understood. By the South laying down their arms, they would hasten that desirable event, save thousands of human lives and hundreds of millions of property not yet destroyed.

Sincerely hoping that all our difficulties may be settled without the loss of another life, I subscribe myself, very respectfully—

Lee was disturbed by this turn of events, but determined to go ahead with the surrender. He had asked Colonel Marshall to take down his reply when a courier dashed up from Longstreet with word that Fitzhugh Lee had found a place where the army could get through the Federal lines. Lee, however, went on dictating his letter to Grant, which read:

I received your note of this morning on the picket line whither I had come to meet you and ascertain definitely what terms were embraced in your proposition of yesterday. With reference to the surrender of this army I now request an interview in accordance with the offer contained in your letter of yesterday for that purpose.

A second courier informed Lee that Fitzhugh Lee was mistaken. Lee then sent word to General Gordon to put up a white flag. He also sent a flag to Sheridan's front and another to Meade, telling them he was about to confer with Grant and asking for a suspension of hostilities until he could find him. The two commanders at first suspected a ruse, then agreed to a two-hour truce. They had to send a messenger through Lee's lines in order to reach Grant, who had left for Sheridan's front. A few miles outside of Appomattox Court House, Grant was overtaken by an officer of Meade's staff with the message from Lee.

Getting notes to their destinations was still a major problem. The Union troops facing Lee had orders to attack, and Lee was warned to withdraw. This caused Lee to send a second note to Grant, which read simply: "I ask a suspension of hostilities pending the adjustment of the terms of surrender of this army, in an in-interview requested in my former communication today." The Federal line still kept moving forward, when he received what Freeman calls "a peremptory warn-ing" to withdraw. He went back to Longstreet's line. The attack did not come, but Lee received a note from Gen-eral Meade suggesting that he send a duplicate letter to Grant through another part of the line. Lee then went to an apple orchard nearby and dictated a new letter, reiter-ating the substance of the first. Lee then tried to get a little rest on some blankets under an apple tree. After a few more messages dealing with the truce a Federal officer arrived with a Confederate escort and was introduced as Lieutenant Colonel Orville E. Babcock, aide to Grant, who presented Grant's reply to Lee's first note of that morning, of which Grant said later: "When the officer reached me I was still suffering with the sick headache, but the instant I saw the contents of the note I was cured." He replied:

Your note of this date is but this moment 11:50 A.M. re-ceived, in consequence of my having passed from the Richmond and Lynchburg road to the Farmville and Lynch-burg road. I am at this writing about four miles west of Walker's Church and will push forward to the front for the purpose of meeting you. Notice sent to me on this road where you wish the interview to take place will meet me.

It was now Colonel Babcock's task to lead General Lee to a meeting with Grant. Colonel Taylor went back to the Confederate lines and only Colonel Marshall ac-companied Lee, followed by a mounted orderly. They proceeded to the village of Appomattox Court House, where they met a man named Wilmer McLean, and Colo-nel Marshall asked him to direct them to a house suita-ble for a meeting. McLean took them to an unoccupied place, but they preferred a better one, and then Mc-Lean led them to his own house, a two-story brick dwell-ing, with a wide wooden porch in the middle and wide steps leading up to it. He ushered them into the living room at one side of the central hall and there Lee and Marshall sat down to await the coming of Grant, while an orderly looked after the two horses.

McLean's contact with the surrender was a peculiar coincidence. During the first battle of Bull Run he was living on a farm near McLean's Ford in a house used during part of the engagement by General Beauregard, while his barn was used to shelter wounded. Preferring a less dangerous location, he had moved his family to the house in Appomattox Court House and a nearby farm. Thus his house became famous as the place of Lee's surrender and he lost most of the furniture of his living room, some of which was paid for and some simply carried off by the soldiers.

Grant arrived a little after 1 P.M. and walked into the room where Lee was sitting, while other Federal officers waited outside. Soon Colonel Babcock invited them in. "We walked in softly and ranged ourselves quietly about the sides of the room," said General Horace Porter, "very much as people enter a sick chamber when they expect to find the patient dangerously ill. Some found seats on the sofa and the few chairs which constituted the furniture, but most of the party stood."

The Federal officers could not but notice the contrast between Lee's fine uniform and Grant's working clothes. Lee was attired as for dress parade; even his topboots had ornamental stitching of red silk. Grant wore a single-breasted blouse of dark-blue flannel, unbuttoned, showing a vest beneath. He wore ordinary topboots, with his trousers tucked inside, and had a pair of dark-yellow thread gloves. Only his shoulder straps designated his rank, and he wore no sword, whereas Lee's sword was apparently new. Grant sat at a large marble-topped table, while Lee used a smaller one. The officers present, who were introduced to General Lee in the course of the meeting, included Generals Sheridan, Custer, Porter, Ingalls, Merritt, and Seth Williams, as well as Colonel Babcock and Colonel Parker. Seth Williams had been Lee's adjutant when Lee was superintendent at West Point, and Lee shook hands with him. Lee started when Colonel Parker, a full-blooded Indian, was introduced to him, and spectators surmised that he must have thought at first that Parker was a Negro.

The words spoken on this dramatic occasion have been read with intense interest by the American people for nearly 100 years and are still a memorable example of democratic intercourse between victor and vanquished. The following transcript reflects a comparison of the best-known sources and rests basically on General Horace Porter's reconstruction of the scene in *Battles and Leaders of the Civil War,* Vol. IV.

GRANT: I met you once before, General Lee, while we were serving in Mexico, when you came over from General Scott's headquarters to visit Garland's brigade, to which I then belonged. I have always remembered your appearance, and I think I should have recognized you anywhere.

LEE: Yes, I know I met you on that occasion and I have often thought of it and tried to recollect how you looked, but I have never been able to recall a single feature. [Some further brief mention of Mexico.] I suppose, General Grant, that the object of our present meeting is fully understood. I asked to see you to ascertain upon what terms you would receive the surrender of my army.

GRANT: The terms I propose are those stated substantially in my letter of yesterday, that is, the officers and men surrendered to be paroled and disqualified from taking up arms again until properly exchanged and all arms, ammunition, and supplies to be delivered up as captured property.

LEE: Those are about the conditions which I expected would be proposed.

GRANT: Yes, I think our correspondence indicated pretty clearly the action that would be taken at our meeting, and I hope it may lead to a general suspension of hostilities and be the means of preventing any further loss of life.

Lee appeared to assent, and Grant made some remarks about the prospects of peace. Then:

LEE: I presume, General Grant, we have both carefully considered the proper steps to be taken and I would suggest that you commit to writing the terms you have proposed so that they may be formally acted upon.

GRANT: Very well, I will write them out.

Grant took up a manifold order book and began writing. As he did so he glanced once at Lee's fine sword, then added something. He asked Colonel Ely S. Parker to look it over, then handed the book to Lee.

Lee placed the book on the little table, took out his steel-rimmed spectacles, wiped them carefully, crossed his legs, and read. He called Grant's attention to the omission of one word and it was corrected. The text:

GENERAL: In accordance with the substance of my letter to you of the 8th inst., I propose to receive the surrender of the Army of N. Va. on the following terms, to wit: Rolls of all the officers and men to be made in duplicate; one copy to be given to an officer to be designated by me, the other to be retained by such officer or officers as you may designate. The officers to give their individual paroles not to take arms against the Government of the United States until properly exchanged, and each company or regimental commander to sign a like parole for the men of their commands. The arms, artillery and public property to be parked and stacked, and turned over to the officers appointed by me to receive them. This will not embrace the side-arms of the officers, nor their private horses or baggage. This done, each officer and man will be allowed to return to their homes, not to be disturbed by United States authority so long as they observe their parole and the laws in force where they may reside.

LEE: This will have a very happy effect upon my army.

GRANT: Unless you have some suggestions to make in regard to the form in which I have stated the terms I will have a copy of the letter made in ink and sign it.

LEE: There is one thing I would like to mention. The cavalrymen and artillerists own their own horses in our army. Its organization in this respect differs from that of the United States. I would like to understand whether these men will be permitted to retain their horses?

GRANT: You will find the terms as written do not allow this. Only the officers are permitted to take their private property.

LEE: No, I see the terms do not allow it; that is clear.

GRANT: Well, the subject is quite new to me. Of course I did not know that any private soldiers owned their animals, but I think this will be the last battle of the war—I sincerely hope so—and that the surrender of this army will be followed by that of all the others, and I take it that most of the men in the ranks are small farmers, and as the country has been so raided by the two armies, it is doubtful whether they will be able to put in a crop to carry themselves and their families through the next winter without the aid of the horses they are now riding, and I will arrange it in this way: I will not change the terms as now written, but I will instruct the officers I shall appoint to receive the paroles to let all the men who claim to own a horse or mule take the animals home with them to work their little farms.

LEE: This will have the best possible effect upon the men. It will be very gratifying and will do much toward conciliating our people.

Lee handed the terms back to Grant, who directed Colonel Bowers to make a copy in ink. Bowers turned it over to Colonel Parker. There was no ink. Colonel Marshall then produced a small boxwood inkstand. Lee asked Colonel Marshall to draw up a letter of acceptance, which Lee signed. It read:

I have received your letter of this date, containing the terms of surrender of the Army of Northern Virginia, as proposed by you. As they are substantially the same as those expressed in your letter of the 8th inst., they are accepted. I will proceed to designate the proper officers to carry the stipulations into effect.

LEE: I have a thousand or more of your men as prisoners, General Grant, a number of them officers whom we have required to march along with us for several days. I shall be glad to send them into your lines as soon as it can be arranged, for I have no provisions for them. I have indeed nothing for my own men. They have been living for the last few days principally upon parched corn and we are badly in need of both rations and forage. I telegraphed to Lynchburg directing several trainloads of rations to be sent by rail from there, and when they arrive I should be glad to have the present wants of my men supplied from them.

GRANT: I should like to have our men sent within our lines as soon as possible. I will take steps at once to have your army supplied with rations, but I am sorry we have no forage for the animals. We have had to depend upon the country for our supply of forage. Of about how many men does your present force consist?

LEE: Indeed, I am not able to say. My losses in killed and wounded have been exceedingly heavy, and besides, there have been many stragglers and some deserters. All my reports and public papers, and indeed, my own private letters, had to be destroyed on the march to prevent them from falling into the hands of your people. Many companies are entirely without officers, and I have not seen any returns for several days; so I have taken no means of ascertaining our present strength.

GRANT: Suppose I send over 25,000 rations, do you think that will be a sufficient supply?

LEE: I think that will be ample and it will be a great relief, I assure you.

GRANT: I started out from my camp several days ago without my sword, and as I have not seen my headquarters baggage since, I have been riding about without any sidearms. I have generally worn a sword, however, as little as possible, only during the actual operations of a campaign.

LEE: I am in the habit of wearing mine most of the time. I wear it invariably when I am moving among my troops, moving about through the army.

Lee asked Grant to notify Meade. At 4 P.M. Lee shook hands with Grant, bowed to the others, and left the room with Colonel Marshall. He stood on the lowest step while his horse was being brought up and smote his hands together several times. When he was mounted, Grant, who was also leaving, came down to the foot of the steps and raised his hat. Lee returned the salute of Grant and the other officers and rode slowly toward his lines. The final act, which he had seen coming for months but had hoped to avert, had taken place.

Grant and Lee met again next morning on the lines. Grant said he hoped the war would soon be over. Lee said he had been anxious for some time to stop and trusted everything would be done to restore harmony and conciliate the people of the South. He said emancipation of the slaves would be no hindrance, as it was not likely that the majority of the Southern people would care to restore slavery even if the opportunity were given. He hoped other Confederate armies would follow his example.

There followed an exchange of visits between officers of both sides, some of whom had known each other in the U.S. service. Longstreet had been present at Grant's wedding and Heth had been his subaltern in Mexico. Gordon and Pickett also called. The impetuosity of General Custer had caused some amusement to Longstreet. When the truce had been announced on Gordon's front, where Custer was in command, Custer had dashed to Longstreet's headquarters and in his "brusque, excited manner" had called out: "In the name of General Sheri-

dan I demand the unconditional surrender of this army."
Longstreet told him he was inside the enemy's lines and
was showing disrespect to General Grant no less than to
Longstreet. Custer explained it would be a pity to have
more blood on that field. Longstreet explained that Lee
had gone to Grant to discuss terms. This satisfied Custer
and he left.

When Lee reached the Confederate lines he was met
by the men of his army, who crowded around him to
find out if they had been surrendered. Lee tried to ride
on, but finding himself stopped he said: "Men, we have
fought the war together and I have done the best I
could for you. You will all be paroled and go to your
homes until exchanged." The anguish of his men was un-
controlled. These were veterans of many hard fights,
poorly clad and half starved, survivors of the costly retreat, who had not run off when they saw the end coming. The testimony from many sources is that some wept,
some spoke with bitterness, others were ready to go out
immediately to "lick the Yankees."

On April 10 Lee had numerous visitors from the
Union lines—General Grant, who talked with him out of
earshot of their staffs; General Meade, to whom Lee, in
answer to a question, said he had 33,000 muskets on his
lines at the time of the Petersburg siege; General Henry
J. Hunt and several others who had known Lee before
the war. Later in the day he dictated a farewell order
to Colonel Marshall, which, after a number of penciled
revisions, read thus:

GENERAL ORDERS NO. 9 HD. QRS. ARMY OF N. VA. APRIL 10, 1865

After four years of arduous service marked by unsurpassed
courage and fortitude, the Army of Northern Virginia has
been compelled to yield to overwhelming numbers and resources.

I need not tell the brave survivors of so many hard fought
battles, who have remained steadfast to the last, that I have
consented to this result from no distrust of them; but feeling
that valor and devotion could accomplish nothing that could
compensate for the loss that must have attended the continuance of the contest, I determined to avoid the useless
sacrifice of those whose past services have endeared them to
their countrymen.

By the terms of the agreement, officers and men can return to their homes and remain until exchanged. You will take with you the satisfaction that proceeds from the consciousness of duty faithfully performed; and I earnestly pray that a Merciful God will extend to you His blessing and protection.

With an unceasing admiration of your constancy and devotion to your Country, and a grateful remembrance of your kind and generous consideration for myself, I bid you all an affectionate farewell.　　　　　　　　　R. E. LEE

GenL.

Generals Longstreet, Gordon, and Pendleton were named commissioners by General Lee, with the duties of arranging for paroles. The surrender of the troops took place on April 12, when General Gordon led the regiments to a field near Appomattox Court House, where they stacked arms and colors. On duty to receive them was Brigadier General Joshua L. Chamberlain and the First Brigade of the First Division of Major General Griffin's Fifth Corps. General Chamberlain ordered his troops to present arms, and General Gordon saluted in turn. Some of the Confederates had concealed their battle flags under their shirts, others had torn them into small bits and passed these around as souvenirs. General Fitzhugh Lee, not wishing to be a party to the surrender, had ridden away with most of his cavalry, which then scattered. About 1,500 Federals who had been taken prisoner were delivered to the Union command.

General Lee did not witness the laying down of arms. He rode out of the camp that day with Colonels Taylor and Marshall and Major Cooke, the latter in Lee's ambulance, since he was ill. It was noted by observers that Lee now wore an old uniform and another sword than the one he had worn when visiting Grant. Lee's sword was not tendered in surrender. Grant had glanced at it when writing the terms and inserted the provision that officers might keep their sidearms. It is now in the Confederate Museum at Richmond.

Lee's report to President Jefferson Davis of the circumstances of the surrender is dated April 12 and probably was prepared before he left camp. In it he describes the situation confronting the army when it arrived at

Amelia Court House on April 4 and did not find the needed supplies awaiting it. This resulted in a waste of twenty-four hours while the troops searched for forage and food, and caused a change of route when supplies were ordered from Lynchburg to Farmville. After describing the final movements toward Appomattox and the ensuing stalemate, Lee said he surrendered "that portion of the Army of Northern Virginia which was on the field."

. . . I deemed this course the best under all the circumstances by which we were surrounded. On the morning of the 9th, according to the reports of the ordnance officers, there were 7,892 organized infantry with arms, with an average of 75 rounds of ammunition per man; the artillery, though reduced to 63 pieces with 93 rounds of ammunition, was sufficient. These comprised all the supplies of ordnance that could be relied on in the state of Virginia. I have no accurate report of the cavalry, but believe it did not exceed 2,100 effective men. The enemy was more than five times our number. If we could have forced our way one day longer, it would have been at a great sacrifice of life, and at its end I did not see how a surrender could have been avoided. We had no subsistence for man or horse and it could not be gathered in the country. The supplies ordered to Pamplin's Station from Lynchburg could not reach us, and the men, deprived of food and sleep for many days, were worn out and exhausted.

Many Confederates who had left returned to be paroled and by April 12, 26,018 had surrendered.

44

JOHNSTON'S SURRENDER
TO SHERMAN

General Sherman was pushing toward Raleigh, North Carolina, with Major General Judson Kilpatrick's cavalry crowding the rearguard of General Wade Hampton's

troops, when Sherman received word from Grant that Lee
had surrendered at Appomattox April 9. On the morning
of April 13, just before Sherman reached Raleigh, three
leading citizens of Raleigh came into his lines on a
locomotive with a white flag and asked protection for the
people in the city. Sherman assured them the war was
practically over and it was best for the civil authorities to
remain at their posts until further notice. When Sherman
entered Raleigh he learned that Governor Vance had
fled, fearing arrest.

General Stoneman's cavalry was reported approaching
Greensboro, North Carolina, and Major General James
H. Wilson's cavalry was operating toward Columbus
and Macon, Georgia. General Sherman made new
dispositions to cut off the retreat of General Johnston's
army by sending Major General Howard's right wing
across the Haw River on new bridges. Sherman now
ordered that there be "no further destruction of railroads, mills, cotton and produce" without specific orders,
and "the inhabitants will be dealt with kindly, looking
to an early reconciliation. The troops will be permitted,
however, to gather forage and provisions as heretofore;
only more care should be taken not to strip the poorer
classes too closely." Sherman realized that with the end
of resistance an impoverished people would have to be
helped to subsistence by the very ones who had laid
the country waste.

On April 14 General Kilpatrick conveyed to Sherman a
note from General Johnston proposing a temporary truce,
and asking him to ask Grant to do likewise with other
armies, "the object being to permit the civil authorities to enter into the needful arrangements to terminate
the existing war." This was a bit roundabout for Sherman,
who replied that he was empowered to make terms, would
observe the conditions that applied to Grant and Lee at
Appomattox, and would halt his advance troops. His
aide-de-camp was sent with instructions to arrange an
interview, and Johnston agreed to meet Sherman between the lines beyond Durham Station, twenty-six miles
from Raleigh, and the end of Sherman's advance.
About to enter his train on the morning of April 17,
Sherman received a telegraph message in cipher from

Secretary of War Stanton telling of the assassination of President Lincoln, the attempt on the life of Secretary of State Seward and his son, and the threat against Grant. Sherman asked the telegraph operator to withhold the information for the moment.

At Durham, General Kilpatrick provided horses for a five-mile ride, at the end of which Sherman met General Johnston and General Wade Hampton. Sherman and Johnston went into a little farmhouse owned by a man named Bennett for consultation. There Sherman disclosed the news of Lincoln's murder. Sherman saw perspiration come out in large drops on Johnston's forehead as he read the dispatch; he called the assassination "a disgrace to the age" and hoped it would not be charged against the Confederate government. Sherman replied he did not think General Lee or the officers of the army would tolerate such an act, but he could not say as much for "Jeff Davis, George Sanders and men of that stripe." Johnston wanted to arrange the surrender of all the Confederate armies still in the field and to the end offered to get authority to do so from President Davis and report the next day. Sherman returned to Raleigh and published the news of Lincoln's assassination to the army, fearing that the war might now take its worst shape, "that of assassins and guerrillas."

When General Johnston returned the next day to the Bennett farmhouse he was ready to drive a bargain. He assured General Sherman that he could order the surrender of all the Confederate armies, but he wanted the political rights of his officers and men guaranteed. Sherman pointed out that President Lincoln's proclamation of amnesty of December 8, 1863, would enable every Confederate below the rank of colonel to get an absolute pardon by laying down his arms and taking the oath of allegiance; that Grant, in addition, had extended this to all officers, including General Lee, and that this pardon would restore all rights of citizenship, in Sherman's opinion. Johnston wanted John C. Breckinridge to add his plea for political rights; Sherman demurred at first because Breckinridge was Confederate Secretary of War, but when Johnston explained that he was also a Confederate major general, Sherman allowed

him to talk. Privately he advised Breckinridge to get out
of the country in a hurry; the North would remember
that, as Vice President of the United States, he had
announced the election of Lincoln to the Presidency
in the Senate. Breckinridge said he would "leave the
country forever."

General Sherman took these objections into account,
then wrote out the terms of surrender personally and
Johnston signed them. But Sherman stipulated that he
would have to get approval from Washington, and
suggested that the truce continue until this was received.
Sherman had a few objects of his own to pursue; he
thought this would give him time to complete the railroad to Raleigh and put him in a better position to strike
again if the surrender failed.

Sherman sent the agreement to Washington, addressing
it "to General Grant or General Halleck." Grant saw it
first and knew immediately that it would not be approved.
There was consternation among the authorities, led by
the President, Andrew Johnson, naturally jealous of his
newly acquired prerogatives. The Secretary of War was
outraged, and General Halleck once more acted the
martinet. Sherman had far exceeded his authority as a
military commander and had dealt with matters reserved
to the Executive, but his intention was reconciliation,
on which his experience had given him definite opinions.

Sherman had guarded against an extreme interpretation; he called the document of April 18 a "memorandum,
or basis of agreement." It specified that the Confederate
armies would go to their state capitals, there deposit their
arms and public property in the state arsenal, and each
man would execute and file an agreement to abide by
state and Federal authority. Arms were to be used to
maintain peace and order only and were to be reported
to the chief of ordnance in Washington, for future disposition by Congress. Other provisions were:

The recognition, by the President of the United States,
of the several state governments, on their officers and legis-
latures taking the oaths prescribed by the Constitution of
the United States, and, where conflicting state governments
have resulted from the war, the legitimacy of all shall be
submitted to the Supreme Court of the United States.

The re-establishment of all the Federal courts in the several states, with powers as defined by the Constitution ... and of the states respectively.

The people and inhabitants of all the states to be guaranteed, so far as the Executive can, their political rights and franchises, as well as their rights of person and property. . . .

The Executive authority of the Government of the United States not to disturb any of the people by reason of the late war, so long as they live in peace and quiet, abstain from acts of armed hostility, and obey the laws in existence at their place of residence.

In general terms, the war to cease; a general amnesty, so far as the Executive of the United States can command, on condition of the disbandment of the Confederate armies, the distribution of the arms, and the resumption of peaceful pursuits by the officers and men hitherto composing said armies.

General Grant recalled, when writing his *Personal Memoirs,* how Sherman quickly cascaded from being one of the most popular generals to one denounced by the President and the Secretary of War "in very bitter terms." Some people even called him a traitor. Even at the distance of nearly one hundred years it is possible to comprehend the irritation among the authorities, especially that of an Executive who had just assumed high office and who often repeated: "Treason is a crime and must be made odious." Sherman had laid down a line of conduct for the President, for the Congress, and for the courts, and apparently had overlooked that he was dealing only with the surrender of a fighting force.

Secretary of War Stanton, in terse instructions to General Grant, stating that Sherman's memorandum was disapproved, said that President Johnson's instructions were identical with those of President Lincoln and added the galling phrase: "The President desires that you proceed immediately to the headquarters of Major General Sherman and direct operations against the enemy." This did not necessarily mean to displace General Sherman, for Grant was already Sherman's superior, and the actual direction was in his hands. Neither did General Sherman so understand matters nor accept the letter "as a serious reproof." That he did not was due to Grant's reasonableness and understanding. Grant respected Sherman's integrity and proceeded to mend matters in his calm, deliberate manner. Secretary Stanton had given him a copy of Lincoln's instructions regarding the surrender of Lee; they said precisely that there was to be no conference with Lee unless for capitulation or solely minor and purely military matters; that Grant was not to touch on political subjects, for the President did not intend to submit them to military conferences or conventions. So Grant went to Sherman's headquarters and tried to keep his presence from becoming known. He showed Sherman Lincoln's message and asked him to resume negotiations, to meet Johnston again and make a plain request for surrender; if not effected the truce would end in forty-eight hours.

This time Sherman went straight to the point. He informed General Johnston that "I am instructed to limit my operations to your immediate command and not to attempt civil negotiations. I therefore demand the surrender of your army on the same terms as were given to General Lee at Appomattox, purely and simply." Johnston was in the same situation as Lee; he had nothing substantial to offer in bargaining. So he met Sherman again at the Bennett farmhouse beyond Durham's Station, and "without hesitation" agreed to the new terms. He had been imposing on Sherman's good nature for better conditions, but he knew his army could not withstand another fight with Sherman. The terms signed April 26 provided that all arms would be delivered to an ordnance officer of the United States Army at Greensboro; rolls of officers and men would be made in duplicate; each officer and man would sign an obligation not to take up arms against the government; officers would retain their sidearms, private horses, and baggage; and all were to return to their homes. The document was signed by Sherman and Johnston, and when Sherman presented it to Grant in Raleigh, Grant appended his approval.

Major General J. M. Schofield took command of the United States forces in North Carolina and as such supervised the paroles of Johnston's army at Greensboro. Supplemental terms to the agreement of surrender provided for field transportation to be loaned to the troops going home; the right to use artillery horses for this pur-

pose; each brigade to retain arms equal to one-seventh
of its effective strength; private horses and private property of officers and men to be retained by them; water
transport to be available from Mobile or New Orleans
for troops from Arkansas and Texas. As an afterthought,
perhaps, it was stipulated that naval forces within the
limits of Johnston's command were included in the
agreement. General Schofield reported the parole of 36,-
817 prisoners of war. General J. H. Wilson reported the
surrender of 52,453 in Georgia and Florida. Thus the total
under Johnston's agreement was 89,270.

Both Secretary Stanton and Major General Halleck were
at fault in their hasty condemnation of General Sherman.
Secretary Stanton published material directly libelous by
innuendo, as when he said in a bulletin: "The orders of
General Sherman to General Stoneman to withdraw from
Salisbury and join him probably will open the way for
Davis to escape to Mexico or Europe with his plunder,"
and then said that Davis and his associates hoped to
make terms with Sherman or some other commander
looking to their escape with the gold from the banks. No
less discreet was Halleck, who advised Stanton that Generals Meade, Sheridan, and Wright had been ordered to
pay no regard to any truce of Sherman's, and that similar
orders were going out to other commands.

General Sherman's reaction was violent. A facile
writer, much more voluble than Grant, he talked and
wrote at length in protest at the indignities put upon him
by his superiors. "General Halleck's measures to capture
General Johnston's army, actually surrendered to me at
the time," he wrote, "simply excited my contempt for a
judgment such as he was supposed to possess." Halleck
had left Washington for Richmond to command the Military Department of the James, and when General Sherman
was proceeding north Halleck invited Sherman to accept
his hospitality there. This Sherman refused. When Sherman's army passed the President at the Grand Review in
Washington, May 24, 1865, Stanton was in the stand
and offered his hand to Sherman, who "declined it
publicly."

The men of Sherman's army, loyal to their commander,
resented the slurs. Major General Henry W. Slocum de-

scribed a scene near Raleigh, where he came upon a group of soldiers standing around a cart that was being burned with its contents. Upon inquiring the reason he was told that the cart was filled with New York newspapers to be sold to the soldiers; that the papers were filled with "the vilest abuse" of General Sherman and the soldiers refused to let them circulate. "That was the last property that I saw destroyed by the men of Sherman's army," wrote General Slocum, "and I witnessed the scene with keener satisfaction than I had felt over the destruction of any property since the day we left Atlanta."

45

THE LAST DAYS OF ABRAHAM LINCOLN

President Lincoln visited Richmond on April 4, the day after its occupation. He walked from the steamboat landing to General Weitzel's headquarters, in the former house of Jefferson Davis, now known as the White House of the Confederacy. On his walk he was followed by a large crowd composed chiefly of Negroes who expressed their happy feelings volubly and tried to touch him. The President also visited Libby Prison and inspected the burned section of the city. He slept that night on a gunboat and returned next day, when he conferred on reorganization with Judge James A. Campbell, former Assistant Secretary of War in the Confederate cabinet and one of the emissaries who had met the President at the Hampton Roads conference. The President gave General Weitzel authority to allow leaders to meet to discuss a new state government. He also visited the battlefield of Petersburg. On April 8 he passed most of the day visiting sick and wounded soldiers in the City Point hospital, shaking hands with over 6,000 and giving each a word of encouragement. He returned to Washington by steamer that night, in the company of Mrs. Lincoln and several members of the cabinet, who had followed him to Richmond.

When the news of Lee's surrender reached Washington, the pent-up feelings of the people led to many demonstrations in front of the White House during the day of April 10. President Lincoln did not wish to make speeches. Excusing himself to one crowd, he said: "I see you have a band. I propose now closing up by requesting you to play a certain air, or tune. I have always thought 'Dixie' one of the best tunes I ever heard. [Laughter] I have heard that our adversaries over the way have attempted to appropriate it as a national air. I insisted yesterday that we had fairly captured it. I presented the question to the Attorney General, and he gave his opinion that it is our lawful prize. I ask the band to give us a good turn upon it."

"Dixie," considered truly to express the spirit of the South, was actually composed by a Northerner, Dan Emmett of Mount Vernon, Ohio, a minstrel. He wrote it because Bryants' troupe needed a "walk-around song," one to be sung as the minstrels paraded around the stage. Utilizing the favorite expression of actors during a northern winter, "I wish I was in Dixie"—that is, below the Mason and Dixon line—he hit upon words and melody that gave him enduring fame.

Lincoln spoke once more that day, and promised to make a longer address on the evening of the next, April 11. That carefully prepared address dealt with the reorganization of Louisiana and hence with his conciliatory attitude toward reconstruction. Opposition had developed to the action of 12,000 recognized voters of Louisiana who had formed a state government that recognized the constitutional amendment abolishing slavery, opened the public schools to whites and Negroes, and empowered the legislature to enfranchise Negroes. While not agreeing in full with what had been done, President Lincoln argued that to discard the new state government would create discouragement and paralyze attempts to get the people into proper working relations with the Union. This, Lincoln's last public speech, closed with the promise: "In the present situation it may be my duty to make some new announcement to the people of the South. I am considering and shall not fail to act when satisfied that action will be proper."

On April 13 President Lincoln ordered a reduction of the military force. The Secretary of War informed Major General Dix that all drafting and recruiting would stop, purchases of arms and commissary supplies would be curtailed, the number of general and staff officers would be reduced to actual needs, and military restrictions on trade and commerce would be removed, consistent with public safety.

An air of rejoicing still pervaded Washington on April 14, 1865. This was the anniversary of the fall of Fort Sumter, and on it Major General Robert Anderson returned to the fort and raised on its staff the identical Stars and Stripes that had been hauled down four years before.

It was also the day for a cabinet meeting, attended by General Grant. The cabinet discussed measures to expedite normal conditions. Secretary Stanton said, "the President was very cheerful and hopeful, spoke very kindly of General Lee and others of the Confederacy and the establishment of the government of Virginia." But it was clear that General Weitzel had exceeded the President's instructions and practically recognized the former Virginia legislature and its governor, William Smith, who had exercised their power in Confederate times. The President revoked General Weitzel's order.

That evening the theaters were decorated and the White House asked Ford's Theatre for the upper right-hand box, customarily used by the President. The theater manager announced in the evening papers that the President and General Grant would attend a performance of Laura Keene's company in *Our American Cousin*. General Grant learned that he would have to go north with his family and could not attend.

As the President left the White House that evening with Mrs. Lincoln, he exchanged a greeting with Isaac N. Arnold, Chicago lawyer and long-time associate who was later to write a book about Lincoln. He also talked briefly with Representative George Ashmun of Massachusetts who had presided at the convention that nominated Lincoln; Ashmun had a request to make and Lincoln gave him a card admitting him to the White House next morning. Then, with him in the carriage, went Major Henry Reed Rathbone and Rathbone's fiancée, Clara Harris.

The entrance to Ford's Theatre was at the south end of the front façade, and in order to reach his box President Lincoln had to pass behind the last row of the dress circle, entering the box by a small stairway. The box was built over the apron of the stage and was decorated with two American flags, which had a framed portrait of George Washington at the point where their staffs crossed. When the party of four entered the box during the first act the audience rose and cheered the President. He sat down in a rocking chair at the edge of the box with Mrs. Lincoln beside him; farther forward sat Miss Harris and Major Rathbone.

Not until the third act did the great tragedy of the evening unfold. The audience heard the sound of a pistol shot; a man leaped from the President's box to the stage, stumbling as his boot caught in the draped American flag, yelled something, flourished a dagger, and ran across the center of the stage and disappeared in the rear. Mrs. Lincoln's shriek as the President slumped back in his chair and Major Rathbone fell back with blood spurting from a flesh wound, awoke the audience to the horror of the moment; men climbed over chairs to the stage and one raced after the man who had left. Surgeons were called and it was found that the President had been shot in the base of the neck and that the bullet had lodged there. He was unconscious, and shortly thereafter was carried across the street to the house of a man named William Peterson, and placed upon a bed in a narrow bedroom just back of the front hallway.

Practically at the same time a ruffian forced his way into the bedroom where William H. Seward, Secretary of State, was lying ill, and stabbed him, also inflicting a knife wound on Frederick W. Seward, Assistant Secretary of State, who tried to intercept him. This suggested that the assassination of the President and the Secretary of State had been part of a conspiracy.

The three-story red-brick building across from the theater soon was crowded with members of the President's family and the government, and cabinet officials insisted on their prerogative to enter the bedroom and remain with the unconscious President, at a time when fresh air was greatly needed. Mrs. Lincoln, who was prostrated, was escorted to a sofa in the front room; in the back parlor adjoining Chief Justice Carter of the District of Columbia took depositions of persons who had seen or heard the tragedy. At 7:22 A.M. on the morning of Saturday, April 15, the President, who had never regained consciousness, died.

An eyewitness of the tragedy was an actor, Hawk, who was on the stage at the moment of the shooting. He wrote in a letter to his father:

I was playing Asa Trenchard, in the "American Cousin." The "old lady" of the theater had just gone off the stage, and I was answering her exit speech when I heard the shot fired. I turned, looked up at the President's box, heard the man exclaim, "Sic semper tyrannis!" saw him jump from the box, seize the flag on the staff and drop to the stage; he slipped when he gained the stage, but he got upon his feet in a moment, brandished a large knife, saying, "The South shall be free!" turned his face in the direction I stood, and I recognized him as John Wilkes Booth. He ran toward me, and I, seeing the knife, thought I was the one he was after, ran off the stage and up a flight of stairs. He made his escape out of a door directly in the rear of the theater, mounted a horse and rode off.

The above all occurred in the space of a quarter of a minute, and at the time I did not know that the President was shot, although, if I had tried to stop him he would have stabbed me.

With John Wilkes Booth identified as the assassin, the government offered a reward of $50,000 for his capture. It also offered $25,000 for each of his fellow conspirators, David E. Herold and John H. Surratt. The hysteria that swept the country also led the government to offer $100,000 for the arrest of Jefferson Davis. In a proclamation of May 2 President Andrew Johnson asserted the Bureau of Military Justice had evidence that

Davis, C. C. Clay, Jacob Thompson, and other Confederates had "incited, created and procured" the assaults on Lincoln and Secretary Seward.

The Military Commission associated these crimes with a far-flung conspiracy, which, it asserted, included a raid on St. Albans, Vermont, on October 19, 1864, when Lieutenant Bennett H. Young and a group of Confederate soldiers in civilian attire seized money in the banks and burned houses there. It also linked up with this the fires started in New York City on November 25, 1864, when ten New York hotels and Barnum's Museum were damaged. A forecast of biological warfare was contained in the charge that a Dr. Blackburn had tried to produce pestilence in northern cities by spreading disease through infected clothing.

But many Southerners realized that Lincoln would have been the most effective leader to "bind the nation's wounds."

John Wilkes Booth survived barely twelve days after shooting President Lincoln. He was tracked to a barn on the Garrett farm near Bowling Green, Caroline County, Virginia, by First Lieutenant E. P. Doherty and twenty-five men of the Sixteenth New York Cavalry on April 26, 1865. As his accomplice, David Herold, was surrendering to Doherty, Sergeant Boston Corbett watched Booth through a crack in the barn, and suspecting Booth was about to fire, shot him. Booth was taken to the porch and died soon after. His body was first interred in the Penitentiary at Washington and four years later removed to the Booth family plot in Baltimore.

Under a ruling of Attorney General Speed the assassination was a military crime—it struck down the commander-in-chief—therefore the trial of the conspirators must proceed before a military commission. A court of ten was presided over by Joseph Holt, judge advocate general, who had been Secretary of War under Buchanan. Eight accused of complicity were found guilty. Four, David E. Herold, Lewis Payne, George A. Atzerodt, and Mrs. Mary E. Surratt, were condemned to death and hanged July 7. Mrs. Surratt had kept the boarding house where the conspirators met and had denied knowing

Payne. Her twenty-one-year-old son, John H. Surratt, who had carried some dispatches for the Confederates, had escaped to Europe. Two men were given life imprisonment—Dr. Samuel A. Mudd, who had set Booth's broken ankle without having been a party to the crime, and Samuel B. Arnold, who had provided vehicles. The stage carpenter, Edward Spangler, was given six years in prison. A boy, Michael O'Laughlin, was given six years. Mudd, Arnold, and Spangler were sent to Dry Tortugas, where they served so unselfishly during a yellow-fever attack that they were pardoned after two years. O'Laughlin died in 1867. John H. Surratt enlisted in the Papal Guards at the Vatican and after two years was brought back to the United States. He was accused of having had knowledge of a plan to kidnap the President. In 1867 he received a civil trial; the jury disagreed and he went free. Within a few years the methods of the military court were severely criticized, and the hanging of Mrs. Surratt was called a miscarriage of justice. President Andrew Johnson had signed the death sentences, apparently not knowing that an appeal for clemency, asking life imprisonment instead of hanging for Mrs. Surratt, had been made by five of the ten members of the court.

Jefferson Davis, moving south by train with Confederate records, was caught May 10, 1865, at Irwinville, Georgia, by Federal cavalry and taken by ship to Fortress Monroe. Indicted for treason, he was held there for two years. On May 13, 1867, he was released on bond of $100,000 furnished by Horace Greeley and nine other citizens. A new indictment for conspiracy was drawn up, but as the feeling for conciliation gained ground, he was never brought to trial. Although neither Davis nor Robert E. Lee ever regained the voting franchise, they were considered included in the General Amnesty proclaimed by President Andrew Johnson on December 25, 1868.

INDEX

Abolitionists, 25-27, 266-277
Adams, Charles Francis, 53, 85, 88, 167, 500, 504, 505
Adams, Pres. John Quincy, 17
Alabama, the, 499-505
Albemarle, the, 570-573
Alcott, Bronson, 291
Alexander, Brig. Gen. E. Porter, 381, 389, 390, 394-396, 461, 476, 598, 631
Amnesty Proclamation of 1863, 413
Anderson, Gen. Richard H., 187, 198, 217, 222, 236, 243-247, 252, 260, 280, 301, 359, 368, 369, 510-514, 520, 528-534
Anderson, Maj. Gen. Robert, 38-47, 122, 650
Andrews, James J., 480-486
Antietam Campaign, 227-263
Appomattox, 623-641
Armistead, Gen. Lewis A., 205, 260, 389, 395, 398-401
Arthur, Pres. Chester A., 227
Articles of Confederation, 11
Augur, Gen. Christopher C., 213, 542-545
Averell, Gen. William W., 206, 209, 279, 292, 299, 300, 489, 538, 550, 554, 556, 596

Bankhead, Cmdr. J. P., 156
Banks, Gen. Nathaniel P., 83, 168, 173, 177, 178, 185, 210-213, 266, 354, 356, 426, 468, 494, 522, 552, 553, 614-621
Barksdale, Brig. Gen. William, 200, 205, 245, 280-282, 284, 319, 382, 387
Barton, Clara, 61
Bate, Edward, 63

"Battle Hymn of the Republic," 273, 274
Beauregard, Gen. Pierre, 35, 37, 42, 44-47, 64, 70, 71, 76, 82, 118, 127, 129, 135-140, 327, 346, 360, 444, 451, 483, 525, 526, 530, 564, 582, 583, 586, 588, 591-595, 598-604, 609, 634
Bee, Brig. Gen. Barnard E., 74, 76, 82
Beecher, Henry Ward, 26
Bell, John, 32
Benjamin, Sec. Judah P., 88, 89, 503
Blair, Francis P., 67, 68, 94, 546, 623, 624
Blair, Montgomery, 41, 62, 67, 99, 158, 174, 410, 547, 549
Blockade, the, 49, 50
Booth, John Wilkes, 652, 653, 654
Braddock, Gen., 235
Bragg, Lieut. Gen. Braxton, 41, 117, 127, 129, 132, 136-140, 346, 432, 449-480, 487, 513, 526, 588, 589, 592, 594, 598, 600, 603, 614, 622
Branch, Gen. L. O'B., 185, 213, 299
Breckinridge, Maj. Gen. John C., 31, 32, 129, 130, 139, 166, 343, 355, 459, 460, 463, 476, 528-540, 546-553, 585, 586, 643, 644
Brooke, Lieut, John M., 154
Brown, Capt. Isaac N., 340-343
Brown, John, 25-27, 65, 272-274, 574
Bryan, William Jennings, 118
Bryant, William Cullen, 274

655